AUDREY M. SHUEY

PROFESSOR OF PSYCHOLOGY, RANDOLPH-MACON WOMAN'S COLLEGE

2nd EDITION

The Testing
of Negro
Intelligence

SOCIAL SCIENCE PRESS   *NEW YORK, 1966*

Library of Congress Catalog Card Number: 66-19037

PRINTED IN THE UNITED STATES OF AMERICA

TO VERA BELTING

FOREWORD

TO THE

SECOND EDITION

The question of Negro-white differences in mental test performance has been the subject of lively debate in recent years. Unfortunately, the subject has often been confused with social and political issues of racial inferiority, desegregation, civil rights and other extraneous matters. Moreover, a number of well meaning but often insufficiently informed writers have taken the untenable position that racial differences ought not to be found; or if found should immediately be explained away as somehow immoral and reprehensible. With this attitude I am in sharp disagreement. I welcome every honest effort to help Negroes improve their lot, but I do not believe it is necessary to "prove" that no racial differences exist, nor to conceal and gloss them over, if found, in order to justify a fair policy toward Negroes. The honest psychologist, like any true scientist, should have no preconceived racial bias. He should not care which race, if any, is superior in intelligence, nor should he demand that all races be potentially equal. He is interested simply in uncovering differences in performance when such exist and in inferring the orgin of these differences. And this is certainly a legitimate scientific enterprise.

The study of Negro-white differences in the United States offers certain distinct advantages to the student of social psychology. Negroes and whites have lived side by side in this country for more than 300 years. The American Negro's native language is English, and he has been exposed in varying degree to the same environmental influences as the American white. As a result, American whites and Negroes are much more alike in background than are racial groups of totally different cultures, e.g., American whites and Congolese.

Two major difficulties arise when Negroes and whites are compared in mental test performance in the United States. First, the American Negro is generally below the white in social and economic status and his work opportunities are more limited. Many of these inequalities have been exaggerated. But inequities in the environment render it difficult to make fair comparisons between many Negro and white groups, though fair comparisons can be - and have been - made by a careful equating of background variables. A second difficulty stems from the fact that many American Negroes have white ancestry. Racial mixture, however, should cause Negro-white differences in the United States, if found, to be even more significant. For then racial differences would probably be much greater if American whites and African Negroes were compared.

The second edition of *The Testing of Negro Intelligence* summarizes the studies of Negro-white differences in mental test performance in the United States over the past 50 years. It is a careful and accurate survey which should command the attention of all serious students of the subject. Dr. Shuey finds that at each age level and under a variety of conditions, Negroes regularly score below whites. There is, to be sure, an overlapping of 10-15 per cent which means that some Negroes achieve high scores. But the mean differences persist and are statistically significant. We are forced to conclude that the regularity and consistency of these results strongly suggest a genetic basis for the differences. I believe that the weight of evidence (biological, historical and social) supports this judgment.

HENRY E. GARRETT
Professor Emeritus of Psychology
Columbia University

ACKNOWLEDGMENTS

The author is indebted to the following publishers for permission to incorporate brief quotations in this book: The American Association for the Advancement of Science; The American Association on Mental Deficiency; The American Journal of Psychology; The American Psychological Association, Inc.; Appleton-Century-Crofts; Columbia University Press; The Gryphon Press; Harper & Brothers; Harvard Educational Review; Henry Holt and Company, Inc.; Howard University Press; The Journal Press; The Macmillan Company; Prentice-Hall, Inc.; Rinehart & Company; Rutgers University Press; Stanford University Press. Permission to reprint selections from his book was kindly granted by Dr. Henry A. Tanser.

The author is grateful to Miss Margaret F. Thomas and to Mrs. William M. Breazeale for their assistance in obtaining for her a number of interlibrary loans including unpublished theses and dissertations. The writer is obligated to the following colleges and universities for lending their manuscripts: Atlanta University; Baylor University; Bryn Mawr College; Columbia University; Fisk University; Fordham University; George Peabody College for Teachers; George Washington University; Hampton Institute; Harvard University; Howard University; Marquette University; North Carolina College at Durham; Northwestern University; Ohio State University; Pennsylvania State University; Prairie View University; Stanford University; State College, Montgomery, Alabama; Temple University; Tennessee Agricultural and Industrial State College; Tulane University; Tuskegee Institute; University of Chicago; University of Cincinnati; University of Colorado; University of Denver; University of Illinois; University of Kansas; University of Louisville; University of Michigan; University of Minnesota; University of Missouri; University of North Carolina; University of Oklahoma; University of Pennsylvania; University of Pittsburgh; University of Tennessee; University of Toledo; University of Virginia; University of Wisconsin; Virginia State College; Washington State College; Washington University; and Western Reserve University.

In addition to the Lipscomb Library of Randolph-Macon Woman's College the author has had occasion to make frequent use of the Alderman Library of the University of Virginia and is appreciative of the hospitality accorded her. The writer also wishes to acknowledge the excellent service rendered her by the University Microfilms, Inc. in their xerographic reproduction of 25 or more unpublished dissertations.

Various individuals have been helpful in supplying information requested by the writer, including Dr. Marcus B. Caldwell, Florida State University; Dr.

Willis W. Clark, Los Angeles City Schools; Dr. Susan W. Gray, George Peabody College for Teachers; Dr. William M. McCord, Harvard University; Dr. Frank C. J. McGurk, Alabama College; Dr. Merritt C. Oelke and Dr. R. Travis Osborne, University of Georgia; Dr. James L. Sartin, University of Cincinnati; Dr. Dorothy M. Sherman, Wichita State University; and Dr. Elizabeth Woods, Los Angeles City Schools.

Her colleagues in the Department of Psychology at Randolph-Macon, Dr. M. Van Voorhees Lloyd and Dr. Frederick B. Rowe, have made helpful suggestions and criticisms and have called attention to pertinent studies that the writer may have overlooked. Dr. Cora L. Friedline has given valued assistance in reading the complete manuscript for the second edition. The author wishes to thank Dr. Henry E. Garrett who obliged her by reading several chapters of the manuscript and generously consented to contribute the Foreword.

Finally, the author wishes to express her indebtedness to many of her present and former students, particularly to Ann Gray Vermooten, Judith Stevens, and Linda Jane Tomlin, and to her daughter, Joan Wobst, for their interest in the progress of the research, their willingness to "lend an ear", and for the special assistance which they so cordially gave.

AUDREY M. SHUEY

Lynchburg, Virginia
March, 1966

CONTENTS

CONTENTS

LIST OF TABLES

Chapter I

INTRODUCTION

It is not the purpose of this book to prove that Negroes are socially, morally, or intellectually inferior to whites; nor is its purpose to demonstrate that Negroes are the equal of or are superior to whites in these several characteristics. Rather, it is the intention of the writer to convey with some degree of clarity and order the results of many years of research on one aspect of Negro behavior and to assess objectively the ever-growing literature on this subject.

A meaningful review of research, obviously, requires not only some evaluation and interpretation of individual studies but an organization of them into various significant categories and a presentation of conclusions — tentative or final. In the area of group comparisons, such as those between Negroes and whites, the interpretations and conclusions of the author are often of great importance to the reader as he relates them to himself, his family, and to larger groups with whom he identifies. If they are found to support his previously-formed attitudes on the subject the book and author are immediately given his approval. If they are in opposition to his attitudes he may reject the book by reading no further; however, if he does continue with it he frequently becomes depressed, annoyed, or outraged, the quality and intensity of the emotion varying, among other things, in proportion to the amount of research presented and the recognized logic of the analyses.[1]

The author, like the reader, is often deeply concerned with the outcome of his research, and would generally find it all to the good if he could knock the props from under old prejudices.[2] But at the same time he is aware that as a scientist he must proceed without wishful thinking, without undue concern for his theoretical interpretations, and without awe of prevalent opinion — whether it be found in the courts, in the pulpit, or in the press. Aware of his responsibilities, he must exercise his freedom to interpret research in fields where he presumes himself to be expert and assume that the reader can bear with him the burden of such interpretation.

The first edition of *The Testing of Negro Intelligence* (1958) has been subjected, not surprisingly, to varying amounts of commendation and adverse criticism.[3] In the latter category there have been comments to the effect that the results only revealed what the reader already knew, or that too much detailed re-

---

[1]As one young social scientist said in conversation with the writer: "If there *are* innate differences between the races that's all the more reason to say that there aren't any."

[2]From Woodworth and Marquis. (1947, p. 187)

[3]For example, see: Bond (1958), I. C. Brown (1960), Dreger and Miller (1960), Gini (1961), Klineberg (1963), Pettigrew (1964), Roen (1960), Tumin (1964), or Vernon (1959).

search was presented,[4] or that some studies were overlooked, or that the work was limited by what appeared to be a polemic attitude.[5] One social psychologist objected to the relative amount of research dated prior to World War II and to the author's ignorance of the "newer conceptions of intelligence" (where the emphasis is placed on nature *and* nurture).[6] As far as the writer knows, only one competent reviewer has indicated that any specific study was reported inaccurately or with bias.[7] It is evident to the writer that some of those who commented upon the first edition of this book read at most no more than its concluding statement.[8]

In addition to incorporating approximately 140 additional investigations with the 240 included in the first edition, we have attempted to examine the new and old researches carefully for such items as percentages of overlapping, age and grade differences, urban-rural differences, socioeconomic factors, testing prior to and after the end of World War II, and to determine the probable effect of specially enriched school programs, the subject's motivation and self-esteem, and the race of the examiner on test performance.

In reviewing the research pertaining to the intelligence of American Negroes we have limited the field primarily to studies dealing with intelligence as measured by standard intelligence tests. The survey includes, however, in addition to the data on mental tests, reports of maximum schooling and school grades of certain migratory and sedentary Negroes, rejection rates among Negroes and whites in World War II, results of certain information and vocabulary tests administered to illiterates in World War II, and research utilizing special tests given to school children and unselected adults.

This book might properly be called *A Comparative Study of the Intelligence of American Negroes and Whites,* since there are continuous references to the scores earned by white groups throughout. Wherever experimenters tested both Negroes and whites comparable statistics have been included; where only Negro groups were examined, there are references to norms that have been derived mainly from standardization on white groups. But because specific studies made on whites alone have not been included, as they were when Negroes were tested, the writer has preferred to place the emphasis upon *Negro* intelligence in the title.

---

[4]Anastasi (*in* Buros, 1959, pp. 1162-1163).

[5]Dreger and Miller (1960). Among the 13 researches cited by these authors as having been overlooked by the writer, eight were genuine omissions; of the others, one was *not* omitted (MacPhee, Wright, and Cummings, 1947); one, an article by Fulk and Harrell (1952) was based upon a Master's thesis (Fulk, 1949) which was included; and three were brief abstracts by Roberts (1946, 1948, 1950) based in part, apparently, upon the unpublished works of two of his students (Rooks, 1946, and L. F. Anderson, 1948) whose researches were included. These and many other studies inadvertently omitted in the 1958 edition have been now combined in the present edition.

[6]Pettigrew (*J. Negro Educ.,* 1964, pp. 6-8)

[7]For various comments by the present writer and by Anastasi on the D'Angelo thesis, see: Anastasi (*op. cit.*) and p. 26 of this volume.

[8]As an example see the various writings of H. C. Dyer, S. Tomkins, R. H. Turner, S. L. Washburn, and M. Tumin (*in* Tumin, 1964, pp. 3-8).

We have employed the terms *Negro* and *colored* interchangeably and have occasionally used the expression *race* or *racial group* when referring to the Negro subjects examined. Probably all social psychologists have been alerted to the fact that the American Negro does not represent a pure racial group but rather one with a predominance of African ancestry[9] yet they frequently allude to American Negroes and whites as races. The justification for this lies, no doubt,[10] in the fact that except for small groups of transitional types, the American Negro constitutes a recognizable and clearly defined group, the criterion of membership in which group being that of more-or-less African ancestry.

The review comprises approximately 380 *original investigations* of Negro intelligence, included in 48 published monographs, books or sections of books, 203 published articles, 90 unpublished Master's theses, 35 unpublished Doctor's dissertations, and four other unpublished monographs; as well as 62 *reviews, interpretations, or research* pertaining to the topic, and 122 books, articles, and monographs dealing with *material related to the tests* used, their interpretation, and standardization.

Negroes living in the United States served as subjects in all but three of the studies; in these three, Canadian or British West Indian Negroes were tested. In addition to the hundreds of thousands of colored men tested in the Armed Forces, the 11,120 Negro adults examined in jails, prisons, reformatories, psychiatric clinics, shelters for homeless men, *etc.*, the literature includes researches made on more than 81,000 colored children, including those examined in special studies of selective migration, hybrids, retarded, and gifted, and on 48,200 Negro high school and college students. Enlisted men, officers, veterans, and other adults tested represent all states except Alaska and Hawaii. Children and students have been examined in all of the Southern states: Alabama, Arkansas, Florida, Georgia, Louisiana, Mississippi, North Carolina, South Carolina, Tennessee, Texas, and Virginia; in the Border states of Kentucky, Missouri, Maryland, Oklahoma, and West Virginia, as well as the District of Columbia; and in many of the Northern and Western states, such as: California, Colorado, Connecticut, Illinois, Indiana, Kansas, Massachusetts, Michigan, Minnesota, Nevada, New Jersey, New York, Ohio, Oregon, Pennsylvania, and Wisconsin. The research covers a period of approximately 50 years. Eighty psychometric tests, excluding different editions or forms of a given measure, each purporting to measure intelligence or some aspect of behavior related to it, were employed.

We have attempted to present the research in a systematic and relatively complete form in the tables. A critical reader will note the numbers of cases and the methods of selection used by the investigators in order to determine whether or not the specific groups studied may be considered to have been randomly selected and representative of larger ones. Wherever possible, pertinent

---

[9]South of the Sahara. A provisional estimate of the amount of accumulated white admixture in the American Negro population is 20 per cent. (D. F. Roberts *in* Garn, 1960, pp. 224-231)

[10]See Garrett (Science, 1945).

information about the home, school attended, and community was included. Without doubt, the Southern studies should be considered separately from the Northern, the rural from the urban, the older subjects from the younger, those who have achieved a high school or college education from those with some or no elementary education, those tested in recent years as compared with those examined during an earlier period, the delinquent and psychiatric cases from the normal, those subjects tested by verbal as compared with those tested by nonverbal tests, and those examined in groups as compared with those tested alone with the examiner. The reader should in every case distinguish the *results* from the *comments or conclusions of the authors* found in the tables or text, and likewise separate the results from the comments or analyses offered by the author of this volume (generally identified as *the reviewer,* or *present writer*). The results are objective, verifiable, and presumably accurate within the limitations of each research; the interpretations or comments are relatively subjective and must be held up to careful scrutiny.

The researches have been grouped into primary divisions according to *Subjects Examined:* (1) Young Children, primarily in Nursery Schools and Kindergartens; (2) Children in the Elementary Schools, on whom the great bulk of the testing has been done; (3) High School Students; (4) College Students; (5) Men in the Armed Forces—World War I, World War II, and the Post-Korean War; (6) Veterans and Other Civilians; (7) Gifted Deviates; (8) Retarded Deviates; (9) Delinquents; (10) Criminals; and (11) Racial Hybrids. In addition, there is a final division on Selective Migration, a problem particularly intriguing to psychologists.[11] In this division we have included studies of colored who have moved from rural areas and small towns to cities in the same region of the country (rural-urban migration) and those of colored who have migrated from one region to another (Southern-Border, or Southern-Northern migration).

The research examined has been compiled into 14 tables, three of which pertain to elementary school children. Within a given table we have usually been able to organize the material with reference to three items: the *test,* the *section of the country* where the research was conducted, and the *year* reported. Where one or very few investigators employed the same test, as in studies of deviates, delinquents and criminals, and the like, we have made no systematic attempt to classify the research according to *test* but only according to *section of the country* and *date.*

Where a number of researchers employed a given test (as in Tables I-VII) the test itself was made a heading in the table, with the studies located in the eleven Southern states first tabulated in chronological order, followed by studies in the Border states and the District of Columbia in chronological order, and

---

[11]See: Calvin *et al.* 1961, pp. 138-141; Geldard, 1962, pp. 318-320; Hilgard, 1962, pp. 440-444; Kendler, 1963, pp. 627-631; Kimble and Garmezy, 1963, pp. 124-129; Krech and Crutchfield, 1958, pp. 578-581; Lewis, 1963, pp. 71-74; Munn, 1961, pp. 177-179; Ruch, 1963, pp. 480-483; Sanford, 1965, pp. 201-203; Whittaker, 1965, pp. 474-475; Wickens and Meyer, 1961, pp. 449-452.

concluding with those conducted in the North and West. Where an author reported the results on more than one test or in more than one part of the country, the results of each were tabulated separately in its appropriate section.

The pattern of reporting pertinent research data within each division of Young Children, School Children, *etc.*, and followed wherever applicable throughout the tables is: (1) *Author* and *Date* of publication; or date of completion of an unpublished work; (2) *Location* of study, including name of city and state, or county and state if so given; the name of college, Army Camp, Induction Station, *etc.*; (3) *Subjects*, including number; age; grade in school, year in college, or highest grade completed; rank if in Armed Forces; and method by which they were selected; (4) *Results* of the research, usually presented in terms of medians or means, standard deviations, ranges, t-ratios, and percentages of overlapping. The overlap, unless otherwise indicated, is given in terms of the percentage of a given group of Negroes whose scores equaled or exceeded the median or mean of the whites with whom they were compared; and (5) *Comments of Author*. Under this rubric we have included no comments or interpretations of our own, the writer's comments being either placed in footnotes to the tables or in the text itself. Sometimes it was necessary for the writer to estimate the number of cases or to calculate measures of central tendency and variability, significance of differences between means, percentages of overlapping, and the percentages of gifted or inferior deviates. It was frequently necessary for her to calculate combined means and combined standard deviations. Whenever estimates or calculations were made by the writer some notation of the fact has been clearly indicated.

Chapter II

YOUNG CHILDREN

Comparative studies on the intelligence of Negro and white children of preschool age form a special group of investigations and will be reviewed separately from those on school children. Young children who have been given mental tests have typically been enrolled in day nurseries, in nursery schools, in kindergartens, or in summer schools; have been brought regularly to free clinics over a period of years; have been tested in order that their parents might start them to school before the age of six; have participated in a voluntary testing program in a first-grade preregistration period; and have been enrolled in school above the kindergarten level at the age of five. Therefore, these children may be considered to have been more highly selected than others of their age and socioeconomic background who were not tested.

In the seventeen studies on young children included in Table 1, the following tests have been utilized: *Stanford-Binet Scale, 1916; Stanford-Binet Scale, 1937, Forms L* and *M; Stanford-Binet Scale, 1960, Form L-M; Peabody Picture Vocabulary; Full-Scale Picture Vocabulary; Van Alystine Picture Vocabulary; Goodenough Draw-a-Man; Wechsler Intelligence Scale for Children; Lorge-Thorndike, Level 1;* and the *Merrill-Palmer Scale.*[1] We have omitted several comparisons of Negro and white children based upon the *Yale* or *Gesell Schedules,* the Buehler *Vienna Babytests,* and the *Northwestern* tests. The exclusion of these latter tests was due to the fact that infant tests are usually considered to be norms and inventories of development and behavior rather than mental tests, and to the fact that they are conspicuously nonpredictive.[2]

The ages of the children whose scores are included in Table 1 ranged from two to six years, the mode being at five years.

STANFORD-BINET, 1916

In its final revision, the *Stanford Revision of the Binet-Simon Tests, 1916 Form* contained 90 tests, 36 more than the *Binet Scale.* The reasons given for undertaking a revision of the *Binet* were that the original tests were too few and too difficult at the upper age levels and too easy at the lower levels, the directions for giving the tests were often inadequate, and many tests were misplaced in the scale. To be included in the *Stanford-Revision,* each test had to show an increase in the percentage of children passing it from one year to the next; furthermore,

---

[1] In this and in the immediately following chapters we have grouped the research according to the particular test employed; and, wherever possible, we have included some brief description of each measure with one or more evaluations in terms of its reliability and validity.

[2] See Freeman (1950, pp. 242-249), also Cronbach (1949, p. 170).

all of the children tested were divided into three groups on the basis of total score—those below 90 IQ, those 90 to 109 IQ, and those 110 IQ or higher—and each test was examined to see if it showed a decidedly higher per cent of passes from the inferior to the superior group and only those tests which met this criterion were considered adequate; finally, a high correlation between IQ and quality of school work was set up, school achievement and teachers' ratings being considered to be valuable indices of intellectual ability. The reliability of the *Stanford-Binet Scale* as measured by self-correlation was found to range usually from .80 to .95. (Garrett and Schneck, 1933, pp. 9-10)

In an early attempt to study the relation between intelligence and age in Negro children, Arlitt (1922) examined colored Ss from public schools near Philadelphia and from playgrounds and public and private schools in New Orleans. Combining the results from the two regions, Arlitt reported that the twenty-eight boys and the twenty-six girls of the five-and six-year age group earned median IQ's of 94.8 and 100.5, respectively, or about twenty points above that of the ten-to fifteen-year age group. She attributed the higher scoring of the five-and six-year group in part to the assumption that at these ages the brighter children found the playgrounds or were sent to school.[3]

Lacy (1926) presented the results of the *Stanford-Binet* given during a three-year period to Oklahoma City kindergarten children and to school children in Grades 1 to 3. The mean IQ of the 212 white kindergarten Ss was 103, that of the 113 Negro kindergarten Ss, 99. From the frequency distributions included in the author's data, the reviewer calculated the median IQ's of the 170 five-year-old white and the 89 five-year-old colored children. The medians of these respective groups of white and colored children were 110.8 and 102.1.[4]

Strachan (1926) similarly reported the results on the *Stanford-Binet* as administered to 10,688 white and 576 colored kindergarten children in Kansas City from 1921 to 1925. The median IQ's of these respective groups of white and colored Ss were 105.2 and 95.4. Strachan observed that the children were admitted to kindergarten at the age of five years, that kindergarten attendance was not required and therefore the Ss were not unselected.

STANFORD-BINET, 1937

The *Stanford-Binet Scale, 1937 Revision* has two equivalent forms, L and M, each of which contains 129 test items; the scale extends from the level of age two through three levels of *superior adult*. The levels below five years and above fourteen have been more carefully standardized, the scoring standards and instructions for administering the tests have been improved, there are more performance and other nonverbal materials at the lower age levels, *etc.* The test items were chosen on the basis of their validity, ease and objectivity of scoring, interest to the subjects, *etc.* Forms L and M were found to correlate from .90 to

---

[3]Since education was not compulsory until the age of 7.

[4]The 5-year-old groups included all Ss from 5-0 to 5-11 months.

.98 with one another. The highest reliability coefficients were found for IQ's below 70 (.98), the lowest for IQ's above 130 (.90). Age levels above six years showed greater reliability (.93) than those below six (.88). (Freeman, 1950, pp. 135-137)

Only American-born white subjects were used in the standardization of the 1937 scale, the total number being approximately 3000; Ss were chosen from eleven states in several widely separated areas of the country, and an effort was made to select them from homes which, occupationally and socially, would be representative of the general population. In the 1937 revision, a criterion of basic importance in judging validity of test items was the increase in percentage of successful performance with increasing age. Another criterion of importance in retention of an item was its correlation with the total scores of the individuals of the age level at which the test item is located. About 78 per cent of the 258 coefficients are .50 or higher. These and other data provide strong evidence that the *Stanford-Binet Scale* measures "general ability" by means of test items that have psychological processes in common to a high degree. (Freeman, 1962), pp. 211-214)

Tomlinson (1944) attempted to find and test with either *Form L* or *Form M* all pairs of Negro siblings living in Austin, Texas, provided one of each pair was between seven and nine years of age and the other was between four and six years. The pairs were located at the two selected age levels through examination of the school census records, the city, county, and state birth records, and through home interviews. From 115 pairs who qualified according to the school census, only 75 pairs were included in the study; the others could not be located, were not full siblings, were not living in the same household, *etc.* As a result, the author suggested that her group of 75 pairs may not have been completely representative of the 115. Of the 75 children between four and six years, 21 were having or had had some kind of school experience. The mean IQ of the four-to six-year group was 92.5, which was about six points higher than that earned by the seven-to nine group. Tomlinson tabulated the IQ's according to the ages of the Ss as follows: four—97.7; five—90.5; six—90.2; with the means of the seven-to nine group decreasing at each successive year. However, except between the four- and five-year-olds the individual means were found to be not statistically significant.

Allinger (1954) compared the performances on 16 items of the *Stanford-Binet* of forty-nine white five-year-old preschool children who had been matched in various ways, including IQ, with forty-nine colored five-year-olds. The matching followed a summer of testing 1225 children in Arlington County, Virginia, the parents of the children having written to request appointments in response to a public announcement through the newspaper. In the announcement, parents were informed that children who would not ordinarily be old enough to enter the first grade in September (birthday after September 30) might enter at five and one half years if they successfully fulfilled certain requirements of intellectual, physical, emotional, and social maturity. The forty-nine colored Ss comprised the total number of Negroes on whom the *Abbreviated Scale* had been completed; from an examination of the fathers' occupations it was estimated that they represented mainly the top 80 per cent rather than a more evenly distributed group of Negro five-year-olds.[5]

The forty-nine Negro children, who had had no kindergarten experience and whose mean IQ proved to be 95.88, were matched with a like number of white children for IQ, test form, age, sex, and absence of kindergarten experience. The whites were described as representing inferior genetic ability as compared with the average of the large group of whites from which they were chosen, since the mean IQ for the total group of whites was *112*. In addition, the matched group of whites was lower than the total white group with respect to their socioeconomic status. While the Negro group represented *lower* socioeconomic status than the white matched group, they appeared to be of *higher* status than the Arlington Negro population.

Analysis of the test performances showed that only in two items were the colored inferior to the matched white Ss: *count four* of *Form L* at the five-year level favored the white boys over the Negro boys, and *bead chain, Form M* (reproducing a pattern when completed bead chain is visible) favored the white group as a whole (p $<$.05). The author considered the differences in behavior on these two items to be due to a lack of purposefulness of the task; the Negro, especially the boy, is believed to be at a disadvantage if the task to be performed is not functional or purposeful.

Brown (1944) reported the mean IQ of 91 Minneapolis Negro kindergarten children to be 100.8 on *Form L*, in contrast to a mean of 107.1 obtained on a sample of 341 white kindergarten children in the same city. The difference between the means was significant at the .01 level. The white sample had been secured by determining the percentage of gainfully employed adults in each of six occupational levels in the city of Minneapolis and then selecting from Ss of Scandinavian ancestry those whose parents were proportionally represented at each of the six levels. Brown further determined the mean IQ's of the white samples at each of the six occupational categories[6] and compared them with the Negroes who were undifferentiated as far as occupation was concerned.[7] As will be observed in Table 1, the colored Ss *taken as a group* scored below the mean of each of the white groups with the exception of Group VI; the difference between the mean of white Group VI and the total colored mean was not significant. Brown observed that a theoretical resemblance between two social groups in terms of socioeconomic status as indicated by occupational rating scales does not necessarily demonstrate real equivalence in cultural drive, moti-

---

[5]Notifying parents through newspaper announcement and requiring requests for appointments be made in writing may have contributed to the selective factor, according to Allinger.

[6]Separated also according to sex groupings.

[7]Did not divide Negroes according to occupational categories; but separated the scores of the males and females.

vation, and aspirational level. He argued that one does not know whether
Negroes grouped in one category would be capable of attaining higher positions
in a free society or whether their positions represent "endowment-limited ceil-
ings". Brown noted that the average IQ of white children who were living in a
Negro neighborhood and attending the same school where most of his Negro Ss
were tested was 104, or just three points above the Negro mean. Moreover, a
comparison of percentiles for colored and white children attending the same
school revealed that the Negro mean IQ was at the 27th and the white mean at
the 35th percentile of the total Minneapolis kindergarten population.

From his results (see Table 1) Brown felt justified in making the following
assertion: *"Negro children at the kindergarten level in the Minneapolis Public
Schools are not inferior to White children of nominally similar socio-economic
status in general intellectual capacity as measured by the Stanford-Binet Scale,
Form L. Negro males compare favorably with White males of higher socioeconomic status than their own."* (p. 168)[8] In the opinion of the reviewer, the
first of the statements may be more nearly correct if the socioeconomic status of
the total group of Minneapolis Negroes was "nominally similar" to that of the
white Ss of the two lowest occupational groups.[9] But the total group of Negro Ss
included at least 14.5 per cent whose fathers were identified with Groups I-III
(professional to skilled labor). As to the second of the above statements, it seems
to the present writer to be misleading to say that Negro males *compare favorably*
with white males of a higher socioeconomic status, since the several white male
groups above the unskilled and slightly-skilled levels earned means of 104.5,
107.7, 115.0, and 114.6 in contrast to the Negro male mean of 103.0.[10]

Rhoads, Rapoport, Kennedy, and Stokes (1945) limited their samples of
Negro and white children to male infants brought to the free clinic at the
Philadelphia Children's Hospital. All of the children were from the three lowest
occupational groups. In return for free milk and vitamin supplements with
which the child was supplied for the first five years of his life, the mother was
required to bring the child to the clinic at regular intervals for various examinations, to receive visits from the nurse or social worker, and in general to cooperate
with the investigators. At three years of age, 113 white and 87 colored were
tested by *Form L,* the mean IQ's of the respective groups being 103.9 and 96.3.
The IQ's, which are higher than those usually found on white and Negro children
of the lower socioeconomic levels, may be attributed in part to some actual
selectivity that existed in the study. The mothers who could not or would not
cooperate were eliminated within the first two years and their children, therefore,
were not included in the mental testing.

The mean of the entire group of white children was significantly above that

---

[8]Brown's italics.

[9]In fact the author does make this qualified statement later (without italics) "The total
Negro group resembles the White semi- and unskilled labor class." (p. 174)

[10]Negro female mean was 98.0.

of the Negro Ss (see Table 1). The children were divided into groups according to the occupation of the father, the largest percentage of the whites falling in Group V and the largest percentage of the colored in Group VII; the mean IQ's of the Negro children in Groups V, VI, and VII were all below the respective groups of whites, the difference being significant only between the racial samples in Group VI. The authors found no relationship between mental development as measured by the IQ and dietary variations in the groups of children studied.

STANFORD-BINET, 1960

The 1960 Revision of the *Stanford-Binet Intelligence Scale* is based on materials and standardization of the 1937 Revision. The more satisfactory items of *Forms L* and *M* have been retained and combined into a single scale, *L-M.* Some items are more satisfactorily located as to age levels. An important innovation has been introduced, *i.e.,* the deviation IQ, a standard score derived theoretically from a mean of 100 and a standard deviation of 16. In addition, IQ tables have been extended to include chronological ages of 17 and 18 since retest findings have indicated that mental development as measured by the *Stanford-Binet* continues that long at least. (Freeman, 1963, pp. 211-238)

The items of the 1960 Revision consist primarily of opposite and direct analogies, comprehension, similarities and differences, vocabulary, verbal and pictorial completions, absurdities, memory of meaningful material and digits, and drawing designs. (Kennedy, Van De Riet, and White, 1963, p. 60)

In the fall of 1960, shortly after the publication of the 1960 Revision of the *Stanford-Binet,* Kennedy, Van De Riet, and White (1963) conducted a broad, normative study of Negro elementary school children in five Southeastern states. A sample of 1800 subjects, stratified according to age, grade, sex, socioeconomic status, and size of community, and randomized within these limits, was tested by a group of twelve examiners from the Human Development Clinic, of Florida State University. In addition to the *Binet,* the *California Achievement Test* and the *Goodenough Draw-a-Man Test* were administered. The children were enrolled in Grades 1 to 6 and ranged in age from five to sixteen years. However, due to the age distribution in the school population, there were 19 5-year-olds tested, 227 6-year-olds, 243 Age 7, 302 Age 8, ... , 30 Age 13, 9 Age 14, and one each at Ages 15 and 16, indicating the operation of some highly selective factors at different age levels, particularly at the extremes.

The mean IQ of the five-year-olds proved to be 86, approximately five points above the mean of the total group of 1800 Negroes. The variability, as determined by the standard deviation, was relatively small, *i.e.,* somewhat more than half that attributed to the entire group. As will be observed in Table 1, the intelligence quotients of the young colored children ranged from 75 to 99, none of the children quite equaling the mean of the standardization group and none being retarded.[11]

---

[11]See Chapter 3, pp. 41-42 for further discussion of this investigation.

Gray and Klaus (1963) have attempted to improve the intellectual function-ing and personal adjustment of culturally deprived children by obtaining special experiences for them in the 15 to 24 months preceding entrance to first grade. Their paper, referred to as an *interim report,* describes the project as it developed in the interval between May, 1962, and August, 1963. The authors selected about 60 per cent of all Negro children living in Murfreesboro, Tennes-see, who were born in 1958, the selection being based upon several criteria related to their homes and the education and occupation of their parents. From the 60-odd children selected as culturally deprived, three groups were formed: T_1, a group that received special training for 10 weeks in the summer of 1962 and 10 weeks in the summer of 1963, supplemented by weekly contacts with the home visitor in the intervening months; T_2, a group that received special training for 10 weeks in the summer of 1963; and T_3, a control group that received no special training. A second control group of 27 Negro children, T_4, born in 1958 and living in Columbia, Tennessee, composed the final group. All subjects were tested four times by *Form L-M* of the *Stanford-Binet* and by either *Form A* or *Form B* of the *Peabody Picture Vocabulary Test.* The four test-ings took place in May, 1962, August, 1962, May, 1963, and August, 1963, the last examination immediately following the summer training programs in which T_1 and T_2 participated.

The ten-week summer schools centered around (1) increasing the child's *achievement motivation,* which involved attempting to get the child to compete, to improve his performance, to persist longer in an activity, to delay gratification, to be interested in school-type activities, and to identify with achieving adults or children, as well as increasing the parents' interest in the child's school achievements; and (2) developing *aptitudes for achievement,* the work of the school being directed toward developing an understanding of the simple and basic concepts needed in schoolwork, toward increasing the child's perceptual discrimination, and toward language development.

The summer school programs differed from the usual preschool program, not so much in the materials and equipment provided for the children, but rather in the high ratio of adults to children (one to every four or five), in the generally superior education of the staff members and their apparent interest in (or even dedication to) the project, and in the fact that the adults were about equally divided as to sex and race. The *uses* made of the equipment and the *amount of time* the children were allowed to devote to the several kinds of materials also distinguished this experimental program from that of the usual nursery school. The authors indicate that the program required the children (T_1 and T_2) to spend a great deal of time with one-inch colored blocks and that these blocks were used for many counting activities and the development of color, size, direction, and other concepts.

The home visitor contacts were intended to provide continuity with the summer sessions. The visitor spent nearly an hour each week with every T_1

child and his mother, bringing supplies such as counting books, picture dictionaries, crayons, and the like, and showing the mother and child together how to make use of them. At this time the mother was given suggestions regarding certain activities that she should carry out with the child and each month was presented with a new copy of *Ebony* which was examined and discussed with her. In addition to these visits, the children met for three hours once a month with the directors and teaching staff in order that those patterns developed in the preceding summer might be reinforced.

As will be observed from Table 1, the two groups who received the special training program (T_1 and T_2) gained from 5 to 10 points between the first and fourth *Stanford-Binet testings;* the control groups (T_3 and T_4) lost from 2.5 to 4 points between these testings. It will also be noted that the group which had had twenty weeks of summer school supplemented by supervised work during the academic year made a larger gain than the group which had had but ten weeks of summer instruction. The mean gains in mental age on the *Peabody Picture Vocabulary Test* proved likewise to have been significantly greater for the experimental than the control groups from May, 1962, to August, 1963.

How permanent the gains of the experimental groups may eventually prove to be, to what extent the intensive summer training programs involved elements of test coaching, to what extent the repeated testings with the same measure may have affected test scores (the same form of the *S-B* being used throughout), and to what extent examiner bias was eliminated may be subject for conjecture. As regards the last item, it would seem that a competent mental examiner in the course of testing would very soon know whether a child belonged to the control group in Murfreesboro or to one of the special training groups in this city. The authors have indicated that experiences during the summer with eight different adults (apart from those at home) probably increased the ease with which the experimental groups of children related to a strange situation. No mention was made of the place of testing, but if it was the school building where the summer programs were held, the greater ease of the T_1 and T_2 groups would most certainly have identified them. In any event, the authors felt that the results could not be fully evaluated at the time of the interim report and the reviewer subscribes to this opinion.

WISC, PEABODY AND FULL-RANGE PICTURE VOCABULARIES

The *Wechsler Intelligence Scale for Children,* a downward extension of the *Wechsler-Bellevue,* is designed for children from ages five to fifteen, and consists of twelve subtests yielding three scores: Verbal, Performance, and Total. The test was standardized on 2200 white boys and girls of wide geographic distribution and was carefully administered and fully reported. However, evidences of the validity of the test as a whole, its subtests, or its items, are missing from the manual. The value of the test for predicting common-sense criteria such as school progress or other evidences of adjustment remains to be established. With

AUTHOR DATE	LOCATION	N	SUBJECTS AGE	GRADE	METHOD OF SELECTION
					STANFORD-BINET
Arlitt,[1] A. H. (1922)	New Orleans, La., and near Philadelphia, Pa.	c- 54	5-6		From NO playgrounds and publ & private schs. From Pa publ schs.
Lacy,[2] L. D. (1926)	Oklahoma City, Okla.	w-212 c- 113	5-6 5-6	Kg Kg	All children entering kindergarten.
Strachan,[2] L. (1926)	Kansas City, Mo.	w-10,688 c-　576		Kg Kg	All kg children tested if present during periods of test administration.
					STANFORD-BINET, 1937
Tomlinson,[3] H. (1944)	Austin, Tex.	c- 75	4-6		All available pairs of c siblings at 2 age ranges, 4-6 & 7-9.
Allinger, D. A. (1954)	Arlington County, Virginia	w-49 c- 49	5 5		Preschool testing program to 1225 Ss including 49 c about 5½ years; testing appointments made at request of parents. If S met various test requirements he was allowed to begin sch before age 6; 49 w were selected to match the c, the 2 groups equated for age, IQ, test form, sex, & no-kg experience.
Brown, F. (1944)	Minneapolis, Minn.	w-341 c- 91		Kg Kg	Selection of w Ss based on percentage of gainfully employed adults in city, acc to Goodenough-Anderson Scale of Occupations. Method of c selection not given. Children tested by teachers.

[1]For results on older children, see Table 2.
[2]For results on children above the kindergarten level, see Table 2.
[3]A study of 75 pairs of c siblings, the younger one of each pair being included in table; for results on the older of each pair, see Table 2.

ONE

CHILDREN

RESULTS	COMMENTS OF AUTHOR

1916 FORM

	IQ		The brighter 5-6 year-olds may find playgrounds or be sent to school. Education compulsory at 7 years.
	c Girls	c Boys	
Mdn	100.5	94.8	
Range	70-129	80-119	

	IQ		Results substantiate theory that mental growth of c is slower than that of w child.
	w	c	
M	103	99	

	IQ		Children admitted to kg at age of 5; not compulsory, therefore groups not unselected.
	w	c	
Mdn	105.2	95.4	

FORMS L AND M

	IQ	Small appreciable relation bet c child's intelligence and character of home; r of .20 bet Sims score and IQ.
	c	
M	92.5	
s	10.2	
Range	65-124	

	IQ		Evidence that Negro group represented a somewhat higher socioeco group than c pop of Arlington Co. Matched w group of higher status than the c but lower than the w pop. Mean IQ of matched groups about 16 points below that of total w tested.
	w	c	
	Matched		
M	95.88	95.88	
s	9.46	9.78	
	Total		
M	112	95.88	

	IQ[4]		Apparent deterioration of c IQ may be the hemming in of intellectual development and efficiency strongly suggesting operation of constrictive factor in Negro intellectual development.
	w	c	
M	107.1	100.8	
s	13.1	12.9	
t =		4.13	

	M IQ		
Occup	w		w
	Girls		Boys
I	109.0		114.6
II	113.7		115.0
III	110.2		107.7
V	106.2		104.5
VI	96.5		101.8
VII	105.4		101.2

[4]Brown breaks down total w (but not the c) according to the occupational level of parents (I-highest, VII-lowest), and compares various mean IQ's with that of the total c group. At least 64% of c parents were in semiskilled labor and below.

TABLE

YOUNG

AUTHOR DATE	LOCATION	N	SUBJECTS		METHOD OF SELECTION
			AGE	GRADE	
Rhoads, T. F., Rapoport, M., Kennedy, R., and Stokes, J., Jr. (1945)	Philadelphia, Pa.	w-113 c- 87	3 3		All children had been brought to free clinic regularly from birth; only males who weighed 5 or more lbs at birth & had no breast feeding were included. All given free milk & vitamin supplements.

STANFORD-BINET, 1960

AUTHOR DATE	LOCATION	N	SUBJECTS		METHOD OF SELECTION
			AGE	GRADE	
Kennedy,[5] W. A., Van De Riet, V., and White, J. C., Jr. (1962, 1963)	Alabama, Florida, Georgia, South Carolina, Tennessee	c- 19	5	Above kg	Part of normative study of c grade-sch pupils; 15 counties chosen as representative, 3 from each state. From total of 1800 Ss selected by stratified random sampling, only 19 were 5 years old.
Gray, S. W., and Klaus, R. A. (1963)	Murfreesboro, Tenn. Columbia, Tenn.	c- T_1-22 T_2-20-22[7] T_3-20-22 c- T_4-27	3.8 3.8 3.9 3.8		Approx 62 c children, comprising the more deprived 60% of colored born in M in '58, were placed in 3 groups by random selection: T_1 rec'd 2 summers of special training & 1 winter of home visitor contacts; T_2 rec'd 1 summer of spec training; T_3, a control group, given no special training. T_4, an additional control group of 27 Ss in C, also born in '58.

PEABODY PICTURE

AUTHOR DATE	LOCATION	N	SUBJECTS		METHOD OF SELECTION
			AGE	GRADE	
Gray, S. W., and Klaus, R. A. (1963)	Murfreesboro and Columbia, Tenn.	See above.			See above.

[5]For results on older children, see Table 2.

[6]This comment is part of authors' Summary and Conclusions, applying to the total group tested, not specifically to the 5-year-olds.

[7]Authors indicated that 22 children were included in T_1, 27 in T_4, and approximately 60 in T_1-T_3 with bet 20 and 22 in each group. The ages listed refer to the average age at the initial testing.

ONE *(continued)*

CHILDREN

	RESULTS			COMMENTS OF AUTHOR
		IQ		All Ss from the three lowest occup groups. Mean IQ of w higher than c for each group. More of w in semiskilled, more of c in day-labor group.
	w		c	
M	103.9		96.3	
s	14.9		15.0	
t =		3.62		

FORM L-M

	IQ	Analysis of item difficulty and a biserial correlation item analysis of data showed that, in general, the abstract verbal items appear at too low a level in the test.[6]
	c	
M	86.00	
s	6.40	
Range	75-99	

	IQ[8]		The culturally deprived child appears to pose some major problems of adequate testing, centering in *rapport*, in use of appropriate language, and in need for sufficient time in which to respond.
Group	c	c	
	1st Testing	4th Testing	
	May '62	Aug '63	
T_1	85.6	95.7	
T_2	91.2	96.3	
T_3	87.4	83.4	
T_4	88.0	85.5	

T_1 & T_2 showed sig greater gains from 1st to 4th testing than did T_3 or T_4.

VOCABULARY

	MA[9]	
Group	c	c
	1st Testing	4th Testing
	May '62	Aug '63
T_1	29.8	45.0
T_2	30.3	50.6
T_3	28.3	38.4
T_4	32.2	38.6

T_1 & T_2 showed sig greater gains from 1st to 4th testing than did T_3 & T_4.

[8]Reviewer has omitted results of second and third testings (Aug, 1962, and May, 1963). In Aug '64 (5th of successive *S-B* testings) after T_1 had received 3 summers of special training and 2 winters of home visitor contacts and T_2 had received 2 summers of special training and one winter of home contacts, the respective mean IQ's obtained on T_1 and T_2 were 95 and 96. In Aug '64 the mean IQ's of the two control groups, T_3 and T_4, were respectively 83 and 82 (Gray and Klaus, 1964).

[9]A normal increase in MA between May '62 and Aug '63 would be 15.

TABLE

YOUNG

AUTHOR DATE	LOCATION	N	SUBJECTS AGE	GRADE	METHOD OF SELECTION
Osborne,[10] R. T. (1965)	Georgia	w-56 c- 50	5-6 5-6		From one c & one w sch in each of 3 counties. During preregistration period in May & June '61 children who were to enter 1st grade in fall were tested if available and parents permitted.

AMMONS FULL-RANGE

| Osborne,[10] R. T. (1965) | Georgia | w-56 c- 50 | 5-6 5-6 | | See above. |

WECHSLER INTELLIGENCE

| Semler, I. J., and Iscoe, I. (1963) | Austin, Tex. | w-26 c- 26 | 5 5 | Nursery- kg | All in private schs. Ss randomly selected from sch lists. Intelligence testing incidental to study of learning. |
| Osborne,[10] R. T. (1965) | Georgia | w-56 c- 50 | 5-6 5-6 | | From one c & one w sch in each of 3 counties. During preregistration period in May & June, '61, children who were to enter 1st grade in fall were tested if available and parents permitted. |

VAN ALYSTINE

| Moore, J. E. (1942) | Tennessee and Kentucky | w-82 c- 78 | 2-6 2-6 | | White from 5, c from 4 private, publ, and WPA nursery schs & kindergartens. |

[10]This study forms part of a longitudinal research project and has not yet been published. Data secured from personal communication with author.

ONE *(continued)*

CHILDREN

	RESULTS		COMMENTS OF AUTHOR
		IQ	One county was identified as large and industrial, one as of medium size and industrial, and one as rural.
	w	c	
Mdn	107.7	88.5	

PICTURE VOCABULARY

		IQ	The same children were administered 3 tests: *Peabody Picture Vocab, Ammons Full-Range,* and the *WISC.*
	w	c	
Mdn	118.0	106.0	

SCALE FOR CHILDREN

		IQ[11]	It seems improbable that intellectual differences alone could explain superior learning of young white Ss. Some consideration is due, therefore, for environmental factors.
	w	c	
M	110.5	82.9	

		Mdn		The same children were administered 3 tests: *Peabody Picture Vocabulary, Ammons Full-Scale Vocabulary,* and the *WISC.* Author generally able to secure cooperation of parents. The median subtest scores are scaled scores.
Subtest	w	*Scores*	c	
Infor	10.3		7.4	
Compr	12.6		10.2	
Dig Sp	10.2		6.9	
Arith	10.7		7.7	
Simil	10.7		9.7	
Vocab	11.9		7.1	
Pic Arr	9.6		6.8	
Pic Com	11.3		7.5	
Block D	10.1		6.6	
Obj Ass	10.3		7.4	
Coding	10.3		7.4	
		IQ		
Verbal	109.5		90.0	
Perform	103.5		85.0	
Full Sc	108.5		87.0	

PICTURE VOCABULARY

Increase in vocab appears slower for c
Growth curve of c flattens
more at upper ages

Eco condition of both c and w ranged from very poor to well-to-do. Test reflects cultural advantages and favors w more than *Eye-Hand Coordination* test.

[11]For results on school children, see Table 2.

TABLE

YOUNG

| AUTHOR DATE | LOCATION | N | SUBJECTS | | METHOD OF SELECTION |
			AGE	GRADE	
					DRAW-A-
Lindner, R. S. (1962)	Alabama, Florida, Georgia, South Carolina, Tennessee	c- 19[12]	5	Above kg	Stratified random sampl from publ schs of 5 states. In each state 3 county systems selected, 1 metrop, 1 urban, 1 rural. Only 19 of 1800 tested, Grades 1-6, were 5 years of age.
D'Angelo, R. Y. (1950)	New York, N. Y.	w-50 c- 50	5 5		From 11 Dept of Welfare day nurseries in mixed and unmixed neighborhoods. Ss within 6 mo of 5th birthday. Day nursery directors provided the Ss, 25 girls & 25 boys from each racial group.
Vane, J. R., and Kessler, R. T. (1964)	New York State	w-44[13] c- 68		Kg	All kg children in 5 NY publ schs in state administered the test. Children retested at 12-month intervals in first, sec, & third grades; only 112 of the original 280 tested 4 times.
					LORGE-THORNDIKE
Katzenmeyer, W. G. (1962)	Jackson, Mich.	w-1061 c- 193	5-3[14] 5-3	Kg Kg	During falls of '57 & '58 test given to all entering kg children of the 16 publ schs; 2 yrs later all Ss in 2nd-grade rooms of these schs were retested with Level 2 of *L-T*. Number of cases includes all Ss present at both testings.
					MERRILL-PALMER
Horton, C. P., and Crump, E. P. (1962)	Nashville, Tenn.	c- 76	3		Children included represent larger group studied from birth to 5 yrs who were brought for 36-months evaluation in 33-month period and whose scores on *M-P* were considered either *superior* or *inferior* according to test norms.

[12]These Ss were also tested on *Form L-M* of *Stanford-Binet* (Kennedy, Van De Riet, and White). For results on older children tested by *Draw-a-Man*, see Table 3.

[13]These numbers deducted by reviewer from information given by authors; they give 112 as total number, 104.1 as the kg mean of the whole group, and 113.0 and 98.4 as the respective

ONE *(concluded)*

CHILDREN

	RESULTS		COMMENTS OF AUTHOR

MAN

	IQ		Test scores, both IQ and MA, decreased con-
	c		sistently when compared by age and also by grade
M	99.3		with Goodenough's means.
s	24.6		

		IQ		No significant race diff in mean IQ. Over-all race
	w		c	diff in mean sentence length slight and insig but
M				favored whites. "Mature" sentence types more
Total	101.8		101.0	frequent among w Ss.
	Mixed			(Anastasi & D'Angelo, 1952)
Boys	97.07		94.29	
Girls	107.60		107.00	
	Unmixed			
Boys	101.45		100.18	
Girls	104.36		100.36	

		IQ		Negro children showed less decline than the w
	w		c	children from kg to 3rd grade. Greater decline
M	113.0		98.4	of w attributed to the narrow range of test which
				makes it difficult for a bright child to maintain a
				high IQ as he increases in age.

LEVEL 1

		IQ[15]		Colored pupils were distributed throughout 11 of
	w		c	the 16 schools, in proportions ranging up to 65
M	102.04		83.06	per cent.
s	13.71		12.28	
t =		19.37		

SCALE

	Distribution of Scores		Racial origin alone is not enough to allow general-
	M-P		izations about children's test performances.
Rating	Norms	c	
Very sup	5%	2.4%	
Superior	15%	2.4%	
Inferior	15%	27.8%	
Very inf	5%	3.8%	

means of the white and colored Ss. Therefore the group must have been divided into 44 c and 68 w.

[14]Median age at entering kindergarten.
[15]For results on Level 2, see Table 3; *t* calculated by reviewer.

its Verbal and Performance IQ's obtainable from one scale and with its interesting possibilities of subtest analysis it will be evaluated by many studies. (Shaffer, *in Buros*, 1953, p. 363)

Wechsler's definition of intelligence is broad enough to include in its measurement any item which is judged to tap a child's capacity "to act purposefully, to think rationally, and to deal effectively with his environment". (Littell, 1960)

The Full Scale, the Verbal, and the Performance IQ's appear to be sufficiently reliable for most testing purposes as indicated by split-half reliability coefficients computed within the 7½-, 10½-, and 13½-year samples; the Full Scale coefficients for the three age levels being, respectively: .92, .95, and .94, the Verbal Scale coefficients being: .88, .96, and .96, and the Performance Scale coefficients being: .86, .89, and .90. Very little evidence relating to the validity of the *WISC* has been reported in the *manual* or elsewhere, and this lack of data remains its principal weakness. (Anastasi, 1961, pp. 315-320)

Semler and Iscoe (1963) employed the *WISC* in their study of the learning abilities of Negro and white children. Using four different experimental conditions: 1) Similar-Concrete, 2) Similar-Abstract, 3) Dissimilar-Concrete, and 4) Dissimilar-Abstract, six pairs of objects were presented in sequence at regular intervals but in a randomized order of pair presentation. When the six pairs of *actual objects* (such as *banana-toothbrush, cup-toy truck*) were presented, the task was designated as *concrete* learning. When *colored photographs* of these same objects were used instead of the objects themselves, but also presented as were the object pairs, the task was one referred to as *abstract* learning. Pairs that were considered by the authors to have high associative value by virtue of conceptual or functional similarity (such as *cup-bowl, banana-orange*) comprised the *similar* category; while other combinations (such as *doll-cigar, glove-bowl*) formed the *dissimilar* task.

All of the subjects were enrolled in the public schools and private nurseries or nursery schools (sometimes referred to as kindergartens) in Austin, Texas, and were between five and nine years of age,—the five-year-olds being in the private schools, since public school kindergartens *per se* did not exist in Austin at this time. The Negro five-year-olds were taken from a setting run by a church with over 120 children ranging in age from three to six years. The majority of them were attending the nursery because their mothers were employed, the children being cared for all day "in less than adequate circumstances". On the other hand, the white children were not generally the offspring of working mothers, the children were given some informal school training, and the plant and staff facilities were described as excellent. The "school" and home environments of the young colored children, therefore, may be presumed to have been less stimulating to learning than those of the white children of this age.

The subjects were randomly selected by age from lists furnished by the schools. Each child was administered the *WISC* by a trained examiner. Approximately a week later, each S was given the paired-associates learning task after having been randomly assigned to one of the experimental conditions. As will be noted in Table 1, the mean *WISC* Full Scale IQ of the white children was 110.5, that of the colored, 82.9, a difference of 27.6 points separating the racial means. Neither frequency distributions nor measures of variability were included in the data for the five-year-olds; however, a proportional analysis of variance of *WISC* Full Scale for 120 of the subjects (60 white and 60 colored) included 12 whites and 12 Negroes at the five-year-level. A highly significant difference in mean IQ in favor of the white Ss was indicated, the difference being most pronounced at the five-year level.

The young Negro children had more difficulty than the young white Ss in learning new paired associates, particularly when cues were reduced by using photographs rather than actual objects. ". . . . in view of the decreasing difference between races in learning ability across age levels, and in spite of continuing significant differences in intelligence, and the low correlations between IQ and total learning score, it seems improbable that intellectual differences alone could explain the superior learning of the young white subjects." (Semler and Iscoe, p. 42)

As a part of a long-range study of mental growth and school achievement, Osborne (1965) obtained test data on 56 white and 50 colored preschool children living in three Georgia counties. The subjects were among those boys and girls who were preregistered on certain days in May and June, 1961, in anticipation of their entering the first grade the following fall. The author had selected one colored and one white school from a large industrial county, a smaller industrial county, and a rural county, the schools drawing from areas or neighborhoods which were considered to be average or racially representative. During the pre-registration period, Osborne supervised the administration of three mental tests to children who were available and *whose parents were willing for them to be tested*. At this time there were no public kindergartens in these areas and none of the children tested had had preschool training.

The *Peabody Picture Vocabulary* and the *Full-Range Picture Vocabulary* were administered to all 106 Ss in conjunction with the *WISC*. On the *Peabody*, the colored averaged 88.5 IQ and the whites 107.7 IQ—which were very close to their *WISC Full Scale* medians of 87.0 and 108.5, respectively. However, on the *Full-Range* test (see pp. 72-73 for comments on this test) the median IQ of the Negro children was 106 and that of the whites, 118. The Negro median on the *Full-range* is puzzling in view of its being between 17 and 18 points higher than that earned by those children on the *Peabody Picture Vocabulary* and in view of the poor showing these children made on the *WISC* Vocabulary subtest.

As will be noted from Table 1, both the white and colored children earned higher Verbal than Performance IQ's on *WISC*, the respective medians of the white subjects being 109.5 and 103.5, the corresponding medians of the colored being 90.0 and 85.0. It is interesting that the colored Ss scored their worst on

Block Design (followed by Picture Arrangement, Digit Span, and Vocabulary) and their best on *Comprehension* (followed by Similarities) since it has been consistently reported that colored school children have also found the *Block Design* to be among the most difficult and the *Comprehension* to be among the easiest of the *WISC*.

Van Alystine Picture Vocabulary

The *Van Alystine Picture Vocabulary Test for Preschool Children* consists of forty-five cards on each of which are four pictures of objects or of experiences common to small children. A child is asked to show the examiner a certain object on each card. No verbalizing is necessary as the child is merely asked to point to the desired object. The score is the number of cards on which the test object is correctly identified. According to R. W. Washburn, the test was standardized on a small group of eighty subjects whose age range was between 33 and 39 months and whose average IQ was high and cultural background similar, making the test of improbable value for other cultural groups. (*in* Buros, 1949, p. 296)

Moore (1942) administered this test to 82 white and 78 colored children between the ages of two and six years who were attending nine private, public, and WPA nursery schools and kindergartens of Tennessee and Kentucky. The background and economic condition of the children was described as ranging all the way from the very poor to the well-to-do. Moore reported the white children to be superior to the colored in eight of the nine age groups compared, the growth curves for word knowledge being very similar in shape and trend.[12] However, the vocabulary curve for the Negro Ss flattened out markedly at the upper age groups. Moore was of the opinion that the white children may have had an earlier advantage of picture books, blocks, and more attention from the parents, resulting in stimulating development of better vocabularies.[13]

Draw-a-Man

The *Goodenough Draw-a-Man Test,* intended for ages from three and one half to thirteen and one half years, presumes to measure a child's mental development in terms of his keenness of observation and his ability to select certain significant items from his environment. The child is asked to make the very best picture of a man that he can, the scoring depending on the presence of certain items, such as legs, nose, *etc.,* and not on art quality. The points emphasized in scoring were chosen because they show a regular increase with age, and differentiate between children of the same age but in different school grades. In general, the test does not correlate highly with other intelligence tests; in one study the correlation with *Stanford-Binet, 1937 Revision* IQ's was .45. Reliability, as determined by odd-even, retest, and rescoring techniques, ranges from .77 to

---

[12]Each age group included a six-months range.

[13]Author regretted that he did not check on the possession of blocks, books, *etc.,* or visit the children's homes.

.94. (Mursell, 1949, p. 174) Lindner (1962) surveyed five studies in which *Draw-a-Man* scores had been correlated with *WISC* or with the 1916, 1937, or 1960 Revision of the *Stanford-Binet*, and found the validity coefficients to range between .41 and .80; he pointed out that they are not significantly different from correlations obtained when other tests of intelligence are validated against the *Stanford-Binet*.

As was indicated,[14] the *Goodenough Draw-a-Man* was administered to some 1800 Negro children in the Southeastern United States in conjunction with *Form L-M* of the *Stanford-Binet* and the *California Achievement Test*. (Lindner, 1962) Included in this normative survey of public elementary school children in the five states of Alabama, Florida, Georgia, South Carolina, and Tennessee were 19 five-year-old children. As will be seen in Table 1, the same children who earned a mean IQ of 86 on the *Stanford-Binet* achieved a mean of 99.3 on the *Draw-a-Man*. The *Draw-a-Man* mean of the five-year-olds compares favorably with that of the total Negro sample which was 91.22, the advantage being due in part to the selective factors operating in the admission of five-year-olds to grade school above the kindergarten level.[15] Although Lindner did not tabulate IQ frequency distributions by age, it is evident from the size of the standard deviation (24.6) that the children were much more variable in their *Draw-a-Man* performance than they were on the *Stanford-Binet* where the s was found to be 6.40.

D'Angelo (1950) investigated the language development of 50 white and 50 colored preschool children and compared the results with those obtained on the *Draw-a-Man* test. All of the children were in attendance in eleven Department of Welfare day nurseries, five of them located in unmixed neighborhoods and six in mixed neighborhoods, all in the New York City Boroughs of Manhattan, Bronx, Brooklyn, and Queens. Only those children whose parents met the requirements of the Department as to financial status were accepted in the Centers, resulting in the children for the most part belonging to occupational groups ranging from *clerical* to *unskilled labor*. The median occupational level of the white and colored parents was very close to the *semiskilled and minor clerical,* and the education completed by both mothers and fathers was between eleven and twelve years.[16]

In order to be included as subjects the children had to be within six months of their fifth birthday and come from homes where no foreign language was spoken. "The day nursery directors were therefore asked to provide as subjects only children from uni-lingual homes." (D'Angelo, p. 12)[17]

---

[14]See Kennedy, Van De Riet, and White, pp. 11 and 41-42 of this book.

[15]Although the authors do not specify the grade, it may be presumed that all of the 5-year-olds were enrolled in the first grade and not a higher one.

[16]Based upon an over-all return of 70 per cent to a questionnaire submitted to the mothers. (Anastasi and D'Angelo, 1952)

[17]". . . . . since the Supervisors of the Day Care Centers had been asked to select for this study only children from unilingual homes." (Anastasi and D'Angelo, p. 153)

Language development was studied by recording and subsequently analyzing samples of spontaneous conversation of the children. From her records, D'Angelo reported that "mature" sentence types including simple complete sentences, simple sentences with phrases, compound sentences, and elaborated sentences, tended to occur more often among white children; "immature" sentence types, including incomplete sentences and functionally complete but structurally incomplete sentences, were more frequent among the Negro children.

On *Draw-a-Man* the white and colored children scored about the same, with the girls averaging higher than the boys of their race; however, the sex differences were significant or nearly significant only in the mixed neighborhoods, while they were small or negligible in the unmixed areas (Table 1). In the previous edition of this book the writer commented as follows upon the mean *Draw-a-Man* IQ's earned by the white and colored Ss: "Unfortunately these results permit no generalization due to (1) the fact that the *directors of the nurseries were asked to provide the Ss* for testing and (2) the fact that the author does not indicate how many children in each nursery would have qualified, had she decided to test all who were within 6 months of 5 years and who heard nothing but English spoken at home." (Shuey, 1958, p. 16)

Anastasi took exception to the above statement and replied as follows: "In actual fact, *all* children who met these two requirements were tested, the nursery directors merely providing the names of those who fulfilled these specifications." (*in* Buros, 1959, p. 1162) The present writer merely wishes to point out that if *all who qualified were tested, i.e.,* all children who were within six months of their fifth birthday and unilingual, it was indeed unusual to have secured as subjects 25 white boys, 25 white girls, 25 colored boys, and 25 colored girls, and in addition to find that in each racial group 25 were living in a mixed neighborhood and 25 in an unmixed neighborhood.

In her review (*in* Buros, *op. cit.*) Anastasi also objected to the writer's not referring to the Anastasi-D'Angelo article of 1952 which "covered more cases and provided more refined statistical analyses" than the original unpublished thesis of D'Angelo. While the reviewer agrees that in the article the statistical analyses employed were more refined as well as more comprehensive, in view of the fact of there being no racial difference between the mean IQ's, in view of the fact that this book is primarily concerned with Negro-white differences rather than sex differences, and in view of the fact that the method of selection seemed unclear, the article was omitted, with no intent to "create misleading impressions." In re-examining the 1952 article, we find no evidence of a coverage of *more cases* than in the thesis report. "The subjects included 25 Negroes and 25 whites living in uni-racial, unmixed neighborhoods, and 25 Negroes and 25 whites living in inter-racial, mixed neighborhoods." (Anastasi and D'Angelo, p. 163)

In an attempt to determine its reliability and validity, Vane and Kessler (1964) administered the *Draw-a-Man* to 280 kindergarten children "in five New

York State public schools". Twelve months later the test was administered again to all of these children who were in the first grade, and after another twelve months to them in the second grade, *etc.,* until the same children had been tested four times, the last being in the third grade. The IQ's of 112 select Ss comprised the data upon which the report is based,[18] comparisons between colored and white children being made only at the kindergarten and Grade 3 levels. At the lower level the mean IQ of the white children was 113.0 as compared with 98.4 for the colored; whereas, at the third grade the mean of the white children dropped to 105.3 I.Q., the mean of the colored Ss to 95.8. In other words, at the kindergarten level the white pupils scored 15.4 IQ points above the colored, but by the time they were in the third grade the difference between the means of the racial samples dropped to 9.5 points. Vane and Kessler attributed the greater decline on the part of the white subjects to the nature of the test, the narrow range of which makes it difficult for a bright child to maintain a high IQ as he increases in age.

Instead of requesting the child to *draw a man,* Machover (1953) developed a projective test requiring him to *draw a person,* and afterward to draw a person of the opposite sex. Completion of the drawings is followed by an inquiry in which S is asked to tell a story about each person he has drawn. In a preliminary report, Machover compared some drawings of Negro and white five-year-olds in New York City kindergartens, the whites (primarily Jewish) being "somewhat accelerated" in IQ ratings, and the colored, "slightly retarded". The drawings of the Negro children were described as in many ways like those of *younger white children;* the colored appeared confused by the task, unable to fix a spot on the drawing sheet, and finally produced drawings more like centipedes than persons. She brought up the question as to whether cultural deprivations and the disordered family constellation of the Negro home are chiefly responsible for this apparent retardation in self-development.

LORGE-THORNDIKE INTELLIGENCE TESTS

The Lorge-Thorndike Intelligence Tests are nonverbal in the two lowest levels. The authors' position is that both verbal and nonverbal types of materials test "abstract intelligence" defined as "ability to work with ideas and relationships among ideas". Authors state that the following mental processes are descriptive of intelligent behavior and sampled by their tests: (a) dealing with abstract and general concepts, (b) interpretation and use of symbols, (c) dealing with relationships among concepts and symbols, (d) flexibility in the organization of concepts and symbols, (e) utilizing one's experience in new patterns, and (f) utilizing "power" rather than speed in working with abstract materials. (F. S. Freeman *in* Buros, 1959, pp. 479-481)

---

[18]*Select* in that they were all kindergarten Ss, remained in the school system for years (were not children of transients), were not absent during any of the testing days, and received yearly promotions.

The standardization population consisted of 136,000 children in 44 communities in 22 states, the communities being selected on the basis of a composite of factors that have been found to be related to tested intelligence, including: per cent of adult illiteracy, number of professional workers per 1000 in population, per cent of home ownership, and median home rental value. With few exceptions, all pupils enrolled in kindergarten through high school were tested in each community. The composite distribution of scores from this representative sample population was used in determining the IQ equivalent for each age group in terms of deviation IQ. The authors followed the practice of assuming a mean IQ of 100 and a standard deviation of 16. Alternate forms of the test correlate between .76 and .90, the coefficients being the more significant since they were computed on the population of a single grade. Except at *Level 2,* the odd-even reliabilities are high, from .88 to .94. Standard errors of measurement in terms of IQ points are given in the manual as an additional and desirable estimate of the tests' reliabilities. The major deficiency appears to be the lack of adequate data on predictive and concurrent validity. On the whole the *Lorge-Thorndike* tests are among the sounder group instruments available, from the point of view of psychological insights shown in selecting and developing materials and from the point of view of statistical analysis of the standardization data. (Freeman, *op. cit.*)

In order to explore the culturally learned aspects of intelligence, Katzenmeyer (1962) tested the hypothesis that there would be no change in the measured intelligence of Negro pupils relative to white pupils over the first two years in a racially mixed program which served to enhance opportunities for social interaction between the two racial groups. Since the first testing occurred during the fall of the kindergarten year and the second two years later when these children were in the second grade, only the results incident to the original testing will be considered at this point, the subsequent testing to be discussed in Chapter III.

During October and November of 1957 and 1958 *Level 1* of *The Lorge-Thorndike Intelligence Tests* was administered to all entering kindergarten children of the 16 public schools in Jackson, Michigan. The subjects of Katzenmeyer's research included all pupils who completed both of the tests in the kindergarten and second grade years. The author was of the opinion that except for the 15 per cent of school age population attending parochial schools and the children who moved into or out of the community during the period in question, his sample included all children of this age group who were enrolled in regular classrooms of the city. The colored subjects were distributed in eleven of the schools, in proportions ranging from one to 66 per cent. The intelligence test was given by the regular classroom teachers to children at the kindergarten level in small groups, the tests then scored by the teachers and subsequently re-scored by the school psychometrist. The *Lorge-Thorndike* had been used in the school system and the teachers who did the testing were familiar with its administration.

One hundred ninety-three colored and 1061 white subjects comprised the experimental and control groups. The mean IQ of the white Ss was 102.04 and that of the colored, 83.06, the difference of 18.98 points being highly significant since the t (calculated by the reviewer) was *19.37*. The standard deviations differed by 1.43 points, an amount which proved to be significant at the .05 level of confidence, the t (calculated by the reviewer) being 2.07. Therefore, the colored and white five-year-olds who entered public kindergarten and two years later were in the second grade of the school system differed significantly in mean IQ and in variability, the whites having the higher mean and being the more variable.

MERRILL-PALMER SCALE

This scale for preschool children makes use of pictures, puzzles, form boards, games, *etc.* Language questions are simple tests of comprehension. A number of the tests involve dexterity, such as cutting with scissors, standing on one foot, and pulling up a string. Speed is emphasized. The technical quality and content compare unfavorably with the *Stanford-Binet.* (Cronbach, 1960, p. 207)

Horton and Crump (1962) conducted a longitudinal study of factors influencing the growth and development of Negro infants and children from birth to five years of age. As a part of the research the subjects were given tests at six-month intervals, after 24 months of age. The children included in this report were among those in the total group who were brought for the 36-months testing between December, 1956, and September, 1959, and whose scores on the *Merrill-Palmer Scale* were rated as superior or inferior according to the test norms. All were in good physical condition at the time of the test.

Of the 209 *Merrill-Palmer* tests administered during the three-year interval, 76, or 36.4 per cent, received scores designated as *inferior or superior.* From the table it will be observed that 4.8 per cent of the colored children scored in the *top* 20 per cent of the norm distribution, and that 31.6 per cent of the colored ranked in the *lowest* 20 per cent of this distribution. Analysis of the data showed certain family characteristics to be associated with *Merrill-Palmer* performance, such as socioeconomic status, education of parents, parents' marital status, and number of siblings, these factors having "long been recognized as affecting test performance of white children."

SUMMARY

In the seventeen studies reviewed in this chapter, approximately 1700 colored and 13,900 white children between the ages of two and six years were given one or more mental tests. The majority of the children were attending kindergarten, nursery school, or day nurseries; some were tested in conjunction with a special training project; some participated in a voluntary testing program in a first-grade preregistration period; some had been brought regularly to clinics; others were tested to determine whether or not they were ready for first grade work, and a very few were already enrolled in the first grade.

In nine of the studies, either the 1916, 1937, or the 1960 Revision of the *Stanford-Binet* was employed. The average IQ of the colored on these tests ranged from 86 to 101, the combined average for the 1153 subjects being 95. White children were tested in five of the nine researches in which a form of the *Stanford-Binet* was used, their averages being without exception above those of the colored with whom they were compared. The averages obtained on the white samples ranged from 103 to 112, the combined average for the 12,579 cases being 106.

As determined by *WISC,* the mean IQ of the 76 Negro children was 85.60 as compared with a mean of 109.14 obtained on the 82 white subjects.

In three studies the *Draw-a-Man* was administered to 137 Negro children; the mean IQ of these Ss proved to be 99.1. In two of the studies the test was also given to 94 white pupils; their mean IQ was 107.0.

On the *Lorge-Thorndike,* the respective mean IQ's earned by 193 colored and 1061 white children were 83 and 102.

IQ's were not secured on all of the groups tested by the three picture vocabularies nor on those children tested by the *Merrill-Palmer;* however, on these tests the colored scored below the white norms or below the specific white groups with whom they were compared.

Combining the means reported in the fifteen studies where IQ's were obtained (and treating Arlitt's and Strachan's medians as if they were means)[19] we secured an average IQ of 94.03 on the colored (1541 cases) and an average of 105.61 on the whites (13,816 cases).

We have compared the IQ's of the young colored children tested in the Northern and Border states with those in the Southern states. The combined mean IQ of the seven groups examined in Michigan, Minnesota, New York, Pennsylvania, Oklahoma, and Missouri (1178 Ss) was 94.62; while the combined mean IQ of the six groups tested in Alabama, Florida, Georgia, South Carolina, Tennessee, Texas, and Virginia (309 Ss) was 91.15.[20] The combined mean of the Northern-Border white subjects was 104.95 (12,509 Ss) as compared with a mean of 111.94 obtained on 1307 Southern children.

The combined average IQ's of 909 colored and 11,241 white children whose test scores were reported prior to 1945 were 96.28 and 105.22, respectively, a difference of nine points; in the 1945 to 1965 period, the average IQ's of 632 colored and 2575 white subjects were 90.79 and 107.33, a difference of 16.5 points.

The research reviewed in this chapter indicates that the average IQ of the colored preschool child tested is twelve points below that of the white child of

---

[19]Excluding these medians, the combined means of the c and w groups are 93 and 109, respectively.

[20]In combining the results of the several studies, the writer has consistently treated the group tested 2 or 3 times (*e.g.,* by the *L-M* of the *S-B* and *Draw-a-Man,* or by *Peabody, Full-Range,* and *WISC*) as one group, by finding a combined mean based upon the 2 or 3 tests before including the results with other data.

the same age; the various colored groups tested have a range in mean IQ from 83 to 101 as compared with a white range of from 102 to 113; that the combined mean of the Southern Ss is about 3.5 points below that of the Northern and Border Negroes; that the racial difference in IQ is decreased when white Ss are selected on the basis of living in the same neighborhood, attending the same school, and having fathers in the same occupational group as the colored; that the disparity between the races has increased rather than decreased in the twenty years beginning with 1945 over the preceding period of comparable length; that Negro and white preschool children tested earn higher IQ's than respective samples of Negro and white grade school children; and that the discrepancy between the mean IQ's of Negro and white young children tested may be somewhat less than that found between Negro and white school children.

The relatively high means obtained on these young children of both races may be attributed in large part to the assumption that they do not represent random samplings of their age group. Other explanations involve the view that the preschool tests are not as valid or reliable as tests for school children, "that an individual IQ obtained before the age of six must be interpreted with discretion."[21] In attempting to account for the smaller differences reported between Negro and white "preschool" groups than between Negro and white school children, explanations such as the following have been given: tests at the school level become increasingly verbal and involve more abstractions and generalizations, the mental growth curves may not be the same for the two races, the tested Negro "preschool" children may make up a more highly selected sample of their age group than tested white "preschool" Ss, and the IQ at the 2- to 6-year level may be less affected by either enriching or constricting environmental influences than at the school level.

---

[21]Here Bradway was referring to the *Stanford-Binet, Forms L* and *M;* quoted by Goodenough (1949, p. 312).

Chapter III

SCHOOL CHILDREN

In this chapter we will review the research directly pertaining to the intelligence of American Negro school children. With very few exceptions standardized psychometric tests have been employed and the studies have been reported by their authors with objectivity. Altogether, 155 studies have been included; 49 or more tests have been administered; and approximately 80,000 colored children have been examined, excluding duplications. The chapter has been divided into three sections according to the type of measuring instrument, *i.e., Individual Tests, Nonverbal Group Tests,* and *Verbal Group Tests.* The research, which is summarized in Tables 2 to 4, extends from 1913 to 1965. Within each section we have grouped the studies according to the particular test administered and have usually included some description and appraisal of the test itself.

INDIVIDUAL TESTS

We have examined 43 studies wherein the authors have reported the testing of 9925 colored school children by means of individual tests (Table 2). Eighty-nine per cent of these Ss were living in urban centers and 11 per cent in villages or on farms; approximately 45 per cent were residing in the South, 31 per cent in the North, and 24 per cent in the Border states. Fourteen individual tests were employed in the testing of the children, ranging from the *Goddard Revision of the Binet-Simon* (1911) to the *Stanford Revision of the Binet, Form L-M* (1960).

GODDARD-BINET

The Goddard Revision of the Binet-Simon Tests was the first translation and adaptation of the *Binet-Simon* to be extensively used in the United States. Goddard shifted the age location of several of the tests, introduced a few new tests into the 15-year group, and adapted the terminology and content for use with American children. This scale was widely used until 1916 when it was supplanted by the *Stanford-Revision.* (Garrett and Schneck, 1933, p. 7)

Five early studies of Negro intelligence made use of the *Goddard Revision* (Table 2); in these studies the percentages of mental retardation and advancement were computed or estimated for the several groups of Negro and white children. In general, the 249 Southern Negroes examined by Strong (1913) and Sunne (1917) and the 482 Northern colored subjects tested by Odum (1913), Phillips (1914), and Wells (1932) showed more retardation and less acceleration than the white groups. Odum and Wells observed that the colored children at the younger ages tested about the same as the whites but the older Negro children became progressively inferior with increase in age.

Morse (1914) believed that native factors were responsible for at least a part of the Negro-white differences obtained by Strong. From an analysis of her data Morse concluded that the colored excel in rote memory, naming words, making rhymes and in time orientation; but that they are inferior to whites in esthetic judgment, observation, reasoning, motor control, logical memory, use of words, resistance to suggestion, and in adjustment to the complexities of civilized society. Phillips argued that a difference in mentality exists between colored and white children if the tests are a gauge of mentality, and raised the question as to whether or not the two groups should be instructed under the same curriculum.

Odum and Wells, on the other hand, were inclined to attribute the mental differences to environmental rather than to native factors. In comparing his Philadelphia white and Negro samples, Odum described the efficiency of the latter as varying inversely with the complexity of the process required. "But they exercise to a high degree of efficiency the simple processes which, if coordinated, would lead to a higher degree of general intellectuality." Both Odum and Wells cited the smaller incentive for the Negro child to continue in school as a consequence of limitation in occupational opportunities, the lower economic position of colored people, the disadvantageous home influences, and the greater percentage of absences from school among the colored.

The importance of environment was recognized by other investigators and attempts were made even in this early period of testing to equate groups for background factors. Strong, for instance, compared cotton mill white children with the total group of Negro Ss after finding that the education and environment of the former were little, if any, better than those of the latter group. Phillips matched colored and white Ss for home rating; and Sunne compared groups of about the same social and economic status since all of her subjects were living in a very poor district. Sunne even attempted to equate colored and white children for *both* age and school grade, an obviously unwarranted procedure which serves to conceal or minimize real differences in mental ability when they occur.

POINT SCALE

The *Yerkes-Bridges-Hardwick Point Scale* consists of twenty tests, nineteen of which were taken from the *Binet Scale*. The separate tests are arranged in an ascending order of difficulty, credit points being assigned for passing each test in the scale. The authors of the *Point Scale* objected to Binet's system of grouping tests into age groups and to his method of scoring a test as either right or wrong, without allowing partial credits. Scores from the *Point Scale* can be changed into mental age equivalents which have much the same meaning as the MA obtained from an age-scale. A correlation of .87 in a group of about 300 female adult delinquents has been obtained between scores on this scale and *Stanford-Binet*. (Garrett and Schneck, 1933, pp. 7-8)

Of the two studies which utilized the *Point Scale* (Table 2), Sunne's (1917) probably merits little further consideration; the colored and white children, tested also by the *Goddard Revision,* were matched for age and grade in so far as possible. The work of Peterson and Lanier (1929), however, will be examined here since Klineberg believed it to have been a significant contribution to the problem of racial differences. "The results give definite indication, therefore, of a marked difference between Southern and Northern Negroes, as well as of a clear tendency for Northern Negroes — at least in New York — to approach very closely the results obtained by the whites." (Klineberg, 1935, p. 3) It is with the latter part of his statement that we are concerned here, since Northern and not Southern Negroes were tested by the *Point Scale.*

As will be noted in Table 2, Peterson and Lanier examined 60 white and 187 colored boys of 12 years of age from Grades 4 to 8 in certain public schools of New York City. The mean scores earned by the white and colored were 74.20 and 74.28, respectively, with *s's* of 9.76 and 9.36; the medians of the respective groups were 76.50 and 73.80, with 59 per cent of the whites above the median of the colored and 43 per cent of the colored above the white median. The investigators offered three possible interpretations of the close similarity between the averages: (1) the New York Negroes make up a highly selected group as compared with the American Negro in general; (2) environmental advantages from living in New York have raised the scores of the Negroes there; and (3) the white sampling in New York may have been inferior in ability to a truly representative one.

The sampling of the white boys may have been a representative one of New York City's 12-year-old boys, at least the reviewer cannot say that it was not. However, it seems important to call attention to the fact that one of the white children tested was foreign-born, and one third of the white boys came from non-English-speaking homes. Eliminating the children from foreign-speaking homes the median of the white boys becomes 79.5 as compared with 73.8 for the colored boys. Since the *Point Scale* is a verbal test it is obvious that children with a language handicap are at a disadvantage on this scale. Yerkes and Foster implied the inapplicability of the indiscriminate use of the *Point Scale* on children from non-English-speaking homes in establishing special norms which they used for such children (1923, p. 164). The norms at the age of twelve years are about five points higher in the English-speaking than in the non-English-speaking homes. Due to these facts the reviewer does not consider either of these *Point Scale* studies to have been a significant contribution to the study of racial differences.

Stanford-Binet, 1916[1]

Fifteen studies which made use of the 1916 Form of the *Stanford Revision of the Binet-Simon Scale* may be separated into three groups: (1) those on selected groups of Negro children, (2) those dealing with unselected groups

---

[1]See pp. 6-8 and 11 for brief descriptions and appraisals of the several *Stanford-Binet* revisions.

of Negro and white children, and (3) those in which attempts were made to equate Negro-white groups for environmental factors.

(1) In the first classification we have included the research of Long (1933) in Washington, D. C., and that of Beckham (1933) in Washington, D. C., Baltimore, and New York City. Long compared intelligence scores of a group of 100 colored children from underprivileged communities with those of a group of 100 colored children from better residential sections. The mean IQ of Group I was 15 points below the mean of 112 obtained on Group II. Group I, the underprivileged group, was selected on the basis of opinions of Washington teachers and supervisors; however, it was only selected by these judges as a *community*. Long did not obtain an estimate of the socioeconomic status of the home of each child. He indicated that the Sims socioeconomic scale had been administered previously to children in the fourth grade with the result that the regions from which a part of the underprivileged group came had a rating of *13*, while the regions from which a part of the privileged group came had a rating of 20. Regarding Group II, Long observed that the five selected schools were large and that he could not take all of the children meeting his initial criteria (having been born in D. C. and in attendance at one of the five schools located in the better residential sections). Therefore he asked principals and teachers to *recommend pupils for testing, who, in their judgment, came from better homes of the school community*.

We have already remarked, in surveying D'Angelo's study of day nursery children selected by their supervisors, that it is to be expected that teachers who are asked to choose pupils for testing purposes will select the more alert children, either with or without the intention of so doing. *Group II* in Long's study, must have been selected on some other basis than that of socioeconomic status since over half of the parents of this group were either unskilled or semiskilled laborers or had no occupation. While we admit the plausibility of Long's argument that one is not justified in making the usual inference with reference to intelligence from social status of economically handicapped groups such as the Negro, we are of the opinion that since his purpose was to analyze test results on the basis of socioeconomic status, he should have selected his subjects much more carefully and much more objectively than he did.

Beckham's large number of 1000 colored youths, 753 of whom were from Washington, D. C., cannot be considered as an unselected sample of Negro adolescents from the areas represented. Beckham did not indicate how the New York City Ss were selected; but he observed that in addition to some Baltimore adolescents who were referred to the laboratory by parents or teachers, all of the Washington Ss (and presumably some of those from Baltimore) were brought to the Howard University laboratory by psychology students as a part of a course project. It may be assumed that the subjects were heavily biased in favor of siblings, neighbors, and friends of the *Howard* students.

(2) There are ten studies in which the samples for the *Stanford-Binet* testing

were apparently saturated or chosen at random. These include the work of Graham (1926), Thurmond (1933), and Lambeth and Lanier (1933) in the South; the research of Lacy (1926) and Strachan (1926) in the Border states; the investigations of Schwegler and Winn (1920), Barnes (1923), and Klineberg (1935) in the North; and those of Arlitt (1921, 1922) where the location was not reported or where the results of both Northern and Southern Ss were combined. The combined mean IQ of the 2236 colored cases proved to be 88, approximately 15 points below that of the 15,145 whites examined.[2] Very similar IQ's of 90, 89, and 87 were obtained on Negro children from the Southern, Border, and Northern states, respectively.

(3) Attempts were made by Arlitt (1921), Pintner and Keller (1922), Sunne (1925), and Bruce (1940) to compare groups of underprivileged white and colored children by means of the *Stanford-Binet*. Pintner and Keller made a beginning in this direction by selecting three schools in Youngstown, Ohio, which were located in sections of foreign-speaking populations. The white children of native parents in these areas secured an average IQ of 95; the colored, a mean of 88. Sunne similarly eliminated from her survey both white and colored pupils from the best schools and residential districts and likely overweighted the retarded element among the whites by including a school which had special classes for retarded white children. The resulting mean IQ for the whites was 91.2, for the colored, 80.56.

Arlitt went further in her attempt to secure children of comparable backgrounds when she eliminated from a group of 191 white children of native American parents all whose fathers were above the semiskilled laboring class and then compared the 43 remaining Ss with 81 children of Italian-born parents and the 71 colored children. Twelve per cent of these two latter groups were from families above the semiskilled group and to this extent were given advantage over the children of native white parents. The median IQ of the 43 white Ss of native parents was 92; the median IQ's of the total Italian and colored groups were 84.3 and 83.4, respectively. Arlitt observed that "The curve of distribution of Intelligence Quotients of the Italian and Negro groups is skewed markedly to the side of inferior ability as compared with that of native-born white children of the same social status. This difference seems to be racial." (*Psychol. Bull.*, 1921, p. 96)

Bruce's study is noteworthy in that she attempted to equate according to the Sims socioeconomic scale the home backgrounds of 49 colored and 49 white children, after she had originally selected a Virginia rural county for the low socioeconomic status of both its colored and white residents. In spite of the low socioeconomic status of the 87 white children originally tested on the *Stanford-Binet*, i.e., Sims score of 6.00, it was higher than that of the 72 colored

---

[2] Average IQ of colored Ss based on the results of the 10 studies. White Ss were included in half of them.

children tested (Sims score of 3.50).[3] Consequently, in matching her colored and white pairs for Sims score Bruce eliminated all white children whose statuses were above that of any Negro child and eliminated some of the Negro children of the lowest status. When the 49 pairs were finally selected there was a significant difference between the white mean IQ of 85.76 and the colored mean of 76.88. However, Bruce was careful to call attention to the difficulty in equating for social status at the low end of the Sims scale, and as a result of this difficulty she felt that her results were not proof of the innate superiority of the white group. While the schools for both Negro and white children were similar in appearance, with practically no distinguishable characteristic, and while the conditions in both white and colored schools were often bad, there appeared to be fewer books and writing supplies in the Negro schools and the Negro teachers were paid less than the white teachers.

If we combine the results of the four studies in which IQ's of underprivileged white and colored children were compared, we find that 1369 white and 1140 colored Ss between the ages of $5\frac{1}{2}$ and 15 years obtained respective average *Stanford-Binet* IQ's of 91.5 and 81, both below the American white norm. If we remove the Italian group from consideration because of their bilingual handicap, we find that the white groups were uniformly higher than the colored with whom they were compared—the differences favoring the whites by 7 points (Pinter and Keller), 9 points (Arlitt), 9 points (Bruce), and 11 points (Sunne). These findings therefore do not lend support to Herskovits' statement (1945) that "certain white groups of underprivileged status test about the same as Negroes," if we are correct in assuming that he meant *Negroes of underprivileged status,* rather than Negroes in general.

It will probably have been noted that an awareness of a cause-and-effect relationship existing between environment and tested IQ was present in the thinking of some of the earliest investigators, and that a number of them made serious though beginning attempts to equate the environments of the Negroes and whites tested (*Goddard Revision,* Strong, 1913, Phillips, 1914, Sunne, 1917; *Point Scale,* Peterson and Lanier, 1929). Likewise, certain psychologists, using the 1916 form of the *Stanford-Binet,* while not matching Negro and white children for parental occupation, socioeconomic status, *etc.,* as did Arlitt (1921) or Bruce (1940) cited above, did imply their appreciation of such need. Thurmond (1933), for example, in appraising her results obtained from administering several tests to 40 Negro 12-year-olds from six Georgia rural schools — securing a mean IQ identical to that later obtained by Bruce in a poor Virginia county — found conditions in the average home of her subjects to be sufficient to cause their irregular school attendance. An inspection of the homes from which many of the children came showed small and inadequate houses for the large families, little food (especially in the homes of the share croppers), an unbalanced diet, and little evidence of "cultural taste" according to white standards.

---

[3]Considerably below the estimated score of Long's underprivileged group: 13. *Op. cit.*

Several of the authors have analyzed the *Binet* performances of their subjects and identified the areas in which their Negro Ss were at their best and those areas where they were at their worst, relative to the whites. Arlitt found colored children to be relatively poor in language but good in *rote memory*. Sunne reported the colored to be worse in tests requiring *accurate training in reading, arithmetic,* and *drawing,* as well as inferior on the more *difficult forms of logical analysis* and some tests requiring *brief timing.* Graham considered the colored to be better in tests of a practical nature and poorer in tests involving discrimination and *critical accuracy.* Schwegler and Winn concluded that the colored are about three fifths as successful in tests of *adjustment to unfamiliar situations* and those involving *abstract reasoning,* but do about as well in *direct reproductive memory,* in *common sense adjustments,* and in *common sense verbal facility.* Barnes observed that the tests where Negroes "most nearly equalled" the performance of whites had certain characteristics in common. They are the essential simplicity and commonness of the situation involved and the consequent demands on the mind of the child, the demands of such tests being for *understanding common sense situations, often concrete in nature.* Likewise Thurmond noted that her Negro subjects showed more proficiency in *manipulating concrete objects* than in *dealing with abstract ideas* or *verbalizations.*

Because these statements appear to have been a result of observation and not of statistical analysis, we wish only to note the recurrence of comment on (1) the relatively good or adequate scores made by the colored in tasks involving *reproductive memory, concrete objects,* and *practical intelligence;* and (2) the relatively inferior scores made by them in tasks involving *language, logical analysis, critical discrimination,* and *abstract reasoning.*

STANFORD-BINET, 1937

In order to determine how IQ and age are related in the Negro child population, Tomlinson (1944) attempted to locate and test with either *Form L* or *Form M* all available pairs of colored siblings living in Austin, Texas. She required that they be full sibs living in the same household, and that one of each pair be between seven and nine years of age and the other between four and six years. Records were obtained on 75 pairs of sibs; the mean IQ of the older group (as determined by a composite of *L* and *M* IQ's) was reported to be 86.7, or about six points below that of the younger group. For successive ages of 7, 8, and 9, the respective mean IQ's were: 88.1, 85.8, and 83.7. The *s* of the distribution for the 7 to 9 year group was 11.5 as compared with that of 16.4 reported by Terman and Merrill on their standardization group. Tomlinson was unable to determine the cause of the apparent deterioration in IQ; neither could she explain to her satisfaction the greater homogeneity among her Ss as compared with the Terman-Merrill norms. However, she was cognizant of the probable cumulative effect of a restrictive environment on the IQ of an underprivileged child.[4] A similar

---

[4]Mean *Sims* score obtained on 72 of the 75 homes was between 4 and 5.

decrease in IQ's of colored children between the ages of seven and nine years was reported by Arlitt (1922) on the 1916 form of the *Stanford-Binet*. Arlitt attributed the decline in part to the presence of fewer rote memory tests at the upper age levels.

Klugman (1944) was interested in determining if there exist race, sex, or age differences in test motivation when money rather than praise serves as the controlled reward. Having decided to make use of the average range of intelligence scores, only *those children who had earned IQ ratings between 90 and 110* on a mental ability test "constructed and administered by the local school system" qualified as potential subjects. These children, Age 7 to 14 and in Grades 2 to 7 of a single public elementary school (probably in Philadelphia, although the author omits the name and location of the city) were given letters to their parents asking permission to test their children. Unless the parents refused, the children were subsequently given *Form L* or *Form M* of the *Stanford-Binet* and *only those who earned IQ's between 90 and 110 a second time* were allowed to take the alternate form of the *Binet* and be included in the final roster of subjects.

Klugman administered all of the *Binet* tests himself, giving the alternate form one week after the first, except in cases of two absences where the interval was two weeks. Praise was given on half the occasions and a penny each for certain correct answers on the other half. Eight different testing situations were used such as: *Form L* with praise followed by *Form M* with praise, *Form L* with money then *Form M* with praise, *Form M* with praise and *Form L* with money,— with a true chance order of testing established by the aid of Fisher and Yates' Table of Random Numbers. When *money* was the incentive to be used, the directions to each S were:

> "I am going to ask you a number of questions and I want to see how well you can answer them. There are certain questions which, if answered correctly, will entitle you to one of these pennies I have here before me. Therefore, the more questions you answer properly the more pennies you will receive and keep for yourself. Don't try to figure out which questions will earn a penny because you will not be able to do so. The proper thing to do is to try to answer all the questions correctly and by so doing that you will be sure to get all the pennies coming to you."

When *praise* was the incentive, these were the instructions:

> "I am going to ask you a number of questions and I want to see how well you can answer them. Try to answer all the questions correctly."

The children earned from 5 to 15 pennies when money was the incentive. The fathers' occupations ranged between unskilled labor and "clerical, skilled trades, and retail business." The combined *L* and *M* IQ's of the 38 white and the 34 colored children averaged, respectively, 99.11 and 98. As will be seen from Table 2, the whites averaged the same under the praise and money conditions; the whites were superior to the colored only under the praise condition (.05

level); and the colored performed better when they were rewarded with pennies than when they were praised (.05 level).

This is an interesting experiment and though not well controlled in certain respects (the author who designed the experiment did all of the testing, the *money* directions seem to be much more interestingly presented than the *praise* directions, and it seems likely that some Ss would tell their friends *which questions produced money*) does suggest that Negro children might do better on tests if they were given concrete rewards.[5]

While Klugman clearly indicated that his samples were not selected at random, at one point he made a true but apparently irrelevant and therefore misleading statement relating to the mental level of his groups. "Terman (17, p. 92) predicts that '. . . . there will be discovered enormously significant racial differences in general intelligence, differences which cannot be wiped out by any scheme of mental culture.' With this statement, the results of this investigation are not in agreement. While it is true that the white children made slightly higher scores (on the average, 1.11 IQ points), the difference is far from statistically reliable since the critical ratio comes to only .81." (p. 264)

Following this lead, Dreger and Miller (1960) end their brief review of Klugman's work by mentioning the essential similarity of the Negro-white means—thereby suggesting to the reader that the two groups were unbiased samples.

> "Klugman (1944) in a study not mentioned by Shuey discovered that money incentives and praise had no demonstrable effects on white children (CA 7-14) in taking the alternate form of the Binet after an initial first form. However, comparable age Negro children given money rewards showed better performance than those given praise as an incentive. (Incidentally the two groups averaged 99.11 for whites and 98.00 for Negroes, with 6.08 and 5.66 SDs, respectively.)" (p. 369)

Higgins and Sivers (1958) compared the results obtained from the testing of 440 white and 349 colored children by the *Stanford-Binet, Form L* and the *Colored Raven Progressive Matrices*. These subjects were described as including all 7-, 8-, and 9-year-olds in Grades 1 to 3 and those from five fourth-grade classes of public schools serving the lowest socioeconomic areas of a Northeastern city. The authors found no differences in intelligence as measured by the *Stanford-Binet,* both groups earning mean IQ's of 90. The present writer is of the opinion that Higgins and Sivers' method of selection probably served to eliminate some children of superior mental ability and that their method may have worked more to the detriment of the whites than the colored.[6] A preferable procedure would have been to test all 7-, 8-, and 9-year-olds throughout the elementary

---

[5]This hypothesis is further explored by Tiber. See p. 42.

[6]Since proportionately there are more gifted white than colored children. See Chapter 7.

schools surveyed rather than to limit their subjects to children of this age-range enrolled only in the lower grades.

The identical means are also interesting and puzzling since on the *Progressive Matrices,* a nonverbal test, the white children were found to be significantly superior to the colored. Several explanations may be cited for this apparent discrepancy: (I) *Progressive Matrices* may be a test of a specific skill; (2) intelligence tests heavily loaded with nonverbal items may discriminate against Negro children; and (3) some of the white children may have come from foreign-speaking homes.[7]

STANFORD-BINET, 1960

Two major investigations making use of *Form L-M* of the *Stanford-Binet* were conducted from Florida State University. As the first of these (Kennedy, Van De Riet, and White, 1961, 1963) included the testing of some five-year-old children, the design of the research has been outlined in Chapter 2. In making a normative survey of Negro children of Alabama, Florida, Georgia, South Carolina, and Tennessee, these authors secured a sample of 1800 colored school children intended to adequately represent the more than one million children of this race in the elementary schools of the Southeast. Three counties were selected from each state, considered to be representative of the states sampled, one of them being metropolitan, one urban, and one rural. Because of the large number of schools in the metropolitan counties—nearly 100 in some instances—a random sampling of them usually resulted in testing at twelve schools; six schools were selected in each urban county and three in each rural county.

After selecting the specific schools to be represented in the sample, the usual randomized techniques were employed to obtain the individual children to be tested. When there was more than one section of a particular grade in the school, equal numbers were chosen from each classroom. A table of random numbers was used to select subjects from an alphabetized roll supplied by the teacher. The resulting sample contained 120 Ss from each of the fifteen counties, 20 children at each grade. The tests were administered by twelve trained examiners, their work being periodically checked and their examining techniques observed from time to time by supervisors.

Using the McGuire-White Index of Social Status (ISS) which was based upon a combination of ratings from three scales: (1) occupation of family's "status parent", (2) source of income of family's "status parent", and (3) the educational attainment of the family's "status parent",[8] the investigators reported

---

[7]The reviewer is of the opinion that an elementary school, located in the lowest socioeconomic area of a Northeastern city with a population 44 per cent colored, would have many bilingual children who would have been handicapped on *Form L.* No information could be obtained on this point. In addition, the authors do not indicate if Puerto Rican children were attending the schools; if they were, there would be the problem of their classification.

[8]Ratings on each of these 3 scales multiplied by appropriate weights and the products summed to provide a total index score. The higher the total index, the lower the social status.

the occupations of their subjects' parents to be distributed in a manner similar to the occupational distribution of the Negro population in the Southeast. In addition, the educational attainment of the status parent was found to be representative of the adult Negro population in these states.

The principal findings of this research[9] may be enumerated as follows: (1) The *mean IQ* of about 81 and *standard deviation* of 12 were below the Terman-Merrill norms, the latter being, respectively, 102 and 16. (2) IQ was found to be negatively correlated with *age,* the mean difference between the age levels being significant at the .001 level. (3) IQ was not significantly related to *school grade,* as will be observed in Table 2. (4) IQ was correlated positively and significantly with *socioeconomic level,* the combined two upper levels having a mean of *94* (6 cases at level 1 and 28 cases at level 2), the mean of the lowest level being *79* (918 cases), and that of the group listed as *unknown, 78* (432 cases). (5) Five IQ points separated the means of the *metropolitan* and *rural* children, the difference being highly significant (see Table 2). (6) The correlation between IQ and teacher ratings obtained on over-all class standing was highly significant. (7) Analysis of item difficulty and biserial correlation item analysis of data showed that in general the abstract verbal items were relatively difficult, and the rote memory items and practical items relatively easy for the children; there did not appear to be any exceptionally high *performance* ability in contrast to low *verbal* ability for the sample.

Tiber (1963) made use of *Form L-M* in investigating the effects of several incentives on the intelligence test performance of Negro and white children in a "Southeastern" public school system. Since he not only wanted to study racial *(caste)* differences but *class* differences in test performance he employed the McGuire-White Index of Social Status,[10] and divided his white subjects into two groups: (1) *middle-class,* who had a mean ISS index of 40, and (2) *lower-class,* whose mean ISS index was 63. The Negro children tested were all identified as *lower-class,* with a reported ISS index of 74. One hundred sixty children composed each of the three groups, all being enrolled in the second and third grades and all being 7 years, one month and 10 years, no months of age.[11] The subjects in each class and racial group were randomly assigned to one of four incentive groups designated as follows: verbal praise, verbal reproof, candy, no incentive.[12] The final experimental design consisted of 12 groups with 40 Ss in each.

Eight examiners administered the *Stanford-Binet,* each E testing the same number of subjects from each of the 12 subgroups to counterbalance examiner effects. A random sequence of testing subjects was used to counterbalance

---

[9]Omitting comparisons with results of the California Achievement Test given to the Ss.

[10]*Op. cit.*

[11]No further information on method of selection of Ss.

[12]The *praise* and *candy* groups would parallel Klugman's *praise* and *pennies* groups.

practice and fatigue effects. All testing procedures recommended in the *Stanford-Binet* manual were followed as closely as possible, and were the same with all Ss "varying only in regard to the incentives employed by the examiners." At the end of each testing period the child was cautioned not to speak to other children "about the type of games we played together." All tests were scored twice, the second time by the author of the study and made "blind" to avoid possible examiner biases.

The incentive used was administered at the end of each subtest but not between the subtest items. In the *Verbal Praise* group, E's statements consisted of: "Good. You're doing well. Very good. That's fine." In the *Verbal Reproof* group, E's statements were: "Bad. You're not doing well. You're not trying. That's bad."[13] In the *Candy* group, uniform pieces of sweet candy mints were given. In the *No incentive* group, E neither praised, reproved, nor gave mints.

The data were treated by an analysis of variance and the Duncan Multiple Range Test. From Table 2 one will observe differences between the three major groups—the white middle class having earned a mean IQ of about 108, the white lower class a mean of approximately 94, and the Negro lower class a mean slightly over 77 — the respective standard deviations being approximately 17, 13, and 10. The differences between the means were highly significant.

No doubt the reader of Tiber's work would agree with him when he observes that the most interesting result of the study is the total lack of significant differences in test performance under the various incentive conditions. This is somewhat in opposition to Klugman's findings that for Negro children money is substantially superior to praise, and to Hurlock's (1924) report that in taking certain intelligence tests, Negro children react more favorably to praise and white children to reproof. Noting that previous investigators have obtained somewhat contradictory results and that the present study corrected for many of the weaknesses noted in previous designs, Tiber argues that his results would seem to place the burden of proof on those who hypothesize differential effects in intelligence test performance due to incentives.

In contrast to the learning studies, however, where significant differences in performance were obtained by the use of incentives similar to those used in his research, Tiber offers as explanation that an intelligence test measures *previous* learning, not the learning process itself. Thus the important motivational differences may not lie within the test situation itself but in the acquisition of knowledge and skills which the intelligence test measures.[14]

WISC

Of the seven investigations employing the *Wechsler Intelligence Scale for Children*,[15] six have included relatively unselected colored subjects in the

---

[13]Only one of these comments following a subtest.

[14]A debatable point.

[15]For a brief description and evaluation of this scale, see pp. 13 and 22.

TABLE

SCHOOL CHILDREN

| AUTHOR DATE | LOCATION | N | SUBJECTS | | METHOD OF SELECTION |
			AGE	GRADE	
					GODDARD REVISION
Strong, A. C. (1913)	Columbia, S. C.	w-225 c- 123	6-12 5-15[1]	1-7 1-7	From all grades in 4 w schs: 2 in city, 1 outskirts, 1 in cotton mill village with only 5 grades. All 7 grades in c sch. Teachers were asked to select children of varying ability from pedagogical standpoint.
Sunne,[4] D. (1917)	New Orleans, La.	w-112 c- 116 c- 10		2-5 2-5 6-7	C & w in 2 schs in one of "very poorest districts"; selected c children of nearly same age & grade as w Ss tested.
Odum, H. W. (1913)	Philadelphia, Pa.	c- 300	5-15	1-8	"Fair chance selection."
Phillips, B. A. (1914)	Philadelphia, Pa.	w-166[6] c- 86	9.6 9.6		From larger groups 57 c matched with 57 w Ss for age, sex & home rating. Mean age was 9.6.
Wells, G. R. (1923)	Oberlin, Ohio	w-267 c- 96	6-16 6-16		Practically all w & c of 6-12 MA in publ schs included in report.

[1]One S Age 5 and one Age 15.

[2]*A* is used in this study to include children who scored *more than one year above* their CA; *B* includes children who scored *more than* one year *below* their CA; *C* includes the *satisfactory* group, all Ss scoring at CA ± 1 year.

[3]Study made under direction of J. Morse who discusses it in separate article (1914).

[4]Results on *Point Scale* administered to these Ss included in this table.

[5]Goddard's norms, based on 1547 w children.

[6]Number of cases taken from Phillips' Table IV.

TWO

INDIVIDUAL TESTS

RESULTS	COMMENTS OF AUTHOR

BINET-SIMON

	% Advanced, Retard.[2]	
	w	c
A	5.3	.1
B	10.2	29.4
C	84.4	69.8

Negro children from 6-12 are mentally different and also younger than Southern w children of corresponding ages; this condition is partly due to native or racial causes (Morse, 1914).[3]

%age retardation of c greater than that of w though the average amount is the same for both.

Negro Ss inferior in coordination, more retarded in tests of abilities commonly demanded in publ schs; but keener sense of rhyme, greater facility in story telling, and originality in combining colors.

	Norms[5]	
% testing:	w	c
1 yr above age	21	5
1 yr below age	20	26
Feebleminded	3.9	6.3

Mdn w "at age"
Mdn c "one yr below age"

In comparison with w children, the efficiency of c varies inversely with complexity of process. Environment alone seems sufficient to account for majority of results.

	% Advanced, Retard.[7]	
	w	c
	Total	
A	20.5	7.0
B	24.7	54.7
	Matched	
A	57.8	29.8
B	42.1	68.4

Unselected c as a class good in memory, poor in tests requiring judgment, less animated, slower. If *Binet* is gauge of mentality must follow that a mental difference exists bet the c and w children.

Total Advance Units[8]	
w	c
224	121

Total Retard Units	
w	c
221	358

Social environment of c not equal to that of w on average. Progressive inferiority on tests with increase in age.

---

[7]*A* is used in this study to include % of children who scored *one year or more* above CA; *B* includes % of children who scored *one year or more below* their CA.

[8]An *advancement unit corresponds* to one S who was mentally advanced for one year or part of year; advancement of a child 3 years ahead of his age level recorded as 3 units; a *retardation unit* corresponds to one S who was mentally retarded for one year or part of year, *etc.;* c & w figures are directly comparable since actual units for c were multiplied by 11/4, the number of w cases being approximately 11/4 that of c.

TABLE

SCHOOL CHILDREN

| AUTHOR DATE | LOCATION | N | SUBJECTS | | METHOD OF SELECTION |
			AGE	GRADE	
					YERKES-BRIDGES-HARDWICK
Sunne, D.[9] (1917)	New Orleans, La.	w-112 c- 126		2-5 2-7	White & c in 2 schs in one of "very poorest districts"; selected c children of nearly same age & grade as w Ss tested.
Peterson,[10] J., and Lanier, L. H. (1929)	New York, N. Y.	w- 60 c- 187	12 12	4-8 4-8	White boys from PS 26 & PS 5; c boys from PS 5 & PS 139. All 12-yr-old boys in PS 5 tested.
					STANFORD-BINET
Arlitt, A. H. (1921)	Not given	w-272 c- 71		Prim. Prim.	"In a single school district."
Arlitt,[12] A. H. (1922)	New Orleans, La., and near Philadelphia, Pa.	c- 189	7-15		From NO publ & private schs & playgrounds; Pa Ss all in publ schs.
Sunne, D.[13] (1925)	New Orleans (probably)	w-947 c- 949	5-15+ 5-15+	Elem. Elem.	Excluded best districts. Tried to test all in schs surveyed; probably overweighted retarded element of w, as all retarded from wide area in special classes of a single sch.
Graham, V. T. (1926)	Atlanta, Ga.	c- 105	6-7	1	"a group of unselected first-graders."

[9]For *Goddard* test results, see preceding section of this table.

[10]For results on other tests reported by Peterson and Lanier, see Tables 3 and 4.

[11]The difference between the white *mdn* of 79.5 and the colored *mdn* of 73.8 is significant at the .01 level ($t = 5.70/2.11$), if we assume that the white *s* remains at 9.76 (calculated by reviewer).

[12]For results on younger children, see Table 1.

TWO *(continued)*
INDIVIDUAL TESTS

RESULTS	COMMENTS OF AUTHOR

POINT SCALE

C slightly more retarded		Negro girls surpass c boys more than w girls surpass w boys; c inferior in motor coordination, and perhaps in capacity for logical analysis.

	Scores		C boys probably representative of NY Negro but uncertain about w boys; if exclude those from non-English-speaking homes, mdn of w (40 cases) is 79.5.[11]
	w	c	
M	74.20	74.28	
Mdn	76.50	73.80	
s	9.76	9.36	

1916 FORM

	IQ		Disparity bet children of same race but inferior and superior social status is greater than that bet children of different races.
	w	c	
Mdn	99.9	83.4	

Age	Mdn IQ	Majority of inferior social status. Decrease in IQ due to a genuine race diff. Also c poor in language and good in rote memory, and there are more rote memory tests at lower ages.
	c	
7	90.9	
8	87.5	
9	83.9	
10-15	78.4	

	IQ[14]		Tendency for c to pass fewer tests requiring accurate training in reading, arith and drawing and to score lower on more difficult forms of logical analysis and on some requiring brief time limit.
	w	c	
Mdn	91.22	80.56	

	IQ[15]		Both groups normal by white standards. C most proficient in tests of practical nature and poorest in tests involving discrimination and critical accuracy.
	c	c	
Age	6	7	
M	103.2	94.8	
s	11.3	10.7	

[13]Used both *Stanford-Binet* and *Y-B-H Point Scale.*

[14]Calculated by writer from Sunne's distributions.

[15]Greater selectivity of 6- than 7-year-olds in first grade. Graham does not report the proportion of c 6-year-olds enrolled in sch; neither does she mention the fact that some of the brighter 7-year-olds would have been in the 2nd or higher grade.

TABLE

SCHOOL CHILDREN

AUTHOR DATE	LOCATION	N	SUBJECTS		METHOD OF SELECTION
			AGE	GRADE	
Lambeth, M., and Lanier, L. H. (1933)	Nashville, Tenn.	w-30 c- 30	12 12		Boys from 3 publ schs; not stated how selected. Grades from 1 "to above 9".
Thurmond,[16] S. (1933)	Clarke Co., Ga.	c- 40	12		From 6 best of 13 rural schs for Negroes in county, selected all who had not reached 13th birthday. Complete data on 40 of the 52 enrolled; others absent during one or more of the testing sessions.
Bruce,[17] M. (1940)	Rural Virginia County	w-87 c- 72	6-12 6-12		All Ss in attendance at 9 pairs of schs had been tested on $K\text{-}A$ & ranked in order of IQ. Every 5th S in distribution was tested on $S\text{-}B$.
Lacy,[18] L. D. (1926)	Oklahoma City, Okla.	w-4947 c- 704	5-12 5-12	1-3 1-3	Tests given to all children over a 3-year period by trained teachers.
Strachan,[19] L. (1926)	Kansas City, Mo.	w- 1-7023 2-2371 3- 444 c- 1- 329 2- 63 3- 16		1-3 1-3	All children who had missed test in kg, all who had not attended kg, & all Ss new to the system were tested in 1st or 2nd grade. Additional Ss tested in 3rd grade as time permitted. Covered 4-year period.
Long, H. H. (1933)	Washington, D. C.	cI- 100[21] cII-100		3A 3A	cI-"Practically all" of c from 5 schs in underprivileged areas, if born in DC. cII-Principals & teachers recommended pupils who came from better homes & attended 5 schs located in better residential sections. Born in DC.

[16]For results on *Arthur Point Performance Scale*, see Table 2. For results on *Illinois General Examination*, see Table 4.

[17]See this table for results on *Arthur* & Table 4 for results on *Kuhlmann-Anderson*.

[18]For results on Ss at kindergarten level, see Table 1.

[19]Excluded from table are children of foreign-born parents tested in 1924. For results on kindergarten Ss, see Table 1.

TWO (continued)

INDIVIDUAL TESTS

RESULTS			COMMENTS OF AUTHOR
		IQ	Hereditary diffs an important causal factor in test diff, but not only factor. Possibly inferior motivation; may be something in living habits making for less carefulness and perseverance.
	w	c	
Mdn	96.43	77.50	
Q	8.75	9.37	
D/PEd	6.46		
4% c above w mdn			
		IQ	It is apparent that our Ss show more proficiency in manipulating concrete objects than in dealing with abstract ideas or verbalizations.
		c	
M		77	
s		8.37	
Range		58-93	
		IQ	When 49 c and w pairs were matched acc to Sims socioeco score, w mean IQ became 85.76, the c mean, 76.88. Diff bet these means significant.
	w	c	
M	90.07	76.33	
Mdn	90.00	74.17	
s	15.66	14.22	
Range	51-130	50-127	
Grade	*M IQ*		*Binet* results substantiate theory that mental growth of c is slower than mental growth of w children.
	w	c	
1	104	93	
2	104	88	
3	102	87	
Grade	*Mdn IQ*		Lower *mdns* in 1st and 2nd grades probably due to method of testing all children in kg if possible.
	w	c	
1	98.5	90.3	
2	97.4	82.5	
3	92.0	71.0	
Total[20]	101.9	92.8	
		IQ	Underprivileged areas selected by consensus of teachers and supervisors. Previously gave Sims Scale to 4th grade c in a part of this area, mean score of 13; regions from which cII came had mean rating of 20 on *Sims*.
	cI	cII	
M	97	112	

[20]Total number includes all who had been tested in kindergarten as well as those tested in Grades 1-3.

[21]For results on *Pintner-Paterson, Dearborn A,* & *Kuhlmann-Anderson* given to these Ss, see Tables 2, 3, and 4, respectively.

TABLE

SCHOOL CHILDREN

| AUTHOR DATE | LOCATION | N | SUBJECTS | | METHOD OF SELECTION |
			AGE	GRADE	
Beckham, A. S. (1933)	New York City Washington, D. C. Baltimore, Md.	c- 100 c- 753 c- 147	12-16 12-16 12-16		Selection in NY not given, "tests were given at several places." DC & Balt Ss were brought to lab by students as course project. Some Balt Ss were referred by parents or teachers.[22]
Schwegler, R. A., and Winn, E. (1920)	Lawrence, Kan.	w-58 c- 58		7-8 7-8	Tested all c in the 2 grades; chance selection from enrollment cards of equal number of w Ss.
Pintner,[24] R., and Keller, R. (1922)	Youngstown, Ohio	w-249 c- 71		Kg-2 Kg-2	Selected 3 schs in which a large majority were foreign-speaking.
Barnes,[25] J. R. (1923)	Lawrence, Kan.	c- 210	5-17	1- JrHS	Data all drawn from city sch records. About 85% from S-B tests given in 1922-23, balance going back to 1920. Author does not report whether or not the records of *all* Negroes tested during the period were included in study.
Klineberg,[27] O. (1935)	New York City	c- 421	10		From Harlem publ schs. In 2 of studies, all who had lived in NY less than 4 yrs were tested, all others chosen at random; does not say how Ss were selected in one study.

STANFORD-BINET, 1937

| AUTHOR DATE | LOCATION | N | SUBJECTS | | METHOD OF SELECTION |
			AGE	GRADE	
Tomlinson,[28] H. (1944)	Austin, Tex.	c- 75	7-9		All available pairs of c sibs at the 2 age levels: 4-6 & 7-9.

[22]Ss obviously not unselected samples.
[23]*t* ratio calculated by writer from authors' data.

[24]Used a revision of *Binet-Simon* prepared & given by members of Children's Service Bur. of Youngstown. This revision correlated .97 with *Stanford-Binet*. Only American-born of native parents included in table. Kindergarten testing was not separated by authors from testing of 1-2 grades.

TWO (continued)
INDIVIDUAL TESTS

	RESULTS			COMMENTS OF AUTHOR

		IQ			*M IQ Taussig's Scale*	
	c	c	c		Professional	98
	NYC	*DC*	*Balt*		Clerical	101
M	104.7	97.7	95.7		Skilled	97
s	9.2	12.5	13.1		Semi-sk	95
					Day Labor	93

		IQ	
		w	c
Mdn		103.3	89.2
Q		15	7
Range		60-139	60-139
t =		3.49[23]	
12% c above w mdn			

C and w in same schs; c seemed more at ease with E. C functioned in terms of obvious, w in terms of related possibilities. C relatively least efficient in tests of Abstract Reasoning and Adjustment to Unfamiliar Situations.

		IQ	
		w	c
M		95	88

Mean IQ of foreign-speaking children was below that of the c.

		IQ	
	c	c	c
Age	*5-10*	*11-17*	*Total*
M	91.2	81.2	86.2
s	15.8	15.2	14.8
Range	42-128	38-130	38-130
t =	4.67[26]		

Negro child tends to function with reasonable degree of efficiency in concrete situations involving common sense, everyday life experiences, where materials do not call for involved manipulation or abstract analysis.

		IQ	
	c	c	c
	NY-born	*So-born*	*Total*
M	89.8	85.6	86.9

Of total group, 294 were Southern-born and 127 were New York-born.

FORMS L AND M

	IQ
	c
M	86.7
s	11.5
Range	55-64
	to
	125-134

Raises question whether c grow progressively duller in accordance with a genetically determined mental growth curve or as cumulative result of repressive surroundings.

[25]For results on *Terman Group & Mentimeter* given to high sch Ss, see Table 5.

[26]Standard deviation for 11-17 age group and *t* calculated by reviewer from author's data.

[27]Part of large study on Selective Migration. *Stanford-Binet* results include the combined studies of J. Skladman, E. Wallach, & H. Rogosin, all directed by Klineberg. See Table 12.

[28]A study of 75 pairs of c siblings; for results on younger pair members, see Table 1.

TABLE

SCHOOL CHILDREN

| AUTHOR DATE | LOCATION | N | SUBJECTS | | METHOD OF SELECTION |
			AGE	GRADE	
Klugman, S. F. (1944)	Not given (probably Philadelphia)	w-38 c- 34	7-13 7-14	2-7 2-7	In order to qualify as a S, each child had to take mental tests on 3 occasions, had to score bet 90-110 IQ on *each of first 2 tests,* & had to receive written permission from parents to participate. All from same sch. (See text for experimental design.)
Higgins,[29] C., and Sivers, C. H. (1958)	A Northeastern City	w-440 c- 349	7-9 7-9	1-4 1-4	From publ schs serving lowest socioeco areas of a Northeastern city. All 7-, 8-, & 9-yr-olds in Grades 1-3 of these schs were studied, plus children from 5 4th-grade classes.

STANFORD-BINET, 1960

| AUTHOR DATE | LOCATION | N | SUBJECTS | | METHOD OF SELECTION |
			AGE	GRADE	
Kennedy,[30] W. A., Van De Riet, V., and White, J. C., Jr. (1961) (1963)	Ala., Fla., Ga., S. C., Tenn.	c- 1800	5-16	1-6	Normative study of c sch child'n in 5 states; 1 metro., 1 urban & 1 rural county from each state. Each co selected for representativeness of state sampled. Ss selected from roster of children in sch systems by use of table of random numbers.
Tiber, N. (1963)	A Southeastern Public School System	w- (1)160 (2)160 c- 160	7-10	2, 3	McGuire-White Index of Social Status used to identify S's social class; 3 groups were selected: (1) 160 middle-class w, (2) 160 lower-class w, & 160 lower-class Negroes. Ss in each class & caste group randomly assigned to 4 incentive groups & tested on *S-B.*

[29]For results on *Progressive Matrices* given to these Ss, see Table 3.

TWO *(continued)*

INDIVIDUAL TESTS

RESULTS	COMMENTS OF AUTHOR

RESULTS

IQ
Praise

	w	c
M	99.54	96.16
s	6.05	5.05

Pennies

	w	c
M	99.68	99.56
s	6.83	6.53

COMMENTS OF AUTHOR: Substantial superiority of scores of *colored* when tested with *money incentive* over those col tested with praise incentive. *W* show substantial superiority over col when *praise* is incentive.

IQ

	w	c
M	90.6	90.3
s	15.1	13.2
t =		0.27

COMMENTS OF AUTHOR: Mean *S-B* IQ's were similar for Negro and white children, boys and girls, and for groupings within the 3 age levels.

FORM L-M

IQ
c
Community Size

	Total	Metro	Urb	Rur
M	80.71	83.97	79.37	78.70
s	12.48	12.63	12.05	11.82

F sig. at .001

Grade

	1	2	3
M	81.81	80.38	80.25
s	12.43	12.79	11.90

	4	5	6
M	79.65	81.20	80.77
s	11.83	12.60	12.87

F not sig.

COMMENTS OF AUTHOR: These normative data make it possible to do an accurate job of counseling and guidance of c elem sch child'n in SE; and present openly and objectively a serious academic, socioeconomic, and perhaps intellectual gap, and a challenge as to how we close the gap.

IQ

	w (1)	w (2)	c
M			
Praise	106.27	93.55	77.42
Reproof	106.27	92.15	75.95
Candy	108.92	91.67	78.65
None	108.88	96.45	77.55
Total	107.59	93.96	77.39
s			
Praise	11.58	12.25	11.53
Reproof	16.50	13.56	13.34
Candy	13.27	14.67	10.50
None	17.10	13.48	9.65

COMMENTS OF AUTHOR: The important motivational differences may not lie within the test situation itself but in acquisition of knowledge and skills which the intelligence test measures.

---

[30]See Table 1 for results on the 5-year-olds.

TABLE

SCHOOL CHILDREN

AUTHOR DATE	LOCATION	N	SUBJECTS		METHOD OF SELECTION
			AGE	GRADE	

WECHSLER INTELLIGENCE

AUTHOR DATE	LOCATION	N	AGE	GRADE	METHOD OF SELECTION
Sartin, J. L. (1950)	Tallahassee, Fla.	c- 45	8-9	3-4	From a Negro Elem Sch in a neighborhood considered representative of c areas in city. All of children in Grades 3-4 included if 8 or 9 yrs, acc to sch counselor's records.[31]
Young, F. M., and Pitts, V. A. (1951)	County, Northeast Georgia	c- 80	6-16		40 congenital syphilitics in Alto Medical Center, hospitalized for treatment; control group attending a rural sch matched with above group for race, age, sex, geographic location, & father's occupation.
Young, F. M., and Bright, H. A. (1954)	Muscogee and Oconee counties, Ga.	c- 81	10-13	4-7	All c in 3 rural schs if within age & grade range. A random sample from 4th sch.
Caldwell, M. B. (1954)	Ala., Fla., Ga., N. C., S. C.	c- 420	5-12	1-7	Six boys & 6 girls randomly picked in each of 7 age groups totalling 84 from each of 5 states. Usually 2 towns were selected from a state, all schs being located within corporate limits. Children with physical handicaps & all "suspected of mental deficiency" were excluded.
Semler, I. J., and Iscoe, I. (1963)	Austin, Tex.	w-115 c- 108	6-9 6-9		All enrolled in 2 publ schs, 1 c, 1 w; attempt to select schs to minimize socioeco diffs. Ss were randomly selected by ages from lists furnished by schs.

[31]The retarded children falling within the CA span may have been already excluded from sch or withheld from sch by their parents (personal communication from author in 1964).
[32]Total mean IQ's computed by reviewer. See Table 1 for testing of 5-year-olds.
    In a study reported by Iscoe & Pierce-Jones (1964) the mean WISC Full Scale IQ (exclusive of Comprehension & Picture Arrangement) of 110 c Ss in Austin, Ages 5-9, was 91.6 (*s*, 12.57);

TWO (continued)

INDIVIDUAL TESTS

RESULTS	COMMENTS OF AUTHOR

SCALE FOR CHILDREN

		IQ	
		c	
	Verb	Perf	
M	85.93	97.31	
s	11.02	18.31	
Diff sig at .01			

Negroes in this study were poor in the fundamental capacity to reason, and were poor in most items relating to verbal ability.

		IQ	
		c	
Syph	Verb	Perf	Full
M	67.75	59.00	59.00
Mdn	65.10	58.25	57.80
s	10.60	12.4	12.40
Control		c	
M	79	67.38	69.80
Mdn	78.25	68.25	71.04
s	14.50	15.15	15.08

Inferiority of syphilitics in learning new material and in comprehending part-whole relationships noteworthy. Unreasonable that controls selected as a representative sample of rural Negro children should be regarded as borderline.

		IQ	
		c	
	Verb	Perf	Full
M	73.92	67.13	67.74
s	8.25	11.45	9.60

Questions suitability of WISC for Southern rural colored children.

		IQ	
		c	
	Verb	Perf	Full
M	90.79	82.74	85.52
Diff's sig at .01			

Group as whole best on Arith, Comprehension, Digit Span, and Similarities; lowest on Picture Completion, Vocabulary, and Block Design.

	M IQ[32]	
	w	c
Age	Full Scale	
6	104.5	97.0
7	97.4	90.7
8	105.5	97.6
9	96.3	87.5
Total	101.36	93.71

Analysis of variance of WISC Full Scale IQ's for 60 w and 60 c randomly selected from total groups indicates highly significant diff's in favor of w Ss (p < .001).

the mean IQ of 110 w Ss was 103.37 (s, 14.01). Although the authors do not refer to the Semler & Iscoe work, the description of the Ss suggests that many of the same children were included in both researches.

TABLE

SCHOOL CHILDREN

AUTHOR DATE	LOCATION	N	SUBJECTS		METHOD OF SELECTION
			AGE	GRADE	
Tuttle, L. E., Jr. (1964)	Gainesville, Fla.	w-25 c- 25	9½-10½ 9½-10½	3-4 3-4	From 1 c elem sch (Duval) & 1 w (Kirby Smith). All c in the 2 grades who had had all of educ in Alachua Co & were bet 9½-10½; of the 49 who proved eligible, 33 were permitted by parents to be tested; from the 33, random selection table used to get 12 boys & 13 girls. Whites selected by same criteria, but instead of using table of random numbers, final selection of 25 Ss based on matching with c for sex, CA & grade. Girls perfectly matched ; boys were matched for grade but not age.
Teahan, J. E., and Drews, E. M. (1962)	Lansing, Mich.	c- No-26 So- 24	13.0* 12.9	Elem & JrHS	All had been referred by their schs at some time during past 2 yrs for intellectual evaluation; child had to be clearly identified as a Negro who had either been born & educated in *North* or who had migrated from *South* within 1 yr previous to testing.
					PINTNER-PATERSON SCALE
Peterson, J., and Telford, C. W. (1930)	St. Helena Isl., S. C.	c- 86 to 100	12		19 Ss from Penn Normal & Industrial Sch; rest from publ schs, 2 of which were crowded shacks.
Klineberg, O. (1928)	Villages in Southeastern W. Va.	w- 25 c- 129	8-15 7-15		w- as random a sample as possible; c- all children found in house-to-house canvass.
Long, H. H. (1933)	Washington, D. C.	c- I-100 II-100		3A	cI- "Practically" all of c from 5 schs in underprivileged areas, if born in DC. cII- Principals & teachers recommended pupils who came from better residential sections. All born in DC.

*Mean age at testing.
[33]Three tests in the P-P series: *Mare and Foal* (100 Ss), *Healy A* (86 Ss), *Two-Figure Form Board* (100 Ss).

TWO *(continued)*
INDIVIDUAL TESTS

RESULTS	COMMENTS OF AUTHOR

	IQ		F-ratio
Verb	w	c	
M	108.2	88.7	27.43
Mdn	104	92	
Perf			
M	103.4	86.7	54.27
Mdn	103.2	86.3	
Full			
M	106.5	86.5	23.91
Mdn	106	91	

All c-w diffs $<$ .01

In addition to the *WISC* the *Peabody Picture Vocabulary Test (PPVT)* and the *Columbia Mental Maturity Scale (CMMS)* were individually administered to the 50 Ss. The *WISC* appeared to measure more consistently for both c and w children than did the *PPVT* or *CMMS*.

	M IQ c		
Bkg	*Verb*	*Perf*	*Full*
No	87.42	88.38	87.04
So	80.29	68.83	72.37

Southern Negroes may be even more hampered on nonverbal (than verbal tests) due to their restricted and impoverished social and educational bkgs.

OF PERFORMANCE TESTS

C sig below w norms on[33] the 3 tests.

Individual tests reflect educational and cultural effects much less than standard group tests.

	IQ[34]	
	w	c
Mdn	88	83
Q	15	12
Range	46-123	40-130

Personal equation of E an important factor in this test.

	IQ cI
M	97

cII about one mental year above cI.

---

[34]12 tests in the P-P series. Klineberg was assisted by a Negro who established contacts with c families and gave tests to colored Ss.

TABLE

SCHOOL CHILDREN

| AUTHOR DATE | LOCATION | N | SUBJECTS | | METHOD OF SELECTION |
			AGE	GRADE	
Klineberg, O. (1928)	New York City	w-100 c- 200	11-16 11-16	6-9 7-8	w- boys from a neighborhood settlement house, Eastside YMCA & Hudson Guild; c- random sampling of boys from a Harlem Jr HS.
Klineberg, O. (1935)	New York City	c- 110	10		Harlem publ sch boys; does not say how selected.
Tanser, H. A. (1939)	Kent County, Ont.	w-211 c- 162	5-15 5-16	1-8 1-8	"As far as practicable all Negro pupils in the one urban and the 6 rural schools were tested." As many whites as possible.

KOHS BLOCK

Graham,[35] V. T. (1926)	Atlanta, Ga.	c- 28	6-7	1	Unselected.
Harris, B. V. (1929)	Columbus, Ohio	c- 345	5-15	1-6	All c from 2 publ schs, Grades 1-6. Because of small number of cases at 5, 14, & 15 yrs, these eliminated in comparisons.

ARTHUR

Thurmond,[36] S. (1933)	Clarke Co., Ga.	c- 40	12		From 6 best of 13 rural schs for Negroes in county; list of every pupil who was under 13 yrs but had reached 12th birthday; 52 enrolled met criterion but 12 absent on one or more of testing days.

[35]Five of P-P tests: *Mare and Foal, Casuist Form Board, Healy A, Triangle Test, & Knox Cube.* IQ's not given; mdn age of both groups was 13; P-P norm for Age 13.
[36]Estimated from average mental ages given by author. Used 6 of P-P tests: *Triangle, Healy A, Two-Figure Form Board, Casuist Form Board, Knox Cube, & Five-Figure Form Board.*

TWO *(continued)*

INDIVIDUAL TESTS

	RESULTS			COMMENTS OF AUTHOR

		Scores[35]		No attempt to get a "typical" NY group of w boys,
	P-P			or to secure w and c groups equal in social status or
	(norm)	w	c	in educational opportunity.
Mdn	224	174	162	

		IQ[36]	Part of series of studies dealing with problem of
		c	selective migration.
M		80.00	

	IQ[37]		No effort spared to have children put forth best
	w	c	effort.
M	109.59	90.98	
Mdn			
Rural	102.00	92.72	
Urban	108.93	87.63	
Total	108.20	91.20	
s	22.45	18.95	
18% c above w *mdn*			

DESIGN TEST

		Scores		C child's Block Design ability lags decidedly behind
		w	c	his general ability and indicates a special racial
M		(norm)		inferiority in the factors that contribute to success
Age 6		4	1.4	at this type of work.
Age 7		8	2.0	

		Mdn		These colored have median performance level
		w	c	considerably lower than that of the group with
Age		(norm)		which Kohs worked, the diff becoming more marked
6		2	0	with increasing age.
7		6	2	
8		11	6	
9		18	10	
10		25	17	
11		35	20	
12		43	25	
13		61	29	

POINT SCALE

	IQ	Poorly trained teachers. Attendance law not rigidly
	c	enforced upon Negro. Children may stay home be-
M	84	cause child or parent dislikes the teacher.
s	12.28	
Range	60-114	

[37]Used *Short Scale* consisting of 10 of P-P tests; for results on other tests see Tables 3 and 4.
[38]For results on *Stanford-Binet* and *Otis*, see Tables 2 and 3.
[39]For results on *Stanford-Binet, 1916* and *Illinois*, see Tables 2 and 4.

TABLE

SCHOOL CHILDREN

| AUTHOR DATE | LOCATION | N | SUBJECTS | | METHOD OF SELECTION |
			AGE	GRADE	
Bruce,[40] M. (1940)	Rural Virginia County	w-87 c- 72	6-12 6-12		All in attendance at 9 pairs of schs tested on K-A; each child was ranked acc to K-A score & every 5th one selected for testing on *Arthur*.
					FULL-RANGE PICTURE
Coppinger,[41] N. W. (1949)	New Orleans and Caddo Parish, La.	c- 80		1-8	One NO sch, 10 rural schs; selected only Ss correctly placed in grade acc to age; in city, sampled also to get correct representation acc to occupation of parents.
					DETROIT TESTS OF
Furlow,[42] F. D. (1954)	Atlanta, Ga.	c- 38	10-14	6	Ss enrolled in one of 3 6th-grades of Carter Elem Sch; does not say whether this group is representative of the 3. Each S given 3 tests.
					DAVIS-HESS INDIVIDUAL
Hess, R. D. (1955)	Chicago, Ill.	w- high-188 low-178 c- low-179	6-9 6-9		Sample of 545 elem sch pupils tested at 4 CA points: 6.5, 7.5, 8.5, 9.5. High-status w from prof & manag occup; low-status w from semi-& unsk; low-status c from unsk & unemploy. All given a standard test & the new one.

[40]For results on *Stanford-Binet, 1916* and *Kuhlmann-Anderson,* see Tables 2 and 4.
[41]See also Coppinger and Ammons (1952).
[42]For results on *Davis-Eells Test & California Test of Mental Maturity,* see Tables 3 and 4.

TWO *(continued)*

INDIVIDUAL TESTS

	RESULTS		COMMENTS OF AUTHOR

	IQ		Significant diff between means; 11% of colored above mdn of whites.
	w	c	
M	94.21	77.10	
Mdn	93.25	74.73	
s	22.11	14.08	
Range	46-173	48-116	

VOCABULARY TEST

	M Scores		Mean scores of colored in general equal to those of white norms about 2 years younger.
	w	c	
M age	(norms)		
6.5	25	18	
7.5	27	21	
8.5	31	25	
9.5	35	29	
10.5	39	33	
11.5	43	36	
12.5	48	40	
13.5	52	44	

LEARNING APTITUDE

	IQ	This sch serves as cultural center for the Negro community.
	c	
M	84.60	
Mdn	82.50	
s	16.44	
Ranges	50-117	

TEST OF INTELLIGENCE

No sig diff bet high-status w and low-status w Low-status w sig above the low-status c at all ages[43]

Results of exper testing project showed marked reduction of socioeco differential bet high and low status groups on standard tests.

[43]Statement is reviewer's, based on author's tables. Author compares high-status & low-status w, high-status w & low-status c, but *not* low-status w & low-status c. In a personal communication, Hess indicated that the standard test was generally *Kuhlmann-Anderson*, that the Ss were from 6 publ schs, & that the new test was developed by himself in collaboration with Davis, and was individually administered. For results on standard test as given to these Ss, see K-A in Table 4.

TABLE

SCHOOL CHILDREN

AUTHOR DATE	LOCATION	N	SUBJECTS		METHOD OF SELECTION
			AGE	GRADE	

PEABODY PICTURE

| Tuttle, L. E., Jr. (1964) | Gainesville, Fla. | w-25 c- 25 | 9½-10½ 9½-10½ | 3-4 3-4 | Administered *PPVT, CMMS*, & *WISC* to all Ss. See method previously outlined, this table, under *WISC*. |

COLUMBIA MENTAL

| Tuttle, L. E., Jr. (1964) | Gainesville, Fla. | w-25 c- 25 | 9½-10½ 9½-10½ | 3-4 3-4 | Administered *PPVT, CMMS*, & *WISC* to all Ss. See method previously outlined, this table, under *WISC*. |

TWO *(concluded)*

INDIVIDUAL TESTS

RESULTS	COMMENTS OF AUTHOR

VOCABULARY TEST

	IQ		F-ratio
	w	**c**	
M	105.5	77.2	54.71
Mdn	103.3	75	
P $<$ .01			

This study indicates that teachers, sch psychologists, *et al.*, should recognize that a Negro child scoring at 110 IQ and above may well represent the higher IQ level of his subcultural group; and that an IQ of 75 on *WISC* or *S-B* may not nec indicate that a c child is a candidate for an educable mentally retarded class.

MATURITY SCALE

	IQ		F-ratio
	w	**c**	
M	87.0	75.0	9.7
Mdn	80.3	69	
P $<$ .05			

Results of data analysis introduces the question of what CMMS measures, how well it measures, and whether or not it does measure any aspect of general intelligence.

states of Alabama, Florida, Georgia, North Carolina, South Carolina, and Texas. Although some selectivity occurred in these studies in the South, whatever was reported would seem to have affected the Negro samples favorably rather than unfavorably.[16] For example, Semler and Iscoe (1963), in reference to the particular Austin public school from which they had chosen their colored subjects, commented that it had "a very adequate physical plant, a good lunch program, and a dedicated, well-trained group of teachers." They considered it to be certainly the equal of that attended by their white school children.[17] M. B. Caldwell (1954), in investigating the adequacy of the *WISC* for measuring the intelligence of Southern urban Negro children, selected nine towns in the Southeast for his testing program. Of these, three were described as containing Negro and white colleges or universities and one as a progressive winter resort. Ss were drawn from the school populations of the elected towns according to a table of random numbers; however, all children suspected of mental deficiency were excluded from his samples, and as most of the schools did not have objective criteria for judging mental deficiency, "the only alternative was teacher judgment."

Sartin (1950) may likewise have excluded the seriously retarded from his sample.[18] At any rate, this investigator appeared to have selected his subjects for *both* age and grade, since he included all of the colored children in a Tallahassee school in Grades 3 and 4, if they were 8 or 9 years of age. Tuttle (1964) not only selected his subjects for both age and grade, thereby eliminating retarded and advanced children; chose only children who had had all of their formal schooling in Alachua County; but required that they have written permission from their parents to participate in the study — referred in a letter to the parents as research "designed to compare test results of Negro and white children."[19] While the schools were not reported as having been chosen because of similarity in socioeconomic class, it is probable that the majority of subjects from both Negro and white schools were of the *middle class*.[20] The reviewer

---

[16]The data on the 40 congenital syphilitics (Young and Pitts, 1951) are exceptional and do not enter into this and the following discussions; their means, *etc.*, may be found in Table 2.

[17]Ss 6 years and older were generally in publ schools. However, some of the 6-yr-olds included in Table 2 were still enrolled in the private nursery-kindergartens, due to the fact that a child had to have reached his 6th birthday when he started in the first grade in public school.

[18]Sartin's Master's thesis was directed by Caldwell. See fn. 31, Table 2.

[19]Although in his letter Tuttle indicated that all information obtained would remain strictly confidential, about 30 per cent of the colored and 35 per cent of the white parents did not permit their children to be tested, possibly affecting the representativeness of the 25 colored and 25 white children finally selected to serve as subjects.

[20]According to their teachers' evaluations, 8 per cent of the colored were from the upper class, 64 per cent from the middle class, and 28 per cent from the lower class; 76 per cent of the white Ss were from the middle class and 24 per cent from the lower class.

might add, finally, that there seems to have been a selective urban-rural factor operating in these studies. Of the 719 colored children tested in the South, 598 were living in urban and 121 in rural areas.[21]

The combined *Full-Scale* mean IQ proved to be 84, based upon 719 Southern colored subjects, just three points above the *Stanford-Binet* mean of 81, secured on a stratified sampling of 1800 Negro children in the Southeast (Kennedy, Van De Riet, and White, 1963).[22] The combined *Performance IQ* is 81, exactly the same as the Kennedy, *et al.* mean on the *S-B,* and six points below their own *Verbal* mean of 87 (611 Southern cases).

Teahan and Drews (1962) compared the test scores of 50 colored children attending elementary and junior high schools in Lansing, Michigan; 26 of them were born and educated in the North and 24 were born in the South and had lived in the North less than one year prior to testing. All of the pupils had been referred to the school psychologists for intellectual evaluation because they were deficient in school work and all had been given the *WISC*. As will be noted in Table 2, the Northern-born-and-reared were not only significantly superior in mean IQ to the Southern-born-and-reared but they differed more from them in their *Performance* IQ than in their *Verbal* IQ. While emphasizing the point that their Negro samples might not be representative of Negroes in general, the authors nevertheless believed that their results suggested that one should use great caution in interpreting the nonverbal IQ's when cultural deprivation is suspected, "especially with respect to the southern Negro".

The findings of Teahan and Drews, though based upon very small and selected samples, in certain respects are in substantial agreement with those investigators who tested Negro children in the South. The large group living in the South (all Ss combined) and the small group living in the North (50 Ss) earned total mean IQ's well below the white norms. In contrast to the white norms, the Southern colored children and the small group living in the North who had spent nearly all of their lives in the South (24 Ss) achieved lower *Performance* IQ's on the average than *Verbal* IQ's.[23] Also, both groups of Teahan and Drews, like those of Caldwell (the author of the major Southern study employing *WISC*) and unlike the normative Ss, were reported as making their better scores on the subtests of *Comprehension* and *Similarities* and making among their poorer scores on the subtests of *Vocabulary* and *Block Design.*

However, Teahan and Drews' results taken *independently* do not enable us to generalize with any degree of confidence. This is due — not only to the

---

[21]After studying the 1950 Census, Kennedy, Van De Riet, and White concluded that by 1960 the Negro school population in the Southeast would be about equally located in the large metropolitan counties, the urban counties, and the rural counties. (1963, p. 59)

[22]In consideration of the factors mentioned which may have biased the *WISC* data the writer is of the opinion that the *Stanford-Binet* IQ is the more valid statistic.

[23]In agreement with findings of Atchison (1955) on *WISC*. The *Verbal* mean IQ of 80 mentally defective Negro boys and girls exceeded the *Performance* IQ.

relatively small numbers of colored tested and to the fact that they were doing so poorly in their schoolwork that their teachers needed an evaluation of their mental ability — but to the fact that no measure of variability was included in the data (nor frequency distributions of age or IQ), to the fact that there was no report on average grade placement, to the fact that there is no indication as to whether the birthplace of the Southern-born group was rural, urban or metropolitan (presumably the Northern-born was urban or metropolitan), and to the fact that no indication was given as to whether the Northern- or Southern-born sampled their Lansing racial group in the same proportion.

PINTNER-PATERSON

The *Pintner-Paterson Scale of Performance Tests,* designed for Ages 4 to 15 years, consists of 15 tests. Seven of these are of the form board type, three are picture completions, and the other 5 include: manikin test, feature profile test, substitution test, adaptation board, and cube test. A *Short Scale* of the *Pintner-Paterson* includes 10 of the tests, those omitted being: triangle test, diagonal test, Healy Puzzle A, substitution test, and the adaptation board. "These and similar performance tests have been found valuable as supplements to verbal tests of mental ability, also with subjects who, though they are English-speaking, have speech defects or reading disabilities." These performance tests are considered more susceptible to practice effects, and chance successes are more frequent than is the case with verbal tests; they correlate moderately with the *Stanford-Binet* at the lower range of ability (.43) and poorly at the upper range (.23); they correlate with other performance test ratings between .50 and .80. A factorial analysis of results obtained on 34 commonly used performance tests indicates that the principal factors measured may be identified as: spatial, perceptual speed, and induction. The first two of these functions are of relatively little significance in determining a person's rating on verbal tests. (Freeman, 1950, pp. 169-174)

Five investigators made use of some or all of the *Pintner-Paterson* tests in studying Negro intelligence. Peterson and Telford (1930) tested children in the South, Klineberg (1928) and Long (1933) in the Border section, and Klineberg (1928, 1935) and Tanser (1939) in the North. Results were not presented in terms of IQ in all of these studies; wherever IQ's were given, however, none of the colored groups averaged more than 91, with the exception of the Washington, D. C., Ss studied by Long. These D.C. pupils are the same children who were tested on the *Stanford-Binet, 1916 Form,* and the reviewer has already commented upon the methods by which they were selected.

The children of St. Helena, an island connected by a bridge to the coast of South Carolina and inhabited principally by colored people, did poorly on this test, as did the New York City Negro groups and the white group examined by Klineberg (Table 2). In one of his New York investigations the mean IQ of a group of Negro boys was 80; while in the other the white boys scored above the colored but both were considerably below the *Pintner-Paterson* norms. In his 1928 research Klineberg did not select his colored and white subjects in the same manner; the colored boys were a sampling from a Harlem junior high school while the whites were chosen from settlement and recreation houses or guilds. In his rural West Virginia survey the Negro children's median IQ was 83, which placed them 5 points below a group of 25 whites from the same area. In neither this study nor in the New York City investigation did Klineberg consider the testing technique to be above reproach.

In preparation for his doctoral dissertation, Tanser[24] studied the mental capacity of Kent County, Ontario, Negro children. Among the four tests he employed was the *Short Scale* of the *Pintner-Paterson* which he gave to 211 white and 162 colored subjects from seven public schools in this county. Tanser was of the opinion that practically all of the colored inhabitants of the county were descendants of early settlers, very few new families having moved into the area within the preceding fifty years. He observed that the adverse conditions which Long (1934) described as existing for the Negro in the District of Columbia were not paralleled in Kent County. In the Canadian county, according to Tanser, the Negro may attend the whites' church, may sit in any seat in the public theatres, may ride side by side with the white man in any public conveyance, be served in any hotel or restaurant, may work where he likes, and may own property and live in any part of the city or country. His children attend the same public schools as white children, and some of the schools are taught by colored teachers. Thus the Negro of Kent County, in contrast to the Negro of the Southern states, is reported to have been subjected to fewer pronounced color prejudices and in general to have been allowed better social, cultural, economic, and educational advantages.[25]

The mean IQ of the white children on the *Pintner-Paterson* was 109.6, that of the colored, 91; the standard deviation of the Negro distribution was 3.5 points less than that of the white. Although the colored mean on this test was higher than that of any of the colored groups reported in the States with the exception of Long's, it is nine points below the American white norm and about 19 points below the mean of the white Canadian group. Eighteen per cent of the Negroes reached or exceeded the median of the white subjects in Kent County, one third of the Negroes reached or exceeded the median of the American whites, and two thirds of the Ontario whites reached or exceeded the median of the American whites. Relative to his findings on this test, Tanser wrote: "From the evidence presented the deduction follows that according to the Short Scale of the Pintner-Paterson Performance Tests the Negroes as a group are low in intelligence and considerably lower than the Whites tested." (1939, p. 129)

---

[24]Superintendent of Schools, Chatham, Kent Co., Ontario.

[25]At one point, Tanser said that, "with few exceptions", the Kent County Negro is on a level with the white man in regard to every political and social advantage. (p. 20)

Tanser stated that the whites attending the Central School[26] (the one urban school included in the survey) came from homes, on the average, of considerably higher socioeconomic status than the homes from which the colored pupils came. However, the colored and white children attending the six rural schools came from homes which were generally of equal status. Parents of most of the rural children, colored as well as white, were employed on the land, many of them owning the farms which they worked. Generally speaking, the farms of the colored were as modern and the owners as prosperous as their white neighbors. The respective medians of the comparable but not equated groups of rural Negro and white children were 92.72 and 102.00.

Tanser noted that the Negroes were considerably over-age and the whites slightly under-age for the various grades, and concluded: "In the light of the present findings it is now readily clear that the main factor responsible for the over-ageness of the Negroes is their low level of intelligence. Other factors, such as low socio-economic status, may be partly responsible, but in view of the prevailing wide difference between the intelligence levels of the Whites and Negroes we feel that the low intelligence of the Negroes plays the major rôle in this connection." (1939, p. 163)

From the above discourse the following points appear: (1) Negro children in Kent County averaged *consistently below* the whites in the county on the various tests administered to them;[27] (2) the socioeconomic status of the urban colored was without doubt *inferior to that of the whites* in the city of Chatham; (3) the socioeconomic status of the rural Negroes was *generally the equal* of that of the rural whites;[28] and (4) the colored as a community possessed all *civil rights* enjoyed by any other Canadians, and had been subjected to *less color prejudice* than have Negroes in the United States.

Tanser's work has been scrutinized and either treated with respect or belittled, depending in part at least upon which of the above cited points (or explanations) the critic had uncovered in the original text or noted in another's review of it. Anastasi, for example, as a part of her brief appraisal and dismissal of this research, said, "Nevertheless significant differences were found in the socioeconomic level of the two groups." (1958, p. 556)[29] This statement would be correct only if qualified to read, "Nevertheless significant differences were found in the socioeconomic level of the *two urban groups*." (See point 2.) In Klineberg's

---

[20]Central School in Chatham furnished one third of total number of colored Ss used in the research, *i.e.*, 65 as compared with 123 from 6 rural schools.

[27]For specific results on other intelligence tests administered, see pp. 77, 87, and 134 of this book.

[28]40% of the rural whtes tested were of non-British birth or descent. (See p. 88.)

[29]Anastasi also noted that ". . . it is reported that the white children attended school more regularly than the Negro, a difference often associated with social class differences." (pp. 556-557) This report from Tanser is correct. However, in the one urban school where the social class differences were reported, the colored were at least as regular in their attendance as the white children, *i.e.*, c, 94.24% and w, 84.17%. (Tanser, p. 78)

review of Negro-white differences in intelligence he cites as "pertinent" Anastasi's statement quoted above — without the proper qualification. (1963, p. 199)

McCord and Demerath referred to McGurk as having *"totally omitted* references to Tanser's own confession that the socio-economic status of Negroes in Kent County *was then and had always been inferior to whites."* (1958, p. 122) This statement to be correct would have to be qualified in two ways: (1) by eliminating the word *confession* (it is absurd to call point 2 *a confession*), and (2) by qualifying the statement to read ". . . . the socioeconomic status of *Negroes attending the urban school* in Kent County . . . ."[30]

In replying to McCord and Demerath, McGurk quoted from a passage in Tanser's book, following it with: "It seems from the above that Tanser felt quite clearly that the socioeconomic opportunities for the Negroes were extremely close to those for the whites:" (point 4) and making a distinction between *socioeconomic opportunities* and *socioeconomic status,* he continued: "if the Negroes' socioeconomic status were so low, relative to that of the whites, it was not because the opportunity for socioeconomic equality was not present." (1959, pp. 57-58)

Garrett, likewise, commented on the Tanser research as follows: "The social and economic conditions of the whites and Negroes were substantially the same." (1962, p. 261) To be exact, it should be qualified to read, ". . . . conditions of the *rural whites and Negroes* were substantially the same." (point 3)

In the 1963 review, Klineberg referred to having lived the first 25 years of his life in Canada and observed that he would have thought that Canada was similar to the Northeastern United States in its prejudices toward the Negro; he cited, in support of his opinion, the work of Chant and Freedman in which they compared nationality and racial preferences of a group of University of Toronto undergraduates with those of Thurstone's Chicago University sample. Klineberg, however, misinterpreted the results of this study relating to the Negro specifically, for this racial group was placed *higher* on the *Toronto scale* than on the *Chicago* scale. In fact, Chant and Freedman conclude with this statement (supporting Tanser, if applicable at all to Kent County): "The higher relative position of the Negro on the Toronto scale can be accepted as indicating a difference of attitude towards Negroes which is readily apparent to anyone familiar with the two cities." (1934, p. 120)

Still another comment on the Tanser study was offered by Smart (1963) which she said was long overdue. Mrs. Smart spent her childhood and youth in Kent County and her remarks about Negro housing, dress and grooming, jobs, *etc.*, indicate that at the time of Tanser's study the Negroes were of much lower status than the whites in Kent County. Actually the statements are not contradictory to Tanser's remarks about the socioeconomic status of the *urban whites,* (it being obvious that Mrs. Smart was referring to the *Chatham* Negroes rather

---

[30]Probably the expression, ". . . and had always been . . . ." is gratuitous; but it does seem important if an established fact.

than to the *rural* Negroes) even though she apparently depended upon her memories dating back some thirty years or more.

KOHS BLOCK DESIGN

The *Kohs Block Design* is a measure of manual activity as well as of accuracy and fidelity of perception of likeness and difference. The test makes use of sixteen colored cubes, the four sides of each cube painted in white, blue, red, and yellow, respectively; the other two sides divided diagonally, one being half blue and half yellow, the other being half white and half red. Seventeen designs on cards, using these colors and ranging in order of difficulty, are to be duplicated by the subject with the blocks. Scoring is done in terms of time and number of moves. (Garrett and Schneck, 1933, p. 82)

Kohs Block Design was administered to a small group of Atlanta colored children by Graham (1926). These first-grade children were found to be very inferior to the Kohs' norms, as will be observed from Table 2. The results of this test were surprising to Graham in view of the normal *Stanford-Binet* scores achieved by 105 Atlanta colored first-graders (1926). She concluded that there was indication of a special racial inferiority in the factors contributing to success at this type of work.

Harris (1929) standardized the *Kohs Block Design* on a group of Northern Negroes, having selected this test because it involved no use of language on the part of the subject; because it involved many of the factors which are considered criteria of general intelligence, such as observation, memory, imagery, attention, autocriticism, and invention; and because the material of the test is such that a child is quickly and easily interested. Harris selected all colored children from two Columbus, Ohio, public schools, Grades 1-6—however, because of the small number of cases at Ages 5, 14, and 15 years, the children at these ages were eliminated in the comparisons. He noted that one school was located in a district rather thickly populated with Negroes who had migrated from the South during the preceding few years; the other school selected had very few newcomers and included a large number from very good homes; and the two schools taken together (he did not separate them in the results) would, the author believed, represent a fair sampling of the Negro population of an average city of the size and location of Columbus. Harris indicated that the conditions under which the testing was done were especially favorable and that all subjects seemed interested and willing to take the test.

The school records showed that 225 of the colored children were in the normal grade for their age, 9 were accelerated one grade, 66 were retarded one grade, 36 were retarded two grades, 7 were retarded three grades, *etc.*

An examination of Table 2 will reveal that in comparison with Kohs norms the colored tested in Columbus were retarded one year between the ages of six and nine, and about two years between the ages of 10 and 12; the 13-year-olds were the most retarded but probably not as representative of their age group since the brighter ones would have passed out of the sixth grade. Harris concluded that his results agreed with those of other investigators in that the performance level of the Negro children at each age was inferior to that of white children.

Thus, there seems to be increasing evidence that the *Kohs Block Design* is a difficult task for Negro children. In conjunction with the above two studies we have the more recent ones of Caldwell (1954), Young and Bright (1954), Teahan and Drews (1962), and Tuttle (1964), who found the *Block Design* to be one of the most difficult subtests of the *WISC* for children of this race.

ARTHUR POINT SCALE

Form I of the *Arthur Point Scale of Performance Tests* is a restandardization of eight of the *Pintner-Paterson Tests* (Knox Cube, Seguin Form Board, Two-Figure Form Board, Casuist Form Board, Manikin, Feature Profile, Mare and Foal, and Healy Picture Completion I) with the two additional tests of *Kohs Block Design* and *Porteus Maze*. A second form of this scale, designed for retest purposes, has been less well standardized. Form I is based upon results obtained with 1100 public school children; and the following validating criteria were applied: parental occupation, age-grade distribution, significant increases in score in successive ages, and degree of correspondence with ratings obtained by means of other scales already considered to be valid, such as *Stanford-Binet*. Correlations reported between *Binet* IQ's and *Arthur Point Scale* IQ's (Form I) between the ages of five and twelve ranged between .68 and .80, with one exception. For clinical purposes the *Arthur* scale is considered as a valuable supplement to verbal tests. (Freeman, 1950, pp. 174-178)

Thurmond (1933) and Bruce (1940) tested Southern colored school children with the *Arthur Point Scale* and other mental tests.[31] Both of these investigators administered the *Stanford-Binet, 1916 Form* to rural children of low socioeconomic status, Thurmond in a county in Georgia and Bruce in a county in Virginia. However, Thurmond examined only 12-year-old colored children from the six best of the thirteen schools for Negroes in the county; while Bruce tested both colored and white children from nine pairs of schools, the children ranging in age between six and twelve years.

Thurmond was very interested in finding that her subjects earned a mean *Point Scale* IQ of 84 which proved to be seven points more than their mean IQ as determined by the *Stanford-Binet*. "Whatever the factors may be which account for the amount of retardation here found as estimated from the three measures of intelligence, we are perhaps safe in assuming that under existing conditions twelve-year-old rural Negroes show decidedly more aptitude for non-verbal performances than they do for verbal activities." Whereas on the *Binet*, only *2.5 per cent* of Thurmond's subjects equaled or exceeded the white norm of 100, on the *Point Scale*, *7.5 per cent* equaled or exceeded this norm.

---

[31]Thurmond gave *Stanford-Binet, Illinois,* and *Arthur;* Bruce gave *Stanford-Binet, Kuhlmann-Anderson,* and *Arthur.*

Bruce found smaller differences than did Thurmond between the mean IQ's earned by her subjects on the *Binet* and *Point Scale,* the mean IQ of her white subjects on the latter being 94.21, or just *four points* higher than their mean on the former test; the mean IQ of her colored Ss on the *Arthur Point Scale* was 77.10, or *one point higher* than their *Binet* mean. The variability of the scores of the whites was greater than that of the colored, the respective *s's* being 22.11 and 14.08 (Table 2). Bruce found the difference between the colored and white *Point Scale* means to be significant; further analysis indicated that *11 per cent* of the Negro children were above the median of the whites of the same county. Upon matching the 49 white and the 49 colored children with respect to Sims socioeconomic scores, the mean white IQ became 89.02 and the mean colored IQ, 76.98, the difference remaining significant at the one per cent level of confidence. Fifteen per cent of the 49 colored Ss equaled or surpassed the median of the equated group of whites. Bruce was of the opinion that the lower mean scores of both racial samples, in comparison with the white norms, were due in part to the fact that very few white or colored children in the county are sent to feeble-minded institutions, regardless of the amount of mental defect.

Bruce ranked the *Arthur* subtests in order of difficulty for each child and computed the average rank of each subtest for the two racial groups. With both Negroes and whites all of the tests identified as *speed tests* were found to be in the upper half of the scale, "while the more discriminating 'Power' tests are in the lower half of the scale." (p. 48) Bruce interpreted the lower scoring on the *power tests* as indicating that the low intelligence quotients are due to innate inferiority, or else the "new situation" type of test is as subject to the depressing influence of environment as other subtests.

FULL-RANGE PICTURE VOCABULARY

The *Full-Range Picture Vocabulary Test,* developed by the Ammonses, consists of 16 4-picture plates, the pictures being cartoon-like drawings of everyday activities and objects. Ss are required to point to one of the four pictures which best represents the word E gives. The test, therefore, requires an understanding of spoken words; but the child does not need to speak or read. These test scores correlated in the .80's with the *Stanford-Binet* vocabulary test in two instances, and about the same with the vocabulary subtest of the *Wechsler-Bellevue.* The authors have, therefore, constructed a test measuring approximately the same factor or factors which underlie the vocabulary tests of Terman and Wechsler. (W. D. Altus, *in* Buros, 1953, p. 340)

The *Full-Range* test was administered to 80 colored children, Grades 1-8, in one urban and ten rural Louisiana schools by Coppinger (1949). To develop normative material for Southern colored Ss, Coppinger selected five girls and five boys who were correctly placed according to their age in each of the first 8 grades. The 41 urban Ss were further sampled so that their fathers' occupations would be correctly represented in accordance with the census reports of Southern

Negro males. As will be seen in Table 2 the mean scores of these children approximated those of a white population about two years younger.

DETROIT LEARNING APTITUDE

The *Detroit Tests of Learning Aptitude* are designed for Age 4 to the adult level, and is a point scale test. "Standardization is inadequate. . . . The whole interpretation lacks statistical foundation" according to Mursell. (*quoted in* Cronbach, 1949, p. 136)

The *Detroit Learning Aptitude Test* was one of three given by Furlow (1954) to a small group of colored pupils in Atlanta. As will be noted in Table 2 these Ss were enrolled in one of the three sixth grades of the E. R. Carter Elementary School, a school which is reported to be a center for various extra-curricular activities and cultural interests of the Negro community. A range of IQ's from 50 to 117 was reported on these children, with a mean of 84.60, and a standard deviation of 16.44.

DAVIS-HESS TEST

In attempting to control the influence of culture on test performance Davis and Hess developed an *Individual Test of Intelligence* which was administered by Hess to Negro and white public-school children in the city of Chicago (1955). The test was made up of 16 items which were believed to be similar to real-life situations and to have intrinsic motivation; likewise, children of different social status were presumed to be equally familiar with the materials, symbols, and verbal content of the instructions. Each S was allowed to proceed at his own speed, and the testers were urged to establish rapport and encourage maximum performance.

In the Chicago study, children were tested at four chronological age points, $6\frac{1}{2}$, $7\frac{1}{2}$, $8\frac{1}{2}$, and $9\frac{1}{2}$. Three groups of children, each group selected from two different schools, were chosen at random within the criteria established. (1) The first group consisted of 188 white Ss whose parents were from professional and managerial occupational levels and identified as *high-status level*. (2) The second group consisted of 178 white Ss whose parents were from unskilled and semiskilled occupational levels, *low-status level*. (3) The third consisted of 179 colored Ss whose parents were unskilled laborers or unemployed, *low-status level*. All of the 545 Ss had been previously tested on a "standard group test" and their scores listed in the school records. Hess tabulated the mean "standard test" MA's for each of the four ages of the three race-status groups; for comparative purposes he tabulated the mean raw scores earned on the *Davis-Hess* test for each of these 12 subgroups. In comparing the white Groups 1 and 2 with one another Hess found significant differences favoring Group 1 on the "standard test" (usually the *Kuhlmann-Anderson*); however, he obtained no significant difference between the white groups on the *Davis-Hess* test. Significant differences occurred between the high-status whites and the low-status colored at various

ages on the *Davis Hess* test, but the several *t's* were much less than those obtained
on the "standard test". Hess included no measure of variability in his data nor
did he compare the means of the low-status whites with those of the low-status
colored groups. However, it is evident from his tables that the colored mean at
each CA point is significantly below the corresponding mean of the low-status
whites. In other words, even when the psychometric measure employed is
"culture-fair", there remains a significant difference in the tested intelligence of
Negro and white children of low socioeconomic status.

PPVT, FORM B AND CMMS, 1959 REVISION

The *Peabody Picture Vocabulary Test* consists of 150 sets of drawings, four
pictures comprising each set. A word is given orally to the child by the examiner
and the child may point to or give the number of the picture in the set which
most closely approximates the word. Raw scores may be converted to MA's, IQ's,
and percentiles by using the tables provided in the manual. The test is untimed
and is thus a power rather than a speed test; it is reported to have high interest
value; and the scoring is completely objective. It has been designed to provide
a well-standardized estimate of verbal intelligence through measuring a subject's
hearing vocabulary. (Tuttle, 1964, p. 13)

The *Columbia Mental Maturity Scale,* designed for the mental age range of
3-12 years, is intended primarily, though not solely, to test mental ability of
children handicapped by cerebral palsy or other defects of motor or verbal
functioning. The scale consists of 100 cards presenting problems graded in
difficulty, each with a series of 3-5 drawings, the child being asked to select from
each series the one drawing that is unrelated to the others on that card. The
scale was validated against the 1937 *Stanford-Binet* as the criteron, the coefficients
varying from .66 at Age 8 to .88 at Age 11; reliability coefficients range from .89 at
Age 4 to .92 at Age 10. Normally a single-type scale such as this is not preferred
to one like the *S-B* or the *WISC* employing several types of test materials.
(Freeman, 1962, pp. 290-291)

Tuttle employed both the *PPVT* and *CMMS* in addition to *WISC* in his
research on the 50 Gainesville, Florida, school children (1964).[32] As will be seen
from the table, the white children achieved a mean IQ of 105.5 on *PPVT,* just
one point below that earned on *WISC;* however, on the *CMMS* the mean IQ
dropped to 87.0. With the Negro children, the larger decrease occurred between
their *WISC* mean (86.5) and their *PPVT* mean (77.2); their *CMMS* mean of 75.0
was only slightly lower than the latter. Using the median as a basis for comparison, the IQ's of the colored children decreased 16 points from *WISC* to *PPVT*
and a further 6 points from *PPVT* to *CMMS*. After comparing several means and
medians and after studying his analysis of variance data and a number of
correlation coefficients, Tuttle concluded that the *WISC* measures mental ability

---

[32]See p. 56 for description of experimental design and results obtained on *WISC*.

more consistently than the *Peabody Picture Vocabulary Test* or the *Columbia Mental Maturity Scale,* that the *Peabody Picture Vocabulary Test* seems to be of doubtful use with Negro children between nine and one half and ten and one half years, and that it is questionable what the *Columbia Mental Maturity Scale* actually measures that may be common to the white and Negro culture.

SUMMARY

Fourteen individual tests have been administered to 9925 colored school children, comprising 43 investigations.

Twenty-three of the studies have included white subjects; in two of these the mean of the colored equaled that of the compared white group.[33]

In the 20 research projects in which no whites were tested, 17 of the authors have reported inferiority to the white norms. Of the three in which the results compare favorably with the norms, the Atlanta group (Graham, 1926) and one of Long's (1933) were apparently unselected, the other group of subjects examined by Long (1933) and the three city groups making up Beckham's data (1933) being selected cases.

There are probably 26 investigations in which the subjects were selected at random within the conditions of the research, the results of which have been presented in terms of IQ. The *combined mean IQ,* based upon more than 7000 Negro school children, falls *between 84 and 85.* The average IQ of the colored pupils living in various *Southern* cities and towns approximates 83; that of the colored in the *Border* urban areas, about 90; and in the *Northern* cities and towns, nearly 86. The North-South comparison is probably the most valid of the three, in part due to there being only three cities included in the Border statistics and in part to their enrollment being exclusively in the lower elementary grades. The age and grade ranges in the Northern and Southern cities are larger, as will have been noted from Table 2.

We have included seven studies on rural colored subjects in which the IQ was a means of comparison, five of these being from the South. The average IQ of the *Southern Negro* children tested in the rural areas is 77, that of *all* colored rural children examined, 79.

In the several studies where whites and Negroes have been selected from the same neighborhoods, where mill whites have been compared with Negro children of varying status, and where whites and colored have been matched for occupational status of father or the socioeconomic status of the home, the colored subjects have, with one exception, scored the lower of the two groups.[34] Where

---

[33]That of Peterson and Lanier (New York City, 1929) in which one third of the w boys came from non-English-speaking homes, and that of Higgins and Sivers (1958) whose Ss were in public schools *serving the lowest socioeconomic areas of a Northeastern* city and may have included children from non-English-speaking homes (reviewer's opinion).

[34]Phillips, Sunne, Strong, Pintner and Keller, Arlitt, Bruce, Tanser, Hess, and Tiber. The exception was Higgins and Sivers.

comparisons were made in terms of IQ, the colored averaged about 9 points below the whites.

Measures of variability were frequently omitted from the data by the researchers. Where s's or Q's were included in the results, those pertaining to the distributions of the white children were the larger in 15 of the 17 comparisons.[35]

NONVERBAL GROUP TESTS

We have examined and summarized 41 studies in which the authors report the testing of approximately 14,800 colored school children (excluding duplications) by nonverbal group tests. Altogether, 17 nonverbal group tests have been employed, ranging from the *Otis Group Intelligence Scale, Primary Examination,* published in 1918, to Raven's *Coloured Progressive Matrices,* revised in 1956.

Pintner-Cunningham

The *Pintner-Cunningham Primary Test,* designed by its authors for kindergarten and Grades 1 and 2, consists of seven subtests: common observation (identifying objects commonly found in the usual environment), esthetic judgment, identification of associated objects, discrimination of size, perception of the elements that constitute a whole picture, picture completion, and copying designs (using a given square of dots). Validity of the test is given in terms of its correlation with the *Stanford-Binet* (1916), the reported coefficients ranging from .73 to .88. Reliability is reported in terms of correlation between the alternate test forms and in terms of the probable error of test scores. The reliability coefficients vary from .83 to .94. (Freeman, 1950, p. 193)

Group tests, such as the *Pintner-Cunningham,* have been used frequently to survey large populations of colored and white school children. In fact, about 2900 colored children have been examined by the *Pintner-Cunningham* alone, all but 330 of them having been included in two surveys. (Boots in 1926, and *Report to the Superintendent — St. Louis,* 1925) Colored Ss from 19 Mississippi counties were reported by Boots to have earned mean IQ's of 79.02 and 72.70 as compared with mean IQ's of 100.51 and 97.91 achieved by white children from 30 counties of the state. The two means for each racial sample are for the first and second grades, respectively, the higher means having been secured by the first-grade children. The differences between the colored and white means were highly significant at each grade level as indicated by the very large t's of 22.5 and 32.4. As will be noted from the table, the first-grade children were the more variable in their test performance, and the colored less variable than the white, particularly in Grade 2.

An attempt was made to test all children entering the first grade of the

---

[35]Lambeth and Lanier reported their colored Ss to be the more variable. In addition, a difference of less than 0.20 was reported by Tiber in one comparison.

St. Louis public schools in 1924-25. As will be observed in Table 3, the median IQ of the colored was eight points below that of the white entrants. Although no measures of variability were computed, the ages of the children were reported as ranging from five to ten years. In both racial groups the younger pupils in the grade obtained the higher IQ's. "We must assume that only the brighter 5-year-olds are allowed to enter school and that children entering school at the age of eight or later are, in general, those who mature at a slower rate physically and mentally, and who are believed to be incapable of taking up school work successfully at a younger age." (1925, p. 51)

Included in a West Virginia testing program were thousands of pupils in Grades 1-12 sampled from five zones of the state in proportion to their numbers. Among those examined were 65 colored and 1477 white children in Grades 1 and 2. Cavins presents a distribution of mental ages for the first two grades as determined by *Pintner-Cunningham*. For the colored, the median mental ages are 5-4 and 6-10; for the whites, the corresponding mental ages are 6-2 and 7-8. Since Cavins included the median chronological ages for the colored and white at each grade, we have estimated the median IQ's as approximately 75 and 88 for the colored and 93 and 97 for the white Ss. Cavins pointed out that the school conditions in the areas tested were decidedly inferior for the Negro pupils— particularly in the case of school buildings and equipment, concluding ". . . . that environmental conditions not only affect school work but reflect themselves in the mental development of the children concerned." (1928, p. 143)

In contrast to the lesser educational advantages enjoyed by colored pupils in West Virginia as described by Cavins, Tanser (1939) pictures the Kent County, Ontario schools as not being separated, the colored and white sitting side by side and being afforded the same classroom privileges. In endeavoring to test all colored children present in Grades 1 and 2 and as "large as possible" sampling of whites, Tanser examined 54 colored and 155 white pupils. The median IQ's on these children secured from one urban and six rural schools were 97.59 and 82.83 for the white and colored, respectively. When the scores were separated, according to Grades 1 and 2, they were found to be, respectively, *white,* 100.13 and 93.75; *colored,* 85.50 and 79.50. When the groups were divided into *urban* and *rural,* the medians of the white became 98.41 and 92.0; those of the colored, 79.5 and 84.5.[36]

The remaining four studies will be described briefly since the numbers of colored tested varied between 41 and 82 and the children tested were not intended to represent a city, county, or state. All of the colored subjects included in the research of Koch and Simmons (1926), Hirsch (1926), Feacher (1947), and Nicholson (1949) were Southern urban children in Grades 1 and/or 2. Where the method of selection was mentioned it was described as unselected, representative of the school, or "all present," except for Grade 2 in Nicholson's study (as

---

[36]About 7.5 points separating the c and w *rural* groups and 19 points separating the c and w *urban* groups. See comments on Tanser's work, pp. 68-70.

will be seen in Table 3). All of the results were given in terms of IQ, except those of Koch and Simmons; these authors reported the Austin and San Antonio 8- and 9-year-old white Ss to have been significantly superior to the colored of the same ages.

The Nashville colored sample, according to Hirsch, achieved a mean IQ of 80.6 in contrast to a mean of 97.8 earned by the Massachusetts mill town white children of the same grade.

Feacher reports a median IQ of 95.83 and a range of scores from 59 to 133 on the *Pintner-Cunningham* given to colored children in one Jacksonville, Florida, school. The occupations of all of the fathers were stated as belonging in the range of skilled to unskilled labor.

Finally, Nicholson tested first- and second-grade colored pupils in one elementary school in Trenton, South Carolina. Although she tested the same children four times with the *Pintner-Cunningham* test, twice with Form A and twice with *Form B,* we have recorded only the results of the first testing. As will be observed in Table 3, the mean IQ of children in Grade 1 was 85; in Grade 2, 71. The latter is probably not representative of the second-grade children in the Trenton school since it is based on only thirteen cases.

Otis Primary

The *Otis Group Intelligence Scale, Primary Examination, Forms A and B,* was designed for children in kindergarten and Grades 1 to 4. It contains eight subtests: following directions, picture association, picture completion, maze tracing, picture sequence, similarities in pictures, synonym-antonym (simple words), and common-sense judgment. Norms are furnished for age and grade, but reliability coefficients are not given in the Manual. (Garrett and Schneck, 1933, p. 94)

IQ's on the *Otis Primary* were not determined for the Southern children in the research reported by Leggett (1921), Peterson (1923), Graham (1926), and Peterson and Telford (1930). The Wilmington, North Carolina, colored subjects (Leggett) scored progressively lower than the whites at each of the four critical age-levels compared, the author estimating the former's efficiency on this test to be from 80 to 81 per cent of the latter's. The amount of overlapping at *Age 10* was 30 per cent; at *Age 11,* 15.9 per cent; at *Age 12,* 16.3 per cent; and at *Age 13,* 10.6 per cent.

The Wilmington and Elizabeth City, North Carolina, groups (there may have been some duplication of subjects from *Wilmington)* examined by Peterson likewise scored lower than the white subjects with whom they were compared, as indicated by the fact that their median was surpassed by 75 per cent of whites from the same communities. At least a part of the difference was attributed by Peterson to the inferior environment of the colored children. The St. Helena group tested much below the white norms and likewise below the means of the Negro children in the United States. As will be seen from Table 3, the medians of the St. Helena children at the older age levels, *i.e.*, 11 to 14, were all below the *Otis* norms at the age of 7 *years*. The consistent low scoring of the St. Helena Negroes in various tests has been reported by Peterson and Telford, but attention must be called to the relative primitiveness of the islanders (in 1930), to the fact that some of the Negroes speak the Gulla dialect, and to the miserably poor schools (the exception being the Penn School). That the children were tested by a Negro psychologist is of little consequence in view of these obvious handicaps.

Graham's study included more than 1600 Atlanta colored school children who were principally in Grades 2 to 4. (*Publ. Health Rep.,* 1926) Her subjects, Age 8 to 10, scored from 7 to 9 points below the norms prepared by Otis, the differences being significant at the one per cent level of confidence. At 11 years the difference still favored the white norms, but was less than that at the 8 to 10 age groups. However, at the 7-year level the colored mean was a fraction of a point *above* the white mean, and at the 12-year level it was about one point above the mean of the whites. Graham accounted for the apparent inconsistency of her results at the 7-year level by the difference in the grade composition of the Atlanta group and Otis' groups. In the former, the Negro group, less than five per cent of the children tested were in the first grade, whereas 32 per cent of the whites were in Grade 1. Presumably more of the duller 7-year-olds among the Negroes were not tested than was the case with the whites, since 7-year-olds in the first grade may be presumed to score lower on an intelligence test than 7-year-olds in Grades 2 and above.

Graham interpreted the higher scoring of the 12-year-old Negroes as compared with the norms as follows: In Otis' data there were 240 10-year-olds in the fifth grade and 306 10-year-olds in Grades 1-4. At 11 years there were 127 Ss in Grades 1-4 and 135 in Grade 5; there were 135 12-year-olds in Grade 5 and 70 of them in Grades 1-4. On the other hand, Graham's data show 328 10-year-olds in Grades 1-4 and 83 10-year-olds in Grades 5-6; 215 11-year-olds in Grades 1-4 and 180 in the fifth grade or above; and 211 12-year-olds in Grades 1-4 and 246 12-year-olds above Grade 4. "If these two lots of data may be taken as typical, school retardation is more prevalent among the Negroes; the average White child of a given age is more advanced in school than the colored child of the same age; and the retarded colored child is a more normal racial representative than is the retarded White." (p. 2763) Accordingly, on the *Otis Primary,* white children of 10 years of age and older who have not progressed beyond the fourth grade are too inferior to be used as racial representatives.

Calculations by the reviewer from Vernon's (1936) IQ distributions of colored and white children of Grades 1 to 4 in two district schools in Muskogee County, Oklahoma, indicate the median of the Negro group to be 92.1 and that of the white group, 111.1. Analysis of his data shows, furthermore, that while the median IQ's of the white groups at each grade remained relatively constant, those of the colored children dropped by eight or more points after Grade 1. Vernon did not account for the decrease in IQ of his colored Ss; nor did he explain the difference between the colored and white medians except indirectly when he observed that there were more colored children enrolled per teacher, that the colored teachers averaged lower salaries than the white teachers, and that the white children had an average of 14 days of absences from school during a year as compared with 31 days of absences for the colored children. In general, however, as contrasted with Bruce's rural groups, the children studied in Muskogee County lived in a relatively prosperous community, the land extending into the rich soil of the Arkansas River bottom. In addition to farming, some of the parents held jobs in the oil fields and in related industrial occupations. Vernon considered the two racial samples to be more nearly equal in opportunity in Boynton than in many other communities within the state.

Adler (1925) analyzed the intelligence scores of over 11,000 white children from one Northern and one Southern county in Illinois and the intelligence scores of nearly 1200 colored children from the Southern county. The *Otis Primary Examination* had been administered to all Ss present in Grades 1 to 3, and the *Haggerty Delta 2* to those in Grades 4 to 8. The results of the two tests were not separated by the author. The urban white children in Northern Illinois had a median IQ of 103.3, the rural whites in this county, 95.2. The median IQ of the urban whites in the Southern county was 96.6, that of the rural whites, 85.8; whereas the median IQ of the urban Negroes in this Southern county was 77.8, that of the rural Negroes, 75.9. The rural Negroes were accordingly ten points below the rural whites on the average, and the urban Negroes were about 19 points below the urban whites in the same county. In discussing the *Pintner-Cunningham* test results we noted that Tanser likewise found rural Negroes to approximate more closely the scores of rural whites in Ontario than did the urban Negroes the urban whites. It seems probable that in Southern Illinois as in Kent County, Ontario, the environments of the groups of country children were more alike than were the environments of the groups of urban children.

Kempf and Collins (1929) compared the *Otis Primary* and *Haggerty* IQ's of 399 Southern Illinois urban and rural Negroes with those of 677 urban and rural white children. The whites in these comparisons were all sons and daughters of unskilled laborers and farmers. As will be noted in Table 3, the urban colored median is 15.5 IQ points below that of the urban white children from unskilled laboring families, the rural colored median about 13 points below that of the whites from unskilled rural families and eight points below that of the whites of the "farmer" group. While the colored medians were below those of the whites in the various comparisons, the authors do not necessarily attribute the lower colored scores to a racial difference; they indicate that the white children of the unskilled laboring class might have more economic and social advantages than the colored group as a whole, regardless of occupational classification.

In all of the 15 studies which made use of either the *Otis Group Intelligence Scale, Primary Examination* or *Pintner-Cunningham Primary Group Test*, therefore, the white groups surpassed the Negro children with whom they were compared.[37]

MYERS MENTAL MEASURE

The *Myers Mental Measure,* a test probably less well known than the majority of the tests employed in comparing Negroes and whites, is primarily a nonlinguistic test including such items as: following oral directions by drawing lines with a pencil, drawing in missing parts in a picture completion test, underlining objects that are similar among pictured items, and indicating similarities by underlining the four that are most alike. Except for the New York City groups of Negro and white boys tested on *Myers* by Peterson and Lanier (1929) all Ss were examined in the South. Median or mean scores were given and the percentages of overlapping were somtimes included; however, none of the comparisons are in terms of IQ.

The 7-year-old colored children examined by Peterson (1923) in Nashville were slightly more than two points below the medians of the white children tested in the same city, in Red Bank, and in Shelby County, Tennessee; the 10-year-old colored children were significantly inferior to the medians of the whites, the colored median being 14.2, and the white, 33.5.

The research of Sunne (1924) included more than 2000 Negroes and whites, probably from New Orleans and vicinity, very few of the subjects being from the professional class. At each age level the colored children scored lower on the average than the white children, but the difference was least at the youngest age tested, *i.e.,* eight years. At 8 years, 40 per cent of the colored equaled or exceeded the median of the whites, whereas at 9 years, 23 per cent of the colored equaled or surpassed the median of the whites.

Koch and Simmons (1926) tested 613 Negro and 594 white children living in the cities of San Antonio, El Paso, and Austin, Texas, and 617 white children living in rural areas of this state. At each of the seven age levels the city whites surpassed both the city Negroes and the rural whites by a large margin; the *urban colored* means, however, were above those of the *rural whites* at four of the age levels. It is apparent from Table 3 that the urban-rural differences are as great as or greater than the white-colored differences on the *Myers Mental Measure.*[38] The authors considered the possibility that there may be more ruthless elimination of the colored from the city schools because of scholastic and intellectual inefficiency than would be the case with the rural whites.

Peterson and Lanier (1929) found the sample of colored boys in New York City performing about as well on the *Myers* as the white sample in this city, with 44 per cent of the colored equaling or surpassing the median of the latter group.[39]

---

[37]In four of the studies the white group used for comparative purposes was the normative group.

[38]Not true of the *National.* On this test, both urban and rural whites were superior to the urban colored. See Table 4.

[39]These boys were also tested on the *Yerkes-Bridges-Hardwick Point Scale.* See Table 2.

Both of the New York City groups scored above the Nashville Negroes on this test; however, *both of the New York City groups* were definitely inferior to the Nashville whites and to Myers' norms.

McGurk (1943) reports the results of *Myers Mental Measure* as given to 890 white and to 561 colored children in Richmond, Virginia. A random sampling of the city's public school population was secured by selecting every tenth name from alphabetized lists of children in Grades 4 to 8. As will be noted in Table 3, large and significant differences were obtained between the average scores at each grade. The colored children of Richmond scored below the *Myers* norms as well as below the Richmond whites.

The results of the *Myers Mental Measure,* therefore, appear to favor with some consistency the white children over the colored in the same localities. In some of the studies neither measures of variability nor significance of obtained differences were given; however, judging from the size of the samples, the amount of the differences, and the percentages of overlapping, it would seem that the differences are significant, except for one age group tested by Peterson where the number of white cases was 26 and the New York City group tested by Peterson and Lanier in which about half of the white parents were foreign-born. The rural white children of Texas compared somewhat unfavorably with Negro children from three large Texas cities.

HAGGERTY DELTA 1

The *Haggerty Intelligence Examination, Delta 1,* designed for Grades 1 to 3, consists of five nonverbal and one verbal subtests: following directions (pictures), copying designs, picture completion, picture comparison, symbol-digit, and word comparison. Since the last two of the subtests employ numbers and words, the test is not considered suitable for children just entering the first grade. The score is in points with norms given for age and grade. The reliability of the test, as determined by retesting a group of 100 children in Grades 1A to 2A, is .79. (Garrett and Schneck, 1933, pp. 92, 94)

The small group of colored children in Elizabeth City, North Carolina, examined by Peterson (1923), ranked below the white children of the same city on *Haggerty Delta 1*. The difference is marked at the age of 7 years, the only age level which should be considered since the children were in the first grade and only two colored children at the age of 6 were tested. Peterson referred to his colored group as *Normal School Negroes* and described them as being a selected group in mental ability.

The St. Helena colored children scored much lower than the Elizabeth City Negroes on *Delta 1*. As is shown in Table 3, the St. Helena Ss at Age 10 did about as well as the Elizabeth City Negroes at Age 7 and the Elizabeth City whites (27 cases) at Age 6. The *Haggerty* results, like those of other tests administered to them, indicate that commonly used intelligence tests are poorly adapted for use with the St. Helena children. As was to be expected, these children earned very low scores on the Digit-Symbol and Symbol-Digit tests. More than one third of the subjects tested made zero scores on these substitution tests. (Peterson and Telford, 1930)

DRAW-A-MAN

Reporting on *Draw-a-Man Test* as administered to 613 Negro children in three cities of Louisiana and Tennessee, the author of the test (Goodenough, 1926) gives an obtained mean of 78.7 on these subjects in Grades 1 to 4.[40] Sixty-nine Negro children in Grades 1 to 3 who were living in various California cities achieved a mean IQ of 85.8. From Table 3 it will be noticed that the California whites, the California Negroes, and the Southern Negroes were about equally variable on this test.

The St. Helena Negroes made their best showing on the *Draw-a-Man Test*. According to Peterson and Telford (1930) the mean IQ's ranged from 60 to 98, with a "weighted average IQ" of 79. None of the nine age groups, with the exception of the five-year-olds, secured an average IQ of more than 80.[41] On the assumption that this test is considered to be less subject to environmental influences, the *Draw-a-Man* is sometimes preferred by psychologists to other measures when they are testing different racial groups.[42] The St. Helena results give some support to this hypothesis, not only because these island Negroes earned their highest scores on this test, but also because their mean IQ proved to be identical to that obtained by Goodenough (1926) on Southern Negro children.

The large stratified sample of 1800 Negro school children from the Southeastern states likewise performed more satisfactorily on the *Draw-a-Man* than they did on the *Stanford-Binet*. Lindner (1962) reported a mean IQ obtained on these elementary school children to be 91 on the *Draw-a-Man,* 10 points above their own *Stanford-Binet* mean (Kennedy, Van De Riet, and White, 1963) and about 10 points below Goodenough's white mean (Table 3).[43] An examination of Lindner's frequency distributions shows that 29 per cent of the Negro children overlapped the mean of the normative group, 12 per cent earned IQ's below 70, and one percent achieved IQ's of 140 or higher. Significant differences in *Draw-a-Man* were found to obtain between the three types of county, *i.e.,* metropolitan, urban, and rural, the mean IQ's for these being respectively, 94.9, 91.0, and 87.8.

---

[40]For comments on *Draw-a-Man* test, see pp. 24-25.
[41]Only three Ss tested at Age 5.
[42]Not a *culture-free* test however (Goodenough and Harris, 1950).
[43]For a brief description of the experimental design of these two research projects see pp. 20, 25 and pp. 41-42.

From Table 3 one can easily observe a drop in mean IQ from 101.8 at 7 years to 67.7 at 13 years. Although not noted in the table, there were fewer cases at the age extremes, particularly above 11 years. There seems to have been some selectivity of six- and seven-year-olds also, since at Age 6 there were 227 cases; at Age 7, 243; at Age 8, 302; the number of cases from 8 to 10 being very similar. Even in the age range from 8 to 10, however, there is a decrease of 5 IQ points. By including the norms on white samples, Lindner enables us to see that a decrement in IQ is found not only among the Negro sample studied but also among Goodenough's validation sample. He concluded that the downward trend is not a function of race, nor is it due to some form of economic deprivation as claimed by Goodenough[44] but rather a function of an error in Goodenough's prescribed method of calculating MA scores from item scores. Lindner found that by computing new weights for the conventional Goodenough weights for scoring, and recomputing the MA, he was able to make a substantial improvement in the correlation with *Form L-M* of the *Binet, i.e.,* .67. In using revised weights the mean IQ drops to 83.1, the drop being due to weighting procedure designed to optimize the prediction of the *Stanford-Binet* IQ.

Detroit First Grade

The *Detroit First Grade Intelligence Test,* in the original form, consisted of ten tests: information, similarities, memory, absurdities, comparisons, relationships, symmetries, designs, counting, and directions. According to Garrett and Schneck (1933, p. 92) the author did not give the reliability of the test. The reliability coefficient of the *revision* of this test, however, was found to be .91. The validity of the items of the revised test was determined by comparing the percentage of passes in three groups of children: bright, average, and dull and then selecting only those items in the final test which showed a satisfactory increase in performance of passes from dull to bright group. A correlation coefficient of .76 was obtained on 116 cases with *Stanford-Binet, 1916.* (P. Cattell *in* Buros, 1938, p. 1044)

Koch and Simmons (1926) found about 77 per cent of the 78 white children tested in San Antonio, Austin, and El Paso scoring above the median of the 128 colored Texas samples on the *Detroit First Grade Test.*[45]

Ellis (1947), using the revision of this test, reports a mean IQ of 87.16 on 64 first-grade colored children living in Baton Rouge. The range of IQ's was large, particularly at the lower end of the scale, *i.e.,* 51 to 116.

In an early study, Berry (1922) analyzed the results of the *Detroit First Grade* test which had been given to all pupils entering the first grade in the Detroit public schools in 1920. Scores were separated into three categories: the superior,

---

[44]Nor presumably primarily due to selective factors operating at Ages *below* 8 and *above* 10 in Grades 1-6, suggested by the reviewer above.

[45]These Ss also tested on *Myers Mental Measure.*

the average, and the inferior. Four hundred forty-three colored children were tested, and, as will be seen in Table 3, a smaller percentage of them scored in the superior group and a slightly larger percentage scored in the inferior group, as compared with white children from English-speaking homes. The white children from foreign-speaking homes had a greater percentage falling in the inferior group than did the Negroes, all of whom came from English-speaking homes.

Dearborn A

Dearborn Group Intelligence Tests, Series 1, designed for children in Grades 1 to 3, is nonverbal except for directions and a knowledge of simple counting. It includes: directions, drawing and counting, simple information, everyday knowledge, and substitution learning. Validity of the scale is given in terms of correlations with *Stanford-Binet, 1916,* the coefficient being .84 for 211 first-grade pupils. Reliability coefficients, determined by correlating odd and even items, are between .80 and .90; when determined by the retest method the coefficients range from .63 to .88. (Freeman, 1950, pp. 191-192) According to Freeman, *Series I* of *Dearborn,* in use since 1922, has been found to have considerable usefulness in educational problems concerning groups of pupils.

On *Dearborn A* the 101 Nashville colored subjects earned a mean IQ of 79 which placed them 18 points below the mean of the Massachusetts mill town whites of the American-born parents. (Hirsch, 1926) Thirteen of the 14 nationality groups of children of foreign-born white parents living in the mill towns secured mean IQ's which were above the Nashville mean. Only the Ss of Portuguese parents averaged below the Nashville Negro mean.

The highest scoring Negro group on any of the nonverbal group tests was that examined in the District of Columbia by Long (1933). The 100 Negro Washington-born children from underprivileged communities and in the 3A grade achieved a mean IQ of 102 on *Dearborn A.* This mean is consistent with the very favorable showing made by these same children on the *Stanford-Binet, 1916,* the *Pintner-Paterson,* and the *Kuhlmann-Anderson.* We have already commented upon the method by which Long selected his subjects. No white children were included in the Washington study.

Minnesota Paper Form Board

The *Revised Minnesota Paper Form Board* is a test which reproduces in printed form the same type of problems as those presented by form boards. The test is designed to measure capacity to visualize and imaginally manipulate geometric forms. Reported research indicates that this paper form board test has a moderately good correlation with quality of mechanical performance and a moderate to low correlation with success in descriptive geometry. (Freeman, 1950, p. 276) According to Drake, it is no longer considered a good test of general intelligence. (*in* Buros, 1949, p. 259)

Bean (1942) gave the *Minnesota* test to 49 colored Ss in the eighth grade of the Baton Rouge public schools and reported the mean to be at the twenty-third percentile of the white norms. Bean observed that "At least we can be sure that this group as a whole is inferior in ability to do the kinds of thinking called for on both tests, whether language is required or not." (p. 348) [46]

ARMY BETA

The *Revised Beta Examination,* intended to serve as a measure of general ability in the case of relatively illiterate or non-English-speaking subjects, includes the subtests of: mazes, symbol-digit combinations, pictorial completion, geometric construction, number checking, picture absurdities, and object similarities and differences. Validity of the revised *Beta* is given in terms of the correlation between its point scores and *Stanford-Binet 1916* mental ages (.78). The reliability of the test as determined by correlation of odd-even items was .987; but for test-retest, the coefficient was .77. Freeman (1950, pp. 197-8) concludes that the *Beta* may be used to supplement verbal scales but should not be substituted for them.

The *Revised Beta* was one of two mental tests administered to all colored boys in the seventh grade of the B. T. Washington High School in Montgomery, Alabama. The mean IQ of the 96 Ss was 91.75 and a large standard deviation of 17.88 was recorded. The range of scores, from 48 to 112, indicated positive skewness. (Lewis, 1947)

PINTNER NON-LANGUAGE

The *Pintner Non-Language Mental Test,* designed for Grades 4 to 8, consists of six nonverbal tests: imitation of movement (an adaptation of the *Knox Cube Test* for group purposes), digit-symbol easy learning, digit-symbol hard learning, picture completion, reproducing reversed figures, and picture reconstruction of picture sequence. The reliability of the test is reported to be .79 by the retest method, based on 201 children, Grades 4 to 6. (Garrett and Schneck, 1933, p. 95)

The *Pintner Non-Language Test* was given to groups of children by Bousfield (1932) and Tanser (1939). The Chicago Negro children from Keith Elementary School (Table 3) scored close to the white norms. They were described as "3 points below normal mentality". Actually they came much closer to the white norms on this test than they did on a verbal test.[47] In general these children were of an inferior socioeconomic status.

---

[46] Test involving language given to these Ss was the *Otis S-A, Intermediate Form.* Woods and Toal (1957) found 120 Negro adolescents to score lower on subtest 4 of revised *Beta* (Paper Form Board) than a group of whites matched on total *Beta* score. Difference was significant at .01 level.

[47] *Otis S-A, Intermediate Form.*

Tanser tested 102 Negro children and 387 whites from Grades 3 to 8 in Kent County and reported the respective mean IQ's to be 95.25 and 110.87; the *s's*, 13.30 and 19.03. The urban and rural groups were separated in order to compare racial samples of very similar socioeconomic status. The medians of the urban white and colored were respectively, 109.76 and 94.81; the corresponding medians of the rural white and colored groups were 110.5 and 96.67. "The important finding is, however, the comparatively small extent to which the Negroes 'overlap' the Whites, whether the environment be rural or urban. In the Pintner Non-Language Mental Test, only 10 per cent of the rural Negroes reach or exceed the median of the rural Whites, while only 14 per cent of the urban Negroes reach or exceed the median of the urban Whites." (pp. 119-20)

CHICAGO NON-VERBAL

The *Chicago Non-Verbal Examination,* designed to measure the nonverbal aspects of intelligence from Age 7 upward, may be administered either orally or by pantomime. Four criteria were employed to determine the validity of the test: correlation with chronological age, comparison of normal and feebleminded children, the normality of the distribution of scores, and the correlation with other tests. As far as can be judged from these criteria, the test seems to be reasonably valid. Reliability coefficients obtained by the split-half and retest techniques on groups with ranges of 2 to 6 grades in school placement vary from .80 to .93. (Bernreuter, *in* Buros, 1941, p. 1387)

Research on the comparative intelligence of Negroes and whites by means of the *Chicago Non-Verbal Examination* has been undertaken in Virginia and Tennessee. Testing 890 white and 561 colored Ss, Grades 4 to 8, in the city of Richmond, all of them having been selected by random sampling, McGurk (1943) found the whites to be significantly superior at every grade.[48] The Richmond whites were found not to differ from the published norms according to an analysis of variance.

Similar large differences between Negro scores and the white norms were recorded by Lawrence (1951) and Newland and Lawrence (1953) in their survey of the colored school population, Ages 6 to 14, in three Tennessee counties. In his unpublished Master's thesis, Lawrence gives the medians of 923 colored children for each age level (Table 3). At the age of 10 years, Lawrence reports that 14 per cent of his Ss' scores equaled or exceeded the white median; at other ages, from 4 to 9 per cent of the colored equaled or exceeded the medians of the normative groups. The *s's* ranged from 9.86 at the 7-year level to 13.94 at the 12-year level; five of the 7 *s's* (for Age Groups 7-13) were between 11 and 12.

In a subsequent published report, Newland and Lawrence included the subjects of the unpublished study together with a "representative sample" from

---

[48]These Ss were also tested by *Myers Mental Measure* and *Otis S-A, Intermediate Form.* Ss in Grades 9-11 included in Table 5.

Knoxville, making the total number of colored examined, 1140. The inferior performance of these children is indicated by the fact that from 3 to 6 per cent of them scored above the norms at the ages of 6 to 9; 10 to 15 per cent of the children at the ages of 10 to 14 were recorded as exceeding the *Chicago* norms. At all age levels, these Negro children scored not less than the equivalent of two years below the respective age norms for this test. At Ages 11 to 14 the disparity increased to three or more years. Unreliable differences were found to exist between the means of the colored in the city of Knoxville and the Blount and Knox county means, the respective measures being 65.85 and 64.00.

SRA Primary Mental Abilities

The *SRA Primary Mental Abilities (Primary)*, intended for children of ages 5 to 7 years, contains tests for five primary mental abilities: motor ability, perceptual speed, verbal meaning, space, and quantitative thinking. Pictures are to be marked according to verbal instructions. For example, verbal ability is measured by tests in which the child shows his understanding of word meanings, sentence meanings, and paragraph meanings by indicating appropriate pictures. Motor ability is measured by drawing lines connecting dots in parallel rows. The battery yields a total score, which is reported to give a measure of the child's general learning ability, and also scores on each of the five abilities. (Mursell, 1949, pp. 212-213)

Johnson (1954) gave this test to 100 colored children entering the first grade of the Clarksville, Tennessee, public schools in 1953. The mean IQ was reported to be 83.50 with a range of from 53 to 133. The lower intelligence scores of the colored in this study were attributed by Johnson to home deficiency.

International Group Rotator

The *International Group Mental Test,* designed for kindergarten level to adult, is nonverbal; the reliability of this test by the split-half method was reported to be .97 for 112 sixth-grade orphans; the reliability determined by the retest method on the same group was .78. (Garrett and Schneck, 1933, p. 94)

Peterson and Lanier (1929) used the rotator forms of this test and reported them to be entirely nonlinguistic, both as to the directions given and as to the situations presented; Ss were not even required to use pencils. The subjects' reactions consist in turning a rotating cardboard piece in the form of a cross until one of the four pictures or groups of pictures on it appears in the particular relationship required and illustrated. Peterson and Lanier used only five of the subtests: cube analysis, picture association, maze tracing, pictorial rhythms, and picture narratives. They tested unselected samples of 12-year-old white and colored children in Nashville. The medians on each subtest for each racial group are included in Table 3. All five of the differences were found to be significant, with 10 to 31 per cent of the colored equaling or exceeding the various medians of the whites.

Davis-Eells Games

The *Davis-Eells Test of General Intelligence or Problem-Solving Ability* (also referred to as the *Davis-Eells Games*) was developed by its authors after they had analyzed a number of commonly used intelligence tests and found the results on all types of test problems to significantly favor the highest socioeconomic group. (Eells, Davis, *etc.*, 1951) Believing that intelligence tests in general mask the real learning ability of children of the lower socioeconomic classes, they developed a new test the purpose of which was to *"afford the teacher a measure of a pupil's mental capacity, of his basic resources of reasoning, insight, problem-organization, etc."* (*Manual*, p. 2) Although the authors insist that the test measures problem solving ability, according to Guilford (*in* Buros, 1959, p. 462) they present no empirical evidence to support this contention.

In this group intelligence test, no reading is required, the material being presented in pictorial form with directions expressed in colloquial language in a relaxed atmosphere of a *game* rather than a *test*. The pictures are relatively large and drawn in semihumorous style assuming a familiarity with the comic strip and "thus bound to handicap the less sophisticated children from the rural areas." Cyril Burt believed the method of presenting tests as games to be an excellent device with younger and duller children. "But with British children aged 9 and upwards better results are secured when tests of intelligence are given quite frankly as an internal examination in which every pupil is expected to take the problems seriously and do his utmost to answer even the more difficult problems." (Burt, *in* Buros, 1959, p. 460)

A number of studies indicate that IQ's obtained with the *Davis-Eells* run lower than those obtained with other tests and that the test differentiates as much between high and low socioeconomic groups as do the verbal tests which it was intended to improve upon. The reliability of the test computed in one study was reported to be .79; validity was checked in two schools against the individual ratings of seven teachers and against standardized achievement scores. These correlations were then compared with the same validity criteria applied to the *California Test of Mental Maturity*, with the results that the *Davis-Eells* was found to be the less valid as a predictive instrument. (Drake, *in* Buros, 1959, p. 461)

Several psychologists (including Drake) have noted that some of the test items have strong emotional loadings which may adversely affect the performance of the child. Cited are these pictures: (1) an adolescent boy being spanked by his father, (2) three boys lying in wait to beat up another boy, (3) a big boy being spanked for breaking a window, and (4) a girl crying at the breakfast table because she thinks she has no Christmas present.

In an attempt to determine whether or not the *Davis-Eells* tests would give teachers insight into the problem solving abilities of children, G. T. Altus (1956) administered a battery of tests including the *Davis-Eells* and *California Test of Mental Maturity* to 184 fourth-grade children in Santa Barbara County, Cali-

TABLE

SCHOOL CHILDREN

AUTHOR DATE	LOCATION	N	SUBJECTS		METHOD OF SELECTION
			AGE	GRADE	
					PINTNER-CUNNINGHAM
Boots, W. E. (1926)	Mississippi	w-4000[1] c- 1000		1, 2 1, 2	W children from 30 and c from 19 counties.
Koch,[2] H. and Simmons, R. (1926)	San Antonio and Austin, Tex.	w-126 c- 82	6-11 7-12	2 2	
Hirsch, N. D. M. (1926)	Massachusetts and Nashville, Tenn.	w-100 c- 47		1 1	W- all children in 1st grade of publ schs in 4 Mass mill towns. C- certain publ schs in Nashville, representative of c pop.
Feacher, J. P. (1947)	Jacksonville, Fla.	c- 41	6-11	1	The 41 pupils in Grade 1 in Lavilla Sch.
Nicholson, L. W. (1949)	Trenton, S. C.	c- 41	5-12	1, 2	Boys and girls in Bettis Academy Elem Sch; only 13 tested in Grade 2; not give basis for selection.
"Report ...." (1925)	St. Louis, Mo.	w-8998 c- 1574	5-10 5-10	1 1	All children entering 1st grade in publ schs, 1924-25.
Cavins, L. V. (1928)	Parkersburg, Martinsburg, and Buffalo Districts, W. Va.	w-1477 c- 65		1, 2 1, 2	Selected groups of Ss representing graded sch systems.

[1]Numbers of w and c Ss estimated by reviewer. Boots noted that there were 13,680 w and 3272 c Ss in Grades 1-8.

[2]For results on other tests given by these investigators, see Tables 3 and 4.

[3]Ss of American-born parents. Of those of foreign-born parents, 11 groups were sig above

THREE

NONVERBAL GROUP TESTS

RESULTS	COMMENTS OF AUTHOR

PRIMARY GROUP TEST

		IQ		t	White Ss sig above c means at each grade.
	w		c		
M					
1	100.51		79.02	22.5	
2	97.91		72.70	32.4	
s					
1	19.05		18.55		
2	16.10		12.55		

Age			Sig diffs bet means at 8 and 9 years in majority of comparisons.
8	77% w above c mdns		
9	85% w above c mdns		

		IQ[a]		Mill Ss from poorer socioeco environments than average urban American child.
	w		c	
M	97.8		80.6	

	IQ	Fathers all skilled laborers, or below.
	c	
Mdn	95.83	
Range	59-133	

	IQ	Common Observation, Associated Objects, Esthetic Differences easiest parts; Dot Drawing the most difficult.
	c	
M		
1	85	
2	71	

		IQ		
	w		c	
Mdn	100		92	

		IQ[4]		For most part, c teachers gave tests to c children. Sch buildings and equipment decidedly inferior for c pupils.
	w			
Mdn			c	
1	93		75	
2	97		88	

the c mean; only the Portuguese below c; comparisons based upon 3 tests. For other results reported in this study, see Tables 3 and 4.

[4]These medians are approximate, having been calculated by reviewer by dividing mdn MA by mdn CA. For results on *Detroit Primary*, see Table 4.

TABLE

SCHOOL CHILDREN

| AUTHOR DATE | LOCATION | N | SUBJECTS | | METHOD OF SELECTION |
			AGE	GRADE	
Tanser,[5] H. A. (1939)	Kent County, Ontario	w-155 c- 54		1, 2 1, 2	Attempted to test all children enrolled in the 1 urban and 6 rural schs; excluded county schs with very few c.

				OTIS GROUP INTELLIGENCE SCALE	
Leggett,[6] J. L. (1921)	Wilmington, N. C.	w-168 c- 191	6-13 8-16	3-5 4-5	Tests given in Grades 3-5 in white schs, in Grades 4-5 in c schs. Only bet ages 10-13 were there enough Ss of both groups for comparative purposes.
Peterson,[7] J. (1923)	Wilmington and Elizabeth City, N. C.	w-357 c- 201		3-4 4	W from 3 schs, c from one.
Graham,[8] V. T. (1926)	Atlanta, Ga.	c- 1591 c- 79	7-12 7-12	2-4 H1	Part of US Publ Health survey; tests given in 5 elem c schs.
Peterson,[9] J., and Telford, C. (1930)	St. Helena Island, S. C.	c- 139	7-14		Penn Normal and Industrial Sch, also 5 publ schs, all but 2 of latter were shacks.
Vernon, J. O. (1936)	Muskogee County, Okla.	w-123 c- 154		1-4 1-4	All w and c children in attendance at the 2 schs.

[5]For results on other tests administered by Tanser, see Tables 2, 3, and 4.
[6]For results on *Otis Group, Advanced* administered to 6-7 grade Ss, see Table 4.
[7]Part of survey of intelligence of w and c children from 6 sch systems in 3 states. For other results, see Tables 2, 3, and 4.

THREE (continued)
NONVERBAL GROUP TESTS

	RESULTS		COMMENTS OF AUTHOR

	IQ		C and w attend same schs; c teachers in 3 of rural schs. In urban, but not rural schs, w of higher socioeco status than c.
	w	c	
Mdn			
Rural	92.00	84.50	
Urban	98.41	79.50	
Total	97.59	82.83	
13% c above w mdn			

PRIMARY EXAMINATION

	M Scores			The Negroes, on the aver, are only 80.5 per cent as efficient as the w as measured by Otis Primary.
	w	c	D/PEd	
Age				
10	58.7	54.5	1.75	
11	56.3	45.7	4.82	
12	59.2	47.5	7.31	
13	62.1	48.3	3.37	

About 75% w above c mdn

Results show that Negroes suffer from inferior environment.

	M Scores		Large sig diffs at 8-10; 7-yr-old c relatively highly selected as few chosen from Grade 1; 11-12-yr-old w in Grades 2-4 relatively more retarded than 11-12-yr-old c in these grades.
	w	c	
Age	(norms)		
7	31.01	31.36	
8	42.45	35.56	
9	50.35	41.26	
10	51.60	43.48	
11	50.02	46.92	
12	48.86	49.80	

Mdn 7 yr w (norm) = 31
75 %ile 12 yr c = 28.25

Ss tested by Negro from Tuskegee Institute.

	IQ[10]		C and w living under similar conditions; occup of people mainly farming, oil-field jobs and industry. C schs more pupils enrolled per teacher; more w teachers with degrees.
	w	c	
Mdn			
1	111.3	102	
2	113.8	94	
3	112	82.5	
4	109	90.1	

[8]For results on other tests reported by Graham, see Tables 2 and 4.
[9]For results on other tests reported by Peterson and Telford, see Tables 2, 3, and 4.
[10]Medians determined by reviewer from author's frequency distributions.

TABLE

SCHOOL CHILDREN

AUTHOR DATE	LOCATION	N	SUBJECTS		METHOD OF SELECTION
			AGE	GRADE	
Adler, H. M. (1925)	DuPage and Alexander Counties, Ill.	w-8360 w-2997 c- 1192		1-8 1-8 1-8	All children in 2 counties, one Northern & urban, other Southern & rural if present in sch when tests given.
Kempf,[12] G. A., and Collins, S. D. (1929)	A Southern Illinois County	w-677 c- 399		1-8 1-8	See Adler, above
				MYERS MENTAL	
Peterson,[7] J. (1923)	Nashville, Red Bank, Shelby County, Tenn.	w-26 c- 90 w-25 w-60	7 7, 10	2, 3 4, 5	All 7-yr-olds in Ross, all 7- and 10-yr-olds in Napier Sch, Nashville; w Ss selected by grade in Red Bank and Shelby.
Sunne,[13] D. (1924)	New Orleans and Vicinity	w-1053 c- 1113	7-16 7-16	3, 4 3, 4	Social status of whites ranged from poor to very good; very few were from professional class.
Koch,[2] H. L., and Simmons, R. (1926)	San Antonio, El Paso, Austin, and Texas Counties	Urban w-594 c- 613 Rural w-617		1-6 1-4 1-8	Both whites and c from the 3 cities; also w from 6 rural counties.

[11]*Otis Primary* given to Ss in Grades 1-3, *Haggerty Delta 2* in Grades 4-8. Adler does not separate the results. The six medians calculated by reviewer from author's frequency distributions.

[12]Part of preceding project; *Otis Primary* results, Grades 1-3, combined by authors with *Haggerty*, Grades 4-8. Total group of w Ss includes a few foreign-born children & children of foreign-born. W Ss in unsk labor and farmer groups include only children of native parents.

THREE *(continued)*
NONVERBAL GROUP TESTS

	RESULTS		COMMENTS OF AUTHOR

	Mdn IQ[11]		Part of survey of handicapped children in state.
Northern	w	c	In both counties country schs have greater %age of
Urban	103.3		inferiors than city schs; c show still greater %age of
Rural	95.2		inferiors.
Southern			
Urban	96.6	77.8	
Rural	85.8	75.9	

	Mdn IQ		C mdn considerably lower than that of children of
Total	w	c	w unsk laborers in both urban & rural areas.
Urban	91.2	70.6	However, w of unsk group may have had many
Rural	84.3	73.8	more eco & soc advantages than c as whole.
Unskilled			
Urban	86.1		
Rural	86.7		
Farmers	81.8		

MEASURE

	Mdn		Sch and home environments of c inferior to those
Age	w	c	of w Ss.
7	14.6	12.3	
10	33.5	14.2	
	D/PEd		
7	1.4		
10	9.8		

		Mdn	% c above w mdn	C had only half-day sessions in lower grades and
Age	w	c		training of teachers very different in the 2 races.
8	26	22	40	
9	30	21	23	
10	34	25	20	
11	39	28	24	
12	45	32	22	
13	46	35	22	
14	51	36	12	
15	48	37	26	

	M Scores[14]			City w more successful on tests than city c; city c
	Urban	Rural	Urban	usually above rural w on *Myers*, rural w higher on
Age	w	w	c	*National*. May have more ruthless elimination of c
7	18.65	12.58	12.10	from schs because of scholastic and intellectual
8	25.75	16.52	19.10	deficiency.
9	31.20	20.24	22.33	
10	33.85	22.91	23.15	
11	36.00	23.93	25.15	
12	36.85	26.18	24.60	
13	33.85	28.08	26.50	

[13]For results on *National*, see Table 4.
[14]Very few Ss of Ages 6, 14, and 15 included.

TABLE

SCHOOL CHILDREN

AUTHOR DATE	LOCATION	N	SUBJECTS		METHOD OF SELECTION
			AGE	GRADE	
Peterson,[15] J., and Lanier, L. H. (1929)	Nashville, Tenn., and New York City	w-119 c- 86 w- 60 c- 187	12 12 12 12	4-8 3-9 4-8 4-8	*Nash* - all 12-yr-olds in 3 w and 2 c schs; also 9 c Ss selected at random in a jr high sch. *NYC* - 50 w from PS *26* and 10 from PS *5;* all the w 12-yr-olds in PS *5;* all c 12-yr-olds in PS *5* and half of c 12-yr-olds in PS *139,* a jr high sch.
McGurk,[16] F. C. J. (1943)	Richmond, Va.	w-890 c- 561	9- 9-	4-8 4-8	Alphabetized names in each grade and selected every tenth.

HAGGERTY

| Peterson,[17] J. (1923) | Elizabeth City, N. C. | w-71 c- 37 | 1 1 | | One c & one w sch. C in Training Sch of a Normal Sch. |
| Peterson,[9] J., and Telford, C. W. (1930) | St. Helena Isl., S. C. | c- 101 | 7-14 | | Ss from Penn Normal and Indus Sch & 5 publ schs. All but 2 were crowded shacks. |

DRAW-

| Goodenough, F. L. (1926) | Chattanooga, Tenn., Mt. Pleasant, Tenn., Natchitoches, La., Cal. Cities | c- 613 c- 69 | | 1-4 1-3 | All c in 3 schs in Southern cities. All c & w in several California cities for whom racial stock information available. W Ss from 3 schs in Southern cities. |

[15]Only boys in the NYC groups. For other test results reported by these authors, see Tables 2, 3, and 4.

[16]For results on other tests reported by the author, see Tables 3 and 4.

THREE (continued)
NONVERBAL GROUP TESTS

	RESULTS			COMMENTS OF AUTHOR

		Mdn		About half of NYC w Ss foreign-born. NYC w
	w		c	below all 3 of Nash w groups and below Myers'
Nash	50.40		29.30	norms. *Myers* given individually in NYC and as
NYC	41.82		40.73	group test in Nash. NYC c may be a select group
		Q		of Negroes.
Nash	9.05		8.14	
NYC	9.33		7.84	

8% Nash c above w *mdn*
44% NYC c above w *mdn*

		M Scores		Large and sig diffs bet aver scores of w and c in
	w		c	Richmond publ schs. Sig diff bet c mdns and
Grade				published norms.
4	38		25	
5	44		30	
6	50		35	
7	51		38	
8	57		42	

DELTA I

		Mdn		Mdn IQ of c in first grade about 77. When cor-
Age	w		c	rected by being multiplied by ratio of c mdn to
6	16.4			w mdn it becomes 92.
7	42.0		16.8	
8	30.0		30.0	

		Mdn[18]		Such standard group tests as this and *Otis* are
	Norm			inadequate for studying innate racial differences.
Age	w		c	
7	59		1.8	
8	68		9.0	
9	76		7.5	
10	80		16.5	

A-MAN

		IQ		Southern Europeans and c groups rank much below
	w	c	c	American w Ss and those of Northern European
	(native	Cal	South	stock.
	parents)			
Mdn	100.3	82.7	76.5	
M	101.5	85.8	78.7	
s	18.3	18.7	17.5	

[17]Scores of first-grade Ss older than 8 years are not included in the table. For results on *Pintner-Paterson, Otis Primary, Draw-a-Man,* and *Otis S-A, Intermediate,* see Tables 2, 3, and 4.
[18]Haggerty's norms given only through Age 10.

TABLE

SCHOOL CHILDREN

| AUTHOR DATE | LOCATION | N | SUBJECTS | | METHOD OF SELECTION |
			AGE	GRADE	
Peterson, J., and Telford, C. W. (1930)	St. Helena Isl., S. C.	c- 361	5-15		Ss from Penn Normal & Indus Sch and 5 publ schs. (See Peterson & Telford above.)
Lindner,[19] R. S. (1962)	Alabama, Florida, Georgia, South Carolina, Tennessee	c- 1800	5-16	1-6	Stratified random sampling used to draw Ss from publ schs of 5 states; final sample of 1800 c, Grades 1 to 6. In each state, 3 county systems selected, 1 metrop, 1 urban, 1 rural. Only 19 of Ss were 5 yrs.

DETROIT

Koch,[2] H. L., and Simmons, R. (1926)	San Antonio, Austin, and El Paso, Tex.	w- 78 c- 128	7-9 6-10	1 1	
Ellis, P. D. (1947)	Baton Rouge, La.	c- 64	6-10	1	Tested first grade of one sch with revised edition.
Berry, C. S. (1922)	Detroit, Mich.	w-6186[20] c- 443		1 1	All pupils entering 1st grade in the publ schs in 1920.

[19]This work also discussed by Kennedy and Lindner (1964). Five-year-olds omitted from this table; for results on this younger group, see Table 1.

THREE *(continued)*

NONVERBAL GROUP TESTS

RESULTS	COMMENTS OF AUTHOR

	M IQ	Compared with w norms Ss about 2 yrs retarded in lower age range and 4 or more yrs retarded above 9 yrs. Very little diff bet isl c and other Southern c on this test. Weighted average IQ is 79.
Age	c	
5	98	
6	78	
7	77	
8	80	
9	76	
10	68	
11	70	
12	64	
13	60	

		IQ			Primary finding of normative data obtained was that means for Negro sample were consistently lower than norms of Goodenough. Practical usefulness of normative data must be viewed as questionable in terms of the consistently low validity correlations.
	M		s		
Age	w (norms)	c	w (norms)	c	
6	108.4	100.6	17.2	23.1	
7	105.7	101.8	17.9	19.3	
8	101.9	93.4	18.3	17.7	
9	100.3	90.0	19.2	17.2	
10	97.9	88.1	17.4	15.4	
11	91.4	85.0	16.6	16.0	
12		77.4		15.1	
13		67.7		16.1	
Total	100.7	91.1	18.8	19.48	
29% c above w *mean*					

FIRST GRADE

	M Scores		Sig diff bet 7-yr-means; nearly sig diff bet 8-yr-means.
	w	c	
Age			
6		34.50	
7	39.40	35.00	
8	40.75	36.85	
9	45.00	38.95	
78% w above c *mdn*, Age 7			
77% w above c *mdn*, Age 8			

	IQ	Ss well developed socially acc to Vineland Scale. Evidently racial discrimination evil does not affect children of this age range.
	c	
M	87.16	
s	18.6	
Range	51-116	

	%age	
	w	c
Superior	30	23
Average	59.6	63.7
Inferior	10.4	13.3

[20]Including only children from English-speaking homes.

TABLE

SCHOOL CHILDREN

AUTHOR DATE	LOCATION	N	SUBJECTS		METHOD OF SELECTION
			AGE	GRADE	

DEARBORN

AUTHOR DATE	LOCATION	N	AGE	GRADE	METHOD OF SELECTION
Hirsch, N. D. M. (1926)	Massachusetts and Nashville, Tenn.	w-284[3] c- 101		2, 3 2, 3	W- all in publ schs of 4 Mass mill towns. C- from certain schs chosen as being representative of c pop.
Long,[21] H. H. (1933)	Washington, D. C.	cI-100		3A	"Practically all" of c from 5 schs in under-privileged communities *if born in DC.*

MINNESOTA PAPER

Bean,[22] K. L. (1942)	Baton Rouge, La.	c- 49	13-18	8	Ss selected at random.

ARMY BETA

Lewis,[23] M. L. (1947)	Montgomery, Ala.	c- 96		7	All boys in 7th grade of one high sch.

PINTNER NON-

Bousfield,[24] M. B. (1932)	Chicago, Ill.	c- 222		5-8	From Keith Elem Sch. Method of selection not given.
Tanser,[5] H. A. (1939)	Kent County, Ontario	w-387 c- 102	6-15 7-16	3-8 3-8	From 7 schs, all rural except one. As far as practicable tested all enrolled.

[21]For results on other tests reported by Long, see Tables 2 and 4. *Dearborn A* results on Group II not given. Note that in I (underprivileged group) neighborhood was rated *fair* or *good* in 49% of cases, that 58% of homes were rated *good* or *fair* in appearance, and that 10% of fathers were skilled laborers or of higher occupational rank.

[22]For other test results, see Table 4.

THREE *(continued)*

NONVERBAL GROUP TESTS

RESULTS	COMMENTS OF AUTHOR

A

	IQ		W Ss, of Amer-born parents, living in same neigh-
	w	c	borhoods as immigrant groups. From relatively
M	97.3	79.1	inferior environment.

	IQ	Previous Sims Scale rating on a part of this com-
	c	munity was 13.
M	102	

FORM BOARD

M at 23rd %ile rank of norms group	This group as a whole inferior in ability to do kind of thinking called for on both tests, whether language required or not.

REVISED FORM

	IQ
	c
M	91.75
s	17.88
Range	48-112

LANGUAGE TEST

	Score	Children mainly from homes of inferior social and
	c	economic status.
M	49.7	
s	13.7	

	IQ		W children surpass c in all grades with decreasing
	w	c	amt after 4th. Probably accounted for by process
M	110.87	95.25	of selection which takes place among the Negroes.[25]
Mdn			
Rural	110.5	96.67	
Urban	109.76	94.81	
Total	109.87	96.02	
s	19.03	13.30	
16% c above w *mdn*			

---

[23]For results on *California Mental Maturity*, see Table 4. For results on delinquents, see Table 11.

[24]For results on other tests, see Table 4.

[25]See Smart (1963) relative to this point.

THE TESTING OF NEGRO INTELLIGENCE

TABLE
SCHOOL CHILDREN

AUTHOR DATE	LOCATION	N	SUBJECTS AGE	GRADE	METHOD OF SELECTION
					CHICAGO NON-
McGurk,[16] F. C. J. (1943)	Richmond, Va.	w-890 c-561	9- 9-	4-8 4-8	Alphabetized names in each grade and selected every 10th.
Lawrence, W. C. (1951)	Anderson, Blount, and Knox Counties, Tenn.	c-923	6-14		All c in sch on testing days if in age range. Included cities in 3 counties, except for Knoxville.
Newland, T. E., and Lawrence, W. C. (1953)	Knoxville and Anderson, Blount, and Knox Counties, Tenn.	c-1140	6-14		All c in attendance in all segregated schs of Anderson, Blount, and the county schs of Knox. "Representative sample" from Knoxville.
					SRA PRIMARY MENTAL
Johnson, S. T. (1954)	Clarksville, Tenn.	c-100[26]	5-11 to 7-0	1	50 boys & 50 girls who entered sch for first time in Sept, 1953.
					INTERNATIONAL GROUP
Peterson,[27] J., and Lanier, L. H. (1929)	Nashville, Tenn.	w-119 c-86	12 12		All 12-yr-olds in 3 w & 2 c schs; also 9 12-yr-olds from a c jr high sch, since one of c schs had only Grades 1-6; random selection.

[26]There were 110 children enrolled in the first grade (personal communication from Superintendent).

THREE (continued)
NONVERBAL GROUP TESTS

RESULTS	COMMENTS OF AUTHOR

VERBAL EXAMINATION

	M Scores		
	w	c	
Grade			
4	86	66	
5	98	78	
6	108	87	
7	114	96	
8	121	98	

Analysis of variance indicates no difference bet published norms and Richmond w means. Sig diff bet c and w means.

	Mdns	
	w	c
Age	(norms)	
6	—	6.5
7	57	23
8	75	42
9	88	65
10	99	72
11	110	84
12	119	90
13	124	93
14	—	94

C %ile ranks of 86-96 correspond to medians of normative sample. Cannot assume that a test measures the intelligence of everyone to whom it is given.

Age	
6-9	3-6% c above w (normative) means
10-14	10-15% c above w (normative) means

C at all ages 2 or more years below norms. Unreliable diff bet city and country groups. Majority of Ss were included in preceding study of Lawrence's.

ABILITIES TEST

	IQ
	c
M	83.50
Range	53-133

Lower intelligence of c attributable to educational deficiency of the home, low economic status, & to a lack of enriching experiences.

ROTATOR

	Mdns	
Test	w	c
1	20.90	14.30
4	17.65	14.60
5	5.33	3.21
6	11.86	8.63
9	17.75	10.50

All w-c diffs sig.
19% c above w mdn

Used only Tests 1, 4, 5, 6, and 9; rotator forms & entirely nonlinguistic.

[27]See Tables 1, 2, 4, and 5, respectively, for results on following tests: *Point Scale, Myers Mental Measure, Binet Group,* and *Otis S-A.*

TABLE

SCHOOL CHILDREN

AUTHOR DATE	LOCATION	N	SUBJECTS		METHOD OF SELECTION
			AGE	GRADE	
					DAVIS-EELLS
Furlow,[28] F. D. (1954)	Atlanta, Ga.	c- 38	10-14	6	Ss enrolled in one of 3 6th-grades of Carter Elem Sch; does not say if this group is representative of the 3. Each S given 3 tests.
Queen, P. M. J. (1954)	Apex, N. C.	c- 30	11-12	6	From Apex jr high sch; "a selected group of Negro sixth graders".
Tate, M. W., and Voss, C. E. (1956)	Pa. Havertown (w) Coatesville (c) S. C. Orangeburg (w) Columbia (c) Richland Co. (w) Orangeburg Co. (w) Richland Co. (c) Orangeburg Co. (c)	Pa.[30] w-177 c- 122 S. C. w-372 c- 209		4-6 4-6	*Davis-Eells & CMM* given by classroom teachers in the 3 grades of selected urban & rural schs, w & c, in Pa & SC.
Clark,[32] G. E. (1957)	St. Louis, Mo.	w-362 c- 361		High 4	All children were taken in complete class units. Schs segregated. Ws from 14 schs, c from 8 schs serving high, middle, & low socioeco class areas. Negro E tested in c schs, w E in white schs.

[28]For results on *Detroit Learning Aptitude* and *California Mental Maturity*, see Tables 2 and 4.

[29]Authors prefer term *IPSA* (Index of Problem Solving Ability) but say *IQ* may be appropriately applied (Manual).

THREE *(continued)*

NONVERBAL GROUP TESTS

	RESULTS		COMMENTS OF AUTHOR

GAMES

	IQ		The fruitfulness of the Davis-Eells test is of fullest import when appraising the intelligence of Ss from a population which is heterogeneous enough to possess inherent culture differences.
	c		
M	81.42		
Mdn	80.50		
s	14.65		
Range	53-117		

	IQ[29]		*California Test of Mental Maturity* also administered to these Ss.
	c		
M	84.8		
s	6.2		
Range	-104		

	M IQ[31]		Neither schs nor sections of US randomly selected. Believed that the schs were fairly representative of urban middle-class & rural schs, but they may not be.
	w	c	
Pa urban			
4	106	85	
5	109	88	
6	107	91	
SC urban			
4	105	89	
5	103	83	
6	104	90	
SC rural			
4	94	63	
5	97	63	
6	93	75	
All c-w diffs sig.			

	IQ		*Davis-Eells* did provide scores and IQs for Negro children which were relatively independent of socioeco level of the 3 groups. Even in most favored socioeco area, *Davis-Eells* failed to provide IQ's which approached a mean of 100.
	w	c	
Socioec		*M*	
Low	88.63	81.75	
Middle	99.74	83.48	
High	106.74	84.32	
Total	98.74	83.40	
		s	
Low	12.65	12.60	
Middle	13.85	13.94	
High	11.56	13.91	
Total	15.13	13.55	

[30]See Table 4 for results on *California Mental Maturity*. Authors also tested 197 rural w Pa children but were not able to secure rural colored in Pa; hence we have omitted the rural Pa whites.

[31]Calculations by reviewer from authors' data.

[32]For results on *Otis Quick-Scoring, Beta*, see Table 4.

TABLE

SCHOOL CHILDREN

AUTHOR DATE	LOCATION	SUBJECTS			METHOD OF SELECTION
		N	AGE	GRADE	
Love,[33] M. I., and Beach, S. (1957)	Cincinnati, Ohio	c- 110		3	110 3rd grade children in one of predominantly lower-class schs tested when their mdn age was 9-0.
Fowler, W. L. (1959)	Detroit and Hamtramck, Mich.	w-285[34] c- 70	10 10		12 elem schs from all major geographic areas in Detroit & 2 schs in Hamtramck supplied pupils. 442 pupils who were born in 1944 to be given 6 mental tests; omitted 87 due to absence from one or more of the tests.
					OTIS QUICK-SCORING MENTAL
Boger,[33] J. H. (1952)	A Rural Virginia County	w--53 c- 51		1-3 1-4	Tested intact classes in 1-2 teacher schs with CMM & Q-S; tests repeated after 3½ months practice on puzzles & other problems.
Wade, A. C. (1954)	Candor, N. C.	c- 32	6-3 to 7-3	1	Tested own class at Brutonville Elem Sch; test repeated after 3 months of enriched program.

[33]For results on *California Mental Maturity*, see Table 4.

[34]This number includes 84 Polish "ethnics" and 201 American white "nonethnics", separated in the author's data but combined by reviewer.

THREE *(continued)*
NONVERBAL GROUP TESTS

RESULTS			COMMENTS OF AUTHOR

	IQ		In the use of familiar problem situations the test might depict some episodes that create a shock situation and handicap S's functioning.
	c		
M	82.5		

	M IQ[35]		Used Warner *et al.* method of status classification acc to parental occupation, house type, and neighborhood type. Since only 3 of the 70 Negro Ss were classed above *Lower-Lower* group, it is only with this socioeconomic level that the principal racial and ethnic comparisons are made.
Cult-Con (3 tests)	w	c	
Total sample	105.57	88.23	
Lower-lower	97.04	87.53	
Specific Tests	*(lower-lower)*		
IPAT—A	94.06	90.8	
IPAT—B	96.74	82.0	
Davis-Eells	100.32	89.8	

ABILITY ALPHA TEST

	IQ		Study indicates that perceptual training will cause an increase in IQ's of rural elementary sch pupils.
	w	c	
M	90	84	
Mdn	92	85	

	IQ	No improvement in mean IQ (82.2) but Ss more variable (*s*, 9.15).
	c	
M	82.8	
s	6.5	
Range	66.5-99	

[35]Three of the 6 tests are referred to as *conventional: California Mental Maturity, Detroit Alpha,* & *Henmon-Nelson* (see Table 4); and 3 as *culture-controlled*, consisting of the Cattells' *IPAT Culture Free* Test, Scale 2, Forms A and B and the *Davis-Eells test.*

TABLE

SCHOOL CHILDREN

AUTHOR DATE	LOCATION	N	SUBJECTS		METHOD OF SELECTION
			AGE	GRADE	

RAVEN'S PROGRESSIVE

| Higgins,[36] C., and Sivers, C. H. (1958) | A Northeastern City | w-440 c- 349 | 7-9 7-9 | 1-4 1-4 | From publ schs serving lowest socioeco areas of a NE city. All 7-, 8-, & 9-yr-olds in Grades 1-3 of these schs were studied, plus children from 5 4th-grade classes. |
| Sperrazzo, G., and Wilkins, W. L. (1958) (1959) | St. Louis, Mo. | Total-480 | 7-11 | | Approx ⅓ of Ss from all-w sch, ⅓ from all-c sch, & ⅓ from sch of 60% c & 40% w. Occup of fathers classed (1) prof & semipro (2) sk, semisk & clerical (3) service, unsk & labor; 160 Ss at each level. |

LORGE-THORNDIKE

| Katzenmeyer,[38] W. G. (1962) | Jackson, Mich, | w-1061 c- 193 | | 2 2 | During fall of '57 & '58 *L-T, Level 1* given to all entering kg children of the 16 publ schs; 2 yrs later all Ss in 2nd grade rooms of these schs were retested with *L-T, Level 2.* Data include only Ss present at both testings. |

[36]For results on *Stanford-Binet, 1937 Form* given to these Ss, see Table 2.
[37]From Jensen's corrections (Jensen, 1959). Sperrazzo's & Wilkins' *F*'s are slightly higher as will be noted from their Table 2.

THREE *(continued)*

NONVERBAL GROUP TESTS

RESULTS	COMMENTS OF AUTHOR

MATRICES

	IQ		The present findings suggest that intelligence tests heavily loaded with nonverbal items may discriminate against Negro children.
	w	c	
M	90.8	80.5	
s	18.9	16.3	
t =	8.23		

Source of Variation	F[37]	Results appear to support validity of Raven's norms on Scottish sch children when applied to the St L population. Sig diff bet c & w in occup groups (1) and (2). Diff in (3) favored w but not significant.
Race	78.28*	
Age	44.13*	
Occup	19.54*	
Sex	2.96	

*p ⟨ .001
Highly sig diff's

Occup Class	*M Scores*		*F*
	w	c	
(1)	26.41	21.46	40.20*
(2)	24.78	18.76	59.58*
(3)	21.13	19.51	3.73

*p ⟨ .001
Highly sig diff's

INTELLIGENCE TESTS

	IQ[39]		Mean IQ of w group increased by 1.87 points from kg to 2nd grade testing; that of c by 6.68 points. Diff in increase significant (t=4.44).
	w	c	
M	103.91	89.74	
s	12.27	10.77	
t =	16.48		

[38]For results on Level 1 of *Lorge-Thorndike,* see Table 1.
[39]t of 16.48 calculated by reviewer.

TABLE

SCHOOL CHILDREN

AUTHOR DATE	LOCATION	N	SUBJECTS		METHOD OF SELECTION
			AGE	GRADE	
Deutsch, M., and Brown, B. (1964)	Not given	w- (1) 52 (2) 68 (3) 104		1, 5	From a sample of 543 urban publ sch children stratified by race, grade level (first & fifth), &
		c- (1) 51 (2) 111 (3) 157		1, 5	social class.

[40]*Occupational class* refers to Institute's SES scale. This scale was derived both from prestige ratings of occupations as well as the education of the main breadwinner of the family. The reviewer has reversed the Institute's class levels of (1) and (3) to make (1) correspond to the *highest* occup grouping, in keeping with the usual procedure of designating the highest status group as (1).

THREE *(concluded)*

NONVERBAL GROUP TESTS

	RESULTS			COMMENTS OF AUTHOR

Occup[40]	*IQ*		*t*[41]	Two possible environmental modifiers of intell test performance that would seem to account for some of racial & other group differences are presch experience (nursery sch or kindergarten) & family cohesion (presence of father in home).
Class	w	c		
(1)				
M	114.92	102.57	4.70	
s	12.05	14.53		
(2)				
M	105.59	94.87	3.96	
s	14.88	14.70		
(3)				
M	97.24	91.24	3.26	
s	15.35	13.25		
Total				
M	103.88	94.32	7.08	
s	16.12	14.53		

	IQ		
	c	c	
Grade	Father present	Father absent	t
1			
M			
comb	96.96	88.95	2.35[42]
s			
comb	13.57	20.12	
5			
M			
comb	92.84	88.02	2.13[42]
s			
comb	14.83	12.18	

[41]t's calculated by reviewer.

[42]Combined means, standard deviations, and the *t's* calculated by reviewer from data in authors' Table 4. Only Ss from two lowest occupational classes included here.

fornia. Her findings coupled with those reported by Havighurst (1953) suggested to Altus that whatever gains the lower-class children make on *Games* as opposed to other tests would be slight. Further, Altus, in discussing the validity of the test, said that problems of test validation are nearly insurmountable if one accepts the assumption of the authors of the test that school grades, reading skill, and other measures of academic success cannot be accepted as validating criteria (since these are strongly culture-bound). Since the authors seem to accept none of the usual external criteria, it would seem, according to Altus, that the validity of the test must be taken on faith. Faith, in turn, would depend upon belief in the reasonableness of the test problems, the care taken in the long period of test standardization, and the extent to which one agrees with the authors' premises.

Three *Davis-Eells* studies specifically relating to Negroes were made in the states of Georgia, North Carolina, and Ohio, respectively, on small groups of sixth- or third-grade children. Furlow (1954) tested a class of 38 colored pupils in Atlanta and reported a mean of 81.42, a standard deviation of 14.65, and a range of 53 to 117. Queen (1954), in another Master's project, obtained a mean IQ of 84.8 and standard deviation of 6.2 on a group of 30 junior high school children in Apex, North Carolina, whom she described as a "selected group of sixth graders". Love and Beach (1957) examined 110 third-grade Negro children "in one of the predominantly lower-class schools" of Cincinnati and secured a mean IQ of 82.5 on this group but did not report its variability (Table 3). The authors also found differences between the mean performances of children of lower, middle, and upper socioeconomic levels which were statistically significant on the *Davis-Eells Games,* even as on the *Kuhlmann-Anderson.*[49]

These three studies are similar in that their experimental designs were relatively simple and straightforward, each group was in a single grade and in a single city, and the mean IQ's obtained were between 81 and 85. We will now examine the experimental designs and results of three larger and more complicated pieces of research in which the *Davis-Eells* was one of the tests employed.

The objective of Tate and Voss (1956) was to determine the extent to which race, residence, and sex influence performance on the *Davis-Eells* as compared with the *California Test of Mental Maturity.*[50] These investigators selected for their subjects white and colored children in Grades 4, 5, and 6 from urban and rural areas of Pennsylvania and South Carolina. Accordingly, the respective towns of Havertown and Coatesville were chosen to provide the urban white and colored Ss in Pennsylvania; the cities of Orangeburg and Columbia were elected to provide the urban white and colored of South Carolina, respectively; whereas both white and colored children were drawn from the counties of Richmond and Orangeburg to represent the rural dichotomy in South Carolina. The Pennsyl-

---

[49]Statement based on other part of authors' study in which c and w were undifferentiated.

[50]The part of the research dealing specifically with this test will be discussed in the next section of this chapter.

vania samples consisted of 177 whites and 122 Negroes, the South Carolina urban samples of 184 white and 115 colored, and the South Carolina rural samples of 118 white and 94 colored. In addition, the authors hoped to secure comparable groups of rural colored and white Pennsylvania Ss; but, although they had located and tested their whites, they were unable to secure rural colored children from this state. Consequently, the reviewer has omitted the data on the rural Pennsylvania whites.

The two mental tests were administered by the classroom teachers to all children present in the 29 classes [51] or sections earmarked for testing, eleven of them being colored. Although the authors report that neither the schools nor the sections tested were randomly selected they had believed that the schools were fairly representative of *urban middle-class and rural schools,* "but they might not be."

The reviewer was able to present the data from this study (see Table 3), particularly the race differences aspects of it, by making various calculations from the authors' Tables 1 and 2 and using the *Davis-Eells Manual* to transform the raw scores into IQ's: (1) all mean chronological ages were presented in months which we changed into *years;* (2) all mean test scores were listed separately for each section, even within the same type of school, and by combining the means we reduced the groups from as many as 18 to 9; (3) variances were likewise listed by class or section and these were changed by the reviewer to *combined standard deviations,* reducing these 18 variances to 9 *s's,* (4) the significance of the differences between the racial groups in *age* and in *mean test score* was determined at each grade level, for each type of school, and within each state; and (5) the several mean scores were changed into the more meaningful IPSA's (IQ's).

As will be observed from Table 3, the mean IQ's of the white children in the three grades of the Northern and Southern cities are very similar to one another, ranging between 106 and 109 in Havertown and between 103 and 105 in Orangeburg. Similarly, the Negro urban samples from these states are very like one another, ranging between the IQ's of 85 and 91 in Coatesville and between those of 83 and 90 in Columbia. The rural South Carolina whites, on the other hand, scored approximately 10 points below the mean of the urban whites, whereas the rural South Carolina Negroes fell on the average about 20 points below the means of the urban Negroes.

In Pennsylvania, the Negro samples scored on the average from 16 to 21 IQ points below the whites of the same grade and state; in South Carolina the urban colored ranged from 14 to 20 points below the urban whites; and in rural South Carolina the colored earned scores on the average from 18 to 34 points below the rural whites. In each of these nine racial comparisons the difference was highly significant, the *t's* ranging from 4.51 to 13.06.

---

[51] 35 classrooms if one included the six Pennsylvania rural white rooms.

Clark (1957) hoped to determine whether or not the *Davis-Eells* would enable St. Louis slum children to obtain higher IQ's than would the highly verbal *Otis.*[50] He administered both tests to 361 Negro and 362 white school children in the high fourth grade, in each case selecting complete class units from the segregated schools. In order to compare the mental abilities of children of different socioeconomic levels he selected for his *Negro sample:* (1) 114 children of low status from two large schools in a district containing slum-type dwellings, (2) 115 Ss of middle status from three large school districts in the midcity area, and (3) 132 of high status from three schools "serving the best residential area of appreciable size available to St. Louis Negroes." Comprising his *white* sample were: (1) 118 Ss of low status from three large schools serving the downtown, river-industrial areas, (2) 109 middle-status Ss from five schools located in midcity white residential areas, and (3) 135 children from six schools, all except one in the southwest part of the city, identified as the *high-status* group.

The schools in the Negro and white communities were selected on the basis of a consensus reached by a committee of seven persons who had served as psychological examiners for the School Board and were well acquainted with the St. Louis schools and their pupil populations. The schools which had been selected subjectively by this committee were analyzed on the basis of the following United States Census data regarding the areas which they served: (1) income (as of 1949) of families and unrelated individuals, (2) monthly rental, (3) per cent of housing very inferior, (4) per cent of male adult workers below craftsmen, (5) per cent of female adult workers below craftsmen, and (6) median school years completed for persons of 25 years or older. In studying Clark's tables giving the range of these six characteristics for the low, middle, and high socioeconomic groups, and is impressed by the marked differences between the high white and high colored, middle-class white and middle-class colored, *etc.* The author said that he did not equate the socioeconomic factors of the Negro and white subgroups; but if one were to make such an attempt from Clark's tables, the reviewer would estimate that the *high socioeconomic* group of the Negroes would be equivalent to some point *between the low and middle socioeconomic groups* of the whites but *nearer the former.*

From Table 3 one will observe that the mean of the total colored sample is approximately 15 IQ points below the mean of the total white sample on the *Davis-Eells Games;* and if the nominally same socioeconomic levels are compared the greatest discrepancy between the mean IQ's is at the *high* level where the difference favors the white group by 22 points. If it be true, as the reviewer surmised, that the "high" socioeconomic status group of Negroes (whose mean IQ is 84) should be more fairly compared with a status position of the white group somewhat above the *low socioeconomic level* (whose mean IQ may be about 92), then this difference of eight points may be thought of as representing the advantage that whites of relatively low socioeconomic status have over Negroes of about the same status level.

Fowler (1959) stated that his purpose was to contrast conventional with culture-controlled mental tests by comparing pupil performance with race, socioeconomic status, ethnic background and sex.[52] In addition to the *Davis-Eells* test the researcher used two forms for the Cattells' *IPAT Culture Free Tests,* Scale 2, as well as three *culture-controlled* measures of mental ability. The *IPAT* constructed by Raymond B. Cattell and A. K. S. Cattell, relies completely upon geometric designs for item content, and consists of four tests: series completion, classification, matrix or pattern completion, and meeting certain conditions.

Split-half reliabilities ranging between .70 and .92 are reported for *Forms A* and *B* combined; immediate retests yielded reliabilities in the .80's, but retests over a longer interval in one sample correlated as low as .53. Factorial validity of the *IPAT* test was determined from its correlations with a pool of intelligence tests, including both verbal and performance types. (Anastasi, 1961, pp. 259-261) There are grounds for claiming that the *IPAT* tests are relatively culture fair, for no significant differences were discovered in the performances of American, Australian, French, and British samples. There were slightly different norms in some other countries but it is possible that these differences were due to sampling artifacts. (I. Macfarlane Smith, *in* Buros, 1959, pp. 473-474)

Fowler drew samples of 70 colored and 285 white children from 10-year-olds attending the public schools in Detroit and Hamtramck, Michigan. Twelve elementary schools were selected from all of the major geographic areas of Detroit: two from the southwest, two from the west, one from the northwest, two from the southcentral, two from the northeast, and three from the southeast sections; in Hamtramck, one school was taken from the northeast and one from the eastern section. From these 14 schools, 442 pupils were originally selected because they were born during the year of 1944; however, the records of 87 of these children were excluded from the author's data because of absences from one or more of the series of tests.

To determine the socioeconomic level of the pupils, the Warner, Meeker, and Eells method of status classification was used. This method, originally designed for white, American-born nonethnics, employs three factors in its classification: *parental occupation, house type,* and *neighborhood type.* To find a sufficiently large number of Negro children for testing, 67 of the 70 members of this racial group had to be drawn from slum areas that were completely *lower-lower* class.[53]

From Table 3, it may be noted that on a combination of the three *culture-controlled* tests the total white Michigan sample earned a mean IQ of 105.57

---

[52]The *conventional* differing most fundamentally from the *culture-controlled* in that the former is verbal, the latter, nonverbal. The three conventional tests used were *California Test of Mental Maturity, Detroit Alpha,* and *Henmon-Nelson* which will be surveyed in the next section of this chapter.

[53]Every S's home was visited by Fowler. He reported that no neighborhoods from which the white pupils were drawn were the equal of the Negro's nighborhoods in over-all decadence.

which placed them about 17 points above the mean of the total sample of Michigan Negroes.[54] The 69 white children making up the *lower-lower socioeconomic group* achieved a mean IQ of 97.04 on a combination of the three *culture-controlled* tests, or approximately 9.5 points above the mean of the 67 Negro children of the *lower-lower* group. At the *lower-lower* level, the mean IQ reported for the whites on *Form A* of the *IPAT* was only four points above that of the colored, whereas on *Form B* the difference in IQ was about 15 points. On the *Davis-Eells* test, the whites at this socioeconomic level achieved a mean IQ of 100, or about 10.5 points above the *lower-lower* Negro mean.

In fine, a total of 940 Negro elementary school children who have been tested on the *Davis-Eells Games* earned a combined mean IQ of 83; the 1196 whites (with whom they were compared in three of the studies) achieved a combined mean of 101. This mean difference of 18 IQ points between the racial samples was reduced to between 7 and 10.5 points when only the *lowest* socioeconomic groups from each race were compared.

OTIS QUICK-SCORING ALPHA

The *Alpha* of the *Otis Quick-Scoring Mental Ability Tests,* designed for Grades 1A to 4, may be given as a verbal or nonverbal test or both. The distinctive features of the *Quick-Scoring* tests are their brevity and scorability; yet the batteries show about the same correlations with other intelligence tests as those ordinarily expected. (Mursell, 1949, pp. 158-59)

In using *Alpha,* Boger (1952) was primarily interested in determining the effect of practicing on pictorial and geometric problems and puzzles; accordingly, he administered the *Otis Quick-Scoring Alpha* and a form of the *California Test of Mental Maturity* before and after a practice period. All white and colored children from the lower grades of one-teacher and two-teacher rural schools selected were tested. The mean *Otis* IQ of the colored Ss was 84, the mean of the whites was 90 (Table 3).

Wade (1954) hypothesized that enriching the program of underprivileged first-grade pupils would effect an increase in IQ. Selecting as subjects her own class (housed in a six-room modern brick building) in a colored school in Candor, North Carolina, Wade administered *Alpha* early in the fall, and three months later repeated the test. During this interval, her pupils — described as mainly coming from tenant farms and large families, with parents averaging no more than elementary education—were given costume parties, had the use of many toys as well as books on small tables, were taken on tours of the school plant and the Fire House, had a playhouse which they painted, *etc.,* all calculated to increase their intellectual and social maturing. Although the children's scores

---

[54]The statistics included in Table 3 result from the reviewer's having combined the author's groups of boys and girls and his samples of Polish and white nonethnics.

were more variable on the second testing, their means were found to be unchanged.

PROGRESSIVE MATRICES

The *Raven Progressive Matrices Tests* (1938-1956) consist of 60 matrices, or designs, a piece of which having been removed from each, the subject must choose the missing part from six or eight alternatives. The designs are grouped into five series, each of which contains 12 matrices of increasing difficulty but similar in principle. The earlier series require accuracy of discrimination; the later, more difficult series involve analogies, permutation and alteration of pattern, and other logical relations. The test is administered without time limit and with very simple oral instructions. Retest reliability in groups of older children and adults moderately homogeneous in age varies between .70 and .90, the reliability falling below these values at the lower score ranges. Factorial analyses indicate that the *Progressive Matrices* are heavily loaded with a factor common to most intelligence tests (identified with Spearman's *g*, or general factor), but that spatial aptitude, inductive reasoning, perceptual accuracy, and other group factors influence test performance. (Anastasi, 1961, pp. 261-63)

Higgins and Sivers (1958), using a public-school population of low socio-economic status, proposed to test the hypothesis that there is no significant difference between the *Stanford-Binet* IQ and an IQ determined by the *Progressive Matrices* (colored form). The authors planned their research to include all 7-, 8-, and 9-year-olds in Grades 1 to 3 and those children from five 4th-grade classes of public schools serving the lowest socioeconomic area of "a northeastern city". As was reported in this book, the authors found no difference in the mean intelligence of the colored and white subjects as measured by the *Stanford-Binet*.[55] On the *Progressive Matrices*, however, the colored children earned a mean IQ which was about 10 points below that of the whites, the difference being significant at the .001 level of significance (Table 3). Higgins and Sivers concluded that there was no evidence found to support the hypothesis that social bias in the verbal items of the *Stanford-Binet* depressed the IQ below the nonverbal, nonsocially biased *Progressive Matrices* IQ. In fact, they suggested, on the basis of their data, that the *Progressive Matrices* cannot be considered as a test of intelligence or a measure of *g*, but is rather a measure of a *specific skill*.

We have already mentioned the fact that in the several studies using *individual tests*, where white and colored children were selected from the same underprivileged neighborhoods, or where they were divided into groups according to the father's occupation or the socioeconomic status of the family, the colored averaged approximately *9 IQ points below* the white groups. In the research utilizing *nonverbal group tests* where white and colored subjects were selected from the same neighborhoods, etc., the colored averaged from *7 or 8 to 15 points*

---

[55]See pp. 40-41.

below the white means. Therefore, the finding of Higgins and Sivers of a *10-point difference* in the *Progressive Matrices* means of his groups is not unexpected.[56]

Sperrazzo and Wilkins (1958) present an analysis of variance of scores of Negro and white St. Louis school children on the *Progressive Matrices*. The normative data on the colored *Matrices* were based on Dumfries, Scotland, children, Ages 7-11; a subsequent study of test scores secured on Rochester, Minnesota, school children (Green and Ewert, 1955) indicated higher median at each age group for the American Ss. Sperrazzo and Wilkins attempted to cross validate the two sets of normative data with the testing of St. Louis school children.

Replicating (except for size of sample) the Rochester sample for age and grade, these investigators selected 480 children, Age 7 to 11, one third of whom came from an all white school, one third from an all Negro school, and one third from a school of 60 percent colored and 40 per cent white. A three-level socioeconomic status classification, based upon occupation of father was employed: (1) professional and semiprofessional, (2) skilled, semiskilled, and clerical, and (3) service, unskilled, or simply 'laborer'. As may be noted in Table 3, very large and significant differences were found with the socioeconomic (or occupational) status, age, and race variables. However, Sperrazzo and Wilkins call attention to the fact that the test was not designed to discriminate racial differences but age differences and that it is apparent from the significant race by socioeconomic status interaction and the third-order interaction that a restriction of the interpretation of the race difference found is necessary. The measured differences in scores between races are related to the age, sex, and socioeconomic status. "The results cannot be interpreted, therefore, as showing differences in intelligence between the races tested here. The differences found seem to depend upon variations of the nonrace factors." (p. 37)

Jensen (1959) indicates that Sperrazzo and Wilkins made an incorrect interpretation of the analysis and that the above conclusion is unwarranted. Jensen noted that the most stringent test of the significance of the main effects is obtained in their case, not by using the residual (or *within group*) variance as the error term, but by including all the interactions (in addition to the within group variance) in the error term. By doing this, Jensen concluded that in spite of the interactions between the variables, the race difference is *highly significant* statistically.

Accepting Jensen's criticism and following his suggestion that it would be desirable to perform an analysis of variance on the three socioeconomic groups and to present the mean scores for each race within each socioeconomic group, Sperrazzo and Wilkins (1959) present statistical data including the mean scores achieved by each racial group on the *Progressive Matrices* according to occupation of father and the significance of the differences between the means. From Table 3 one may observe that not only was the white group as a whole significantly

---

[56]For reviewer's interpretation of the *Stanford-Binet results,* see pp. 40-41.

superior to the total colored group on this test, but that at each occupational level the whites surpassed the colored, the differences being highly significant except in the case of the lowest groups (unskilled, service, and laborer). The authors remind one that the Negro and white socioeconomic groups were not equated as this term is defined in the usual treatment of social classes and that American Negro class structure and American white class structure are not directly comparable. The researchers were surprised, even so, that a relatively nonverbal performance test is *demonstrably sensitive* to differences in socioeconomic level.

Lorge-Thorndike Intelligence Test

Katzenmeyer[57] proposed to test the hypothesis that significant changes occur in the measured intelligence of Negro children after two years in a racially mixed public school. At the beginning of the kindergarten year, the 193 colored children averaged 19 IQ points below the 1061 white children in Jackson, Michigan, when tested on Level 1 of the *Lorge-Thorndike Intelligence Test*. Two years later the teachers again administered the *Lorge-Thorndike* test, but Level 2 instead of Level 1, to the same children who were then in the second grade (thereby excluding children who were accelerated and retarded, the transients, and the absentees). Katzenmeyer (1962) reports that on the second testing the whites were still significantly superior but that the difference was decreased to 14 points, the colored having *gained 6.68 points* on the average, and the whites having *gained 1.87 points* on the average. The investigator's explanation for the significantly greater gain on the part of the Negro children and the contrast between his findings and those of other experimenters who have noted a tendency for the Negro child's IQ to *decrease* and for the *disparity* between races to *increase with increase in age* is the presence of *social interaction* among the racial groups in the two-year interval. He stated that the Negro in Jackson has free access to movies, most restaurants, parks, golf courses, cultural events, and school, but that assimilation has not occurred in housing, church membership, community leadership, and social patterns. "Thus, for most Negro children, entry into the racially mixed public school program represents the beginning of a period of increased social contact." (p. 64) Katzenmeyer strongly believes that equalization of educational opportunity lies only partially in "integration" *per se;* and that the basic problem of the school relates to the guiding and encouraging of the assimilative process. "It may be inferred that the size of the difference between the measured IQ of Negroes and whites will be inversely proportionate to the degree of social freedom and cultural assimilation afforded the Negro group." (p. 71)

Katzenmeyer includes tabulated data for the 16 schools itemized separately, such as: the number and percentage of children in the colored and in the white groups, the mean IQ's and *s's* for the colored in kindergarten and for them in the

---

[57]For a description and appraisal of this test, see pp. 27-28. For summary of Katzenmeyer's experimental design, see p. 28.

second grade, the mean IQ's and standard deviations for the white Ss in kindergarten and in the second grade, and the like. From these tables it can be noted, with a minimum of calculations, that (1) at five of the schools there were 337 white but no Negro children in the second grade (who had also been tested in kindergarten); (2) at five schools there were 368 white children and nine Negro children tested (with no more than from 1 to 3 colored tested in a single school); and (3) at six schools there were 356 white and 184 colored tested, and colored subjects from a single school varying from 20 to 50. In other words, the tables reveal that all except nine of the 193 colored subjects in the research were present in but six of the 16 schools where about one third of the white subjects were enrolled. The reviewer analyzed the data a little further—from the five schools that were all white, the mean IQ at the kindergarten level was 103.37 and the mean gain in the two years was 3.21, the percentage gain being 3.11; from the six schools that were about one third colored (those that included all except nine of the colored Ss), the whites averaged 99.38 in kindergarten and achieved a mean gain of only 0.60 IQ points (percentage gain, .60 also) by Grade 2. The obtained difference between these two percentages, *i.e.*, 2.51, divided by the standard error of the difference between the percentages, *i.e.*, 1.02, results in a *t* of 2.46 which is significant at the .02 level of confidence. *This means of course that the whites who were experiencing no assimilation in the schoolroom made gains significantly larger than those white children who had been assimilated.* If, as the author suggests, the greater improvement in IQ of his Negro subjects (as compared with his white subjects and as compared with Negroes in other cited studies) is attributable to the *presence of social interaction* between Negroes and whites, would it not follow that the greater improvement in IQ of white children in certain of his schools (as compared with those in other schools) is traceable to the *abence of social interaction* between the two races?

Deutsch and Brown (1964) report the study of white and Negro IQ differences in relation to such variables as grade in school, socioeconomic class level, preschool training, and presence of father in the home. Without indicating the locale, the number of schools surveyed, or the precise method of selection of subjects within the school(s), the authors state that the data had been collected on cross-sectional samples of 543 urban public school children stratified by race, first and fifth grade levels, and social class (measured by a 12-point SES scale devised by the Institute for Developmental Studies, Department of Psychiatry, New York Medical College). The SES is an occupational scale derived both from prestige ratings of occupation and the education of the main breadwinner, and yields a weighted index of these two factors for each subject. The index scores were broken down into twelve levels and subsequently grouped into three, the comparisons in this study being made among the three levels.[58]

---

[58]The authors designate Level 1 as the lowest group and 3 as the highest; however, the reviewer has reversed this numbering, in accordance with the usual procedure of referring to I as the highest class.

The *Lorge-Thorndike Intelligence Test,* Level 1 was administered to the first-grade subjects and Level 3 to fifth graders, in small groups during school hours. The authors do not give the number of white and colored children tested at each grade, but do include the number of each racial group at each of the three SES (occupational) levels. A three-way analysis of variance indicated the presence of highly significant differences in IQ between the racial groups and between the SES levels but no significant differences between the grades. The differences between the colored and white means proved to be highly significant at each of the three occupational levels with the difference increasing with increase in SES (Table 3).

Deutsch and Brown interpret the lesser (but still highly significant) Negro-white differences at the lower occupational levels to be related to a more homogeneous environment of social deprivation in which the influence of race is reduced by the pervasiveness of poor living conditions. Believing that the amount of family participation may be related to "participation in the cultural mainstream" the authors observed that their data indicated fewer variegated family activities in the Negro than in the white group; in fact, one of the most striking differences between the Negro and white groups was the greater frequency of broken homes among the Negroes. In studying the relation between the presence of the father in the home (since it may be related to need achievement and aspiration level of the children, especially of the boys) and intelligence scores, Deutsch and Brown tabulated the data on 168 Class 2 and Class 3 Negro children whose fathers were present in the home and on 101 Negro children from these two classes whose fathers were absent from the home. From these data there appears to have been a consistent trend for the children whose fathers were living at home to score higher on the *Lorge-Thorndike* in Grade 1 and in Grade 5; however, there is no greater disparity between the mean IQ's of the father-present father-absent groups at the fifth-grade level (as the authors suggest) than at the first grade. As will be seen in Table 3, the *t*'s at both grades were very similar and point to a significance at the five per cent level of confidence.

The other background variable which the authors thought might be positively related to intelligence test performance is the presence of some formal preschool education. Consequently, they compared the *Lorge-Thorndike* IQ's of all children who were reported as having had kindergarten and/or nursery school experience with the IQ's of children who had had no preschool experience. Analysis of variance at the fifth-grade level (both races combined and the highest SES omitted) indicated that children who had had preschool training scored significantly above those without this training. However, when the same analysis was made for the *first-grade* group, children with preschool experience did not score significantly above children without this experience, the *t* ratio being only 1.53 (calculated by reviewer from authors' Table 6).

Deutsch and Brown interpret the fact that preschool experience appears to have been more closely related to intelligence test scores at Grade 5 than at Grade 1 to be consistent with the father-in-the-home evidence and to be in support of the cumulative deficit hypothesis, *i.e.*, that deprivational influences have a greater impact at later than at earlier developmental stages. This theory, earlier advanced by Fred Brown in 1944 (see Table 1), may have much to recommend it, but, in the opinion of the present writer, it appears that Deutsch and Brown's findings have given it frail support. We have already shown that at the fifth-grade level the lack of father in the home was no more detrimental to the intellectual development of the child than was the lack in the first grade (Table 3); as regards the importance that should be attached to their finding that preschool experience is more closely related to intelligence at Grade 5 than it is at Grade 1 (for the lower two SES classes), it should be noted that there were 53 Ss (both races) who were included in the group without preschool education in Grade 5, whereas in Grade 1 there were only 23 Ss (both races) included in the group who had not had preschool training. Since the mean difference between the groups (with and without preschooling) at Grade 5 was only *1.22 IQ points above the mean difference between comparable groups* at Grade 1 (authors' Tables 5 and 6) and since the standard deviations are very similar it would seem that a tripling of the number of cases at Grade 1 would probably be sufficient to remove any significance that is attached to the authors' findings in this instance.

Deutsch and Brown conclude that their data on *family cohesion* and *preschool experience* represent two possible environmental modifiers of intelligence-test performance that would seem to account for some of the differences found between ethnic and class groups. The authors have certainly shown that racial differences persist within given class levels to significant degrees, and that among the two lower-class groups of children those who had had preschool training and those whose fathers were present in the home earned IQ's on the average from 5 to 8 points above children who did not have these advantages. However, it seems to the reviewer that the authors are as much in error in their concluding statement as they would be if they had observed instead that their data showed that the *intelligence of the parents* represented a possible *hereditary modifier* of intelligence test performance of the children; that the 22 per cent who were not sent to preschool and the 28 per cent who had no father in the home represented a poor sampling of the entire group, with the definite implication that their parents had less mental energy, less general intelligence, and less competency than the parents of other children.

SUMMARY

In the preceding section we have reviewed 41 studies which have made use of 17 nonverbal group tests in the examination of approximately 14,800 colored school children, excluding duplications. About 75 per cent of the subjects were living in urban areas and 60 per cent were living in the Southern states.

White children were included in 22 of the investigations. In all of these the white Ss secured higher averages than the colored of the same localities. In some instances the differences were reported to be significant; in others, though no measures of variability were included, the sizes of the samples and the amount of differences separating the measures of central tendency were highly indicative of significance. Among these 22 reports, there are included three in which children of different localities were compared. Hirsch found the obtained differences between the *Northern mill town white* children and the *colored Nashville* sample to favor the whites. The South Carolina *rural white* children scored higher at each grade than the *South Carolina urban colored* and the *Pennsylvania urban colored* subjects (Tate and Voss). Koch and Simmons, however, in one comparison of *urban colored* and *rural whites* from Texas, reported the colored to surpass the whites in four of the seven subtests of *Myers Mental Measure*.

In the 19 experimental studies where the scores of the colored were compared with white norms, all except Long (1933)[59] reported inferiority to the norms. In general, the children seem to have been selected by random or stratified sampling or else saturated samples have been secured.[60]

In twenty-eight of the investigations, including 9300 colored children, the results were presented in terms of IQ. From the various averages reported, we have calculated a combined average, which proved to be 85. When the subjects were categorized according to residence, *i.e.*, North, Border, or South, and rural or urban, the following combined average IQ's were obtained: *Northern rural,* 77 (987 cases); *Southern rural,* 80 (1535 cases); *Northern urban,* 83 (1953 cases); *Southern urban,* 86 (2442 cases); *Border rural,* 89 (219 cases); and *Border urban,* 91 (2035 cases).

When measures of overlapping were included among the data,[61] typically 75 to 80 per cent of the whites tested equaled or surpassed the medians of the colored. On the other hand, from 0 to 44 per cent of the colored were reported to equal or exceed the corresponding white medians.

Where measures of variability were reported for white and colored groups, the white children were the more heterogenous in 15 comparisons, the colored were the more variable in six comparisons, and there was no difference in three of them.

VERBAL GROUP TESTS

More than twice as many colored children have been examined by verbal group tests as by nonverbal group and individual tests together. In Table 4 are summarized the results of 103 studies in which approximately 60,850 colored

---

[59]See p. 85. These Ss were likewise tested on *Stanford-Binet, Pintner-Paterson,* and *Kuhlmann-Anderson*.

[60]In a few of the studies reviewed the method of selection of subjects was either ambiguously reported or omitted.

[61]Or IQ frequency distributions included so that the overlap could be determined.

children (excluding duplicates) have been examined by one or more of these tests. At least 18 verbal psychometric group tests have been employed, beginning with the *Otis Group Advanced* and the *Pressey,* 1918, and ending with the *California Test of Mental Maturity,* 1963, S-Form.

KUHLMANN-ANDERSON

The *Kuhlmann-Anderson Intelligence Tests,* a very significant test, has gone through five revisions since its first appearance and has a range of application from Grades 1 to 12. It comes in nine booklets, the various booklets being for designated age and grade levels. The subtests involve use of pictures, geometrical figures, mathematics, new associations, and verbal relations and information—the subtests having been selected from 100 possibilities on the basis of definite increase in scores attained at successive age levels. Mental ages are obtained from tables of equivalents for each subtest and the MA of the subject is his median subtest MA. (Mursell, 1949, p. 161)

The *Kuhlmann-Anderson* tests (1952 revision), beginning with Grade 4, are: scrambled words, substitution of letters for numbers, word classification, word meanings and information, word opposites and similarities, word analysis, accuracy of perception (using the alphabet), scrambled sentences, number series, arithmetical problems, perception of details, following increasingly complex verbal instructions, and logical analysis of brief statements. The reliability of the *Kuhlmann-Anderson* as determined by the *odd-even* items method is reported to be from .88-.95, by the *test-retest* method, .90. Evidence of the validity of the test is indicated in: differentiation among average, retarded, and accelerated pupils; relative uniformity of means, standard deviations, and ranges of IQ's at the several grade levels; subtest intercorrelations; and correlations with school achievement—the coefficients ranging from .60 to .80. (Freeman, 1962, pp. 385-86, 389-90)

Altogether 4061 Southern Negro school children have been examined by these tests, and except for a group of 112 seventh-grade pupils tested in Nashville (Willis, 1939) they may be considered to have been unselected. Willis utilized both the *Kuhlmann-Anderson* and the *Stanford Reading* test scores for the purpose of selecting colored and white children for a remedial reading program. For this program, no pupils were included who had IQ's of *under 80* or *over 115* and none who had reading scores of under 4 or over 9.5; consequently, the respective IQ's of 98 and 89 obtained on the white and colored children cannot be regarded as typical of larger Nashville groups.

Bice (1938) tested colored subjects in one town and whites in another, both towns being located in a county in the central part of North Carolina.[62] This county had been selected previously as average for the state, based on a combined

---

[62]The tests were administered by white and Negro examiners, by strangers and by home room teachers.

rating of social and economic factors. Pupils from Grade 1 through high school in the two school units were examined on *Kuhlmann-Anderson;* any child whose IQ was found to be under 80 was given a *Stanford-Binet.* The mean IQ's were 94 and 83, respectively, for the white and colored subjects, the difference between them being highly significant as will be seen in Table 4. Eighteen per cent of the colored Ss overlapped the median of the whites. Fifteen per cent of the colored and four per cent of the white pupils earned IQ's below 70; two white children (.46 per cent) obtained IQ's in the 140's and one Negro child secured an IQ in the 120's. Noting that the colored may be of a culture different from that of those on whom the tests were standardized, Bice nevertheless points out that the teachers and principal of the Negro school have repeatedly indicated that the results of the objective tests confirm their own conclusions — "conclusions that were often reached after the pupils had failed one to five or more times." (p. 14)

The other three studies on Southern Negro children were surveys of rural areas. Bruce (1940) administered the *Kuhlmann-Anderson* to relatively large groups of Negro and white children in the Piedmont section of Virginia, on the basis of which she selected smaller groups for testing by the *Stanford-Binet* and the *Arthur Point Scale.* The principal facts relating to the socioeconomic character of this county as they affect test results have already been considered. The population of the county at the time of the testing was about 41,000, somewhat less than half of which was colored, with 86 per cent of the people living on farms. The white and colored enrollments represented practically the same proportion of their respective school populations, *i.e.,* 69 and 70 per cent of the school census; the white average attendance was 80 per cent of its enrollment, and the colored, 76 per cent. The average white child was entered in school at 6 years 9 months, the colored at 7 years 0 months. The mean IQ's of the total numbers in attendance at the nine pairs of schools were about 88 for the whites and 72 for the colored. When the children were matched for socioeconomic score the difference in mean IQ was reduced to 10 points but was still significant. Twenty per cent of the Negroes equaled or exceeded the median of the matched whites. A positive skewness, *i.e.,* a piling up of IQ's at the lower end of the distribution, was observed in the results of each of the intelligence tests as given to the Negroes; positive skewness did not characterize the distributions of the white subjects.

Bruce divided the children into 14 age groups of 6 months each and computed the mean IQ for each group. The results showed considerable fluctuation with a general lowering trend but with no greater Negro than white decline. Bruce did not consider the loss of ten points with increasing age to have been significant since it is approximately the decline to be expected in IQ's around 80. Because the two racial groups resembled each other more closely in social status than in IQ, she did not believe a difference in socioeconomic status to be sufficient explanation of the Negro-white IQ difference. She suggested the possibility of selective migration as an alternative to innate racial differences as a factor responsible for the Negro-white difference. According to this interpretation, one would assume either *no* selective migration on the part of whites from this county or else *a more gradual* one due to their advantageous position in the social order.

Marks directed the *Kuhlmann-Anderson* testing of 2250 rural Negro children in eight counties in the states of Alabama, Georgia, Mississippi, North Carolina, and Tennessee. The mean IQ's for the various counties ranged from about 74 to 80. (Johnson, 1941) No county mean (both sexes combined) was below the colored mean obtained by Bruce. No measures of variability were included in Marks' data. The latter attributed the differences in mean IQ's to cultural and educational differences between the counties; he was of the opinion that the results showed the *type of area* determining very largely the character of the school and the outlook of youth, the type of area being more important than the socio-economic classification of the family alone in the determination of children's alertness and interest in learning.

The research of Chapanis and Williams (1945) formed a part of a mental hygiene study of children in a fairly rich agricultural county of Tennessee. Testing more than 90 per cent of the white and 73 per cent of the colored children between the ages of 6 and 14, the authors found a significant difference between the racial samples. From a listing of mean IQ's for the separate age groups of 3-months range, the reviewer determined the total average IQ—which proved to be about 87 for the whites and 74 for the Negroes. The various distributions of mental ages of white children are reported by the authors as showing no great asymmetry, with about an equal amount of positive and negative skewness indicated; whereas the mental age distributions of both the younger and older Negro children were asymmetrical, with two thirds of the Negro age groups showing positive skewness. With both racial groups there was a decrease in IQ with increase in age, the mean IQ of the whites decreasing from 95 at the age of 6 years to 79 at the age of 14, the mean IQ of the colored decreasing from 85 at 6 years to 66 at 14 years. The greatest drop in IQ during a one-year interval was five points, a drop which occurred between the ages of 6 and 7 for both the whites and Negroes. In general, the authors emphasized the role that social and economic advantages played in a mental test performance, and questioned whether or not rapport had been established with the children in their own study.

The low average scores achieved by the Southern rural samples on the *Kuhlmann-Anderson* are in marked contrast to the essentially normal scores earned by the Washington, D. C., samples reported by Long (1933, 1934) and Robinson and Meenes (1947). It had been the practice over a period of years to test all District of Columbia 3A colored children with the *Kuhlmann-Anderson*. Robinson and Meenes selected somewhat less than one third of the records of these children tested in the school years of 1938-39 and 1945-46, securing at least two schools from each section of the city and eliminating all children who were born outside of the District. The mean IQ's are approximately 97 and 100 for the two years canvassed. Both of these means are somewhat higher than that of all 3A colored children previously tested in the District as reported by Long. The 3A mean of all colored was nearly 96 (Long, 1934), whereas the 1A and 5A means were approximately 93.

The higher average IQ's obtained by Negro children born in Washington as compared with those born outside the District have been reported by McAlpin (1932) and Long (1933).[63] The means secured by Long on the two relatively small groups of 3A colored children were about 99 and 110.[64] The higher scoring of the former group, *i.e.*, the one from underprivileged communities, as compared with the total Washington 3A group (IQ of 96), could hardly be attributed to the fact that the underprivileged were born in the city. The reviewer is inclined to interpret the difference as due to the small number in the underprivileged group and to the method by which the subjects were selected. The evidence does, however, rather consistently indicate that the District of Columbia Negro children do better on intelligence tests than Negro children in other parts of the United States.

In comparing the mental ability of juvenile delinquents and nondelinquents, Charles (1936) selected for the latter group an equal number of colored and white boys from the public schools of St. Louis of the age range of the institutionalized delinquents. An attempt was made to test boys in about equal numbers from each age range and from schools located in different parts of the city. Charles did not indicate how many schools were included among his comparisons, nor how he picked the boys within the school selected. However, he reports that the *schools* were chosen in such a way that the social environments of the white and colored were similar. Unfortunately, we are not informed further about the social environments of the areas in which the schools were located, but it may be presumed that they were below average for whites in the city. As will be observed in Table 4, the mean *Kuhlmann-Anderson* IQ obtained on the white boys was about 10 points above that of the 172 Negroes. The St. Louis Negroes likewise scored from 6 to 10 points below large groups of District of Columbia Negro children.

Charles has included measures of variability in his data (Table 4). The scores of the whites were the more variable, as suggested by the sizes of the ranges and indicated by the standard deviations.

Chicago was the site of three investigations in which 2225 colored school children were examined by the *Kuhlmann-Anderson* test. They include the work of Lichtenstein and Brown (1938), Hess (1955), and Boylan and O'Meara (1958). In two of the studies underprivileged children were tested, and in one, middle-class children; in two, whites of similar status or living in the same area were compared with the colored, in one, no direct comparisons were made with white children.

---

[63]McAlpin reported the *Kuhlmann-Anderson* average IQ for 3A Negro Ss born in DC to be 98. Numbers were not given but Ss were not from underprivileged communities. See Table 14.

[64]These were the same Ss tested on *Stanford-Binet, Pintner-Paterson,* and *Dearborn A.* For comment upon the method of selection of Ss, see p. 35.

As noted in Table 4, Lichtenstein and Brown selected four public schools in an area adjacent to central business and industrial districts and characterized by physical deterioration, decreasing population, and high rates of dependency as well as of foreign and Negro populations. Crime and delinquency were prevalent; about 20 per cent of the boys in this area were under police surveillance as alleged delinquents in 1926. Four hundred eighty white children and 178 colored children in Grades 4 to 6 served as subjects. The respective mean IQ's of the white and colored pupils were reported to be 91.6 and 88.1, the standard deviations, 12.7 and 13.9, the difference between the means being highly significant. Two conditions which may have operated to affect the means should be mentioned. First, no recognizable mental defectives, particularly if they presented classroom problems, were included among the subjects as they had been placed in schools for the retarded or in ungraded divisions of the city schools. Second, the authors described the area where the subjects lived as being about 27 per cent Negro and the remaining whites principally Italian. It may be presumed that if the white school children were composed principally of Italian pupils that many of them were working under a language handicap and were improperly tested by the *Kuhlmann-Anderson*.

Hess reports the results of testing colored and white Chicago school children by means of the *Davis-Hess* test (Table 2) and a standard test, generally the *Kuhlmann-Anderson*. Hess examined the scores of children in four chronological age groups: 6½, 7½, 8½, and 9½, and separated into the following race-status categories: whites of high status, whites of low status, and colored of low status. From the mean mental age for each of the twelve subgroups as presented by the researcher, the reviewer has calculated mean IQ's for the three race-status groups. The average IQ's for the high- and low-status whites proved to be about 109 and 103, respectively; the average for the low status colored, about 90. No measures of variability were included with the means. Hess was of the opinion that socioeconomic differences between high and low status samples in this country are exaggerated by the use of standard intelligence tests.

Boylan and O'Meara (1958) attempted to answer the question as to whether or not Southern-born Negro children are lower in tested mental ability than Chicago-born Negro children enrolled in the Victor F. Lawson School. A survey of this school, which is located in a middle-class Negro neighborhood on the South Side, showed low achievement in reading in all grades and a slow rate of improvement from any one grade to the next. The *Kuhlmann-Anderson* and the Thurstone *Primary Mental Abilities* have been used for a number of years in this school and many of the children had been tested more than once, a small number of them having been additionally tested on the *Stanford-Binet*. The authors tabulated and compared the IQ's of 667 Southern-born (including children tested in kindergarten) and 1201 Chicago-born (including no children tested in kindergarten), in each case using the latest test whenever a child had been examined more than once. The mean IQ's of the Southern-born and the Chicago-born were remarkably close together as were the standard deviations, the former being 94.29 and 95.15 and the latter, 11.8 and 11.9, respectively. The authors conclude that they have reason to doubt that the school-wide reading problem can be explained on the basis of inferior mental ability of the 770 Southern-born among the 2300 pupils.

McCord and Demerath (1958) report the results of the testing of 562 white and 50 Negro 10-year-old boys living in Cambridge and Somerville, Massachusetts, (Table 4). Following some preliminary testing with the *Stanford-Binet* in 1937, the *Kuhlmann-Anderson* tests were administered mainly in 1938 in conjunction with an experiment in the prevention of juvenile delinquency. (Powers and Witmer, 1951) In this project, approximately 325 predelinquent boys from the two cities were selected as subjects from a large number of referrals by teachers, principals, playground supervisors, police, youth leaders, and others, when directed to find the "worst" boys in the community, nuisances in the schoolroom or on the playground, *etc.* More than three fourths of all school referrals were from the third grade and below with no referrals being accepted from grades above the fifth. These *predelinquent boys* were matched with *normal boys* (from a file secured from youth leaders, teachers, *etc.*) for IQ plus or minus 10 points, as well as for many other variables. Most of the parents belonged to the lower class or to the lower-middle class, and an appreciable number of them seem to have been foreign-born. The *Kuhlmann-Anderson* medians for both the colored and white groups were located between 95 and 99 and the *Stanford-Binet* medians for both groups were located in the class interval, 90-95. The authors conclude that the present study supports the argument that equalization of educational and social opportunities will result in the equalization of mental test performance of Negroes and whites.

McGurk (1959) directed several criticisms against this research which may be summarized as follows: (1) The authors did not test their central tendencies for statistically significant differences; instead, they inspected their data. From inspection, they found that the median scores for both racial groups fell in the same large interval of scores and that therefore the median scores for both races were generally of the same size. Since inspections are not demonstrations of significant differences, the statements about significant differences are without factual support. (2) McCord and Demerath presented the data in a few very large class intervals, *i.e., 84 and below, 85 to 94, 95 to 104, 105 and above,* with both ends of every frequency table open. This makes it impossible for any reader to verify the conclusions. (3) The authors' use of chi-square is confusing. Beneath each of the tables of data, there is some statement about the significance of chi-square, but no data about that statistic. Further chi-square is not an appropriate statistic for the determination of the significance of differences between measures of central tendency (mean or median).

The reviewer wishes to make an additional comment or two about the McCord-Demerath report. The normal boys were paired with the predelinquents in a number of ways, *one of them being race*. That is, Negro normals were paired with Negro predelinquents for IQ, and since no predelinquents who satisfied the several criteria set up were eliminated,[65] this meant that normals would be selected who matched the *predelinquent in IQ* among other things. It seems to the present writer, then, that McCord and Demerath were essentially comparing a group of 25 Negro boys who appeared to have some delinquent tendencies with 281 white boys who likewise showed delinquent tendencies. At any rate, it is very interesting that these colored and white predelinquents should have earned IQ's that on the average are *substantially above* those earned by colored and white delinquents (see Chapter 7). Possibly the descrepancy lies in the method by which the predelinquent were finally selected. The families as well as the children themselves had to be relatively stable and cooperative to permit regular and continued counseling lasting in some cases over a period of years.[66] Furthermore, the very fact that only one (2 per cent) of the 50 colored boys ultimately selected had an IQ below 85 (the approximate mean of American Negro children) and only 6.6 per cent of the total group of white boys earned IQ's below this point would suggest that the Selection Committee was interested in rehabilitating essentially normally intelligent children rather than the borderline or the mentally retarded.

Brown (1955) was interested in studying a selected group of the population, the *nonpromoted* in the public schools of York, Pennsylvania. There were 4271 pupils who were enrolled in Grades 1-9 and had failed one or more grades during the 10-year interval beginning in 1943-44. Since intelligence was among the factors that Brown was to examine in connection with the failures, he obtained the IQ's of all the nonpromoted during this period from the permanent record file. The IQ's were derived from the following tests: *Detroit Intelligence Test* (the specific one not indicated) and the *SRA Primary Test of Mental Abilities* given in Grade 1, the *Kuhlmann-Anderson* administered in Grade 4, and one of the *Otis Quick-Scoring* tests in Grade 6. We have noted some of the author's findings relative to the topic with which we are concerned: (1) the colored children made up 6.6 per cent of the total grade-school enrollment during the decade and accounted for 11.7 per cent of the children receiving nonpromotions; (2) the median IQ's of the white and colored nonpromoted differed by 8 points (Table 4), that of the whites being significantly the higher; and (3) the nonpromoted Negro children came relatively more frequently from broken homes, from the unskilled laboring group, and from "worst quality houses" than did the nonpromoted whites.

---

[65]Whenever possible a Negro was matched with a Negro, a boy of Irish parentage with one of Irish parentage, *etc*. Ths variable was disregarded only when the cultural pattern of the home was considered to be of greater significance than parental nativity. (Powers and Witmer)

[66]Only the experimental group received counseling or treatment. However, these personal or family characteristics if important would be required of the whole group, since placement of every matched pair of boys in the treatment or control group was determined by the toss of a coin.

KUHLMANN-FINCH

As a supplement to verbal group tests or the *Stanford-Binet*, the *Kuhlmann-Finch* tests are useful over the range of elementary and high school grades. They are virtually alternate forms of the *Kuhlmann-Anderson* tests. The tests are not designed to be used in differential diagnosis of scholastic strengths and weaknesses. (Garrett, *in* Buros, 1959, pp. 477-78)

McQueen and Churn (1960) attempted to compare a matched sample of Negro and white subjects for intelligence, academic achievement, and classroom behavior. Fifty-five Negro public-school children, in Grades 3 to 8, living in a Western city of approximately 60,000, were selected for the comparative study.[67] Presumably all Negro children in these grades of the public schools were included, but the authors do not say so. McQueen and Churn do indicate, however, that for nearly two generations the city has had a small but relatively stable colored population, that there is no history of racial strife, that the schools have never been segregated, and that all attend schools nearest their place of residence.

These children were matched with white pupils according to the following variables: age, sex, school grade, years enrolled in the school system, father's occupation, and residence (members of the pairs living within one block of one another and almost always in the same type of home). The mean IQ's reported for the white and colored matched groups were 101.7 and 94.89, respectively, the difference between the means being significant at the .05 level of confidence. The standard deviations were very similar, being respectively, 13.67 and 13.08 (Table 4). The authors indicate that the raw data reveal a large measure of overlapping on the *Kuhlmann-Finch* between the groups (but they do not give figures showing the amount of this overlapping) and in general consider the racial difference to be negligible. However, the reviewer wishes to call attention again to the impropriety of equating for *both* age and school grade.[68] Selecting simultaneously for both variables serves to eliminate some of the retarded and advanced pupils— an elimination which does not necessarily operate to the same degree or in the same direction for the two groups compared. Thus racial differences may be concealed or minimized.

NATIONAL INTELLIGENCE TESTS

The *National Intelligence Tests*, designed for Grades 3 to 8, consist of Scales A and B, each including five tests. *Scale A* is composed of tests of arithmetic reasoning, sentence completion, logical selection, synonym-antonym, and symbol-digit. The tests of *Scale B* are: computation, information, vocabulary, analogies, and comparison. The reliability of these scales is reported by Garrett and Schneck

---

[67]Sixteen first- and second-grade Negro children were also studied but were not given mental tests and are therefore excluded from this review.

[68]This procedure would be correct only if there were no children in the elementary grades who had ever repeated a grade and if there were none who had ever been given a double promotion or had started to school before the usual age.

(1933, p. 41) to be about .70 for a single grade, about .93 for Grades 3 to 8; *A* and *B,* Grades 3 to 8, correlate .94.

Thousands of colored school children have been tested by the *National.* About 6000 colored Ss from six Southern states, an undetermined but probably very large number from one Border city, and about 4000 colored from the North have been examined by this test, the results of which are summarized in Table 4. Except for some of Boots' and Tanser's Ss the children were drawn from cities, and in nearly all of the investigations the children were enrolled in Grades 3 to 8. The results on the Southern and Border children are typically given in terms of raw scores for age or grade groups; and in some instances racial comparisons are indicated by the amount of overlapping of scores. The results of all the Northern studies included in Table 4 are in IQ units.

Jordan (1922) found pronounced racial differences between random samples of 1502 white and 247 colored Arkansas school children. At the age of 10, the colored averaged one and one half year behind the whites of Fort Smith; at 14, the colored dropped to three years below the whites of this city. Between 20 and 26 per cent of the Fort Smith colored scored above the median of the whites of this locality. At the age of 10, the respective white and colored medians were 77.5 and 57.5; at the age of 14, the respective medians were 105 and 79. All of these medians compare unfavorably with the 10- and 14-year white norms of 91 and 131, respectively. As determined by the standard deviation, the Fort Smith whites were slightly more variable at the two lowest age levels than the Fort Smith colored children but became progressively less variable with increase in age.

Sunne (1924) reported that between 10 and 31 per cent of the 1112 Negro children of New Orleans and vicinity reached or exceeded the medians of the whites in the same area. Young (1929) noted that 20 per cent of the Baton Rouge and Lake Charles white Ss scored below 50, whereas 60 per cent of the colored tested in these two cities scored below this point.

Klineberg (1935) described the results of the testing of 776 colored 12-year-old children in three Southern cities. The results on the *National Intelligence Test* included in Table 4 of this review are incidental to the author's work on selective migration. Klineberg presents his results in terms of group averages and gives the number of cases for each group. From these the reviewer has calculated an average score of 66.3 for the total group. The average score of Klineberg's 12-year-old Negroes, therefore, appears to have been below the *National* median attained by the *white 10-year-olds of Fort Smith* and below the medians reported for *white 9- and 10-year-olds of Baton Rouge and Lake Charles;* it was very close to the *median of Baltimore white pupils in Grade 4* (Strayer, 1921).

The 1272 Dallas and Fort Worth Negro children were reported by Garth and Whatley (1925) as having a median IQ of 75.2, with a range from below 50 to 129. Boots (1926), surveying large samples of Mississippi colored and white children from 19 and 30 counties, respectively, found the mean IQ's of the former to be more than 20 points below the means of the latter. In this study the critical ratios were very large, ranging from 22 to 32. Boots categorized all children according to the size of the community in which they lived. *Group I* included all Ss living in cities of 10,000 or more, *Group II* included all Ss living in towns of from 2500 to 10,000, *Group III* included farm children and those living in villages of less than 2500. The approximate mean IQ's, estimated by the reviewer from Boots' grade means, for the Negroes in Group I, II, and III, were 79, 73, and 70, respectively; the corresponding average IQ's for the groups of white children were 103, 100, and 90.

The National Intelligence Test was given as a part of an elaborate testing program to Negro, white, and Mexican children in three cities and six counties of Texas by Koch and Simmons (1926). The scores of the Mexican children, whose racial ancestry includes Indian stock, are not included in this review. Koch and Simmons do not report the testing of rural Negroes; however, they compare the results of testing *city Negroes* with scores made by *city whites* and *rural whites*.[69] At each age level the mean of the urban whites was higher than that of the urban colored, the difference obtained being significant except at the age of 8 where there were only 15 white subjects. Beginning with the age of 9 and up, from 63 to 88 per cent of the city whites equaled or exceeded the medians of the comparable Negro groups. The authors did not indicate whether or not the differences between the white rural and urban means were significant. However, on this test, from 58 to 96 per cent of the *rural whites* equaled or surpassed the medians of the *city Negroes*. The last percentage is of no importance, however, since the figure is based on but 14 colored and 43 white cases. Koch and Simmons found the differences between the several groups, *i.e.*, urban white and urban Negro, urban white and rural white, and rural white and urban Negro, to be greater at the ages of 11 and above than between the ages of 8 and 10. They interpreted this fact to be a result of the cumulative effect of environmental handicaps.

Koch and Simmons have not, in the opinion of the reviewer, sufficiently accounted for the superiority of the rural white child over the *city Negro* child on the *National* test. It would seem gratuitous to assume as they did that the rural white child is stimulated to do more extensive reading because of his isolation in living on a farm. Living on farms is not usually considered to be a cultural aid in the development of children, white or colored. It is of course possible, if not probable, that the rural white children's schools were superior to those attended by Negro children in the cities of San Antonio, Austin, and El Paso; it is also possible that the rural child's socioeconomic status and accompanying cultural opportunities have placed him at an advantage over the Negro urban child. However, these factors, if they existed, were not investigated.

In his survey of the Baltimore school system, Strayer (1921) included medians of white and colored pupils, Grades 4 to 8, as determined by the *National* test

---

[69]These Ss also tested by *Myers Mental Measure*.

(Table 4). He observed that the Baltimore whites did just as well on the test as pupils in the same grades in other cities. When the Baltimore Ss were grouped according to age the whites were uniformly superior to the colored. At the age of 10, the medians of the whites and colored were 69 and 55, respectively; at the age of 14, the medians of the two racial groups were 112 and 78. At Age 11, the colored appeared to be about 2 years retarded; at Age 14, their retardation (as measured by the *National*) increased to 4 years.

We have included in Table 4 six studies in which Northern Negro children are reported to have been examined on the *National*. Four of these testings involve New York City children from Grades 5 through the junior high school. In two of them, which comprise all but 361 of the 3404 cases tested in this city, Klineberg (1935) secured a mean IQ of 88.5 and Pintner and Maller (1937) a mean IQ of 88.[70] In the latter study the white subjects consisted of Italian and Jewish public-school children who were reported as having a mean IQ of 98. Hurlock (1924, 1930) reported slightly higher IQ's for both of her smaller groups of white and colored children in New York City, the colored groups averaging between 93 and 94, and the whites, 102.

The above difference of 8 to 10 points found between tested groups of Negroes and whites in New York City is less than that separating the Kent County, Ontario, Negro and white Ss. The 103 Canadian colored children (Tanser, 1939) earned a mean IQ of 89 as opposed to a white mean of nearly 104. Twenty per cent of the Kent County Negroes reached or exceeded the median of the whites in the same locality; and 29 per cent of the colored and 56 per cent of the whites reached or surpassed the *National* test norms.

Urban and rural groups were separated by Tanser with practically no change in the median IQ's of the Negro groups. The urban white group, however, proved to be superior to the rural whites, as indicated by the respective medians of 105 and 96. Tanser believed the white urban-rural difference may have been attributable partly to the fact that "a fairly large proportion of the rural Whites tested are of non-British extraction and consequently adversely affected in a test such as the National Intelligence Test in which knowledge of the English language plays such an important part." (p. 102) Approximately 19 per cent of the urban Negroes reached or exceeded the median of the urban whites and about 33 per cent of the rural Negroes reached or exceeded the median of the rural whites. "It would appear, therefore, that generally speaking, the findings of the present investigation indicate that on the basis of such intelligence tests as the National, Kent County Negroes rank in intelligence roughly half-way between Southern and Northern Negroes." (p. 137)

The data which we have just presented on the New York Negroes obviously do not support Tanser's statement. In fact, the mean IQ of 89 obtained by Tanser is practically identical with that secured by the large majority of the

---

[70]Pintner and Maller used both *National* and *Pintner Rapid Survey*, but did not separate the results in their report.

New York Negroes. The higher average of Northern Negroes to which Tanser was implicitly referring was that secured by Clark (1923) on Los Angeles Negro children. Here 510 colored subjects, from 5 to 16 years of age and attending five elementary schools, earned a median IQ of 104.7 which was but slightly less than the 106.0 secured on 4326 children of 15 representative Los Angeles schools. The latter number included all children tested, *i.e.*, white, Chinese, Mexican, Negro, *etc.*, but the majority of the number were white.

Since this study of Clark's was given special emphasis in a review of Negro intelligence testing by Klineberg (1944, p. 35) and since *less than one page* was given to the original report in 1923, the reviewer asked Clark for further information about his method of selection of subjects and for any other details that he could give relating to this research. In addition to commenting that the *National* norms available in 1922 were probably about 5 per cent too high, Clark wrote that the five schools were largely in the Central Avenue neighborhood, an area not considered the "better" section of the city occupied by Negroes, and that all pupils with *Stanford-Binet* IQ's below about 75 were enrolled in special developmental schools. However, it seems that some of these schools and classes may have been included in this particular group of five schools.

The reviewer was referred by Clark to Elizabeth Woods, Head Supervisor, Educational Research and Guidance, of the Los Angeles Public Schools. Upon further inquiry, Woods wrote that in about 1928 Alice McAnulty Horn, a statistician in her department, did research on the intelligence of Los Angeles Negro children. Although this work was not published, Woods reported that Dr. Horn was certain "that the median IQ for our Negro children came out .95. This was found by drawing out of our files the group intelligence data on a thousand Negro children and comparing with a thousand cases of Japanese, a thousand of Mexican, and a thousand of Anglo-American children."

Haggerty Delta 2

Haggerty Intelligence Examination Delta 2, for Grades 3 to 9, consists of five verbal tests: reading and vocabulary, arithmetic problems, same-opposites, practical judgment, and information; as well as a nonverbal exercise in picture completion. The reliability of this test based on a single grade was reported to be about .60; for Grades 3 to 9 it was found to be about .90. (Garrett and Schneck, 1933, p. 40)

In making a survey of rural and urban school children from nine cities and 18 counties in Virginia, Haggerty (1921) tested white and colored children in Grades 3 to 7 or 3 to 8. The data are presented in terms of grade medians rather than age or IQ medians, and have been further divided into three categories: 1-teacher rural schools, 3- or 4- teacher noncity schools, and city schools. It will be noted in Table 4 that in each of the 16 comparisons the white median is higher than the corresponding colored median. The medians of the colored children of the city schools, Grades 3 to 6, were higher than those of the whites in the 1-teacher schools, but lower than the medians of the 4-teacher white noncity schools. However, since the colored were on the average older at each grade, one cannot conclude from this study that the urban colored child is superior on the Haggerty test to the rural white child of the state.

Daniel (1932) and Walker (1946) compared the mean IQ's and *s*'s of problem and nonproblem colored children from the same schools. Both found the mean IQ of the Southern samples to be about 91, and both reported the problem children to have lower IQ's and to be less variable than the nonproblem Ss. The mean IQ of the Richmond nonproblem boys was about 94, nearly eight points above that of the problem boys from the same five schools; whereas the mean IQ of the Fayetteville group of nonproblem children was 98, 14 points above that of the problem Ss. However, we wish to comment briefly on the method used by Walker in selecting her subjects. She did not simply choose nonproblem cases at random; but she selected 15 from each of two grades who had been given the best ratings by their teachers on the *Haggerty-Olson-Wickman Behavior Scale.*

Treacy (1926) reports the median IQ of 205 colored children from Grades 3 to 12 in the Minneapolis public schools to be 97.5. *Haggerty Delta 2* was given to the majority of the Ss who were in Grades 3 to 6. In evaluating his results one should be cognizant of the fact that, although somewhat more than one third of the colored children in the grades covered were tested, Treacy does not indicate how the selections were made; also the scores of 22 high school pupils were included in the above median; further, *Stanford-Binet* ratings had been made on 50 Negro children who were doing unsatisfactory work, and in no case was a *Binet* score averaged in with the *Haggerty* scores. Even if a child was tested by the group test his score was not included if he had been tested on the *Binet*. Treacy suggests that in determining an IQ which would be representative of the colored pupils of Minneapolis one would have to include about 36 per cent of those tested by the *Stanford-Binet*.[71] According to the author, "The colored children in Minneapolis seem to be slightly below the general average in the abilities measured by intelligence tests; and from this can be predicted that they will have more difficulties in accomplishing the tasks required of pupils than will the school population as a whole." (p. 38) Treacy observed that much larger proportions of colored than white children were in the lower grades and in special and vocational classes; furthermore, that over half of the colored were over age for their grade and 60 per cent were making slow progress, failures

---

[71]Inclusion of 18 of the *Stanford-Binet* scores which averaged 73.6 with the 205 scores of the main sample results in an average IQ of approximately 95.6. Excluding the 12 high school Ss (Grades 10-12) who were in the main sample, the average IQ of the remaining 211 would be about 94.8. Estimated by reviewer from Treacy's tables.

being twice as prevalent among Negro children as among the total school population.[72]

OTIS SELF-ADMINISTERING

The *Otis Self-Administering Tests of Mental Ability, Intermediate Examination,* were designed for Grades 4 to 9 and consist of 75 items of different types in mixed order. For purposes of prediction of school success these tests are reported as comparing favorably with other measures of general ability. When the *Otis* IQ's and those determined by individual intelligence tests are compared it appears that the former correspond more closely with those of the *Wechsler-Bellevue* than with the IQ's of the *Stanford-Binet.* (Kuder, *in* Buros, 1949, p. 250)

The *Intermediate Examination* of the *Otis* was employed in 15 studies of Negro intelligence (Table 4). The seven conducted in the South between 1926 and 1943 indicate a rather large variation in average scores and IQ's, ranging from the very low ones obtained in St. Helena (Peterson and Telford, 1930) and Baton Rouge (Bean, 1942), through a median IQ of 72 secured in Athens (Patrick, 1926), an estimated IQ of about 82 in Richmond (McGurk, 1943), a mean IQ of 86 in Atlanta (Beavers, 1935), to mean IQ's of 95 in Atlanta (Mazique, 1934) and 91 to 98 in Charlotte, Raleigh, and Atlanta (Evans, 1934). As will be noted from the table, the highest of the above average IQ's were obtained on children in private schools of Atlanta. Beavers included a class from the Atlanta University Laboratory High School, Evans a group of 20 from Oglethorpe University Experimental School, and Mazique two groups of private school children from Chadwick's Elementary School and Atlanta University Laboratory School. The mean IQ's of 95 to 98 secured on these colored private school children are nearly the equal of those obtained on groups of unselected white children. They are from 15 to 20 points below mean IQ's typically found when white private school children are tested. It is, of course, a well-established fact that private school children on the average score significantly above public school pupils on tests of intelligence.

With the omission of the private school subjects, it appears that the highest mean IQ's were obtained by Evans in a small town in South Carolina, and in Charlotte, Atlanta, and Raleigh, where the colored means ranged between 88 and 92. These means are likewise higher than those reported in the Border states by Lacy (1926), by Garth, Lovelady, and Smith (1930), and by Ries (1940). Lacy found the mean IQ earned by 411 Oklahoma City Negro children in Grades 5-8 to be 82. Garth, Lovelady, and Smith recorded a mean IQ of 78, based on the testing of more than 2000 colored Ss in Grades 4-9 from the cities of Dallas and Tulsa and from some Oklahoma towns. Ries reported that 380 colored junior high-school pupils in Louisville had been tested by the *Otis S-A* when they were in the sixth grade; the median of this group was 85.3, as compared with a median

---

[72]In 1923, W. S. Miller supervised the testing of all Minneapolis 6A pupils on *Haggerty.* The mean IQ was 108.3, according to Treacy.

of 99 recorded for a large group of white children in the Louisville junior high schools who had also been tested in the sixth grade. As will be seen in Table 4, the variability of the white group was the greater and the difference between the medians highly significant. Approximately 16 per cent (62) of the IQ's of the Negro subjects overlapped the median of the whites.

The white junior high schools of Louisville were located in nine districts which, according to Ries, afforded a convenient means of comparing the intelligence of *white children* living in various sections of the city. The approximate average rental in these districts ranged between $50 and $15 and the median IQ's ranged between 114.5 and 91. Ries said that the living conditions (of the whites) in most parts of *District 9,* the lowest rental district, would most nearly approximate those of the Louisville Negro. The 255 white children attending the school in *District 9* achieved a median IQ of 91, or 5.7 points above that earned by the Negro pupils attending the two junior high schools from the entire city of Louisville. This difference proved to be significant at the .01 level.

In addition to his Southern samples, Evans tested 121 Negro boys from the seventh grade of a junior high school in New York City and recorded a mean IQ of nearly 92, which placed the group slightly below his colored sample from Raleigh. An inferior mean score (not IQ) of 28.5 achieved by 413 12-year-old colored girls of the Harlem (New York City) public schools was reported by Klineberg (1935); this mean may be compared with the higher one of 40 earned by 12-year-old Negro school children in Richmond, Virginia. (McGurk, 1943)

Two University of Chicago Master's theses, those of Bousfield (1932) and Doran (1934), include the results of testing Chicago Negro school children in the upper grades. Bousfield obtained a median IQ of 87.15 and a s of 12.82 on 222 Keith Elementary School children, the subjects being described as mainly of inferior socioeconomic status. Testing a somewhat more selected group of Phillips Junior High School children, Doran reported an IQ of 90.66 and a s of 13.78 (Table 4). These children were all in the eighth grade, had had all of their education in the Chicago public schools, their schooling had not been interrupted, and they were all about six years of age when they started to school. The reviewer could not determine whether or not all qualified school children in *Phillips* were included in the Doran study; it would have been interesting if she had noted the percentage her group was of the total eighth grade in the junior high school. Bousfield did not describe her method by which she selected the 222 fifth-to eighth-grade subjects in the *Keith* school.

Williams (1935), in an unpublished thesis from Marquette University, includes results on the *Otis S-A* which had been administered to 270 sixth-grade children in Milwaukee, Wisconsin. The investigator, a principal of an elementary school in this city, was interested in examining the problems of colored children, particularly in relation to their promotion failures. The subjects, upon whom the analysis is based, were attending three schools: *Garfield Avenue, Fourth Street,* and *Ninth Street,* about half of the children dealt with in the report being Negro.

Williams did not give the total enrollment of the sixth-grade classes in the three schools, and we are not informed if his work was based on a saturated sample, or if not, how his selections were made. He did observe, however, that the class of whites studied was not representative of the Milwaukee white population, citing as evidence for his statement the larger percentage of the white families (represented by the children in the three schools) receiving county relief than the colored families. Although he had difficulty in obtaining complete records on his Ss, Williams secured mean IQ's which placed the colored children 4.6 points below the whites. In each school the white median was above that of the colored, but the colored median in one school was higher than the white medians in the other two schools. As a rather curious explanation for the latter point, the author pointed out that "the test was not administered by the same person to each group of children in the three schools." If this is a pertinent criticism, then the relatively high measures of central tendency obtained on both white and Negro groups are invalid.

Griffith (1947) obtained a mean IQ of 91 on seventy-six colored Ss and a mean of about 100 on thirty-nine white children in the upper grades of an elementary school in Portland, Oregon. Both white and colored parents were categorized in the three *lowest* occupational groups, with a single exception; and both groups were given very similar ratings on the Sims Score Card. All children were described as living in a deteriorated neighborhood that was rapidly becoming all colored.

Otis Group Test Advanced

The *Otis Group Intelligence Scale (Advanced Examination)* was designed to test children in Grades 5 to 12, and consists of ten tests: following directions, opposites, disarranged sentences, proverb matching, arithmetic, geometric figures, analogies, similarities, narrative completion, and memory. A reliability of .97 is reported for Grades 4 to 8. (Garrett and Schneck, 1933, p. 42)

From Table 4 it will be noted that the colored subjects generally achieved relatively low scores on the *Otis Advanced Examination*. Five of the seven researches were conducted in the South, beginning with Leggett's (1921); this investigator analyzed the results of the test that had been administered to sixth and seventh grade white and colored children in Wilmington, North Carolina. As was to be expected, some decline in scores was recorded above the age of 11 for both racial samples, due to the fact that older children in the sixth and seventh grades would begin to show some retardation. Leggett estimated that the colored children were about 76 per cent as efficient on the *Otis* as the white. The percentages of the colored reaching or exceeding the white means at the ages of 11, 12, 13, and 14 were 22, 17, 21, and 22, respectively. From Peterson's research (1923) on Arkansas and North Carolina school children it is evident that the colored in Grade 8 were only slightly below the white median; whereas, in Grades 5 to 7 the colored earned from less than half to about two thirds as much as the whites. Although Peterson selected schools which he considered to be representative of the colored and white, he believed the colored schools were the less efficient.

As a part of the survey made by the United States Public Health Service, Graham (1926) tested 881 colored children in Grades 5 and 6 from five elementary schools of Atlanta. She found a highly significant difference between the colored means and the Otis' norms for the various age groups from 10 to 14; at Ages 10 to 12 the colored means were from 68 to 77 per cent of the standard white means. Gray and Bingham (1929) reported a median index of brightness of the 58 Texas Negro children to be 76 as contrasted with a median brightness index of 108 attained by the Texas white subjects. Although the numbers were small the difference between the medians proved to be significant.

Slivinske (1949) designed an experiment to test the hypothesis that environmental conditions affect the IQ. From one Virginia county he utilized the results of a county-wide intelligence testing program administered or supervised by the County Supervisor during the fall of 1948. The individual tests, the results of which were not separated in the data, include: the *Pintner-Cunningham Primary, Form B,* in Grades 1 and 2; the *Otis Group Intelligence Scale, Primary, Form B,* in Grades 3 and 4; and the *Otis Group Intelligence Scale, Advanced, Form B,* in Grades 5, 6, and 7.[73]

The tests were administered to 1764 children in the elementary white schools (Grades 1-7) and to 1190 pupils in the elementary Negro schools (Grades 1-7). All children enrolled in the county elementary schools were tested except 34 white and 17 colored pupils who were absent, these constituting 1.9 per cent and 1.4 per cent of their respective school populations. The IQ's were categorized according to three different criteria: (1) *size of school,* the *small* schools comprising the one- and two-teacher schools, the *large,* the three-or-more-teacher schools; (2) the *socioeconomic level of the community* from which each school derived its pupils. Seven principals, two county supervisors, the county visiting teacher, and the county superintendent of schools were instructed to rate a community (or perhaps communities) as *superior, above average, average, below average,* and *inferior,* taking into consideration prevalent occupations, educational, cultural, social and economic status of the adult members, opportunities for contact with urban and other communities, availability of desirable literature, newspapers, radio programs and motion pictures, and opportunities for public gatherings and meetings. The white school communities were to be rated only with respect to their position among other white communities, the Negro . . . . with respect to other Negro communities; (3) the *socioeconomic level of the home* as rated by the teacher. Each teacher was asked to classify the socioeconomic backgrounds of the children in her own room by checking *superior, above average, average, below average, inferior,* or *no information* for each pupil's home background, the ratings in each case to be relative to the particular classroom group. Only the

---

[73]Tabulated data in the monograph is classified according to *age* (in 12-month intervals) rather than *grade.*

extreme groups of *superior* and *inferior* were included in Slivinske's tabulated material on *home background*. He observed that this procedure was decided upon to eliminate, as far as possible, the unavoidable errors in teacher ratings. Also, throughout the monograph, the author eliminated from his data the scores of all children who at the time of testing were either *under six years of age or had reached their thirteenth* birthday, because these extremes were found to be unrepresentative of their age groups.[74]

Size of School. The white mean IQ proved to be 96.3 as compared with a colored mean of 78.1. When the racial samples were dichotomized according to large and small schools, the colored mean IQ's became 78.9 and 77.1, and the white means 96.7 and 91.4, respectively.[75] The difference between the mean IQ's of the whites and Negroes attending the large schools was 18 points, between the means of the whites and colored attending the small schools, 14 points, both of these differences being highly significant (Table 4). In both types of schools the variability of the whites was the greater.

The reviewer compared the combined mean IQ's of children divided into two groups, the *6 to 8 age group* and the *10 to 12 age group*. The colored subjects scored about the same— the children in the *small schools* earning respective mean IQ's of 77.73 and 77.21 at the two age levels, those in the *large schools* achieving means of 78.03 and 79.85, respectively. The whites in both types of schools, however, seemed to improve in their mental test rating from the 6 to 8 to the 10 to 12 age group. In the small schools the mean IQ of the younger group was 87.59, of the older group, 94.85; similarly, in the large schools the respective means of the younger and older groups were 93.51 and 100.25.

Socioeconomic Level of the Community. The mean IQ's of the colored pupils attending schools located in communities rated as *superior, above average, average, below average,* and *inferior* were respectively, 80.2, 81.2, 73.3, 75.4, and 76.6, the corresponding *s*'s (computed by the reviewer) being 14.99, 16.69, 13.53, 12.40, and 15.59. The mean IQ's of the white children were respectively, 95.2, 102.5, 96.2, 93.1, and 90.9, their corresponding standard deviations (also calculated by reviewer) being, 18.70, 18.00, 17.87, 18.35, and 19.54.

Socioeconomic Background of Home. The mean IQ of the 245 white children whose home backgrounds were rated by their teachers as *inferior* was 82.74, the mean of the 254 white Ss whose home backgrounds were rated as *superior* was 108.29; the corresponding means for the 186 (inferior) and the 99 (superior) colored children were 70.09 and 88.52. The difference between the means of the white and colored from *inferior home backgrounds* was about 13 points, the difference between the racial means from superior homes, 20 points, both of these differences being significant at the .001 level (Table 4).

In the three major comparisons, size of school, socioeconomic level of the

---

[74]His number of cases becomes thereby reduced to less than 1500 (whites) and to fewer than 900 (colored).

[75]The apparent discrepancy due to the small number of white Ss in small schs, *i.e.*, 80.

TABLE

SCHOOL CHILDREN

AUTHOR DATE	LOCATION	N	SUBJECTS		METHOD OF SELECTION
			AGE	GRADE	
					KUHLMANN-
Bice, H. V. (1938)	A Central North Carolina County	w-438 c- 457		1-11 1-11	All Ss in attendance in 2 schs tested.
Willis, L. J. (1939)	Nashville, Tenn.	w-112 c- 112		7 7	Ss from 2 jr high schs. Selected only pupils with IQ's bet 80-115 with reading test grades bet 4-9.5.
Bruce,[2] M. (1940)	A Rural Virginia County	w-521 c- 432	6-12 6-12		All pupils in attendance at 9 pairs of Negro and white schs.
Marks, E. (1941)	Counties Alabama (2) Georgia (1) Mississippi (2) North Carolina (1) Tennessee (2)	c- 2250			Rural c children in the 8 counties.
Chapanis, A., and Williams, W. C. (1945)	Williamson County, Tenn.	w-3501 c- 810	6-14 6-14		Tested over 90% of w & 73% of c in the various age groups.

[1]The *s's* and *t* calculated by reviewer.
[2]For results on *Stanford-Binet* and *Grace Arthur,* see Table 2.

FOUR

VERBAL GROUP TESTS

	RESULTS			COMMENTS OF AUTHOR

ANDERSON

		IQ^1		The tests were not given to prove innate diff in inferiority. Interested in a program of education that will enable c and w to adjust successfully to their life situations.
	w		c	
Mdn	95		85	
M	94		83	
s	12.94		12.56	
Range	50-149		40-129	
t =		13		

		IQ		No Ss with high or very low K-A scores included. White families had more books, magazines and newspapers in homes than c.
M	w		c	
High 7	98.55		87.61	
Low 7	96.65		89.50	

		IQ		When 49 pairs of c and w Ss were matched acc to Sims socioeco score, mean IQ of w became 83.31; mean of c, 73.20. This diff sig ($t = 3.33$).
	w		c	
Mdn	88.48		71.64	
M	88.10		71.80	
s	13.60		12.43	
Range	52-129		39-130	
t =		19.31		
10% c above w mdn				

		M IQ		It is apparent that the relative excellence of the consolidated schs of N.C. is of great benefit to rural Negro youth.
	c		c	
	Boys		Girls	
NC	79.15		80.65	
Tenn	78.54		86.30	
Tenn	80.20		80.43	
Miss	77.62		81.24	
Miss	75.23		77.38	
Ala	77.18		77.09	
Ala	75.00		75.24	
Ga	70.65		77.73	
Total	77.47		79.60	

		IQ^3		Scores consistent with hypothesis that mental test performance reflects to considerable extent the social and eco advantages of the children tested.
	w		c	
M	86.6		74.0	
Sig diff bet means				

[3]Authors give medians, means *etc.*, for age groups of 3-months range. Reviewer calculated IQ's for groups as whole.

TABLE

SCHOOL CHILDREN

AUTHOR DATE	LOCATION	N	SUBJECTS		METHOD OF SELECTION
			AGE	GRADE	
Long,[4] H. H. (1933)	Washington, D. C.	c- I 100 II 100		3A 3A	cI—"Practically all" pupils from 5 schs in underprivileged communities, if born in DC. cII—Principals & teachers recommended pupils who came from better homes & in 5 schs in better residential sections. All born in DC.
Long,[5] H. H. (1934)	Washington, D. C.	c- 2103 - 1323 - 1258		1A 3A 5A	All 1A, 3A, & 5A c children tested in 1930.
Charles,[6] C. M. (1936)	St. Louis, Mo.	w-172 c- 172	12-16 12-16		W & c boys selected in about equal numbers for each age group from schs in diff parts of city; schs sought in which social environ of w & c similar. Method of selection within a sch's age group not given.
Robinson, M. L., and Meenes, M. (1947)	Washington, D. C.	c- 935		3	Secured IQ's of pupils in 12 c publ schs during 1938-39 or 1945-46; at least 2 schs from each section of city. All born in DC for whom IQ's could be obtained. Scores taken from office records.
Lichtenstein, M., and Brown, A. W. (1938)	Chicago, Ill.	w-480 c- 178		4-6 4-6	K-A administered to all in Grades 4-6 in 4 publ schs. Area adjacent to central business & industrial districts, characterized by physical deterioration, decreasing population, high rates of dependency, foreign born & Negro population.

[4]For results on *Pintner-Paterson, Stanford-Binet,* and *Dearborn A,* see Tables 2 and 3.
[5]For studies on Selective Migration, see Table 14.

FOUR *(continued)*
VERBAL GROUP TESTS

	RESULTS			COMMENTS OF AUTHOR
M	IQ c			Underprivileged communities selected by teachers and supervisors. Previous giving Sims Scale to 4th graders in a part of this community showed a rating of 13; regions from which cII came had rating of 20.
I	98.7			
II	110.18			
		IQ		Decr in IQ explained by incr inadequacy of home, sch, and community for maturing Negro child.
	c	c	c	
	1A	3A	5A	
M	93.35	95.71	92.72	
s	17.10	15.80	15.75	
		IQ		Cannot determine whether superiority of w boys is due to inherent factors, to training, to environment, or to possible deficiencies in test used.
		w	c	
M		98.31	88.60	
s		12.25	11.00	
Range		60-135	55-114	
		IQ		
M		c		
1938-39		97.02		
1945-46		99.76		
Sig diff bet means				
		IQ		Mentally defective, especially the problem cases, when detected are put in schs for retarded or in "ungraded divisions". They were not included.
		w	c	
M		91.6	88.1	
s		12.7	13.9	
$t =$		4.54		
Diff bet means sig				

[6]For results on juvenile delinquency, see Table 11.

THE TESTING OF NEGRO INTELLIGENCE

TABLE

SCHOOL CHILDREN

AUTHOR DATE	LOCATION	N	SUBJECTS		METHOD OF SELECTION
			AGE	GRADE	
Brown, W. W. (1955)	York, Pa.	w-3771 c- 500		1-9 1-9	Studied IQ's from permanent record file of all w & c who had failed one or more grades during a 10-year period beginning with 1943-44.[7]
Hess, R. D. (1955)	Chicago, Ill.	w- High 188 Low 178 c- Low 179	6-9 6-9		Sample of 545 elem sch pupils. High-status w from prof & manag occup; low-status w from semi & unsk; low status c from unsk & unempl. All given a standard test & a new test.[8]
McCord, W. M., and Demerath, N. J., III (1958)	Cambridge and Somerville, Mass.	w-562 c- 50	10 10		10-yr-old boys had been tested as a part of a research project in attempt to prevent juvenile delinquency. Half considered *pre-delinquent* and half *normal*. K-A given mainly in 1938.
Boylan, F. T., and O'Meara, R. B. (1958)	Chicago, Ill.	c- South-born 667 Chicago-born 1201			Survey of Victor F. Lawson School located in middle-class Negro neighborhood on South Side in 1957-58. Used latest mental test scores when child tested more than once. Usually K-A or Thurstone Primary Mental Abilities recorded.

KUHLMANN-

AUTHOR DATE	LOCATION	N	SUBJECTS		METHOD OF SELECTION
			AGE	GRADE	
McQueen, R., and Churn, B. (1960)	A Western Community[10]	w-55 c- 55		3-8 3-8	Negro pupils were matched with w acc to: age, sex, sch grade, yrs enrolled in sch system, residence (members of pairs living within 1 block of each other) & father's occupation.

[7]Ss had been given a variety of tests over the years, incl *K-A*. Since Brown did not separate results acc to test used we have tabulated his pertinent statistics with *K-A*.

[8]In a personal communication, the author indicated that the standard test used was generally

FOUR *(continued)*

VERBAL GROUP TESTS

	RESULTS			COMMENTS OF AUTHOR
		IQ		Colored comprised 6.6% of total sch enrollment in Grades 1-9, and 11.7% of the nonpromotions from these grades. Publ schs were segregated at the elem level.
		w	c	
Mdn		88.9	80.7	
		IQ[9]		Results suggest that socioeco differences bet high and low status samples in this country are exaggerated by standard intelligence tests.
M		w	c	
High		108.88		
Low		102.83	90.21	
		IQ		The present study lends weight to the argument that equalization of educational and social opportunities (as has partially occurred in Mass) will result in the equalization of Negro and white test performance.
		w	c	
Mdn		95-99	95-99	
		IQ		Have reason to doubt the ready answer (of sch teachers) that the sch-wide reading problem can be explained by the inferior mental ability of the Southern-born among our pupils.
	c		c	
	So-born		Chi-born	
M	94.29		95.15	
s	11.8		11.9	
Diff bet means not sig				

FINCH

	RESULTS			COMMENTS OF AUTHOR
		IQ		From a statistical point of view, the obtained difference in mean IQ of the 2 groups seems very large. From a practical psychometric point of view, however, 6.18 points represent a negligible diff.
	w		c	
M	101.07		94.89	
s	13.67		13.08	
t $=$		2.43		
P $=$		$< .05$		

the *Kuhlmann-Anderson* and that the Ss were from 6 publ schools. For results on the new test, see *Davis-Hess Test*, Table 2.

[9]Author tabulates mean MA for each of the 12 CA groups; IQ's calculated by reviewer.

[10]Probably Las Vegas, Nevada.

TABLE

SCHOOL CHILDREN

AUTHOR DATE	LOCATION	N	SUBJECTS		METHOD OF SELECTION
			AGE	GRADE	

NATIONAL

Jordan, A. M. (1922)	Fort Smith, Ark.	w-1502 c- 247	10-14 10-14	4-8 4-8	Random samplings; 52% of w and 71% of c sch children.
Sunne,[11] D. (1924)	New Orleans and Vicinity	w-5834 c- 1112	8-17 8-17	5-8 5-8	
Garth, T. R., and Whatley, C. A. (1925)	Dallas and Fort Worth, Tex.	c- 1272	-16	3-8	
Koch,[11] H. L., and Simmons, R. (1926)	San Antonio, Austin, El Paso, and Rural Counties, Texas	Urban w-294 c- 242 Rural w- 324	8-13 8-15 9-14	3-5 3-5 3-5	"Representative samples". Only rural whites tested in the 6 counties.
Boots,[13] W. E. (1926)	Mississippi	w-9500 c- 2000		3-8 3-8	
Young, P. C. (1929)	Baton Rouge and Lake Charles, La.	w-282 c- 277	9-10 9-10	3- 3-	All 9- and 10-yr-olds in the third grade and above in the schools surveyed.

[11]For results on *Myers Mental Measure,* see Table 3.
[12]From Garth's Table 8 (1931).

FOUR *(continued)*

VERBAL GROUP TESTS

RESULTS	COMMENTS OF AUTHOR

INTELLIGENCE TESTS

	Mdn Scores		Pronounced racial diff found; c were 2 yrs behind w at 10 yrs, 3-4 yrs behind w at 13-14 yrs.
	w	c	
Age			
10	77	57.5	
11	91.4	66.7	
12	104	70.6	
13	106	82	
14	105	79	

20-26% c above w *mdn*

10-31% c above w *mdn*

Will not estimate how much the diffs are due to race and how much to sch training and social conditions. Both c and w found among highest and lowest 3% at each age.

	IQ	Increase in education exercises no constant influence on IQ's of these c children.
	c	
Mdn	75.2	
Range	"below 50"—129	

7.5% c above w *mdn*[12]

City w
  M above city c at each age
  M above rural w at each age
Rural w
  M above city c

Isolation of rural w may cause them to read more than city c.

	IQ		All diffs highly sig at every grade level. There are indications that training plays a large part in the differences in the intelligence test scores.
	w	c	
Grade	*M*		
3	89.64	67.28	
4-8	95-98	70-79	
	s		
3	24.05	15.30	
4-8	18-22	14-18	

	Scores		Attempted to get equivalent eco status by taking c and w schs in same wards.
	w	c	
Mdn	75	35	
Range	8-164	0-125	

[13]Whites from 30 counties, c from 19. Reviewer has estimated the number of cases in Grades 3-8 from Boots' total number, Grades 1-8. *Pintner-Cunningham* given in Grades 1-2; see Table 3.

TABLE

SCHOOL CHILDREN

AUTHOR DATE	LOCATION	N	SUBJECTS		METHOD OF SELECTION
			AGE	GRADE	
Klineberg,[4] O. (1935)	New Orleans, Atlanta, and Nashville	c- 776	12		Colored boys in publ schs.
Strayer, G. D. (1921)	Baltimore, Md.	Not given	8-16	4-8	Not given. Probably all in these grades who were present on testing days.
Clark, W. W. (1923)	Los Angeles, Cal.	c- 510	5-16	Elem, mainly 3-6	All c in mixed regular classrooms from 5 schs. A total number of 4326 includes all pupils of all races (incl Negroes) from 15 schs.
Hurlock,[15] E. B. (1924)	New York City	w-257 c- 151		3, 5, 8 3, 5, 8	Tried to get random sampling with %age from each of grade sections and a few from ungraded classes of PS 5 and PS 119.
Hurlock, E. B. (1930)	New York City	w-194 c- 210	10-17 10-17		All Ss attending PS 5.
Klineberg,[5] O. (1935)	New York City	c- 1697	12		Attempted to secure every c child of 12 yrs of age at various elem and jr high schs.

[14]Calculated by reviewer from various group averages given by author.
[15]Used *National Scale B* for 5th and 8th grades Ss; *Otis Primary* for 3rd grade; Hurlock

FOUR (continued)

VERBAL GROUP TESTS

	RESULTS			COMMENTS OF AUTHOR
	Score[14]			Part of project to determine effect of city
	c			environment on test scores of country-
M	66.3			born Ss.

	Mdn Scores			
	w		c	
Grade				
4	67		44	
5	84		61	
6	105		84	
7	123		106	
8	139		110	

	IQ			
	All		c	Probably *National* norms too high; if not,
Mdn	106.0		104.7	achievement norms too low or pupils not being well taught.
Percentage				
Above 140	4.3		2.4	
110-139	37.0		35.3	
90-109	40.5		43.9	
70- 89	17.2		15.7	
Below 70	1.0		2.7	

	IQ			
	w		c	W Ss sig superior to c in all 3 comparisons.
Groups	M			About 40% of children in each sch were
Control	101.69		93.70	c; c and w of same social status.
Praise	101.29		94.40	
Reproof	102.35		92.74	
	s			
Control	17.06		16.49	
Praise	18.36		16.55	
Reproof	17.12		17.20	

	IQ			
	w		c	All children lived in same general
M	102.17		93.14	neighborhood.
s	17.91		16.91	

	IQ			
	c			Results incl combined works of Lapidus,
M	88.5			Yates, and Marks, whose studies were directed and reported by the author.

combined IQ's. Purpose of study was to determine value of praise and reproof as incentives, with intelligence being incidental.

TABLE

SCHOOL CHILDREN

| AUTHOR DATE | LOCATION | N | SUBJECTS | | METHOD OF SELECTION |
			AGE	GRADE	
Pintner,[16] R., and Maller, J. B. (1937)	New York City	w-5007 c- 1346		5 5	C pupils in central Harlem. W pupils in schs where pop was 85-100% Italian or Jewish.
Tanser,[18] H. A. (1939)	Kent County, Ontario	w-386 c- 103	6-15 7-16	3-8 3-8	Attempted to test all w and c enrolled in one urban and 6 rural schs; excluded county schs with very few c pupils.

HAGGERTY INTELLIGENCE

Haggerty, M. E. (1921)	Virginia	w- I 250 II 5077 III 3541		3-7 3-7 3-8	From 9 cities and 18 counties: w I 1-teacher rural schs II 4-teach noncity schs III city schs
		c- I 361 II 201 III 976		3-7 3-7 3-8	c I 1-teach rural schs II 3-4 teach noncity schs III city schs
Daniel, R. P. (1932)	Richmond, Va.	cI- 80 cII-120	9-16 9-16	4-5 4-5	cI behavior probl boys from 5 schs. cII nonproblem boys from same schs.
Walker, M. B. (1946)	Fayetteville, N. C.	c- 60	10-16	6-7	80 pupils were rated by their 2 teachers on Haggerty-Olson-Wickman Beh Schedule. E selected 15 from each grade with highest scores (probl) and 15 from each grade with lowest scores (nonprobl Ss).

[16]Tested Ss with *National* and *Pintner Rapid Survey* and combined IQ's on the two tests.
[17]Calculated by reviewer. Authors give means for Jewish and Italian Ss in 6-month groups acc to month of birth.

FOUR *(continued)*
VERBAL GROUP TESTS

	RESULTS			COMMENTS OF AUTHOR

	IQ[17]			Purpose was to study relation bet month of birth and aver intelligence of several ethnic groups.
	w		c	
M	97.8		87.7	

	IQ			Urban w from higher socioeco status than c; in rural schs w and c of equal status. Educ environment equal for both races.
	w		c	
M	103.59		89.19	
s	16.49		15.89	
Mdn				
Rur	96.29		90.06	
Urb	104.68		89.08	

20% c above w *mdn*

EXAMINATION DELTA 2

		Mdn Scores					C older on aver for each sch grade; IQ discrepancy would be greater than score diffs tabulated by grade.
	w			c			
Grade							
	I	II	III	I	II	III	
3	24	31	38	17	28	25	
4	38	49	57	31	39	44	
5	61	68	78	40	55	64	
6	70	80	93	55	66	74	
7	90	93	105	75	83	86	
8			117			97	

19.9% rural c (I, II) above *mdn* of rural w
14.3% city c above *mdn* city w

	IQ		
	cI		cII
M	86.4		93.6
s	12.9		14.4

	IQ			Problem Ss about one year older than the nonproblem pupils.
	c		c	
	M		s	
Rating				
Probl	83.6		13.9	
Nonprobl	97.7		18.8	
Total	90.65			

---

[18]For results on other tests employed by Tanser, see Tables 2 and 3.

TABLE

SCHOOL CHILDREN

AUTHOR DATE	LOCATION	N	SUBJECTS		METHOD OF SELECTION
			AGE	GRADE	
Treacy, J. P. (1926)	Minneapolis, Minn.	w-1949[19] c- 205		6A 3-12	*Haggerty* and other tests given to 36% of c children. Does not say how selected Ss.
					OTIS SELF-ADMINISTERING
Patrick, J. R. (1926)	Athens, Ga.	w-47 c- 47		7 7	All c in one sch in Grade 7; 42% of w in Grade 7, does not say how selected.
Peterson,[21] J., and Telford, C. W. (1930)	St. Helena Island, S. C.	c- 53 c- 21	11-16 16-		Penn Sch and 5 inferior public schs.
Mazique,[22] E. C. (1934)	Atlanta, Ga.	c- 125		Elem	2 private c schs incl Atlanta U Lab Sch. In this sch Ss from 7th grade only.
Evans, C. A. (1934)	New York City, Atlanta, Charlotte, Raleigh, and South Carolina	c- 121 c- 100 c- 100 c- 98 c- 69 ——— 488[23]		7 7 7 7 7	*NYC*-cross-section of 10 classes in *Jr HS 139*. *Atlanta*-20 from OglethorpeU sch, 80 from publ sch. *Charlotte & Raleigh*-at least ⅔ of 7th grades. *SC-small town*-all available.
Beavers, L. L. (1935)	Atlanta, Ga.	c- 100		9	Whole class in Atl U Lab sch. From 2 publ jr high schs from which Ss were selected at random. Only girls from the 3 schs.

[19]This number includes all of the 6A pupils tested in 1923 under direction of W. S. Miller. *Mdn IQ* (108.3) is likewise based on total group.

[20]*Stanford-Binet* ratings obtained on those who had been doing unsatisfactory work and those in special classes. No group scores were included by Treacy if Ss had been tested on *Binet*. Treacy observed that c had, in proportion to their numbers, about half as many children in

FOUR (continued)

VERBAL GROUP TESTS

RESULTS			COMMENTS OF AUTHOR
	IQ^{20}		In determining IQ representative of c
	w	c	pop, one would have to include 35.6%
Mdn	108.3	97.5	(18) of those tested on *Binet* whose aver
			is 73.6. Would reduce mdn IQ of group
			test results.

INTERMEDIATE EXAMINATION

	IQ		12.8% of c were above the 25th %ile of
	w	c	w Ss.
Mdn	98	72	
None of c reached w *mdn*			

	Mdn Scores		Great test deficiency of isl c compared
	w	c	with w norms. Little encouragement or
	(norms)		motivation for speed and accuracy in publ
11	35	21.00	schs.
12	41	18.75	
13	46	18.00	
14	51	10.50	
15	55	13.50	
16	57	21.00	
Adult	59	12.75	

No c overlapping w *mdns*

	IQ		Forty-six % of parents in prof and busi-
	c		ness, 12% clerical and skilled, 38%
M	94.96		semisk and unsk, 3% unemployed.
s	15.81		

	IQ		IQ is in large measure proportional to
	c		immediate educational environment in
	M	s	which child is living.
NYC	91.5	12.0	
Atl-Pri	98	9.9	
-Pub	88	14.9	
Charl	90.7	14.4	
Ral	92.2	10.7	
SC	88.5	10.6	

	IQ	Tested by Atl Univ teacher. Low aver
	c	IQ may be accounted for by limited
M	85.95	opportunities. Incredible that 15 should
s	15.45	be feebleminded.
Range	50-132	

Grades 10-12 and about 3 times as many in special classes as the Minneapolis pop on the whole.

[21]For other test results reported by Peterson and Telford, see Tables 2 and 3.

[22]Atlanta Univ Laboratory Sch has small classes, varied program, well-equipped classrooms and library; each pupil has 4 teachers.

[23]All samples included both sexes, except NYC sch which had boys only.

TABLE

SCHOOL CHILDREN

| AUTHOR DATE | LOCATION | N | SUBJECTS | | METHOD OF SELECTION |
			AGE	GRADE	
Bean,[24] K. L. (1942)	Baton Rouge, La.	c- 49	13-18	8	Selected at random.
McGurk,[25] F. C. J. (1943)	Richmond, Va.	w-890 c- 561	9- 9-	4-8 4-8	Alphabetized names in each grade and selected every 10th.
Lacy,[26] L. D. (1926)	Oklahoma City, Okla.	c- 254		5-8	All c in city schs tested except for those in Grades 5-7 in one sch.
Garth,[27] T. R., Lovelady, B. E., and Smith, H. W. (1930)	Dallas, Tex., Tulsa, and Smaller Oklahoma Cities	c- 2006	9-17	4-9	
Ries, A. J. (1940)	Louisville, Ky.	w-1871 c- 380		6A 6A	Results of S-A secured from Off Board Educ for all pupils entering 7th grade, '38, but all tested in 6A in spring of '38. From 44 w & 13 c elem schs; Ss attending 9 w & 2 c jr high schs.

[24]For results on revised *Minnesota Paper Form Board,* see Table 3.
[25]Intermediate form to both racial groups in Grades 4-6, higher form to all above 6. For results on *Myers Mental Measure* and *Chicago Non-Verbal,* see Table 3.

FOUR (continued)

VERBAL GROUP TESTS

RESULTS				COMMENTS OF AUTHOR

M of c at 11.8%ile rank of w norms 6% of c above w *mdn*

Fundamental capacity to reason probably low in most of members of this group. Warns against interpreting any low score on usual type of test as entirely accounted for by lack of cultural opportunity.

		M Scores	
	w		c
Grade			
4	37		32
5	42		35
6	48		38
7	50		42
8	54		44

Large and statistically reliable diffs bet aver scores of w and c publ sch children.

	IQ
	c
M	80

C below norms in reading achievement which may account for lower scores on *Otis* than on *Binet*.

	IQ
	c
M	77.9

From percentage overlapping, appears that c grow less and less like w with increase in age.

	Scores		% c
	w		overlap
Mdn	(norms)	c	w mdn
9	15	12.3	32
10	23	14.2	20
11	31	16.2	9
12	38	18.1	8
13	44	19.6	7
14	49	22.3	7
15	53	23.8	8
16	56	24.3	3
17	58	26.3	1

	IQ	
	w	c
Mdn	99	85.3
Q	12.5	9.5
Range	50-149	50-139
D/PEd =		19.0

16% c above w mdn

Environmental opportunities, extra-curricular activities, cultural experiences of parents and chance to acquire education in wider sense, all contribute to final results of any test.

---

[20]For results on *Stanford-Binet*, see Tables 1 and 2.
[27]Used the intelligence test of the *Otis Classification*.

TABLE

SCHOOL CHILDREN

AUTHOR DATE	LOCATION	N	SUBJECTS AGE	GRADE	METHOD OF SELECTION
Bousfield,[28] M. B. (1932)	Chicago, Ill.	c- 222		5-8	From Keith Elem Sch.
Doran,[27] A. T. (1934)	Chicago, Ill.	c- 212	12-18	8	Negro pupils in Phillips Jr HS, spring of '33. All had begun sch in Chicago publ schs at about 6 yrs & had been enrolled continuously. None had obtained any educ outside of Chicago.
Williams, H. J. (1935)	Milwaukee, Wis.	w-133 c- 137		6 6	Intelligence test scores obtained on 270 6th-gr pupils in 3 schs: Garfield Ave., Fourth St., & Ninth St. Tests given in 1934-5.
Klineberg, O. (1935)	New York City	c- 413	12		From Harlem schs.
Griffith, W. R. (1947)	Portland, Ore.	w-39 c- 76		6-8 6-8	From Eliot Elem Sch.

OTIS GROUP

Leggett,[32] J. L. (1921)	Wilmington, N. C.	w-209 c- 161	9-15 10-17	6-7 6-7	Test given to children in publ schs. Ss were "a fair representation" of those of city as whole.

[28]For results on other tests reported by Bousfield, see Tables 3 and 4.
[29]Mean and s calculated by reviewer from author's frequency distribution.
[30]s's and t calculated by reviewer.

FOUR *(continued)*
VERBAL GROUP TESTS

	RESULTS			COMMENTS OF AUTHOR

		IQ		
		c		Ss mainly of inferior socioeco status; 46% from broken homes, 48% help from charity, 41% no daily newspaper.
Mdn		87.15		
s		12.82		

		IQ[29]		
		c		Interest in the tests was very keen. Attention prevailed throughout.
M		90.66		
s		13.78		
Range		55-125		

	w	*IQ*[30]	c	
Mdn	102.02		97.87	Class of whites studied is not representative of Milwaukee w population; a larger %age of white families represented in these 3 schs receive relief than colored families.
M	103.21		98.59	
s	11.75		12.70	
Range	70-129		65-124	
t =		3.10		
Sig at .01 level				

		Score		
		c		This research, with girls as Ss, was conducted by Traver, directed and reported by Klineberg.
M		28.5		

	w	*IQ*[31]	c	
M	99.63		91.08	Sch in district progressively becoming colored. Mean socioeco rating by Sims Score of w-13, of c-14. All parents, with one exception, in 3 lowest occup ratings.
s	15.17		14.19	
t =		2.93		
Sig at .01 level				

ADVANCED EXAMINATION

		M Scores		D/PEd	
Age	w		c		On average, the c are 75.6% as efficient as the w children in performing exercises in the *Otis Advanced Exam*.
11	76.6		61.0	3.47	
12	76.1		52.9	5.27	
13	70.8		56.9	2.84	
14	69.5		49.4	4.28	

[31]All calculations by reviewer.
[32]For results on *Otis Primary* given to 4-5th grade Ss, see Table 3.

TABLE

SCHOOL CHILDREN

AUTHOR DATE	LOCATION	N	SUBJECTS		METHOD OF SELECTION
			AGE	GRADE	
Peterson,[33] J. (1923)	Ashley County, Arkansas, and Elizabeth City, N. C.	w-171 c- 115		5-8 5-8	Tested in schs judged to be representative of c & w.
Graham,[34] V. T. (1926)	Atlanta, Ga.	c- 881	10-14	5-6	Part of Publ Health Survey. Psychol tests given in 5 c elem schs.
Gray, C. T., and Bingham, C. W. (1929)	Port Arthur, Beaumont, and South Park, Tex.	w-112 c- 58	6-8 6-8		
Slivinske, A. J. (1949)	A Virginia County	w-1764 c- 1190	6-12 6-12	1-7 1-7	All in elem schs tested except 34 w & 17 c who were absent; all tested during 1st 3 wks, Nov '48. County Supervisor gave or supervised all tests. Schs classed into large & small. *Small* = 1 or 2 teach. *Large* = 3 or more teach. Homes rated by classroom teachers. Only extremes are included to reduce errors. Various tests given but results undifferentiated.
Gound, H. D. (1938)	Bryan County, Oklahoma	w-190 c- 38		4-12 4-11	w: about ⅔ of those enrolled in *Achille Sch*. c: about ½ of those enrolled in *Colbert Sch*. Only 14 c above 8th gr.

[33]For results on *Otis Primary, Myers MM*, and *Haggerty*, see Table 3; for results on *Pressey Group*, see Table 4.

[34]*Otis* norms for w children, Grades 5-6 based on about 13,000 cases. For results on *Stanford-Binet, 1916* and *Kohs Block*, see Table 2; for *Otis Primary*, see Table 3.

FOUR (continued)

VERBAL GROUP TESTS

	RESULTS			COMMENTS OF AUTHOR
		Mdn		Schs of c and w not equally efficient.
Grade	w		c	
5	75.0		34.4	
6	86.3		42.2	
7	98.6		61.0	
8	108.3		105.0	

	M Scores		On *Advanced Otis,* 5th and 6th-grade
	w	c	selections do not give fair w averages
Age	(norms)		beyond 11th year.
10	76.11	52.23	
11	79.22	54.22	
12	77.02	59.02	
13	71.18	57.43	
14	66.48	55.47	

Diff's bet means highly sig

	IQ^{35}		Mdn CA of c a few months less than that
	w	c	of w; mdn MA almost 3 years below w
Mdn	108	76	mdn. No w Ss tested in Port Arthur.
s	22.67	11.42	

Sig diff bet mdns

IQ^{36}
Size of School

	Small		*Large*		Negro home environments and sch en-
	w	c	w	c	vironments in any type community or
M	91.4	77.1	96.7	78.9	home are probably more nearly alike
s	21.0	13.7	18.6	15.9	than that found in similar white
t	= 5.74		= 19.78		situations.

IQ
Home Rating

	Inferior		*Superior*		
	w	c	w	c	
M	82.7	70.1	108.3	88.5	
s	15.4	13.3	20.2	14.6	
t	= 9.17		= 10.19		

	IQ^{37}		Farming chief occup. Consolidated schs,
	w	c	both sch busses, same salary schedule, free
M	98.19	74.87	books and hot lunches; w teachers more
Mdn	99.05	72.50	training and have more pupils.
Range	50-144	45-114	

[35]Index of Brightness.

[36]Calculations by reviewer. Author tabulates throughout acc to chronological age in 12-month intervals.

[37]Calculated by reviewer from frequency distributions.

TABLE

SCHOOL CHILDREN

| AUTHOR DATE | LOCATION | N | SUBJECTS | | METHOD OF SELECTION |
			AGE	GRADE	
Wallace, E. B. (1932)	Cincinnati, Ohio	c- 226[38]		6	Test given each year to all publ sch children in 6th grade. Obtained records from 4 schs.

					DEARBORN
Hirsch,[39] N. D. M. (1926)	Massachusetts Mill towns and Nashville, Tenn.	w-682 c- 301		4-9 4-9	w: all pupils in publ schs of 4 mill towns. c: in publ schs "fairly representative of the Nashville colored pop."

					BINET
Peterson,[40] J., and Lanier, L. H. (1929)	Nashville, Tenn.	w-119 c- 86	12 12		All 12-yr-olds in 3 w & 2 c schs; 9 12-yr-olds from a c jr high sch since one of c schs had Grades 1-6 only.

					ILLINOIS GENERAL
Hewitt, A. (1930)	In South	w-85 c- 90	11-16 10-19	7 7	Three groups from 1 w sch; 5 groups from 2 c schs.
Farr, T. J. (1931)	Newton County, Tennessee	c- 200		3-7	Those in attendance at 2 largest village schs.
Thurmond,[41] S. (1933)	Clarke County, Georgia	c- 40	12		From 6 best of 13 rural county schs, selected every child from rolls who had reached 12th but not 13th birthday; 12 of 52 absent from one or more testing sessions.

[38]Fewer than half of Ss enrolled in Grade 6 in the 4 schs included in report; does not say how made selection. See Table 4 for results on *Detroit Alpha*.

[39]*Dearborn C* is both verbal and nonverbal, as is true of a number of other tests included in this table, such as *California Mental Maturity, Kuhlmann-Anderson, etc.* For other results reported by Hirsch, see Table 3. Ss in table are children of American-born parents.

FOUR *(continued)*
VERBAL GROUP TESTS

	RESULTS			COMMENTS OF AUTHOR
		M		54 per cent of parents below skilled labor
	Sims		*IQ*	group.
School	*Score*		c	
1	12.32		89.63	
2	8.09		80	
3	8.47		76.66	
4	6.82		82.85	

C TEST

		IQ		Whites from poorer socioeco environ than
	w		c	that of aver urban American child.
M	98.8		87.1	

GROUP TEST

		Scores		Simple organization of c mentality might
	w		c	be due to less specialization of c
Mdn	25.81		15.07	environment.
Sig diff bet *mdns*				
94% w above c *mdn*				
7% c above w *mdn*				

EXAMINATION

		IQ		C markedly below w in analogies, sentence
	w		c	vocab, verbal ingenuity, and synonym-
Mdn	107.5		90	antonym ability.
Range	70-144		50-145	

		IQ		Low scores may be due to lack of ability
	Girls		Boys	to read with enough understanding for
	c		c	tests to be valid, to poor homes and
Mdn	64.4		67.5	inferior teaching.
Range	40-110		40-100	

		IQ		*Stanford-Binet* and *Illinois* depend to a
		c		great extent upon sch training; the per-
M		69		formance scale does so very slightly if at
s		12.40		all.
Range		49-100		
2.5% equaled norm of 100				

[40]For results on *Yerkes Point Scale,* see Table 2; for *Myers MM & International,* see Table 3.
[41]For results on *Stanford-Binet, 1916* and *Arthur Point Scale,* see Table 2.

TABLE

SCHOOL CHILDREN

AUTHOR DATE	LOCATION	N	SUBJECTS		METHOD OF SELECTION
			AGE	GRADE	
					DETROIT
Jenkins, T. A. (1932)	Goldsboro and Selma, N. C.	w-37 c- 37	12-13 12-13	5- 8 3-10	Twelve-yr-olds & some who had just reached 13. Method of selection not given.
Smith, M. (1953)	Chambers County, Alabama	c- 200	9-15	5-6	5th & 6th grade pupils from 5 elem schs. Implies that all were tested.
Wallace, E. B. (1932)	Cincinnati, Ohio	c- 239		5	Selected ⅓-¾ of pupils from each 5th grade in 4 publ schs. Method of selection not given.
Fowler, W. L. (1959)	Detroit and Hamtramck, Mich.	w-285 c- 70	10 10		Twelve Detroit schs & 2 in Hamtramck supplied Ss, each pupil taking 6 group mental tests. Tests divided into *Conventional* and *Culture-Controlled. Alpha* one of latter.
					McCALL MULTI-
Mazique, E. C. (1934)	MacDonough, Union City, and Hampton, Ga.	c- 125	8-	1-7	Four rural schs near Atlanta; 1 of 2 in MacD is county training sch; Hampton is Rosenwald sch.
Vernon, J. O. (1936)	Muskogee County, Oklahoma	w-222 c- 200		3-10 3-10	Tested w & c of 2 schs. (Only 27 of c were above 8th grade.)

[42]Mean socioeconomic score. The first is described by Wallace as "median or average", while the other 3 are "medium low". For results on *Otis Advanced*, see Table 4.

[43]For results on Culture-Controlled tests and further information about selection of Ss, see Table 3, under *Davis-Eells* tests, and pp. 115-116.

FOUR *(continued)*

VERBAL GROUP TESTS

	RESULTS		COMMENTS OF AUTHOR

ALPHA

	Scores		Tested by teachers and supervisors. Study
	w	c	indicates slight racial diff in intelligence
M	126	119	and language ability acc to present
Mdn	121	107	measures.
Range	84-221	31-202	

	IQ		All schs located in rural area, sparsely
	c		populated; cultural agencies limited and
Mdn	82.8		schs inadequately equipped.
Q1	79.11		
Q3	85.25		

School	Sims[42]	M IQ	About ¾ of teachers had degrees; over ¼
	Score	c	parents had attended high sch; 11-12%
1	11.66	86.66	had attended college.
2	9.44	84.73	
3	7.88	79.56	
4	7.09	88.03	

	M IQ[43]		Culture-Control tests included: *Cattell, A*
Test	w	c	*and B,* and *Davis-Eells.* Conventional tests
Conven	104.21	88.02	included: *Detroit Alpha, California*
Cult-con	105.57	88.23	*Mental Maturity,* and *Henmon-Nelson.*

MENTAL SCALE

	IQ		Fathers mainly farmers. One sch is 8
	c		months, others 6 months. Mean salary of
M	77.46		teachers below $200.
s	13.75		
Range	50-124		

	IQ[44]		The capacities of the 2 groups are de-
	w	c	cidedly different, and the Negro pupils
Mdn	106	95	are below the w.

[44]Totals calculated by reviewer from Vernon's frequency tables. For results on *Otis Primary,* see Table 3.

TABLE

SCHOOL CHILDREN

AUTHOR DATE	LOCATION	N	SUBJECTS		METHOD OF SELECTION
			AGE	GRADE	
Bousfield,[28] M. B. (1932)	Chicago, Ill.	c- 222		5-8	From Keith Elem Sch; no report as to method of selection, or if all tested or not.
					PRESSEY GROUP
Pressey, S. L., and Teter, G. F. (1919)	Two Small Indiana Cities	c- 120	10-14	3-12	All children in the 2 c schs tested; w norms based on one of the 2 cities.
Murdoch, K. (1920)	New York City	w-1473 c- 129	9-16	5-8A	From 5-8A grades selected all c boys & every 3rd w boy from one sch in upper East Side; rather undesirable locale. Also Italian & Jewish boys of foreign-born parents in another sch.
Peterson,[33] J. (1923)	Nashville, Tenn., Wilmington, N. C., Hamilton County and Shelby County Tenn.	w-326 c- 223 w-108 c- 91 w-207 c- 196 w-131 c- 263		3-8 4-7 2-7 6 6 3-6 4-8 4-9 6-8 4-5 4-8 3-8 4-8	Selected only acc to grade. Two w & 2 c schs in Na; 1 w & 1 c sch in Wil; 3 w & 2 c schs in Ham; 1 w & 2 c schs in Shelby Co. The 7 w & 7 c schs of same sections to get nearly same social status.
					OTIS QUICK-SCORING
Younge, S. L. (1947)	Tuskegee, Ala.	c- 27	9-13	6	All 6th-grade pupils of Tuskegee Laboratory School, on campus.

FOUR (continued)
VERBAL GROUP TESTS

RESULTS			COMMENTS OF AUTHOR

		Scores		Only 3 families in good circumstances, rest in main of inferior socioeco status. Great care should be used in selecting mental tests.
		w	c	
		norm		
M		50	45.1	

INTELLIGENCE TEST

14% c above w mdn
54% c below w 25%ile
3% c above 75%ile

C best in rote memory; poorest in verbal ingenuity and knowledge of abstract terms. Suggests more elementary and less highly developed ability among c children.

	% w (Amer-born parents) & c above Jewish Mdn		Rel few white children above age of 14 in Grades 5-8A; rel few c below age of 11 in these grades.
Age	w	c	
10	54	61	
11	53.5	33.3	
12	50	24	
13	57.5	33.3	
14	66.5	30	
15	30	30	

W mdns sig above c at each age bet 11-16; at age 10 diff of 3 points not sig

C inferiority greatest in logical relations.

MENTAL ABILITY BETA TEST

	IQ	Socioeco status ranged from medium to very high; 63% had one or both parents who had attended college.
	c	
M	92.22	
s	17.04	
Range	62-132	
30% c overlapped w norm		

TABLE

SCHOOL CHILDREN

| AUTHOR DATE | LOCATION | N | SUBJECTS | | METHOD OF SELECTION |
			AGE	GRADE	
Cliff,[45] E. M. (1949)	Atlanta, Ga.	c- 110	10-16	7	Selected Ss from 7th grade acc to "normative survey method"; one sch was used: *Edmund A Ware Elem.* Approx 5 weeks later, retested half under timed condit & half under untimed conditions. See text for results of retest. (p. 188)
Hunt, W. B. (1950)	Hardeman County, Tennessee	c- 134	8-18	4-5	All fourth & 5th grade pupils in 6 of the 38 county schs; varied in size from 1-teacher to 10-teacher schs.
Allman,[47] R. W. (1953)	Birmingham, Ala.	c- 457		8	All of the available 8th-grade Negro pupils in the Birmingham publ schs.
Clark,[48] G. E. (1957)	St. Louis, Mo.	w-362 c- 361		High 4 High 4	All children taken in complete class units. Schs segregated. W from 14 schs, c from 8 schs serving high, middle, & low socioeco class areas. Negro E assigned to about ½ Negro schs.

[45]Ss also tested by *California Mental Maturity.* See Table 4.
[46]*s* calculated by reviewer.
[47]For her report on college Ss in Alabama, see Table 6.

FOUR *(concluded)*

VERBAL GROUP TESTS

RESULTS			COMMENTS OF AUTHOR
		IQ	31% below 70 IQ
	c	c	
	boys	girls	
M	76.30	80.70	
s	14.62	15.60	
Range	50-119	50-139	
10% c overlapped w norm			
		IQ[46]	48% from broken homes; 84% with heads of homes having only grade-sch education.
		c	
M		70.87	
s		15.27	
Range		43-111	
0.7% c overlapped w norm			
		IQ	
		c	
M		84.06	
Range		44-117	
		IQ[49]	For children in less favored areas included in this research, the *Davis-Eells* test provided no apparent advantage over the more verbal *Otis.*
		M	
Socioeco	w	c	
Low	94.65	85.25	
Middle	107.86	92.36	
High	110.33	93.40	
Total	104.51	90.41	
		s	
Socioeco	w	c	
Low	8.61	10.29	
Middle	10.78	10.22	
High	9.97	10.98	
Total	12.48	10.82	

[48]For results on *Davis-Eells,* see Table 3. Races about equally represented in the 3 socioeconomic groups- w: 118 low, 109 middle, 135 high; c: 114 low, 115 middle, 132 high.

[49]Author gives a number of IQ's tabulated acc to test and socioeconomic status; these reported in table have been estimated by reviewer from author's tabulations

TABLE

SCHOOL CHILDREN

AUTHOR DATE	LOCATION	N	SUBJECTS		METHOD OF SELECTION
			AGE	GRADE	
Murray, W. I. (1947)	Gary, Ind.	c- 193 c- 208	10 14		*Alpha* form given to 10-yr-olds, Grades 1-4; *Beta* to all 14-yr-olds above Grade 4; *Kuhlmann-Anderson* to 10-yr-olds; *Henmon-Nelson* to 10-yr-olds above Gr. 2. Does not say how many schs were surveyed. Method of selection not always clear. Ss in "Opportunity Room" not tested on *H-N*.
					PINTNER GENERAL ABILITY
Jordan, A. M. (1947)	North Carolina County	w-1980 c- 1214	6-17 6-19	1-8 1-8	Tested all pupils present in every sch in a predominantly rural county.
Jordan, A. M. (1948)	Winston-Salem, N. C.	w-5429 c- 4856		1-8	More than 95% of elem sch children were tested. All tests administered with care by one E; all scored by one person & checked by another.

[50]From author's Tables 4 and 9; reviewer includes all Ss' mean IQ's acc to parental occupa tion wherever the same occupation is listed for both racial groups.

FOUR (continued)
VERBAL GROUP TESTS

	RESULTS			COMMENTS OF AUTHOR
		IQ		Ss were divided into 3 social classes, 22% being in middle class, rest below; the higher the class the higher the mean IQ on each test.
	c		c	
	(10)		(14)	
M	86-91		87-91	
s	7-15		12-16	

VERBAL SERIES

		IQ		The real intelligance of Ss tested would be 7-12 IQ points above that actually achieved.
	w		c	
M	91.4		74.3	
s	17.95		13.5	
Range	—170		—120	

		IQ			In general the Negro scores are low because as a whole they occupy low socioeco levels.
		M		*s*	
Age	w	c	w	c	
6	107.9	83.8	16.6	9.0	
7	103.7	83.3	15.4	11.6	
8	98.4	81.7	16.3	11.1	
9	98.7	82.7	16.9	11.8	
10	99.3	84.3	16.3	13.0	
11	97.2	83.7	17.4	13.2	
12	98.1	81.6	17.3	11.9	
13	99.4	78.1	18.2	12.2	
14	92.7	76.6	17.3	11.1	
Total	97.7	80.9	17.4	12.6	

9% c above w mean

	M IQ^{50}	
	w	c
Professional	113.9	92.0
Railroad wkr	102.2	83.7
Salesman	100.9	82.3
Barber, Beaut	95.6	87.3
Factory wkr	93.6	80.7
Truck Driver	89.9	81.0

TABLE

SCHOOL CHILDREN

AUTHOR DATE	LOCATION	N	SUBJECTS		METHOD OF SELECTION
			AGE	GRADE	
					CALIFORNIA TEST
Lewis,[51] M. L. (1947)	Montgomery, Ala.	c- 96	12-18	7	Tested boys in 7th grade of *B. T. Washington High Sch. Intermediate Form.*
Johnson, C. N. (1948)	Conecuh County, Alabama	c- 195	10-16	6	Tested all 6th-grade children present in the 43 c rural schs. *Elem Form.*
Cliff,[53] E. M. (1949)	Atlanta, Ga.	c- 116	10-16	7	Selected Ss from 7th grade of *Edmund A. Ware Elem Sch* acc to "normative survey method"; about 5 wks later, retested half under timed conditions & half under untimed conditions.
Harper, R. M. (1950)	Atlanta, Ga.	c- 44		1-7	Each of the 22 pupils in Bush Mt Sch who had not been absent first semester was paired for age, sex, & grade with one absent 10 or more times. *Primary & Elem Forms.*
McPherson, L. A. (1951)	Waco, Tex.	w-67 c- 82	6-8 6-8	1 1	All Ss in first grade of 2 schs in East Waco; c & w schs in same area; c & w Ss of similar socioeco status (D level).
Boger, J. H. (1952)	Rural County, Virginia	w-53 c- 51		1-3 1-4	Tested intact classes in 1-2 teacher schs; *CMM Primary Form & Otis Q-S, Alpha.* Tests repeated after 3½ months practice on puzzles & other problems.

[51]For results on revised *Beta*, see Table 3; for results on delinquents, see Table 11.
[52]Calculated by reviewer from author's frequency distribution. Obtained mean corresponds to an average grade placement of 3.1.

FOUR (continued)
VERBAL GROUP TESTS

	RESULTS		COMMENTS OF AUTHOR

OF MENTAL MATURITY

	IQ		An analysis of scores of random sample of 60 Ss gives:
	c		
M	83.7		M Language IQ = 85.1
s	11.83		M Non-L IQ = 79.8
Range	54-117		

	Scores[52]		Low sch achievement due to poor eco status, nonstim environ, low mental ability, inferior teacher preparation.
	c		
M	44.54		
s	5.81		
Range	35-63		

	IQ		Data suggest that time is probably not an important factor in determining one's IQ on CTMM.
	c	c	
	Boys	**Girls**	
M	86.80	85.60	
s	10.70	12.09	
Range	60-104	50-129	

	IQ		On Cal Test of Personality, those without absences also sig higher in *Sense of Personal Worth, Feeling of Belonging, Family Relations & School Relations*.
M	c		
Perfect attend	88.59		
Irreg attend	72.18		

	IQ		Of the 149 Ss, 24 w & 24 c were matched for scores on *CMM* & other items; these c sig low on *Performance Scale* of *WISC*.
	w	c	
M	101	91	

	IQ[54]		Gain in IQ due to practices:		
M	w	c		w	c
Language	87.0	77.7	Language	3.9	0.4
Nonlang	95.2	81.9	Nonlang	11.1	15.0

[53]Ss also tested by *Otis Q-S, Beta* (Table 4).
[54]These IQ's based on first testing. See Table 3 for results on *Otis Q-S, Alpha.*

TABLE

SCHOOL CHILDREN

AUTHOR DATE	LOCATION	N	SUBJECTS		METHOD OF SELECTION
			AGE	GRADE	
Dendy, A. P. H. (1952)	Landrum, S. C.	c- 45		7	Tested the 45 7th grade pupils of Mountain View Elem Sch, 1951-52; writer assisted by principal.
Sutton, L. J. (1954)	Duplin County, North Carolina	c- 20		8	All 8th-grade pupils in Chinquapin Elem Sch given *Intermed Form*. Home envir rated *fair* or *good* generally. Also tested 25 7th-gr pupils who had good grades.
Parker, L. M. C. (1954)	Macon, Ga.	c- 238	12-17	8	Ballard-Hudson Jr High Sch pupils who had attended 3 c elem schs located in diff parts of city. *Elem Form*.
Furlow,[56] F. D. (1954)	Atlanta, Ga.	c- 38	10-14	6	Ss enrolled in one of the 3 6th grades of Carter Elem Sch; does not say whether or not this group is representative of the 3. Each S given 3 tests.
Freeman, R. L. (1954)	Americus, Ga.	c- 84	11-16	7	*Elem Form* given to all present in 7th grade of the Negro elem sch.
Queen,[57] P. M. J. (1954)	Apex, N. C.	c- 30	11-12	6	"A selected group of Negro sixth graders" from Apex jr high sch. Method of selection not given.
Hammer, E. F. (1954)	Madison Heights, Va.	c- 207		1-8	Surveyed entire sch pop of c elem & high sch. (*N* includes high sch Ss.)

[55]*s* calculated from frequency distribution by reviewer.
[56]For results on *Detroit Learning* and *Davis-Eells,* see Tables 2 & 3, respectively.

FOUR *(continued)*
VERBAL GROUP TESTS

	RESULTS	COMMENTS OF AUTHOR
	IQ^{55} c	Test results show these pupils to be well below the average in native capacity, to be below mean of normal progress in sch and within range of normal personality adjustment *(Cal Test of Pers)*.
M	76	
s	7.52	
Range	63-92	
0 equaled norm of 100		
	IQ c	Only a few seemed to possess the interests, intel, and other assets necessary for training and entering the vocations they desired.
Mdn	81	
	Scores c	The 3 schs provide stimulating and profitable learning experiences for pupils altho they are markedly retarded in mental develop.
M	74.58	
s	21.30	
Grade placement acc to intell should be 5.3		
	IQ c	IQ's on *CMM* and *Davis-Eells* suggest that either the discriminating diff bet the 2 tests is not of high degree, or that whenever a test-pop is homogeneous as to culture, the diff bet the types of tests is nil or slight.
M	98.71	
Mdn	97.30	
s	14.25	
Range	75-140	
	Scores c	All but 2 of 25 teachers have degrees. Most of parents factory workers, farm laborers and domestics. Consistent inferior level in intell, achieve, and personality of pupils suggests advisability of diagnostic testing program.
M	68.55	
s	11.55	
Grade placement acc to intell should be 5.2		
	IQ c	
M		
Language	89	
Nonlang	94.5	
Total	94.0	
s	8.5	
Range	—100	
	M IQ c	Significantly higher means on language than on nonl parts of test. Suggests a factor responsible for the lower c IQ may be emotional disturbance.
Grade		
1	71.04	
2	77.33	
3	67.74	
4	79.74	
5	72.49	
6	61.62	
7	76.75	
8	75.50	

[57]For results on *Davis-Eells,* see Table 3.

TABLE

SCHOOL CHILDREN

AUTHOR DATE	LOCATION	N	SUBJECTS GRADE	METHOD OF SELECTION
Osborne, R. T. (1960)	County in a Southern State	w-1388 c- 723 w- 815 c- 446	6 6 6, 8, 10 6, 8, 10	*CMM* in *Elem, Interm,* or *Adv Form* given in '54, '56, & '58 to all w & c who were in 6th gr in '54, 8th in '56 & 10th in '58; 1388 w & 723 c in original testing; 815 w & 446 c were tested on all 3 dates (or make-up testing periods).
Tullis, D. S. (1964)	A West Texas Community	w-56* c- 56	4-7 4-7	*Henmon-Nelson* given in Gr 4 & *CTMM* in Gr 5, 6, & 7, all integrated & in one central area. All 7 c boys & 7 c girls in Gr 6 used as Ss; by random sampling selected 7 of each sex from each of 3 ethnic groups per grade, totaling 56 c, 56 *Latin,* & 56 *Anglo* Ss. Social status (SS) determined by McGuire-White Index.
Swan, D. A. (1965)	St. John the Baptist Parish, Louisiana	w- 988 c- 2244	1-8 1-8	All pupils enrolled in Grades 1-12 of parish sch system tested if present when tests administered in fall of 1963.
Osborne,[59] R. T. (1965)	County in a Southern State	w-6518 c- 4123 w-5719 c- 3407	5 8	All pupils, Grades 5 & 8, if present on testing days, were examined in 3 successive years beginning with 1963.

[58]Calculations by reviewer from author's data.
*White pupils called *Anglos* & Ss of Mexican parents, *Latins*. Results on *Latins* omitted by reviewer since they were bilingual; *s's, t's,* & overlap calculated by reviewer.

FOUR (continued)

VERBAL GROUP TESTS

RESULTS	COMMENTS OF AUTHOR

		IQ		Negro teachers administered tests to c pupils, w teachers to w pupils. On the culturally weighted verbal tests c children held their own, but on nonverbal items involving only number combinations the overlap bet the 2 racial groups was virtually eliminated at the last testing.
	w	M	c	
Total	97.71		75.31[58]	
Grade				
6	101.28		78.78	
8	100.58		84.35	
10	102.28		78.60	
		s		
6	13.37		13.90	
8	10.73		9.93	
10	8.38		9.64	
8% overlap at Grade 8				

		IQ		Mean SS of Anglos was 45.6 that of c, 72.4, favoring former. There is no substantiation for the statement that the Latin or Negro ethnic group is inferior to Anglo group in the ability to learn or to perform.
	w		c	
M	108.46		87.00	
s	13.65		11.07	
$t =$			8.94	
4% c above w mean				
		IQ**		
	w		c	
M	101.14		79.71	
s		11.01		
t		3.64		

		IQ[58]			No evidence that cumulative effects of segregated education result in lower ability-achievement correlations in the higher than in the lower grades.
	w		c		
	M	s	M	s	
Language	96.52	17.20	77.69	15.04	
Nonlang	93.14	18.19	73.63	15.68	
Total	95.04	15.69	75.86	13.47	
All diffs bet racial means highly sig					

		M IQ		CTMM, Elem Level administered to w & c pupils in 5th gr; Junior High Level to w and c in 8th grade.
Grade 5	w		c	
Language	108.8		88.4	
Nonlang	104.6		85.1	
Total	106.8		86.8	
Grade 8				
Language	102.1		81.5	
Nonlang	97.5		81.0	
Total	100.0		81.3	

[59]From unpublished data supplied by Osborne. For results on high sch Ss tested, see Table 5.
**From Tullis' frequency tables the reviewer found 7 w & 7 c of the same social status score. These were from all 4 grades (w: 2-2-2-1 and c: 1-2-2-2). The mean SS's of these groups were 60.86 and 60, resp, their mean IQ's differing by 21.43 points.

TABLE

SCHOOL CHILDREN

AUTHOR DATE	LOCATION	N	SUBJECTS		METHOD OF SELECTION
			AGE	GRADE	
Tate, M. W., and Voss, C. E. (1956)	Pa. Havertown (w) Coatesville (c) S. C. Orangeburg (w) Columbia (c) Richland Co. (w) Orangeburg Co. (w) Richland Co. (c) Orangeburg Co. (c)	Pa. w-177 c- 122 S. C. w-372 c- 209		4-6 4-6	*CMM* & *Davis-Eells* given by classroom teachers in the 3 grades of selected urban & rural schs, w & c, in Pa & SC.
Love,[61] M. I., and Beach, S. (1957)	Cincinnati, Ohio	c- 110		3	Children in one of predominantly lower-class schs tested when their mdn age was 9.0. All in 3rd grade.

DETROIT

| Cavins,[62] L. V. (1928) | West Virginia | w-3567 c- 230 | | 3-4 3-4 | Part of state survey. Ss in Grade 4 were from 1- & 2-room schs only. |

[60]See Table 3 for results on *Davis-Eells*. Authors also tested 197 rural w Pa children but were not able to secure rural c in sufficient numbers in this state. Calculations by reviewer from authors' data.

[61]For results on *Davis-Eells*, see Table 3.

FOUR (continued)
VERBAL GROUP TESTS

RESULTS					COMMENTS OF AUTHOR

Language Scores[60]

	M		s		t
	w	c	w	c	
Pa urban					
4	45.9	32.3	13.0	9.2	6.07
5	55.9	42.0	10.8	11.8	4.62
6	65.3	42.6	12.8	12.2	9.73
SC urban					
4	43.1	30.8	13.7	13.6	4.49
5	50.5	39.7	11.9	9.3	5.05
6	60.1	45.3	14.5	14.1	4.87
SC rural					
4	39.6	24.1	11.2	8.1	8.03
5	58.9	30.8	12.0	9.5	11.00
6	54.7	35.0	12.1	10.8	8.32

All 9 diff's bet means highly sig

Non-Language Scores

	M		s		t
	w	c	w	c	
Pa urban					
4	91.2	76.4	10.8	11.7	6.68
5	100.8	90.2	9.4	10.0	4.16
6	103.8	87	10.0	12.7	7.68
SC urban					
4	87.2	74.0	12.3	14.7	4.74
5	95.6	84.4	10.7	14.1	4.23
6	100.0	89.1	12.5	14.6	3.91
SC rural					
4	84.6	50.6	10.7	20.0	9.68
5	90.8	72.0	10.1	13.4	6.10
6	96.0	79.0	10.8	16.0	5.48

All 9 diff's bet means highly sig

M	IQ
	c
Language	87.2
Nonlang	91.9
Total	89.2

Ss rated consistently higher on *CMM* than on *Davis-Eells*, the diff bet means significant.

PRIMARY TEST

Grade	Mdn IQ[63]	
	w	c
3	88	76
4	84	79

Large number of over-age pupils. Among c schs the yearly promotion is 76%, among w schs, 84%.

---

[62]For results on *Pintner-Cunningham,* see Table 3. Grade 3 represents all schs in the 41 tested districts except for "distinctly graded school systems. . . ."

[63]Approximated IQ's; obtained by reviewer by dividing the median MA's by the respective CA's.

TABLE

SCHOOL CHILDREN

AUTHOR DATE	LOCATION	N	SUBJECTS AGE	GRADE	METHOD OF SELECTION
					SRA PRIMARY
Swan,[59] D. A. (1964)	Jackson, Miss.	w- gr 2-1815 5-1485 8-1186 c- gr 2-1224 5-1070 8- 817	2, 5, 8 2, 5, 8		A standardized testing program including PMA tests given to all Ss present in 2nd, 5th, 8th, & 10th grades. Data for 1960 included here.
Wylie, R. C. (1963)	A small highly industrialized Pennsylvania city	w-739 c- 84	7-9 7-9		All children who were present on testing day included. Each had been previously given PMA test & IQ's from this used as estimate of "ability to do schoolwork." From the only jr high sch in city.
					PHILADELPHIA TESTS
Soifer, M. W. (1937)	Philadelphia, Pa.	w-159 c- 152	6B 6B		Pupils from Holmes Jr High Sch were measured & given physical tests in physical educ classes. *E* secured mental test records of all who had been enrolled in 6B in city schs where these tests universally given.
					OTHER
Hartill, R. M., and Loretan, J. O. (1940)	New York City	c- 1715	Kg-6		*PS 5* including 63 classes, all of pupils c, which was 1 of 20 selected "problem schs" studied.

[64]Means separated acc to father's occupation, 1-4 being the higher. Means of w Ss listed acc to occupation calculated by reviewer; *t* calculated by reviewer.

FOUR (continued)
VERBAL GROUP TESTS

	RESULTS				COMMENTS OF AUTHOR

MENTAL ABILITIES

	M		IQ	s	
Grade	w	c	w	c	
2	106.5	93.5	8.6	11.9	Teacher qualifications, as measured by number of yrs of professional training and advanced degrees substantially equivalent for w and c schs. Academic curricula basically the same.
5	109.3	89.4	13.2	13.7	
8	107.1	78.4	18.0	16.4	

$t's = 32.5, 36.7,$ and 37.3
6-13% c above w means

	IQ[64]		
	w	c	
Mdn	103.95	85.88	Evidence presented that sex, race, and occup level of father all associated with children's estimates of their ability to do schoolwork.
M			
Total	103.30	88.30	
1-4	111.0	88.4	
5-7	100.6	90.6	
Unclass	102.2	87.0	
s	17.30	15.11	
t (totals) =		8.47	

MENTAL AND VERBAL ABILITY

	IQ[65]		
	w	c	
M			White girls and boys more intelligent than c girls and boys of same age; but c are superior to w of same sex in jumping, throwing, and running.
Boys	110.5	98.9	
Girls	109.2	98.6	
Total	109.9	98.8	
s	11.3	12.5	
t =		8.2	

18% c overlapped w mean

TESTS

	IQ	
	c	
M	85	

---

[65] *s's* and *t* calculated by reviewer.

TABLE

SCHOOL CHILDREN

AUTHOR DATE	LOCATION	N	SUBJECTS		METHOD OF SELECTION
			AGE	GRADE	
Bird, C., Monachesi, E. D., and Burdick, H. (1952)	Minneapolis, Minn.	X w-81 c- 10 Y w-63 c- 20		3-5 3-5	Ss enrolled in 2 publ schs, in diff city districts; X is physically less desir- able, closer to industry & business than Y. Residents of both generally belonging to middle & lower-middle class. Test scores from sch records, all of c who had been tested; meth of select of w from the 393 enrolled not given.
Dinitz, S., Kay, B. A., and Reckless, W. C. (1958)	Columbus, Ohio	w-447 c- 270		6 6	All 6th-grade pupils in 24 rooms of 11 schs. Schs chosen on basis of pop & dwelling area characteristics of census tracts in which located. Ranged from schs in least desirable through schs in most desirable tracts.
Price, A. C. (1962)	Gainesville, Fla.	w-90 c- 90	6, 10, 14 6, 10, 14		30 c & 30 w pupils selected from each of 3 ages. On basis of sch gr, sch grades, *K-A, P-C, Draw-a-Man*, & in some cases the high sch form of *ACE*, children were classed as *Below aver, Aver,* & *Above aver* in intelligence. In each age-race group were 20 of *Aver intel,* 5 in *Below aver,* & 5 in *Above aver* categories. All of these Ss given *Rorschach*, using Beck's scoring procedures.

[96]Calculated by reviewer.
[97]Significant at .01 level at 14 years only.

FOUR *(concluded)*

VERBAL GROUP TESTS

	RESULTS			COMMENTS OF AUTHOR
		IQ		Negro and white residents did not differ sig in social status.
District X	w		c	
M	105.48		92.30	
s	10.84		12.43	
District Y				
M	109.79		103.55	
s	10.81		12.79	
t (w-c, Dist X) =		3.21[66]		
t (w-c, Dist Y) =		1.97		

		IQ		
	w		c	The Negro youngsters averaged 15 points lower in IQ scores, were over 1½ grade levels lower in aver reading scores, & slightly over a year behind in arith. These diff's all highly significant.
M	101.21		85.98	
s	15.3		14.5	
t =		15.86		

		Intellectual Factors		
	w		c	The older child and the white child are better able to organize the stimulus field, are more imaginative, and less stereotyped in manner of handling intellectual problems. Older and white children appear to be more energetic and creative than younger and Negro children.
		Response Total		
M	25.97		24.98[67]	
s	7.61		4.93	
		Z Score		
M	16.85		11.87[68]	
s	11.97		11.50	
		F+ %		
M	78.29		78.08	
s	11.94		14.62	
		A %		
M	51.66		52.84	
s	12.85		13.75	
		M Determ		
M	1.41		.91[68]	
s	1.67		1.33	
		FM Determ		
M	1.27		.82[68]	
s	1.47		1.35	
		% R's to W or D		
W	14.7		10.4	
D	76.8		82.0	
Dd	8.5		7.6	

[68]Significant at .05 level. For interpretation of *Intellectual Factors*, see p. 201.

community and socioeconomic level of the home, the differences were significant and in favor of the whites. Furthermore, the mean of the whites from the *small schools* compared with the mean of the Negroes from the *large schools* and the mean of the whites from schools in *relatively inferior communities* compared with the mean of Negroes from *relatively superior communities* still favor the white groups. Only when one compares the mean IQ of white children from homes rated as relatively *inferior* with the mean IQ of Negro children from homes rated as relatively *superior* do we find the difference reversed in favor of the Negroes.

Gound (1938) examined a small number of rural Negro children attending a school which in general compared favorably with that attended by white children in the Oklahoma county. The mean IQ of the colored children was about 75, which was 23 points below that of the white Ss. Wallace (1932) obtained *Otis* test records of 226 sixth-grade Negro children from four Cincinnati public schools. The mean IQ's of these children ranged from 77 to 90, the latter mean attained by pupils living in a "better" neighborhood, as judged from their mean Sims score of *12*.[76] The *Otis* score was found to correlate .26 with the socioeconomic score. While the Cincinnati schools attended by the colored children were probably superior to those attended by the Southern Negroes, it is doubtful if the home environments of the Ohio Ss were above those of the Southern children, judging from the relatively low Sims scores of Wallace's groups.

DEARBORN C

The *Dearborn Group Tests of Intelligence, Series II*, designed for use from Grade 4 to Grade 10, consist of verbal and nonverbal subtests. The greater part of the maximum possible score is determined by the verbal or numerical items which are included in subtests of: word sequences, opposites sentence completion, proverbs, and number completion. Reliability coefficients have been reported between .87 and .93 for single ages and between .84 and .92 for single grades. Validity is reported in terms of correlation with *Stanford-Binet*, r's being .87 and .82, respectively, for 196 and 1924 Ss varying in age from 4 to 5 years. (Freeman, 1950, pp. 211-12)

Hirsch (1926) examined 301 Nashville colored children from Grades 4 to 9 who were in schools considered to be fairly representative of the city's Negro population. These children achieved a mean IQ of 87 which placed them 12 points below the mean of the 682 Massachusetts mill town white children (Table 4).

BINET GROUP

The *Binet Group Test* is described by Peterson and Lanier (1929) as including 10 subtests, composed of items drawn from the individual *Binet* scales

---

[76]While this rating is much better than those of *7 or 8* characterizing the other three schools, it is about the same as the *deteriorating neighborhood* in Portland (Griffith) and the neighborhood from which Long's *underprivileged* group came in District of Columbia (1933).

but adapted to group use. Among the subtests are: finding rhymes, making change, ball and field, ingenuity, free association, *etc.*

Peterson and Lanier tested the intelligence of 86 colored and 119 white Nashville 12-year-old Ss by means of the *Binet Group* as well as by the *Myers Mental Measure* and the *International Group* (Table 3). On all of these tests the colored were inferior to the whites. The Negro Ss earned an average score of 15 points in contrast to one of about 26 points secured by the whites (Table 4). Ninety-four per cent of the white Ss scored above the median of the colored. Peterson and Lanier concluded that the Negroes on the whole were somewhat more variable than the whites; an explanation offered by the authors for the greater variability was that the colored may have had a larger percentage of dullards in their group.

ILLINOIS GENERAL

The *Illinois Examination, General Intelligence* is a group test requiring ability to read and to follow written directions. It includes tests of analogies, sentence vocabulary, verbal ingenuity, synonym-antonym, arithmetic problems, arithmetical ingenuity, and substitutions. The *Illinois* scale was given to 203 pupils whose mental ages had been determined by *Stanford-Binet*. The correlation between the mental ages by these two scales was .74. (Thurmond, 1933, p. 4)

Hewitt (1930) reported a median IQ of children from the seventh grade of two colored schools in a Southern community to be 90 on this scale; this placed them about 17 points below the median of white children from another school in the same system. Farr (1931) and Thurmond (1933) obtained much lower IQ's on the *Illinois General* when they tested village and rural colored school children in Tennessee and Georgia. Not only were their averages below those obtained by Hewitt (Table 4) but their range of scores was between 40 and 110 in one instance and between 49 and 100 in the other. In Thurmond's group, only 2.5 per cent overlapped the white norm of 100. The investigators commented upon the difficulty in reading with understanding and upon the inadequacies in the home and school environments of these Negro children.

DETROIT ALPHA

The *Detroit Alpha Intelligence Test,* designed for Grades 5 to 9, includes tests of information, opposites, classification, block design, generalization, analogies, number relations, and disarranged sentences. The reliability of the test, based on a retesting of 251 unselected sixth-grade pupils was found to be .91. (Garrett and Schneck, 1933, p. 40)

Jenkins (1932) recorded a mean score (not IQ) of 119 achieved by thirty-seven 12- and 13-year-old colored children in two North Carolina cities on the *Detroit Alpha;* this mean compared with one of 126 earned by 37 white children of the same age. The author did not indicate how she selected her small number of cases from these towns.

Wallace (1932) and Smith (1953) report their research in terms of IQ. It is interesting to note that the average IQ of the 200 *rural Alabama* colored Ss tested by the latter proved to be about 83, only some two points lower than the average given for 239 Cincinnati Negro children. Wallace tested colored subjects from the fifth grade of four public schools, giving each school a mean socio-economic score according to Sims method.[77] The mean IQ obtained for the several schools ranged from 79.56 to 88.03, the highest mean having been attained by the school sample with *lowest* socioeconomic rating. Unfortunately, Wallace did not test the whole fifth grade in any school and does not indicate the method by which she selected her cases.

Fowler (1959) administered six mental tests to 10-year-old Negro and white children in twelve Detroit schools located in different parts of the city and to 10-year-old Negro and white children in two Hamtramck, Michigan schools. Administering the *culture-controlled* tests of *Davis-Eells Games* and two forms of Cattells' *IPAT,* and the *conventional* tests of *California Mental Maturity, Henmon-Nelson Tests of Mental Ability,* and the *Detroit Alpha,* the author was able to determine whether or not a combination of the *culture-controlled* tests would produce higher IQ's (particularly on underprivileged Ss) than would the *conventional* tests. Fowler observed that the latter tests are similar in that they all draw heavily upon reading, mathematical concepts, word definitions, geometric designs, or general reasoning from a culturally loaded situation. As will be seen from Table 4, the Negro children achieved a combined mean of 88 on each of the two types of tests, some 16-17 IQ points below the test means of white children attending the same schools.[78] When the IQ's of the 69 white children of lower-lower socioeconomic status were compared with the IQ's of the 67 colored children of lower-lower status, the *Detroit Alpha* means were found to be respectively, 93.24 and 83.88.

McCall Multi-Mental

The *McCall Multi-Mental Scale, Elementary School Form,* designed for Grades 2 to 9, is composed of 100 groups of words; in each group the subject is to cross out the word that does not belong with the others. The relationships to be looked for vary and may be verb objects, opposites, modifiers, nouns, sequences, and identical elements.

The relatively low IQ of 77.46 was earned by the average colored child attending village or rural schools near Atlanta. (Mazique, 1934) Some of the teachers of these children were inadequately trained and the average salaries were reported to be low. The fathers of the pupils were mainly farmers, semiskilled and unskilled laborers. In spite of these apparent handicaps one child scored in the class interval of 120 to 124. Vernon (1936), likewise using

---

[77]See p. 163.
[78]See p. 165.

the *McCall Multi-Mental,* tested the colored and white children of two schools in Boynton, Oklahoma, which he considered to be nearly equal in educational opportunity provided. These Ss, some of whom were tested by *Otis Primary,*[79] scored higher than many groups tested, the medians of the whites and colored being 106.3 and 95.2, respectively.

Bousfield (1932) administered the *McCall Multi-Mental,* in addition to the *Otis Self-Administering Intermediate* and the *Pintner Non-Language*[80] to 222 Chicago Negro elementary-school pupils, the majority of whom were of inferior socioeconomic status. The subjects, whose method of selection was not given, scored five points below the *McCall* norm of 50 (Table 4).

Pressey Group

The *Pressey Group Intelligence Tests,* consisting of: rote memory, practical judgment, practical arithmetic, controlled association, logical memory, word completion, knowledge of moral terms, practical information, *etc.,* making 10 in all, were given to colored children in two small Indiana cities. These Ss were reported by Pressey and Teter (1919) to average the same as white children 2 years younger, with 14 per cent of the colored equaling or exceeding the norm medians. The colored were at their best in the test of rote memory and worst in tests of verbal ingenuity and knowledge of abstract terms. The authors observed that the test of rote memory had been found to be the poorest of the 10 in differentiation of subnormal and feebleminded, and Test 8 (disarranged sentences requiring verbal ingenuity) most differential.

In Peterson's study (1923), where both urban and rural Ss were examined by the *Pressey tests,* the white medians were significantly higher at each age level between 11 and 16 years, but not reliably superior at the 10-year level. While three of the seven colored schools were good ones, according to Peterson, in general the schools of the colored tested were not as efficient as those of the whites.

Murdoch (1920) gave the *Pressey* tests to large numbers of colored and white boys in Grades 5 to 8A in two New York City public schools. In Table 4 her results are given in terms of the percentage of the white (non-Jewish of American-born parents) and colored above the Jewish medians. At Age 10 the colored were superior to the whites and at Age 15 they were their equals; but at the intervening ages of 11, 12, 13, and 14 the colored were noticeably inferior. Relatively little significance was attached to the comparisons at Ages 10 and 15, since at Age 10 there were but 18 colored subjects and at Age 15 there were only 16 white Ss. Apparently children of these two ages in Grades 5 to 8A are not representative of their age groups.

---

[79] See pp. 79-80.

[80] See pp. 86 and 138.

Otis Quick-Scoring Beta

The *Otis Quick-Scoring Mental Ability Tests, Beta Form,* for Grades 4-9 are a revision of the *Otis Self-Administering, Intermediate Examination.* The reliability coefficient for the grade levels taken separately is about .79. (Kuder *in* Buros, 1949, p. 249)

This test was given by Younge (1947) to all of the sixth-grade pupils of the Tuskegee Institute Laboratory School in an attempt to determine the inter-relationship of intelligence, socioeconomic status, and achievement. The author described the status of these children as ranging from medium to high, the *Sims* median being 20 and the majority of the children having one or both parents who had attended college. The colored Ss achieved an average IQ of 92.22 with an *s* of 17.04; about 30 per cent of the group overlapped the white norm.

Cliff (1949), in a comparative study of the test performance of Negro children in "speed" and "power" situations, administered *Otis Quick-Scoring Beta* to 110 pupils in Grade 7 of an Atlanta elementary school under standard conditions with specified time limits. When they were first tested the colored boys and girls earned mean IQ's of 76.30 and 80.70, respectively. After the IQ's were recorded, the children were divided into two sections matched for sex and initial test score. Approximately five weeks later, all subjects were retested by the *Otis,* one group timed under standard instructions and the other group permitted to have as much time as desired. The boys and girls whose work was *untimed* scored 8.70 and 6.40 IQ points higher than the respective groups of boys and girls tested under conditions of *speed.*

In selecting fourth- and fifth-grade pupils from six Negro schools in Harde-man County, Tennessee, Hunt (1950) studied the relationship between intelligence, home background, and achievement of the pupils in attendance. These 134 Ss were less favored than the Tuskegee group as indicated by the following: 48 per cent were from broken homes, the heads of the households were typically sharecroppers or small farm renters, and the heads of the homes had no more than sixth-grade education in 84 per cent of the cases. However, home interviews showed that all of the children had 10 hours of sleep and had time provided for play, that 91 per cent ate three meals every day, that 70 per cent lived in un-crowded homes, that in 70 per cent of the homes there was a radio, in 52 per cent there were magazines, and in 33 per cent, newspapers. The range of IQ's of these children was from 43 to 111 with a mean of 71.

In a study of the competency of the prospective Negro teacher in Alabama, Allman (1953) included for purposes of comparison the mean IQ of 457 Birmingham colored pupils. Reporting on "all of the available eighth grade Negro pupils" in the public schools of this city, she indicated the mean as 84.06, the range from 44 to 117.

G. E. Clark (1957), whose experimental design has been previously reviewed in some detail,[81] found (as did Fowler in 1955) that underprivileged urban Negro children do not improve their IQ ratings when measured by tests such as the *Davis-Eells* over those obtained from the more conventional tests. In comparing the mean IQ's of St. Louis school children, Clark noted that at every socioeconomic level the *Otis Quick-Scoring Beta* mean was above the *Davis-Eells,* and that when the IQ's of all Negro children were combined, the difference of 7.01 points between the means on these two tests was highly significant (*t,* 10.29). As will be seen in Table 4, the white groups surpassed the colored at each socioeconomic level by 9 to 17 points. The colored children identified with *high socioeconomic level* (their status *actually closer* to that of the *low level whites* than to that of the *high level whites*) earned a mean IQ of 93.40 as compared with 94.65 earned by the *low level* whites.

Another investigation making use of the *Quick-Scoring Beta* was that of Murray (1947). Like Younge, Hunt, and Clark, Murray was interested in relating intelligence test performance to socioeconomic status. Murray reported that he classified his 401 Gary, Indiana, ten- and fourteen-year-old Negro subjects according to W. Lloyd Warner's technique used in his study of Yankee City. Accordingly, Murray identified his three classes as: *upper-* or *lower-middle, upper-lower,* and *lower-lower.* To varying numbers of 10-year-olds (131 to 193) the author administered three tests: *Kuhlmann-Anderson, Otis Quick-Scoring Alpha,* and *Henmon-Nelson, Elementary Examination;* to the 208 14-year-olds, he administered *Henmon-Nelson, High School Examination* and *Otis Quick-Scoring Beta.*[82] Murray did not say how many schools were surveyed, nor was his method of selection within a school always clear to this writer. Since Murray presented his data separately for the tests and for each status group, we have averaged the status groups as given for each test. As will be noted in Table 4, the mean IQ's of the 10-year-olds ranged between 86 and 91 on the several tests; the mean IQ's of the 14-year-olds were between 87 and 91. On *Quick-Scoring Beta,* the highest of the three status groups averaged 99.77, while the lowest averaged 82.67. These means are respectively higher than those obtained on the good-status groups in Tuskegee and St. Louis and on the low-status group in Hardeman County.

PINTNER GENERAL ABILITY: VERBAL

Three of the four batteries of subtests making up *Pintner General Ability Tests: Verbal Series* were employed by Jordan (1947, 1948) in his two North Carolina surveys. These include: a slightly modified version of the original *Pintner-Cunningham Primary Test* (involving responses to pictures); the *Elementary Test,* composed of two scales, the Picture Content and the Reading

---

[81]p. 114.

[82]The *Chicago Tests of Primary Mental Abilities* were reported as having been given to 14-year-olds who were in the 7th grade or above. However, no data on this test seem to have been included.

Content, the latter including vocabulary, number sequence, analogies, opposites, *etc.;* and the *Intermediate Test,* which includes the six subtests of the elementary battery and, in addition, a classification test and a best-answer test. As reported by Marzolf (*in* Buros, 1949, p. 255) the median intercorrelation for the intermediate battery is .58; the Picture and Reading Content correlate about .70; for fifth and seventh-grade samples, the batteries correlate .84 and .785, respectively, with total scores on the *Metropolitan Achievement Test;* and the reliabilities obtained by the split-half and interform methods for the various batteries are generally above .90.

Jordan (1947) tested 1980 white and 1214 Negro children in Grades 1 to 8 in a North Carolina county described as "predominantly rural". Although he attempted to examine all school children in the county, he found that he was able to test only 73 per cent of the white pupils and 65 per cent of the colored, those untested having been absent on the testing days. In fact, he found that in the case of some small schools for Negroes it was necessary for the examiner to return two or three times in order to have present enough children to be representative of them. As will be seen in Table 4, the mean IQ of the whites was 91.4 and that of the Negroes, 74.3. The whites proved to be the more variable as indicated by the sizes of the standard deviations. IQ's up to 120 were discovered among the Negroes, and those up to 170 among the whites.

In Jordan's Winston-Salem study (1948), 5429 white and 4856 colored children, comprising more than 95 per cent of the public elementary school enrollment in this city, were tested on the *Verbal Series of the Pintner General Ability.* As will be seen in Table 4, the mean IQ of the total white group was about 98, that of the colored, 81, the respective standard deviations being 17 and nearly 13. Nine per cent of the IQ's of the colored children overlapped the Winston-Salem white mean. The mean IQ's listed in Table 4 according to chronological age show reasonable stability and consistency except at the extremes where the factor of selection may be operative.[88] The standard deviations of the colored are markedly smaller at each age level than the corresponding values of the white pupils.

Jordan commented upon the fact that Winston-Salem is a manufacturing city and that many of the parents of the pupils tested (probably more than half of the parents of the colored and nearly one fourth of the parents of the whites) were employed as factory workers. He made a not uncommon observation that the homes of the Negro children were apt to be in the poorest section of the city and to have in them few of the appurtenances of our modern culture. In an attempt to control cultural differences, Jordan compared the mean IQ's of white and

---

[88]Noting the lower IQ's of Ss at 14-17 years, Jordan said that in general the normal and superior at the upper ages are either in high school or have dropped out of school. There were very few colored and white children in the 6-yr-old group, and relatively few at the ages of 14 and over as compared with those in the 7-13 age groups. Reviewer has omitted from the table the scores of members of both races who were 15 years of age or more.

colored pupils attending different schools. The mean IQ's of children attending the 13 white schools ranged from 90.2 to 108.3, the mean IQ's of children attending the six colored schools ranging from 79.1 to 82.6—the colored range being obviously smaller. The difference between the lowest mean of the white schools and the highest mean of the colored schools proved to be highly significant, the value of t being 9.27.[84]

Believing that the Negro IQ's are low because as a whole they occupy low socioeconomic levels and that those Negroes who are at higher socioeconomic levels produce children whose IQ's approach those of the whites, Jordan tabulated the mean IQ's of colored and white children according to the occupations of their parents. He was able to find the occupations of the parents from the record cards of approximately 3500 white and 4400 colored among his subjects. The present writer has included in Table 4 whatever occupational listings were common to both Negro and white parents. As will be noted, the white children were found to be superior to the colored in each category; in fact, all of the colored groups, with the exception of the professional which averaged above the white truck drivers, were below all of the white groups, in so far as they were represented by the IQ's of their children.

CALIFORNIA MENTAL MATURITY

The *California Test of Mental Maturity,* designed to test a mental age range from kindergarten to college and consisting of language and nonlanguage sections, presumes to measure five factors: memory, spatial relationships, logical reasoning, numerical reasoning, and vocabulary. Validity is chiefly implied, but a correlation of .88 with the *Stanford-Binet* is stated, for an unspecified level and range. The large amount of nonverbal material, especially at the higher levels, is distinctive of this test. (Garrett, *also* Line, *in* Buros, 1949, p. 223)

A review of the *Short Form* of this test indicates that total score reliabilities range from .92 to .95, and part-score reliabilities from .81 to .95, being higher at the upper age levels. Norms are based on very large groups, controlled with respect to age and school progress; however, no evidence is given about the geographic or socioeconomic distribution of the normative Ss. (Shaffer *in* Buros, 1953, p. 282)

Nineteen studies, using one or more forms of the *Mental Maturity,* were reported on colored children between 1947 and 1965 (Table 4). Of these, seventeen researches included Southern, one both Southern and Northern, and one Northern children; seven studies included white as well as Negro children; and eleven included urban, four both rural and urban, and four rural children. Ten of the 19 investigations have been reported in unpublished theses or dissertations from Southern Negro colleges and universities, the *California Mental Maturity* test scores having been studied in relation to a variety of items, such as: personal-

---

[84]Calculated by reviewer.

ity, interests, occupational choices, regularity of school attendance, delinquency, high rate of dropouts, home status, *Davis-Eells Games,* and speed *vs.* power.

The average IQ's of 75, 80, and 81 achieved respectively by three groups of colored children from the *rural South* (Hammer 1954, Boger 1952, and Sutton 1954) would appear to be indicative of the range of ability represented by the mean scores (not IQ's) reported by Johnson (1948) and Tate and Voss (1956).[85] Selected groups of *Southern urban* or *Southern urban and rural* children earned mean IQ's as follows: those irregular in school attendance, 72.18, those with perfect attendance, 88.59 (Harper, 1950); those who received regular promotions from the sixth to the tenth grades and had not left the school system, 80.58 (Osborne, 1960); "a selected group of Negro sixth graders", 94.00 (Queen, 1954); and a sample of colored children whose method of selection was not specified, 98.71 (Furlow, 1954).

In the Southern studies where all pupils in attendance were tested or where a random sampling was indicated, the mean IQ's of the colored children were recorded as follows: 76 (Dendy, 1952); 83.7 (Lewis, 1947); 86.20 (Cliff, 1949); 91 (McPherson, 1951); 87.00 (Tullis, 1964); 75.86 (Swan, 1965); and 84.36 (Osborne, 1965). Where the IQ's were not given, as in the researches of Parker (1954), Freeman (1954), and Tate and Voss (1956), the reported scores of the colored were lower than those of the white norms *below* their own grade, as will be seen in Table 4.

The Negro children tested in Cincinnati by Love and Beach (1957) achieved a mean of 89.2 on the *California Mental Maturity,* this IQ being significantly above the mean of 82.5 earned by the same children on the *Davis-Eells.* It likewise compares favorably with the mean IQ's of 85.0 and 88.2 earned on the *CTMM* by 470 boys and girls, respectively, all of whom reported as living in a culturally deprived area "more than 90% Negro" and enrolled in Grades 6, 7, and 8 of three Syracuse public schools.[86]

The Pennsylvania colored subjects (Tate and Voss) were significantly below the white pupils in another town of the same state at each grade tested and on the nonlanguage as well as the language portion of the scale. The *Davis-Eells* proved to have been more difficult for both the Northern and Southern colored pupils than the nonlanguage section of the *California Mental Maturity* but less difficult than the language section of this test.

In comparing *language* and *nonlanguage* scores on *Mental Maturity,* Boger (1952), Queen (1954), Sutton (1954), Tate and Voss (1956), and Love and Beach (1957), all found the nonlanguage scores to be the higher, a finding which was apparently anticipated and needed no explaining. On the other hand, Lewis (1947), Hammer (1954), Swan (1965), and Osborne (1965) found the reverse to be true; with them one might tentatively include McPherson (1951) who

---

[85]See Tables 3 and 4 and pp. 112-113 for design and results of the Tate and Voss research.

[86]Information supplied by David E. Hunt of Syracuse University to V. C. and V. J. Crandall and reported in their article. (Crandall and Crandall, 1965)

noted that colored matched with white children on *Mental Maturity* score, socioeconomic status, *etc.*, scored lower than the whites on the *Performance Scale* of *WISC*.

Hammer interpreted the lower scores made by Southern Negroes on intelligence tests and the significantly poorer showing of the Madison Heights Negroes on the nonlanguage than on the language tests as due in part to emotional disturbances. Noting that Wechsler found intellectual functioning in performance areas to be significantly lower than intellectual functioning in verbal areas among neurotic subjects, and observing that his own Ss appeared to be more neurotic as measured by the *H-T-P* (House-Tree-Person) projective test than he would have anticipated in a like group of white school children, Hammer concluded with suggesting the hypothesis that at least some of the lowering of the Negro IQ may be attributed to the presence of emotional disturbances presumably produced in part by the pressures, social, economic, cultural and interpersonal, to which the Negroes, as members of a minority group, are subjected.

Tullis (1964) attributed the significantly lower mean IQ earned by Negro children in a West Texas community to: (1) their low socioeconomic status, and (2) the use of culturally based intelligence tests, *i.e.*, tests measuring much the same learned skills as the Metropolitan Achievement Tests. "Taking into consideration the fact that the Anglos also rated significantly higher in such areas as social status, reading, word knowledge, and spelling but did not show this same span of difference in the less culturally based test of arithmetic computation, the theory of racial superiority or inferiority cannot be supported by these data." (p. 94)

Tullis assumes rather than demonstrates from his data a relation between social status and mental test score. The reviewer, using the author's frequency distribution tables, was able to match seven colored with seven white subjects for socioeconomic status. As will be observed in Table 4, their SS means were practically the same—60 and 60.86—but their mean IQ's differed by *21.43 points,* a difference significant at the .01 level of confidence.

Regarding his point that the colored Ss rated significantly lower in the culturally based Metropolitan Achievement Tests of Reading, Word knowledge, and Spelling, but that the difference between the racial samples was less in Arithmetic Computation, we wish to call attention to the fact that Tullis at no point reports the ages of his subjects. Since the colored were likely older at each grade than the white pupils the true amounts separating these ethnic groups in various achievements are probably masked. Further, in the opinion of the reviewer, Tullis should have indicated that the colored-white difference in Arithmetic Computation was also significant (at the .01 level). On the AC test we have found that the means of the 56 white and the 56 colored subjects were 6.06 and 5.26, respectively, the comparable standard deviations, 1.51 and 1.39, and the *t*, 2.91.

Osborne's work (1960) differs from the others in that he studied the mental-

and school achievement-growth of the same white and colored children over a four-year period. Selecting one county of a Southeastern state he administered the *Elementary Level* of the California Test Battery to children in the sixth grade; two years later the *Intermediate Level* of the same edition of the test was administered to the children in the eighth grade; and two years later the *Advanced Level* of the edition was used for the 10th grade white children and the *Intermediate Level for the Negro* tenth grade pupils. "When the advanced levels of the tests were used for the Negro 10th grade pupils of a previous year, it was found that the test was too difficult for the group as a whole and that the test scores were therefore spuriously low." (p. 234) Eight hundred fifteen white and 446 colored children were tested on the three dates. Students who dropped out, who were retarded, who were accelerated, or were absent on both the regular and make-up testing dates of any year were excluded, resulting in the samples being not unselective. In fact, 1388 white and 723 Negro pupils completed the California Reading, Arithmetic, and Mental Maturity Battery in the original 1954 testing, indicating an attrition rate over the succeeding four-year period of 41 per cent for the white and 38 per cent for the colored.

As may be observed from Table 4, the white children's mean IQ's were approximately 101, 101, and 102 when tested at two-year intervals, the colored means being 79, 84, and 79 during the same intervals. The mean IQ's for both racial groups remained relatively constant over four years but the range and variability decreased significantly "and the overlap all but vanished." During the four years the range of IQ's for each racial group was reduced by about 33 per cent. Osborne believed that the environmental interpretation of Negro-white differences in intelligence leaves unexplained the reason both Negro and white groups of the lowest initial intelligence earn higher IQ's at later ages while the bright children of both races tend to earn lower scores on subsequent testings. "The parsimonious explanation of the apparent change in IQ's from the 1954 to the 1958 testing seems to be the normal decrease in variability between ages 12 and 16 and the regression phenomenon of tests of less than perfect reliability." (p. 239)

DETROIT PRIMARY

The *Detroit Primary Intelligence Test,* for Grades 2 to 4, is one of a series of somewhat traditional type; the tests are satisfactory in form and the instructions appear to be adequate and clear. There is some evidence in the manual that the various sections of the test are less homogeneous than might be desired if the test is used beyond the local setting in which it was constructed. (Line, *in* Buros, 1941, p. 1393)

Cavins (1928) conducted a survey of the mental abilities of West Virginia third-and fourth-grade children as a part of a larger project in which children from Grades 1 to 12 were tested. The *Detroit Primary* was administered to samples of 230 colored and 3567 white children in Grades 3 and 4. Cavins describes the selection of his Ss as follows: "The first two grades . . . represent distinctly graded school systems including Parkersburg, Martinsburg and Buffalo districts; grade three represents all other schools in the forty-one tested districts; grade four contains pupils of one and two-room schools in the same districts;—." (p. 26) Cavins gives median chronological and median mental ages for his Negro and white groups according to grade. The reviewer, using these data, has estimated approximate IQ's which are included in Table 4. As will be seen from this table, at Grade 3 the estimated median IQ difference is 12 points, whereas at Grade 4 (including 1- and 2-room schools only) the estimated difference is but 5 points.

SRA PRIMARY MENTAL ABILITIES

Five factors are measured at each of the test levels in the present battery, only two of them, *verbal meaning* and *space,* being common to all three levels. The 7 to 11- and 11 to 17-year tests measure in common two additional factors, *reasoning* and *number,* the fifth factor at the 11-17 year level being *word fluency.* The 5 to 7 and the 7 to 11 level batteries measure in common the *perceptual speed* factor, in addition to *verbal meaning* and *space.* Factors measured only at the 5 to 7-year level are *quantitative* and *motor.* Tests bearing the same name at different levels do not necessarily utilize the same types of items. For example, the verbal meaning factor is measured at the 5 to 7 level by requiring the child to choose the picture corresponding to a word or idea stated orally. At the 7 to 11 level this factor is measured partly by a printed synonyms test and partly by a picture-choosing test. At the 11 to 17 level, the factor is measured entirely by a printed synonyms test. Reasoning, likewise, is measured by two subtests at the 7 to 11 level: "Which word does not belong?" and "Which picture does not belong?" At the 11 to 17 year level, reasoning is measured by a letter series test. (Frederiksen *in* Buros, 1959, pp. 709-714)

The test items are well written and the directions are almost always clear. The timing of the test is probably too brief. The best current estimates of the reliabilities of the five subtests are .72, .75, .83, .87, and .90, lower than most test specialists would like. We do not yet know much about the validities of these tests. (Kurtz *in* Buros, 1959, pp. 714-717)

The two investigations utilizing the *SRA Primary Mental Abilities Tests* include saturated samples of colored and white school children of certain grades who were living in Jackson, Mississippi, and in a small industrialized Pennsylvania city. In an unpublished study, Swan (1964) describes the results of a standardized testing program administered over a period of years to Jackson public-school children in various grades. In addition to the *Primary Mental Abilities* the testing program in recent years has included the Metropolitan Readiness Tests and the Metropolitan Achievement Tests. Only the *Primary Mental Abilities Tests* which were administered to all children (who were present) in the second, fifth, and eighth grades will be reviewed at this point, leaving the results of the testing of the tenth-grade pupils for the next chapter. In addition it should be noted that, although Swan obtained mean IQ's for the colored and white groups tested in 1960, 1961, and 1962, only in 1960 was he able to secure complete frequency distributions; hence his analysis of the *Mental Abilities* data pertains specifically to the 1960 testing.[87]

Altogether, 4486 white and 3111 colored pupils in the second, fifth, and eighth grades from the 25 elementary white schools and the 12 elementary colored schools were examined on the *Primary Mental Abilities* in 1960. As may be observed from Table 4: (1) the numbers in the eighth grade of both racial groups are about two thirds of those in the second, the attrition presumably due in the main to promotion failures and to dropouts; (2) the mean IQ's of the white children (107, 109, and 107) being relatively constant at Grades 2, 5, and 8, and the mean IQ's of the colored (94, 89, and 78) showing a decline from Grades 2 to 8, it follows that the difference between the racial means of 13 points in the second grade and the 29 points in the eighth is due to a decline in mean IQ of the older Negro children; (3) the differences between the mean IQ's at the three grade levels were highly significant, all of the critical ratios being over 30; (4) the children of both races seem to have become more heterogeneous in their test performance from Grade 2 to 8 (in contrast to the findings of Osborne that the *same* children who were promoted regularly *decreased* in variability from Grades 6 to 10);[88] and (5) the amounts of overlapping were not large, varying from 13 per cent in the second grade, to 6 and 7 per cent in Grades 5 and 8, respectively.

From Swan's tabulated frequency distributions the reviewer noted that the percentages of colored children scoring at the low end of the distribution, *i.e.*, *below 70 IQ,* were 2.7, 7.0, and 30.7, respectively, at the three grade levels, the corresponding percentages of the white children at these grades being 0.1, 0.3, and 1.5. At the other extreme, the percentages of the colored earning IQ's of *135 or more* at the three grades were 0, 0.2, and 0.1, the corresponding percentages of the white children being 0, 1.0, and 8.9. It is rather obvious now that the increase in variability, particularly at the eighth-grade level, was due in some measure to the increase in the percentage of high-scoring white children as well as to the great increase in the percentage of low-scoring Negro children. In the description of the three levels of the *SRA Primary Mental Abilities* at the beginning of this section, there were comments made to the effect that as the test advances from the primary level (Ages 5-7), through the elementary (Ages 7-11) to the intermediate level (Ages 11-17), the test items change from the pictorial type to a highly verbal one. It may be that the Jackson data reinforce the view that Negro children, particularly at the eighth-grade level or in the

---

[87]The respective mean colored-white differences at Grades 2, 5, and 8 for the three years are as follows: *1960*—13, 20, 29; *1961*—13, 23, 29; *1962*—13, 17, 30.

[88]See p. 177.

adolescent years, as a group are inferior in test performance that consists primarily in dealing with material that is of a complex verbal nature.

Wylie (1963) made a study involving the self-estimates of ability to do schoolwork and the ability for college work, using the IQ as a criterion of this kind of ability. The subjects were all children who were present on the testing day in the seventh, eighth, and ninth grades of the one junior high school in an unnamed Pennsylvania small city described as being highly industrialized and containing a four-year college. All of the pupils, 84 of whom were colored, had been tested previously by the *SRA Primary Mental Abilities.* Self-estimates of ability were secured simultaneously from the various groups of children toward the end of the school year. They included: (1) the child's chosen subjective equal, (2) the child's estimate of his standing in his home room, (3) the child's estimate of his ability for college, and (4) the child's expressed desire for college, assuming that he had the ability.

The occupation of the father was identified from the child's record card and was rated on a scale from one to seven, using Hollingshead and Redlich's socioeconomic scale positions, with one being the highest category. Nine and one half per cent of the Negro children and 21.8 per cent of the whites were thus located in occupational levels 1 to 4; 50 per cent of the Negro and 48.3 per cent of the white pupils were grouped in levels 5 to 7; the unclassifiables (fathers deceased, or records incomplete or ambiguous) included 40.5 per cent of the colored and 29.9 per cent of the whites.

As will be noted from the table, the mean IQ of the total colored group was 15 points below that of the white; the difference between the means is highly significant, the critical ratio being 8.47. Among the whites, the higher occupational levels are associated with a mean IQ of 9-10 points higher than the means of the lower and the unclassified groups; however, the small group of colored subjects at the higher occupational levels did not earn higher IQ's on the average than did the lower level. Wylie found that white girls, Negro children, and those of the lower socioeconomic levels made more modest estimates of their abilities than did white boys, white subjects, and children of higher socioeconomic levels, respectively. The author concluded that, in line with other studies and with the assumption that the mechanism of denial is widely used, her results indicate a highly significant self-favorable bias in the group as a whole.

PHILADELPHIA TESTS

The *Philadelphia Tests of Mental and Verbal Ability* are described as a series of group intelligence tests that have been standardized on Philadelphia school children and are somewhat similar to the *Otis* series of tests. For a number of years they have been given regularly to all pupils in attendance in Grades 1A, 2B, 4B, 6B, and 9A of the Philadelphia public schools and the several group IQ's are inscribed on each pupil's cumulative record card. (Lee, 1951)

Soifer (1937) in an unpublished Master's thesis attempted to determine whether or not colored children as a group are physically superior to white children and whether physical superiority is accompanied by lower intelligence. Soifer's subjects were pupils from the Holmes Junior High School in Philadelphia, all of whom were measured or tested in their physical education classes. All of them, except for an additional sample of 13-year-old white boys, were 14 years of age and all had been tested by the *Philadelphia Tests of Mental and Verbal Ability* in the sixth grade. One hundred fifty-nine white children and 152 colored children, about equally divided as to sex, served as the subjects. These children may be considered as relatively unselected junior high school students of 14 years of age, rather than unselected sixth-grade pupils, even though they took the test in the sixth grade, since only those pupils who had progressed to the junior high school were included.

As will be seen from the table, the mean IQ of the whites was 11 points above that of the colored children, the difference being highly significant; 18.4 per cent of the colored overlapped the white mean, and conversely, 83.7 per cent of the white children overlapped the colored mean. The author concluded that white girls and boys are more intelligent than colored girls and boys of the same age, but that colored are superior to whites of the same sex in jumping, throwing, and running.

OTHER TESTS

Hartill and Loretan (1940) reported briefly of an attempt to help antisocial boys in the New York City public schools. One of the 20 selected *problem schools* with 63 classes included only Negro pupils. The authors, without giving the name of the test used or the ages of the 1715 Ss tested, reported an average IQ of the pupils of this school to be 85 as based on group tests.

Bird, Monachesi, and Burdick (1952) in a study of racial attitudes, selected a group of 152 white and 31 colored subjects in Grades 3 to 5 from two public schools in Minneapolis, described as being located in middle-class and lower-middle economic class neighborhoods. One school was located in District *X* which had older houses and was closer to industry and business than was the school located in District *Y*. Two judges, employing the Chapin Social Status Scale, rated the residences — with the result that those of the white children received an average higher rating in both districts than those of the Negro children. However, both Negro mothers and fathers were found to have had slightly more formal education than the white mothers and fathers of the children tested.

Bird *et al.* did not indicate on what basis the white children were selected from the large group of 393 in these three grades, but they did note that all of the available colored children were included. Intelligence quotients (name of test or tests not given) were secured from the school records on 144 of the white and 30 of the colored children. As will be observed from Table 4, approximately 13 points separated the mean IQ's of the colored and white children in District X and 6 points separated the mean IQ's of the racial groups in District Y. The first of these differences, as calculated by the present writer, was significant to the .01 level of confidence, the second, not quite significant at the .05 level.[89]

Dinitz, Kay, and Reckless (1958), in a study of social background and delinquency proneness, report the administration of an unidentified intelligence test to 447 white and 270 colored children in the sixth grade of the Columbus, Ohio, public schools. The research included all of the children present at this grade level in 24 rooms of 11 elementary schools, the schools having been chosen on the basis of the Columbus population and dwelling area characteristics of the census tracts in which the schools were located. The schools, as a result of this design, ranged from those in the least desirable through schools in the most desirable tracts. School achievement tests and a structured schedule containing a section on social background, the delinquency scale, and social responsibility scale of the California Psychological Inventory were administered in the classrooms to all children present. In addition, the 24 teachers were interviewed and asked to place each of their pupils' names in one of three specific categories according to their estimation of his delinquency proneness.

The mean IQ achieved by the colored pupils was 86, or about 15 points below that earned by the whites; this difference was highly significant, the t ratio being 15.86. The IQ's of the whites seemed just slightly the more variable (Table 4). Finding that Negro students, regardless of sex, scored much higher on the delinquency measures, were much lower in school achievement, and were below the whites in mean IQ, the authors interpreted the results as reflecting more or less favorable growth of children (up to the sixth grade) which is determined in large part by a differential socialization impact in the various milieux in which they have been reared.

Price (1953) hypothesized that intellectual and emotional personality differences exist between Negroes and whites that are reflected in the *Rorschach*. Since Price depended upon a number of group tests in the selection of his subjects and since his findings and interpretations are related to the topic of Negro intelligence, the present writer is completing the survey of intelligence testing of Negro and white school children with a review of his research.

Price selected 90 white and 90 colored school children from the public schools of Gainesville, Florida, 30 of each race being at each of three age groups: 6, 10, and 14 years (Table 4). Since it was of primary importance that the selected

---

[89]It will be noted that these several mean IQ's are above those usually obtained on unselected groups of white and colored public school children in the United States. In this connection, the reviewer wishes to call attention to the mean IQ of 107 obtained on white kindergarten Ss in Minneapolis (F. Brown, 1944) and the mean of 108 obtained by W. S. Miller from testing of all 6A pupils in Minneapolis (Treacy, 1926). In light of these statistics the Bird *et al.* IQ's obtained in Minneapolis do not seem excessive.

subjects be representative of their age and racial groups, each group of 30 was to consist of 20 of average intelligence (in comparison with others of *same age and race*), 5 of above average intelligence, and 5 below average, resulting in a total of 60 children of average mental ability, 15 of above average ability, and 15 of below average ability for their respective races. The sex ratio was to be about one half male at each age level. Specifically, the subjects were selected as follows:

White 6-year- and 10-year-olds (from four elementary schools) — *above average,* random selection from lists of pupils scoring above 110 IQ on *Pintner-Cunningham* or *Kuhlmann-Anderson* and subsequently scoring above 110 IQ on *Goodenough Draw-a-Man; average,* random selection from lists of pupils earning between 90-110 IQ on the above tests; and *below average,* the random selection from lists of those scoring below 90 on the tests.

White 14-year-olds (from the Gainesville High School) — *above average,* selection based upon pupil's being "on grade for age or above grade for age," a year's average grade of B or higher, and a superior rating on *Draw-a-Man.* A check by author indicated that all Ss thus selected attained scores on the *American Council Examination* which placed them at least one standard deviation above the norm mean; *average,* subjects were on age for grade, had grade averages from C to B-, and were in average range on *Draw-a-Man; below average,* grade averages were below C and the *Draw-a-Man* IQ's were below average.

Negro 6-year-olds (from the Williams and Lincoln Schools) — *above average,* random selection of children whose *P-C* IQ's were above 95, based upon a plotted distribution of scores made by colored first-grade children in these schools; in addition, the Ss had to be above average on *Draw-a-Man; average,* random selection of Ss who had a *P-C* IQ ranging between 80-95 and who were average on *Draw-a-Man; below average,* selected in same way from those whose IQ's were below 80.

Negro 10-year-olds (from Lincoln School)—*above average,* selected from those having a year grade average of B or more, were on age for their school grade, and scored above 110 IQ on *Draw-a-Man; average,* selection from those having a year grade average of C to B-, were on age for their school grade, and earned between 90 and 100 IQ on *Draw-a-Man; below average,* presumably selected in the same way, *i.e.,* grade averages below C, overage for grade, and below 90 IQ on *Draw-a-Man* (this section seems to have been omitted by author).

Negro 14-year-olds — selected in the same manner as were the 14-year-old white Ss.

Rorschach was subsequently administered to the 180 subjects according to standard procedure. Beck's scoring methods were used throughout, and the data were treated under the headings of *intellectual factors* and *emotional factors.* A list of intellectual factors has been included in Table 4 with the means and standard deviations for each factor separated according to the colored-white dichotomy. The three age groups have been combined, making the number of cases 90 for each sample throughout. The first factor is the *total number of responses* which S gives to the series of cards and called "one of the most important indicators of intellectual functioning". Age, but not race, seems to have been a significant influence. In an analysis of variance the differences between age groups were significant at the .001 level of confidence, with the 6-year-olds having the lowest *response total*. The difference between races in the response total proved to be significant (.01 level) only at Age 14. "We see there an indication of a possible difference in intellectual functioning between the two races which is very slight or non-existent at the lower age levels but which begins to emerge as a definite difference in favor of the white group as they enter adolescence." (p. 18)

The Z score values, *representing the ability to perceive the elements of a situation and to combine them into a meaningful context,* indicate a difference significant at the .05 level between the two racial samples, the white subjects having the superior organizing ability. Analysis of variance performed on Z, or organizational total, showed age differences to be significant at the .001 level with the younger children having the lowest mean.

The F plus per cent is reported to give some indication of the agreement between an individual's perception and reality. There was little or no difference on this variable among the various age-race groups. The A, or animal, per cent indicates the percentage of the total number of responses that have animal content. The analysis of variance here indicated no significant age or race differences.

M or human movement response on the *Rorschach* is said to be the amount of intellectual energy a person brings to bear on adjustmental problems. The human movement response is also characterized as showing a subject's recourse to fantasy and is possibly an index to creativity. FM refers to animal movement responses. The analysis of variance on both of these factors shows differences between the races to be significant at the .05 level. The last factor refers to the percentage of responses based on the whole blot *(W)*, on a major detail of the blot *(D)*, or on a minor detail of the blot *(Dd)*. Although the differences were not significant, there was a tendency for the white subjects and the older subjects to give a slightly greater emphasis to the *W* responses.

In conclusion, the author found that the older child and the white child were better able to organize the stimulus field, were more imaginative, and were less stereotyped in the manner of handling intellectual problems. Also older and white children appeared to have been more energetic and creative than younger and Negro children. Racial and developmental differences were also noted in the *emotional sphere.* There seemed to have been a general trend toward introversion with increasing age and this was somewhat more pronounced among the whites. "Generally speaking, the younger children and Negroes seem to function in a somewhat less inhibited or controlled and less complex manner in the emotional sphere." (p. 38)

SUMMARY

We have tabulated and reviewed 103 studies of colored school children in which eighteen or more psychometric verbal group tests have been employed. Altogether, about 60,850 colored children were examined by these tests, about four fifths of them living in urban areas and one fifth in villages or on farms. Approximately 64 per cent of the subjects were tested in the South, 17 per cent in the Border states and 19 per cent in the North.

IQ's have been obtained on approximately 50,000 Negro school children. Aware of the fact that IQ's based on different group tests are not always comparable, we have calculated, nevertheless, a combined mean IQ on all the Negro children. This proved to be 84.01. Separating the colored into South, Border, and North, the respective averages proved to be 80.6, 89.8, and 89.7.

White children were examined in addition to the colored in 58 of the researches; the whites were found to have earned higher scores, on the average, in every investigation except one.[90] The differences between the measures of central tendency were typically large, and where t ratios were calculated (by the authors or reviewer) the differences proved to be significant.

In 45 studies the colored averages were compared only with established norms, either directly or by inference. In all but one of these the Negro averages were inferior to the norms, the exception being Long's District of Columbia group of 100 selected subjects.[91]

In 17 comparisons involving more than 13,000 Negro children, the results have included statistics on the amount of overlapping. The mean overlap of the colored on the white was 10 per cent.

Where measures of variability were calculated from the data, the white children proved to be the more variable in 45 comparisons, the colored the more variable in 21 comparisons, with no difference larger than 0.20 in three.

GENERAL SUMMARY

1. One hundred fifty-five investigations relating to the intelligence of Negro school children have been reviewed in this chapter. Some of the authors have reported on more than one group of subjects and on more than one test. At least 35 different group tests and 14 individual tests have been employed and approximately 80,000 colored children have been examined, excluding duplications.

2. These investigations include some 539 Negro-white comparisons,[92] direct or implied, since a particular researcher may have examined subjects in more than one city, county, or grade, or many have categorized mental test scores according to age, sex, or father's occupation. In order to detect the presence of

---

[90]McCord and Demerath (1958). For review and appraisal of this report, see pp. 129-130.

[91]Group II. For method of selection, see p. 35.

[92]Some of these Ss were involved in more than one comparison.

good-scoring small groups of Negroes at any specified age, grade, school, *etc.,* the reviewer has examined these 539 comparisons for relative standing of the colored and white S. Where whites were also examined in the same community, school, city, or state, as was the case in half of the comparisons, the position of the colored is related to the particular white group; otherwise the colored means are compared with the test norms.

In 522 of the comparisons the colored children scored the lower; in 291 of these their means were below those of the white groups tested, in 231 they were below the norms.

In seventeen of the 539 comparisons the colored scored the equal of or better than the whites with whom they were compared. In two of the comparisons it may be that the verbal test employed was not a valid instrument for measuring intelligence. Peterson and Lanier (1929) included white boys from foreign-speaking homes in their New York City group;[93] and Higgins and Sivers (1958) may have included few or many white subjects from foreign-speaking homes (in the opinion of the reviewer) since they indicated that all children of certain age and grade groups in public schools "serving the lowest socioeconomic areas of a northeastern city" had been tested.

In two instances the numbers tested were too small to allow one to attach significance to the findings (which the authors did not). Peterson (1923) found one group of *eight* colored 8-year-olds in Grade 1 to average the same as a group of *ten* 8-year-old white children in this grade;[94] and Kennedy *et al.* (1963), in their survey of mental abilities of Negro children in the Southeastern states, reported a mean IQ of 105 for a group of *six* children from the highest socioeconomic level.

In four comparisons (three of them being Long's) the subjects do not appear to this writer to represent a random sample of their respective populations. Long (1933) administered three tests to a group of 100 colored children in the District of Columbia, *the children being selected upon the recommendation of teachers and principals.* Klugman (1944) included in his analysis only the scores of colored and white subjects who scored between 90 and 110 IQ on each of two tests.

In four comparisons, those of Murdoch (1920) and Graham (1926), the particular samples do not represent their respective age groups, as these authors have noted. Murdoch, testing New York City children in *Grades 5 to 8A,* reported that at *Age 15* the percentages of native whites of American-born parents and of colored overlapping the Jewish medians were the same; at the age of *10 years* the colored boys showed a greater percentage of overlapping (61 *vs* 54) than the whites of American-born parents. Murdoch observed that 10-year-old colored

---

[93]Excluding these, the New York City white mean was the higher. For reviews of the Peterson and Lanier study and others referred to in this section, see pp. 34, 40-41, 96-7, 42, 35, 39-40, 187, 79, 35, 129-30, 46-47, 85, 126.

[94]Neither were these children representative of their age group.

and 15-year-old white children in Grades 5 to 8 are probably not representative of their respective age groups. Graham, using the *Otis Primary* with Atlanta colored children in Grades 2 to 4 with a few added at High 1, reported the colored to be slightly better than the norms at 7 years and also at 12 years. She was of the opinion that her 7-year-old colored Ss were probably rather highly selected since few were chosen from Grade 1; she also noted that 11- and 12-year-old whites in Grades 2 to 4 were relatively more retarded than 11- and 12-year-old colored in these lower grades.

Beckham (1933) reported the mean IQ of 100 Negro adolescents living in New York City to be about 105 when tested on the *Stanford-Binet;* and McCord and Demerath (1958) found *Kuhlmann-Anderson* median IQ's of selected colored and white boys living in Cambridge and Somerville, Massachusetts, to be between 95 and 99. In our opinion Beckham and McCord and Demerath have omitted pertinent data and/or have presented their results in a manner confusing to the reader. As a result, their findings are less meaningful and significant than they otherwise might be.

In three comparisons the Negro children seem to have been the equal of, or superior to, the norms group, without qualification. These include: the 54 unselected 6-year-old colored children in the first grade of Atlanta public schools who were reported by Graham (1926) as earning a mean IQ of 103; the 100 Ss of Long's Group I (1933) selected from a District of Columbia community identified as underprivileged, who secured a mean IQ of 102 on the *Dearborn* A; and a random sample of 491 colored children, all of whom had been born in the District of Columbia and tested on the *Kuhlmann-Anderson* in 1945-46, who achieved a mean IQ of 100. (Robinson and Meenes, 1947)

3. It is evident that all of the studies are by no means of equal significance. Certain of the tests have greater validity and reliability than others; certain of them are considered to be better measures of intelligence where the home and school environments are poor or inadequate. In some of the research work large numbers of subjects were tested; in other, smaller numbers were employed but efforts were made to secure random samplings of the given population areas; while in still other reports, either no mention was made of the method of selection of Ss or if the technique was recorded, it is obvious that the groups did not represent unbiased samplings of the school, community, or city. In some of the studies the data were treated analytically, including not only averages, measures of variability, critical ratios, percentages of overlapping, but analyses of test items.

Where results have been presented in terms of IQ, we have attempted to give a picture of the test data by calculating a combined mean of the colored subjects and relating it to the type of test administered, to the section of the country, and to the rural or urban character of the group. The combined mean IQ of the approximately 66,000 Negro school children tested (excluding duplications) proved to be 84.20; on the individual, the nonverbal and verbal group tests the respective means were 84.45, 85.00, and 84.01.

The combined mean IQ of 39,450 Southern colored school children was 80.5, that of 11,360 Border children was 90.8, while the mean of 15,450 Northern Negro children was 87.6. A qualifying factor here is the relative size of the Southern, Border, and Northern cities. The Southern urban children were selected less frequently from very large cities than were the Border and Northern urban children tested. The Border State average, furthermore, is heavily weighted by the great number of District of Columbia test scores (making up half of those of the Border region as a whole) and is therefore probably not representative of the Negro Border state children; with the exclusion of the District subjects their average IQ would be about 87.

At least 13,000 of the 66,000 colored pupils were living in rural areas or in small villages of less than 2500, about 84 per cent of them being in the rural South. The combined mean IQ of these children was 77.8, as compared with a mean of about 86 attained by Negro urban children on whom intelligence quotients were reported.

It appears that the Southern rural Negro child averages about 5 to 6 points below the Negro child of the urban South (respective IQ's being 77.0 and 82.6), and that the urban Southern Negro child averages about 5 to 9 points below the urban Negro child of the Border and Northern States (the latters' average IQ's being 91.1 and 88.3, respectively). If the rural and urban groups are combined, the average IQ of the Southern Negro child (80.5) is approximately 7 points below that of the Northern Negro child (87.6).

4. We have recorded or calculated the amount of overlapping in 37 studies in which white and colored school children were compared. By *overlap* we refer here to the percentage of Negroes' scores that equaled or exceeded the median or mean test score of the white group. Following each of the 37 investigations listed below, the number of colored subjects tested has been included. In eight of the researches the amount of overlapping ranged from *0 to 4 per cent*. They comprise the results of: Patrick (1926) 47; Peterson and Telford (1930) 74; Lambeth and Lanier (1933) 30; Thurmond (1933) 40; Hunt (1950) 134; Dendy (1952) 45; Wade (1954) 32; Tullis (1964) 56. In seven other studies the overlap was between *5 and 9 per cent:* Garth and Whatley (1925) 1272; Bean (1942) 49; Jordan (1948) 4856; Newland and Lawrence (1951) 1140; Osborne (1960) 446; Kennedy, Van De Riet, and White (1963) 1800; and Swan (1964) 3111.

In the following eight investigations the overlap was from *10 to 14 per cent:* Pressey and Teter (1919) 120; Schwegler and Winn (1920) 58; Peterson and Lanier in Nashville (1929) 86; Garth, Lovelady, and Smith (1930) 2006; Bruce (1940) 432; Cliff (1949) 116; Caldwell (1954) 420; and Tuttle (1964) 25.[95]

---

[95]The mean overlap on the 3 tests administered to one group of c and to one group of w Ss by Tuttle (1964) was 12 per cent.

In eight of the studies the overlap was from *15 to 19 per cent:* Haggerty (1921) 1538; Leggett (1921) 267; Peterson (1923) 115; Barnes (1923) 210; Soifer (1937) 152; Bice (1938) 457; Tanser (1939) 162; and Ries (1940) 380.

In two researches the overlapping was between *20 and 24 per cent:* Jordan (1922) 247; and Sunne (1924) 1113; in two the overlap was between 25 and 29 per cent: Younge (1947) 27; and Lindner (1962) 1800.[96] There was one in which an overlap between *30 and 34 per cent* was observed: Murdoch (1920) 227; no overlap between *35 and 39 per cent* was recorded; and there was one in which the overlap was between *40 and 44 per cent,* that of Peterson and Lanier, New York (1929) 187 Ss.

Among the various investigations the overlap ranged from 0 to 44 per cent, the total number of Negro cases, excluding duplications, being 21,477. The mean overlap based upon the total number of cases was found to be 12.3 per cent.

5. Variability appears to have been greater among the white than among the Negro subjects tested. Where samples of both racial groups were examined and the measures of dispersion recorded in terms of *s* or *Q,* the white children were more heterogeneous in 76 of the 111 comparisons, the colored were the more variable in 28 of them, and there was no appreciable difference noted in the remaining seven.[97]

6. One hypothesis that appears somewhat frequently in the literature and is supported by the findings of various investigators is that the IQ's of Negro children decline as they grow older. However, we have observed that "evidence" pointing to a decline in IQ at the elementary school level may be misleading, due in part to the presence of young children in the lowest grades (below compulsory school age and therefore not representative of their age group) and in part to the presence of over-age children in the upper grades (children who have neither left school nor have been promoted into high school and are therefore not representative of *their* age group.)

In attempting to verify this hypothesis, we have compared the mean IQ's of Northern and Southern Negro elementary school children Age *6 to 9* with those of other Negro school children from the same regions, Age *10 to 12.* We found 19 studies including about 9350 cases that appeared to meet our criteria: the records were in IQ units, the children were selected by saturated or random sampling, if children of only one age were tested (*e.g.,* 7 years) they were selected from the entire school or at least from several grade levels, and if more than one age group was tested (*e.g.,* 11 to 12 years) the results were tabulated separately for each age or were within either of the two age ranges employed. This meant, of course, eliminating studies where records of children were combined in other groupings (such as 7 to 12, 8 to 10, and the like) as well as eliminating all Ss

---

[96]Lindner (1962) tested the same Ss on *Draw-a-Man* that Kennedy *et al.* examined on the *Stanford-Binet.* Hence, in calculating a mean overlap for the total number of Ss, their overlapping percentages were first averaged and subsequently treated as one group of 1800.

[97]Any difference between the *s*'s or *Q*'s of 0.20 or less was arbitrarily disregarded.

whose IQ's were combined with those of children over 12 years of age. The resulting average obtained on the younger group was 84.03, that secured on the older group, 82.98. Being of the opinion that the presence of the six-year-olds may have effected the slightly higher average of the 6- to 9-year group (since education is frequently not compulsory until the age of seven) the reviewer excluded the IQ's of the 710 six-year-olds from the eight researches, with the result that the younger group's combined IQ was reduced to 83.33, just 0.35 above the combined mean of the 10- to 12-year group.

The present writer has also compared the mean IQ's of Negro children enrolled in Grades 1 to 3 and 4 to 7, selecting all Southern and Northern studies in which school children appeared to have been chosen by random or saturated sampling within these grades;[98] in addition, it was necessary for the results to have been tabulated separately for each grade or so combined that children in any of the first three grades could be separated from those in the last four. Grade 8 was excluded from the comparisons since some Southern school systems did not offer more than seven grades in the elementary schools. Accordingly, forty-three studies, comprising approximately 19,000 Negro school children, were divided into Grades 1 to 3 and 4 to 7. The respective averages proved to be 83.11 and 84.54.

Twelve of the above researches were conducted in the North, comprising 3315 colored Ss in Grades 1 to 3 or 4 to 7. The combined averages of these two groups proved to be 87.82 and 88.24, respectively. These averages, based upon the testing of relatively few colored school children in the North, are very close to that derived from the testing of 15,450 Northern Negro school children, i.e., 87.6.[99]

It seems, therefore, that between the ages of seven and twelve and between grades one and seven there is a marked stability in the IQ of colored children enrolled in the public schools.

7. A number of investigators have attempted to control environmental factors by selecting white subjects from relatively inferior or lower-class neighborhoods, or from public schools located in poor areas, and comparing their test performances with those of colored children living in either the same or in comparable neighborhoods. In at least fourteen studies, which are listed below, students in the field have singled out this factor of *neighborhood* in relation to Negro-white differences in IQ.[100]

Pintner and Keller (1922) selected for comparative purposes three schools from relatively poor neighborhoods in which a large majority of the residents

---

[98]The Border States were omitted from these particular comparisons because the colored children tested in this area were in large part from Grades 1-3, about 4500 of them being from these lower grades in the District of Columbia.

[99]See p. 205. Only six studies, involving a total of 2820 colored Ss and conducted in the North, could be separated into the two age groups, according to our criteria. The respective combined means of the 6 to 9 and the 10 to 12 age groups were 87.09 and 87.78.

[100]In this section we have included only studies where results were given in IQ units.

were foreign-speaking; Hirsch (1926) compared a "representative sampling" of Nashville Negro children with white Massachusetts mill town children of below-average environment; Hurlock, in two studies (1924, 1930) selected New York City schools, 40 per cent of the enrollments being colored and the children in attendance described as of the same social status; Williams (1935) obtained IQ's on pupils attending three Milwaukee schools, a larger percentage of the white than the colored being from families on county relief; Charles (1936) selected St. Louis schools in which the social environments of the white and colored were "similar"; Lichtenstein and Brown (1938) tested colored and white children living in a Chicago slum area characterized by a decreasing population, high rates of dependency, delinquency, and crime; Tanser (1939) compared *rural* colored and white school children in a county of Ontario, both racial samples considered to be of approximately equal socioeconomic status and from a community where racial prejudice was at a minimum; Ries (1940) compared the mean IQ of white pupils attending a Louisville junior high school in the least desirable of nine districts with the mean of Negro pupils attending the two junior high schools available to them at this time and located in districts approximating the living conditions in the poor white district; Mc-Pherson (1951) chose two public schools in East Waco, Texas from the same neighborhood because of the similarity between the living conditions of the people in the area; Bird, Monachesi, and Burdick (1952) compared colored and white middle- and lower-middle-class children from two Minneapolis public schools, the racial samples reported as not differing significantly in social status; Clark (1957) separated all white and colored children into *high, middle,* and *low* socioeconomic classes according to the characteristics of the neighborhoods in which the schools were located; Higgins and Sivers (1958) compared white and Negro pupils enrolled in public schools serving the lowest socioeconomic areas of a Northeastern city; and Semler and Iscoe (1936) selected particular schools for testing in order to minimize socioeconomic differences between the Negro and white school children of Austin.

The above fourteen studies have included data on approximately 2264 Negro school children and a larger number of whites. Differences between the various Negro and white means were determined and a combined mean difference was found to be 8.02 points.

In other investigations the authors have attempted to control environmental factors by "equating" the socioeconomic status of the colored and white homes according to some device such as the Sims Scale or according to the occupational status of the father, both parents, or status-parent. In the following thirteen researches, Negro and white children reported to be of the same or of somewhat similar socioeconomic status, or whose parents were of the same occupational status, have been compared. In certain instances, whites of low occupational status were compared with the colored group as a whole. Arlitt (1921) compared a group of white children of native-born parents whose fathers were either *semiskilled* or *unskilled laborers* with the total Negro group, 88 per cent of whose parents were of inferior or very inferior social status; Kempf and Collins (1929) examined the IQ's of Southern Illinois white children of native-born parents of the *unskilled laboring group* and those of the total group of colored subjects from the same urban and rural localities; Bruce (1940) matched a group of colored and white children living in a rural Virginia county according to their *Sims socioeconomic scores;* Griffith (1947) examined colored and white children from the *three lowest occupational groups* (with one exception) and who had been given very similar ratings on the Sims Score Card, all of these Ss attending one school in a predominantly Negro district of Portland, Oregon; Jordan (1948) compared the mean IQ's of his colored and white subjects living in Winston-Salem, North Carolina, according to the *occupation of the father;* Slivinske (1949) compared Negro and white rural school children of relatively superior socioeconomic status and those of relatively inferior status after the teachers had classified their homes according to a five-point scale with *superior* and *inferior* being at the extremes; Hess (1955) compared the test scores of groups of *low status* whites and colored in Chicago; using the Warner method of status classification, Fowler (1956) compared *lower-lower class* colored and white children of Detroit and Hamtramck, Michigan; McCord and Demerath (1958) compared the test scores of Cambridge and Somerville, Massachusetts colored and white children from *lower* and *lower-middle* socioeconomic levels, half of whom were believed to be predelinquent and half normal; McQueen and Churn matched colored and white children living in a Western city for residence, *occupation of father,* grade, age, and some other items; Tiber (1963), employing the McGuire-White Index of Social Status, compared the mean IQ's of a *lower-class* group of whites and a *lower-class* group of Negro subjects from a Southeastern public school system; Wylie (1963) analyzed the data secured on colored and white children enrolled in the one junior high school located in a small Pennsylvania city, after she had separated the Ss into *lower* and *higher* scale positions according to the Hollingshead and Redlich classification; and Deutsch and Brown (1964) compared the mean IQ's of colored and white public-school children who had been placed at about the same position on a socioeconomic scale derived from occupational prestige and amount of education of the main parent supporting the family.

The average difference in IQ between Negro and white children whose fathers were of approximately the same occupational group, or whose homes were comparable as to socioeconomic status, proved to be 12.80 points.[101]

From the several comparisons it would seem that, by selecting for testing colored and white school children who live in the same or similar neighborhoods *and* by reducing socioeconomic-status differences between them, there is a corresponding reduction in IQ differences from the usual 15-16 points to 8-13

---

[101]Based upon 4303 colored Ss whose means were compared with those of white pupils in the 13 studies.

points, or an approximate mean difference of about *11 points*. The size of this remaining difference (11 points) does not warrant our assuming that racial differences in IQ would be eradicated with further steps toward equality or opportunity. In the first place, the authors' statistics relative to parental occupational and socioeconomic ratings—based as they were upon information secured from the child, mother, other relatives, or teacher—included omissions and likely some inaccuracies. Also, in some of the comparisons, the authors indicated that the colored children were at a disadvantage in that their neighborhoods or homes were inferior to those of the white pupils, in spite of their attempts to match them. Even among those areas where both white and colored were living we would not consider the neighborhoods as representing the same status for the white as for the colored. This writer is inclined to think of mixed neighborhoods as districts where selective migration takes place more rapidly than in other neighborhoods and where it takes place in reverse order for the white and colored. As vacancies occur in white residential areas, those allowed to move in may include a few Negroes that are acceptable to the whites, perhaps because they are better educated, more enterprising, holding better jobs, and at least as able as themselves, "the talented tenth".[102] As they move in, comparable white families in the area, who are not only "talented" but perhaps prejudiced, may find reasons for moving to another area in the city or to the suburbs, thus making room for colored families in addition to the original arrivals. Hence any area in the process of becoming mixed would be one representing higher status for its colored than its white inhabitants, and would be accompanied by a reduction of mental differences among them. This theory has some support from the investigations which included Negroes and whites living in the same or in similar neighborhoods. In these neighborhoods the Negroes achieved a mean IQ of 88 which placed them about as much *above* the mean of colored school children in general[103] as the mean IQ of 96 earned by white children in the same or comparable neighborhoods placed them *below* the mean of white children in general.

8. A number of authors have analyzed their test results and have indicated areas in which the colored children seem to have the most and the least difficulty. Several of them, notably Pressey and Teter (1919), Schwegler and Winn (1920), Arlitt (1922), Graham (1926), and Kennedy, Van De Riet, and White (1963) found the colored to be at their best in certain *rote memory* or *immediate memory* tests. Schwegler and Winn (1920), Graham (1926), Thurmond (1933), and Nicholson (1949) found the Negro children to do relatively well in tests of a *practical* nature. Perhaps with this group might be included Caldwell (1954) and Teahan and Drews (1962) who reported their colored subjects as performing relatively well on the *WISC* subtest of *Comprehension* which depends upon a

---

[102]An aspect of the familiar selective migration hypothesis.

[103]In contrast to a mean IQ of 81 earned by the colored children who were matched with white children for socioeconomic status of the home or for occupation of parent.

certain amount of practical information and general ability to evaluate past experience.

Sunne (1917) described her subjects as having a keener sense of rhyme and a more fertile imagination than the whites tested, the latter point contradicted by the findings of Price (1953) on the *Rorschach*. Sunne also observed that her subjects had facility in *control of words,* a comment not at variance with subsequent reports of the following investigators: Lewis (1947), Hammer (1954), Young and Pitts (1951), Young and Bright (1954), Caldwell (1954), and Teahan and Drews (1962), all of whom found that Southern Negro school children[104] earned higher mean IQ's on the *language* (or *verbal*) sections of the *California Mental Maturity* (or *WISC*) than they did on the *nonlanguage* (or *performance*) sections of these respective tests. Likewise, Clark (1957) and Fowler (1959) reported that their Negro samples did not achieve higher IQ's on the pictorial type of test, such as the *Davis-Eells*, than they did on the more conventional or *verbal* tests.[105]

On the other hand, several authors have referred to *verbal difficulties* or *deficiencies* of their colored subjects; among these are Pressey and Teter (1919), Arlitt (1922), Sunne (1925), Graham (1926), Lacy (1926), Hewitt (1930), Jenkins (1932), Thurmond (1933), Murray (1947), and Kennedy *et al.* (1963). Young and Bright (1954), Caldwell (1954), and Teahan and Drews (1962) noted the poor scores earned by their subjects on the *vocabulary* test of the *WISC*.

The *Kohs Block Design,* the *Block Design,* and the *Coloured Progressive Matrices,* all of which involved working with colored abstract forms, seem to be difficult tests for colored children. Relatively low scores on these tests have been obtained by Graham (1926), Harris (1929), Young and Bright (1954), Caldwell (1954), Higgins and Sivers (1958), Teahan and Drews (1962), and Tuttle (1964).[106]

Difficulty with questions involving *logical analysis* and *abstract reasoning* was noted by Schwegler and Winn (1920), Peterson (1923), Sunne (1925), Graham (1926), Thurmond (1933), Bean (1942), and Sartin (1950). Price (1953), likewise, found that his colored subjects were less able than the whites to organize the elements of the *Rorschach* blots into a meaningful context and showed indications of being more stereotyped in the handling of intellectual problems.

9. Three investigators, Hurlock (1924), Klugman (1944), and Tiber (1963), have studied the relative effect of different incentives upon mental test perform-

---

[104]In Teahan and Drews' work the "southern" Ss were *Southern-born* but living in the North.

[105]Clark's colored samples achieved higher means on the *verbal* test employed.

[106]The researches of Young and Bright, Caldwell, Teahan and Drews, and Tuttle utilized the *WISC* which includes the *Block Design* as a subtest.

Tuttle's 25 Negro Ss, for example, earned about half the total *Block Design* raw score credited to his group of 25 white Ss of the same age and school grade.

ance of Negro school children.[107] If one were to combine the results of the first two researches one would conclude that the incentives of the Negro children rank in the order of: money,[108] praise, reproof, and none; whereas, for white children the rank order of the incentives would be reproof, praise or money (no difference), and none; the only significant differences appear to have been between the effects of *praise or reproof* as against *none* for both racial groups (Hurlock) and between *money* and *praise* for the colored children (Klugman). If, however, one were to substitute candy mints for pennies and to improve upon the experimental design in several ways as Tiber did, he would find that for the colored subjects the rank order of incentive would probably be: candy, praise or none, and reproof; and for the white Ss: candy or none, and reproof or praise — with none of the differences being significant. By omitting the *no incentive* category[109] throughout we note that for the mean Negro child the pattern is the same in the three studies — being, money or a reward of candy, followed by praise, followed by reproof. We also observe that the differences between the mean IQ's of the colored children, when one rather than another of these incentives was employed, vary from about one to 3.4 points. This seems to be an area in which further research is desirable.

---

[107]For a summary of the designs of these experiments see pp. 39-40 and 42-43.

[108]A penny given to a child following certain specific correct answers; no child earned more than 15 cents and no one earned less than 5 cents.

[109]We do not mean to infer that there was actually *no incentive*, of course, rather that there was no *specific* incentive under the control of the investigator.

Chapter IV

HIGH SCHOOL AND COLLEGE STUDENTS

HIGH SCHOOL STUDENTS

Fifty-five studies, in which the authors have reported the testing of more than 23,600 colored high school pupils, excluding duplications, are summarized in Table 5. Of these, 33 were conducted in the South, six in the Border states, 14 in the North, and two in more than one section of the country. Twenty tests were employed, including eight which have been administered to school children.[1]

TERMAN GROUP

The *Terman Group Test of Mental Ability* consists of the following ten subtests: information, best answer, word meaning, logical selection, arithmetic, sentence meaning, analogies, mixed sentences, classification, and number series. For any item to be included in the test it had to distinguish between children of known brightness and children of known dullness. "This was a good test when it was first published in 1920, both in terms of its intrinsic and relative values. There were no other group tests which were unmistakably better." (Easley, *in* Buros, 1941, p. 1424)

Boots (1926) and Davis (1928) obtained *Terman Group Test* IQ's on Mississippi and Texas colored pupils and found the respective averages in the two states sampled to be 81.33 and 78. The large number of white high school pupils tested by Boots in the same state earned a mean IQ which was 13 points higher than that attained by the Negroes. The standard deviation of the whites' distribution was likewise larger than that of the colored. When he separated his subjects into *city, town,* and *rural* groups, Boots noted that the city whites were about 15 IQ points above the city Negroes on the average, the town whites 20 points above the town Negroes, and the rural whites 10 points above the rural colored. It is possible that the rural white and colored schools were more nearly alike than the city or town white and colored schools; or it may be that the cities of Mississippi exerted a greater "pull" on the brighter rural whites than upon the brighter rural Negroes.

---

[1]The 8 tests are: *International Group, Otis Self-Administering Intermediate, Myers Mental Measure, Chicago Non-Verbal, Otis Group Advanced, Kuhlmann-Anderson, California Test of Mental Maturity,* and *SRA Primary Mental Abilities.* Brief descriptions and appraisals of these tests have been included in Chapter III and are not repeated in this chapter.

In the spring of 1922, the *Terman Group Test* was administered to all pupils of the junior and senior high schools in Lawrence, Kansas. Selecting all papers of the colored and every third paper of the whites after they had been arranged alphabetically by school grade, Barnes (1923) calculated means and medians and found those of the colored to be approximately two thirds of those of the whites. The standard deviations were unusually large for both groups, as will be noted in Table 5. While Barnes observed a marked deficiency on the part of the colored subjects in all of the ten subtests, he found the disability to be greater in the following four: word meaning, sentence meaning, arithmetical reasoning, and completion of number series. This author pictured the Negro child tested in Lawrence as having a marked vocabulary difficulty, as being weak in reasoning (as shown in mathematical situations), and as being at a great disadvantage in problems calling for quick analysis of new situations and for the manipulation of abstractions (such as presented in subtest 10).

In his Master's thesis, H. L. Jones (1940) compared the physical skill and intelligence of 200 Denver, Colorado, junior high school boys. A total of 485 boys from the Carlos M. Cole Junior High School, all of whom having been previously tested by the *Terman Group,* were given the *Johnson Skill Test* in their regular gymnasium classes. From this number a random sampling of the records of 100 Negro and 100 Spanish-American boys was selected for comparison. Both groups averaged below the norm of 100 on the *Terman Group,* with the Spanish-American mean being 4.5 points below that of the colored. Although he indicated that both samples came from rather poor and inadequate environments and that the junior high school was located in a neighborhood tending toward a large and increasing proportion of Negro- and Spanish-Americans, Jones did not mention whether or not the children of the latter group (presumably of Porto Rican and/or Mexican stock) were from Spanish-speaking homes. It may be assumed that some or many of them were bilingual, and if so, the *Terman Group* may not have been a valid test for them.

INTERNATIONAL GROUP

Peterson and Lanier (1929) administered several tests to colored students attending the Agricultural and Industrial Normal College in Nashville and to white students at the State Teachers College in Murfreesboro, Tennessee. Since both schools surveyed included high school as well as college level Ss the results of the three tests have been placed in Table 5. On the *International,* the 135-138 colored students were below the 100 whites on the average in each of the five subtests, the differences in four of them being large and significant. In terms of overlapping, 81.4 per cent of the whites equaled or exceeded the combined test scores of the colored. The authors considered it highly probable that real innate differences in intelligence, as well as environmental differences, were shown between the two racial groups on these tests.

Otis Self-Administering

Eleven studies summarized in Table 5 include the measurement of intelligence by the *Otis Self-Administering Tests of Mental Ability*. The *Higher Examination* was usually given, but some authors did not specify the form of the *Otis;* in these instances, if a junior high school group was tested we have inferred that the *Intermediate Examination* was administered.

Williams (1938), Gray (1945), Dunn (1946), and Johnson (1946) gave the *Otis S-A* to colored high school pupils in Mexia, Texas, in 22 Louisiana parishes, in Montgomery, Alabama, and in Houston, Texas, respectively, and secured mean IQ's of 93.45, 85.77, 89.85, and 82.70. With the exception of Gray's subjects they represent from three to four high school grades; in all instances the numbers tested are reasonably large (104-508) and the standard deviations small (where calculated); with the exception of William's subjects the students were reported to have been selected either by the saturated- or by the random-sampling method. However, attention should be called to the fact that the Montgomery pupils (Dunn, 1946) were enrolled in the State College Laboratory High School and therefore were probably not representative of the colored high school students of that city.

Gray (1945) was interested in securing a sampling of high school seniors who were expected to graduate in June, 1942. With the aid of some Fisk University research fellows, Gray administered the *Otis S-A* to this class in 29 Louisiana high schools, representing 22 parishes in the state and typifying all major economic, social, and geographic categories. About two thirds of the subjects tested were girls and they came from families whose children numbered 4.2, on the average, and lived in homes of 4.5 rooms, on the average; the vast majority of their parents had not been beyond the elementary schools and relatively few had gone to college, indicating "a barren educational background". In addition, the pupils seemed to be inexperienced in taking mental tests and not only their cultural but their geographic background was very different from the norms group. In general, the Louisiana subjects seemed to be handicapped by a lack of energy, drive and ambition, *esprit de corps,* and the ability to cooperate.

Peterson and Lanier (1929), McGurk (1943), and Stainbrook and Siegel (1944) tested Southern groups of high school students, but did not report their results in terms of IQ.[2] Peterson and Lanier found a significant difference between the medians of the 243 Negroes at the Agricultural and Industrial Normal College and the 301 whites at the Middle Tennessee State Teachers College, with 93.5 per cent of the whites overlapping the colored. After selecting every tenth name from alphabetized lists of colored and white children attending the Richmond public schools[3] McGurk gave a number of tests to grade and high school Ss. The mean *T* scores of the 535 white high school pupils were found to

---

[2]McGurk translated the raw scores on the *Otis* into *T* scores.
[3]Alphabetized within each grade.

be about the same as the *Otis* norms; the means of the 145 Negroes were significantly below the Richmond whites as well as the *Otis* norms.

Testing small groups from the tenth grade of two high schools of a "Southern city", Stainbrook and Siegel found the colored mean score to be below that of the white. The *Otis* testing was incidental to the *Group Rorschach* administered to these subjects. An analysis of the latter showed *less productivity* of responses among Negroes than among the whites. The responses of the colored were also described as *less fluid* and having "less differentiation in association" than those of the whites. Finally, the colored were found to be more emotionally stable, less impulsive, and less anxious than the white pupils.

In a National Survey of colored high school seniors, the *Otis S-A* was administered to Ss in 15 urban and 19 rural high schools; the urban high schools were located in nine Southern states, the rest being in Border and Northern cities; the rural schools were all located in the Southern states. All seniors present were tested except in "schools with large enrollments, in such cases one-half of the group was chosen by selecting every other name from alphabetically arranged class rolls." The median of all of the 2097 Ss was reported to be 34, which was 10 points below the national median for high school seniors. The medians of the 15 urban high schools varied between 30 and 43; the medians of the 19 rural high schools ranged between 20 and 40. The lower performance of the rural Ss on the *Otis* was attributed in large part to the poorer schools and inadequate facilities provided the rural pupils.

Lacy (1926) and Anderson (1947) utilized the *Otis S-A* in the testing of Oklahoma colored high school students. As a part of an Oklahoma City testing program Lacy examined all colored high school Ss, obtaining mean IQ's of from 81 to 85. Lacy was of the opinion that his Ss were highly selected, owing to the large amount of retardation among colored children below the high-school level. Anderson, testing 153 colored high school pupils in Okmulgee, reported the range of IQ's to be from 80 to 124 with a relatively high mean of 103.25.

Testing 155 white and 122 colored subjects, described as unselected,[4] Clinton (1931) noted that the mean IQ of the former was about 16 points above the latter, the respective means being 100.5 and 84.5.

MYERS MENTAL MEASURE

The *Myers Mental Measure* was used to compare the intelligence of Murfreesboro and Nashville Ss (Peterson and Lanier, 1929) and Richmond students (McGurk, 1943). All of these subjects were tested on the *Otis S-A*. As will be noted in Table 5, the difference between the Tennessee groups on the *Myers* was significant, with 88 per cent of the whites overlapping the colored median. The Richmond whites were likewise significantly superior to the colored.

---

[4]Probably in New York City. See fn. 6 to Table 5.

CHICAGO NON-VERBAL

McGurk tested the Richmond white and colored high school pupils by the *Chicago Non-Verbal Examination,* in addition to the *Otis S-A* and *Myers,* and reported the difference between the means to be significant.

OTIS QUICK-SCORING GAMMA

The *Otis Quick-Scoring Gamma Test* is a revision and extension of the *Otis Self-Administering, Higher Examination.* It consists of 80 items, mainly verbal, including: analogies, vocabulary, opposites, mixed sentences, reasoning, proverbs, *etc.* The test is reported to correlate about .86 with the *Otis S-A, Higher Examination.* (Pintner, *in* Buros, 1938, p. 1053)

Seven studies, six of them located in the South, have dealt with the testing of colored high school students by *Otis Q-S Gamma.* McClain (1948) used this test in measuring the intelligence of junior and senior high school students of Montgomery County Training School, in Waugh, Alabama. The mean IQ was 79.43, the standard deviation, 8.92, and the range, 45-103. Dividing the subjects into three age groups, 11-14, 15-18, and 18-24 (identified as preadolescent, adolescent, and postadolescent, respectively) McClain reported the IQ's to be 84, 74, and 72.

Without revealing the method of selection, Petway (1948) reported testing 50 Negro boys and 50 Negro girls from the ninth grade of a junior high school in Nashville, Tennessee, obtaining a mean IQ of 84.1, a standard deviation of 9.7, and a range from 67 to 114. Royster (1954) was interested in determining the difference between the intelligence of urban and rural seniors in eight high schools in four Alabama counties. The mean IQ of the urban subjects was 84.09, that of the rural, 74.46. No measures of variability were included in the results. Royster mentioned the advantages experienced by the urban groups when compared to the rural, among them—better qualified teachers, higher economic status, and a longer school term.

Berry (1954) examined the relationship between mental ability as measured by the *Otis Quick-Scoring Gamma* and mechanical and art aptitude among colored high school girls attending Pike County Training School. Having selected 50 of the 450 pupils enrolled in the school by a method of random sampling, Berry reported a mean *Otis* IQ of 78 and a standard deviation of 6.6 (Table 5). Only one S scored above 98, *i.e.,* between 99-101, indicating that no more than two per cent equaled or exceeded the median of the norms group. While noting that the socioeconomic status of the colored girls approximated that of most Negroes living in rural Alabama communities the author observed that in this Training School they were taught by 18 well-qualified instructors.

Geisel (1962) studied the potential ability of Negro and white pupils as measured by their *Lorge-Thorndike* or *Otis Q-S* test scores and their educational and occupational aspirations. From a "Southern city" of approximately 150,000 population, Geisel selected subjects from one white and one colored high school and from two white junior high schools and two colored junior high schools, the junior high schools being so chosen that one for each racial group would be in a lower socioeconomic area of the city and one for each in a higher socio-economic area. All of the 1245 white and the 777 colored subjects were divided into two socioeconomic status groups according to the education attained by the parents, *i.e., lower,* if the completed education was less than the 12th grade, and *higher,* if it was the 12th grade, or more. As will be seen from the table, the total group of white pupils earned a mean IQ of 108, the colored, a mean of 89.7; the means of the *upper* colored and white Ss differed by 21 points, the difference between the *lower* means was 12.5 points; all of the three differences were highly significant. Although their IQ's were lower on the average, the colored subjects scored significantly *higher* than the whites on *self-evaluation* and had higher educational and occupational aspirations.

Roland and Swan (1965) have compared the *Otis Q-S* IQ's of colored and white high school pupils of Wilmington, North Carolina. As a part of the regular testing program all 7th, 8th, and 9th grade pupils in attendance were examined in 1956. Three years later, all of these pupils who remained in the school system and had advanced to the 10th, 11th, or 12th grade were retested. The colored and white students were attending separate schools and were tested by teachers of their own race. The mean IQ's of the white and colored Ss at the junior high school level were 99.55 and 81.24, respectively, their means at the second testing were somewhat higher, *i.e.,* 101.98 and 84.62, both of these differences being highly significant.

Approximately five per cent of the whites and no colored pupils reached or exceeded an IQ of 120 in Grades 7-9, whereas 18 per cent of the colored and about two per cent of the white students scored below 70. In Grades 10-12, seven per cent of the whites and no colored Ss earned an IQ of 120 or more, while seven per cent of the colored and 0.2 per cent of the white pupils earned IQ's below 70.

In studying the relationship between intelligence and frustration-aggression patterns, McCary and Tracktir (1957) administered the *Otis Q-S Gamma* and the Rosenzweig Picture-Frustration Study to 188 white and 87 colored pupils in an integrated high school in Pittsburgh, Pennsylvania. All of the subjects were described as being from *middle, middle-class families.* Separating the sexes, the authors found the colored males to average significantly below the white males in IQ, the respective means being 96.8 and 104.8, the *t* ratio, 4.60; similarly, the colored females averaged significantly below the white females, the respective mean IQ's being 93.9 and 105.5, the *t* ratio being 4.56. On the other hand, the differences between the sexes *within* the races were not significant. McCary and Tracktir further divided the four race-sex groups into subgroups of *high, middle,* and *low* intellectual levels, and compared the subgroups to ascertain the relationship between frustration-aggression patterns and level of intelligence. The *low IQ Negro males* were *more overtly aggressive,* the *low IQ white males* being *more self-blaming* and also *conforming more closely* to the group; the *middle IQ white females* exceeded the *middle IQ Negro females* in *need-persistence,* these differences being the only ones reported as significant at the .01 level of confidence.

OTIS GROUP ADVANCED

Collum (1937) employed the *Otis Group Advanced Examination, Form B* in comparing the abilities of white and colored high school students in Southern Oklahoma. The two schools selected were of similar size, fully accredited, of the same length of term, and had teachers with qualifications above the average for schools of their size. Both offered the same subjects in grade and high school; other factors such as buildings, equipment, and library facilities were equal. The mean IQ's of the white and colored groups were 101 and 88, respectively; 13 per cent of the colored overlapped the mean of the whites.

CALIFORNIA CAPACITY

The *California Capacity Questionnaire,* a short and revised form of the *California Test of Mental Maturity,* was administered by Smith (1942) to 95 colored pupils of Grades 10 to 12 in the Atlanta University high school. A wide range of scores from 65 to 130 was reported, as well as a relatively low mean of 92.25, considering the fact that these university high school pupils were a selected group.

In a study of the sociocivic and religious attitudes of high school pupils, Fallin (1949) gave the *California Capacity Questionnaire, Form A* to 194 Dunbar High School pupils in Bessemer, Alabama. The median IQ proved to be 78, the quartile deviation 8.5, and the range from 60 to 108. Fourteen per cent of the subjects were below 70 IQ and 2.1 per cent equaled or exceeded 100. The author found that in most cases the pupils were in the correct grade for their age and that the compulsory attendance law was being complied with in this school area.

AMERICAN COUNCIL ON EDUCATION

The *American Council on Education Psychological Examination for College Freshmen, Form 1939,* provides two scores, a *linguistic* value based on a composite of same-opposites, completion, and verbal analogies, and a *quantitative* value based on a composite of arithmetic, number series, and figure analogies. The linguistic score is weighted about twice as heavily as the quantitative. No evidence is offered as to the reliability of the test. Validity of the 1938 form is shown in the correlation of about .50 with results of each of four 6-hour examinations in introductory courses in biology, the humanities, physical sciences, and social sciences. (Dunlap, *in* Buros, 1941, p. 1377) "This is perhaps the test that one is likely to recommend to anyone who is looking for a 'good' intelligence test to give to a group of college freshmen." (Commins, *in* Buros, 1949, p. 217) The *ACE* for *High School Students* has similarly a language and a quantitative section. Validity is based on the a priori relevance of the material to scholastic aptitude and the similarity of the tests to others which have been validated in the school room. Hovland (*in* Buros, 1949, p. 218) quotes from the Thurstones in their Manual, 1946 Edition: "While the scores do show roughly the mental alertness of the student, they should not be thought of as measuring mentality with high accuracy . . .".

Brooks (1942) tested 285 seniors enrolled in the Negro high schools of the Portsmouth-Norfolk area on the *1939 College Form* of the *ACE*. These seniors, who were examined one month before graduation, earned a mean score which corresponded to the *3.5 percentile rank* on the national norms for college freshmen. A small number of Ss whose fathers were in the professions scored at the twelfth percentile on the college freshman norms. Dozier (1946) gave the *1944 High School Form* of the *ACE* to girls in the first year mathematics course at a colored high school in Davidson County, Tennessee. The mean raw score of 39.75 and range of 13 to 67 compare unfavorably with the high school norms; according to the norms the mean score for eleventh grade pupils on the total test is 79.61, the author estimating that the average score for the ninth and tenth grades would be between 65 and 73. There was apparently no overlap of the colored on the norms. It should be noted that although the Haynes High School is only four miles from downtown Nashville it was the only one for Negroes in the county in 1946 with the result that the majority of the pupils came to the high school from rural schools. The parents were described as farmers, factory workers, domestics and janitors, railroad workers, skilled workers, grocers, preachers, and housewives.

The very poor showing of Negro high school students on the *ACE* is emphasized by the results of Williams' study in Alabama (1946). Testing 457 Negroes representing the *upper half* of their class at a state academic meet for high school seniors, Williams secured a mean of 19.35 and scores ranging from 0 to 32. The norm for college freshmen on the *1945 College Form* given to these Ss was *101.5*. It is obvious that there was no overlapping on this test.

Bottosto (1959) investigated the relationship between certain median county-wide socioeconomic measures and median county-wide intelligence and academic achievement levels of high school seniors throughout the state of Florida. During the academic years of 1955-56 and 1956-57 nearly all of the state's *white* high school seniors participated in the Florida State-Wide Twelfth-Grade Testing Program shortly before graduation; as a result, Bottosto was able to include in his dissertation data pertaining to 19,749 white pupils from 213 public and 32 private high schools located in 67 counties of the state. Fewer of the nonwhite high schools participated in the Testing Program Battery (the program being voluntary); however, the author succeeded in obtaining adequate data on 4277 high school seniors enrolled in one private and 86 public nonwhite high schools in 50 of the 67 counties.[5]

In the absence of scaled scores for the intelligence portion of the test battery, the original raw scores of the *ACE* were given a mean and standard deviation comparable to those of the achievement test scores. Since the Florida achievement scores had been scaled with reference to national norms, the procedure followed produced a set of county median intelligence scores comparable to the county median achievement scores and the national norms. With 50 representing the national average according to the scaled scores, the median-county score of the Florida whites was 46.8, the median-county score of the Florida nonwhites, 37.4. The range in county medians, as will be noted in Table 5, was 41 to 52 for the whites and 29 to 44 for the nonwhites; in the 50 counties where both whites and nonwhites were included in the report, the *lowest median-county* score of the whites was *above* that of the *highest median-county* score of the nonwhites; however, among the 17 additional counties (where nonwhite scores were excluded because of insufficient or inadequate data) there were *four median-county* scores of the whites *below* that of the one highest nonwhite county median (among the 50).

The correlations calculated by Bottosto for the *white* population indicate a high degree of association between intelligence and the socioeconomic factors of: median years of school completed by adults, median annual family income, and measure of schooling and income combined. Intelligence, schooling, and family income were all intercorrelated and presumably exert a reciprocal influence on each other, according to the author's findings; in fact, Bottosto considered it "quite possible that high levels of schooling and intelligence are powerful contributors to the development of high income and social status levels among the counties of Florida." (p. 178) He found notably *lower* correlations for the *nonwhite* population and interpreted the fact as probably attributable to the particular measures of socioeconomic factors and intelligence employed, since these revealed less variability among the nonwhites than among the whites. An interesting finding reported by the author was that *nonwhite county income-level* was more highly associated with *nonwhite pupil intelligence* than was the *nonwhite county level of schooling.*

KUHLMANN-ANDERSON

In reporting the unusually low *ACE* scores on the 74 Davidson County Negro girls, Dozier referred to the fact that these pupils had scored relatively better on another test. Each year all children entering the high schools in this county were given an intelligence test and during the preceding years the *Kuhlmann-Anderson* had been used. The average IQ obtained in 1944 and 1945

---

[5]Bottosto noted that according to the 1950 Census the Negro population for the state of Florida was 603,101, while the total for other nonwhite races was 2153. The colored, therefore, made up nearly the whole of the nonwhite population, *i.e.*, 99.6 per cent.

on the *K-A* was 85 for this group. Eight per cent of the Negro girls overlapped the white norm.

Lawson (1945) gave the *Kuhlmann-Anderson* to all members of the ninth-grade general science class of the East Highland High School in Sylacauga, Alabama, in an attempt to determine the effect of specific science teaching on superstitious beliefs.[6] The mean IQ earned by these 25 colored pupils was 81.6, the standard deviation, 8.02, and the range of scores was from 62 to 96. No colored score equaled or exceeded the mean of the norms group.

CALIFORNIA MENTAL MATURITY

Nine Southern studies, three of them reported in unpublished Masters' theses from Atlanta University, describe the results of administering the *California Test of Mental Maturity* to Negro high school students. Using the *Advanced Short-Form* of this test, Howard (1947) compared unselected students attending day classes in the Booker T. Washington High School and those enrolled in the David T. Howard Evening High School and the B. T. Washington Evening High School. In spite of the fact that the groups were not homogeneous in chronological age, the age range extending from 14 to 45, only about three points separated the *Mental Maturity* IQ's. The day students earned a mean of 85.97, the evening Ss, 82.64. The scores of the evening group were the more variable as will be noted in the table.

Flemister (1950) related the intelligence of 100 Negro pupils in Grades 9 to 12 to their personality adjustment and achievement. She selected her subjects by random sampling from 280 enrolled pupils in the Upchurch High School, Raeford, North Carolina, allowing for proportional representation from each class and for the sexes. The mean *Mental Maturity* IQ (*Advanced Short-Form*) was 83, the range of scores varying from 56 to 104.

Thomas (1954), using the *Intermediate Short-Form* of the test, compared ninth-grade pupils of a Negro high school in Alexandria, Virginia, who had been continuously enrolled in either the city schools or in the rural schools up to this grade. The results were reported in terms of raw score rather than IQ; however, the rural and urban means of 37.05 and 39.57 corresponded to grade placements of 5.1 and 5.4, respectively.

In two Alabama State College theses intelligence was related to scholastic achievement in junior and senior high schools for colored pupils in the State of Alabama. A. S. Brown (1951) reported a mean IQ of 79 on the *Intermediate Short-Form* of *Mental Maturity*, earned by 173 pupils from eight junior high schools in Pike County. The range of scores was from 43 to 117, with about 14 per cent overlapping an IQ of 100. Reese (1951) tabulated the Mathematics,

---

[6]The acceptance of superstitious beliefs ranged from four Ss who believed that "If a person is burned others can talk the fire out of him", to 24 who believed that "If a bird flies into the window, there will be a death in the family."

Reading Comprehension, and *California Mental Maturity* scores (*Short-Form—* author does not indicate whether it was *Intermediate* or *Advanced*) of 55 senior high school students selected by the normative survey method from the Elmore County Training School at Wetumpka. The mean IQ, calculated by the reviewer, was 86.91 and the range, 67 to 102, with six per cent overlapping a norm of 100.

We have previously reviewed Hammer's survey (1954) of the Madison Heights, Virginia, Negro school children, Grades 1 to 8. In Table 5 we have included the results on Grades 9 to 11, the school system operating on an 11-year basis at this time. No measures of variability were recorded, nor was the amount of overlapping given. However, the mean *Mental Maturity* IQ's of the pupils in Grades 9, 10, and 11 were, respectively, 71.50, 81.25, and 80.87.

Osborne (1962) was interested in comparing the mental growth and achievement curves of colored and white pupils living in Chatham County, Georgia. Following the initial testing of 1388 white and 723 colored sixth-grade children in 1954 (whose respective mean IQ's were found to differ by 22.4 points) Osborne matched Negro and white girls and Negro and white boys in IQ; six years later there remained 59 matched pairs of boys and 81 matched pairs of girls, all now in the twelfth grade, all of whom had been tested when in the eighth and tenth grades. Since the total groups from which the equated Ss were drawn differed by 22.4 IQ points, it is obvious that the majority of the white children used in matching were well below the mean of their classmates and the majority of the colored were well above the mean of their groups. As will be noted in Table 5, the equated groups had an average IQ of 89.77; in the six subsequent years the white children increased on the average from five to eight points, their means at the 8th, 10th, and 12th grades being approximately 95, 98, and 97, respectively; the corresponding Negro means dropped from less than one point to about five points, their means at the 8th, 10th, and 12th grades being approximately 89, 84, and 89, respectively.

Osborne pointed out that the divergence in the mental growth curves of the two racial groups was not attributable to a difference in the training and qualifications of the Negro and white teachers. His own survey in 1957 of more than 800 Chatham County teachers indicated that: Negroes had completed a greater number of years of college training, had completed college work more recently, had a higher proportion of their group holding five-year teaching certificates, had relatively more with Master's degrees, and were earning a higher mean yearly salary. The Negro teachers, furthermore, (in 1957) for the most part had received their training "at the better colleges of the North, East, and Midwest", the white teachers having generally attended their state university or local teacher training college. "What the administrator needs to know is how to assimilate into white school systems Negro children who in spite of better trained and higher paid teachers still learn at a rate only one-half to three-fourths that of the white children in the same school district." (pp. 16-17)

In conjunction with projects aimed at studying the relationship between intelligence and school achievement among Southern biracial groups, Swan (1965) and Osborne (1965) have reported the results of the testing of high school pupils in two Southern counties. Data for the Swan study were obtained from the administration of a form of the *California Test of Mental Maturity* to all high school pupils, if present on the testing days, in the Louisiana parish of St. John the Baptist. In the Georgia county of Chatham, surveyed by Osborne, a form of this test was administered under the direction of the county supervisors to all tenth-grade pupils in 1963, 1964, and 1965, provided they were present on the particular testing days. As will be noted in Table 5, the colored means were 15 IQ points below the means of the white pupils in the Louisiana county, and from 13 to 21 points below the means of the white pupils in the Georgia county; the racial differences between the several language means appear to be about the same as the differences between the nonlanguage means; and when the groups were compared in variability, the colored was the more homogeneous.

Excluding Osborne's 1962 research with groups matched for IQ, we have calculated a combined mean IQ from the seven *CTMM* studies in which 3914 Southern Negro high school pupils were examined. This proved to be 81, approximately eight points below the mean IQ reported by Hickerson on an unbiased sample of California Negroes (1963, 1965).

Hickerson, investigating the kind and amount of Negro participation in a Northern integrated high school, selected an unidentified industrial town of 30,000 located in the San Francisco-Bay area. Enrolled in the one three-year school serving this small city were: nonethnic whites, Negroes, Mexican-Americans, Filipinos, and a very few "others" (Table 5). As was probably predicted, the Negro students were found to participate fully in certain interscholastic sports such as football, basketball, and track in the year in which the school records were examined (probably in 1961-1962), but rarely in certain other sports, such as baseball, tennis, swimming, and golf. Negro students were proportionally well-represented in the high school band, the "pep-band", the Girl's Athletic Association, and the Homemaking Club. However, they were poorly-represented in academic clubs, in elective college preparatory classes, in the college preparatory program track, and in assignments to Class A sections in English (even when they were compared with the non-Negro groups who scored in the same quarter of the total IQ distribution and whose fathers were of the same occupational class as their own).

As indicated in the table, the white seniors scored on the average about 13 IQ points above the colored seniors (numbers not given), and the white juniors and sophomores scored about 10 points above the colored Ss in these two classes (numbers not given). When the pupil were equated for occupation of fathers— thereby of necessity including only parents in skilled-and semiskilled-laboring positions and those serving as noncommissioned officers in the United States Armed Forces — the difference between the white and colored seniors was reduced to 10 points on the average, and that between the white and colored sophomores and juniors (always combined by the author) was reduced to seven points. Again, the numbers of cases and measures of variability have been omitted by the author making it impossible for a reader to determine the reliability of these reported differences.

Since Hickerson does report the number of each racial or ethnic group located in each quarter of the total IQ distribution (all three classes combined), the present writer has converted these numbers into percentages and believes that a comparison of them may provide the more meaningful data relative to IQ. From these percentages as presented in Table 5, one can readily observe, for example, that instead of the expected 25 per cent in the *highest or first quarter,* there is, for the whites, 32 per cent; for the Mexican-Americans, 15 per cent; for the Filipinos, 9 per cent; and for the Negroes, 8 per cent. And conversely, in the *lowest quarter* of the IQ distribution, instead of the normal 25 per cent, we find for the whites, 16 per cent; for the Mexican-Americans, 26 per cent; for the Filipinos, 34 per cent; and for the Negroes, 45 per cent. Comparing only Negro and white pupils, we note that proportionally the former had one fourth as many members in the highest quarter of the IQ distribution, one half as many in the second quarter, one and one third times as many in the third quarter, and three times as many in the lowest quarter.

HENMON-NELSON

The *High School Examination* of the *Henmon-Nelson Tests of Mental Ability,* like the other *Henmon-Nelson* tests, yields a single global score; at all three levels the tests measure scholastic aptitude. It may be considered as ranking among the better group tests of general intelligence. However, there has been an apparent lack of continuous research and the tests need rejuvenating; the norms appear to give mental ability estimates that are too high; the manuals need revising, and percentile norms by age groups could profitably be added. (Fowler, *in* Buros, 1953, p. 299)

In Table 5 we have included summaries of four studies which utilized the *Henmon-Nelson* tests. Congehl (1946) analyzed the records of 122 Negro girls who were enrolled in the senior class of the two St. Louis high schools for Negroes. Sixty-one of these girls had withdrawn from school during the academic year and 61 girls (randomly selected) remained in school. The mean IQ determined by the *Henmon-Nelson* or "other group tests" of those who dropped out of school was 91.6, while that of the graduates was 96.5.[7] In addition to having

---

[7]The difference in mean IQ between the dropouts and the graduates is exactly the same as that obtained between two groups of New York City Negro boys tested in the ninth grade of a *general high school.* The 79 dropouts earned a mean group IQ (also *Henmon-Nelson*) of 93, in contrast to a mean of 98 secured on 159 Negroes who remained in school. However, in a *vocational high school* the mean IQ (*National Intelligence Test*) of 66 Negro boys in school proved to be the same as that of the 127 dropouts, *i.e.,* 80 (calculated by the reviewer from separate means for 1937 and 1938 given by the author, E. Silverglied, 1940).

TABLE

HIGH SCHOOL

AUTHOR DATE	LOCATION	SUBJECTS		METHOD OF SELECTION
		N	GRADE	
				TERMAN GROUP
Boots, W. E. (1926)	Mississippi	w-9785 c- 1621	9-12 9-12	White from 49 & c from 17 counties of Mississippi.
Davis, R. A., Jr. (1928)	Texas	c- 222	8-12	A Negro Normal and Industrial School.
Barnes,[2] J. R. (1923)	Lawrence, Kan.	w-1093 c- 122		Test given to all pupils enrolled in jr & senior high sch. No separation of races; selected every third paper of w pupils after alphabetically stacked by sch grade.
Jones, H. L. (1940)	Denver, Colo.	c- 100	7-9	Random sampling of 100 cases from c boys and 100 from Spanish-American boys in Cole Jr High Sch.
				INTERNATIONAL
Peterson,[3] J., and Lanier, L. H. (1929)	Murfreesboro and Nashville, Tenn.	w-100 c- 138	Last yr high sch and college	w-Middle Tenn State TC; c- Agric & Indus Normal College.
				OTIS SELF-
Peterson,[3] J., and Lanier, L. H. (1929)	Murfreesboro and Nashville, Tenn.	w-301 c- 243	Last yr high sch and college	w-Middle Tenn State TC; c- Agr & Ind Normal Coll.

[1]Cities if population of 10,000 or more; towns, 2500 to 10,000; rural, under 2500; z computed by reviewer.

[2]See this table for results on *Mentimeter; t* calculated by reviewer.

FIVE

STUDENTS

	RESULTS			COMMENTS OF AUTHOR
TEST				
		IQ^1		In so far as these tests are valid measures of intelligence, data show that w pupils in common and high schs far superior to Negro pupils.
M	w		c	
Cities	98.46		83.83	
Towns	97.52		77.15	
Rural	90.90		80.47	
Total	94.43		81.33	
s	12.95		10.30	
z =		45.33		
		IQ		Four-yr accred high sch; teachers well trained. Should not draw lines bet races in intell until have equalized the character as well as amt of education of the races.
		c		
Mdn		78		
Range		55-105		
		Scores		Marked disability as compared with w in all of the 10 tests of *Terman Group*.
	w		c	
Mdn	106.15		65.00	
M	106.16		71.06	
s	41.50		40.02	
t =		9.16		
19% c overlap				
		IQ		Both groups came from rather poor and inadequate environments.
	S-A		c	
Mdn	85.8		90.3	
M	85.0		89.7	
s	13.3		14.3	
GROUP				
		Mdn		From 65.5 per cent to 81.4 per cent of w students above c mdns on various tests used.
Tests	w		c	
1	25.81		18.28	
4	18.61		16.94	
5	10.09		5.92	
6	14.57		9.65	
9	19.50		13.08	
ADMINISTERING				
		Mdn		Highly probable that some real innate differences in intelligence bet groups on tests.
	w		c	
	47.25		32.25	
93% w above c mdn				
Sig diff bet mdns				

[1]See this table for other tests given to Ss in these two schools; some duplication of Ss.

TABLE

HIGH SCHOOL

| AUTHOR DATE | LOCATION | SUBJECTS | | METHOD OF SELECTION |
		N	GRADE	
Williams, L. B. (1938)	Mexia, Tex.	c- 300	8-11	Many of the advanced high sch pupils from surrounding communities. Method of selection not given.
National Survey— (1942)	Southern, Border, and Northern States	c- Urb-1689 Rur- 408	Senior	Urban c schs from 3 North, 3 Border, & 9 South cities in diff states; rural in 11 Southern states.[4]
McGurk,[5] F. C. J. (1943)	Richmond, Va.	w-535 c- 145	9-11 9-11	10% of stratified sample by selecting every 10th name from alphabetized lists.
Stainbrook, E., and Siegel, P. S. (1944)	A Southern City	w-40 c- 40	10 10	From one w & one c high sch; all in first semester classes.
Gray, W. H., Jr. (1945)	Louisiana	c- 508	Senior	Sampling of the probable Negro high sch graduates in state, '42; 29 high schs representing 22 parishes typical of all major economic, social, & geographic aspects of state.
Dunn, F. H. (1946)	Montgomery, Ala.	c- 104	10-12	All State Teachers Coll Laboratory High School pupils tested.
Johnson, W. L. D., Jr. (1946)	Houston, Tex.	c- 228	9-11	Random sampling of 3 grades in Jack Yates High Sch. Higher S-A form used.

[4]Tested all prospective graduates, except those in large schools where every other name was selected.

FIVE *(continued)*

STUDENTS

	RESULTS		COMMENTS OF AUTHOR
	IQ c		Mexia the trade center of an oil field region.
Mdn	93.45		
Q	4.31		
Range	60-119		

	Scores		Lower performance of rural Ss attributed in large part to poor types of schs and facilities provided.
	Urban	Rural	
	c	c	
Mdn	36	27	
Range	6-71	3-56	

	M Scores		
Grade	w	c	
9	60	49	
10	62	52	
11	67	58	

	Scores		All c tested by c graduate student. On *Rorschach*, c less productive in responses than w.
	w	c	
M	41	27	

	IQ c		. . . . a lack of energy, drive, and ambition, *esprit de corps* and ability to cooperate are recognizable problems facing Negro high school students in Louisiana.
M	85.77		
s	10.70		
Range	61-120		

	IQ c		Wide range of intelligence due to the varied environmental and social bkg of pupils.
M	89.85		
s	9.75		
Range	71-115		

	IQ		No relation between intelligence or personality adjustment, as measured by *Bell* and academic averages.
M	82.70		
Mdn	80.05		
Range	60-119		

[5]Part of a testing project in the Richmond publ schools. For other tests given to these pupils, see this table.

TABLE

HIGH SCHOOL

AUTHOR DATE	LOCATION	SUBJECTS		METHOD OF SELECTION
		N	GRADE	
Lacy, L. D. (1926)	Oklahoma City, Okla.	c- 157	9-12	All c in school tested.
Anderson, W. E. (1947)	Okmulgee, Okla.	c- 153	9-12	Currently enrolled pupils in Dunbar High Sch.
Clinton, R. J. (1931)	New York City[6]	w-155 c- 122		Unselected within the high sch.

MYERS MENTAL

Peterson,[2] J., and Lanier, L. H. (1929)	Murfreesboro and Nashville, Tenn.	w- 87 c- 130		w-*Middle Tenn State Teach Coll.* c-*Agri and Indus Normal Coll.* Ss from last yr of high sch and from college.
McGurk,[5] F. C. J. (1943)	Richmond, Va.	w-535 c- 145	9-11 9-11	Selected every 10th name from alphabetized lists.

CHICAGO NON-VERBAL

McGurk,[5] F. C. J. (1943)	Richmond, Va.	w-535 c- 145	9-11 9-11	Selected every 10th name from alphabetized lists.

[6]Location omitted in article reporting study. However, R. M. Clark (1933) noted that Clinton's Ss were all from a New York City high school.

FIVE (continued)
STUDENTS

	RESULTS		COMMENTS OF AUTHOR
Grade	M IQ		Highly selected group in upper grades due to high percentage of retardation in c schools.
	c		
9	81		
10	84		
11	85		
12	85		
	IQ		Cal Test of Ment Maturity correlated .92 with Otis when given to these Ss; 68% of boys and 89% of girls made higher scores on language than nonl sections of CTMM.
	c		
M	103.25		
Range	80-124		
	IQ		Tests show unselected w high sch pupils to be superior mentally to unselected c high sch pupils.
	w	c	
M	100.5	84.5	

MEASURE

	Scores	
	w	c
Mdn	72.95	53.94
Sig diff bet mdns		
88% w above c mdn		

	M Scores	
	w	c
Grade		
9	60	47
10	61	52
11	70	49

EXAMINATION

	M Scores	
	w	c
Grade		
9	130	108
10	134	116
11	141	116

TABLE

HIGH SCHOOL

AUTHOR DATE	LOCATION	SUBJECTS		METHOD OF SELECTION
		N	GRADE	
				OTIS QUICK-SCORING
McClain, B. M. (1948)	Waugh, Ala.	c- 182	7-12	Jr and sen high sch pupils of Montgomery County Training Sch.
Petway, J. K. (1948)	Nashville, Tenn.	c- 100	9	Method of selection not given; 50 of each sex from one jr high sch.
Royster, E. W. (1954)	Calhoun, Etawah, St. Clair, and Talladega Counties, Ala.	c- 320	12	Four urban and 4 rural high schs for c; 22-58 seniors tested in each sch. Does not how Ss were selected, probably all present were tested.
Berry, B. Y. (1954)	Brundidge, Ala.	c- 50	10-12	Ss selected by normative survey method from Pike County Training Sch. All girls.
Geisel, P. N. (1962)	A Southern City	w-1245 c- 777	7, 8, 12 7, 8, 12	Ss from one w & one c high sch; also 2 w junior high schs from diff socioeco bkgs & 2 c junior high schs from diff socioeco bkgs. Divided all Ss into lower or higher socioeco status acc to educ attained by parents. If less than 12th, "lower", if 12th grade or more, "upper".
Roland, H. M., and Swan, D. A. (1965)	Wilmington, N. C.	w-2440 c-1145	7-9 7-9	All junior high sch pupils tested in '56.
		w-1631 c- 730	10-12 10-12	All senior high sch pupils tested in '59; number includes all present who had been tested in '56.

[7]Mean and *s* calculated by reviewer.

FIVE *(continued)*

STUDENTS

	RESULTS		COMMENTS OF AUTHOR

GAMMA TEST

	IQ[7]		Preadolescents $M\ IQ$, 84
	c		Adolescents $M\ IQ$, 74
M	79.43		Postadoles $M\ IQ$, 72
s	8.92		
Range	45-103		

	IQ		
	cB	cG	
M	85.0	83.2	
s	9.6	9.8	
Range	69-109	67-114	

	IQ		Urban students had longer sch term, more
	c		qualified teachers, more social opportunities,
M			and were of higher eco status.
Urban	84.09		
Rural	74.46		

	IQ		Socioeconomic status of c approx the same as
	c		in most rural Ala communities; employment
M	78.0		mainly maids, janitors, and unsk laborers.
Mdn	76.6		
s	6.6		
Range	66-101		

	IQ[8]		Although Negro IQ's average sig lower than
Upper	w	c	whites' their scores are higher on factor of
M	113.2	92.1	self-evaluation; they have higher mean educ-
s	15.6	12.8	and occup-aspirations.
t =	19.01		
Lower			
M	101.1	88.6	
s	13.4	10.0	
t =	15.43		
Total			
M	108.2	89.7	
s	15.9	11.0	
t =	28.03		

	IQ		Tests administered by teachers; white teach-
	w	c	ers examined pupils in w schs, colored
M	99.55	81.24	teachers the pupils in c schs.
s	13.74	13.45	
t =	37.75		
8.3% c overlap[9]			
	w	c	
M	101.98	84.62	
s	12.59	11.20	
t =	31.74		
8.4% c overlap[9]			

[8]IQ's on 7th and 8th grade Ss determined by *Lorge-Thorndike.*

TABLE

HIGH SCHOOL

AUTHOR DATE	LOCATION	SUBJECTS		METHOD OF SELECTION
		N	GRADE	
McCary, J. L., and Tracktir, J. (1957)	Pittsburgh, Pa.	w-188 c- 87		Rosenzweig Picture-Frustration and *Otis Q-S* administered to 275 pupils in one high sch. All were described as being from middle middle-class families.

OTIS GROUP

| Collum, M. C. (1937) | Woodville and Ardmore, Okla. | w-70 c- 80 | 9-12 9-12 | C in Ardmore, w in Woodville; both in same locality in southern part of state. |

CALIFORNIA CAPACITY

| Smith, W. N. (1942) | Atlanta, Ga. | c- 95 | 10-12 | Ss in the 3 years of the Atlanta Univ Laboratory High Sch. |

| Fallin, W. (1949) | Bessemer, Ala. | c- 194 | 10-12 | Test administered to 194 Dunbar High Sch pupils, 1948-49. |

AMERICAN COUNCIL ON

| Brooks, L. B. (1942) | Portsmouth and Norfolk, Va. | c- 285 | Senior | All seniors in Negro high schs in P-N area tested in 1941. |

| Dozier, M. C. (1946) | Davidson County, Tenn. | c- 74 | 9-10 | Girls in first yr math class of Hayes High Sch. Used 1944 high sch form. |

[9]Calculated by reviewer from author's frequency distribution. In the Wilmington testing probably *Beta* was used in junior high schs and *Gamma* in senior high schs.

FIVE *(continued)*

STUDENTS

	RESULTS		COMMENTS OF AUTHOR
		IQ	Significant differences in intelligence between the Negro and white groups. No significant diff *within* the racial groups.
M	w	c	
Males	104.8	96.8	
Females	104.5	93.9	
s			
Males	10.9	10.4	
Females	10.8	12.2	

ADVANCED

		IQ	C and w schs similar size, same term length, equal in bldgs and equip. Tester w. Capacity to learn much less than that of w children.
	w	c	
M	101	88	
Range	80-119	65-114	
13% c overlap[9]			

QUESTIONNAIRE

	IQ	Acc to IQ rating, 4 were very superior, 7 superior, 41 average, 31 dull, 11 borderline, and one feebleminded.
	c	
M	92.25	
s	14.13	
Range	65-130	

	IQ	Pupils are in most cases enrolled in correct grade, indicating that they are not retarded and that compulsory attendance law is complied with in sch area.
	c	
Mdn	78	
Q	8.5	
Range	60-108	
2% c overlap 100 IQ		

EDUCATION EXAMINATION

	Scores[10]	Mean of 10 Ss whose fathers were in professions was 62.90.
	c	
M	47.72	
s	16.68	
Range	10-105	

	Scores	Unusually low scores; mean for 9th and 10th grades should be bet 65-73. These same pupils had mean IQ of 85 on *Kuhlmann-Anderson* on entering 9th grade.
	c	
M	39.75	
s	13.1	
Range	13-67	

[10]Used 1939 *College Form*. Score of 48 corresponds to 3.5 %ile rank on coll freshman norms; score of 63, to the 12th %ile rank on these norms.

TABLE

HIGH SCHOOL

AUTHOR DATE	LOCATION	SUBJECTS		METHOD OF SELECTION
		N	GRADE	
Williams, H. S. (1946)	Alabama	c- 457	Senior	Ss, representing 58 high schs and ranking in upper half of classes, were attending state-wide academ meet for high sch seniors. Used 1945 coll form.
Bottosto, S. S. (1959)	Florida	w-19,749 c- 4,277	12 12	Nearly all of state w high sch seniors take Testing Program Battery shortly before graduation; fewer of non-w high schs participate; data incl 213 w publ & 32 w private high schs in 67 counties & 86 non-w publ and one private high schs in 50 of the counties.

KUHLMANN-

Lawson, R. E. (1945)	Sylacauga, Ala.	c- 25	9	Tested all 9th grade science class, East Highland HS.

CALIFORNIA TEST OF

Howard, M. E. (1947)	Atlanta, Ga.	c- Day-95 Eve- 75	9-12	Unselected Ss from day and evening high sch classes.
Flemister, R. C. (1950)	Raeford, N. C.	c- 100	9-12	Random sampling.
Brown, A. S. (1951)	Pike County, Alabama	c- 173		Colored pupils from 8 junior high schs.
Reese, H. S. (1951)	Wetumpka, Ala.	c- 55	10-12	From the senior high sch of the Elmore County Training Sch. Used normative survey.

[11]Scaled scores; for interpretation, see p. 221. Seventeen counties omitted by author from c data because of insufficient or inadequate results.

[12]Calculations by reviewer.

FIVE (continued)
STUDENTS

	RESULTS			COMMENTS OF AUTHOR
		Scores		The 457 pupils represent a superior sampling
		c		of the 2253 c high sch seniors in Alabama.
M		19.35		
s		7.75		
Range		0-32		

		Scores[11]		W mdns above c in each of 50 counties where
	w		c	both groups tested. Two non-w county mdns
Mdn County	46.8		37.4	of the 50 were higher than the lowest mdn of
Range Co Mdns	41-52		29-44	the 67 white county mdns.

ANDERSON

		IQ		
		c		
M		81.6		
s		8.02		
Range		62-96		

MENTAL MATURITY

		IQ		
	cD		cE	About ⅔ of both groups had higher IQ's on
M	85.97		82.64	the language than on the nonlanguage
s	13.5		15.3	sections.
Range	51-111		50-118	

		IQ		
		c		
M		83		
Range		56-104		

		IQ[12]		
		c		
M		79		
s		16.04		
Range		43-117		
13.9% overlap w norm				

		IQ[13]		
		c		Agriculture the chief occup of parents; live
M		86.91		from 2-25 miles from sch. About 95%
s		8.97		transported by bus.
Range		67-102		
6% overlap w norm				

[13]Mean, standard deviation, and percentage of overlapping determined by reviewer from author's list of individual scores.

TABLE

HIGH SCHOOL

| AUTHOR DATE | LOCATION | SUBJECTS | | METHOD OF SELECTION |
		N	GRADE	
Thomas, T. E. S. J. (1954)	Alexandria, Va.	c- 67	9	Study of c coming from rural & urban elem schs. Tested all 9th-grade pupils in Peabody HS who had been continuously enrolled in either the city or rural schs.
Hammer, E. F. (1954)	Madison Heights, Va.	c- 207	9-11	Surveyed entire sch population. Number includes elem as well as high sch Ss.
Osborne, R. T. (1962)	Chatham County, Georgia	w-140 c- 140	8, 10, 12 8, 10, 12	*CMM* in *Elem, Interm,* or *Adv Form* given in '54, '56, '58, & '60 to all w & c who were in 6th gr in '54, 8th in '56, 10th in '58, & 12th in '60. From 1388 w & 723 c in orig testing, selected all w & c who were tested on all 4 dates (or makeup dates) and who were *equated on basis of IQ's earned in 6th grade.*
Swan, D. A. (1965)	St. John the Baptist Parish, Louisiana	w-615 c- 541	9-12 9-12	All pupils enrolled in Grades 1-12 of parish sch system tested if present when tests administered in fall of '63.
Osborne,[16] R. T. (1965)	A County in Southeastern United States	w- 1876 1924 1702 c- 902 983 890	10 10	All pupils from one county in Grade 10, if present on testing days, examined in successive years.

[14]Author gives *Intell Grade Placement* for her means as 2.4 and 2.6, respectively. She inadvertently used the Scoreze for *Elementary Form* which lists these grade placements. Scoreze No. 110 for *Intermediate S-Form* gives *Intell Grade Placement* for scores 37 and 40 as 5.1 and 5.4, respectively.

FIVE (continued)
STUDENTS

	RESULTS				COMMENTS OF AUTHOR
	Scores[14]				Grade placements acc to intelligence: 5.1
M	c				and 5.4.
Rural	37.05				
Urban	39.57				
s					
Rural	11.00				
Urban	12.00				

	M IQ				A Negro of 75 IQ is at about the middle of
Grade	c				his group in Virginia. May be that a neurotic
9	71.50				factor is operative.
10	81.25				
11	80.87				

		M IQ[15]			In order to match the 81 pairs of girls and
Grade	w		c		the 59 pairs of boys it was necessary to select
6	89.77		89.77		the majority of children from opposite ends
8	94.61		89.34		of the 2 distributions, w being considerably
10	98.42		84.44		below their w classmates and majority of c
12	96.83		88.92		above 75th %ile of their group.

		IQ[12]			No evidence that ability-achievement correla-
	w		c		tions are significantly lower among the c
	M	s	M	s	than among the w pupils in a segregated sch
Language	97.40	14.89	82.26	10.47	system.
Nonlang	95.26	13.34	80.06	12.09	
Total	96.44	11.10	81.29	9.66	
All diffs bet racial means highly sig					

		M IQ		CTMM, Advanced Level, administered to
	w		c	white pupils at all testings; Junior High
		1963		Level to Negro pupils in '63 and '64, and
Language	100.5		79.9	Advanced Level to Negro pupils in '65.
Nonlang	100.0		80.2	
Total	100.3		80.2	
		1964		
Language	101.0		80.3	
Nonlang	99.7		79.2	
Total	100.3		79.8	
		1965		
Language	101.8		85.4	
Nonlang	98.8		85.9	
Total	100.3		85.6	

[15]Mean IQ's acc to race & sex reported by author in personal communication; IQ's of males & females combined by reviewer. See Table 4 for Osborne's complete study (1960) of which this is a part.

[16]Unpublished data communicated by author to reviewer. See Table 4 for results of sch children tested in Grades 5 and 8.

TABLE

HIGH SCHOOL

AUTHOR DATE	LOCATION	SUBJECTS N	GRADE	METHOD OF SELECTION
Hickerson, N. (1963) (1965)	San Francisco-Bay Area, Cal.	w- 561 c- 167 MA-118 F- 44	10, 11, 12	Selected a 3-yr high sch with enrollment of 960 in a river city of about 30,000 pop (an industrial center). Data taken on all pupils who had lived in town for at least 2 yrs & on whom there was sufficient inform. Included w, c, Mexican-Amer, Filipino & 6 others. *CTMM* and/or *Otis Q-S* had been given; author used IQ of last administered in each case.

HENMON-NELSON TEST

Congehl, I. H. (1946)	St. Louis, Mo.	c- 122	12	*Drops:* girls withdrawing in 12th gr from 2 publ academic high schs for c, 1943-45. *Grads:* equal number girls who later graduated; took names immed following those of drops. Used H-N "or other group tests".
Byrns, R. (1936)	Wisconsin	w-about 132,800 c- 124	10, 12	Data a part of information collected by Wis Coop Testing Commission.
Beckham, A. S. (1939)	Chicago, Ill.	c- 912	9-12	Selected every 10th name in some classes, every 5th among seniors in Du Sable High Sch.
Brown,[20] W. W. (1955)	York, Pa.	all-3362	10-12	Studied IQ's from permanent record file of all w & c who had failed one or more senior high sch subjects bet 1943-44 and 1952-53.

[17]Group A includes total number of Ss whose records comprised research data. Numbers of seniors, juniors, and sophomores omitted by author throughout.

[18]Group B selected from Group A. Fathers of Group B Ss were either skilled or semiskilled workers or were noncommissioned officers in U. S. Army. These numbers were likewise omitted by author.

[19]Calculated by reviewer from author's data in which seniors, juniors, and sophomores were combined. Author uses term *quartile* throughout for *quarter,* the reviewer substituting the

FIVE *(continued)*

STUDENTS

	RESULTS				COMMENTS OF AUTHOR

	M IQ				Negroes as compared with non-N in same IQ quartile and whose fathers are in comparable employment are less apt to be enrolled in class A sections of English and are less often in college preparatory and secretarial programs.
Group A[17]	w	M-A	F	c	
Sen	102.87	94.12	92.73	90.00	
Jr, Soph	99.41	94.73	92.74	89.11	
Group B[18]					
Sen	102.40	92.41	92.73	92.61	
Jr, Soph	97.05	95.10	92.17	89.76	
	%ages in IQ Quarters[19]				
Quarter	w	M-A	F	c	
1	32	15	9	8	
2	29	28	30	15	
3	23	31	27	31	
4	16	26	34	45	
Total	100	100	100	99	

OF MENTAL ABILITY

	IQ		On average, those who dropped out in senior year made lower grades, had lower IQ's, were older, and of lower eco status than graduates.
	cD	cG	
M	91.6	96.5	
Range	65-125	68-128	

35.4% c above w mdn.
Of 84 groups of w strains, 82 were above c mdn.

29 w groups each representing a diff nationality. Other w groups, making up total of 84, included combinations of European strains.

	IQ	21% from unsk families; 25% semiskilled; 36% skilled; 18% professional and semiprof.
	c	
M	92.0	
s	11.9	
Range	62-144	

	IQ		It appears that intelligence factor operates much more precisely upon Negro pupils in the determination of promotion or nonpromotion than upon Caucasian pupils.
	w	c	
Mdn	98.9	86.7	

correct term here. (See Guilford, J. P., Fundamental Statistics in Psychology and Education, McGraw-Hill, 1956. Pp. 80-81.)

At each quarter the Negro-white percentages differ significantly from one another, the *t* ratios for the 4 quarters being as follows: *1* - 6.15, *2* - 3.60, *3* - 2.08, and *4* - 7.84. (reviewer's calculations)

[20]See Table 4 for Brown's data on nonpromotions among sch children.

TABLE

HIGH SCHOOL

AUTHOR DATE	LOCATION	SUBJECTS		METHOD OF SELECTION
		N	GRADE	

IER TESTS OF RELATIONAL THINKING,

| Thorndike, E. L. (1923) | Large North Central City | w-1656 492 505 c- 151 114 84 | 9 10 11 9 10 11 | Tested all c available in Grades 9-11 in publ high schs; retested following year in Grades 10-12. Tested available w's in 9th gr; all w's in Gr 10-11 chosen by random sampling. |

ARMY

| Feingold,[21] G. A. (1924) | Hartford, Conn. | w-2295 c- 58 | 9 9 | All of 4 freshman classes tested on entering high sch. |

| Adler, H. M. (1925) | Alexander and DuPage Counties, Ill. | w- 389 c- 82 w-1363 | 9-12 9-12 9-12 | All publ high sch pupils tested; no c tested in DuPage County. |

MENTIMETER

| Barnes,[24] J. R. (1923) | Lawrence, Kan. | w-1027 c- 103 | | Tests given in both jr & senior high schs. Results of all Negroes and of large random sample of w included (secured by taking every 3rd paper from piles alphabetically stacked within sch grades). |

SCHOOL AND COLLEGE

| Anderson, T. M. (1958) | Mississippi | c- 948 c- 468 | 9 12 | Sampling drawn by districts; in each of 8 dists all of high schs were arranged in alphabetical order & the schs were selected so that a 10% sample of all 9th and 12th grade Ss was represented. |

[21]Modified form adapted by Feingold especially for high school pupils.
[22]When w freshmen were separated acc to parents' nativity, all means were above that of the c.

FIVE *(continued)*

STUDENTS

	RESULTS		COMMENTS OF AUTHOR

GENERALIZATION & ORGANIZATION

	M Scores		
	w	c	
Grade			
9	393	227	
10	413	280	
11	426	296	

Less than 4% c above w *mdn* at a given grade

C perhaps more likely to include very best minds of their race since fewer in private schs. Substantially as familiar with taking exams as w pupils.

ALPHA

	IQ^{22}		
	w	c	
M	102.18	95	

C favored by positive selection, for larger proportion of poor material among c leave grammar sch to work than among other groups.

	Mdn IQ^{23}		
County	w	c	
Alex	102.6	87.3	
DuP	107.8		

Southern county large rural; Northern, urban. All tests scored by Chicago bureau.

EXAMINATION

	Scores		
	w	c	
Mdn	105.2	86.3	
M	105.6	87.6	
s	16.2	15.3	
Range	21-180	31-150	

14% c above w mdn

As long as the problems remain comparatively simple in nature the c child functions adequately; where type of activity called for is of more abstract and involved types he drops woefully to the rear.

ABILITY TESTS

	Scores		
		M	
Grade 9	(norm)	c	
Verbal	269	248.5	
Quant	287	263.0	
Total	278	259.9	
Grade 12			
Verbal	283	258.6	
Quant	293	276.6	
Total	287	265.4	

4-8% c in Gr 9 above national means[25]
5-6.4% c in Gr 12 above national means

There seems to be little relation bet the measured ability and measured interests of the boys and girls tested in this study.

[23]Calculated by reviewer from Adler's frequency tables.
[24]These Ss were also examined by the *Terman Group* test.
[25]4% verbal, 7.6% quantitative, and 4% total.

TABLE

HIGH SCHOOL

| AUTHOR DATE | LOCATION | SUBJECTS | | METHOD OF SELECTION |
		N	GRADE	
				COLLEGE BOARD
Stalnaker, J. M. (1948)	Seventeen[26] Southern States and D. C.	w-[27] I-130 II-507 c- I- 18 II- 80	12 12	A special program devised to identify superior Negro high sch seniors in "southern" states and DC by Pepsi-Cola Scholarship Board. (See pp. 251-2 for method.) The 98 c winners selected from among 1875 c. Ss who had been nominated and tested from 652 segregated high schs in 1948; the 637 w winners used for comparison were from all states.
				SRA PRIMARY
Swan,[29] D. A. (1964)	Jackson, Miss.	w-813 c- 548	10 10	A standardized testing program including *Primary Mental Abilities* given to all Ss present in 2nd, 5th, 8th, & 10th grades in city publ schs. Only data for 1960 complete and included here.
				WECHSLER-BELLEVUE
Grandison, F. L. (1951)	Central and Southern Ohio	w-21 c- 21	11-12 11-12	From 3 high schs located in industrial cities; c and w pupils were matched for age, education, and *Verbal intell* of *W-B*, minus *Arithmetic* and *Vocabulary* tests. These matched pairs were then compared for diffs on the 5 performance subtests & *Arith*.

[26]In addition to the 11 Southern states of Ala, Ark, Fla, Ga, La, Miss, NC, SC, Tenn, Tex, and Va, author probably has included the following Border states: Del, Ky, Md, Mo, Okla, and WVa.

[27]*I* refers to the 4-year scholarship winners; *II*, to the college entrance award winners (a $50 prize for each runner-up).

FIVE *(continued)*

STUDENTS

RESULTS	COMMENTS OF AUTHOR

SCHOLASTIC APTITUDE TEST

	SAT Scores[28a]			Lowest possible score on either the *verbal*
	Verbal Section			or *mathematical* section of this test is 200;
	M			maximum score attainable on either section
Groups	w	c		is 800. The College Board norm is based on
				the scores of college applicants throughout
I	762	488		the country (not upon winners of scholar-
II	696	355		ships) who comprised a selective group since

Distrib of Winners' Scores[28b]

SAT	Verbal	Math
	c	c
600-699	1	1
500-599	12	9
400-499	23	32
300-399	44	45
200-299	18	11
	—	—
	98	98

many were applying to Eastern colleges.

13% c winners overlap College
Board norm of 500

MENTAL ABILITIES

	IQ			Mean IQ's of w relatively constant in the 4
	w		c	grades (2, 5, 8, 10), while mean IQ's of
M	104.4		74.0	Negroes showed a sharp decline from 2nd to
s	15.9		15.4	10th grade.
z =		34.9		

4% c overlap w mean

INTELLIGENCE SCALE, FORM I

	M Scores		p	The higher the IQ score of the Negro stu-
	w	c		dent, the more culturally unacceptable is his
Arithmetic	10.19	9.71	—	Level of Aspiration (acc to Rotter's test),
Pic Arrang	10.48	10.00	—	*i.e.,* lacking in consistency, desires not to
Pic Comple	11.19	8.86	.02	take a chance, shifts in upward direction
Block Design	12.05	9	.01	only, level constantly changing to conform to
Obj Assembly	10.67	9.57	—	previous performance, *etc.*
Dig Symbol	11.66	10.14	.05	
	M IQ			
Verbal	109.71	109.33	—	
Perform	109.67	94.86	.01	
Full Scale	111.29	103	.05	

[28a]Scores on the mathematics section for white winners not given.
[28b]The *winners* here include both Groups I and II.
[29]For results on grade sch children tested, see Table 4.

TABLE

HIGH SCHOOL

AUTHOR DATE	LOCATION	SUBJECTS		METHOD OF SELECTION
		N	GRADE	

UNIDENTIFIED

AUTHOR DATE	LOCATION	N	GRADE	METHOD OF SELECTION
Ball, J. C. (1960)	Two Central Kentucky Towns	w-169 c- 31	9 9	Personality test administered to all 9th graders present; 200 valid profiles completed, all of Ss having been previously given an intelligence test. Negro & w Ss attended same classes & lived in same sch districts. From 2 publ schs.
Lott, A. J., and Lott, B. E. (1963)	Lexington and Fayette County, Ky.	w-185 c- 116	12 12	In a study of values & goals of high sch seniors, 2 county & 2 city schs were selected, one of county & one of city schs being entirely c, the others being predominantly w. All seniors present were Ss in 3 of schs; in the city w sch however, only Ss enrolled in psychol or sociol elective classes were tested.[30]
Oldham, E. V. (1935)	Chicago, Ill.	c- 319		From 4 schs in Near South Side with diff socioeco levels. A "sampling of 319 cases." Name of test not given.
McGurk, F. C. J. (1951)	New Jersey and Pennsylvania	w-213 c- 213	12 12	Tested a total of 2863 seniors in 14 high schs. Each c S was then matched with a w from same sch; also matched for curriculum, age, and revised Sims score. Developed a special test with half cultural and half noncul questions.

[30]Authors subsequently obtained for each S his most recent score on a sch-administered group test of intelligence.

FIVE *(concluded)*

STUDENTS

TESTS	RESULTS			COMMENTS OF AUTHOR
		M IQ		Whites as a rule from higher socioeco status families than Negroes on *Minnesota Parental Occupational Scale.*
	w		c	
Boys	104.5		96.4	
Girls	105.3		93.6	
		IQ^{31}		Difference in average IQ's not surprising in view of lower stability within c families, less formal education of c parents, and less desirable jobs held by major provider in Negro families.
	w		c	
M	105.58		88.89	
s	8.68		11.65	
Range	71-134		64-131	
t =		12.67		
		M IQ		A study of adjustments of adolescent c girls.
		c		
Status[32]				
I		100.7		
II		95.6		
III		87.4		
		Scores		Racial diff greater for noncultural than for cultural questions. No evidence that Negroes' lower scores due to their lower status or to their inability to handle culturally weighted test material.
	w		c	
		Cultural		
M	10.5		9.0	
s	5.3		4.6	
t =		3.57		
		Noncultural		
M	15.6		12.6	
s	5.7		4.6	
t =		7.30		

[31]In the 2 predominantly w schs Negroes were tested but their scores were excluded from the analysis.

[32]*I* here refers to better or good status; III to low or lowest status.

lower group IQ's, the dropouts were of lower economic status, were older, and had earned lower grades on the average than the girls who were later graduated.

Beckham (1939) took a random sample of the Du Sable High School colored subjects by selecting every tenth or every fifth name from the rolls of the four classes. The mean IQ obtained from the large sample of 912 students was 92, the standard deviation, 11.9, and the range from 62 to 144. Nearly half of these pupils were from families of unskilled or semiskilled wage earners, the others being children of skilled laborers or of parents in the semiprofessional and professional occupations.

In a survey of the mental abilities of Wisconsin high school students, thousands of seniors were tested in 1931 on the *ACE* and thousands of seniors and sophomores were examined in 1932 and 1933 on the *Henmon-Nelson* test. Byrns (1936), separating the white subjects according to the nationality of parents, found twenty-nine groups reporting parents of the same nationality and fifty-five groups reporting two or more strains. When she compared the test scores made by these eighty-four groups with those of 124 Negroes, Byrns found the medians of *eighty-two groups* to be above the colored median. She concluded that a wide range of statistically reliable differences exists between the average mental ability of natio-racial groups.

Brown (1955) attempted to determine the causes of nonpromotions in the public schools of York, Pennsylvania. Anticipating that the level of intelligence would be an important factor in the realization of success or failure in school, he obtained the IQ's of all nonpromoted pupils during a 10-year period (1943-44 to 1952-53) from the permanent record file. Among these, there were 3362 boys and girls who had failed *one or more high school subjects* in Grades 10-12. Colored pupils composed 6.5 per cent of the average daily attendance as opposed to 7.3 per cent of the high school retentions, *i.e.,* failure in one or more subjects. The median IQ of the nonpromoted or "retained" colored children was 86.7, the mean of the "retained" white pupils, 98.9,[8] five per cent of the nonpromoted whites and 26.8 per cent of the nonpromoted colored Ss earning IQ's below 80. The fact that the median IQ of the Negroes who had failed one or more subjects was 12.2 points below that of the "retained" whites led the author to conclude that intelligence is more often the determining factor in promotion or nonpromotion of colored than of white pupils. In addition, Brown found that the nonpromoted Negro children came in greater proportions from broken homes, from the unskilled laboring group, and from housing areas described as "blighted".

IER TESTS

Thorndike (1923) was one of the first psychologists to call attention to the inferior test scores earned by colored high school pupils. He administered the *IER Tests of Selective and Relational Thinking, Generalization and Organization*

---

[8]The mean IQ of all *promoted* senior high school pupils tested on the *Henmon-Nelson* in 1951-52 was 106.75.

to a large number of whites and to 349 colored pupils in Grades 9 to 11, the racial samples attending separate high schools of a "large city of the North Central Division". While the white subjects were chosen by random sampling all available colored pupils were tested. The three mean scores of the colored were all less than three fourths of the corresponding white means (see Table 5); only four per cent of the colored subjects overlapped the medians of the whites. Although the scores of the white Ss in the three respective grades went up as high as 719, 659, and 659, no colored child achieved a score above 530 and only one earned more than 419 in Grade 9; no colored pupil scored above 499 in Grade 10; and no colored subject achieved a score above 476 in Grade 11. When the test was repeated 12 months later the colored children were found to have gained three fifths as much as the white pupils. Thorndike pointed out that since so few of the colored attend private schools, those in the public schools are even more likely than whites to include the very best minds of their race.

ARMY ALPHA

The *Army Alpha Intelligence Examination* was one of the tests developed in World War I because of the need for a group test of general ability—to sift out from the draft men unfit for military service through lack of intelligence, to select the more intelligent men for further training, and to provide more nearly balanced companies and regiments. Each form includes eight subtests: following directions, arithmetic problems, common sense judgment, synonym-antonym, disarranged sentences, number series completion, analogies, and information. *Alpha* was validated against various criteria including teachers' ratings for intelligence, school marks, officers' ratings of their men, and *Stanford-Binet* MA's, with resulting correlations ranging from .50 to .90. The reliability coefficients of *Alpha* are about .95 for unselected male groups. (Garrett and Schneck, 1933, pp. 32-33)

Feingold (1924) and Adler (1925) have reported results of the testing of colored and white pupils on *Army Alpha*. Using a modified form of *Alpha* adapted by himself "especially for high school pupils" Feingold found the mean IQ's of 58 colored and 2295 white freshmen entering the Hartford, Connecticut, high school to be, respectively, 95 and 102. More than half of the white freshmen were of foreign-born parents and these Ss were categorized into nine groups according to the nativity of the parents. All nine means proved to be above that reached by the colored Ss.

Adler tabulated the distributions of intelligence scores of white high school students in two Illinois counties and of Negro pupils in one Southern Illinois county. From these data we find that the median of the colored subjects was 87.3 and that of the whites in the same county, 102.6.

MENTIMETER

The *Mentimeter, School Group 2a Examination* was administered by Barnes (1923) in conjunction with the *Terman Group Intelligence Test, Form B* to Lawrence, Kansas, Negro and white junior and senior high school students. Since the *Terman Group* depends upon language ability, Barnes thought that a test such as the *Mentimeter,* about one third of which is made up of nonlinguistic items, would be more favorable to the Negro subjects. Utilizing the records of all Negro pupils present on the testing days and selecting a random sample of the white students by taking every third test from papers that had been alphabetized within the school grade, Barnes compared the performances of the two racial groups. Whereas the whites earned a mean score of 106 on both the *Terman Group* and the *Mentimeter,* the colored pupils achieved a mean of nearly 88 on the *Mentimeter* as compared with a mean of 71 on the *Terman Group.* Barnes found the colored subjects to function generally adequately in intellectual tests of a concrete, simple, or common-sense type, but to be very inferior in dealing with abstractions of an analytic or language type. He concluded that the Negro child brings to learning situations a mental, social, and racial endowment of his own, but that one has no right on the basis of present information and measures of ability to say that his endowment is inferior, *but rather that it is different.*

School and College Ability Tests

Cooperative School and College Ability Tests (SCAT) for Grade 4 to college is offered to replace the *ACE* as a means of predicting academic success. A *Verbal* score measures vocabulary and reading comprehension, and a *Quantitative* score measures arithmetic reasoning and the understanding of arithmetic processes. Both are intended to measure school-learned abilities and should serve well in the selection of potential college students. The tests are well prepared, but validity, stability, and discriminating power in exceptional groups need to be further investigated. (Cronbach, 1960, p. 230)

T. M. Anderson (1958) sought to determine the incidence of talent for science and mathematics among Negro students enrolled in the high schools and colleges of Mississippi.[9] As representative of the high school population she selected for testing 948 ninth- and 468 twelfth-grade pupils in 26 public schools in the state. To secure these schools she first separated the state into eight districts; all high schools located in each district were then alphabetized and the particular schools were randomly selected "so that a ten per cent sample of all ninth and twelfth grade subjects was represented." (p. 27)

Anderson incorporated her *School and College Ability* test data in six frequency distributions according to *Verbal, Quantitative,* and *Total* Scores earned by the ninth- and twelfth-grade pupils, and for interpretative purposes included the national percentile norm opposite each scaled score. In addition the usual measures of central tendency and variability were presented. As will be noted in

---

[9]Author administered and scored the following tests: *SCAT; Cooperative Science Test for Grades 7, 8, and 9, Form R; Cooperative Mathematics Test for Grades 7, 8, and 9, Form Y; Cooperative General Achievement Test in Natural Science, Form XX; Cooperative General Achievement Test in Mathematics, Form XX;* and the *Kuder Preference Record, Form BM.*

Table 5 the various means were below the national norms.[10] At Grade 9, 4.1 per cent of the pupils' *Verbal* scores, 7.6 per cent of their *Quantitative* scores, and 3.9 per cent of their Total scores overlapped the national means. At Grade 12, the overlappings were, respectively: 4.9 per cent, 6.4 per cent, and 6.0 per cent. At the ninth grade, the mean *Verbal, Quantitative,* and *Total* scores all fell at the 10th percentile of the normative sample; at Grade 12, the mean Verbal and Total scores fell at the 8th percentile and the mean Quantitative score at the 22nd percentile of the norms group. The six modes (in one instance making up 29 per cent of the scores) all fell in the lowest percentile band of the respective ninth- and 12th-grade norms, indicating that this test was highly unsuitable for these subjects.

The author found little relationship between the *measured ability* and *measured interests* of the colored subjects, the interests of the students being *more idealistic* than their abilities and opportunities appeared to warrant.

College Board Scholastic Aptitude

The *Scholastic Aptitude Test (SAT)* of the College Entrance Examination Board has been in use since 1926, appearing in a somewhat revised form annually for use with high school seniors as one of the college admission criteria. Three sections of the test make use of familiar types of *Verbal* items, such as completion, opposites, analogies, and paragraph meaning, which yield a *Verbal* score; two sections, including arithmetic, algebra, and geometry problems, give a *Mathematics* score. It is a test of "abstract intelligence", designed to estimate the potential for higher education among the upper ability levels of high school seniors. The *SAT* is among the most useful of this type of test, being sensitive enough to measure relatively fine differences among individuals within a selected group. Separate norms are provided for public and private schools in addition for all schools combined, for boys and girls, and for students in several types of curricula. (Freeman, 1962, pp. 392-93)

Recognizing that the environment of many Negro high school students is inferior, that their schools are likely to be substandard, and that these and other factors adversely affect the psychometric intelligence of such pupils, the Pepsi-Cola Scholarship Board developed a special program by which they might identify the superior Negro high school student of the Southern and Border States and the District of Columbia (Stalnaker, 1948).[11] Accordingly, Negro high schools throughout this area were encouraged to register for participation in the special program; once a school was registered, candidates for scholarships were

---

[10]The several *s*'s (not listed in Table 5 but reported by Anderson) are as follows for the Verbal, Quantitative, and Total scores, Grades 9 and 12, respectively: 4.6, 6.3, 3.9, and 6.4, 6.3, and 5.3.

[11]Stalnaker refers to the *17 Southern States* and the D. C.; therefore, in addition to the 11 states usually considered "Southern" he must have included the six Border states of Delaware, Maryland, Kentucky, Missouri, Oklahoma, and West Virginia.

chosen by their senior class election on the basis of being "most likely to make an important contribution to human progress." Any Negro school, no matter how small the senior class, may have had two representatives. In the larger schools, up to five per cent of the senior class could be entered as representatives. These candidates (or representatives) were then required to take a preliminary selection test, a test prepared and scored especially for this program by the College Entrance Examination Board, in their own schools and administered by a member of the school staff. Approximately eight of the highest scoring pupils in each state were asked to take the supervised test of the College Entrance Examination Board (the *SAT*)—the Board paying the fee for this test. On the basis of the second (and last) test, the highest scoring Negro pupil in each state and the District of Columbia, regardless of his score, received a *four-year scholarship*.[12] The next several in order, up to five per cent of those participating, or a maximum of five students from any one of the states or the District, received *College Entrance Awards,* paying $50 on the winner's entrance into college. Even low-scoring contestants, if they were the best in the state, received these awards.

Stalnaker reports that 1875 students were thus nominated and tested in 1948; that they came from 652 high schools which included 40 per cent of the Negro secondary schools in the 17 states and the District of Columbia; and that a total of 28,140 seniors took part in the class elections, comprising 73 per cent of the Negro seniors in the participating schools. From among the nominated and tested students in 1948 there were 98 winners, 18 of them earning 4-year scholarships (Group I) and 80 receiving $50 each as runners-up on entrance into college (Group II). Their mean *Verbal* scores are included in Table 5 along with the *Verbal* means of 637 white winners in 1948, also separated into Groups I and II.[13] The colored Groups I and II earned respective means of 488 and 355, the corresponding means of the white groups were 762 and 696, both based upon a possible score of 800. None of the 98 colored winners equaled the *Verbal* mean attained by either Group I or Group II of the white winners (no overlapping); however one S did earn a *Verbal* score of 690, just a few points below the mean of the white Group II. Both Negro Groups I and II averaged below the norm of 500;[14] in fact about 13 per cent of the 98 colored Ss overlapped the norm. However, the norm was based upon a highly selected group of college applicants, for in 1948 *SAT* was required of applicants to many of the Eastern colleges and universities "and is taken by what is probably the most highly selected group of comparable size seeking admission to college."

Another of the comparisons shown in Table 5 is related to the distributions

---

[12]Resulting in 18 4-year scholarship winners altogether.

[13]Scores of the white scholarship and award winners on the *Mathematical Section* were not available.

[14]College applicants' norm, not scholarship winners' norm.

of the *Verbal* and *Mathematics* scores of the 98 colored winners. Although the author used large class intervals of 100 the distributions are strikingly similar and show marked positive skewness.

SRA PRIMARY MENTAL ABILITIES

A standardized testing program, including *Primary Mental Abilities*, has been administered for several years to all pupils present in the tenth as well as in certain lower grades of the Jackson, Mississippi, public schools. Swan (1964) describes the results of this testing program as conducted in 1960, 1961, and 1962, with emphasis upon the 1960 data since it is complete (relative to distribution of IQ's, *s's*, and the like). In this year the 813 white subjects earned a mean IQ of 104.4 on the *Primary Mental Abilities*, the colored a mean of 74.0, the difference between the means being highly significant. The groups appear to have been equally variable. Four per cent of the colored overlapped the mean of the white pupils and 97.2 per cent of the white Ss exceeded the mean of the colored. Swan called attention to the constancy of the IQ's of the white children from the lower to the higher grades in contrast to the decline in the mean IQ's of the colored from the second to the tenth grade.[15]

WECHSLER-BELLEVUE

The first form of the Wechsler scales, the *Wechsler-Bellevue Intelligence Scale*, published in 1939, was intended to provide an intelligence test that was suitable for adults. Providing norms down to the age of 10 years, its total standardization sample included 670 children (between the ages of 7 and 16 years) and 1081 adults. This scale is very similar to the *Wechsler Adult Intelligence Scale* (the *WAIS*) which later supplanted it. The chief weaknesses of the *Wechsler-Bellevue* lie in the normative sample having been drawn largely from New York City and its environs, the relatively small number of adults making up the sample, the low reliability of some of the subtests, the obsolescence of some of the items, the meager validity data, and the inadequacies of the manual. (Anastasi, 1961, pp. 303-305)

In studying the relation between level of aspiration and Negro-white differences on certain of the *Wechsler-Bellevue* tests, Grandison (1951) selected 21 white and 21 colored high school pupils in Grades 11 and 12 in industrial cities (unnamed) located in central and southern Ohio.[16] The white and Negro subjects had been matched for age, education, and *Verbal* intelligence of the *Wechsler-*

---

[15]For further discussion of Swan's report, see pp. 195-196. In 1961 and 1962 both the white and colored 10th-grade means were larger than in 1960. The 1256 w in '61 and the 1520 w in '62 earned means of 106.2 and 110.1, respectively, while the means achieved by the 735 c in '61 and the 700 c in '62 were 75.4 and 80.8.

[16]Among the Negroes, there were 12 boys and 9 girls; among the whites, there were 14 boys and 7 girls.

Bellevue minus the *Arithmetic* and *Vocabulary* tests. These matched pairs were then compared for differences on the five *Performance* and the *Arithmetic* subtests. The pupils were given Rotter's Level of Aspiration test[17] individually, and subsequently were classified as to whether they had obtained patterns of aspiration that were culturally acceptable or unacceptable in relation to their previous performances. A biserial *r* was applied to determine if a correlation existed between the Arithmetic subtest plus *Performance* scores and the Level of Aspiration patterns.

As will be seen in the table, the *Verbal* IQ's were the same, which was to be expected from the matching technique; on the *Performance* subtests, where Ss were not matched, the colored mean was about 15 IQ points below that of the white mean, the difference being significant at the .01 level of confidence; on the *Full Scale,* a difference of eight points separated the mean IQ's, this difference being significant at the .05 level. The matched groups did not differ significantly on the *Arithmetic* subtest nor on two of the *Performance* subtests, the *Picture Arrangement* and the *Object Assembly;* however, the differences were significant on the *Block Design* (.01 level), the *Picture Completion* (.02 level), and the *Digit Symbol* (.05 level).

Time bonuses earned by each subject on the four *Wechsler-Bellevue* subtests which grant extra points for speed of performance were tabulated by the author. He found that the white Ss were allowed a higher number of bonus points on all four subtests *(Arithmetic, Picture Arrangement, Block Design,* and *Object Assembly),* the white-colored differences in bonus points being significant on *Picture Arrangement* and *Block Design* and on the four subtests taken together. Grandison noted that in this respect his data sustain the position of Davidson, Gibby, McNeil, Segal, and Silverman (1950) in pointing to the effect of speed as a partial factor in colored-white differences on timed tests.

Among the white subjects the relationship between the Level of Aspiration patterns and the *Arithmetic plus Performance* subtest scores was low and insignificant ($.19 \pm .26$), as was the relation between the Level of Aspiration patterns and the *Full Scale* IQ ($.14 \pm .27$[18]). Among the colored Ss, the relation between the Level of Aspiration patterns and *Arithmetic plus Performance* subtest scores was a little higher, negative, and insignificant ($-.43 \pm .23$), while the relation between the Level of Aspiration patterns and the *Full Scale* IQ proved to be higher, negative, and *significant* ($-.72 \pm .16$). The culturally unacceptable patterns of aspiration shown more often by the Negro subjects at higher than lower levels of intelligence include: level of aspiration constantly changing to

---

[17]Involving hitting a steel ball along a groove in a board by means of a stick so that the ball will come to rest as close as possible to a unit marked *10.* Before each trial S estimates the score he expects to make.

[18]A positive biserial *r* indicates that "acceptable" aspiration patterns would be likely to accompany higher *W-B Full Scale* IQ's or higher *W-B Arithmetic* plus *Performance* subtests scores.

conform to the previous performance; shifts in the upward direction only; phantasy responses; desiring not to take a chance; the *absence of shifts* regardless of achievement; and impulsiveness and inconsistency.

Grandison also found that the Negro group as a whole had higher D-scores (greater discrepancy between achievement and aspiration) than the white group, and in this connection cited the publications of Frank (1935) and Sears (1940) wherein they related high D-scores to ego involvement. According to the former, if the ego-level is involved there is a tendency for a person to set his level of aspiration consistently either higher or lower than his level of performance would warrant; the subject thereby protects the ego-level by either ignoring failures or by avoiding their occurrence. Sears suggested that with some subjects a statement of the goal may be in itself gratifying and consequently substitute for the actual attainment of the goal. Believing that his Negro group considered itself to be different from other members of their race who had not attained their educational status, Grandison interpreted their statements revealing a high level of aspiration as a likely attempt to provide to others and to themselves that they were as good as anybody else. At the same time, he cautioned against applying either the *Wechsler-Bellevue* or the Rotter Level of Aspiration results without considering cultural differences and social pressures which might make these tests established on white norms impractical for use with colored students.

UNIDENTIFIED TESTS

Ball (1960) compared the Minnesota Multiphasic Personality Inventory profiles of Negro and white ninth-grade students in two integrated public schools in Central Kentucky. Although 224 pupils were tested on the MMPI, valid profiles were completed by only 200; Ball, accordingly, included the mental test records of the 200 whose MMPI profiles were usable rather than those of the entire group of 224.[19]

The mean IQ of the white girls was about eight points above that of the colored girls; the mean IQ of the white boys was about 12 points above that of the colored boys. Some other differences mentioned by Ball were: lower academic grades of the colored Ss coupled with no significant difference in the numbers of children one or more years retarded, the greater percentage of colored from broken homes, the lower socioeconomic status of the colored, the relatively high incidence of neurotic tendencies found among Negro boys, and the tendency for the Negro girls to be more withdrawn and introverted than the white girls.

In order to compare the educational and vocational goals and values of Negro and white high school seniors, Lott and Lott (1963) selected four schools in

---

[19]The 24 children whose profiles were invalid included 26 per cent of all colored tested and 7 per cent of all whites tested; a study of their records indicated that they were inferior in academic achievement and in IQ; if their scores had been included, the mean IQ's, particularly those of the colored, would have been lower.

Lexington and Fayette County, Kentucky. One of the county and one of the city high schools were Negro, the other two schools being predominantly white. All seniors present in the two rural schools and in the Lexington Negro school served as subjects, but in the Lexington "white" school only students enrolled in the psychology and in the sociology elective classes were selected. One hundred eighty-five white and 116 colored pupils participated in the research, the authors eliminating the records of the colored seniors attending the predominantly white schools. The authors subsequently obtained for each of the pupils his most recent school-administered group intelligence test score.

The mean IQ of the colored pupils was 88.89, that of the whites, 105.58, the difference of about 17 points being highly significant since the t ratio was 12.67. The standard deviation of the colored's distribution proved to be larger than that of the whites (Table 5). The difference between the colored and white IQ's the authors considered not to be surprising in view of the lesser stability within the Negro families, the less formal education of the Negro parents, and the less desirable and lower income jobs held by the major providers in the Negro households, coupled with the cultural bias present in our typical methods of testing general intelligence.

A sample of adolescent girls in Chicago scored about the same on an unidentified test as the Hartford Negro pupils tested by *Alpha*. Oldham (1935) gave the unnamed test to colored girls from four high schools on the "near South Side". She did not indicate her method of sampling, merely stating that she had a "sampling of 319 cases". Since Oldham was interested in the relation of adjustment and status, she divided her Ss into three groups determined by reference to the Sims classification. The respective means, ranging from lower to higher status, were 87.4, 95.6, and 100.7, the average being about 95.

McGurk (1951) attempted to determine whether or not socioeconomic differences are sufficient to account for the consistently lower average intelligence test scores obtained by Negroes. The psychometric test employed by McGurk consisted of 74 questions similar to those found on verbal group tests and selected in the following way: 226 questions were rated by 78 judges (31 were professors of psychology or graduate students in psychology) according as to whether they appeared to be *least cultural, neutral,* or *most cultural.* The questions were ultimately accepted as belonging to one of the categories whenever 50 per cent or more of the raters agreed in their judgments. If there was less than 50 per cent agreement, chi square was calculated between the ratings given by the judges and chance expectancy. When the value for chi square was below that value equal to a probability of 10 per cent, the question was rejected. Following this procedure 103 questions were obtained for category I, 7 for II, and 81 for III. The 103 and 81 questions were administered to a sample of 90 high school seniors to determine the difficulty level of each question, computed by the percentage of Ss answering each item correctly. By a process of matching categories I and III so they would be within two per cent of the same difficulty level, 37 pairs of matched questions were obtained. These sets of *cultural* and *noncultural* questions were subsequently given to the high school seniors.

McGurk's subjects were selected from a total of 2863 seniors in 14 high schools in Northern New Jersey and Southeastern Pennsylvania, seven of the high schools being urban, five suburban, and two rural. In three large schools only academic and commercial pupils were tested; in the other eleven schools all members of the senior class who were present were examined. Except for 20 Negroes who were either absent on the testing days or whose records were not sufficiently complete for classification, all Negro seniors enrolled in the 14 high schools were included in the sample. An equal number of whites was matched with the 213 Negro subjects for age, curriculum, and school attended.[20] In addition, each Negro was matched with a white pupil whose revised Sims score was either equal to or lower than the Negro's score.[21]

The principal findings of McGurk's research are as follows: (1) *Total test performance*—the mean score of the 213 colored was significantly below the matched group of 213 white Ss, the *t* ratio being 5.18; 28 per cent of the Negroes overlapped the mean of the whites and no Negroes scored as much as the best 9 per cent of the whites. (2) *Cultural vs noncultural questions*—the mean of the 213 colored was significantly below the mean of the matched group of 213 white Ss on the cultural questions, the difference being significant at the one per cent level (*t* = 3.57); 39 per cent of the Negroes overlapped the mean of the whites and no Negro scored as much as the best 5 per cent of the whites. The difference between the groups was greater on the noncultural questions, the critical ratio being 7.30; 29 per cent of the Negroes overlapped the mean of the whites and no Negro scored as much as the best 10 per cent of the whites. (3) *Negroes and whites of high status* — the means of the 53 Negroes comprising the high status group[22] were significantly below the means of the matched group of 53 high status whites on both the cultural and the noncultural questions, the respective *t* ratios being 3.59 and 5.44; the Negro overlap on the cultural and noncultural questions was 32 per cent and 25 per cent, respectively. No Negro scored as much as the best 6 per cent of the whites on either set of questions. (4) *Negroes and whites of low status*—the mean of the 53 Negroes comprising the low status group was *slightly above* the mean of the matched group of 53 low status whites on the *cultural questions*, the difference being insignificant (*t* = 0.87) and the colored overlap, 53 per cent. On the *noncultural* questions, however, the situation was reversed with the difference favoring the

---

[20]With a few exceptions. Wherever the matchings were not exact an attempt was made to give the advantage to the Negroes.

[21]Matching on basis of 11 of the 23 items on Sims Record Card. A point biserial r of .40 was adopted as the standard for item acceptance; the 11 were the items which were found to meet the criterion of internal consistency.

[22]Highest 25 per cent after ranking in order on "revised" Sims designated as *high status;* lowest 25 per cent—designated as the *low status* group. Mean "revised" Sims score of total colored group was 4.4, for the group of matched whites, 4.1.

whites being significant at the one per cent level ($t = 3.59$); 30 per cent of the colored overlapped the mean of the whites on the noncultural questions. The data indicate that the colored were significantly inferior on the average to the equated group of white subjects on the test as a whole, and that in the several comparisons the racial differences were *greater for the noncultural* than for the cultural questions. McGurk concluded that "There is no evidence here that culturally weighted test material discriminates against the Negro. There is no evidence that as the socio-economic status of the Negro increases, racial test-score differences decrease." (1953, p. 450)

SUMMARY

We have reviewed fifty-five studies in which psychometric tests have been administered to colored high school students. Approximately 85 per cent of the 23,600 pupils were tested in the South.[23]

1. In 26 of the investigations white students were also examined, the white subjects always achieving higher average scores than the colored.[24] The differences between the measures of central tendency were generally large and where indices of reliability were computed the differences proved to have been significant. Measures of variability were not usually reported in these 26 studies; where the standard deviations were included, the variability of the whites was the greater in 15 of 17 comparisons.[25]

2. In 29 studies the colored scores were compared with the norms rather than with those of a particular white group; of the separate 45 means reported from these researches, 43 were below the norms. One of Oldham's groups in Chicago, identified as belonging to the *better-or good-status category,* earned a mean IQ of 100.7 (1935), and W. E. Anderson's Okmulgee, Oklahoma, subjects achieved a mean IQ of 103.25 (1947).

3. In many of the studies the testing was administered and the research reported by colored men and women. Sixteen of the investigations were described in unpublished Masters' theses from higher institutions of learning for Negroes. Several other authors in this area of testing are also known to be colored. There seems to be no evidence that the race of the examiner materially affected the testing *rapport*.

4. IQ's have been obtained on about 13,250 Negro high school pupils and from the various averages a combined IQ has been calculated. This proved to be 84.14, which is essentially the same as the combined mean IQ obtained from the

---

[23]Including the 1435 Jackson, Mississippi, 10th-grade pupils tested in 1961 and 1962 (Swan, 1964).

[24]However, Bottosto (1959) reported that the 2 highest county medians of colored to be above the lowest one of the 67 county medians of the whites.

[25]Reliability of difference between *s*'s not computed. The two comparisons in which the *s*'s were larger for the c Ss were: McCary and Tracktir (1957) colored girls and white girls, and Lott and Lott (1963) combined groups.

testing of approximately 66,000 Negro school children (84.21). The combined mean IQ earned by 10,600 Southern Negro high school students is 82.42, that of the 2750 Northern and Border colored high school subjects, 90.77.

5. The amount of overlapping appears to be less among Negro high school students than among Negro grade school children. Whereas the overlapping at the grade school level was estimated to be *12.3 per cent,* the overlapping at the high school level, based upon the average overlap present in 26 comparisons, is 9.7 per cent.[26] The larger overlappings were obtained in the Northern or Border states; in fact, the two studies in which the overlap was 30 or more per cent were either conducted in a Border or a Northern state. In each of the following researches the number of cases is given after the year in which the work was reported.

An *overlap of 0-4 per cent* occurred in 11 studies: Thorndike (1923) 349; Davis (1928) 22; Lawson (1945) 25; Williams (1946) 457; Dozier (1946) 74; McClain (1948) 182; Stalnaker (1948) 98; Fallin (1949) 194; Berry (1954) 50; T. M. Anderson (1958) 948; and Swan (1964) 548. In five studies the *overlap was from 5-9 per cent:* Gray (1945) 508; Dozier (1946) 74; Reese (1951) 55; Anderson (1958) 468; Roland and Swan (1965) 1145. The amount of overlapping in the other investigations was as follows—*10-14 per cent:* Barnes (1923) 103; Adler (1925) 82; Collum (1937) 80; and Brown (1951) 173; *15-19 per cent:* Barnes (1923) 122; *20-24 per cent:* Williams (1938) 300; *25-29 per cent:* Jones (1940) 100; and McGurk (1951) 213; *35-39 per cent:* Byrns (1936) 124; and *65-69 per cent:* W. E. Anderson (1947) 153.[27]

6. Negro and white high school pupils of high and low status differed less from one another on the *cultural* than on the *noncultural* items of a psychometric test (McGurk, 1951). Likewise, it appears that at the high school level there is some evidence that the *California Test of Mental Maturity* may be less difficult for colored subjects in its language section than in its nonlanguage section. (Howard, 1951, Hammer, 1954, and Swan, 1965) These findings seem to be in agreement with those of Grandison (1951) who reported that colored pupils who had been matched with whites on four subtests of the *Verbal Scale* of the *Wechsler-Bellevue* were significantly below the whites on the *Performance Scale* of this test.

COLLEGE STUDENTS

Studies on approximately 24,640 Negro college students are included in Table 6. The students were attending colleges and universities located in many states and the District of Columbia and ranged in class standing from the

---

[26]If no white Ss were tested, the overlap is given in terms of norm or per cent of colored equaling or exceeding 100 IQ.

[27]References to the results of 3 investigations have been reported twice: the researches of Barnes (1923) and Dozier (1946) because the overlap varied with the tests employed, that of T. M. Anderson (1958) because the overlap (total scores only) varied with the high school grade tested.

freshman year to the graduate level. Sixteen different mental tests were administered to the subjects, the *Higher Form* of the *Otis Self-Administering Test* or one of the editions of the *American Council on Education Psychological Examination* for *College Freshmen* being most frequently utilized.

STANFORD-BINET

Probably the first test used in comparing the intelligence of Negro and white American college students was the 1916 Form of the *Stanford-Binet*. Derrick (1920) examined unselected Negroes attending Benedict College and Allen University and whites at the University of South Carolina. The class and age ranges were greater for the Negro than for the white Ss and a greater percentage of the colored was reported as coming from an inferior environment. The mean IQ of the colored Ss was 103, that of the whites, 112. One Negro and ten white students scored above 120, with 90.7 per cent of the whites overlapping the colored mean and 16.4 per cent of the colored overlapping the white mean.

MYERS MENTAL MEASURE, BINET GROUP, ARMY ALPHA

Graham (1930) describes the results of a number of tests given to colored students attending classes in education, history, and psychology at Fisk University and to groups of white Ss at the George Peabody College for Teachers and the Middle Tennessee State Teachers College at Murfreesboro. Graham noted that "a definite attempt was made to insure a random sampling in each race" and that an effort was exerted to increase motivation among the colored by selecting as *administrators* of the tests those people who "had been several years at Fisk and were well-known." The respective medians (not IQ's) attained by the white and colored groups on *Myers Mental Measure* were 75.4 and 66.2, the respective *Alpha* medians were 127.6 and 118.3. On the *Myers* 30 per cent of the colored overlapped the white median, on *Alpha* the amount of overlap was 36 per cent. As will be observed in Table 6, the colored median was slightly above that of the whites on the *Binet Group Test,* the respective medians being 36.2 and 35.5 with 55 per cent of the colored above the white.

TERMAN GROUP

Bond (1926) reports the testing of 175 students above the freshman class in a Negro college at Langston, Oklahoma by means of the *Terman Group Test.* The investigation was undertaken by a class in mental testing under the direction of the author, the method of selectivity not being given. The twenty-fifth, fiftieth, and seventy-fifth percentiles of the total Negro group were compared with Terman's norms; as is indicated in Table 6, the colored group's fiftieth percentile was six points above the twenty-fifth percentile of the normative group, and the seventy-fifth percentile of the colored was eight points below Terman's median.

Ohio State

The *Ohio State University Psychological Test,* for Grades 9 to 16 and adults, has appeared in a number of forms. Practically every item has been subjected to validation and the validities of the various forms are reported to be mostly in the .60's; the reliability of the 1937-38 form is about .94. The test consists of the subtests of same and opposites, analogies, and reading comprehension. The test is a work-limit rather than a time-limit test, usually taking about 2 hours but slow workers may take longer. (Pintner, *in* Buros, 1938, p. 1051)

The *Ohio State* test scores of Negro and white students at the Ohio State University and at the University of Toledo were compared by Grigsby (1929) and Solomon (1941), respectively. In Grigsby's research the 131 colored freshmen who entered the university in 1926, 1927, and 1928 were contrasted in test standing with the total freshman classes of these three years. From the table it will be noted that 42 per cent of the Negroes scored among the lowest 25 per cent of their classes while 11 per cent ranked among the highest 25 per cent; 12 per cent of the colored were in the lowest 5 per cent of their classes; and no Negro scored among the top 5 per cent of his class. "The median percentile of these Negroes is 39.5 instead of 50 as it would be if the Negro distribution were the same as that for all entering freshmen — the great majority of whom are white."

In Solomon's study the 47 Negro students and the 181 whites of foreign-born parents, together with the 19 whites with one foreign-born parent, were paired with a random sample of 247 white students of American-born parents. Each colored student or white S of foreign parentage was matched with a white of native parents according to the S's education. For example, a student who had graduated was matched with one who had graduated, one who had dropped out of college at the end of one year with one who had left college at the end of one year, *etc.,* and their freshman scores on the intelligence test compared. Although from 12.5 to 81 per cent of the students of foreign parentage reported that a foreign language was spoken at home, the mean intelligence scores of all of these white groups were higher than that earned by the Negro group. While in general the occupational ratings of the white parents were higher than those of the colored, the Polish group was in no higher category, on the average, than the colored. Just above the Polish in socioeconomic status were the Balkan, Hungarian, and Russian parents, one third of whom were listed as unskilled or semiskilled laborers. In spite of the relatively low occupational rating of their fathers, the Ss of Russian-born parents had a mean test score which placed them at the sixty-fourth percentile of the whole distribution, in contrast to a mean test score at the fifty-fifth percentile for children of native white parents and one at the thirty-ninth percentile for children of native colored parents.

Otis Self-Administering

Eleven studies, in which Negro college students were examined by the *Higher Form* of the *Otis Self-Administering Test of Mental Ability,* are summarized in Table 6. The students were enrolled in 11 or 12 different colleges for Negroes, all but four of which are located in the Southern states.[28] The college averages range from 35.2 to 49.3, all of them being below the *Otis* norm of 53. Five of the investigations were conducted at Fisk University, *i.e.,* those of Graham (1930), Caliver (1931), T. E. Davis (1933), M. H. Johnson (1940), and Brunschwig (1943). Caliver, Davis, and Johnson reported the means of 272, 273, and 109 respective freshmen to be 36.4, 41, and 42.6. From among their subjects Caliver and Davis selected all students who had been graduated from *Northern city high schools;* these Negroes were found to have earned respective means of 44 and 46. Caliver and Davis concurred in their finding that *Fisk* students whose fathers were employed in clerical work achieved higher means than those attained by *Fisk* freshmen from any other occupational category. Graham and Brunschwig tested groups of Negroes enrolled in certain *Fisk* classes totaling 181 and 88 students, respectively; they secured average scores of 49.3 and 45.5.[29]

Three of the other studies which utilized the *S-A Higher Form* were made on unselected groups of freshmen or new students. R. C. Davis (1932) tested all new students entering Virginia State College for Negroes in a given year and reported their median to be at 35.2; Sumner (1931) secured a median of 203 Howard University freshmen in the class interval of 40-44; and Price (1929) found the median of 857 freshmen from seven Negro accredited colleges to be 38.85. The medians for the several institutions ranged between 35.4 and 47.5. A very great range of individual scores was reported, with three Ss scoring in the class interval of 5-9 and one S earning a score in the interval of 70-75. Twenty per cent of the colored in these seven institutions overlapped the white norm, the percentages of overlapping for the individual colleges being as follows: 9, 10, 12, 23, 27, and 43.

Price secured the *Ohio State Psychological Examination* scores of 70 Ohio State Negro freshmen which he transmuted into equivalent *Otis S-A* scores and compared these with the *Otis* scores earned by the freshmen in the seven Negro colleges; he found the difference between the medians to be less than one point. Price was also able to obtain the scores on the *ACE* of 42 colored Ss in *Cornell, Dartmouth, Indiana, Northwestern,* and *Purdue* and those of 433 Ss attending the Negro universities of Atlanta, Fisk, and Howard; the difference between the averages of the two groups was insignificant.

Stainbrook and Siegel (1944) tested small numbers of white and colored students enrolled in psychology or sociology classes in a large Southern university and students in a Southern Negro college. They secured mean IQ's on the respective white and colored subjects of 120 and 99.

---

[28]Eleven colleges for Negroes identified. In addition, Stainbrook and Siegel tested Ss in a "southern Negro college".

[29]Maximum score obtainable, 75. Some of Graham's Ss tested on *Alpha,* etc., Graham gave Ss 20 min. on S-A; on a 30-min. basis his w and c medians of 42.4 and 38.3 would be approximately 54.4 and 49.3.

Incidental to their study of personality differences between Northern and Southern Negroes and Northern and Southern whites, Patrick and Sims (1934) compared the scores of 204 white students attending the state universities of Ohio and Alabama with 177 colored students from *Wilberforce* (Ohio) and *Tuskegee*. All classes were included and an effort was made to secure "representative samples". The respective averages of the white Ss were 52.16 and 50.70, and those of the colored were 45.75 and 37.10. The differences between the Negro and white means were significant; in addition, the Southern Negro mean was significantly below the mean of the Northern Negro college.

Wheatley and Sumner (1946) compared the most neurotic quarter with the least neurotic quarter, as determined by the *Bernreuter* test, of 100 students in the School of Music of Howard University. The 25 most neurotic Ss earned a mean *Otis S-A* score of 39.1 which placed them about four points below the mean of the least neurotic group.

Approximately 2470 Negro students, all of whom were attending various institutions of higher learning for members of their race,[30] have been tested by the *Otis S-A* and included in the above survey. The combined mean score earned by these colored students is 40.49 which corresponds to the 13.2 percentile rank of the norms group.

OTIS QUICK-SCORING GAMMA

Three standardized tests, including the *Otis Quick-Scoring Mental Ability Test, Gamma,* were administered by Virginia State College during freshman week, 1945. Droughn (1946), in an attempt to describe various characteristics of these students, selected a sample of them by taking every third name from an alphabetized list of records until she had secured 100 cases, consisting of 62 female and 38 male, from the total of 353. The mean Otis IQ was 90.9 and the standard deviation, 11, the mean of the women being very close to that of the men, the standard deviation of the women being somewhat the larger. Although Droughn tabulated the education of the fathers and mothers of these subjects, she made no attempt to relate years of parental schooling to intelligence of their offspring.

In order to study the relative competencies of prospective teachers and other students in Negro colleges in Alabama, Allman selected at random subjects from four colleges in the state, 100 from each college with 25 from each class; one of the colleges was a Liberal Arts College, one a Teachers College, and two were Industrial Colleges. From this number the author compared the means and standard deviations on several achievement tests as well as on the *Otis* of 149 "potential teachers" and 200 "non-teachers".[31] As will be noted in Table 6, the

---

[30]Including the Virginia State College study of R. C. Davis, and estimating the number of new students tested as 100.

[31]Not accounting for the 51 other cases. It is possible that the records of these students were incomplete.

students in the Teacher Education Program earned a mean IQ of 95.75, those in other college programs, a mean of 93.50.

AMERICAN COUNCIL ON EDUCATION

The test scores of more than 15,600 Negro college students who were examined by various editions of the *American Council on Education Psychological Examination for College Freshmen* have been summarized in Table 6. The Ss with one exception were attending Negro colleges and wherever the form of the test was given their averages have been compared with the norms. Boots (1926) tested a small number of Negro college freshmen from three colleges in Mississippi and 1681 white freshmen from thirteen colleges in the same state. Although the colored freshmen were on the average two years older than the whites and had spent more than a year longer in school, their mean was markedly below that of the whites, *i.e.*, 37 in contrast to 93. This appears to be the largest discrepancy found between the Negro and white means on the *ACE*.

According to Caliver (1931) the average scores made on the 1927 and 1928 forms of the *ACE* by 76 men and 114 women entering Fisk University during these years were 69.95 and 88.90, respectively, for the two sexes; the freshman norms for these same years were 124.88 and 138.[32] The *Fisk* freshmen who were graduates of Northern city high schools earned a mean score of 96.90 which was superior to that achieved by the freshman class as a whole but inferior to the national norms. As with the *Otis,* Caliver found that students whose fathers were in clerical work attained the highest mean of any occupational group. The absence of higher academic training as a requirement for entering the ministry— which probably was the occupation of a sizeable proportion of fathers who were in the professions—coupled with the relatively high prestige held by clerical workers among Negroes, may have accounted for the higher means achieved by Negro children whose parents were of clerical rather than professional occupations. At *Fisk,* the mean of the offspring of clerical employees was 103.54, whereas the mean of students whose fathers were listed as being in the professions was 86.13.

T. E. Davis (1933) reported the median of about 100 *Fisk* freshmen on the 1929 form of the *ACE* to be 103.18, which placed it about 37 points below the national median of 140.67. Like Caliver, Davis found the highest average among the *Fisk* students to be secured by students whose fathers were employed in clerical positions.

---

[32]A gross score of 69.95 is located at the 11th or 13th percentile rank of the norms distribution depending upon whether the form was 1927 or 1928; a gross score of 88.90 lies between the 20th and 24th percentile ranks of the norms, depending upon the form. A score of 96.90 (mean of graduates of Northern city high schools attending *Fisk*) is between 24th and 30th percentiles of the norms distribution, depending upon the form, and a score of 103.50 (highest mean of Ss separated according to occupation of father) lies between the 28th and 34th percentile ranks of college Ss.

In evaluating certain tests as predictive measures of academic grades, M. H. Johnson (1940) examined the *ACE*, as well as the *Otis S-A*, records of 109 freshmen who entered Fisk University in 1933 or in 1934. The mean gross scores earned by the students on the 1933 and the 1934 forms of the *ACE* placed them at about the 22nd and 25th percentile ranks of the respective norms groups. As will be noted from the table the standard deviations were unusually large.

Rooks (1946) and L. F. Anderson (1948) separated the respective scores of 143 and 101 women who came to *Fisk* directly from high school in *North* and *South* categories, the latter group described as including all states and the District of Columbia where separate schools were required for Negroes and whites. Anderson further limited his group to include only those Ss who remained at *Fisk* for four successive semesters. The Northern mean, as reported by Rooks, was 88.16, which was significantly higher than the Southern mean of 67.57, both of them being lower than the national median of 101.5 (1945 form).[33] Anderson's Northern group earned a mean of 90.5, a score 20 points higher than the Southern mean and 11 points below the national median.

In investigating the performance on the *ACE* of 253 college freshmen who entered Fisk University between 1945 and 1947, Roberts (1948) compared the scores of males: (1) of different socioeconomic status, (2) who were veterans and nonveterans, and (3) who came from the North and from the South. The freshmen whose fathers were in the upper socioeconomic levels, who were non-veterans, and who were from the North earned higher scores on the average than their counterparts, the regional origin being the most important of the three factors. Roberts (1950) likewise examined the *ACE* scores of 54 Fisk women who entered college in 1945 directly from high school and were graduated four years later; he divided them into two socioeconomic levels according to their fathers' occupations and into two regions depending upon whether they came from the North or the South. All of the women had been tested by three forms of the *ACE* between their freshman and senior years. As with the men, the women from the North were consistently superior to those from the South even when matched for socioeconomic status. Roberts concluded that the greater gains made by the Fisk women relative to the national norms for a comparable period of time suggested the need for a general re-examination of conclusions based upon freshman testing alone.

Brooks (1942) found the mean gross score of 184 Negro college freshmen and sophomores at the Norfolk Division of Virginia Union University to be 59.55 on the 1939 form of the *ACE*. This score is in contrast to the published norm of 94 and corresponds to about the ninth percentile rank in the normative distribution.

Craft (1943) was interested in comparing the *ACE* scores of freshmen and upperclassmen enrolled in Morehouse College of Atlanta University. Since some

---

[33]Mothers' occupations were more closely associated with variable performance than were fathers' occupations. (Roberts, 1946)

form of the *ACE* had been administered to all entering freshmen at this college for Negro men Craft was able to select from the files the scores of 169 new students who had been tested as freshmen in 1942 by the 1941 form. These scores were compared with those of the following small groups of advanced students, all of whom had been tested in their freshman year:[34] (1) 35 sophomores, retested on the 1941 form; (2) 31 juniors, retested on the 1941 form; and (3) 16 seniors, retested on the 1941 form. As indicated in Table 6, the standard deviations all appear to have been somewhat larger than that of the normative group with the means of the several upperclass groups being significantly superior to the freshman mean. According to the Thurstones' norms for this form, the mean score of some 70,263 college freshmen was 105.49. The *Morehouse* freshman mean corresponds to the 4th percentile rank, and the respective sophomore, junior, and senior means to the 22nd, 27th, and 24th percentile ranks of the normative distribution.

Roberts (1944) administered the 1940 form of the *ACE* to students attending the Agricultural, Mechanical and Normal College at Pine Bluff, Arkansas, in conjunction with a larger study of the adjustments, opinions, and preferences of Negro college students. He was able to secure complete data on 188 of the 474 students enrolled in the college, 116 of them being in their freshman year. The freshman mean proved to be 54.40, about four points below the mean of the total Negro group tested. The Negro freshman mean is very close to the 4th percentile rank in the Thurstones' sample. Roberts cautioned the reader to bear in mind the definitely substandard situations to which the students had been subjected all of their lives.

In a study of the recreational interest, intelligence, scholastic achievement, personality, and vocational interest of male students at Virginia State College for Negroes, Boone (1945) tabulated the *ACE* scores of 222 students on the 1937, 1938, 1939, and 1940 editions.[35] The mean of 72.73, calculated from the author's data by the reviewer, may be compared with the norm of 94 on the 1939 edition of the test.

Kenyon (1946) included in his data the frequency distributions of the *ACE* scores of Prairie View University freshmen who were enrolled as majors in English, mathematics, history, science, and home economics. The median, calculated by the reviewer, was 94.5. Unfortunately the author did not give the test form employed; however, the *Prairie View* median was below all norms for the years 1940 to 1945.

Caliver (1933) reported the results of the administration of the 1930 form

---

[34]The scores of the advanced students were not compared with their own *ACE* scores achieved as freshmen but with the test scores earned by the 169 Ss of another freshman class. Craft does not indicate how she selected her subjects above the freshman level; she implies that the 169 freshmen tested composed the entire class in 1942-43.

[35]He first converted the scores into equivalent 1939 scores.

of the *ACE* to 1987 freshmen in 33 colleges for Negroes, the colleges being located in the District of Columbia and in 16 states.[36] The average score obtained for the total group of freshmen was 76.01, the median, 65.1, the former being somewhat more than half the norm of 141.5 reported for this edition. The medians of the 33 colleges ranged from 26.33 to 131, the median point of the highest ranking school being some ten points below the national median reported by the Thurstones.[37] Caliver summarized his findings as follows: "The typical Negro college freshman is 20 years of age, has a mean psychological score of 76; and comes from a family of 5 children of which one has already graduated from college. His father and mother have respectively, 8 and 9 years of schooling . . . . he comes from a home having a monthly income of $95. The home he comes from contains 5 or 6 rooms and is occupied by 4 or 5 persons. His parents have 96 books in their home and take two magazines." In contrast to the typical Negro student, the *typical* white S of the depression period was younger, had a significantly higher psychological score, came from a smaller family, had parents with more schooling, had a higher ratio of rooms to the number in the household, and came from a home having a higher monthly income.

In a national survey of the higher education of Negroes, a testing program was administered to a representative sample of 3684 freshmen students in the fall of 1940 (*National Survey* . . . ., 1942). The Ss were enrolled in 27 Negro colleges, 19 of them located in the South; 13 of the colleges were Liberal Arts, seven were Land-Grant, four were Teachers Colleges, and three, Junior Colleges. Those tested included approximately one third of the total number of freshmen attending institutions for the higher education of Negroes during the year. A mean total score of 56 was obtained on the 1940 edition of the *ACE* in contrast to the norm of 103.55; the mean of 56 placed the average freshman in a Negro college at the *fourth percentile* of the national distribution. The scores of the Ss were classified according to location of their secondary education and the following respective medians were secured: North, 82.5; Border, 64.0; urban South, 49.8; and rural South, 43.0. The medians of the groups who had attended public schools in the North, Border, urban South, and rural South were, respectively, at the twenty-second, eighth, third, and first percentile ranks according to the national norms. About two thirds of the colored freshmen had attended Southern elementary and secondary schools which were known to have short school terms, poorly prepared teachers, insufficient equipment, and inadequate school plants. According to the authors of this survey "There can be little argument with the validity of the conclusion that the subaverage educational background offers sufficient explana-

---

[36]Four of the states are Northern.

[37]On the basis of records of 36,479 Ss (Thurstone and Thurstone, 1931) a raw score of 65.1 corresponds to a percentile rank of 8.4; 26.33 to a percentile rank of 0.7; and 131 to a percentile rank of 45.5.

tion of the subaverage achievement without introducing the question of racial differences." (p. 51)[38]

In attempting to determine the means by which academic achievement may be predicted in the freshman year of college, Lowry (1957) analyzed the *ACE* and other records of freshman students entering a Texas college for Negroes during a ten-year period. This college, described as a church-related liberal arts college, was formed by a merger in 1952 of *Tillotson* and *Samuel Huston,* two private colleges located in the city of Austin. The research began with the records on Negro students entering *Samuel Huston* between 1946 and 1951 and continued with those on students entering *Huston-Tillotson,* the college resulting from the 1952 merger. The majority of the freshmen were recent high school graduates, between the ages of 17 and 19; in the earlier years included in the analysis there were reported to be some veterans in the freshman classes, but "very few veterans entered as freshmen after the colleges had merged."

The means (Table 6) may be directly compared with one another, and except for the year 1951, range from 41 to 50. This range corresponds to the first or second percentile rank of American college students who were given this test.

Canady is the author of three studies utilizing West Virginia State College Negro students. In the first of these (1936), all new Ss entering the college during three successive years were tested by the 1931, 1932, or 1933 form of the *ACE*. The 517 students were reported as having secured a mean gross score of 78.65, a median of 69.80, and a standard deviation of 40.05 on these forms.[39] The amount of overlapping was 5.43 per cent. Canady, for comparative purposes, tabulated the median gross scores of his three freshman groups according to the test edition and included 209 subjects tested in 1930. For the four successive years of 1930, 1931, 1932, and 1933, the respective West Virginia State College medians and the National medians were as follows: 1930—63, *139;* 1931—64, *147.37;* 1932—92, *163.72;* and 1933—78.89, *155.20.*

In his second study (1942) Canady included the combined scores of all new students entering West Virginia State College in 1935, 1936, and 1937. The mean score of the 497 Ss was 92.12, in contrast to the college freshman norms of 182, 177.23, and 167.08 for the three editions employed. When he divided his subjects into three groups according to their Sims socioeconomic status scores Canady found those of the upper status to have a mean of 98.90 on the *ACE;* this was higher than the means of the other two groups. In view of the fact that the mean achieved by the highest socioeconomic status group is still far below the

---

[38]Median *ACE* of freshmen of College of Liberal Arts of Howard University from 1938-1945 was within the 20th and 25th %ile ranks of the national norms. Phillips (1946) was interested in studying the characteristics of superior Negro students and did not include in her data the number tested, the test editions, or medians.

[39]All 517 scores combined into one frequency distribution by author.

national norm (only about 60 per cent of it) the reviewer does not consider that Canady's results justify his conclusion that "The evidence presented . . . lead to the conclusion that reported Negro-white differences in intelligence test performance are due in all probability to the Negro's position in the American social system." (p. 170)

Canady further grouped the test results of the West Virginia freshmen into seven categories according to size and location of their home towns. He found the group from large Northern cities to have secured the highest mean score, 113.15; those from large cities in the South to rank second with a mean of 110.87; the Ss from large cities in West Virginia to rank third with a mean of 93.74; Ss from small cities and towns in the North fourth with a mean of 92.62; and Ss from small cities and towns in the South and in West Virginia whose means were 79.00 and 77.36, respectively.

The results of the two preceding studies were of course included in Canady's subsequent report (1943) in which he presented averages and standard deviations for Negro men and women entering West Virginia State College from 1931 to 1937. The mean *ACE* scores for the men and women were 84.50 and 81.50, respectively. Canady did not indicate whether or not the individual scores were transmuted into equivalents of one form; the means, nonetheless, are far below any of the national means between 1931 and 1937.

In comparing various characteristics of Negro college seniors who were education majors with those who were noneducation majors, Richardson (1963) examined the *ACE* records of 200 members of the class of 1957 of Morgan State College, Baltimore, Maryland. All subjects were voluntary participants in the study and included about 90 per cent of each department's majors; furthermore, all had been tested on the 1949 form of the *ACE* at the beginning of the freshman year. Richardson divided the students according to three college divisions: Humanities, Social Sciences, and Natural Sciences. As will be noted in Table 6, the mean gross scores on the *ACE* of the three divisions were very close to the Morgan State College combined mean of 75.69, with the males being superior to the females only in the Natural Sciences Division. The standard deviations varied between 17.75 and 25, the combined standard deviation being 21.94. Ten per cent of the Negro students were above the mean of the norms group of 103.69, based upon more than 43,000 freshmen attending 229 colleges. The Morgan College mean of 75.69 corresponded to a percentile rank of 14 in the normative distribution.

We have found few reports on the *ACE* scores obtained by Negroes attending nonsegregated colleges. We have already noted that Price (1929) reported no significant difference between the mean score of colored Ss enrolled in *Northwestern, Indiana, etc.*, and the average of students attending Fisk, Howard, and Atlanta universities. The *National Survey* authors (1942) tabulated medians secured on small groups of Negroes at the Ohio State University, Chicago University, and the University of Kansas. These medians were found to be above those usually obtained on freshmen attending Negro colleges. However, a saturated sampling of Negroes was not secured, the authors reporting that psychological test scores were available for some of the Negro students in the three nonsegregated universities. The number reported for *Chicago,* for example, was 25; yet grade point averages were given for 98 Negroes at the University of Chicago.

Shuey (1942) reported a higher mean for the 43 colored students entering New York University's Washington Square College from 1935 to 1937 than has usually been obtained on colored students. The mean of 170.61 is relatively close to the national norm of 182 reported by the Thurstones and far above the mean of 92 secured on the West Virginia State College Negroes.[40] Instead of comparing the total number of whites in the college with the Negroes, Shuey selected 43 white Ss after having matched a white with a colored student according to test edition, sex, age (plus or minus one year), country of birth if the Negro's birthplace was in the United States (for the six Negroes born in the West Indies there were obtained six whites of the same age, sex, *etc.,* who were foreign-born), country of birth of parents in so far as Negro parents were United States-born (otherwise a Negro was matched with a white student of foreign-born parents), occupation of father, and academic standing of the student. As will be seen in Table 6, the 43 white students thus selected to match the colored Ss achieved a significantly higher mean of 214.67 and were more variable than the Negroes. No Negro scored within 70 points of the highest scoring white. When ten pairs were eliminated on the presumption of inequality of educational opportunity, the majority of the ten Negroes having had some of their previous education in segregated schools, the test scores of the remaining 33 pairs were compared. The resulting means were 177.00 and 217.76 for the respective Negro and white groups, the standard deviations being practically unchanged. The difference between the means was still significant at the one per cent level of confidence. No colored S equaled or exceeded the seventy-fifth percentile of the 33 white subjects.

DIGIT-SYMBOL

Katz, Epps, and Axelson (1964) attempted to determine if anticipated comparison with whites is detrimental to Negro mental test performance. Since it is often implicit in the testing situation that comparisons will be made with norms or white standards the lower scores obtained by Negro subjects may in part be due to the presence of *too much drive* for efficient responding or to *fear of failure* which may disrupt performance by producing task-irrelevant defensive reactions.

---

[40]Although all new students had been sent written requests to appear for testing on a certain date in the beginning of the school year, about one fourth of colored and white absented themselves and were never tested. Probably the averages would have been lower if these Ss' scores had been included. Not all of the Ss were freshmen, some of them being transfers from other colleges.

Accordingly, hard or easy digit-symbol tasks were administered to Negro college students enrolled in Florida Agricultural and Mechanical University under one of three types of instructions: *no test, test with own college norms,* and *test with national norms.* A Negro faculty member administered the tests. White students in attendance at Florida State University were given the hard task only under the same three conditions, the tests being administered by a white faculty member. As will be seen from Table 6, Negro students scored their best when told that they would be compared with other students at *their own college* and worst under *no test* instructions. Upon completing the tasks the Negro Ss indicated that under all three conditions they felt calm rather than nervous while working; and that the Ss cared more about doing well under the *national norms* condition than did those who worked under *local-norms instructions* (p<.001). In other words, although the *national norms* group obtained *lower digit-symbol scores* than the *local norms* group, the reports of the former indicate that they were *the more highly motivated.*

In the white sample, the digit-symbol scores were about the same under *national norms* as under *local norms* conditions, both being higher than those working under *no test* condition. The white Ss were superior to the colored under each of the three conditions, the difference being the greatest under the *national norms* instructions.

SCHOOL AND COLLEGE ABILITY TESTS

At least three researches on Negro students, all of whom were attending colleges in the Southern states, have made use of the *Cooperative School and College Ability Tests (SCAT).* The first of these was concerned with determining the incidence of talent for science and mathematics among colored students enrolled in schools and colleges of Mississippi. (Anderson, Tommie, 1958)[41] Securing a sample of 260 freshmen from four Negro colleges of this state, two of them designated as private liberal arts colleges, one a state junior college, and the other a four-year state college, Anderson administered not only the *SCAT* but also certain General Achievement tests and the Kuder Preference Record.

The mean Total Score on *SCAT* was reported to be 274.6 as compared with the norms mean of 300; the Verbal and Quantitative means were respectively, 267.5 and 277.7 as opposed to the norms means of 295 and 305 (Table 6). The colored Ss performed somewhat more effectively on the Quantitative than on the Verbal tests, their mean on the former being within the 8-15th percentile band of the norms group, their latter mean within the 4-12th percentile band. The mean Total Score of the colored students placed it within the 5-8th percentile band of the norms group. The amount of overlapping was as follows: Verbal, 5.5 per cent, Quantitative, 6.9 per cent, and Total, 2.3 per cent. The author

---

[41]For a review of Miss Anderson's research on high school pupils as examined by *SCAT,* see pp. 251-252.

TABLE

COLLEGE

AUTHOR DATE	LOCATION	N	SUBJECTS CLASS	METHOD OF SELECTION
				STANFORD-BINET
Derrick, S. M. (1920)	Univ. South Carolina, Benedict College, and Allen Univ.	w-75 c- 55	Mainly 1-2 All	Unselected. C from all college classes and "a few" from the two upper classes of the high sch.
				MYERS MENTAL
Graham, J. L. (1930)	George Peabody, Middle Tenn State Teachers College, and Fisk Univ.	w-106 c- 168	Mainly 1	54 w at *Peabody* & 52 w at *Middle Tenn State TC.* C from classes in Educ, Psychol, & Hist at *Fisk Univ.*
				BINET
Graham, J. L. (1930)	Middle Tenn State Teachers College and Fisk Univ.	w-115 c- 99	Mainly 1	w- *Middle Tenn State TC.* c- *Fisk Univ classes.*
				ARMY
Graham, J. L. (1930)	George Peabody College and Fisk Univ.	w-108 c- 120	Mainly 1	w- *Peabody Coll.* c- *Fisk Univ* classes.
				TERMAN
Bond, H. M. (1926)	Langston Univ.	c- 175	2-4	Ss all students at *Colored A & N Univ* at Langston.[2]

[1]Described by the author as an adaptation to group administration of the individual Binet tests.

SIX

STUDENTS

	RESULTS		COMMENTS OF AUTHOR

1916 FORM

	IQ		Negro better in memory and concrete and
	w	c	routine problems than in those involving
M	112	103	abstractions and reconstruction. Average
Range	91-128	76-125	home environ of c inferior to that of w Ss.
16% c above w *mean*			

MEASURE

	Scores		Should use caution in interpretation of
	w	c	results obtained from individuals with
Mdn	75.4	66.2	unequal social surroundings.
Q	10.8	10.4	
30% c above w *mdn*			

GROUP[1]

	Scores		Results of these studies indicate that
	w	c	about 36-37% of this Negro coll group
Mdn	35.5	36.2	reach or surpass median intell of tested
Q	3.0	3.5	w students.
$D/PEd =$		1.3	
55% c above w *mdn*			

ALPHA

	Scores		Unsolved question of how much the dif-
	w	c	ference bet races is innate and how much
Mdn	127.6	118.3	due to more stimulating w milieu.
Q	16.4	17.3	
$D/PEd =$		3.3	
36% c above w *mdn*			

GROUP

		Scores		White Ss, acc to norms, have an increment
%ile		w	c	of approximately 25% over the colored
Rank		norm		in this test.
25		122	95	
50		147	128	
75		169	139	

[2]Now called *Langston University*.

TABLE

COLLEGE

AUTHOR DATE	LOCATION	N	SUBJECTS CLASS	METHOD OF SELECTION
				OHIO STATE
Grigsby, J. E. (1929)	Ohio State Univ.	c- 131	1	All c entering as freshmen in 1926, 1927, and 1928.
Solomon, S. J. (1941)	Univ. Toledo	w-447[4] c- 47	1 1	All w of foreign-born parents and all c in univ; a random selection of equal number of w of Amer parents, each of whom was paired with a c S or with a w of foreign-born parents, acc to educ; *e.g.*, graduate with grad, 1-yr dropout with 1-yr dropout.
				OTIS SELF-ADMINISTERING
Price, J. St. C. (1929)	Negro Colleges and Ohio State Univ.	c- 857 c- 70[6]	1 1	Ss entering the following 7 Negro accredited colleges in 1927: *Fisk, Hampton, Lincoln* (Pa), *Morehouse, NC State, Va Union,* and *WVa State.*
Graham, J. L. (1930)	George Peabody Coll. and Fisk Univ.	w-126 c- 181	1 1	Effort to get random sampling of each racial group, *mainly* freshmen; c from classes in Hist, Educ, and Psychol. Used 20 min time limit on test.
Caliver, A. (1931)	Fisk Univ.	c- 272 c- 47	1 1	cI-freshmen, 1926-28. cII-entering with advanced standing, 1926-28.
Davis, R. C. (1932)	Virginia State Coll.			All new students entering during the year. Number not given.

[3]Distribution of scores of c is compared with norms secured on all freshmen. *Class 1* includes the lowest scoring 5 per cent of the three classes; 12 per cent of c earned scores in this range.

[4]The 447 w Ss included 181 children of foreign-born parents, 19 with one foreign-born parent, and 247 of American-born parents. All were enrolled bet 1935-1940.

[5]The lowest scoring w Ss, *i.e.*, those of Hungarian-born parents, had a mean intelligence %ile of 44.1, while the highest, *i.e.*, those of Russian-born parents, had a mean %ile rank of 64.

SIX (continued)
STUDENTS

RESULTS			COMMENTS OF AUTHOR

UNIVERSITY PSYCHOLOGICAL

		Scores[3]		
Class	Total		c	
1	5%		12%	
2	20%		30%	
3	50%		47%	
4	20%		11%	
5	5%		0%	

Mdn %ile of Negroes is 39.5 instead of 50 as it would be if the distribution of c were the same as that for all entering freshmen.

	M %iles[5]		
	w	c	
Parent's birth			
Native	55	39	
Foreign	44-64		

Foreign lang spoken in homes of 12.5% of Scan and 80-81% of Hungar and Balkan groups. Polish and c of lowest occup; Balkan, Hungar, Russian next; all others higher ratings.

HIGHER FORM

	Scores	
	c	
Mdn		
Negro coll	35.4-47.5	
Ohio State	38.85	
20% c above w mdn		

As meas by *ACE*, no sig diff bet the 42 c in *Cornell, Dartmouth, Indiana, Northwestern,* and *Purdue* and the 433 c attending *Atlanta, Fisk* and *Howard.*

	Scores[7]	
	w	c
Mdn	42.4	38.3
Q	6.1	5.9
D/PEd =	4.8	
28% c above w mdn		

Fisk Ss tested by teachers who had been there several years. Good cooperation.

	Scores	
	cI	cII
M	36.4	36.6
s	10.6	
Range	2-67	15-54

Mean of graduates of Northern high schs, 44. Means of Ss whose fathers in clerical wk, 40.5; sk labor, 39.5; prof, 37.5; in unsk labor, 33.8.

	Score	
	c	
Mdn	35.2	

Purpose of study was to determine presence of relation bet intelligence and speed of conduction over a reflex arc.

[6]The *Ohio State* freshmen had been given the *Ohio State University Intelligence Test* and the scores transmuted into *Otis* scores.

[7]Median of 2516 college Ss from 21 colleges and universities, based upon a 30 min time interval, is 53, as reported by Otis.

TABLE

COLLEGE

AUTHOR DATE	LOCATION	N	SUBJECTS CLASS	METHOD OF SELECTION
Davis, T. E. (1933)	Fisk Univ.	c- 273	1	Tested *Fisk* freshmen entering bet 1928 and 1930.
Patrick, J. R., and Sims, V. M. (1934)	Ohio Univ.,[8] Univ. Alabama, Wilberforce Univ., and Tuskegee Inst.	w-103 w-101 c- 125 c- 52	1-4 1-4 1-4 1-4	Study made in connection with survey of personality differences. Tried to secure represent samples. Relatively more from first 2 yrs of coll.
Johnson,[9] M. H. (1940)	Fisk Univ.	109	1	From records of entering freshmen where academic records and entrance test scores were complete; 48 in 1933 and 61 in 1934.
Brunschwig, L. (1943)	Fisk Univ.	c- 88	1-4	Ss enrolled in Introductory Psychol. Majority were sophomores.
Stainbrook, E., and Siegel, P. S. (1944)	Large Southern University and a Southern Negro College	w-45 c- 45	2-3 2-3	w- Elem Psychology Class c- Elem Sociology Class
Sumner, F. C. (1931)	Howard Univ.	c- 203	1	
Wheatley, L. A., and Sumner, F. C. (1946)	Howard Univ.	c- 50		Compared most & least neurotic ¼ (determined by *Bernreuter)* among 100 Ss in Sch of Music; the 100 included little over ⅔ of enrollment in Music Sch.

[8]Two colleges in Ohio and two in Alabama including one coll for Negroes in each state.
[9]See this table for results on *Amer Council Psychol Examination* administered to these Ss.

SIX *(continued)*
STUDENTS

	RESULTS		COMMENTS OF AUTHOR
	Scores		M of graduates of Northern mixed high schs, 46; mean of graduates from South, 38.
	c		
M	41		
Range	11-72		

		Scores		Negro functions on lower level than w in situations of abstract nature; in concrete social adjustments to everyday life, w superiority is not consistently shown.
	w		c	
Section		M		
North	52.16		45.75	
South	50.70		37.10	
		s		
North	6.88		7.84	
South	8.70		7.72	
All diffs bet *means sig* except bet the 2 w groups				

	Score[10]		
	c		
M	42.59		
s	11.60		

	Scores		Test given in connection with analysis of popular misconceptions.
	c		
M	45.5		
Range	22-69		

		IQ		Negroes tested by a c graduate student. On Group *Rorschach* c showed more rigidity and less fluency in responses than w.
	w		c	
M	120		99	

	Scores		In connection with mental health survey.
	c		
Mdn	40-44		

	Scores	
	Most "N"	Least "N"
M	39.1	42.9
s	7.65	5.35

Author does not give the number of freshmen on whom data were incomplete.

[10]The *Fisk* mean is at the 18th percentile of the 2516 coll Ss in normative sample.

TABLE

COLLEGE

AUTHOR DATE	LOCATION	N	SUBJECTS CLASS	METHOD OF SELECTION
				OTIS QUICK-SCORING
Droughn, K. P. (1946)	Virginia State College	c- 100	1	Selected every other name from alphabetically arranged student record cards until secured 100 from the 353 entering freshmen, 1945.
Allman,[12] R. W. (1953)	Alabama Colleges	c- 397	1-4	397 Ss selected from 4 Negro colleges, 100 from each, with 25 Ss from each class, selected at random. One coll was Liberal Arts, one Teachers Coll, and two Industrial Colleges.
				AMERICAN COUNCIL ON EDUCATION
Boots,[14] W. E. (1926)	Mississippi Colleges	w-1681 c- 38	1 1	White Ss in 13 colleges, colored in 3 colleges.
Caliver, A. (1931)	Fisk Univ.	c- 190	1	In addition to *Otis S-A,* the *ACE* was administered in 1927 and 1928.[15]
Davis, T. E. (1933)	Fisk Univ.	c- 100[16]	1	1929 form used.
Caliver, A. (1933)	33 Negro Colleges in 16 States and D. C.	c- 1987	1	US Commissioner Educ wrote to presidents of 95 Negro colleges; 42 participated. Deans or Heads Dept Educ in charge of giving & scoring exams. A variety of inform obtained. 1930 form used.

[11]Means and medians calculated by reviewer from author's frequency distributions. Author erred in size of total *mdn* & *m*.

[12]For results on tests given to 8th grade Ss, see Table 4.

[13]Numbers of these not given and presumably not included in results as tabulated.

[14]For results on sch children tested, see Tables 3 and 4.

[15]Thurstones' medians for the 1927 and 1928 forms, based on tests administered to 5077 and 30,653 college Ss are 124.88 and 138, respectively.

SIX *(continued)*

STUDENTS

RESULTS	COMMENTS OF AUTHOR

MENTAL ABILITY TEST

	c Male	IQ[11] c Fem	c Total
Mdn	92.5	90.8	91.5
M	91.1	90.7	90.9
s	9.8	11.7	11.0

36% fathers had only grade-sch educ; 40% had some high sch; 17% had one or more yrs college; 3.5 had additional professional sch.

	IQ c
Teach Educ	
M	95.75
s	9.2
Range	74-120
Other Coll	
M	93.50
s	9.5

In addition 2 senior classes were included, the entire class of *Miles* and every 5th in class at Ala State Teach College.[13]

PSYCHOLOGICAL EXAMINATION

	Scores w	c
M	93	37

Negro freshmen average 2 years older than w and have spent 10 months more in previous schooling.

	Scores c Male	c Female
M	69.95	88.90
s	46	36.60

Mean of Ss graduated from North-city high schs, 96.90; mean of Ss from large South-city high schs, 82.10. Mean of Ss fathers in professions, 86.13; in clerical, 103.54; business, 87.54; unsk labor, 69.55; sk labor, 97.57.

	Score[17] c
Mdn	103.18

Mdn at 24%ile rank of normative sample

Highest aver score obtained by c whose fathers in clerical occup; next in prof, lowest by children of domestics, farmers, and unsk lab. Diffs bet groups not sig.

	Scores[18]
Mdn	65.1
Range Mdns	26-131

Mdn of 65 at 8%ile rank of normative sample.

Typical c S has parents with 8-9 yrs schooling and earning $95 monthly. About 73% from Southern publ schs, 16% from Border, and 11-12% from North.

[16]Estimated by reviewer.

[17]Thurstone and Thurstone report a median on this form, based on scores of 34,507 students from 131 colleges to be 140.67.

[18]The median of 36,479 college Ss on the 1930 form was reported as being 141-142. A score of 131 corresponds to a %ile rank of 45.5 acc to these norms. (Thurstone and Thurstone, 1931)

TABLE

COLLEGE

AUTHOR DATE	LOCATION	N	SUBJECTS CLASS	METHOD OF SELECTION
Johnson,[19] M. H. (1940)	Fisk Univ.	c- 109	1	48 freshmen entering in '33 tested by 1933 form; 61 entering in '34 tested by 1934 form. Selection both years based on availability of complete academic records and entrance test scores.
Brooks, L. B. (1942)	Virginia Union Univ.	c- 184	1, 2	105 freshmen and 79 sophomores in Norfolk Div of Univ tested in May; 1939 form used.
National Survey (1942)	27 Negro Colleges	c- 3684	1	Representative sample of colleges including 19 in South and one third of all c entering higher institutions of learning. 1940 form.
Craft, P. M. (1943)	Morehouse College	c- 251	1-4	169 freshmen tested in Sept '42, 1941 form; 35 sophs who had taken 1941 form as fresh retested on same form, Sept '42; 31 juniors, tested on 1940 form as freshmen & retested with 1941 form in Sept '42; 16 seniors previously tested by 1939 form as freshmen and retested by 1941 form in Sept '42 or Feb '43.
Roberts, S. O. (1944)	Agricultural, Mechanical and Normal Coll, Pine Bluff, Ark.	c- 188	1-4	*ACE* was administered as a minor part of a larger study of social preferences, survey of opinions, adjustment, *etc.*, of Negro college students. Complete data on 188 of 474 enrolled; 116 being 1st year. Used 1940 form.
Boone, E. B. (1945)	Virginia State College for Negroes	c- 222	Mainly 1	Male Ss enrolled in 1941-42 on whom records were available. Tested an additional number (method of selection not given). Used 1937, 1938, 1939, and 1940 forms.

[19]*Otis S-A, Higher Examination* also administered to these Ss.

[20]Norms of '33 *ACE*, based on records of 40,229 Ss in 203 colleges indicate that a score of 109.20 corresponds to a %ile rank of 22. (Thurstone and Thurstone, 1934)

[21]A total gross score of 128.40 corresponds to a %ile rank of 25, based on records of 52,435 Ss in 240 colleges, 1934 norms. (Thurstone and Thurstone, 1935)

[22]A score of 60 on the 1939 form used falls at the 9th percentile on the national norms for college freshmen. Mean for the 1939 form, based on national norms, was 94. (Thurstone and Thurstone, 1940)

SIX *(continued)*

STUDENTS

RESULTS				COMMENTS OF AUTHOR
	Scores			
	c			
M				
1933	109.20[20]			
1934	128.40[21]			
s				
1933	56.80			
1934	51.20			
	Scores[22]			A Negro junior college serving the
	c			Norfolk-Portsmouth area.
M	59.55			
s 1	17.25			
2	20.82			
	Scores[23]			Mean at 4th percentile of college norms.
	c			Low scores reflect cumulative effect of
M	56			subaverage educational and experiential
Range	below 4-165			bkg.

	Scores[24]				All of upper-class means were sig higher
	c	c	c	c	than the mean of the 169 freshmen, CR's
	Fr	Soph	Jr	Sen	being respectively: 7.27, 7.39, and 6.00.
M	56.52	85.64	90.63	88.25	
s	28.22	32.76	36.07	29.13	

	Scores			The present freshman group is representa-
Total	c			tive of the average freshman in *National*
M	58.50			*Survey* where mean of c freshmen was
s	23.30			56, placing it at the 4th %ile rank acc to
Freshmen				coll norms.
M	54.40			

	Scores[25]			Scores converted into equivalent 1939
	c			scores.
M	72.73			
s	13.20			

[20]Thurstone and Thurstone (1941) report a mean of 103.55, 1940 form, based on 54,228 freshmen from 318 colleges. Median of highest 4 per cent of c Survey freshmen was 117, or at the 68th %ile of test norms; 0.5 per cent of Survey freshmen scored above the 90th %ile of national norms (Jenkins and Randall, 1948).

[21]Thurstone and Thurstone (1942) report a mean of 105.49 and s of 25.69 on 1941 ACE, based on 70,263 freshman cases in 373 colleges. The %ile ranks corresponding to the several Morehouse means are: freshman, *4;* sophomore, *22;* junior, *27;* senior, *24.*

[25]Calculated by reviewer from author's frequency table. Median for 1939 form, based on national norms, was 94.

TABLE

COLLEGE

AUTHOR DATE	LOCATION	N	SUBJECTS CLASS	METHOD OF SELECTION
Rooks, A. R. (1946)	Fisk Univ.	c-[26] No-55 So- 88	1 1	Only women who came directly from high schools. Used 1945 form.
Kenyon, H. C. (1946)	Prairie View Texas Univ.	c- 132	1	Second semester Ss who were enrolled as majors in English, Math, Home Ec, History, or Science.
Anderson, L. F. (1948)	Fisk Univ.	c- 101	1	Only women who came directly from high schs in 1945 and were in residence for 4 successive semesters. 1945 form.
Roberts, S. O. (1948)	Fisk Univ.	c- 253	1	Male freshmen entering bet 1945-47; 141 veterans of World War II and 112 nonveterans, 20% from North, 80% from South. Parental occup's were classified acc to Minnesota Occup Scale.
Roberts, S. O. (1950)	Fisk Univ.	c- 54		All were women who entered directly from high sch in Sept '45 and graduated in May '49; 19 from North, 35 from South. All given 1945 ACE form in '45, the 1946 ACE in May '47, and 1948 form in May '49. Two socio levels established, using Minnesota classif of father's occupation.
Lowry, C. E. (1957)	Huston-Tillotson College	c- 1297	1	Negro freshmen who entered *Samuel Huston College* from 1946-51 and *Huston-Tillotson Coll* from 1952-55.

[26]*South* group included all Ss who attended high schs in D.C. and states where separate schools were required for Negroes and whites. *North* group included others.

[27]Median of 55,134 college freshmen from 329 colleges on the 1945 form was 101.5. A score of 88 corresponds to a %ile rank of 31, a score of 68 corresponds to the 12th %ile rank. (Thurstone and Thurstone, 1946)

[28]Calculated from author's frequency distributions. Form of test not given.

SIX *(continued)*

STUDENTS

RESULTS	COMMENTS OF AUTHOR

	Scores[27]	Ss whose parents in upper socioeco levels whether *North* or *South* do better on *ACE* than Ss whose parents in lower levels.
M	c	
North	88.16	
South	67.57	
North group sig superior to *South*		

	Score[28]
	c
Mdn	94.5

	Scores[29]	
	c	c
	North	South
M	90.5	70.6
s	22.0	26.4

Better ACE Scores if Ss:	Results suggest that regional origin is a factor that carries with it a superiority of performance on an intell test for which neither socioeco status nor effect of serving in armed services can compensate.
Of upper socioeco levels	
Nonveterans	
Northern origin	

Ss from North consistently superior to those from South even when matched for socioeco status. Diff's favor upper socioeco level, but these sig only for Southern group. Gains made by these Ss in terms of norms for comparable periods of time suggest need for general re-examination of concl based on freshman tests alone.	Differences in academic achievement, originally in favor of the Northern Ss, had vanished at the end of 4 years when the total record was evaluated.

Year Entering	*Scores*[30]		ACE 1946 form given to entering freshmen in fall of 1946; 1947 form administered to all entering from 1947 to 1955. Converted 1946 scores into equivalent ones for 1947.
	M	*s*	
1946	43.15	20.85	
1947	41.83	21.60	
1948	41.40	17.85	
1949	45.60	21.60	
1950	46.00	21.50	
1951	36.40	20.90	
1952	45.80	19.95	
1953	47.60	20.10	
1954	49.90	22.55	
1955	49.15	20.20	

[29]Mean scores obtained on the Northern and Southern Ss correspond to respective national percentile ranks of 33.5 and 14.

[30]The various 10-year college means correspond to national %ile ranks of 2 or below. Beginning with the 1940 edition the test items of the *ACE* have been selected in order that gross scores in the successive forms are directly comparable. (Cooperative Test Div., Educational Testing Service, 1950, p. 3).

TABLE

COLLEGE

AUTHOR DATE	LOCATION	N	SUBJECTS CLASS	METHOD OF SELECTION
Canady, H. G. (1936)	West Virginia State College	c- 517	1	All new students entering in a 3-year period tested by 1931, 1932, or 1933 form.
Canady, H. G. (1942)	West Virginia State College	c- 497	1	All new students in a 3-yr period tested by 1935, 1936, or 1937 form.
Canady, H. G. (1943)	West Virginia State College	c- 1306[33]	1	All new students entering college from 1931 to 1937.
Phillips, M. V. (1946)	Howard University	c- 4105[34]	1	All Liberal Arts Coll Ss tested from 1938-1945. Interested in those scoring at or above 90th %ile of national norms.
Richardson, J. F., III (1963)	Morgan State College	c- 200	1	From '57 grad-class who were enrolled in Day Session. All Ss were voluntary participants in project that included about 90% of each dept's majors. *ACE* had been administered during first week of freshman year.

[31]National median of the 1932 form (based on 36,665 freshmen in 173 colleges) was 163.72; 5.4 per cent of c freshmen above national mdn. *West Va State Coll* median corresponds to national %ile rank of 4; its mean to a national %ile rank of 6.3.

[32]National *mdns* of the 1935, 1936, and 1937 forms, based upon scores of 39,119; 65,737; and 68,899 coll freshmen were, respectively: 182, 177, and 167. (Thurstone and Thurstone, 1936, 1937, 1938) Used Sims Score Card for socioeco status; theoretical range is 0-36, in this study, 4-35. Canady placed postal workers, high sch teachers, and morticians in professional group because of high status they enjoy within c group.

[33]National *median* on the 1934 form was above 170.

SIX (continued)
STUDENTS

RESULTS	COMMENTS OF AUTHOR

	Scores[31]	
	c	
M	78.65	
Mdn	69.80	
s	40.05	
Range	8-224	

	M Scores[32]	
	c	Sig diffs bet *ACE* means of upper and lower and bet middle and lower status groups. Lower scores of Negroes probably due to their position in social system.
Status		
Upper	98.90	
Middle	94.03	
Lower	80.6	
Total	92.12	

	Scores	
	c	c
	Men	Women
Mdn	76.34	75.77
M	84.50	81.50
s	43.36	41.40

c *mdn* at 20-25 %ile rank in normative distribution

	Scores		A report of a comparison between secondary education- and noneduc- majors, with respect to mental levels, scholarship, interests, personality, *etc.*
	M	s	
Division[35]	c	c	
Human			
Males	74.06	23.54	
Females	78.19	20.71	
Soc Sci			
Males	72.73	17.75	
Females	74.35	25.00	
Nat Sci			
Males	79.65	23.79	
Females	75.10	19.87	
Total	75.69	21.94[36]	

[34]Total number of freshmen in College of Liberal Arts, 1938-1945 was not given by Phillips. Number was estimated by Howard Univ. librarian in private communication. About 2.58 per cent of the Ss scored equal to or above the 90th percentile on the national distribution.

[35]Humanities Division, Div of Social Sciences, Div of Natural Sciences. Education majors are included in these divisions acc to areas in which Ss were preparing to teach.

National mean of the 1949 form, based upon 43,358 scores of freshmen in 229 colleges, was 103.69, with s of 25.66 (E.T.S., 1950). *Morgan Coll* mean of 75.69 falls at the 14th percentile rank of national distribution. The 1949 form was used.

[36]Combined mean and s computed by reviewer. The number of cases in each of the six groups, reading down, were: 17, 21, 41, 37, 43, and 41, totaling 200.

TABLE

COLLEGE

AUTHOR DATE	LOCATION	N	SUBJECTS CLASS	METHOD OF SELECTION
Shuey, A. M. (1942)	Washington Square College, New York Univ.	w-43 c- 43	All All	From new Ss entering, 1935-37, c were paired with w acc to test form; sex; age ± 1 yr; US nativity, or if foreign-born they were matched with foreign-born; nativity of parents if US-born; occup of father; academic standing.[37]

DIGIT-

| Katz, I., Epps, E. G., and Axelson, L. J. (1964) | Florida State University and Florida Agricultural and Mechanical University | w-96 c- 53 -63 | Mainly 2 Mainly 2 Mainly 2 | C_1—*Easy digit-symbol* tasks given to Ss in 3 elem sociology classes. Each S had 5 sheets to work on, 60 sec allowed per page. For one group there was a *no test situation;* Ss being informed that it was an experiment to find out what students thought about the task. In another, it was a *test situation with local norms.* Ss told that they would be compared with other A & M students; in 3rd, it was a *test situation with national norms.* Test introduced as part of National Examination. After finishing tasks Ss indicated on 2 scales the degree to which they had felt nervous or calm and had cared about doing well on the task. Instructor of same race administered tests. Only papers of the males were scored. C_2—*Same procedure for difficult* d-s tasks given to 3 other sociol classes. W—*Same procedure,* except (1) only the *hard* task was used, (2) within each class approx ⅓ received each type of instruction, & (3) task was described in local-norms condition as *Fla State Univ* Exam. |

SCHOOL AND COLLEGE

| Anderson, T. M. (1958) | Mississippi Colleges | c- 260 | 1 | Sample was drawn from those Negro freshman college students enrolled in 2 private liberal arts colleges, a state junior college, and a 4-year state college. |

[37]All individual scores were recorded in terms of their 1935 equivalents. If parents were foreign-born the c S was matched with a w whose parents were also foreign-born.

[38]*Easy digit-symbol* task omitted by reviewer as it was not administered to white students. The c *hard task* means were taken by reviewer from authors' fig. 1 b.

SIX (continued)

STUDENTS

	RESULTS		COMMENTS OF AUTHOR

	Scores		
	w	**c**	
M	214.67	170.61	
s	66.28	47.60	
Range	54-325	50-255	
t =		3.72	

c mean at 40%ile of norms group
w mean at 69%ile of norms group

Such equating as has been done has decreased but not eliminated the diffs usually found bet Negro and w college Ss. The subtest proving most difficult for the Negroes was Artificial Language, followed in order by Arithmetic, Analogies, Opposites, and Completion.

SYMBOL

	Hard Task Trials Comb[38]		
		M	
Instructions	**w**	**c**	
No test	23.5	20.3	
Local norms	26.9	24.9	
National norms	26.5	21.4	

If the self-ratings reports are accurate, the poorer performance of c under *national norms* than under *local norms* cannot be attributed to weaker motivation. Also have no direct evidence that *national-norms Ss* were more anxious about failing than men in other conditions.

ABILITY TESTS

	Scores[39]		
M	Norms	**c**	
Verbal	295	267.5	
Quant.	305	277.7	
Total	300	274.6	
s			
Verbal		7	
Quant.		7.8	
Total		4.36	

2.3% overlap nat'l total mean score

Subjects in this study tend to perform lowest on tests requiring verbal ability. This holds true on *Verbal Section* of the intell tests and on the *Comprehension* and *Interpretation* of the Science test.

---

[39]A *Verbal* score of 268 lies in the 4-12 %ile band of the norms group; a *Quantitative* score of 278 lies in the 8-15 %ile band, and a *Total* score of 275 lies in the 5-8 %ile band of the norms group, based on 1180 students in 99 colleges. (Cooperative Test Div., Educ. Testing Serv., 1957).

TABLE

COLLEGE

AUTHOR DATE	LOCATION	N	SUBJECTS CLASS	METHOD OF SELECTION
Anderson, T. H. (1961)	Alabama State College	c- 669	1	All entering freshmen at the coll had been given *SCAT* in fall '59. Using this file of scores author selected 48 pairs of Ss (high- and low-achievers) from among upper ⅓ for special study of personality, study habits, and attitudes.
Jones, A. L. (1960)	Three Colleges in a Southern State	College- A- 697 B- 622 C- 807 ——— 2126 A- 314 B- 296 C- 450 ——— 1060	1	Three coed 4-yr colleges with enrollments bet 2500-3000, *A* being all white, *B predominantly* w, & *C* all Negro. All were given *SCAT* in fall '59 as freshmen. The 2126 total test scores were tabulated to form a single distribution; then authors removed middle 50%, leaving only lowest & highest quarters for data analysis. These "extreme" groups to be referred to as *Upper* and *Lower*.[41]

---

[40]A score of 273 is within the 4-7 %ile band of the normative distribution which was based upon a sample of 1180 freshmen in 99 colleges. A score of 312 is within the 84-89 %ile band of the norms group. (Cooperative Test Div., Educ. Testing Serv., 1957)

[41]All Ss tested in the *predominantly white coll B* included in data as *white*. The number of nonwhites was not given in either the dissertation nor in article by Cheers and Sherman

SIX *(continued)*

STUDENTS

RESULTS				COMMENTS OF AUTHOR

		Scores[40]			Main purpose of study was to determine whether or not there are measurable diffs bet dimensions of the nonintellectual characteristics of selected groups of low- and high-achieving Ss.
Total		c			
Group					
M		273.3			
s		13.35			
Range		245-312			

		Scores[42]			For this sample, the strength of the positive relationship bet *Sentence Understandings* and *Word Meaning* differentiated: (1) *Upper-lower level of SCAT* regardless of race, and (2) Negro-white test performance within the two levels.
	w	"w"	c	Norm	
	A	B	C		
Mdn	292	290	272	300	

0.6% C overlap norms' mdn
3.5% C overlap A's mdn
18.5% B overlap norms' mdn
43.7% B overlap A's mdn
23.2% A overlap norms' mdn

Number Comprising:

	w	"w"	c	Total
Quarter	A	B	C	
Upper	283	233	14	530
Lower	31	63	436	530

Per Cent Comprising:

	w	"w"	c	Total
Quarter	A	B	C	
Upper	13.4	11.0	0.6	25
Lower	1.5	3.0	20.5	25

r bet *SU* and *WM*[43]

	w	"w"	c
Quarter	A	B	C
Upper	0.64	0.63	0.33
Lower	0.20	0.15	0.007

(1963). Neither the colleges nor the state was identified by name. The present writer infers that the state is Louisiana.

[42]Medians and overlappings calculated by present writer from Jones' frequency distributions.

[43]*Sentence Understandings* and *Word Meaning.*

TABLE

COLLEGE

AUTHOR DATE	LOCATION	N	SUBJECTS CLASS	METHOD OF SELECTION
				SCHOOL AND COLLEGE ABILITY TESTS
Bindman, A. M. (1965)	A Large Midwestern State University[44]	w-2822[45] c- 100	1 1-4	161 male undergrad c students enrolled during first semester, 1963-64; 100 of them had been tested (and scores preserved in university records) by *ACT* and/or SCAT, since the univ strongly urges each S to provide such test scores prior to admission or shortly after enrollment. All *SCAT* scores of Ss who had not taken the *ACT* were converted into *ACT* standard scores with aid of special tables.[46] Of the 100 Ss, 44 were freshmen; scores of 2822 non-Negro freshman males enrolled at the same time comprised the norms group.
				COLLEGE BOARD
Hills, J. R., Klock, J. A., and Bush, M. L. (1964)	Georgia	w-6598 c- 796	1 1	*SAT* given yearly to all freshmen entering any of the undergraduate units of University System incl all tax-supported inst's of higher learning in state. Excluded all whose data were incomplete, enrolled in a terminal program, were foreign, or in some other ways atypical. This study includes those entering in fall of 1962.

[44]Not further identified by author. Assumed by the reviewer to be the University of Illinois, Champaign-Urbana campus.
[45]This number includes all beginning male freshmen tested with the exception of the colored.
[46]A r of .90 was obtained by the author bet *SCAT* and *ACT* scores of 19 colored Ss examined by both tests.
[47]With the exception of the c group mean these statistics were calculated by reviewer. The

SIX *(continued)*

STUDENTS

RESULTS	COMMENTS OF AUTHOR

AMERICAN COLLEGE TEST

	Standard Scores[47]	
	w	c
M	24.66	20.00
s	3.52	4.57
t =		10.13

17% c above w mean
No c equal to highest 13% of w

M Standard Scores[48]
c

Occup	Father	Mother
1	20.5	20.4
2	21.2	20.3
3	20.1	20.1
4	19.4	18.7

M Standard Scores
c

Educ	Father	Mother
Coll	20.8	20.4
HS	18.7	19.7
Grade	20.7	17.5
Omit	18.0	22.0

Among a total of 154 Negro male under-graduates, 40% earned grades below the minimum required for graduation; 44% earned grades in the marginal area of academic performance (C to C+) and 16% were in the letter B category. Negro students whose *ACT* scores indicated adequate college preparation did as well academically as "others". It is primarily those c Ss who are inadequately prepared who do less well than "others" equally inadequately prepared. This disparity in academic performance bet inadequately prepared c and w students suggests that the social system of the university operates differentially on Negro students, cutting them off from the kinds of academic supports taken for granted by white students.

SCHOLASTIC APTITUDE TEST

	Scores *Verbal*	
	w	c
M	436.7	260.1
Range of coll means	346-529	253-264
s	97.3	49.4

	Mathematics	
	w	c
M	469.4	291.4
Range of coll means	389-610	281-294
s	103.9	45.2

1% c above *Verbal* mean of w
0.25% c above *Math* mean of w

Requirement of *SAT* was introduced in the anticipation of a greater number of applicants to Ga colleges than could be accomodated and the desire of admitting only best academic risks.

diff bet the means of the 100 c Ss and the c males identified as freshmen was not significant (t=0.74).

[48]Means of Ss acc to occupations of parents and educational attainments of parents reported by Bindman. Category *1* includes professional and management, *2*—clerical and sales, *3*—crafts and skilled, and *4*—operatives, service, labor, in addition to housewife.

TABLE

COLLEGE

AUTHOR DATE	LOCATION	N	SUBJECTS CLASS	METHOD OF SELECTION
Hills, J. R., Klock, J. A., and Bush, M. L. (1965)	Georgia	w-7135 c- 845		See above. This report includes those entering in fall of 1963.

CALIFORNIA TEST

AUTHOR DATE	LOCATION	N	SUBJECTS CLASS	METHOD OF SELECTION
Holston, O. L. (1946)	State Teachers College, Montgomery, Ala.	c- 85		*CTMM* and Bernreuter given to summer sch students, all college graduates. Author does not report method of sampling, nor whether or not all students were tested.
Buck, J. R. (1964)	Mississippi	c- 944	1	*CTMM*, California Reading Test, American Home Scale, and Kuder Preference Inventory administered to total freshman population of the 6 Negro senior colleges in 1960-61.

[49]Combined by reviewer from author's Table 36.
[50]*None* includes 10 fathers or mothers who had no schooling.
   Att Sch includes 385 fathers and 217 mothers who had varying amounts of elementary schooling but no high sch.
   Ent HS includes 304 fathers and 348 mothers who entered but did not finish high school.

SIX *(continued)*

STUDENTS

	RESULTS		COMMENTS OF AUTHOR

	Scores		
	Verbal		
	w	**c**	
M	446.6	268.3	
Range of coll means	354-539	261-278	
s	98.4	51.0	
	Mathematics		
	w	**c**	
M	478.6	301.6	
Range of coll means	388-622	297-306	
s	104.2	47.7	

0.4-0.5% c above *Verbal* mean of w
0.4%c above *Math* mean of w

Data included all freshmen in 3 Negro and 16 white or predominantly w colleges.

OF MENTAL MATURITY

	IQ	
	c	
M	95.12	
s	11	
Range	80-156	

A study of the first summer students of Graduate Div of the State Teachers Coll. All Ss were engaged in profession of teaching, as supervisors, principals, and teachers.

	IQ		
	c		
M	90.03		
s	9.56		
Range	50-129		

M IQ Reading Level & Home Score acc to Education of Father or Mother[49]

Parent's Educ[50]	IQ	Reading	Home
None	93.0	7.7	26.0
Att Sch	89.0	8.1	29.2
Ent HS	90.3	8.3	33.7
Fin HS	89.6	8.3	38.6
Ent Coll	90.6	8.3	41.5
Fin Coll[51]	93.0	8.6	45.9

It is evident that there is little or no correlation bet IQ of the men and women students and the educational level of their parents, or bet reading achievement of students and the educational level of their parents. No escaping the conclusion that the scores of Negro college students on national tests mirror bkg or environmental conditions rather than racial ability.

Fin HS includes 126 fathers and 182 mothers who were high school graduates.
Ent Coll includes 65 fathers and 82 mothers who entered but did not finish college.
Fin Coll includes 62 fathers and 107 mothers who were college graduates.
[51]All of the six educational levels are mutually exclusive.

TABLE

COLLEGE

AUTHOR DATE	LOCATION	N	SUBJECTS CLASS	METHOD OF SELECTION
				WECHSLER-BELLEVUE
Fortson, C. B. H. (1956)	Atlanta Univ.	c- 50		16 males & 34 females enrolled in Graduate Sch of Education. Every S was tested by both forms, the second approx 24 hours after first. All tested in summer; no information as to how Ss were selected.
				MEDICAL COLLEGE
Reitzes, D. C. (1958)	Various Negro Colleges	c- 1123		All were applicants to US medical schs from Negro undergraduate colleges. Data from Assoc Amer Medical Colleges summary of mean scores & distrib of students from Negro undergraduate colleges having 10 or more students who took *MCAT* bet May '53 and Nov '55.
	Various Colleges	All- 14,656 How- 325 Meh- 476		Includes applicants to Howard U Coll of Medicine '56-'57; applicants to Meharry Med Coll '55-'56; & applicants of all races (but about 95% w) to all medical colleges '55-'56.

[52]In addition to Verbal and Quantitative sections, the *MCAT* includes sections on Understanding Modern Society and Science. These last two sections are omitted by reviewer from the table and discussion. The norms mean and distribution are based upon the total number of medical school applicants taking the *MCAT*, about 95 per cent of whom were white. The norms group mean on the Verbal, Quantitative, and other sections of the test is 500.

SIX *(concluded)*

STUDENTS

RESULTS	COMMENTS OF AUTHOR

INTELLIGENCE SCALE

	First Administration				*Digit Span* and *Picture Completion* were

	Form I		Form II		
	c		c		
	M	s	M	s	
		Scores			
Inform	11.20	2.76	10.84	1.76	
Compre	12.44	3.26	13.32	2.75	
Dig Sp	3.88	3.06	6.32	3.67	
Arith	9.60	2.19	9.32	1.21	
Simil	12.52	3.31	11.08	1.72	
Vocab	10.52	2.19	10.84	1.26	
Pic Ar	9.68	2.86	8.80	2.33	
Pic Co	8.68	2.76	9.60	1.91	
Bl Des	9.20	3.17	7.28	2.79	
Obj As	9.88	2.66	8.52	2.90	
Dig Sy	10.32	2.52	10.28	2.58	
		IQ			
Verbal	106.12	11.13	106.84	8.61	
Perf	104.56	11.01	97.48	11.23	
Full Sc	105.28	11.32	101.44	7.64	

Digit Span and *Picture Completion* were found to be significantly more difficult on Form I; the *Similarities* and *Object Assembly* were sig more difficult on Form II.

ADMISSION TEST

	Verbal & Quantitative Scores[52]		
	c	c	w
	V	Q	norm
	Means		
	389	376	500
	Percentage Distribution		
700-99	0	0	2.0
600-99	1.9	0.4	14.0
500-99	9.5	7.2	34.0
400-99	31.0	29.5	34.0
300-99	45.1	46.5	14.0
200-99	12.5	16.4	2.0

11.4% *Verbal* scores overlap w mean
7.6% *Q* scores overlap w mean

In 1955-56, from a total of 28,639 Ss enrolled in medical colleges in US, 741 (2.59%) were Negro. Of these, 70.9% were in either *Howard* or *Meharry*, and 29.1% in 48 predominantly white med schs; none in 32 exclusively w medical colleges.

	Verbal & Quantitative Scores[53]			
	Mean			
	Accepted		Rejected	
	V	Q	V	Q
Howard (c)	481	444	394	374
Meharry (c)	462	451	371	366
All US Med Schs	524	528	466	459

Applicants to *Howard* & *Meharry* from predominantly white undergrad colleges earned higher scores on the average than those from predominantly Negro colleges.

[53]Reitzes obtained these statistics from Helen H. Gee, The study of applicants, 1955-56, *J. Med. Educ.*, 1958, *31*, 865-66 and from the Registrars' office at *Howard* and *Meharry*.

observed that two of the 260 freshmen scored above the 80th percentile of the norms group.

Thelma Anderson (1961) investigated some of the characteristics of high- and low- achieving Negro college students. All entering freshmen at Alabama State College had been given *SCAT* in the fall of 1959. From this file of 669 names Anderson selected 48 pairs of subjects, which she identified as high- and low-achievers, for a special study of personality, study habits, and attitudes. Although the author selected her paired Ss from the top third of the *SCAT* scores she included in her data the mean, standard deviation, and range of Total Scores for the entire group of freshmen. The mean of 273.3 (just one point below the mean Total Score of the Mississippi Negroes) was within the 4-7th percentile band of the normative sample. The Alabama students appear to have been relatively variable, the lowest 46 scores being below the lowest percentile band of the norms distribution and the highest three scores being within the 80-89th percentile bands.

The doctoral dissertation of A. L. Jones (1960) was designed to determine the patterns of responses which might differentiate the performance of selected groups of Negroes and whites on *SCAT, Form I.* The sample consisted of Negro and white students enrolled in three state-supported colleges during 1959-60; the colleges were described as all accredited, coeducational, four-year institutions, with enrollments ranging from 2500 to 3000; the students were mainly graduates of public high schools within the state. *College A* enrolled only white students, *College B* enrolled *predominantly white* students, and *College C,* only Negro students. All of the entering freshmen were given *SCAT* in the fall of 1959 as a part of the testing program following which a total of 2126 test scores secured from the three colleges were tabulated to form a single frequency distribution. The author, wishing to make an analysis of the highest- and the lowest-scoring groups of students, removed the middle 1066 scores, leaving 530 in the highest 25 per cent and 530 in the lowest 25 per cent of the entire distribution.

Among the 530 Ss in the highest group, 283 were from College A, 233 from College B, and 14 from College C—the white and predominantly white colleges contributing 24.4 and the Negro college contributing 0.6 of the 25 per cent. Conversely, of the 530 freshmen in the lowest group, there were 31 contributed by College A, 63 by College B, and 436 by College C—the white and predominantly white colleges contributing 4.5 and the Negro college 20.5 of the 25 per cent. In other words, *41 per cent* of the entire freshman class of College A, *37 per cent* of this class of College B, and *2 per cent* of this class of College C were drawn to comprise the *highest quarter;* whereas, *4 per cent* of the freshman class of College A, *10 per cent* of the class of College B, and *54 per cent* of the class of College C were drawn for the *lowest quarter.*

While observing that the average scores of the upper white samples only approximated the median of the norms group[42] and consequently supported the view that the average performance of Southern whites is usually below that of whites in other sections of the country, Jones noted that the performance of the Negro students on *SCAT* was "poor indeed" and that their lack of facility in the use of the English language of the test was "astounding". She attributed this deficiency, in part at least, to the common use of dialects by the average Southern Negro, the dialects being a mixture of American English words, word-remnants of African dialects, words coined by slaves according to their American English sounds and "functional expressions" which served as a medium of slave communication — the undue perpetuation of the dialects being probably a consequence of desocialization fostered by American social practices.[43] These dialects are substantially *oral short-hand* and form an underdeveloped language which may restrict the average Negro's perceptual discriminations and concept formulations "in ways that impede both verbal and non-verbal test performance as well as educational achievement." (p. 108)

The only consistent patterning of responses was found in the relationship between *Sentence Understandings* and *Word Meaning*. "Out of numerous implications suggested by the divergent combinations of response patterns, one definitive finding emerged with clarity. For this sample, the strength of positive relationship between Sentence Understandings and Word Meaning differentiated: (1) upper and lower level test performance regardless of race; and (2) Negro and white test performance within the upper and lower levels." (p. 107)

An article by Cheers and Sherman (1963) is essentially a résumé of the Jones dissertation and although they present much of the data to be found in the monograph they conclude that there was no evidence of a racial response pattern.[44] Emphasizing the fact that a direct relationship exists between the size of the mean score of a group and the strength of the positive relation between *Sentence Understandings* and *Word Meaning* and noting that successful performance on *SCAT* was evidenced by all who possessed skills of *Word Meaning* and *Sentence Understandings,* they concluded that there were revealed *successful*

---

[42]This statement does not appear to be accurate, since the midpoint of the upper group of *A* (304) was within the 62-74th percentile band of the norms group and the midpoint of the upper group of *B* (302) was within the 55-68th percentile band of the norms group. (These figures determined by reviewer from author's frequency distributions.)

[43]In this discussion, Jones cites the works of: A. S. Artley, Research concerning interrelationships among the language arts, *Elem. Engl.,* 1950, 27, pp. 527-37; R. I. McDavid, The relationship of the speech of American Negroes to the speech of the whites, *Amer. Speech,* 1951, 26, pp. 3-17; R. A. Hall, The African substratum in Negro English, *Amer. Speech,* 1950, 25, pp. 51-54; L. D. Turner, Africanisms in the Gullah Dialect. Chicago Univ., 1949; and others.

[44]The dissertation was prepared under the supervision of Dorothy M. Sherman; Arlynne L. Cheers is the same person as Arlynne L. Jones.

and *unsuccessful* patterns of responses but that there was *no evidence of a Negro or a white response pattern.*[45]

Jones also included the frequency distributions of the 2126 *SCAT* Total Scores for the three groups of college freshmen from which the highest and lowest quarters were subsequently drawn. The college medians of *A, B,* and C (Table 6) were respectively: 292, 290, and 272, the median of the white college freshmen being within the 28-37th percentile band of the normative sample, that of the predominantly white college freshmen being within the 24-32nd percentile band, and that of the colored freshmen being within the 4-7 percentile band. The median of the colored freshmen proved to be practically the same as the *SCAT* averages reported on Negro freshmen attending colleges in Mississippi and Alabama. (T. M. Anderson, 1958, and T. H. Anderson, 1961)

In attempting to determine why a racially integrated state university in the Midwest[46] seemed to attract such a small number of Negro students and why the quality of academic performance of the average Negro student enrolled there was inferior to that of other students, Bindman (1965) examined in detail various evidences of participation among Negro males attending this university during the first semester of 1963-64. With the aid of several counselors in the university dormitories and the assistance of three hired Negro students who conducted a census for him, the author was able to locate 161 undergraduates. Thereupon he developed a questionnaire which was subsequently administered to these students by four competent Negro men (a graduate student, a law student, and two undergraduates) who were employed not only to interview the subjects but to encourage them to reveal their experiences involving acts of discrimination at the university. The author supplemented these data with his own "participation-observation" and with university records.

Completed interviews were obtained on 154 of the Negro men, as were grade-point-ratios (Table 6). From the university records, Bindman was likewise able to secure 63 *American College Test* scores and 56 *SCAT* scores on 100 of the respondents — 19 of the subjects having taken both tests and 54 having taken neither of them. The author converted all *SCAT* scores into equivalent *ACT* standard scores; and included the *ACT* frequency distributions of 2866 males entering the university as freshmen in 1963 and those of the 100 Negro men *enrolled in various classes* in the university during this year — but all (presumably) having been tested at the beginning of their freshman year. From the author's distributions the present writer calculated the mean of the non-Negro freshmen (24.66) and found it to be more than one standard deviation above the

---

[45]The correlations included in Table 6 do not differ significantly (between the racial samples) at either the upper or the lower level. This may have been due to the relatively small number of Negroes in the upper level and to the relatively small number of whites in the lower level. (Comment by reviewer)

[46]Although the author does not name the university, the reviewer identifies it as the University of Illinois, Champaign-Urbana campus.

mean of the 100 Negro students, a highly significant difference (Table 6). Seventeen per cent of the colored subjects overlapped the mean of the total group of entering freshman males.

In his Table 16, Bindman includes the mean *ACT* scores (with numbers of cases) categorized according to several socioeconomic factors, such as: parent's ability to finance son's education, father's occupation, mother' occupation, father's schooling, and mother's schooling, the latter four factors being contained in our Table 6. There seems to be no reason to contest the author's statement that: "In all of the major categories of the variables used to indicate the socio-economic background of the student, the mean ACT scores were not substantially different." (p. 93)

Among the 154 Negro men interviewed, 16 per cent came from high schools located in the Border or Southern states, the rest from Northern states—with 46 per cent of the total group having received their secondary education in the public schools of the state's "major city" (Chicago). Some 57 per cent of the respondents came from *integrated* high schools and 43 per cent from *predominantly Negro* high schools.[47] Upon analyzing his data Bindman observes: "The racial composition of the respondents' high schools did not explain inadequate preparation for college since those from both integrated and predominantly Negro high schools were found equally distributed above and below the 50th percentile rank of their college and in the G.P.A. categories above and below the required 3.0 minimum for a college degree." (p. 103)

Although the "overwhelming number" of Negro students were living in integrated housing with white roommates, in general they are reported to have mixed socially only among themselves. The prevailing norms proscribing close contact between Negro and white peers and limiting their association to impersonalized activities—and these between those of the same sex—have resulted in the Negro males perceiving themselves as isolated and rejected from meaningful participation with whites in extracurricular affairs. They have tended to seek company only among themselves where they feel at home, and have avoided asking "others" (whites) for academic help, probably in part because they feared being rebuffed and in part because they did not want to admit their shortcomings. Since the 154 Negro men on campus were in widely dispersed curricula there were few, if any, other Negroes in their classes; consequently the poor student was rarely able to find important information about his course or other help from members of his own racial group. Furthermore, when groups of Negro students congregated as they do at various places on the campus, their common topic of conversation related to the *Negro Varsity* rather than to the *academic*.

The author thus attributes the low mental test scores, the lower grade-point-ratios, and the relatively large number of students dropped by the university, not

---

[47]Bindman uses the term *integrated* high school to indicate one with less than 50 per cent Negro enrollment, and a *predominantly Negro* high school to mean one with more than 50 per cent Negro enrollment.

to inferior mental ability on the part of the Negro, but to his being separated from the "mainstream of life".

Scholastic Aptitude Test

Beginning in 1957, the Board of Regents of the University System of Georgia required that all freshmen submit their scores on the College Entrance Examination Board's *Scholastic Aptitude Test (SAT)* prior to admission to any of the undergraduate units of the University System. The University System includes all tax-supported institutions of higher learning in the state. Hills, Klock, and Bush (1964, 1965) have presented various statistics concerning the freshmen who entered the sixteen white colleges and the three Negro colleges in the fall of 1962 and 1963. Excluded from the tabulated data are students whose records were incomplete, those enrolled in a terminal program, foreign students, and other students who were considered to be atypical in some way.

The mean *Verbal* score of the white students tested in 1962 was 436.7, that of the colored Ss, 260.1; the means of the white colleges ranged between 346 and 529, the means of the colored colleges between 253 and 264. The standard deviation of the whites' distribution was about twice that of the colored (Table 6).

The mean *Mathematics* score of the white Ss was 469.4, that of the colored, 291.4, the means of the white colleges ranging between 389 and 610, those of the colored colleges between 281 and 294. The standard deviations of the distribution of the whites was more than twice that of the colored.

Approximately one per cent of the colored were above the *Verbal* mean of the whites, and about 0.25 per cent of the colored were above the *Mathematics* mean of this group. Both the *Verbal* and *Mathematics* means of the colored students fell at the first percentile rank of the whites' distributions.

As will be observed in Table 6, the mean *Verbal* and *Mathematics* scores of the Negro and white students entering the state colleges in 1963 were from 8-10 points higher than the respective means of the Negro and white students entering the same colleges the preceding year. The standard deviations of the colored distributions were in 1963, as in 1962, about half the size of those of the whites. The percentage of overlap was very slight as in the previous year, being from 0.4 to 0.5 per cent. Again, in 1963 as in 1962, the *Verbal* and *Mathematical* means of the colored students fell at the first percentile rank of the Georgia white's distributions.

California Test of Mental Maturity

In connection with a study of personality characteristics of summer school graduate students, Holston (1946) administered the *California Test of Mental Maturity* to 85 Negroes attending the State Teachers College at Montgomery, Alabama. All were employed as teachers, supervisors, or principals during the academic year. Although Holston did not report the number of graduate students enrolled during this summer session nor the method by which he selected his subjects, he indicated that the mean IQ of his Ss was 95.12, the standard deviation, 11.00, and the range from 80 to 156. Twenty-five of the graduate students earned IQ's between 80 and 89 and eight achieved IQ's above 109. Of this group, seven were reported to have secured IQ's between 110 and 119 and one between 150 and 156.

In a study designed to determine various characteristics of Southern Negro college students in order to develop a college program suited to their needs, interests, and abilities, Buck (1964) administered the following tests to 944 college freshmen: *California Test of Mental Maturity,* California Reading Test, Kuder Preference Record, and the American Home Scale (a socioeconomic status scale combining cultural, aesthetic, economic, and miscellaneous scores). His subjects comprised entire freshmen classes enrolled in the six *Negro senior colleges* in the state of Mississippi during 1960-1961. These measures together portray the average Negro college freshman in this state as having an IQ of 90, a reading placement at the eighth-grade level (8.25), and a home score of about 35.[48]

More interesting than the combined means earned by the students on the *CTMM,* Reading, and Home Scales is the relationship between these variables and the education of the students' parents. Using the educational level attained by the fathers or mothers as the independent variable, the parental educational levels were recorded in six mutually exclusive categories, consisting of: *no schooling* (10); *attended school* — any amount of schooling below high school — (602); *entered high school* — any amount of high school but not graduating — (652); *finished high school* (308); *entered college* — any amount of college but not graduating — (147); and *finished college* (169).[49] The dependent variables were IQ, reading level, and home score. As will have been noted in the table, the *home means* increase (varying between 2.9 and 4.9 points) with each increase in the father's or mother's educational level; this increase was to be expected, of course, since it indicates that the higher the educational level attained by the father and/or mother the higher the cultural, aesthetic, and economic status of the home. However, neither the *IQ means* nor the *reading level means* of the students show consistent improvement with increase in parental education. Above the *none* level (where the very small number of cases makes generalization meaningless) there is practically *no difference in reading level,* and only *1.6 points difference in mean IQ,* separating those Ss whose parents had merely had *some*

---

[48]This statement does not necessarily apply to Negro freshmen in Mississippi *junior colleges.* The author describes the American Home mean as "at the 59th percentile, indicating that they come from fairly adequate homes." (p. 125) The scores on the Kuder Preference Record were reported to be of doubtful validity and have not been included by the reviewer.

[49]See Table 6. Buck employed all of these categories but subsumed them under four major divisions: men's fathers' education, women's fathers' education, men's mothers' education, and women's mothers' education, making 24 items. Present writer reduced these to 6 by combining data on men and women students and on education of fathers and mothers.

elementary education and those whose parents (one or both) had had *some college education.* In other words, although one or both parents differed by at least five years of schooling (from elementary school to college) and their homes presumably varied correspondingly, both the reading level and IQ level seem to be relatively unchanged. Not until one or both parents have been graduated from college is there an appreciable increase in reading level (0.5 year) and IQ (4 points).[50]

These findings do not appear to support Buck's concluding statement: "There is no escaping the conclusion that the scores of Negro college students on national tests mirror background or environmental conditions rather than racial ability." (p. 151) Probably one is required only to accept the postulate that going to college is more selective (for Negroes as for whites) at the lower than at the upper socioeconomic levels.

Wechsler-Bellevue

Fortson (1956), in attempting to determine the relative difficulty of the subtests and scales of Forms I and II of the *Wechsler-Bellevue,* gave both forms of this test, one form approximately 24 hours after the other, to 50 Atlanta University students. Like Holston, Fortson examined students attending a summer school, all of whom were college graduates and enrolled in a Graduate School of Education. Like Holston, also, Fortson included neither information regarding the total number of graduate students in attendance nor his method of sampling. Only the results of each form when it was administered *first* are presented in Table 6. It will be observed that Form I produced higher Full Scale IQ's on the average than Form II, the advantage having been due to a difference in the Performance rather than to a difference in the Verbal Scale. The mean Full Scale IQ's of 105 and 101 are, respectively, about 10 and 6 points above Holston's mean.

Medical College Admission Test

The *Medical College Admission Test (MCAT),* administered for the Association of American Medical Colleges by the Educational Testing Service, consists of four tests: two of general ability (*Verbal* and *Quantitative*), one in Understanding Modern Society, and an achievement test in Science.

The *Verbal* and *Quantitative* Ability Tests are general scholastic aptitude tests, designed to measure abilities related to success in postgraduate professional studies. The only requirements are ordinary reading and arithmetic abilities, but these skills are used in new problems. High scores indicate that candidates should be able to perform adequately at the postgraduate level, regard-

---

[50]The author has not computed the significance of any of the mean differences relative to parental education, nor has he included the various standard deviations necessary for their calculation.

less of the specific pattern of courses they have taken. The test in Understanding Modern Society (omitted in this review) is designed to measure general social awareness in fields of history, economics, government, and sociology, and emphasizes the understanding and application of basic concepts in social science. The Science Test (also omitted in this review) purports to evaluate a candidate's grasp of fundamental principles of science, and samples concepts and problems from basic college courses in biology, chemistry, and physics. *(Medical College Admission Test,* Confidential Report of Scores, *etc.* Educational Testing Service, Princeton, N. J., *in* Reitzes, 1958, pp. 376-377)

The scores on the *MCAT* are reported in intervals of 10 on a standard scale with a mean of 500 and a standard deviation of 100; the range of scores is from 200 to 800. The *Medical College Admission Test* is rated as technically among the best of the available standardized tests. Its reliability is satisfactory but its validity for aiding in the selection of medical students has not been demonstrated. (Wantman, *in* Buros, 1953, p. 817)

Reitzes (1958), at the request of Dr. Franklin C. McLean, founder of National Medical Fellowships, Inc., an organization providing assistance to Negroes for education and training in medicine, attempted to make a systematic study of the status of integration in medicine and to analyze the factors contributing to or blocking integration. In conjunction with this study, Reitzes examined the scholastic aptitude scores of applicants to United States medical schools from Negro undergraduate colleges, all of the colleges having ten or more students who took *MCAT* between May, 1953 and November, 1955.

The mean *Verbal* score of the 1123 applicants from colored colleges proved to be 389, their mean *Quantitative* score, 376, in contrast to the norm of 500 which was based upon the total number of applicants taking *MCAT,* about 95 per cent of whom were white. The *Verbal* mean of the Negro applicants was at the 13th percentile rank of the total group of applicants, the *Quantitative* mean being at the 12.5 percentile rank of the large group. From Table 6, it will be seen that 1.9 per cent of the applicants from Negro colleges earned a *Verbal* score of 600 or more, 0.4 per cent of these applicants earned a *Quantitative* score of 600 or more, whereas among all applicants taking the *MCAT,* 16 per cent earned a score of 600 or more on either the *Verbal* or *Quantitative* tests. More than 11 per cent of the *Verbal* scores and about eight per cent of the *Quantitative* scores of the colored Ss overlapped the respective means of the total group of applicants. Approximately 58 per cent of the applicants from Negro colleges earned *Verbal* scores below 400 on *MCAT,* about 63 per cent of them earned *Q* scores below 400 on the test, and 16 per cent of the total number of medical school applicants earned scores below this point (one SD below the mean).

Reitzes examined the scores of applicants to the two Negro medical colleges, Howard University College of Medicine and Meharry Medical College, and compared their scores with those of applicants of all races (about 95 per cent white) to all United States medical colleges in 1955-1956. The 325 Howard

University applicants represented 99 colleges and the 476 Meharry applicants represented 113 colleges — the Negro applicants to both schools attending predominantly white colleges as well as Negro colleges. The *Verbal* means of Ss applying to *Howard* and *Meharry* were respectively, 417 and 405; the *Quantitative* means of the applicants were respectively, 392 and 385. The *Verbal* overlaps of the applicants to *Howard* and *Meharry* on the national means were 19 and 11 per cents, respectively; the *Quantitative* overlaps of these respective colleges were 11 and 7 per cents. Reitzes observed that it is entirely possible that scores of applicants to some other medical schools may have been as low as or lower than the scores of applicants to *Howard* and *Meharry*. Also, the fact that the mean *MCAT* scores of *accepted applicants* at *Howard* and *Meharry* did not differ significantly from those of *rejected applicants* to all United States medical schools does not indicate that there may not have been other medical schools for which this may have been equally true. (See Table 6 for mean *Verbal* and *Quantitative* scores of accepted and rejected applicants at *Howard, Meharry,* and all United States medical schools combined.)

It is likely that relative to whites, Negroes who are admitted to medical schools compose an even more highly selected portion of their race than those admitted to higher educational institutions in general. Thompson (1953) has reported that the enrollment of white students in higher institutions of learning comprises about two per cent of the total white population and that of the Negro students about 0.7 per cent of the total Negro population. In other words, in the early 1950's there were proportionately 2.7 times as many white persons as Negroes in higher institutions of learning in the United States. From the statistics presented by Reitzes relative to the early or middle 1950's, there seems to have been nearly four times as many white as Negro students in the medical schools of this country in proportion to their numbers in the population.

SUMMARY

1. Of the 24,640 Negro college students included in the survey, approximately 61 per cent have been examined by the *American Council Psychological Examination for College Freshmen* (ACE); 10 per cent have been tested by the *Otis Self-Administering Test of Mental Ability (Otis S-A)*; 21 per cent have been examined by the *School and College Ability Tests (SCAT)*, the *College Board Scholastic Aptitude Test (SAT)*, or the *Medical College Admission Test (MCAT)*; and about 9 per cent have been tested by one of the other tests employed. About 98 per cent of the subjects were enrolled in colleges for Negroes.

2. The obtained averages were typically much lower than the norms provided and below the means of the specific white groups with whom they were compared. On the *Otis S-A* the colored students earned an average score which placed them at about the *13th percentile rank* of the norms distribution. On the *ACE* the

colored achieved an average score locating them at about the *12th percentile rank*, according to the norms. On the *SCAT*, the *SAT*, and the *MCAT*, the Negro students secured average scores placing them at about the *6th percentile rank* according to the norms.[51]

3. Fisk University students coming from Northern high schools were found to have achieved higher scores on the average than *Fisk* students from Southern high schools.[52] However, the averages of the colored from the urban North were unequivocally below the norms. Similarly, both the New York University and the University of Illinois means attained by colored students (educated for the most part in the North) were significantly below comparable means of white groups enrolled in these institutions of higher learning.

4. In eleven of the studies the researchers either reported the amount of overlapping or included their frequency distributions among their data. From these studies, comprising 7130 colored Ss, the average overlap was found to be *7.2 per cent,* considerably less than that previously noted in the elementary and high school comparisons.

In each of the eleven investigations listed below the number of cases follows the author and date. An *overlap of 0-4 per cent* occurred in four studies: T. M. Anderson (1958) 260; Hills, Klock, and Bush (1964) 796; Hills, Klock, and Bush (1965) 845; and A. L. Jones (1960) 2126. In two studies the *overlap was from 5-9 per cent:* Canady (1936) 517; and Reitzes (1958) 1123. In one, the *overlap was 10 per cent:* Richardson (1963) 200; in two, it was *between 15-19 per cent:* Derrick (1920) 55; and Bindman (1965) 100; in one, *28 per cent:* Price (1929) 927; and in the investigations of Graham (1930) 99-181, *about 35 per cent.*[53]

5. It is evident that Negro college students, on the average, have earned lower scores on mental or scholastic aptitude tests than have white students. It is also evident, judged from comparisons of average scores, mean percentile ranks, and amounts of overlapping, that they do not approach the white norms as closely as do Negro children, in spite of the fact that Negro college students probably represent a relatively highly selected sampling of their racial group. In 1933, for example, there was about one Negro college student for every 49 of the Negro population of college age, in contrast to one college student

[51]Compare these %ile ranks with those reported in the Project Talent research (Burket, Table 99, 1963); 12th year students in the 48 all-Negro high schools in the Southeast earned mean scores which placed them at the following %ile ranks of representative samples of American 12th grade pupils on the several tests designated as primarily measures of aptitude: Arith Computation, 7; Abstract Reasoning, 9; Reading Comprehension, 9; Arith Reasoning, 14; and Mechanical Reasoning, 21.

[52]Finding supported by the *National Survey* . . . . . . (1942). However, at West Virginia State College, colored students from large Southern cities scored higher on the average than those from small cities of the North.

[53]Graham tested many of the same *Fisk* students on four different tests (Table 6). Their average overlap on the several medians of white Ss from two Tennessee colleges was 35 per cent.

for every 15 of the total population of college age. (C. S. Johnson, 1935) In 1947, whereas Negroes represented about ten per cent of the total population, they accounted for only 3.1 per cent of the total student enrollment in institutions of higher education. (Bonds, 1948) In 1952, Negroes accounted for about four per cent of the total student population in institutions of higher learning in the States (Thompson, 1953); and in 1955-56, they comprised 2.6 per cent of all students enrolled in medical colleges. (Reitzes, 1958)

Thompson (1953) observed that the proportion of Negroes between 5 and 24 years of age attending schools closely approximated that of the white population of the same age range, *i.e.*, 54.8 per cent as compared with 58.6 per cent. However, over half of the Negro public school enrollment (elementary and secondary) was below the fifth grade, while only one third of the total public school enrollment was below this level. Also, the percentage of Negroes enrolled in high schools was only a little more than half that of the total public school population, in spite of the fact that proportionally seven times as many of the total school population as of the Negro school population were enrolled in kindergartens.

The present writer is of the opinion that these statistics suggest that relative to the white population (except at the kindergarten level) the higher the educational level the less is the Negro school population representative of its age population.

One explanation for the increased discrepancy in white and Negro scores at the college level may lie in the abstract nature of the test material used. In connection with the testing of school children, several authors were quoted as finding the colored relatively better on *common-sense, concrete material* than on tests involving *abstract concepts*. Some observations of a similar nature have been made on college students. Derrick (1920) found Negro Ss to be better in memory and in concrete and routine problems than in problems involving mental abstraction and reconstruction. Patrick and Sims (1934) believed that Negro college students function on a lower level than whites in situations of an abstract nature; in concrete social adjustments to everyday life the white superiority was not consistently evident. Stainbrook and Siegel (1944) reported that colored students tested by them on the group *Rorschach* were more rigid and less fluent in their responses. In Graham's study (1930) furthermore, where a variety of less abstract tests was used, the differences appear to have been considerably less than those usually obtained between white and Negro students. In support of this line of reasoning one could cite tests such as the *Scholastic Aptitude*, the *School and College Ability*, and the *Medical College Admission tests* administered to colored students in recent years which consistently show the average Negro student to be at a marked and serious disadvantage,[54] these tests being highly verbal and abstract in nature.

---

[54]The mean overlap being approximately 4 per cent.

Jones (1960) has effectively discussed the relationship between the poor showing of Southern Negro students on this type of test and their common use of dialects in everyday life, the Negro dialects composing a simple undeveloped language which would serve to seriously restrict concept formations, verbal and nonverbal, probably throughout life. Jones referred to dialects as characterizing the speech of *Southern* Negroes, in the main. In this connection, the present writer wishes to make note of the fact that in the studies of elementary and high school pupils it was no problem to separate the scores or IQ's of the Northern, Border, and Southern Negro subjects. The situation, of course, is different with the Negro college student. Although the great majority of colored students were tested in Negro colleges, predominantly in the South, it is well known that many Negroes from the North attend these colleges. However, we cannot determine whether or not the Northern Negro has been included in the Negro college research to the same extent that the Northern Negro child has been included in research dealing with Negro school children.

Another factor which enters into college comparisons that was not present in those of school children and high school pupils relates to the presence of an undetermined number of previously trained private school individuals among the white college Ss. In the comparative racial studies of school children, whites attending private schools were not included—resulting in the removal of a selected group from the Negro-white comparisons.[55] Therefore, it is to be expected that the inclusion of these subjects in the college groups would result in greater differences between Negro and white college students than between Negro and white grade school pupils.

A final and reasonable explanation for the poorer showing of Negroes at the college level rests upon the assumption of a cumulative effect of early poor schooling of many Negro college students and to the probable cumulative effect of a more restricted, less complex environment, and to substandard situations to which these students have been subjected during their lives. However, the following points, namely— (1) the low scoring of colored students in institutions of higher learning for Negroes, (2) the inferior showing of Negroes attending mixed Northern universities as compared with whites in the same universities, (3) the unfavorable averages of colored coming South to college from mixed Northern secondary schools as compared with the norms, (4) the evidence that greater interracial differences occur in the more highly abstract tests than in those dealing with concrete or practical problems, and (5) the greater selectivity of the Negro as compared with the white college student — cast serious doubt upon the assumption that the obtained differences are completely or primarily due to inferior patterns of speech and to the cumulative effect of an inferior environment.

---

[55]Average IQ of private school pupils generally estimated to be between 110 and 120. On the other hand, the *ACE* norms have not included the scores of a number of predominantly white colleges whose students are reputed to be highly selected.

Chapter V

THE ARMED FORCES

Following the widespread mental testing programs of World War I and World War II many psychologists have used the extensive data collected to compare Negroes with whites at the adult level. The racial comparisons have involved rejections, inductees, cadets, and officers; enlisted men of varying education and occupation; men included in the Special Training Program for illiterates; problem and neuropsychiatric cases; and enlisted men from different states, camps, and commands. Since the same scores were included in different analyses of the data, since in some important instances the number of men examined was not given and in other instances the number of colored tested included many thousands, we have not attempted to estimate accurately the total number of Negroes whose test scores are included in Table 7. A rough estimate is between 300,000 and 500,000.

WORLD WAR I

The World War I investigations have been grouped according to the test employed, *i.e., Army a, Army Alpha, Army Beta, Stanford-Binet,* and the *Combined Scale,* and will be discussed in the order named.

ARMY A

Army a, a long scale of more than 400 items, was the forerunner of *Army Alpha* and was used in some of the earlier comparisons of Negroes and whites. It contained two tests that were subsequently discarded, those of immediate memory and cancellation.

Ferguson (1919) compared the medians of 39 Negro companies tested at Camp Lee with the medians of white recruits from 125 companies. The 3285 Negroes were recruited mainly from the states of Pennsylvania, Virginia, and West Virginia, with smaller numbers from North and South Carolina and the District of Columbia. The comparative white draft, likewise, was drawn principally from Pennsylvania, Virginia, and West Virginia. The median of the Negroes' scores was 42, less than one third of the median of the whites (which was placed at 142), the median of the highest Negro company being slightly above that of the lowest white company. Ferguson attributed the lower scores of the Negroes in part to their poorer quality and lesser quantity of schooling. He attempted to eliminate the latter factor by examining the *a* scores of 2000 colored and 4000 white men who had completed the same number of school grades. The colored in this comparison scored approximately 65 per cent of the amount earned by the average white enlisted man.

Yerkes (1921) compared the *Army a* medians obtained from testing large numbers of colored and white recruits at Camp Dix and Camp Lee. The Negro soldiers tested at the former camp were drawn from New York and New Jersey, those at Camp Lee having been recruited mainly from Virginia. The inclusion of illiterates, who comprised about 40 and 24 per cent of the colored tested in Camps Lee and Dix respectively, accounts in part for the very low medians of 14.8 and 53 secured by the Negroes in the two camps. The higher median of 171 attained by the Camp Dix whites as compared with that of 116 secured on the Camp Lee whites may likewise be attributed in large part to the inclusion of a smaller percentage of illiterates in the former camp.

The Devens Literacy Test was administered to 590 whites and 409 Negroes at Camp Dix; the Negroes and whites were matched for literacy scores, and their *Army a* scores were then compared with one another. Yerkes reported that the colored made lower grades on *a* than did the whites of equal literacy. "The interpretation of these results appears to be that negroes of the same degree of intelligence are relatively better in dealing with words than whites, whereas, the whites excel in tests which involve other abstract operations." (p. 353)

Army a was employed in the testing of 1052 white and 106 colored officers at Camp Dix (Yerkes, 1921). The median of the Negro officers was approximately midway between the median of the white officers and that of the white draft. The percentages of the white and colored officers scoring in the respective *A* and *B* categories were 76 and 31.1.

ARMY ALPHA

Various investigators have analyzed the *Army Alpha* scores earned by Negroes and whites in World War I. Trabue (1919) compared the medians of literate colored and English-speaking white recruits at Camp Grant. The Negroes were divided into two groups, North and South, the Northern Negroes coming from the St. Louis and Chicago areas, the Southern Negroes from various Southern States. The Northern Negroes' median of 40.5 was closer to the whites' median of 57.9 than to the low Southern Negro median of 14.4. About 67 per cent of the whites overlapped the median of the literate Northern Negroes and approximately 86 per cent of the whites overlapped the median of the literate Southern Negroes. (Peterson, 1923) Trabue commented upon the large percentage of Louisiana and Mississippi Negroes making inferior or very inferior ratings on this test. He observed that Army test comparisons may have been somewhat favorable to the colored race because of the greater possibility of intelligent white men obtaining commissions or entering some essential industry which would have exempted them from the draft. Trabue, however, was of the opinion that this removal of many of the more able white men from the drafted group was not particularly important and was probably compensated for by the fact that less care was taken by draft boards in eliminating unfit Negroes than was the case with white recruits.

Ferguson (1919) compared the medians obtained on *Alpha* by Negroes and whites at Camp Lee, the men tested having been drafted principally from the states of Pennsylvania, Virginia, and West Virginia. The white median was 51, the colored, 17, with five per cent of the whites and 0.3 per cent of the Negroes scoring in the highest class, *i.e., A*. The Northern Negroes scored midway between the Virginia Negroes and the total white group, their median being higher than that of "a few companies of mountain whites".

At Camp Dodge, Yerkes (1921) compared the letter-grade distributions of 273 colored officers' training camp candidates and 95 colored and 1385 white officers who were below the rank of major. From Table 7 it will be observed that nearly 50 per cent of the white officers earned the grade of A, while about 15 per cent of the colored officers and less than 4 per cent of the colored officer candidates scored in the highest category. Likewise, only 0.4 per cent of the white officers scored below C-, while 13 per cent of the Negro groups were below this level. Yerkes noted that the distribution of the Negro officers' training camp candidates corresponded to the distribution of the white draft, except for a somewhat smaller percentage of inferior men among the former group.

Bagley (1924) was probably the first to point out that the Negro draft from certain Northern states exceeded the white draft from certain Southern states on the *Alpha,* a point later emphasized by Klineberg, Benedict and Weltfish, and Montagu. Bagley observed that the literate Negroes from Illinois achieved a higher median than the literate whites from nine Southern states; that literate Negroes from New York had a higher median than the literate whites from five Southern states; and that the median of the literate Negroes from Pennsylvania was above that of the literate whites from two Southern states. For all Northern Negroes whose scores were included in the comparison, the median *Alpha* surpassed the median of the whites of Mississippi, Kentucky, and Arkansas. Bagley presented a program which he described as that of the "rational equalitarian". "Because it is rational this program does not quarrel with facts; hence it does not deny racial differences in intelligence-levels. It recognizes a high degree of probability that the Negro race will never produce so large a proportion of highly gifted persons as will the white races . . . . It holds furthermore that the level of effective intelligence in any group of whatever race can be substantially raised through education." (p. 186)

Klineberg (1935, 1944) selected from Yerkes' Tables 200 and 262 the four Southern states where the white *Alpha* medians were *lowest* and the four Northern states where the colored *Alpha* medians were *highest*. He tabulated the medians of these eight groups and observed that Northern Negroes were superior to the white groups from a number of Southern states. However, Klineberg did not mention that the eight states were selected as being those where the respective medians were lowest or highest for the white and colored groups, that the median of the highest scoring Negroes (Ohio) was based upon only 152 cases, or that it was *Alpha* that was used as a basis for comparison. Myrdal (1944),

referring to Klineberg and similarly mentioning none of the above points, said:
"In the Army intelligence tests during the first World War, for example, the
Negroes of the Northern states of Ohio, Illinois, New York, and Pennsylvania
topped the whites of the Southern states of Mississippi, Arkansas, Kentucky and
Georgia." (p. 148)[1]

Garrett (1945) reported that these comparisons have often been cited as
evidence that education and economic opportunity are more important than
racial origin, that all psychologists would agree that these data clearly indicate
the influence of education, but that it is doubtful if any conclusion concerning
race differences can be drawn on the basis of these facts alone.[2] When he compared
the *Alpha* medians of Negroes and whites from the four Northern states of Ohio,
Pennsylvania, Illinois, and New York, Garrett found that the Negroes scored
about as far below the white soldiers of these states as they scored below the
whites in the country as a whole. He observed, therefore, that one might argue
that given better education the Negro does improve his *Alpha* score but not his
position relative to the white, and that since white Southerners did about as
well as Northern Negroes in spite of marked educational handicaps, had they
the same advantages as the Northern Negro they would exceed the Negro
medians on *Alpha* just as the Northern whites did, education affecting the whites
as well as Negroes.[3]

Garrett (1945) selected from Yerkes' tables three groups of *Northern*
colored recruits with different amounts of formal school training, including 555
men who had completed eight grades, 457 who had completed high school
training, and 111 who were college graduates.[4] In Table 7 are given the median
Alphas of these groups as well as the median *Alphas* of thousands of whites who
had the same on a less amount of formal school training. The median of the

---

[1]No mention is made in any of these studies of the percentages of white and colored
commissioned officers, none of whom were included in the draft comparisons. In World War II
(*Report of the President's Committee*) there was one commissioned white officer for every
9 white men in the Armed Services, whereas there was only one commissioned Negro officer
for every 125 Negroes. If these men had been included with the draft it would obviously have
increased the test differences in favor of the whites. A removal of 14 superior white men out
of a group of 125 (one out of 9) significantly lowers the average of the remaining 111. However,
the removal of one superior colored man out of 125 affects only nominally the average of the
remaining 124.

This discrepancy was even greater in World War I. Ginzberg (1956) reported that in WWI
over 400,000 Negroes served in the Army including more than 1300 officers—resulting in an
officer-enlisted man ratio of about one in 300.

[2]*J. Abnorm. & Soc. Psychol.*

[3]Pastore (1949) believed that the large number of zero scores made by the Negro draft on
Alpha subtests indicates that the test is unsatisfactory as a measure of intelligence at the
lower extreme and that the Army test results, therefore, should no longer be used in attempts
to compare the intellectual status of the Negro with that of the white.

[4]*Amer. J. Psychol.*

Negroes who had completed eight school grades was 77 per cent of that of the whites of the same amount of formal education, while the medians of the Negro high school and college graduates were lower than the respective medians of the whites who had one year of high school or one year of college training.

Montagu (1945) made comparisons from Yerkes' data between the *Alpha* medians obtained from white samples of nine Southern states and Negro samples from New York, Ohio, Illinois, and Indiana; in addition he compared the "Comprehensive Alpha"[5] medians obtained from white samples of eleven Southern states and Negro samples from four Northern states. As will be noted in the table, only the Ohio Negro medians were larger than all of the given white medians; the Illinois Negro medians were larger than seven of the white medians; the New York Negro medians were larger than five and three of the respective white medians; and the Indiana Negro medians were larger than two and seven white medians, respectively. It will be observed that the Ohio and Indiana samples were very small and that Montagu calculated "average median" scores, resulting in misleading comparisons between Southern whites and Northern Negroes. Montagu concluded that the evidence he presented, on the whole, indicated no significant inherent psychical differences between the colored and white races but that the differences between racial groups could better be explained on the basis of differences in socioeconomic conditions. In addition to attributing the lower Southern test scores to the depressed socioeconomic conditions of the South, Montagu related the lower scores of recruits from the states of Delaware and New Jersey to the fact that these states were in many ways socially backward.

Garrett (1945), in commenting upon Montagu's interpretation, said that since *Alpha* is known to correlate with schooling from .50 to .75 it is not surprising that small groups of presumably better educated Northern Negroes scored higher than small groups of presumably less well educated Southern whites.[4] "It is, however, both important and significant as a prognosis of what education and perhaps selective migration may be expected to accomplish." Garrett, further, found Montagu to be in serious error in reporting "average median scores", in that he disregarded the numbers of the contributing samples. Garrett gave as another possible explanation of the higher *Alpha* scores earned by some Northern Negroes—as compared with some Southern Negroes—the larger proportion of Negro-white mixtures in the Northern group. When Negroes of two battalions at Camp Lee, for example, were separated on the basis of skin color, the lighter men were reported to have an *Alpha* median of 50, the darker, 30; furthermore, the percentage of darker Negroes was greater among the illiterates than among the literates.

---

[5]Including samples of Ss who took *Alpha* only, *Alpha & Beta* and/or an individual examination.

Army Beta

Beta was administered to men who had been identified as illiterate or non-English speaking and to those who were recalled because of having made low grades on *Alpha*.[6] Yerkes described several different methods used to divide the Negroes into literate and illiterate groups so they could be properly sent to *Alpha* and *Beta,* respectively. In some cases the method was to make all step out who could not read and write. Usually a standard of proficiency was adopted, as "to read a newspaper and write a letter home". In some cases an added qualification was employed, such as 3, 4, or 5 years of schooling. "In some cases literacy tests were used, though generally as a supplement to the simpler and more direct method of segregation mentioned above. In some cases the negroes were all sent in a body direct to examination beta." (1921, p. 705) Yerkes indicated that authorities in different camps disagreed as to the value of giving Negroes the *Beta.* "It appears definitely from camp reports that beta is unsatisfactory for use with negro drafts because its use results in such a large percentage of failures that they can not be recalled for individual examination." (1921, p. 706)

Ferguson (1919) compared Negro troups from eight companies drawn mainly from Virginia, Pennsylvania, the Carolinas, and the District of Columbia. He found the Negro *Beta* median to range from 19 for the troops from the District to 13 for the troops from Virginia, in contrast to the white median of 33.

Trabue (1919) calculated weighted *Beta* medians for more than 5000 Negro recruits from Camp Grant, the majority of the men coming from the South but more than 1500 of them from the St. Louis and Chicago areas. In contrast to the white *Beta* median of 100.8, the Northern Negro median was about 62, and the Southern Negro median approximately 33. About 80 per cent of the illiterate whites were above the median of the illiterate Northern Negroes and 93 per cent of these whites overlapped the median of the illiterate Southern Negroes (Peterson, 1923). In commenting upon the use of *Beta* with Negroes, Trabue said that it is probable that the white illiterates had somewhat more experience in making check marks with a pencil and that a few of the pictures presented were not as familiar to the colored men as to the Northern whites. Nevertheless, he considered it evident from the tabulation of *Beta* scores and from the performance of the two races with guns, beds, tent rolls, and squad formation, that the white race is tremendously more capable in matters requiring ability to learn and think than the Negro race.

Using Yerkes' tables, Montagu (1945) determined the Beta "average median scores" of the colored draft from nine Northern and fourteen Southern states and the District of Columbia and compared them with the *Beta* "average median score" of the white draft. The "average medians" obtained on the two colored groups were 32.72 and 17.58, respectively; on the whites, 40.70. In addition, Montagu calculated "average median score" of the colored from six Northern

---

[6]If a man was tested on *Beta* as well as *Alpha,* his *Alpha* score was disregarded.

states and found it to be 34.63, as compared with an "average median score" of 31.11 for whites from fourteen Southern states.[7] Montagu, in presenting *Beta* medians of Negro and white recruits by states, showed that Negroes from some Northern states did as well as whites from some Southern states; he interpreted these findings, as he did those on *Alpha*, as strongly supporting the socioeconomic explanation of racial differences. Garrett, on the other hand, proposed that Montagu did not understand the sampling problems in the Army data and that his method of comparing *Alpha* and *Beta* medians was invalid and misleading.

Some of Garrett's specific criticisms of Montagu's techniques and interpretations are as follows:[8] (1) Comparison of *Beta* medians by states works to the disadvantage of the Southern Negro because of his large number of zero or near-zero scores. About 16 per cent of the Negroes from Alabama, Georgia, Louisiana, Mississippi, and South Carolina scored from zero to 4 and were actually unmeasured by this test. "A large number of zero scores means that Beta was not a suitable test for a great many southern Negroes. These illiterate men may have been of low-grade intelligence or they may not have understood the directions. In any event they were unmeasured, and we cannot tell what they might have done upon a test better adapted to their level of ability." (p. 482) Only two per cent of the Negroes from Illinois, Indiana, New York, New Jersey, and Pennsylvania scored from 0 to 4; hence dropping these does not appreciably affect their medians. (2) Only 28 Kansas Negroes and 77 Ohio Negroes were used in securing their respective state medians, while the Florida white median was based on *12 cases*. (3) Montagu stated that the lowest *Beta* medians among the Northern states (Pennsylvania and New Jersey) came from states bordering on the South, but did not notice that the highest Negro *Beta* median was secured on recruits from Ohio, just across the river from Kentucky. (4) With regard to the statement that the 188 white draftees from Kentucky had a median *Beta* of 12.30, while the 330 colored from the same state had a median of 17.20, it may be observed that the badly skewed distributions and the small samples provide little basis for racial comparison. Similarly, the higher median *Beta* obtained by the 77 Ohio Negroes as against that of the 68 Ohio whites is not significant. (5) There were six states which had *Beta* medians for the whites lower than that of the Negro sample taken to be representative of the *North*. The six states were Kentucky, Virginia, Alabama, North Carolina, Connecticut, and New Jersey, two Northern and four Southern states. (6) Montagu commented upon the lower scores of whites and Negroes in New Jersey and Delaware, referring to the states as being in many ways socially backward. He apparently accepted without question the low score of the New Jersey white sample; actually the real cause lay in the different procedure followed at Camp Dix, where the New Jersey

---

[7]To obtain his "average median score" for the Northern Negroes, Montagu added the six medians and divided by six, thereby weighting all medians equally, regardless of the size of the respective samples. Correct mdn acc to Garrett is 32.39. (*Amer. J. Psychol.*, 1945)

[8]Numbering is reviewer's.

sample was examined, as compared with Camp Lewis, where the highest scoring whites were examined. At Camp Dix, 28 per cent of the men were foreigners and 20 per cent were Negroes, most of these men calling for *Beta* rather than *Alpha*. Since the job of the examining staff was to provide certain minimal information in a short period of time, with the large demand for *Beta* at Camp Dix, it was necessary to minimize the sending on of low-scoring men from *Alpha* to *Beta*. Therefore, men who scored even just a few points on *Alpha* were kept in the *Alpha-only* group, thus tending to lower the median of this group. At Camp Lewis, *Beta* was in less demand and the low-scoring men (up to about 30 points) were transferred to *Beta* and removed from the *Alpha-only* group, with the resulting effect of raising the median of the *Alpha-only* group. Owing to the difference in the selection of *Alpha* and *Beta* samples in the two camps, the states sampled at Camp Lewis (Pacific and near-Pacific) were practically certain of making a better showing than states (New Jersey and Delaware) sampled at Camp Dix.[9]

Yerkes (1921) compared samples of Negro and white soldiers at Camp Sevier after equating them for mental ability as measured by the Army tests. The scores of 200 Negroes tested by *Alpha,* whose percentages of A's, B's, *etc.,* were the same as those of the total Negro draft, were selected; each Negro was paired with a white man with the same *Alpha* score. *Beta* matchings were made in the same manner. Eighty-two Negroes were paired with the same number of whites of equal mental age as determined by the *Performance Test.* Finally, 188 Negroes and 188 whites were equated for mental ability by means of the *Point Scale.* Yerkes found that "the negro as compared with the white man of equal intelligence is relatively strong in the use of language, in acquaintance with verbal meanings, in perception and observation; and that he is relatively weak in judgment, in ability to analyze and define exactly, and in reasoning." (p. 738)

STANFORD-BINET

In addition to reviewing the comparative abilities of white and Negro children, Peterson (1923) reported the median mental ages of samples of white and colored members of the draft. In the first of the comparisons, 653 white and 403 Negro men from nine camps selected as representative of the draft were tested on the *Stanford-Binet, 1916 Form,* in order to evaluate their *Beta* scores. The median mental ages of the respective white and colored enlisted men were 13.33 and 9.18. In the second of the comparisons included in Peterson's survey were the median mental ages of 690 white and 514 colored men from Camp

---

[9]The reviewer is of the opinion that studies on *Beta* alone contribute very little in a discussion of Negro-white differences in intelligence since we have no certain knowledge whether or not men were sent to *Beta* because of illiteracy or because of mental inferiority. Due to the fact that white troops were tested by *Beta* relatively less often than were colored recruits it might be expected that the small number of illiterate and/or dull whites would score as low as or lower than a large number of illiterate and/or dull Negroes.

Sheridan. These men had been recalled for individual examinations because of failure to pass a group examination. "They may fail because of defective intelligence or because of some social maladjustment that renders them unable or unwilling to cooperate in the group examination." (Yerkes, *Memoirs,* p. 791) On the *Stanford-Binet* the median mental ages of the white and colored draftees proved to be 9.6 and 8.6, respectively.

COMBINED SCALE

The Army psychologists recognized the fact that scores obtained from *Alpha* and *Beta* must be equated if the general intelligence level of a comprehensive cross section of the population was to be determined. Hence a *Combined Scale* was developed which would include men who were examined by *Alpha only,* by both *Alpha and Beta,* by *Beta only,* or by *Beta and certain individual tests,* with all test scores converted into a common scale. This eliminated the breakdown of state samples into Alpha and Beta groups.[10] Accordingly, Yerkes (1921) included the percentages of 93,973 white and 23,596 colored recruits making Grades of A, B, C+, *etc.,* on the *Combined Scale.* As will be noted from Table 7, not only was the white draft markedly superior to the principal colored sample which was selected by states on a prorata basis, but it was also superior to the additional sample of Negroes from Illinois, Indiana, New Jersey, New York, and Pennsylvania. The relative standing of the three groups, *i.e.,* the white sample, the additional sample of Northern Negroes, and the principal colored sample, is indicated by their respective percentages of A and B grades, which were 12.1, 3.6, and 0.7, as well as by their percentages of D and D— grades, which were 24.1, 45.3, and 78.7, respectively.[11]

Using the above principal samples Wallis (1926) compared the percentages of *inferior, average,* and *superior* recruits from nine camps. We have included the percentages of *inferior* (D and D—) and *superior* (A and B) white and colored men for each camp listed as well as the number of cases in Table 7. For the white draft the percentage of *inferiority* ranged from 8.4 to 34.4, for the Negro draft the percentage ranged from 23.6 to 92.8; for the white draft the percentage of *superiority* ranged from 9.5 to 18.7, for the Negro draft the percentage ranged from 0.1 to 9.4. Examination of the table will show that there were very few Negroes included from Camps Lewis and Devens. If these two camps were to be excluded from the comparisons we would find fewer differences within a race from camp to camp and greater differences between the races, with the camp making the poorest showing for the whites being superior to the camp making the best showing for the Negroes.

Brigham (1923), likewise using the Hollerith sample, calculated average scores on the *Combined Scale* of 93,955 white and 23,596 colored recruits, as

---

[10]Garrett, *Amer. J. Psychol.,* 1945.

[11]See Table 7, fn. 16, for method of selection of cases.

well as the average of 15,543 white officers. From the table it will be observed that these averages were 13.54, 10.41, and 18.84, respectively, the difference between the means of the colored and white recruits being highly significant. Slightly more than *13 per cent* of the colored earned scores equal to or above the average of the white draft. Brigham concluded that at the present state of development of psychological tests we cannot measure the actual amount of difference in intelligence due to race or nativity, but can only prove that differences do exist and can interpret these differences in terms that have great social and economic significance. "The average negro child can not advance through an educational curriculum adapted to the Anglo-Saxon child in step with that child. To select children of equal education, age for age, in the two groups, is to sample either superior negroes or inferior whites." (p. 194) Brigham (1930) later rejected completely his own and others' findings in the field of natio-racial differences in intelligence on the grounds that the subjects were handicapped by not having been brought up in homes where the vernacular of the test was used (or used exclusively) and that intelligence tests do not measure a unitary trait. As regards the latter point Garrett believes that Brigham attached too much importance to test purity. *Alpha* contains verbal, numerical, and spatial elements, but the intercorrelations of the subtests are sufficiently high at the ability levels of Brigham's subjects to indicate considerable "generality" in the battery.[2]

Using the white draft as a frame of reference with a mean of 100 and a standard deviation of 16, D. M. Johnson (1948) was able to convert Brigham's Negro scores on the *Combined Scale* into standard-score IQ's. He reported a mean IQ of 83 on the sample of 23,596 colored men which placed it slightly more than one standard deviation below the white norm. A mean IQ of 83 relative to a norm of 100 is easily evaluated as compared with a mean of 10.41 relative to a norm of 13.54.

Alper and Boring (1944) compared average scores obtained on the *Combined Scale* by Negroes and whites from four Southern and four Northern states. These eight states had been previously selected by Klineberg (1935, 1944) for *Alpha* comparisons, since the four Northern states were those in which Negroes had secured their highest medians and the four Southern states were those in which whites had secured their lowest medians.[12] Alper and Boring observed that neither Klineberg nor Benedict and Weltfish had presented a total picture of the Army scores which they (Alper and Boring) intended to do: (1) by including scores of the Negroes from the four Southern states and those of the whites from the four Northern states, (2) by including scores on *Beta* with those on *Alpha,* and (3) by performing an analysis of variance with respect to geography and skin color. Referring to their results, Alper and Boring commented as follows: "They are what one might expect from what is already known. It was

---

[12]Benedict and Weltfish (1943) emphasized the *Alpha* differences by eliminating the Southern state where whites scored highest and the Northern state where the colored scored lowest.

a disadvantage in the Army tests of 1918 for a white or a Negro to come from a southern state where education and economic opportunities are few instead of from a northern state where they are better, and also a disadvantage, whether northern or southern, to be a Negro and not white. Thus the average score for the southern Negroes is lowest of the four because southern Negroes work against both these disadvantages, and the average score for the northern whites is, conversely, highest of all. Benedict and Weltfish might have avoided the criticism of selection of states had they given all four of these averages instead of only two, for then they would have avoided the false implication that skin color made no difference in the states under consideration." (pp. 472-473)

An analysis of variance of the data showed that both skin color and geography affected the scores, that skin color had more effect than geography, and that the two factors interacted to enhance each other. In other words, the authors found the average score on the *Combined Scale* for the Northern Negroes to be not quite as high as for the Southern whites, contrary to Klineberg's and Benedict and Weltfish's findings with *Alpha only*. Therefore the inclusion of the *Beta* scores helped the whites more than the Negroes. "Our only suggestion in explanation of this fact is that Beta is less culture-free than even we had supposed, that Beta is better adapted to whites than to Negroes . . . . Of course, it is possible to say that Beta overcomes illiteracy more than stupidity, and that the proportion of Negroes who went to Beta because of stupidity was greater than the proportion of whites who went for stupidity, a conclusion fully consistent with the common prejudice about the low level of Negro intelligence. We should not, however, wish to draw this conclusion in view of the fact that cultural differences are known to have such a large effect on test scores." (p. 474)

Garrett, likewise, was of the opinion that a comparison of Negro and white soldiers to be most impartial should be in terms of the *Combined Scale,* noting that when test data are available for men and women in the Armed Forces of World War II much larger samples, measured on better tests, will be accessible to the students of race differences. "Perhaps the environmental hypothesis will be strengthened by a study of these data, and Negro-white differences no longer stand out so clearly as they did in 1917-1918. That marked differences did appear twenty-five years ago is established beyond any reasonable doubt; and the inference is strong that such differences cannot be explained in socio-economic terms." (p. 495)[10]

WORLD WAR II

The *Army General Classification Test* of World War II which was designed "to determine a soldier's general intelligence and his ability to learn" largely supplanted the tests used in World War I.[13] Pennington, Hough, and Case (1943)

---

[13]Bingham (1944) noted that perhaps the chief cause for anxiety among the Committee members was the tendency on part of some officers to place undue reliance on test scores alone as indicators of ability to learn and to perform.

describe three forms of this test: a verbal form for men who could both read and write English, a nonverbal form for illiterates and foreigners, and a form designed for men who could not understand English or who were unable to take the first or second test forms because of certain deficiencies. This form, as distinguished from the first two forms which are group tests, is an individual test. All forms of the *General Classification Test* were constructed so that earned raw scores could be translated into *grades*. Grade I—*Very Superior Intelligence*—included about 7 per cent of the men. "The services of these men should be required in those posts demanding the maximum of insight and intelligence." Grade II—*Superior Intelligence*—included about 24 per cent of the men. "These men are known to make excellent noncommissioned officers. Many are capable of profiting from extensive training in officers' candidate schools." Grade III—*Average Intelligence*—included about 38 per cent of the men. "The average soldier of good all-round mental ability is usually found in this class." Grade IV—*Inferior Intelligence*—included about 24 per cent of the cases, and this group was described as "slow in thinking, hard to teach, and who have great difficulty in analyzing a complex situation." Grade V—*Very Inferior Intelligence*—including about 7 per cent of the draft ". . . occasionally slip through the *screening examinations* at induction and reception centers. . . . Inasmuch as their lack of general intelligence may endanger the lives of other men, they should be placed under special observation. If they are found unqualified to carry out simple tasks, they should be recommended for an honorable discharge from the Army, or to special duty with labor battalions." (p. 166)

Rejection Rates

Rowntree, McGill, and Edwards (1943) investigated the rejection rates of young Negro and white men of 18 and 19 years of age whose order numbers were reached between December, 1942, and February, 1943. All of these men were called for examination unless they had entered the Armed Forces by direct enlistment prior to December 12, 1942, unless they were in school or college under programs supported by the Army or Navy, or unless they had been given occupational deferment. From Table 7 it will be observed that 42,273 whites (a term used here to include all men examined except colored) and 3312 colored were given physical and psychometric tests at local boards and induction stations during the period covered in the survey. The total rejection rates were high, *i.e.*, 23.8 per cent for the whites and 45.5 per cent for the colored, with the majority of rejections being due to physical defects. About 12 per cent of the colored and one per cent of the whites were excused from military service because of educational deficiency, whereas only 0.68 per cent of the whites and one per cent of the colored were rejected because of mental deficiency.[14]

---

[14]Where several defects were listed on a man's record, any one of which would have exempted him from service, only one, and usually the one listed first, was taken by the authors as the cause of rejection. Doubtless the mental deficiency rates would have been higher had more than one cause for rejection been included.

TABLE

ARMED FORCES

AUTHOR DATE	LOCATION	N	SUBJECTS RANK	METHOD OF SELECTION
				ARMY
Ferguson, G. O., Jr. (1919)	Camp Lee	c- 3285	Enlisted	Recruits mainly from Pa, Va, and WVa, also some from DC and Carolinas. Literate c of 39 companies compared with w of 80th Division.
Yerkes, R. M. (1921)	Camp Dix	w-1052 c- 106	Officers Officers	
Yerkes, R. M. (1921)	Camp Dix	w-10,936 c- 1111	Enlisted	Recruited from NY and NJ; c from 2 field artillery regiments. C mainly from Va.
	Camp Lee	w-26,640 c- 5774	Enlisted	C represented 39 companies.
				ARMY
Trabue, M. R. (1919)	Camp Grant	w-26,605 c- No-1970 So- 1336	Enlisted Enlisted	Literate and English-speaking recruits. Northern c from St. Louis and Chicago and surrounding area sent to camp in July, 1918.
Ferguson, G. O., Jr. (1919)	Camp Lee	c- 1616	Enlisted	Literate and Engl-speaking at camp, mainly from Pa, Va, WVa, and some from NC, SC, and DC. From 8 companies. Men given *Alpha* or *Beta*.
Yerkes, R. M. (1921)	Camp Dodge	w- I- 1385 c- I- 95 II- 273	Officers Officers Officers in training	I-Officers below rank of major. II-Officers' training camp candidates.

[1]Illiterates were included; they comprised 8.6 per cent of w and 23.9 per cent of c recruits at Camp Dix, and 17.7 per cent of w and 39.6 per cent of c at Camp Lee. These were counted as falling in lower halves of their distributions.

SEVEN

WORLD WAR I

	RESULTS		COMMENTS OF AUTHOR

a

	Scores		Mdn sch: w- 6.6 gr, c- 3.8 gr; *r* bet *a* and sch grade completed .67 to .71; 2000 c scored 65% of aver of 4000 w who had same number grades in sch. Scores would be more nearly equal if schs more nearly equal.
	w	c	
Mdn			
Highest Co.	210	93	
Lowest Co.	90	20	
Total	142	42	

	Scores	
	w	c
Mdn	294	218
% A or B Grade	76.0	31.1

	Scores[1]	
	w	c
Mdn		
Dix	171	53
Lee	116	14.8

ALPHA

		Scores		7.4% of all w and 52.9-63.3% c from La and Miss given inferior or very inf ratings; 10.7% total w and .2-.5% c from these 2 states rated as superior or very superior.
	w		c	
		No	So	
Mdn	57.9	40.5	14.4	

	Scores		Northern c scored midway bet the Va w and c on *Alpha;* their mdn was above that of a few companies of mountain whites.
	w	c	
Mdn	51	17	
% A Grade	5	0.29	

	% age Distribution			The distribution of Negro officers' training camp candidates just about corresponds to the distrib of the w draft with somewhat smaller %ages of inferior men among the Negro officers' training camp candidates.
	w	c	c	
Grade	I	I	II	
A	49.2	14.7	3.4	
B	31.2	24.2	8.1	
C+	12.3	21.0	19.4	
C	6.2	22.1	35.6	
C—	0.7	5.3	20.8	
D	0.3	10.0	10.5	
D—	0.1	3.3	2.2	

TABLE

ARMED FORCES

AUTHOR DATE	LOCATION	N	SUBJECTS RANK	METHOD OF SELECTION
Klineberg, O. (1944)	w- Mississippi Kentucky Arkansas Georgia c- Illinois Pennsylvania New York Ohio	w-665 832 618 702 c-578 498 850 152	Enlisted[2]	Selected 4 Southern states where w mdns were lowest & 4 Northern states where c mdns were highest (from Yerkes' Tables 200 & 262). Tables included men who took *Alpha* only. C recruits from Group V only.
Garrett,[3] H. E. (1945)	United States	w-51,620 c- No-2850 So- 1709	Enlisted	From principal samples.
Garrett, H. E. (1945)	United States	w-14,899 c- 555 w- 3793 c- 457 w- 1060 c- 111	Enlisted	All c were from the North. C and w men selected for educational attainment. The 3 groups of w men had completed 8 yrs, 1 yr high sch & 1 yr coll; the 3 c groups had completed 8 yrs, 4 yrs high sch, & 4 yrs coll.
Garrett,[5] H. E. (1945)	Ohio Illinois Pennsylvania New York	w-2318 2056 3089 2843 c- 152 578 498 850	Enlisted	Men who took *Alpha* only in 1918.
Montagu, M. F. A. (1945)	w- Mississippi Kentucky Arkansas Georgia North Carolina Louisiana Alabama Tennessee South Carolina c- Ohio Illinois New York Indiana	w- 665 832 618 702 607 641 697 654 540 c- 152 704 1021 269	Enlisted	Men who took *Alpha* only, w from Groups I & II, c from Gr IV & V. Further selected c from 4 Northern & w from 9 Southern states.

[2]Numbers not given by Klineberg. Included in Yerkes' tables and cited by Garrett, *J. Abn. & Soc. Psychol.*, 1945.
[3]*Amer. J. Psychol.*
[4]From data in *Memoirs* (Yerkes, 1921).
[5]*J. Abn. & Soc. Psychol.* From data in *Memoirs*.

SEVEN *(continued)*

WORLD WAR I

	RESULTS		COMMENTS OF AUTHOR

Mdn		*Scores*	Northern c below Northern w but they are superior to the w groups from a number of the Southern states.
w			
Miss		41.25	
Ky		41.50	
Ark		41.55	
Ga		42.12	
c			
Pa		42.00	
NY		45.00	
Ill		47.35	
Oh		49.50	

		Scores			Part, but not all, of diff found must be attributed to better education of w recruits.
	w		c		
		No		So	
Mdn	58.9	38.6		12.4	

About 25% No c above w *mdn*

Maximum		*Mdn Scores*		Northern c highly selected for education compare unfavorably on *Alpha* with w of considerably less formal schooling.
Schooling	w		c	
8th gr	64.70		50.00	
1 yr hs	80.50			
4 yrs hs			74.50	
1 yr col	106.70			
4 yrs col			97.00	

Mdn		*Scores*[4]		Evident that Negroes in these 4 states scored as far below w soldiers in same states as they scored below w in country as a whole.
Oh	w	c	
Ill	66.7	48.8	
Pa	63.0	46.9	
NY	64.6	41.5	
	64.0	44.5	

22-32% c above resp w mdns

		Scores[6]		Important that literate c from some Northern states did no better than literate whites from some other states all of them Southern. *Av Mdn Score* of c from 14 Southern states and DC was 21.31; *av mdn score* of c from 9 Northern states was 39.90.
Mdn	w	*Mdn*	c	
Miss	41.20	Oh	48.30	
Ky	41.50	Ill	46.85	
Ark	41.55	NY	44.55	
Ga	42.10	Ind	41.55	
NC	43.15		———	
La	45.20	*Av Mdn*	45.31[7]	
Ala	46.20			
Tenn	47.15			
SC	47.40			
Av Mdn	43.94[8]			

[6]From data in *Memoirs*.

[7]Garrett (*Amer. J. Psychol.*, 1945) reports Montagu to be in error, that the correct mdn for the combined group of Negroes from the 4 states is 44.70 instead of 45.31.

[8]Garrett observed that Montagu regularly averaged medians, disregarding the number of cases in the contributing samples.

TABLE

ARMED FORCES

AUTHOR DATE	LOCATION	N	SUBJECTS RANK	METHOD OF SELECTION
Montagu, M. F. A. (1945)	w- Arkansas Mississippi North Carolina Georgia Louisiana Alabama Kentucky Oklahoma Texas Tennessee South Carolina c- Ohio Illinois Indiana New York	w- 710 759 702 762 702 779 837 865 1426 710 581 c- 163 804 269 1188	Enlisted	*Comprehensive Alpha*, a slightly diff sampling on *Alpha*, the great majority of Ss being same as in above study. In addition were samples of men who were recalled for *Beta* and/or an individ exam. Only their *Alpha* scores included here.

ARMY

Ferguson, G. O., Jr. (1919)	Camp Lee	c- 829[11]	Enlisted	Eight companies drawn mainly from Va, Pa, DC, & the Carolinas.
Trabue, M. R. (1919)	Camp Grant	w-8387 c- No-1556 So- 3382	Enlisted	Northern c mainly from St. Louis and Chicago & vicinity who were sent to Camp in July, '18.
Montagu, M. F. A. (1945)	United[12] States	w-15,308 c- 14,643	Enlisted	White recruits from Groups I & II; c from Groups IV & V.

STANFORD-BINET

Peterson,[14] J (1923)	Various States	w-653[15] c- 403	Enlisted	From 9 Camps, selected as representative of draft.

[9]From the *Memoirs*. Note that Montagu includes 2 Border states and omits 2 Southern states.
[10]*Beta* was given to all men selected as illiterate or non-English speaking and to men who took *Alpha* and failed it.
[11]Approximate number, estimated by reviewer.
[12]From *Memoirs*, Tables 206 and 267. Whites from all states and DC, c from 9 Northern and 14 Southern states and DC. Montagu included Md, Ky, and WVa with Southern states.

SEVEN *(continued)*

WORLD WAR I

RESULTS				COMMENTS OF AUTHOR

		Scores[9]		Evidence on whole indicates no significant
Mdn	w		c	inherent psychical differences bet c and
Ark	35.60	Oh	45.35	w. Differences bet c and w best explained
Miss	37.65	Ill	42.25	on basis of differences in socioeconomic
NC	38.20	Ind	41.55	history.
Ga	39.35	NY	38.60	
La	41.10		———	
Ala	41.35	*Av Mdn*	41.94[8]	
Ky	41.50			
Okla	43.00			
Tex	43.45			
Tenn	44.00			
SC	45.05			
	———			
Av Mdn	40.93			

BETA[10]

		Scores		Percentage of illiteracy of c in the Pa
Mdn		w	c	companies was 39; that in the Va
		33		companies, 72.
Va			13	
Pa & Car			15	
DC			19	
Pa			16	

		Scores		Av Northern Negro has the ability to
	w		c	learn new things about equivalent to
		So	No	that of av 11-yr-old w sch boy; av South-
Weighted Mdn	100.8	61.9	32.9	ern Negro mental capacity of 9-yr-old.

		Scores[13]		Important that any group of Negroes
Av Mdn		w	c	from some states should have done better
14 So states & DC		31.11		than whites from some states.
6 No states			34.63	
9 No states			32.72	
So states & DC			17.58	
Total		40.70	19.34	

1916 FORM

		MA		Tested on *S-B* in order to evaluate *Beta*
	w	c		scores.
Mdn	13.33	9.18		

[13]Correct median for c from the 6 Northern states should be 32.39 according to Garrett (*Amer. J. Psychol.*, 1945).

[14]Data from *Memoirs*, pp. 391 and 717.

[15]Whites were born in English-speaking countries.

TABLE

ARMED FORCES

AUTHOR DATE	LOCATION	N	SUBJECTS RANK	METHOD OF SELECTION
Peterson,[14] J. (1923)	Camp Sheridan	w-690 c- 514	Enlisted	Men recalled for individual examinations due to failure to pass a group examination.

COMBINED

| Yerkes, R. M. (1921) | Various States | w-93,973 c- IV-18,891 V- 4705 | Enlisted[17] | Hollerith sample of scores of c and w recruits.[18] |

| Wallis, W. D. (1926) | Camps Lewis Devens Upton Dodge Custer Travis Grant Taylor Wadsworth All Camps | w 834 8247 7876 4575 4933 6514 7671 7363 8243 93,973 | c 118 114 326 831 819 1375 1129 2416 1634 18,891 | Enlisted | Hollerith sample; did not include cV. |

| Brigham, C. C. (1923) | Various States | w- Enl-93,955 Off- 15,543 c- Enl-23,596 | Enlisted and Officers | Both c and w enlisted men; all officers were w. Hollerith sample of scores of recruits, w & c.[18] |

[16]Including men who took *Alpha, Alpha* and *Beta, Beta,* and certain individual tests. All test scores were converted into a common scale described in *Memoirs,* Ch. II by Yerkes.

[17]The first group of c resulted from a prorata selection by states; the second is the number of additional c from Ill, Ind, NJ, NY, and Pa.

[18]From total number of w soldiers approximately 41,278 cards were drawn, prorated by states. Prorata basis was one man per 1000 w male population, 1910 census. In addition, selected 14,684 (Group II) to increase the numbers from states with small populations, and 40,392

SEVEN *(continued)*

WORLD WAR I

RESULTS	COMMENTS OF AUTHOR

	MA		In general, they constituted a low grade group.
	w	c	
Mdn	9.6	8.6	

SCALE[16]

%age Distributions

Grade	w	c	
		IV	V
A	4.1	0.1	0.8
B	8.0	0.6	2.8
C+	15.0	2.0	7.2
C	25.0	5.7	18.0
C—	23.8	12.9	25.9
D	17.1	29.7	31.1
D—	7.0	49.0	14.2

Grades

Camp	% age A & B		% age D & D—		Fluctuation in Negro rating suggests that the diff bet Negroes and whites is to be credited to social heritage rather than to race.
	w	c	w	c	
Lew	18.7	9.4	8.4	23.6	
Dev	16.7	1.8	20.1	32.4	
Upt	11.3	2.1	22.1	44.1	
Dod	11.1	2.2	18.3	50.5	
Cus	12.5	3.1	20.6	58.3	
Tra	9.5	0.6	34.4	70.2	
Gra	12.2	0.9	18.2	76.3	
Tay	14.5	0.8	22.6	80.3	
Wad	11.8	0.1	27.0	92.8	

Scores

	w		c	Results showing marked inferiority of Negro are corroborated by practically all E's who have tested w and c groups.
	Off	Enl	Enl	
M	18.84	13.54	10.41	
s	2.10	2.92	2.79	

z^{19} = 153

3.61% w draft & 0.25% c scored
19 or more

(Group III) selected from the main camps used for w draft. States of men in Group III unknown. The principal sample of 18,891 Negroes (Group IV) drawn from total population of Negro soldiers to obtain representation of Negro male population. Prorated on basis of one per 250 Negro male population, 1910 census. The additional sample of 4705 Negroes (Group V) was drawn from five Northern states on prorated basis of one per 50 Negro males to get a bigger sample from North. (Yerkes, *Memoirs*, pp. 555-560)

[19]Calculated by reviewer.

TABLE

ARMED FORCES

AUTHOR DATE	LOCATION	N	SUBJECTS RANK	METHOD OF SELECTION
Alper, T. G., and Boring, E. G. (1944)	Mississippi Kentucky Arkansas Georgia Illinois Pennsylvania New York Ohio	w- No-13,110 So- 3904 c- No- 4455 So- 5425	Enlisted	Used 8 states Klineberg selected for *Alpha* comparisons, but took c & w from all 8 states & used *Alpha* & *Beta* scores instead of *Alpha* only.

ARMED FORCES

AUTHOR DATE	LOCATION	N	SUBJECTS RANK	METHOD OF SELECTION
Rowntree, L. G., McGill, K. H., and Edwards, T. I. (1943)	Local Boards and Induction Stations	w-42,273[20] c- 3312	18-19 18-19	All registrants examined at Local Boards & Induction Stations, Dec. '42 to Feb. '43.
Hyde, R. W., and Chisholm, R. M. (1944)	Boston Armed Forces Induction Station	60,000	18-44	Consecutive selectees from Eastern Mass, within 35 m of coastline, examined in winter '41 to spring '42.[22]

[20]All young men of 18-19 years whose order numbers were reached from Dec. '42 to Feb. '43 were called for examination unless (1) they had entered the Armed Forces by direct enlistment prior to Dec. 12 '42, (2) they were in school or college under programs supported by the Army and Navy, or (3) they were given occupational deferment.

[21]Including physical and mental defects. If 2 or more defects were present the one listed first was used as the cause of rejection unless "clearly misleading". W includes all except c.

SEVEN *(continued)*

WORLD WAR I

RESULTS	COMMENTS OF AUTHOR

<table>
<tr><td colspan="5" align="center">*Scores*</td><td rowspan="2">Skin color as well as geography affected the test scores of recruits in 1918.</td></tr>
<tr><td></td><td colspan="2" align="center">w</td><td colspan="2" align="center">c</td></tr>
<tr><td></td><td>No</td><td>So</td><td>No</td><td>So</td><td></td></tr>
<tr><td>M</td><td>14.1</td><td>12.7</td><td>12.0</td><td>9.8</td><td></td></tr>
<tr><td>s</td><td>2.60</td><td>2.41</td><td>2.41</td><td>1.82</td><td></td></tr>
</table>

So w mean sig above that of No c
$z = 13.26$[19]

WORLD WAR II

	Rejection Rates		Educational and mental deficiency determined at Induction Centers by psychometric tests designed to measure capacity to absorb military training.
	% w	% c	
Defects			
Educ Def	1.15	12.17	
Mental Def	.68	1.00	
Total[21]	23.80	45.50	

	Rejection Rates for[23] Mental Deficiency	Exceptionally high rate of mental disorders among Negroes cannot be explained merely on basis of population density or socioeconomic level.
	%	
Group		
Old American	0.7	
Jewish	1.0	
Irish	1.2	
Portuguese	3.1	
Italian	3.9	
Negro	11.7	
Chinese	24.5	

[22]Including Boston. Most of area highly industrialized, but sectors of farming and fishing included. Negroes in a moderately dense area of Boston; many came from South during the depression.

[23]"Old American", Jewish, Irish, Portuguese, and Italian identified by communities in which lived. Negroes and Chinese identified by race.

TABLE

ARMED FORCES

AUTHOR DATE	LOCATION	N	SUBJECTS AGE	METHOD OF SELECTION
Davenport, R. K. (1946)	Nine Service Command Areas[24]	w-2,110,292 c- 220,750		Preinduction examinations from Sept. '44-Aug. '45. High sch graduates accepted without mental test; nonhigh-sch grads given verbal group test; failures were tested by a non-verbal group test; failures of 2nd test were given individual test. No limits placed on number of illiterates to be inducted.
Smith, M. (1948)	Induction Stations	Not given	18-44	Rejection rates of Selective Service Registrants given physical exams '40-43. Based upon 10% sample of first exams recorded on certain forms, Nov. '40-Sept. '41, & approx 7% of those recorded on another form, Apr. '42-Dec. '43.

[24]States allocated in the 9 Service Commands are: I- Maine, NH, Vt, Mass, Conn, RI; II- Del, NY, NJ; III- Pa, Md, Va; IV- NC, SC, Ga, Fl, Ala, Tenn, Miss; V- Oh, Ind, WVa, Ky; VI- Mich, Ill, Wis; VII- Minn, Ia, Mo, ND, SD, Nebr, Kan, Wy, Colo; VIII- Ark, La, Okla, Tex, NM; IX- Utah, Nev, Ariz, Cal, Ore, Wash, Mont, Ida.

SEVEN *(continued)*

WORLD WAR II

RESULTS	COMMENTS OF AUTHOR

*Disposition of Men per 1000
of Each Race Processed*

Recommended for Induction

Probability that failure to qualify on military tests of mental capacity indicates only that the total experience of the individual has been so devoid of experiences basic to military success that Armed Forces could not profitably undertake to train him for military service.

Command	Total		As Accept Illit	
	w	c	w	c
I	611	446	26	67
II	699	650	23	141
III	675	631	45	214
IV	592	390	99	210
V	668	606	51	155
VI	704	520	25	136
VII	644	443	10	71
VIII	649	481	93	240
IX	642	522	25	140

Not Recommended

Command	Phys Disqual		Nonaccept Illit	
	w	c	w	c
I	351	354	38	200
II	287	237	14	113
III	295	190	30	179
IV	333	217	75	393
V	292	257	40	137
VI	280	259	16	221
VII	337	394	19	163
VIII	277	200	74	319
IX	343	316	15	162

*Ratio of Accept Illiterates
to Total Illiterates*[25]

Command	w	c
I	.41	.25
II	.62	.56
III	.60	.54
IV	.57	.35
V	.56	.53
VI	.61	.38
VII	.34	.30
VIII	.56	.43
IX	.63	.46

Reject Rates

Excluded reports on registrants examined and later deferred for other than physical or mental reasons.

	% w	% c
Defects		
Educ & Ment D[26]	3.3	15.0
Total	27.6	41.1

---

[25]Calculated from author's table by reviewer.

[26]*Educational and Mental Deficiency* (not separated in author's table.) *Total* refers to %age of all registrants sampled who were rejected because of physical and/or mental defects.

TABLE

ARMED FORCES

AUTHOR DATE	LOCATION	N	SUBJECTS AGE	METHOD OF SELECTION
Harms, H. E., Kobler, F. J., and Sweeney, F. J. (1945)	Mental Hygiene Clinic of an Army Air Base	c- 100	M- 25.72	First 100 completed c cases handled by Clinic. Men a part of Engineer Corps & trained primarily for special engineering work. Admission to clinic in 91% of cases was through medical dispensary or sick call.
Freedman, H.L., and Rockmore, M. J. (1946)	Mental Hygiene Clinic	w- 39 c- 271	M- 26.1 M- 24.5	Soldiers referred to Clinic because of problems. All were users of marihuana; used drug on av of 7.1 yrs. All parts of US represented. Whites a mean sch of 7.5 yrs; c, mean of 6.6 yrs.
Teicher, M. I., and Singer, E. (1946)	General Hospital, Assam, India	w-74 c- 54	Mdn- 26 Mdn- 25	Patients hospitalized in neuropsychiat section, as well as outpatients & patients being treated in other parts of hospital who were referred for psychiatric exam bet June-Sept. '45.
Gardner, G. E., and Aaron, S. (1946)	Naval Hospital	w- I-100 c- I-100 II-100	Under 20 to Over 34	wI- unselected admissions to psychiatric wards. cI- 100 consecutive admissions to psychiatric wards. cII- 100 normal sailors selected at random at Naval Receiving Station. They had never been admitted to psychiatric ward or treated for "nervous condition". Used Kent EGY; also Wechsler Bellevue if suspected of feeblemindedness.

[27]*Army General Classification Test.* Grades I and II include *superior and above average* scoring Ss; III, . . . *average* scoring Ss; and IV and V, *below average* scoring Ss.

SEVEN *(continued)*

WORLD WAR II

	RESULTS			COMMENTS OF AUTHOR

	Percentage			One of major factors in group's inability to function adequately in Army was lack of sufficient native intellectual ability to perform simplest task of soldier. Av length of service in Army, 10.68 months; one third born in North; 84% from marginal or submarginal eco level.
	c			
Maximum Schooling				
8th gr	52			
4 yrs hs	13			
Some col	5			

84% below normal intell

	AGCT[27]			Two recent Army studies showed that 78% of c and 29% of w were on a working level with an ability to learn considered to be below average.
	% ages			
AGCT Grades	w		c	
I, II	5		1	
III	41		8	
IV, V	54		91	

	IQ		Included among Ss:
	w	c	13 psychotics
Mdn	91	80	62 psychoneurotics
			22 psychopaths
			12 normals
			10 alcoholics
			9 mental defectives
			Testing conditions poor.

	MA Distributions[28]			Negro patients more frequently classified in psychotic and feebleminded groups than w.
	w	c		
	I	I	II	
Mental Age				
Below 9		3		
9	4	7	1	
10	9	15	7	
11	9	29	26	
12	14	21	24	
13	21	15	25	
14	32	5	11	
Above 14	11	5	6	
Total	100	100	100	

---

[28]Greater frequency of lower mental ages among c psychiatric than among other two groups.

TABLE

ARMED FORCES

AUTHOR DATE	LOCATION	N	SUBJECTS RANK	METHOD OF SELECTION
Hunt, W. A. (1947)	Not given	w-989 c- 521		Random selection of consecutive cases of 6 groups of c separated from Naval service due to neuropsychiat unfitness; all had some period of service. After each c case took next w case in files. In Group 6, took all w cases during period covered by Negro discharges.
MacPhee, H. M., Wright, H. F., and Cummings, S. B., Jr. (1947)	Great Lakes Naval Training Center	c- 432	Enlisted	*Wechsler-Bellevue, Verbal Scale,* given to all c referred to Neuropsychiatric Unit because they appeared to be of subnormal mentality. All reared on Southern farms & had had an average of 3 yrs of schooling.
Trudeau, A. G. (1945)	Reception Centers	Not given	Enlisted	One year's sampling of recruits: Jan.-Dec. '43. 14 months' data, Aug. '43-Oct. '44.
Altus, W. D. (1946)	Ninth Service Command Special Training Center	w-2721 c- 2142		Each incoming illiterate given *Terman Vocabulary* test, certain tests of *Army Wechsler,* & certain written group tests for selective purposes.

[30]*AGCT* Grade V, the equivalent of slow-learning; identified Ss of *very inferior intelligence.*

SEVEN (continued)
WORLD WAR II

RESULTS	COMMENTS OF AUTHOR

	Mental Deficiency % ages		Incidence of mental deficiency over-whelmingly greater among c group. Same selective standards must not have been enforced for both groups.
	w	c	
Group			
1	1.0	18.1	
2	0.0	4.0	
3	3.0	42.0	
4	0.0	20.2	
5	0.0	14.3	
6	1.9	34.7	

	IQ	Dividing Ss into 7 groups acc to test performance, find at lower levels that *Similarities* contributes most to total score and *Arithmetic* least; not until higher levels does pattern approach uniformity of subtest contribution.
	c	
M	67.11	
s	10.86	
Range	48-92	

Bulk of c at lower end of curve; 2½ times as many c as w in IV-V in proportion to numbers; proportionally 10 times as many w as c in I-II. Proportionally 8 times as many c as w entering Army classed as V.[30]	*AGCT* scores do not necessarily reflect inherent capacity of individual.

	Vocabulary Scores[31]		The *Stanford-Binet Vocab* test (1937 Rev) is most important part of this instrument's component parts . . . it furnishes an easily obtained sampling of language repertoire, particularly of those verbal concepts which set limits upon capacity for abstract thinking.
	w	c	
M	12.27	11.32	
s	3.48	2.77	
$z =$		10.67	

---

[31]Only monolingual groups included in this table. Author also includes 4 bilingual groups for comparative purposes: Mexican, Filipino, American Indian, and Chinese.

TABLE

ARMED FORCES

AUTHOR DATE	LOCATION	N	SUBJECTS AGE	METHOD OF SELECTION
Altus, W. D., and Bell, H. M. (1947)	Ninth[32] Service Command Special Training Center	w-2564 c- 2069		Beginning Sept. '43 incoming illiterates given tests for measuring adjustment, *Terman Vocabulary* in a battery of indiv tests, and the *AB Information* as supplement to *Terman* & *Army Wechsler*.
Davenport, R. K. (1946)	Nine Service Command Areas[24]	Probably 3 million or more[34]		Inductees processed from June '43 to May '45 in Nine Service Commands. Data from Adjutant General's Office, War Dept.

[32]Comprising the Western eighth of the United States.
[33]Mean score for total flow of men processed at Los Angeles Induction Station was 25.

SEVEN (continued)

WORLD WAR II

RESULTS	COMMENTS OF AUTHOR

	AB Information[33] *Test Scores*		
		w	c
M		6.32	5.36
s		3.19	3.06
z =			10.66

Inaptness of illiterates on questions conventionally supposed to derive primarily from schooling was but little greater than for items which are not essentially school items.

%age Distribution of AGCT
Grades

w

Command	I	II	III	IV	V
I	6.6	34.9	37.3	20.9	0.3
II	8.8	37.0	33.8	19.7	0.7
III	6.0	30.5	35.0	27.3	1.2
IV	3.1	17.7	28.1	46.9	4.2
V	5.5	27.4	32.3	32.2	2.6
VI	10.0	37.4	32.5	19.6	0.5
VII	8.8	33.7	32.8	24.1	0.6
VIII	3.5	21.1	30.0	42.1	3.3
IX	7.3	35.3	34.1	22.5	0.8

c

	I	II	III	IV	V
I	0.6	8.3	32.5	55.6	3.0
II	0.4	6.3	24.6	59.8	8.9
III	0.3	4.4	16.0	64.1	15.2
IV	0.1	1.0	4.0	61.7	33.2
V	0.4	4.7	19.7	61.4	13.8
VI	0.8	8.0	23.2	60.6	7.4
VII	0.7	7.0	21.5	62.6	8.2
VIII	0.1	1.0	5.8	66.5	26.6
IX	0.3	5.1	19.9	66.5	8.2

Imbalance in proportions of Negro inductees scoring in extreme grades. Education and social experience cannot be ignored in interpreting the differences obtained.

[34]Estimated by reviewer. Author notes that 2,331,042 selectees were given preinduction examinations from Sept '44 through Aug '45; about one third of these were not inducted.

TABLE

ARMED FORCES

AUTHOR DATE	LOCATION	N	SUBJECTS RANK	METHOD OF SELECTION
Stewart, N. (1947)	United States and Overseas	w- 2550 c- 138 w- 444 c- 114 w- 474 c- 130 w-7416 c- 1149 w-1973 c- 197 w-3919 c- 260 w-5003 c- 1300 w- 723 c- 105 w- 244 c- 448 w- 418 c- 339	Enlisted men	Based on Military Occup Specialty classifications & *AGCT* Standard Scores secured from War Dept Machine Records Survey #4 of 9-30-44. These surveys taken every 3 months & yielded data for about 2% of all Army personnel incl those overseas. *AGCT* scores not available for officers.
Star,[36] S. A., Williams, R. M., Jr., and Stouffer, S. A. (1949)		Not given	Enlisted men	From Adjutant General's Office which had secured data on a 2% sample of the Army in March '45.
	United States	c- 7438	Enlisted men	Special tabulation by Research Branch of data collected while sampling for survey in March '43. In addition to a representative cross section of 3000 c the Negro sample was incr to 7438 to provide additional cases of better educated & of Northern c for intragroup comparisons.

[35]From Stewart's table which included 220 Military Occupational Specialities, the reviewer selected all M.O.S.'s that included 100 or more colored enlisted men (10 categories in all); she found the s's from the author's Q's and computed the significance of the several w-c medians.

There were 41 of the 220 occupational specialities that included 25 or more c men, the numbers in these occupations totalling 5663 c and 40,137 w; the combined medians of the

SEVEN *(continued)*

WORLD WAR II

		RESULTS					COMMENTS OF AUTHOR	
M. O. S.		*Selected %ile Points for AGCT Distributions*[35]						
		P_{90}	P_{75}	P_{50}	P_{25}	P_{10}	*s*	*t*
Clerk-Typist	w	134	127	117	108	99	14.08	9.93
	c	120	113	103	91	80	16.30	
Foreman, Constr	w	129	120	109	95	81	18.53	16.81
	c	99	89	71	59	48	22.24	
Duty NCO	w	128	116	105	90	75	19.27	13.94
	c	108	92	76	63	57	21.50	
Basic	w	127	118	104	85	69	24.46	69.64
	c	99	79	65	57	44	16.31	
Automotive	w	120	111	99	88	75	17.05	15.69
Mech (2nd Ech)	c	104	90	75	62	51	20.76	
Rifleman	w	124	112	95	78	66	25.20	20.51
	c	99	85	71	61	48	17.79	
Truck Driver	w	117	107	93	79	67	20.76	48.15
Light	c	96	80	67	58	46	16.31	
Cook	w	116	105	90	66	41	28.91	12.90
	c	86	78	66	57	46	15.57	
Longshoreman	w	117	106	90	78	67	20.76	16.45
	c	89	77	65	56	46	15.57	
Duty Soldier	w	111	99	84	71	60	20.76	14.69
III	c	89	77	63	52	42	18.53	

AGCT Grade	*%age Distribution of AGCT Grade*	
	w	c
I	6	1
II	32	6
III	32	14
IV	23	45
V	3	28
Unk	4	6
	100	100

The atmosphere in which c took the tests was not always satisfactory. Community and Negro soldier morale entered into the problem by creating non-cooperative attitudes on part of registrants.

Last Sch Grade Completed	*%age in AGCT Grade V*[37]	
	c South	c North
Below 5	90	86
5	77	57
6	70	55
7	58	48
8	43	37
Some H.S.	32	21
H.S. grad	17	13
College	16	10

Consideration must be given to the probability that quality of education received by Negro was inferior, grade for grade, to that received by whites.

colored and white recruits based upon these were respectively, 70.09 and 101. 56 (calculated by reviewer).

[36]From chapter 10 in The American Soldier: Adjustment during Army Life, vol. I, by Stouffer, S. A. Suchman, E. A., *etc.* See References at end of this book.

[37]Statistics estimated with a fair degree of accuracy by reviewer from authors' graphs showing relation of Negro *AGCT* scores to grade completed in school by region of origin.

TABLE

ARMED FORCES

AUTHOR DATE	LOCATION	N	SUBJECTS RANK	METHOD OF SELECTION
Fulk, B. E. (1949)	Army Air Force Service Command	w-2174 c- 2010	Enlisted men	*AGCT* scores obtained from Manning & Information Rosters of Army Air Forces. Only used scores of enlisted men; c includes all available; w selected by random sampling.
Michael, W. B. (1949)	Army Air Force	w-815 c- 356	Cadets	Two samples of West Point and Negro Cadets were administered resp the *Classification Battery* (consisting of 12 pencil-and paper tests & 6 apparatus tests) in Nov. '43 and the *Classification Battery* (consisting of 15 pencil-and-paper tests, 7 of which were identical to those of 1st battery, & same 6 psychomotor tests) in Sept. '44.

[38]Norms were based upon scores of two representative white aviation-cadet populations.

SEVEN *(continued)*

WORLD WAR II

	RESULTS		COMMENTS OF AUTHOR

School Grade Completed	AGCT Scores				% over-lap
	w		c		
	M	s	M	s	
0	82.45	16.5	59.35	13.3	4
1	91.20	16.2	58.40	19.6	10
2	88.45	20.5	57.75	18.6	9
3	91.20	23.2	57.60	18.1	6
4	90.65	23.8	59.80	20.0	8
5	90.35	25.2	54.65	11.6	2
6	87.95	21.3	59.60	14.0	6
7	85.40	15.2	64.45	14.7	9
8	94.50	15.4	69.25	17.3	7
9	100.70	15.2	73.35	16.6	6
10	102.50	14.2	78.95	17.0	11
11	107.95	14.4	85.95	16.2	11
12	109.20	15.4	93.05	17.8	17
13&up	119.5	14.8	97.50	16.7	11
Total	95.10	21.2	68.95	20.7	

Negroes appear to be farther below whites on *AGCT* in War II than they were on combined Alpha & Beta scale in War I. Rosters providing data contained no information of the soldier's place of birth or address; therefore, no information concerning possible differences due to regional origin or quality of schooling can be derived.

	Stanine Composite Scores[38]	
	M	s
Norms	5	1.96
West Point Cad		
Fighter Pilots	6.21	1.80
Bomber Pilots	7.09	1.59
Negro Pilots	3.95	1.61
Diff's bet means highly sig.		

The factor of spatial relations was valid for all 3 populations in prediction of pilot success. The intellectual factors of reasoning, number, & verbality were not valid.

TABLE

ARMED FORCES

AUTHOR DATE	LOCATION	N	SUBJECTS RANK	METHOD OF SELECTION
Moynihan, D. P. (1965)	Six Army Areas[39]	w-235,678[40] c- 50,474 w c I 49,171 7937 II 48,641 9563 III 30,242 20,343 IV 15,048 4796 V 51,117 5723 VI 41,459 2112		*Armed Forces Qualification Test* — a preinduction examination administered to draftees in 1962. Data on Continental United States only.
Roen, S. R. (1960)	Army Post in the Southwest	w-50 c- 50	Enlisted men	Personnel files of hundreds of soldiers stationed in Army post in SW were examined for biographical data & *Army Classification Battery* scores. About 500 were selected for testing & interviews by eliminating those of extremely low *ACB* scores & those whose biogr data would be hard to duplicate. Gave 3 personality tests to the 98% who would cooperate. Then 50 c & 50 w soldiers were closely matched on 10 variables: age, educ, parents' occup, parents' income, geogr area of childhood, Army rank, number years in service, marital status, urban or rural bkg, & plans for re-enlistment. Matching was accompl by categorizing & sub-categorizing the variables & then pairing a c & w soldier most closely resembling him in biographical pattern.

[39]In the 6 Army Areas allocations are as follows- I—Conn, Me, Mass, NH, NJ, NY, RI, Vt; II—Del, DC, Ky, Md, Oh, Pa, Va, WVa; III—Ala, Fl, Ga, Miss, NC, SC, Tenn; IV—Ark, La, NM, Okla, Tex; V—Colo, Ill, Ind, Ia, Kan, Mich, Minn, Mo, Nebr, ND, SD, Wis, Wy; VI—Ariz, Cal, Ida, Mont, Nev, Ore, Utah, Wash.

SEVEN *(concluded)*

POST-KOREAN WAR

	RESULTS			COMMENTS OF AUTHOR

	Rejection Rates			The rejections are due to failure to pass Armed Forces mental test. The test roughly measures the ability that ought to be found in an average 7th- or 8th-grade student. The Negro rejection rate almost four times that of the whites.
Area	% w		% c	
I	26.4		50.1	
II	12.1		44.5	
III	19.1		67.7	
IV	13.5		62.3	
V	8.9		46.9	
VI	12.1		31.1	
Total	15.4		56.1	

	Scores[41]			Negroes as a group, lacking support from pride in significant historical achievement, & developing in an environment of negative experiences, may incorporate intellectually defeating personality traits that play a significant role in their ability to score on measures of intelligence.
	w		c	
		Mean		
ACB	101.2		91.3	
PA	103.0		89.2	
		s		
ACB	19.0		16.5	
PA	21.6		20.2	

Diff's bet c & w means
highly sig.

[40]Referring to the total numbers tested in '62.
[41]*Pattern Analysis* (PA) score, one of *ACB* tests, was used as a second measure of intelligence, since it has been found to correlate .81 with *Wechsler-Bellevue*.

Hyde and Chisholm (1944) reported on the rejection rates for various ethnic and nationality groups of 18 to 44 years of age examined at the Boston Armed Forces Induction Station during the winter of 1941 and the spring of 1942. The 60,000 consecutive selectees were drawn from eastern Massachusetts including highly industrial areas such as Boston as well as some sectors of farming and fishing. The white groups, such as "Old American", Jewish, Irish, Portuguese, and Italian, were roughly identified by the communities in which they lived and therefore percentages of mental deficiency attributed to them cannot be considered as exact; the Negroes and Chinese were identified by race. The rejection rates for mental deficiency among the white sections of the population ranged between 0.7 and 3.9 per cent; the rate for Negroes was 11.7 per cent; the rate for the Chinese was 24.5 per cent. The authors attributed the high rejection rate among the Chinese not to the presence of mental deficiency as such but rather to language and cultural handicaps. They were of the opinion that the Chinese, and to a lesser extent, the Negroes and the Portuguese, seemed to have insufficient familiarity with the materials used in some of the tests to make the results valid. Although Hyde and Chisholm believed that the high rate of mental deficiency among the Negroes could not be attributed solely to their lower socioeconomic status, they thought that in many cases apparent mental deficiency might be a reaction to emotional stress. The frustrated Negro, unable to find aggressive outlet for his stress, may unconsciously assume an attitude of stupidity and thereby incur revenge and exempt himself from disagreeable responsibilities.[15]

Smith (1948) analyzed the rejection rates of Selective Service Registrants according to race, section of the country from which they came, and occupation. Smith's report is based upon: (1) a 10 per cent sample of first examinations recorded on DSS Forms 200, Reports of Physical Examination, for November, 1940, to September, 1941, and (2) an approximate 7 per cent of those recorded on DSS Forms 221, Reports of Physical Examination and Induction, April, 1942, to

---

[15]The unconscious assumption of an attitude of stupidity may be related to the tendency to fall asleep easily. Kanner (1937) has reported this tendency in Negro boys of 8 to 15 years of age who were physically healthy but intellectually retarded "because they had nothing more pleasant to do." Bender (1939) refers to the ease with which Negroes go to sleep or simply do nothing for long periods when it fits the need of the situation. She found that children brought to the Psychiatric Division of Bellevue City Hospital because of sleeping attacks or so-called narcolepsy invariably have been Negro boys of pre- or early adolescent age. She reported that it could be produced not only by boredom but by emotional conflicts and can be used as a means of escape from a frustrating situation. Solomon, finding the incidence of narcolepsy among Negro recruits (especially Southern Negroes) to be more than 60 times that detected in white recruits, suggested the presence of a constitutional predisposition toward its development—related in some Negroes to a faulty resistance toward sleep or to an increased readiness for sleep. The balance between the sleep-promoting factors and those favoring wakefulness may be "permanently prejudiced toward the side of sleep because of an impoverished environment and resultant lack of interest in the outside world." (1945, p. 183)

December, 1943. The total rejection rate due to physical and/or mental defect among the colored registrants was 41.1 per cent, in contrast to a rejection rate of 27.6 per cent for the noncolored. Fifteen per cent of the colored and 3.3 per cent of the noncolored rejected were defective educationally or mentally. In fact, it appears that only in the incidence of educational and mental defect, venereal disease, and foot defects did the Negro surpass the "white" registrant to a marked degree. When the rejection rates were tabulated according to section of the country the Negro rates proved to be the higher in each instance. In three of the regions the Negro rates were from 31 to 34 per cent and the non-Negro rates from 26 to 27 per cent. In the fourth region (identified as Southeastern and South Central) the respective Negro and white rejection rates were about 45 and 32 per cents.

Davenport (1946) gave for each of the Nine Service Commands the numbers of colored and white men recommended for induction, the numbers rejected for physical disqualifications, and the numbers rejected as nonacceptable illiterates, in terms of 1000 of each racial group processed. The dispositions resulted from the preinduction examinations given to more than 2,000,000 men during the 12-month-period beginning in September, 1944. Mental tests were administered to all men who were non-high-school graduates. Following the initial verbal group test, all failures were tested by a nonverbal group test; failures on the second group test were given a nonverbal individual test; finally, all selectees who failed the above series of tests were interviewed by military psychologists who determined the validity of their scores.

If one compares the induction and rejection rates of the three Northern Commands with those rates for the Southern Command, he will observe: (1) that the total rejection rates in the Southern Command were higher than in the Northern Commands; (2) that the Negroes from the Southern Command were less frequently rejected because of physical disqualifications than were the Northern Negroes; (3) that in three of the four Commands the Negroes were less frequently rejected because of physical disqualifications than were the whites from the same Commands, and (4) that in every Command there was a high rate of Negro rejections because of inability to pass the mental tests. The percentage of white recruits classed as "nonacceptable illiterates" was generally small in the Northern Commands, i.e., 1.5 to 3.8, whereas the nonacceptable illiterate Negroes varied in these Commands from a percentage of 16.2 to one of 22.1. In the Southern Command the percentages of nonacceptable illiterates were 7.5 and 39.3 for the white and colored recruits, respectively. It would appear, therefore, that there was *two to three times as high a rejection rate for low mental test scores among Northern Negroes as among Southern whites* and that the lower induction rate of Negroes in general, as compared with whites in general, was not due to a greater number of physical disqualifications but to a preponderance of low mental test scores.

Clinic, Hospital, and Special Problem Cases

Several studies, dealing with relatively small groups of World War II recruits or veterans who were admitted to mental hygiene clinics or hospitalized in psychiatric or neuropsychiatric wards, are included in Table 7. In general, the maladjusted Negroes made poorer showings on the psychometric tests than the maladjusted whites. Harms, Kobler, and Sweeney (1945) selected the first 100 completed cases handled by the mental hygiene clinic of an Army Air Base; all of the men were a part of the Engineering Corps and were trained primarily for special engineering work. Over 50 per cent of the Ss had finished grade school, 13 per cent had completed high school, and 5 per cent had entered college. Eighty-four were below average on the *Army General Classification Test (AGCT)*. According to the authors, "This serves to indicate that one of the major factors in the group's inability to function adequately in the Army was a lack of sufficient native intellectual ability to perform the simplest tasks of the soldier." (p. 310)

Freedman and Rockmore (1946) administered the *AGCT* to 39 white and 271 colored soldiers, all of whom were marihuana users who had been referred to the Mental Hygiene Division because of "inability to get along". The white soldiers averaged approximately a year more of schooling than the Negroes. In terms of their "ability to learn", five per cent of the whites and one per cent of the colored Ss were classed in the *Superior and Above Average* category, 41 per cent of the whites and 8 per cent of the Negroes scored in the *Average* group, while 54 per cent of the whites and 91 per cent of the Negroes were in the *Below Average and Inferior* group.

Teicher and Singer (1946) administered *Form I of the Wechsler-Bellevue* scale to 74 white and 54 Negro patients in the Twentieth General Hospital at Assam, India, between June and September, 1945. The group had a median length of overseas service of 18 months with a range of 4 to 42 months; the whites had had 8½ years of formal schooling, the Negroes, 8 years on the average. Included among the patients were psychotics, psychoneurotics, psychopaths, alcoholics, mental defectives and "normals"; the median IQ's for the respective groups of white and colored were 91 and 80. The authors explained the low IQ's partly in terms of the adverse testing conditions.

Gardner and Aaron (1946) gave the *Kent EGY* test to three groups of sailors, including 100 consecutive colored patients admitted to the psychiatric wards of a naval hospital, 100 unselected whites admitted to the psychiatric wards of the hosptial, and 100 colored men selected at random at a naval receiving station.[16] This last group had never been admitted to a psychiatric ward, nor had any of them ever been treated by a physician for a "nervous condition". The *Wechsler-*

---

[16]The Kent *EGY* (emergency) test is a short test, presented orally, and intended for clinical use when a quick estimate of ability is desired. It consists only of a series of questions on objects and matters of common occurrence. Four overlapping scales. (Freeman, 1950, p. 358)

Bellevue scale was, in addition, administered to all individuals suspected of being feebleminded. The results showed relatively more Negro than white patients or Negro controls to be in the lower mental age groups. Of those in the upper mental age levels (14 or over) 43 were white patients, 17 were colored controls, and 9 were Negro patients.

Hunt (1947) studied the incidence of mental deficiency among Negroes and whites discharged from the Navy because of neuropsychiatric unfitness after some period of service. The Negroes included 521 consecutive cases from six different groups; the same number of whites were selected by taking the white case immediately following each colored S in the files; in addition, 468 whites in Group 6 were included. As will be noted in the table, the incidence of mental deficiency among the discharged Negro groups was from 4 to 42 per cent; that among the discharged whites, from zero to 3 per cent. Hunt concluded that the same selection standards were not enforced for the two races, that the Negro service group was permitted a higher proportion of mental deficiency than allowed in the white group, and that any comparison between the two racial groups becomes biased in favor of the white recruits.

MacPhee, Wright, and Cummings (1947) examined 432 Negro recruits at the Great Lakes Naval Training Center, all of them having been referred to the Neuropsychiatric Unit because of the appearance of subnormal mentality. All of the men had been reared on Southern farms and had had an average of three years of formal schooling. The low *Wechsler-Bellevue* IQ's which ranged from 48 to 92 with an average of 67 would tend to support the view that Negroes who were mentally deficient were recruited in the Armed Forces.

Special Training Units

From the beginning of World War II the problem of raising the quality of the Negro combat units was of special concern to the Army Ground Forces, the concentration of Negro troops into all-Negro units generally resulting in a far greater proportion of low *AGCT* grades than in the Army Ground Forces as a whole.[17] "Under the provisions of the Selective Service Act and a presidential directive, the War Department required all arms and services to absorb Negro enlisted men on the general basis of the proportion of Negroes in the population of the country." (Palmer, Wiley, and Keast, 1948, p. 53) This figure was set at 10.6 per cent, the percentage of Negroes registering in the draft. Since Negro personnel could not be shifted except to other Negro units, large numbers of

---

[17]In the two Selective Service Registrations prior to Pearl Harbor there were 347,000 men who were unable to write their names, and of these over 125,000 were white and 220,000 were Negro (Aptheker). On May 14, 1941, the Army announced that no registrants possessing an education less than that attained by one who had completed the fourth grade in an American elementary school were to be inducted. The percentage of Negroes rejected from May to September, 1941, because of illiteracy, was 12.3, or about 11 times that of the white rejection rate. (Aptheker)

Class IV and V personnel, averaging from 75 to 90 per cent, were concentrated in Negro units.[18] The view of the Army Ground Forces was not that Negro combat units could not be trained effectively but that units with disproportionately low *AGCT* grades could not be trained under normal methods in a normal period of time. Various proposals to improve the quality of enlisted personnel in the Negro combat units were examined by the War Department and discarded finally in favor of a plan which involved the establishment of Special Training Units (STU's), discharging men found to be unteachable, and ordering the transfer of excess high-intelligence personnel to the group combat troups. Accordingly, "intelligent illiterates", *i.e.*, those illiterates who had survived the intelligence tests administered to them, were to be inducted, if, with a minimum of literacy training they might be expected to become better soldiers than the eliminated group.[19] Special Training Units, receiving more Negro than white selectees, were established in June, 1943, at reception centers to teach these illiterates and Class V men the minimum vocabulary and other fundamental skills needed for military training. At the end of an intensive training period of 13 weeks (later reduced to 8 to 12 weeks) draftees were assigned to regular Army training if they could demonstrate a certain degree of military proficiency and an achievement of at least a fourth-grade standard in reading and arithmetic.[20] If they could not, they were discharged from the Army.

Trudeau (1945), Aptheker (1946), Davenport (1946), Erickson (1946), Witty (1945, 1946), Altus (1945, 1946, 1948), Altus and Bell (1947), Altus and Clark (1949), and Palmer, Wiley, and Keast (1948) have discussed the results of the Special Training Program given to large numbers of men classed as

---

[18]On July 1, 1943, the following numbers and types of units were within continental United States:

218	Negro and 32 white aviation squadrons
13	Negro and 12 white engineer general service regiments
3	Negro and one w engineer separate battalions
87½	Negro and no w medical sanitary companies
40	Negro and 2 w quartermaster service battalions
18	Negro and 10 w quartermaster truck regiments
4	Negro and no w quartermaster fumigation and bath battalions
33	Negro and 13 w troop transport companies

(Palmer, Wiley, and Keast, 1948)

[19]As of June 1, 1943. All restrictions on acceptance of illiterates were removed "provided they met the established standards of mental ability." The tests were revised again "the better to identify and bar out the mentally deficient while admitting bright illiterates." (Bingham, 1944, p. 277)

[20]There was a varying degree of literacy among the illiterate trainees received at the STU's. In one study of all trainees received for a period of 5 weeks, it was found that 31.2 per cent could pass the 2 graduation tests the day of their arrival at the Training Center and therefore were literate in the Army sense of the word. Also many more of the very *maladjusted* tended to be discharged for inaptness, regardless of literacy or of measured aptitude, than was the case with the well-adjusted. For the Indian and for the Negro of intermediate literacy, *adjustment* was of marked significance in the type of disposition he obtained. (Altus, 1945)

illiterates or Grade V, particularly in reference to Negro-white differences in mental ability. From June, 1943, through October, 1944, about 180,000 men were placed in the Army Special Training Units; 84 per cent of the whites given the Special Training, as compared with 87 per cent of the colored, were later assigned to regular Army service, with 76 per cent of the whites and 72 per cent of the Negroes completing the training in fewer than 60 days. About 16 per cent of the whites and 13 per cent of the Negroes were found to be unable to reach the minimum level required and were discharged from the Army. Trudeau concluded from these data that, "Given a learning situation in preliminary instruction, which is comparable to that provided for whites, Negroes do about as well as whites in their accomplishments." (p. 14) Witty, moreover, considered that Trudeau's findings offer strong support for the hypothesis that, given similar opportunities and motives, Negroes and whites of comparable background appear to learn about equally effectively.

Erickson, in commenting upon Witty's conclusion, observed that the people sent to the Special Training Units were a selected group, chosen on the basis of both illiteracy *and intelligence*. Those men not considered capable of learning were eliminated at the induction stations, were never inducted into the Army, and never reached the Special Training Units. "Moreover, as there is probably a larger percentage of bright illiterates among Negroes than among whites, due to lack of opportunity, it would be surprising if Negroes did not do better than whites. The higher rejection rate of Negroes should not be ignored." (p. 481)

Palmer, Wiley, and Keast reported that of the 39,521 men released from STU's for assignment to regular training in the first six months of operation, 98.7 per cent were in Classes IV and V, with 40 per cent of the Negroes and 21.3 per cent of the whites in Class V and 0.8 per cent of the Negroes and 2 per cent of the white men in Classes II and III. They concluded that while the STU's increased the total manpower available to the Army they did little to increase that portion of ability from which leadership might be expected to come.

In substantial agreement with the above findings on the *AGCT* is the report by Altus and Clark (1949) that white men (English-speaking) tended to score higher than the colored tested at the Special Training Centers on *Terman Vocabulary, Altus-Bell Information,* and *Army Wechsler.* Since their graduation rates were about the same, in order to graduate the "old-line" whites needed a higher aptitude score than did the Negro.

On the *Terman Vocabulary* (taken from the *Stanford-Binet, 1937 Revision*) administered to 2721 white and 2142 Negro monolinguals sent to the Ninth Service Command Special Training Center, the mean score of the white selectees was 12.27 and that of the colored, 11.32, the difference between the means being highly significant as will be noted in the table. (Altus, 1946) The respective mean *Vocabulary* scores of the whites who were subsequently graduated or discharged from the service were 12.64 and 10.67, the critical ratio being 11.94; the mean scores of the Negroes who were graduated or discharged were respectively,

11.82 and 9.59, the t being 17.29. Altus was of the opinion that the significant differences existing between the means and s's of the white and Negro men may have been due to cultural factors, in that about 19 of 20 colored selectees were born and reared in the South, mainly in the states west of the Mississippi. He concluded that the markedly depressed *Vocabulary* scores of the illiterate, whether white or colored, show him to live in a conceptual world quantitatively so far removed from that of the average literate person that the difference is almost qualitative; that concepts which to the normally literate person are basic and fundamental, are and likely will forever remain unverbalized for the illiterate.

Altus and Bell (1947) developed a 50-item test, the *AB Information Test,* standardized it on the normal flow of inductees processed at the Los Angeles Induction Station,[21] and used it as a supplement to the *Army Wechsler* and the *Terman Vocabulary* in the testing of men sent to the Special Training Center for the Ninth Service Command. In contrast to a mean of 25 attained by the normative group, the means of 2564 white and 2069 Negro selectees at the Special Training Center were 6.32 and 5.36, respectively. The t was highly significant, as will be observed in Table 7. When the white draftees were separated into *graduated* and *discharged* categories, the mean *AB* score of the former, 6.74, was significantly higher than the mean of the latter, 4.65. The respective means of the colored who were graduated and discharged were 5.90 and 3.28, a difference also highly significant ($t = 21.83$).

In the opinion of the present writer the several studies of enlisted men sent to the Special Training Units do not contradict, but probably support, the findings of other Army studies. Some of the facts to be taken into consideration in evaluation of the Negro-white comparisons are: (1) a much larger percentage of Negroes than whites were illiterate and therefore met a chief requirement for admission to the STU's; (2) all illiterates were not directed to the training centers, but rather the *brighter* of the illiterates (mean *Verbal* IQ on *Army Wechsler* was 67); (3) although from 84 to 87 per cent of all men sent to STU's were later graduated and assigned to Army service, *nearly one third of those sent to the Special Training Units were literate when they arrived* there (could pass the necessary tests at the fourth-grade level); (4) the very maladjusted tended to be discharged, regardless of literacy or measured aptitude — the ability to adjust being a particularly important consideration in the disposition of Negroes of intermediate literacy; (5) in general, white English-speaking draftees in the STU's earned higher scores (than did colored and non-English-speaking draftees) on the *AGCT,* the *Terman Vocabulary,* the *Altus-Bell Information,* and the *Army Wechsler;* and (6) since practically all of the men released for assignment

---

[21]Reduced from 105 questions by item analysis. The odd-even stepped-up reliability of the 50-point test was .94± .003. Its correlation with the number of years of schooling claimed by the inductee was .64± .02. It correlated with the *AGCT* to the extent of .78± .02. (Altus and Bell)

to regular training scored in the two lowest classes of the *AGCT* they swelled the Army manpower but did not affect the intermediate or higher levels from which leaders could be drawn.

AGO SAMPLES

Probably the most inclusive single report of Negro-white testing in World War II was contributed by Davenport (1946). Securing his data from the Office of the Adjutant General of the War Department, this investigator gave the percentage distribution of the *AGCT* grades for several million white and colored inductees processed in the two years between June, 1943, and May, 1945. Included are men actually inducted into the Army and excluded are a probable third of the whites and a half of the Negroes who registered for service, these men having been given preinduction examinations and subsequently discharged. The percentage distributions of the *AGCT* grades, ranging from I (highest) to V, are tabulated separately for the Nine Commands and for the Negroes and whites of these Nine Commands.[22]

As will be observed in Table 7, the white Commands were uniformly superior to the Negro Commands. The percentage of whites scoring in Grade I varied with the Command from 3.1 to 10.0, while the percentage of Negroes in Grade I varied with the Command from 0.1 to 0.8; in Grade II, the white percentages ranged from 17.7 to 37.4, the Negro percentages in Grade II ranging from 1.0 to 8.3; in Grade III, the white percentages ranged from 28.1 to 37.3, the Negro percentages from 4.0 to 32.5; in Grade IV, the white percentages ranged from 19.6 to 46.9, those of the Negroes from 55.6 to 66.5; in the lowest Grade, the white percentages ranged from 0.3 to 4.2, and the colored from 3.0 to 33.2.

Since the 48 states were included in the Nine Commands, and since some of the Commands are exclusively Northern whereas one of them is exclusively Southern, it is possible to make comparisons between Northern Negroes and Southern whites as was done in World War I. The states allocated to the Nine Service Commands are given in footnote 24, Table 7. Commands I, VI, and IX include 17 Northern States; Command IV includes seven Southern States; Commands II, V, and VII include twelve Northern and four Border States; and Commands III and VIII include two Northern, two Border, and four Southern States. As was previously stated, we have classified as *Southern* the 11 states of: Alabama, Arkansas, Florida, Georgia, Louisiana, Mississippi, North Carolina, South Carolina, Tennessee, Texas, and Virginia; as *Border*, the states of Delaware,

---

[22]From the *Report of the President's Committee on Civil Rights* (1947) we note that the Armed Forces at peak strength in 1945 included 7.2 per cent Negroes. Since Negroes numbered 9.77 per cent of the United States population (1940 census) and 10.6 per cent of the draft registrants (Palmer, Wiley, and Keast, 1948) it is evident that, in proportion of their numbers, between 70 and 74 per cent as many Negroes as whites were accepted for induction.

Stouffer *et al.* indicate that in the Army the proportion of Negroes increased from 6.03 per cent in Mar '42 to 8.62 per cent in Mar '45.

Kentucky, Maryland, Missouri, Oklahoma, and West Virginia; and as *Northern,* the remaining states.

In the three exclusively Northern Commands the percentage of whites in Grade I outranks the Negroes by more than 10 to 1, and the percentage of Negroes in Grade V outranks the whites by at least 10 to 1. In the Command including only Southern States, the percentage of whites in Grade 1 is 30 times that of the colored, and the percentage of Negroes in Grade V exceeds the whites in the ratio of 8 to 1.

A comparison of the *AGCT* Grade distribution of the whites in the all Southern Command (IV) with the Grade distribution of the Negroes in the particular Northern Command (I) *where their scores were best* shows that proportionally, five times as many Southern whites as Northern Negroes were in Grade I, and proportionally, two times as many Southern whites as Northern Negroes were in Grade II; at the lower end of the scale, there were relatively fewer Negroes than whites in Grade V but more Negroes in Grade IV. Combining Grades I and II, and similarly Grades IV and V, it appears that about *21 per cent* of the Southern whites and *9 per cent* of the Negroes of the best Northern Command scored in the two highest Grades, and about *51 per cent* of the Southern whites as opposed to *59 per cent* of these Northern Negroes scored in the two lowest Grades of the Army test.[23] Further, it will be recalled that in these comparisons some advantage was given to the Negroes in that: (1) there had been more Northern Negro rejections as *unacceptable illiterates* than Southern white, the number of Negroes in Command I rejected having been 200 for every 1000 processed (Sept '44-Aug '45), the number of whites in Command IV thus rejected having been 75 in every 1000 processed; and (2) there was one commissioned Negro officer for every 125 Negroes in the Armed Services and one commissioned white officer for every nine white men in the Services, these having been excluded from the Command figures.[24]

Stewart (1947) presented the findings relative to *Military Occupational Specialty* and *AGCT* Standard Score for 68,325 white and colored enlisted men in 220 military occupational specialties. The basic data were obtained from the War Department Machine Records Survey No. 4, taken on September 30, 1944. The War Department surveys were made every three months and yielded data for approximately two per cent of all Army personnel, including men stationed

---

[23]Command I was the New England Command. In Command VI (the all Northern Command which included Chicago and Detroit) 9 per cent of Negroes were in Grades I and II and 68 per cent of the Negroes were in Grades IV and V. In Command II (including New York City) the percentage of Negroes in the two highest Grades was approximately 7, in the two lowest Grades the percentage was about 69.

[24]In Dec '41, 7.38 per cent of w males in Army were officers as compared with 0.47 per cent of Negro males; proportions increased with course of war, so that by Mar '45, 11 per cent of white males and 0.87 per cent of Negro males were commissioned officers. (Stouffer *et al.*, 1949, pp. 500-501)

within the United States as well as overseas. Distributions of the *AGCT* scores were broken down by *Military Occupational Specialty* and also by race within each M.O.S. The author reported medians for all M.O.S.'s in use on the above date for which data on at least 25 cases were available. For those M.O.S.'s for which data on at least 50 cases were obtainable, the quartile deviation as well as the 10th, 25th, 75th, and 90th percentiles of the *AGCT* was determined.

There were 41 of the 220 M.O.S.'s that included 25 or more colored enlisted men; their scores were therefore tabulated separately from those of the whites.[25] The total number in these 41 military occupational specialties comprised 5663 colored and 40,137 white men. The combined medians of these colored and white enlistees were, respectively, *70.09 and 101.56*. In Table 7, the reviewer has included all of the M.O.S.'s along with the selected percentiles of the *AGCT* distributions for white and colored men where the number of cases was not less than 100, listing each M.O.S. in descending order of the *AGCT* median. In addition, we have determined the significance of the differences between the various colored and white medians. As will be observed, each colored median was significantly below the corresponding white M.O.S. median, the *t* ratios ranging between 9.93 and 69.64. In none of the ten military occupational specialties were the *medians* of the colored above the 25th percentiles of the whites, while in six of the occupational specialities they were not above the 10th percentiles of the whites. An examination of the tabulated material will permit a number of other comparisons.

Star, Williams, and Stouffer (*in* Stouffer, Suchman, *etc., 1949*) report the percentage of *AGCT* Grades of white and colored enlisted men secured from an AGO two per cent sample of the Army in March, 1945. As will be seen in the table, 7 per cent of the colored as compared with 38 per cent of the white recruits earned scores that placed them in Grades I or II; while 73 per cent of the colored as contrasted with 26 per cent of the whites achieved scores that placed them in Grades IV or V. Selective Service officials, noting that a larger proportion of colored failed to pass standardized tests than would have been expected on the basis of education, observed that in some instances morale entered into the problem by creating non-cooperative attitudes on the part of the registrants.

These authors also included a graph, based upon a special tabulation by the AGO Research Branch, of data collected while sampling for the March, 1943, survey. In addition to a representative cross section of 3000 men in the United States, the Negro sample was increased to 7438 to provide additional cases of the better educated and the Northern Negro for intragroup comparisons. The graph shows the percentage of Northern and Southern colored enlisted men in *AGCT* Grade V, who had completed varying amounts of schooling from under five years to college. From this graph the reviewer estimated the statistics which are included in Table 7. Approximately 86 per cent of the Northern and

---

[25]Tabulated by Stewart.

90 per cent of the Southern colored men *who had completed fewer than five years of schooling* were in Grade V; 21 per cent and 32 per cent of the respective Northern and Southern colored recruits *who had had some high school* training were in Grade V; and about 10 per cent and 16 per cent of the Northern and Southern colored men, respectively, *who had had some college work* scored in Grade V. These statistics may be compared with the report (p. 17) that 7 per cent of the *draft as a whole* were classified in Grade V.

Fulk (1949)[26] obtained the *AGCT* scores of 2174 whites and 2010 Negroes in the Army Air Force Service Command. Included were such organizations as Headquarters Squadrons, Service Squadrons, Chemical Sections, Signal Companies, Quartermaster Companies, and other organizations concerned with activities at an air base other than actual flying. All records were those of enlisted men, the number of Negroes including all cases, the whites selected by random sampling. Fulk divided the men according to their school grade completed — from 0 to 13 or more grades — and recorded the mean *AGCT* score of each.

As will be seen from the table, at all education levels the white means were above those of the Negroes. In fact, Fulk and Harrell report that all of the differences were highly significant, the lowest *t* value being 9.1. Not until the Negro had reached the eleventh grade was his mean score as high as that of any group of whites, no matter how little their previous training. Fulk and Harrell included the percentages of Negroes whose scores exceeded the median of the whites at each grade completed. From the table it may be noted that the overlapping ranged from 17 per cent at Grade 12 to two per cent at Grade 5. In comparing the *Combined Alpha and Beta Scale* results of World War I with the *AGCT* results of War II, Fulk found the colored to have been further below the whites in War II than in War I.

CADETS

Michael (1949) attempted to determine the contributions of various factors both to the description of tests and to the predictive value of these tests in two pilot samples of the United States Army Air Forces. One sample of 815 West Point Cadets was administered the *Classification Battery* consisting of 12 pencil-and-paper tests and six psychomotor (or apparatus) tests in November, 1943; a sample of 356 Negro cadets was given a second *Classification Battery* consisting of 15 pencil-and paper tests, 7 of which were identical to those of the first *Battery*, and the same 6 psychomotor tests in September, 1944.

The *Classification Battery* of November, 1943, consisted of the pencil-and-paper tests of Reading Comprehension, Spatial Orientation, Dial and Table Reading Test, Mechanical Principles, General Information, Mathematics, Instrument Comprehension, and Biographical Data. The six apparatus tests included:

---

[26]See also Fulk and Harrell (1952).

Rotary Pursuit, Complex Coordination, Finger Dexterity, Discrimination Reaction Time, Two-Hand Coordination, and Fernald Rudder Control. For each new *Classification Battery*, stanines were established for scores of bombardiers, navigators, and pilots. Norms for these stanines were based upon scores of several representative groups of cadets taking the *Battery* at various training centers. Scores of all groups were converted to scale values determined from these standardizing groups.[27]

Michael found that the Negro and white samples were nonhomogeneous as demonstrated by the application of the *t*-test to differences between the mean scores of tests identical to the two batteries. All differences were significant beyond the one per cent level of confidence (Table 7). For the West Point Cadets the three most valid factors contained in the *Classification Battery* were pilot interest, spatial relations, and psychomotor coordination; for representative white aviation cadets (from previous analysis) the most valid factors were spatial relations, mechanical experience, and psychomotor coordination; for the Negro cadets the three most valid factors were kinesthesis, perceptual speed, and spatial relations.

POST-KOREAN WAR

REJECTION RATES

In discussing the breakdown of the Negro family and factors contributing to its deterioration, Moynihan (U. S. Dept. Labor, 1965) cites the high unemployment rate of the Negro male and the failure of a very large proportion of this racial group to qualify for military service. The Armed Forces, according to the Moynihan Report, provide the largest single source of employment in the nation; and, if Negroes were represented in the same proportions in the military as in the population, they would probably number 100,000 more than at present — thereby serving to reduce the Negro male unemployment rate from 9.1 to 7.0 per cent.

However, Negroes continue to constitute about 8 per cent of the Armed Forces personnel, even though they now comprise 11.8 per cent of the nation's population. In 1962, for example, 56.1 per cent of the 50,474 Negroes, as opposed to 15.4 per cent of the 235,678 whites examined for the draft, were rejected because of failure to pass the *Armed Forces Qualification Test*. This test is described in the report as "not quite a mental test, nor yet an education test", but rather a test of a man's ability to perform at an acceptable level of competence. It roughly measures ability that is found in an average seventh-or eighth-

---

[27]The stanine scale is a condensed form of the T-scale. It consists of nine scaled score intervals. In the lowest interval is included 4 per cent of the scores; in the second, 7 per cent; in the third, 12 per cent; in the fourth, 17 per cent; . . . fifth, 20 per cent, . . . sixth, 17 per cent, . . . seventh, 12 per cent, *etc.* The middle 20 per cent of scores are all given the stanine value of 5.

grade student. "A grown young man who cannot pass this test is in trouble." (p. 40)

As will be noted in Table 7, the draft figures apply only to Continental United States, the 48 states and the District of Columbia having been allocated in six Army Areas. Using footnote 39 as a guide, one can easily compare the rejection rates of colored men from certain areas of the country with those of whites from other areas. It will be observed, for instance: (1)that the rejection rates for colored draftees range from 31.1 to 67.7 per cent according to the Army Area, the white rejection rates ranging from 8.9 to 26.4 per cent; (2) that the highest rejection rate for Negroes is in the Third Army Area (all Southern states) and the highest rejection rate for whites is in the First Army Area (all Northern states); and (3) that the lowest rejection rate for the colored occurs in the Far West where the smallest number of colored men were registered.

MATCHED SAMPLES OF ENLISTED MEN

Hypothesizing that Negroes would score lower on the *Army Classification Battery* than would whites, that Negroes would manifest a greater lack of self-confidence than whites, and that several personality variables would correlate more highly with intelligence test scores in Negroes than in whites, Roen (1960) studied the test records of 50 white and 50 colored soldiers who had been painstakingly matched on a number of items. These 100 enlisted men were selected from the personnel files of hundreds of men stationed in an Army Post in Southwestern United States. By *eliminating those of extremely low Classification Battery scores* and those whose biographical data would be difficult to duplicate, there remained about 500 men who were available for testing and interviews. The following personality tests were administered under conditions of anonymity to the ninety-eight per cent who would cooperate: California Test of Personality, Taylor Manifest Anxiety Scale, and the Bernreuter Personality Inventory.[28] Subsequently, 50 colored and 50 white soldiers were matched on ten variables: age, education, occupation of parents, income of parents, geographical area of childhood home, Army rank, number of years in the service, marital status, urban or rural background, and plans for reinlistment.

Two measures of intelligence, derived from the *Classification Battery,* were employed: the *combined intelligence measure* (obtained by averaging the scores on three tests of the *Battery* — Reading and Vocabulary, Arithmetic Reasoning, and Pattern Analysis) and the *Pattern Analysis (PA) score,* since this test had been found to correlate the highest of the three with the *Wechsler-Bellevue.* On both the *combined intelligence* and the *Pattern Analysis* the 50 Negroes scored

---

[28]Only the Self-Confidence score showed a significant difference between the two groups. A measure of test-taking "integrity" was used by selecting items on the tests that in the judgments of three clinicians appeared to be contradictory. All who responded in a contradictory manner to three or more pairs of items were eliminated from the sample.

significantly below their 50 white counterparts (Table 7). No significant difference was found between the groups in Total Adjustment (California Test), or in Anxiety (Taylor Manifest Anxiety); however, the Negroes were significantly lacking in Self-Confidence (Bernreuter). Roen concluded that statements of causality could not be made from the data but that further research is warranted on the hypothesis that Negroes as a group incorporate intellectually defeating personality traits that play a significant role in the ability to score on measures of intelligence.

SUMMARY

We have found no evidence which would indicate less discrepancy in the mental test scores of Negroes and whites in World War II than in World War I. In World War II the colored draft may be said to have represented a higher mental sampling of its male population of military age than did the white draft. This was due, in large part, to the fact that only about three fourths as many Negroes as whites in proportion to their numbers were accepted for induction into the Armed Forces, to the fact that the differential rejection rate is not explainable on the basis of relatively more physical disqualifications among the Negroes but to there being more unintelligent illiterates among them, to the fact that relatively fewer occupational deferments were given to Negroes because of special abilities or skills, to the fact that some advantage was given to Negro enlisted men in several comparisons,[29] and to the fact that there was a much larger percentage of superior whites than superior Negroes who made up the commissioned officer group and were not included in the statistics for enlisted men. In spite of these advantages given to the Negro soldier in the Negro-white comparisons, we have found a better showing of whites consistently indicated in every study in World War II, and in the Post-Korean period as well. This holds true in comparisons between the Northern Negro and the Southern white draft, although the difference between these groups is less marked than between the Northern Negro and the Northern white or between the Southern Negro and the Southern white.[30]

---

[29]White men in 14 specific M.O.S.'s averaging *highest* in *AGCT* scores could not be included in the comparisons because there were very few (under 25) or no Negroes in these M.O.S.'s (Stewart, 1947). White men in 7 of the 9 M.O.S.'s averaging *lowest* in *AGCT* were included because there were Negroes listed in these Military Occupation Specialities.

Also see Roen's method of matching c and w enlisted men (1960) and note that he eliminated all men who made very low *Army Classification Battery* scores.

[30]For a number of years the reviewer has been of the opinion that the Southern states, owing perhaps to their military tradition, may have contributed more than their "share" of officers to the two World Wars. If this assumption is correct, the South thereby has eliminated relatively more men of above-average and superior intelligence from its rank and file of enlisted men to whom the mental tests were administered. Support for this hypothesis, as it pertains to WW I, was found first in a pilot study in which we made use of the *World Almanac for 1926*, Cummings' *Negro Population: 1790-1915*, and *Official Army Register*, January 1, 1940. (In this discussion we are referring to *white officers*. Racial designation was not included in the

Official Army Registers consulted for WW I data; however, as the ratio of officer to enlisted man was 1 to 9 for the whites and 1 to 300 for Negroes in WW I, it is believed that treating all officers as "white" did not result in biasing the South-Border-North data to a significant degree. See Chapter 5, fn. 1.)

From the *Official Army Register*—which includes data on active and retired Army officers *living in 1939* — one half of the 1200 pages were chosen by arbitrarily examining all numbered pages ending in 1, 3, 6, 7, and 9. From these pages the name of every man was tabulated if he fulfilled these three requirements: (1) born in one of the 48 states or the District of Columbia, (2) born between 1883-1900, making him between 17-35 years of age in 1917-1918, and (3) listed as a cadet or commissioned officer between April 6, 1917, and November 10, 1918. These names were tallied in *Southern, Border,* or *Northern* categories, totaling for the three respective areas: 841; 418; and 2281. The three totals were multiplied by two (since each included one half) and divided by the respective number of white males living in the region of their birth in 1900. According to the 1900 census, there were 5,954,385 white males living in the 11 Southern states of Ala, Ark, Fla, Ga, La, Miss, NC, SC, Tenn, Tex, and Va; 3,934,882 in the six Border states of Del, Ky, Md, Mo, Okla, and WVa, and DC; and 23,882,049 in the 31 Northern (all other) states; the numbers of WW I officers between the ages of 18-35 per 100,000 white males living in the region of their birth in 1900 were: Southern, 28.2; Border, 21.2; and Northern, 19.1.

Subsequently, the reviewer secured an *Official Army Register,* January 1, 1924—which includes comparable data on active and retired Army officers *living in 1923*—and replicated the above procedure, examining all 784 numbered pages ending in 1, 3, 6, 7, and 9, and employing the same three criteria for inclusion of names. Fulfilling these criteria, there were 996 officers born in the South, 464 born in the Border states and the District of Columbia, and 2597 born in the Northern states. Multiplying these numbers by two and dividing each by the number of white males living in the region of their birth in 1900 we secured data comparable to those derived from the 1940 edition: *Southern, 33.5; Border, 23.6;* and *Northern, 21.7.*

According to statistics available in the *Official Army Register* of 1940, (pertaining to *officers who survived WW I by 21 years or more*) it seems that the Southern states contributed proportionally 1.48 times as many Army officers as did the Northern states, and 1.33 times as many officers as did the Border states and DC. According to statistics available in the *Official Army Register* of 1924, (those officers who survived WW I by 5 years or more) the Southern states contributed proportionally 1.54 times as many officers as did the Northern states, and 1.42 times as many officers as did the Border states and DC.

The Registers also include some factual information about officers retired for disability or other reasons. Upon examination of the January 1, 1924, *Official Army Register* we found that the Southern states contributed proportionally 1.64 times as many Army officers retired because of *Disability in line of duty* or *Disability from wounds received in action* as the Northern states, and 1.20 times as many Army officers so disabled as the Border states and DC.

Chapter VI

SPECIAL GROUPS OF VETERANS AND OTHER CIVILIANS

It will have been observed that Negro school children, high school pupils, college students, and enlisted men in the Armed Forces have been subjected to widespread testing in the United States. Particular groups of Negro deviates, such as the gifted, the mentally retarded, delinquents, and criminals have also been frequently examined. In addition to these, there are a few other groups, composed of individuals not readily classifiable according to any of the above categories, whose testing will be considered in this chapter. They include a somewhat miscellaneous assortment of (1) veterans, the majority of whom were examined in Vocational Guidance Programs, (2) mental patients and employees of a state hospital, (3) transients and homeless men, and (4) samples of individuals chosen to represent the "general population".

Veterans

Davidson, Gibby, McNeil, Segal, and Silverman (1950) were interested in determining whether or not there are consistent Negro-white differences in IQ and subtest scores on *Form I* of the *Wechsler-Bellevue Scale*. These researchers examined the test records of 44 Negro and 41 white psychoneurotic patients at the Detroit Mental Hygiene Clinic, having ascertained that their subjects had attained no more than the twelfth-grade level of schooling and had all been clearly diagnosed as psychoneurotic. As will be noted in Table 8, the two racial groups were also of the same average age and the Negroes had achieved a mean school grade at least equal to that of the whites.

The Negro group was significantly inferior to the whites on the *Full Scale* IQ (.01) and on the *Performance Scale* (.01), but not on the *Verbal Scale* (.10). The authors' analysis of subtest scores indicates that the Negro Ss were likewise significantly inferior to the whites on the *Verbal* subtest of *Arithmetic* (.05) and on four *Performance* subtests: *Picture Arrangement* (.05), *Picture Completion* (.01), *Block Design* (.01), and *Digit Symbol* (.01).

Davidson *et al.* attempted to explain the relatively poor showing of the Negro group on *Arithmetic* and on the *Performance* subtests as follows: (1) *Arithmetic* measures the ability for active concentration whereas *Digit Span* — the subtest on which the Negro group did best (in fact slightly surpassing the white mean with a score of 10.66 *vs.* 10.48) — involves the capacity for a more passive attention. (2) *Picture Arrangement* involves a time element as well as ability to plan, anticipate, and grasp the meaning of social situations, and (3) *Performance* subtests in general depend upon psychomotor speed. The slower psychomotor speed of the Negroes may have been due to their lack of anxiety to get things done (essentially a more passive adjustment, a "Why hurry?" attitude) which in turn may be attributed to a relative lack of attainable socioeconomic goals and the particular cultural role the Negro is expected to fulfill.[1]

The studies of Young and Collins (1954) and Scarborough (1956) are similar in that both deal with the administration of *Form I* of the *Wechsler-Bellevue Scale* to venereally infected males being treated at the Alto, Georgia, Medical Center and matched in certain ways with veterans of their racial group. Young and Collins paired, on the basis of education, 52 Negroes who were undergoing treatment for primary or secondary syphilis during a two-month period in 1950[2] with 52 Negro veterans, some of whom were being tested at the Guidance Center of the University of Georgia and others who were in attendance at a vocational training school.

The mean IQ of the Negro veterans was 81.27, that of the Negro syphilitics, 67.96. The subjects in both groups were reported to have been especially inferior to the norms on the subtests of *Information, Arithmetic, Similarities,* and *Digit Span.*[3]

Scarborough (1956) compared white patients infected with venereal diseases with white veterans as well as Negro patients with Negro veterans (Table 8). The experimental groups consisted of 16 white and 24 colored venereally infected persons tested in 1949 on the *Wechsler-Bellevue* and *Rorschach* and a control group of 59 white and 59 colored veterans whose names were selected from the files of the Guidance Center of the University of Georgia, the patients having been matched as a group with the veterans of their race for intelligence and school grade attained. The mean grade reached by the white groups was 7 years, that reached by the colored being 5.5 and 5.9 years for the respective veteran and patient groups. Among the controls there were eight white and seven colored men with a diagnosis of neurosis and two colored with a diagnosis of psychosis in remission. Some of the controls may also have had venereal infections.

As will be noted in the table, the *Verbal, Performance,* and *Full Scale* IQ's of the white veterans were approximately 10 to 11 points above the respective means of the colored veterans, all of these differences being significant at the .01 level of confidence. The respective differences between the *Verbal, Performance,* and *Full Scale* IQ's of the treatment groups were between 8 and 10 points. The white veterans were superior to the colored veterans on the following subtests at the .01 level: *Information, Block Design, Object Assembly,* and *Digit*

---

[1] In support of their interpretation the authors give due credit to D. Rapaport, Diagnostic Psychological Testing. Chicago: Year Book Publ., 1945, I, pp. 176-179, 215-220, and to A. Davis, Socialization and adolescent personality. *Yearb. nat. Soc. Stud. Educ.,* 1944, *43,* pp. 207-211.

[2] They came from VD Control Regions of the State, all participation being on a voluntary basis.

[3] Mean subtest scores were not included in Young and Collins' data.

Symbol; at the .05 level the white veterans were superior to the colored in: *Comprehension, Digit Span, Similarities,* and *Picture Arrangement.*

Due to there being fewer cases in the experimental groups, their mean differences were less frequently significant. At the .01 level the white venereal disease group was superior to the colored in *Information;* at the .05 level the former was superior to the latter in *Digit Span, Picture Completion, Block Design, Digit Symbol,* as well as in *Performance* and *Full Scale* IQ's.

Oelke (1959), observing the dearth of published material on the testing of Negro adults and desiring to secure adequate information for normative data on Negroes who had had cultural problems during early development,[4] decided to report the results of some data which had been obtained on colored veterans from the Veterans' Administration files. The Ss included 684 Southern Negro veterans of World War II; 513 of them had been tested under the vocational guidance program of the VA "at a white university near the Gulf of Mexico" and 171 at the VA Guidance Center of a Negro university in the same state (Table 8).

The subjects included all Negro veterans, provided: (1) they were of military service age during World War II; (2) they received vocational testing and guidance between June, 1946, and June, 1948, at one of the two VA contract guidance centers cited above; (3) their level of education completed at the time of testing was at least equal to that required for testees as stated in the test manuals; and (4) they had no compensable disability that would have materially affected the test results.

The test administrators were white at the white university and Negro at the Negro university. The median grade completed by those tested at the white center was eight, with a range of from two through college; at the Negro center, the median grade completed was twelve, with a range of from Grade I through College. The median grade completed by the total group of Negroes and whites was 8.6. The mean score on the *Otis Quick-Scoring Beta,* which was administered to 157 subjects who had completed school work equivalent to Grades 4 to 9, was 28.2, which corresponded to a mean IQ of 71. The mean score on the *Otis Quick-Scoring Gamma,* administered to 181 subjects who possessed high school or college education, was 26, corresponding to a mean IQ of 84.[5] The author observed that the scores on the several mental tests tended to be concentrated toward the lower end of the scales so that a large portion of the subjects received scores approaching simple guesswork. In fact, the only test which did not show a tendency for the scores to concentrate at the lower end of the scale was the

---

[4]Personal communication.

[5]The Otis IQ's were not reported by Oelke, but secured by the reviewer from Otis' tables. Included in Table 8 are average scores obtained on the *Scovill Classification Test, Survey of Space Relations,* and *Minnesota Test of Spatial Relations.* The author does not have the manuals or general norms which would enable one to interpret these averages. (personal communication from Oelke)

Minnesota Mechanical Assembly Test, Set 2. This was among four tests administered as a part of the testing program at the two centers designed to measure clerical or mechanical aptitude. The test consists entirely of items such as a spring clothespin, pliers, spark plug, and rope coupling which are to be assembled; all of the items are such that they might be relatively familiar to the Ss or could be readily assembled by one possessing a reasonable degree of mechanical insight. "By using items which are not abstract but are to some extent drawn from the familiar, perhaps the subject is motivated to perform better, or perhaps it may be due to the cultural familiarity with concrete operations." (Oelke, 1959, p. 324) The author suggests that a test to be used with a cultural group such as Negro veterans should be constructed of items more closely related to the criterion performance, or perhaps the items should be drawn exclusively from reasonable experiences of the cultural group and used in ways that are more meaningful and less remote to them.

Peters (1960) proposed to compare the performances of white and Negro males on the *Wechsler-Bellevue Verbal Scale* (excluding *Vocabulary*) and to investigate the possibility of consistent Negro-white differences attributable to the lack of equal educational opportunities for Negroes. From the files containing the testing results of thousands of male veterans who had reported to the Veterans Administration Regional Office in Chicago for vocational and educational guidance over a period of five years, Peter excluded all who had more than 13 years of schooling and all who had not been tested on the *Wechsler-Bellevue*. From the remaining, he selected 100 white and 100 colored veterans' reports which he matched for school grade completed, age, and *Digit Span* subtest score. Only *Verbal* IQ's (minus *Digit Span* and *Vocabulary*)[6] were then compared, in addition to the scores on the four subtests of *Information, Comprehension, Arithmetic,* and *Similarities*.

The subjects were further divided into the *educationally-retarded* and the *educationally-normal* groups of 50 each, the point of separation being the completion of fewer than eight years of schooling. Peters did not report the size of the *Verbal IQ's* nor the mean subtest scores. However, he included the *t*'s for seven of the ten Negro-white comparisons. In all of them the white means were above those of the colored, the difference between the Verbal IQ's of the white and Negro educationally-retarded being significant at the .01 level and that between the Verbal IQ's of the two groups of educationally-normal being significant at the .05 level.

The groups of educationally-normal Negro and white veterans, selected for age, educational level, and *Digit Span* showed significant differences favoring the whites on the subtests of *Information* and *Arithmetic* as well as in *Verbal* IQ. The groups of educationally-retarded Negro and white veterans selected for age, educational level, and *Digit Span* showed significant differences favoring the

---

[6]The *Vocabulary* subtest had been omitted from a number of *W-B* examinations.

whites on the subtests of *Information, Arithmetic,* and *Similarities,* as well as in *Verbal* IQ. There were reported to be no significant differences between the white and colored educationally-retarded groups in *Comprehension,* nor between the educationally-normal groups in *Similarities.*

Peters concluded that factors of education and motivation should be taken into consideration when interpreting the performance of Negroes on the *Wechsler Verbal Scale* and that this should be done with an awareness of the culturally restricted background from which the Negro has come, no matter how high his educational achievement.

STATE HOSPITAL PATIENTS AND EMPLOYEES

Davis (1957) hoped to study a sufficient number of *Wechsler-Bellevue* protocols of Southern Negroes to determine the areas and skills in which they had achieved greatest development. He selected 27 colored employees and 33 colored mental patients at a Florida state hospital who were given the *Wechsler-Bellevue, Form II.* The education of the groups ranged from no formal schooling completed through that of one year of college, the median of the employees being 6.2 years, that of the patients, 5.2 years. The *Full Scale* IQ's of both groups were low, *i.e.,* 67-68, with the patients being somewhat the more variable (Table 8). The subtests which were the most difficult for the employees were: *Digit Symbol, Similarities, Digit Span, Information,* and *Block Design;* those most difficult for the patients included three of the above (*Digit Symbol, Similarities, Digit Span*) and *Picture Arrangement.* The four tests in which the employees performed to best advantage are: *Vocabulary, Comprehension, Picture Completion,* and *Object Assembly,* these being the same subtests on which the patients made their best showing. Davis pointed out that the low scores earned by his groups on *Similarities* indicated that they had difficulty in differentiating between essential and superficial likenesses, suggesting an immaturity of thought. However, he believed that environmental factors could account for this lack of maturity and indicated that he was making no attempt to conclude that race *per se* is a limiting factor in intelligence.

TRANSIENTS AND HOMELESS MEN

In an effort to discover whether or not the mental ability of transients differs markedly from that of the population as a whole and whether this difference, if it exists, is great enough to affect their employability, Bryan (1936) sampled 500 cases of male transients. Of these, 250 whites were "clients" of the Durham, North Carolina, Transient Bureau between April and June, 1934; 100 white and 50 colored were among those registered at the same bureau between January and April, 1935; and 50 white and 50 colored were tested at the Cincinnati Bureau in September, 1934.

In Durham, all cases registered on a given day were assembled for tests after

TABLE

VETERANS AND

AUTHOR DATE	LOCATION	TEST	N	SUBJECTS AGE	METHOD OF SELECTION
Davidson, K. S., Gibby, R. G., McNeil, E. B., Segal, S. J., and Silverman, H. (1950)	Detroit, Mich.	*Wechsler-Bellevue, Form I*	w-41 c- 44	30[1] 30	Matched groups of w & c psychneurotic patients at Detroit Mental Hygiene Clinic. All Ss with clear diagnoses; none with schooling beyond high sch. Mean schooling: w-9.04, c-9.43 grades.
Young, F. M., and Collins, J. J. (1954)	Georgia	*Wechsler-Bellevue, Form I*	c- 52 c- 52	26[1] 23	35 Ss at Guidance Center, U. Ga. & 17 attending Vocational Training Sch. Paired on basis of educ with 52 syphilitics being treated at Alto Medical Center from all VD Control Regions of state.
Scarborough, B. B. (1956)	Georgia	*Wechsler-Bellevue, Form I*	VD w-16 c- 24 Vet w-59 c- 59	31.25[1] 29.50 29.99 29.04	In Aug '49 *W-B* & *Rorschach* given to 40 patients who had venereal infections as result of sexual contact. Came from all over state, most from lower income families. Controls of veterans who were matched with VD groups for intelligence & sch grade. Controls from files of Guidance Center of Univ Ga.
Davis, J. C. (1957)	Chattahoochee, Fla.	*Wechsler-Bellevue, Form 2*	c- 27 c- 33	22[1]	Two Southern Negro groups, one consisting of 33 mental patients and the other of 27 employees at a Fla State Hospital, all tested on *W-B*. Method of selection not given.

[1]Mean age in years.

EIGHT

OTHER CIVILIANS

RESULTS				COMMENTS OF AUTHOR

		IQ		Cause of the significant poorer showing of c group
	w	c	t	on Arith and Performance subtests may be found in
M				slower performance of psychomotor perceptual
Verbal	97.10	92.18	1.72	functions which in turn may be related to his
Perf	102.42	91.89	2.75	limited opportunities for achievement and conse-
Full Scale	101.71	91.98	2.84	quent lower level of aspiration.
s				
Verbal	13.96	12.08		
Perf	18.20	16.50		
Full Scale	16.00	14.17		

	IQ		Ss in both groups especially inferior in Informa-
	Vet	VD	tion, Arith Reasoning, Similarities, and Memory
	c	c	Span. Veterans sig superior in 9 of 10 tests. Educ
M	81.27	67.96	program for vets probably most effective at 4th-or
s	14.60	13.60	5th-grade level.

	M-Veterans			It appears that the main diffs in intell among the
	w	c	t	groups were associated with race; true for both
		Scores		VD patients and controls. *W-B* of doubtful validity
Inform	7.56	5.47	.01	when used for study of Southern whites and Negroes
Compr	9.08	6.93	.05	primarily of low socio groupings.
Dig Sp	6.99	5.79	.05	
Arith	6.96	6.17	—	
Simil	7.50	6.36	.05	
Pic Arr	7.07	5.96	.05	
Pic Com	7.10	6.55	—	
Block D	8.97	5.88	.01	
Obj Ass	9.32	7.58	.01	
Dig Sym	7.10	4.91	.01	
	IQ			
Verbal	90.14	79.54	.01	
Perform	90.90	80.22	.01	
Full Sc	89.71	78.44	.01	

	IQ		Supportive evidence of the influence of environ-
	Empl	Pat	mental factors can be drawn from the higher
	c	c	scores obtained on Comprehension & Vocabulary
M	68	67	than on Information & Arith.
Range	51-99	45-108	

TABLE

VETERANS AND

AUTHOR DATE	LOCATION	TEST	N	SUBJECTS AGE	METHOD OF SELECTION
Oelke, M. C. (1959)	Texas[2]	Otis Quick-Scoring Gamma	c- 181		Southern Negro veterans of World War II; 513 were tested under Vocational Guidance program of VA at a w univer, 171 tested at a VA Guidance Center of Negro univer in same state. All were referred to the 2 centers for vocational appraisal bet June '46-June '48. Sample considered representative of those taking tests. Majority of Ss were not required to take all tests.
		Otis Quick-Scoring Beta	c- 157		
		Scovill Classification Test, Part 1	c- 226		
		Survey of Space Relations	c- 64		
		Minnesota Test of Spatial Relations	c- 298		
Peters, J. S., II (1960)	Chicago, Ill.	Wechsler-Bellevue, Form I	w-100 c- 100		Ss were selected from male veterans who had reported for vocational & educ guidance over 5-year period to VA Regional Office. Excluded all who had more than 13 yrs of sch. White & c were matched in terms of sch grade completed, age, & Digit Span subtest score.

[2]Inferred by reviewer.

EIGHT *(continued)*

OTHER CIVILIANS

	RESULTS		COMMENTS OF AUTHOR

	Scores		Examination of results on both Otis tests and Survey of Space Relations indicates that the scores tend to be concentrated toward lower end of scale so that a large portion of Ss receive scores approaching simple guesswork.
	c		
Mdn	24.2		
M	26.0		
s	10.1		

	Scores		Culture, rapport, and lack of familiarity with test situations may be contributors to condition of concentration of scores.
	c		
Mdn	27.2		
M	28.2		
s	13.5		

	Scores		Counselor and employment officer must be extremely cautious in making vocational decisions involving tests with this group.
	c		
Mdn	131.9		
M	132.1		
s	15.8		

	Scores		It may be argued that the tests are not adequate to measure the type of individual represented in this group.
	c		
Mdn	35.9		
M	36.8		
s	21.3		

	Scores	
	c	
Mdn	1292.2	
M	1342.1	
s	341.0	

Verbal Subtest	t[3]	The several differences noted favor the white groups; it may be inferred that their superior cultural and educational opportunities contribute greatly to these differences.
Information		
Educ retard	3.82	
Educ normal	3.25	
Arithmetic		
Educ retard	3.09	
Educ normal	2.46	
Similarities		
Educ retard	2.64	
Educ norm	——	
Comprehension		
Educ retard	——	
Educ norm	——	
Verbal Scale IQ		
Educ retard	4.11	
Educ normal	2.21	

[3]In each instance where a *t* is listed the w mean was significantly greater than that of the c. Author does not report size of *t*'s for the 3 comparisons omitted.

TABLE

VETERANS AND

AUTHOR DATE	LOCATION	TEST	N	SUBJECTS AGE	METHOD OF SELECTION
Bryan, J. Y. (1936)	Durham, N. C., and Cincinnati, Ohio	*Henmon-Nelson*	w-400 c- 100		250 w: clients of Durham Transient Bureau, Apr-June '34. 50 c & 100 w: tested at Durham center, Jan-Apr '35. 50 c & 50 w: registered at Cincinnati Transient Bur, Sept '34.
Levinson, B. M. (1964)	New York, N. Y.	*WAIS*	w-50 c- 32	49[1] 35	Whites were tested in '55, c tested in '62; among c there were 9 Northern-born & 23 Southern-born. All were native-born, homeless men, in receipt of shelter care administered by NYC Dept Welfare.
Miner, J. B. (1957)	United States	Vocabulary Test	w-1347 c- 153	10 and over	Sample collected by interviewers of Publ Opinion Surveys, Inc. of Princeton, N. J. using sample design similar to that employed in national surveys. Excluded inmates of institutions & members of Armed Services on post, those unable to speak English, and those who could speak some other language well but handicapped in use of English.

EIGHT *(concluded)*
OTHER CIVILIANS

	RESULTS		COMMENTS OF AUTHOR

	IQ		
	w	c	
M	73	58	
Yrs sch			Investigation of individual cases suggests that the
1-7	63	53	IQ difference has its partial explanation in native
8 & over	89	70	ability.
Range	45-124	45-124	

	M		Differences in scores reflect to some extent the
	w	c	effects of subcultural, caste, and socioeco differences.
	Scores		
Inform	10.51	7.88	
Compr	10.50	7.81	
Arith	10.31	6.56	
Simil	9.47	7.03	
Dig Sp	10.32	8.13	
Vocab	10.86	6.66	
Pic Arr	9.07	7.53	
Pic Com	9.78	6.94	
Block D	8.54	6.89	
Obj Ass	7.45	7.66	
Dig Sym	7.59	6.28	
	IQ		
Verbal	101.30	85.91	
Perform	91.62	82.31	
Full Sc	96.79	83.78	

	Scores		The racial difference (in educational underplace-
	w	c	ment) is largely the result of our philosophy of
M	11.06	8.08	education that favors age rather than performance
s	3.41	2.72	as a basis for promotion, combined with whatever
t =		12.41	conditions may operate to restrict Negroes as a
p =		$< .001$	group to a relatively low intellectual level.

the evening meal as a part of the routine before receiving a bed for the night. If they indicated themselves as being too tired the men were excused until the following morning. Actually, 20 per cent of all whites and 40 per cent of all colored present were unable to take the test at any time, due to inablity to read, to alcoholism, to poor eyesight, or to the inability to comprehend the test requirements. Approximately 80 per cent of those excluded were illiterate. In Cincinnati, 100 literate cases were selected at random from the total number who appeared for meals on the one day during which the tests were given. All men in both cities were examined by the *Henmon-Nelson Test of Mental Ability*.

All subjects were separated into two groups according to the years of schooling completed. The average IQ of the 247 whites who had completed fewer than eight years of schooling was approximately *63*, regardless of where or when tested. Similarly, the average of the 153 whites who had completed eight or more years was virtually the same for the three samples, *i.e., between 88 and 90*. The average IQ of the 70 colored men who had completed fewer than eight years of schooling was *53* (52 in Durham and 54 in Cincinnati); while the average of the 30 colored who had completed eight or more years was *70* (71 in Durham and 69 in Cincinnati). Bryan observed that the difference between the Negroes and whites in the better-educated group is somewhat deceptive since the actual number of grades which these Negroes had completed was definitely lower than was the case with the whites; also, there were probably appreciably lower standards of education in the schools which Southern Negroes attended than in the Southern schools attended by whites.

In addition to inferior education that should be considered in interpreting test scores of both racial groups, Bryan mentions alcoholism, advancing age, and effects of disease (prevalent among transients) and suggests the need for caution against interpreting any of his results too simply. In general, however, the author must have thought that his test results had some validity, for he observed that usually the men possessing the greatest versatility, skill, self-directive capacity, and originality were found to rank in the upper IQ levels.

Wishing to learn what effect the feeling of hopelessness, believing oneself worthless, and lacking drive might have on Wechsler test performance, Levinson (1964)[7] analyzed the results of the *WAIS* which had been administered to Negro and white homeless men in New York City. These men were all native-born, homeless, and in receipt of shelter care administered by the New York City Department of Welfare.[8] The 50 white men whose mean age was 48 years were tested in 1955; the 32 Negroes whose mean age was 35 were tested in 1962.

As will be seen in Table 8, these homeless men earned impressively higher IQ's on the average than the transients tested by Bryan. Various factors may have been responsible for the 25 points separating the two groups of the same race,

---

[7]*J. Clin. Psychol.*

[8]The reviewer has omitted the results of the *W-B* given to two other groups of white homeless or domiciled men because two fifths to four fifths of them were foreign-born.

such as: (1) the fact that Bryan employed a *group* rather than an *individual* test, (2) the lack of information about the *ages* of the men in Bryan's study and about the *educational level* of the men in that of Levinson, and (3) the probability that Bryan's groups were examined under more unfavorable conditions of fatigue, intoxication, illness, and the like. It is interesting that Levinson's homeless men, who were disadvantaged socially, familiar with hopelessness, despair, and malnutrition, whose scores may have been affected by alcoholism and psychopathology, scored about the same as the average of their race. On the *Full Scale,* the mean IQ's earned by the whites and Negroes were 96.79 and 83.78, respectively. It is also interesting to note that the *Verbal* and *Performance* IQ's of the Negroes were about the same, *i.e.,* 85.91 and 82.31, but that the *Verbal* IQ of the whites was about 10 points higher than their *Performance* IQ, *i.e.;* 101.30 and 91.62.

The homeless whites seemed to perform about equally well on all of the *Verbal* subtests, while the Negroes appeared to have scored relatively better on *Digit Span* and most poorly on *Vocabulary* and *Arithmetic.* On the *Performance Scale* the differences on the various subtests all favored the white group, except for *Object Assembly* where the mean score was slightly higher for the Negroes. On this subtest, the colored scored their best and the whites their worst.

In another article,[9] Levinson (1964) further analyzed the data described above as follows: (1) He included the standard deviations of the 50 white and 32 colored subjects on the *WAIS Verbal, Performance,* and *Full Scales* as well as on its various subtests. The colored proved to be the more variable in all 14 comparisons with the exception of *Digit Span,* the standard deviations of the Negroes' distributions ranging between 18.34 and 18.92 on the *Verbal, Performance,* and *Full Scales,* those of the whites' between 10.90 and 12.34. (2) He excluded from his Negro scores those six Ss who had earned *Full Scale* IQ's above 100 in order to compare more adequately the psychometric patterns of the remaining 26 with those reported on colored subjects by Machover (1943) and Teahan and Drews (1962). His analysis of their subtest averages did not indicate a patterning corroborating that found by these investigators.[10] (3) Levinson also separated the 32 Negroes according to their birthplace, 9 in the North and 23 in the South. The mean *Verbal, Performance,* and *Full Scale* IQ's of the Northern-born were 93.11, 89.67, and 91.11, respectively, while the comparable IQ's of the Southern-born were 83.09, 79.43, and 80.91. It appears[11] that the Southern-born Negroes performed relatively well on the subtests of *Digit Span, Information, Picture Arrangement,* and *Object Assembly,* but relatively poorly on the subtests of *Arithmetic, Digit Symbol, Block Design,* and *Picture Completion.* (4) In in-

---

[9]*J. Genet. Psychol.*

[10]The psychometric patterns found by both Machover and Teahan and Drews included relatively high scores in *Comprehension* and *Similarities* and relatively low scores in *Block Design.* For a review of these studies, see pp. 448-449, 65 and 71.

[11]From Levinson's Table 3.

terpreting his findings Levinson emphasized the *Verbal-Performance* differences obtained. He noted that performance tests usually demand a longer period of sustained attention and depend less on habit and more on the ability to attack new problems,[12] that the Negro child is exposed to large objects in his environment and has few toys, and that he is not rewarded for his ability to note small differences so he learns to evaluate objects by means of verbal cues rather than through emphasis on perceptual observation. The status of being homeless (for both colored and white), in addition, may indicate a withdrawal from reality, producing differences between verbal and performance tests; likewise, homeless men may be more field dependent than the domiciled population.[13]

Unselected Samples

Miner (1957) endeavored to obtain a picture of the intelligence of Americans by employing public opinion interviewing techniques. The testing was carried out as a part of a two-research program devoted to the standardization of the Tomkins-Horn *Picture Arrangement Test;* early work with this test had suggested the desirability of determining the effect of a subject's intelligence on his responses, "and for this reason a vocabulary test was included in the standard interview."[14]

The sample was collected by interviewers of Public Opinion Surveys, Inc. who used a sample design similar to that employed in national surveys conducted by this organization. The design provides stratification by seven regions, and within each region stratification by geographical distribution of the population, urban-rural strata, U. S. Census economic areas, and size of locality. Interviewers were assigned selected areas or clusters of blocks and were required to work within the boundaries of such areas, where they chose respondents on the basis of quota assignments by sex and age. In all, 1896 completed protocols were obtained during December, 1953, and January, 1954, from which a representative sample of 1500 cases was selected. The survey included 329 sampling areas in 228 localities (cities, towns, and counties), and in each sampling area from five to seven interviews were assigned. Among the 1500 cases, 153 were colored and 1347 white. Excluded from these samples were all inmates of institutions, members of the Armed Services living on the post, those individuals *completely unable* to speak English, and all who could speak some other language but were handicapped in the use of English.

---

[12]Levinson quotes from L. J. Cronbach, Essentials of Psychological Testing. New York: Harper, 1960.

[13]Thus bringing about a lowering of certain performance test scores. Levinson cites the work of Witkin reported in H. A. Witkin *et al.,* Psychological Differentiation; Studies of Development. New York: Wiley, 1962.

[14]Many psychologists hold the view that, unless there have been unusual developmental factors, a vocabulary test is one of the most valuable kinds of material used in deriving an index of a person's general intellectual ability. (Freeman, 1950, p. 158)

Form A of a 20-word, multiple-choice, steeply graded vocabulary test, which R. L. Thorndike had adapted from the longer vocabulary section of the *I. E. R. Intelligence Scale CAVD,* was administered to all persons interviewed.[15] Two words from each of the ten levels of the *CAVD Vocabulary* were included with five alternative answers for each. Form A was selected because Thorndike considered it to be slightly easier than Form B at the lower levels and somewhat more difficult at the higher levels. As will be observed in Table 8, the mean *Vocabulary* score of the white subjects was 11.06, a score significantly higher than the mean of 8.08 attained by the colored subjects. The variability of the whites also proved to be larger than that of the Negroes.

Miner tabulated the *Vocabulary* scores of all of his employed subjects, combining the races, and listed them according to their occupational group. The means of the nine groups ranged from a high score of 14.56 (Professional) to the low scores of 9.63 (Laboring) and 9.19 (Service). The Negro mean of 8.08 words was significantly below those of the *two lowest occupational groups* of the total population.[16]

In applying his results to the problem of utilizing our intellectual resources in the educational system, Miner estimated the percentage of nonstudents who could probably return to school at a higher educational level — if we should change from our age-grade system to an intelligence-grade system of promotion. Assuming that the intelligence-grade system is based upon verbal ability as measured by the *Vocabulary Test,* approximately 21 per cent of the whites and only 8 per cent of the Negroes would be capable of performance at a higher educational level. "There are apparently very few Negroes who left school at an educational level markedly below that which they might have attained."[17] Miner believed that the racial difference found may be largely the result of our philosophy of education that favors age rather than performance as a basis for promotion together with whatever conditions that may operate to restrict Negroes as a group to a relatively low intellectual level.

---

[15]Thorndike and Gallup (1944) have described the test as one of *verbal power,* noting that a vocabulary test may be criticized on the grounds that it depends heavily upon education and experience, "though many test users have felt that the effects of formal schooling upon word knowledge are much less than would seem superficially to be the case." However, it does investigate the nature of past learning rather than the ability to make novel adaptations. From a practical standpoint, the test has the advantage of maintaining the cooperation and good-will of the tested person, it is short, simple to administer, and sensible to the person being tested. Thorndike and Gallup found the median of college freshmen to be about 12.6 words on Form A. These authors expressed their firm conviction that data from this test as they stand do not provide a certain basis for judging innate intellectual differences between groups.

[16]t (Negro and Service groups) = 2.64; t (Negro and Laboring groups) = 3.48. Calculated by reviewer from author's Table 8.

[17]See Miner's original publication for thorough analysis of his work and the implications that he drew from it. For various criticisms of it, see reviews of A. W. Heim, John B. Carroll, and Harold Goldstein. (*in* Buros, 1959, pp. 1114-1116)

Summary

The nine studies surveyed in this chapter are varied in that they have included mental patients, men receiving voluntary treatment for venereal diseases, veterans tested under vocational guidance programs, hospital employees, transients and homeless men, and individuals selected to represent the general population above the age of nine years.

The colored averaged from 11 to 17 IQ points below the whites with whom they were compared, or from 16 to 32 points below the white norms; where the results were not given in terms of IQ the mean scores of the Negroes were below comparable groups of whites.

In six of the studies, either the *Wechsler-Bellevue* or the *WAIS* was the measuring instrument. There appears to be no evidence that the colored subjects scored consistently better or worse on the *Verbal* than on the *Performance Scale*.[18]

The Wechsler subtests of *Digit Symbol* and *Block Design* proved to have been the most difficult for the Negro groups on the whole, followed by *Arithmetic* and *Similarities*. The Negroes scored at their best on *Object Assembly* and *Comprehension*, followed by *Picture Arrangement*. Negroes tested on 20 words of the *CAVD Vocabulary* were found to be significantly inferior to the various groups with whom they were compared.

It is not improbable, as various authors have suggested, that the relatively inferior educational background of the colored subjects may have been partially responsible for the lower performances on *Arithmetic* as compared with some of the other subtests. And it may be that this test, as well as the *Digit Symbol* and *Block Design,* depends to a relatively large extent upon the manipulation of symbolic and abstract materials, in contrast to *Comprehension* and *Object Assembly* which emphasize practical information and concrete problem solving.[19] Other explanations offered for inferior performance upon some of the subtests assume a deficiency in active and sustained concentration, inferior ability to plan, inferior skill in separating the superficial and essential likenesses, and difficulty in reacting effectively to situations requiring psychomotor speed. While nature and nurture have not been separated as causative agents, it is evident that the investigators have leaned toward (or accepted outright) nurture as the principal factor contributing to these difficulties and deficiencies.

---

[18]Davidson *et al.* reported a *smaller difference* between white and colored veterans on the Verbal Scale; Scarborough found the *same difference* between white and colored veterans on the two scales; while Levinson found a *greater difference* between white and colored homeless men on the Verbal Scale.

[19]*Comprehension (WAIS)* is designed to test practical judgment and common sense. (Anastasi, 1961, p. 305)

Chapter VII

DEVIATES

In a majority of the studies of Negro intelligence emphasis has been placed upon *average* scores.[1] A review that attempts to be relatively complete should include the atypical individuals, those whose scores are *least* likely to be represented by their group means. Special consideration will be given here to the deviates, *i.e., the very superior or gifted* on the one hand and the *retarded or mentally defective* on the other. The former group will include, with a few exceptions, Ss whose IQ's are 140 or more; the latter, with certain exceptions, Ss with IQ's below 70.

THE GIFTED

A number of investigators have reported the presence of inferior deviates among Negro groups, a fact which apparently surprised neither psychologists nor laymen; however, it took Witty and Jenkins to impress psychologists with the presence of the gifted Negro child. In a survey of elementary textbooks published between 1947 and 1965 we found *Gifted Girl B* to be one of the favorite citations of the authors when they dealt with the topic of intelligence and race. She has been described not as a phenomenon but as evidence that the very highest ability may be found among Negroes and that "Negro blood is not always the limiting specter so universally proclaimed."

In Table 9 we have recorded two groups of studies: (1) those in which the frequency distributions of Negro and white IQ's were given by the authors,[2] the interest in the gifted being only incidental, and (2) the studies of the gifted child *per se,* including the work of Terman (1925), Proctor (1929), Terwilliger (1934), Jenkins (1936), Jones (1948), and Lucas (1948).

INCIDENTAL DISCOVERY OF GIFTED NEGROES[3]

In the majority of studies on *Southern* school children where IQ distributions were recorded there were no very superior Negroes. Among relatively large groups of colored children tested in the South by Garth and Whatley (1925), Hirsch (1926), Young (1929), L. B. Williams (1938), Bruce (1940), Marks

---

[1]Except in World War II where comparisons were usually made between white and colored deviates. In the studies of elementary, high school, and college Ss measures of variability and the amount of overlapping were frequently included in the authors' data.

[2]Enabling the reviewer to calculate percentages of high-scoring Ss. In certain instances these percentages were reported by the investigators.

[3]These are mainly *group IQ's,* as will be noted in Table 9.

(1941),[4] Gray (1945), Jordan (1947), Allman (1953), Caldwell (1954), and Kennedy, Van De Riet, and White (1963) there were no Ss scoring as high as 140.[5] Nor were gifted found among the small groups of Southern Negroes examined by Arlitt (1921), Patrick (1926), Farr (1931), Thurmond (1933), Beavers (1935), Bean (1942), Tomlinson (1944), Lawson (1945), Ellis (1947), Feacher (1947), Lewis (1947), Younge (1947), McClain (1948), Petway (1948), Fallin (1949), Hunt (1950), Reese (1951), Brown (1951), Dendy (1952), Sutton (1954), Berry (1954), and Wade (1954). There were, however, very superior group IQ's reported on Southern colored children by Goodenough (1926), Hewitt (1930), Mazique (1934), Jordan (1948), Cliff (1949), Lawrence (1951), Lindner (1962), and Swan (1964).

In the *Border* states and the District of Columbia, Klineberg (1928), Vernon (1936), Charles (1936), Gound (1938), and Ries (1940) found no IQ's above 139 among their Negro subjects. However, Lacy (1926), Strachan (1926),[6] and Long (1933) discovered gifted children among the colored tested.

In the *Northern* states, Clark (1923), Wallace (1932), and Canady (1936)[7] reported high-scoring colored children; whereas Schwegler and Winn (1920), Adler (1925), Lichtenstein and Brown (1938), Tanser (1939), Fensch (1942), and Griffith (1947) reported no gifted among their colored subjects.

Combining the above studies made in the three sections of the United States and the one in Canada, we find that there were approximately 61,000 white and 33,300 colored school children and high school pupils who were administered standard intelligence tests and on whom IQ frequency distributions were reported.[8] As will be noted in Table 9, there were 627 white and 41 colored subjects testing at 140 or above, the percentages of gifted among the respective white and colored groups being 1.03 and 0.12.

SPECIAL STUDIES OF THE GIFTED

Of the special studies of gifted children, Terman's was the pioneer and model and is by far the best known of them. The elementary public schools, principally Grades 3 to 8, of five California cities, including 164,640 white and

---

[4]Reported in Johnson, *Growing up in the Black Belt* (1941).

[5]For numbers of c and w Ss where no IQ's above 139 were found, see fn. 1, Table 9.

[6]Strachan's Ss are included, although she did not classify the high IQ's further than "above 135".

[7]*J. Negro Educ.*

[8]Excluding Clark's 163 white and 12 colored Ss who comprised 4.3 per cent and 2.4 per cent of their respective Los Angeles distributions, since the *National* IQ's obtained on these children have been reported as being incorrect. If one includes his cases the white and colored percentages of gifted become 1.22 and 0.16, respectively.

Where one group was tested twice (*e.g.*, the 1800 Negro Ss in the 5 Southeastern states were examined both by Lindner on *Draw-a-Man* and by Kennedy, Van De Riet, and White on *Stanford-Binet*) the total number of cases has been tabulated only once, the number of gifted in the two studies being averaged.

3360 colored pupils, were surveyed in an attempt to select the gifted. From each class the teacher was asked to name the most intelligent child, the next brightest, the third brightest, and the youngest child in her room; in addition, she was to name the child who, in her opinion was the brightest in the building during the previous semester. All of these nominees were given a group test and those children scoring in the highest 5 to 20 per cent of unselected samples were retained and given an abbreviated *Stanford-Binet* test. The complete *Stanford-Binet* was administered to all children making an IQ of 120 or more on the abbreviated form. A *Stanford-Binet* IQ of 140 was taken as the lower limit for inclusion among the gifted if the child was below 11 years of age. For those Ss from 11 to 14 years the lower limit was decreased correspondingly from 139 to 132. However, it should be noted that only 22 of the total group of 643 gifted children had IQ's below 140 and only one of them had an IQ below 135.

Only two gifted children were discovered among the Negroes, the percentages of gifted among the colored and white populations surveyed being 0.06 and 0.4, respectively. Therefore, gifted white children in the public schools of California were found about seven times as frequently as gifted colored children in proportion to their number. "Negroes represent 2 per cent of the total of the combined population of Los Angeles, San Francisco, Oakland, Alameda, and Berkeley, and furnish three-tenths of one per cent of our gifted group (two cases). As these cases are both part white (exact proportion of white blood is not known) they account for less than three-tenths of one per cent of the ancestral units in Table 8." (Terman, 1925, v. 1, p. 56) No doubt the difference between the percentages of gifted among the white and colored populations would have been greater had the numerous private schools been included in the study.

Washington, D. C. In an attempt to find the gifted in a part of the Negro population of Washington, Proctor (1929) examined the 1925 and 1926 *Dearborn* test records of the children in 26 colored elementary schools located in various neighborhoods in the District. In addition, teachers were requested to name children in their classes whom they considered bright, who were up to age and grade or were accelerated in grade placement. To the children thus recommended and to the pupils who had earned a score of 70 or more on the *Dearborn* the *Stanford-Binet* was administered. According to Terman's criteria for the gifted, there proved to be 13, or 0.2 per cent of the 8178 Negroes surveyed, who were very superior.

Lucas (1948) was able to find 187 colored pupils with IQ's of 120 or more, after searching the files of the *Research Department for Divisions 10-13* (Negro schools) for children with good intelligence test records. These pupils ranged from nursery school to senior high school, a number of them having been subjected to a variety of tests, usually of the verbal group type. Unfortunately, Lucas does not give the exact number of test records examined; his listing of 2 nursery school, 24 elementary schools, 5 junior high schools, and 3 senior high schools would suggest that half of the District of Columbia's schools for Negroes

TABLE

THE

| AUTHOR DATE | LOCATION | TEST | N | SUBJECTS | |
				AGE	GRADE
Goodenough, F. L. (1926)	Chattanooga, Mt. Pleasant, Tenn., Natchitoches, La., and California Cities	*Draw-a-Man*	w-1262 c· 682		1-4 1-4
Hirsch, N. D. M. (1926)	Massachusetts Mill Towns and Nashville, Tenn.	*Dearborn A, Dearborn C, Pintner- Cunningham*	w-5055[3] c- 449		1-9 1-9
Hewitt, A. (1930)	South	*Illinois General*	w-85 c- 90		7 7
Mazique, E. C. (1934)	Atlanta, Ga.	*Otis S-A, Intermediate*	c- 125		Elem, 7
Bice, H. V. (1938)	A North Carolina County	*Kuhlmann- Anderson*	w-438 c- 457		1-11 1-11
Jordan, A. M. (1947)	A North Carolina County	*Pintner Gen'l Ability: Verbal Series*	w-1980 c- 1214		1-8 1-8
Jordan, A. M. (1948)	Winston- Salem, N. C.	*Pintner-C,[4] P-Durost, P Intermed.*	w-5429 c- 4856		1-8 1-8

[1]The majority of the studies included in Tables 9 and 10 have been more fully summarized in Tables 1-5. Because no children with IQ's above 139 were located among them, the following have been omitted from Table 9: 58 w and 58 c (Schwegler and Winn, 1920); 124 w and 71 c (Arlitt, 1921); 47 w and 47 c (Patrick, 1926); 25 w and 129 c (Klineberg, 1928); 133 w and 137 c (Williams, H. J., 1935); 172 w and 172 c (Charles, 1936); 373 w and 354 c (Vernon, 1936); and 39 w and 76 c (Griffith, 1947). Likewise in the following studies *where only c were tested* and where no IQ of 140 or more was obtained: 243 c (Arlitt, 1922); 210 c (Barnes, 1923); 1272 c (Garth and Whatley, 1925); 200 c (Farr, 1931); 40 c (Thurmond, 1933); 212 c (Doran, 1934); 100 c (Beavers, 1935); 300 c (Williams, L. B., 1938); 100 c (Jones, 1940); 432 c (Bruce, 1940); 2250 c (Marks, 1941); 49 c (Bean, 1942); 31 c (Fensch, 1942); 150 c (Tomlinson, 1944); 25 c

NINE

GIFTED

METHOD OF SELECTION		IQ's 140 and Over[1]	
		N	PER CENT[2]
Bulk of w in foreign sections of cities. All c tested who were enrolled in the grades; all w tested who were enrolled if facts regarding racial stock available.	w	20	1.6
	c	2	0.3
Unselected.	w	29	0.6
	c	0	0.0
Three groups from one w sch, 5 groups from 2 c schs of a "southern school system".	w	1	1.2
	c	2	2.2
Two private schs; 46% had parents in professions & business.	c	2	1.6
All Ss in attendance in two schs tested.	w	2	0.5
	c	0	0.0
County predominantly rural. Tested in every sch & included all present.	w	24	1.2
	c	0	0.0
More than 95% of elementary sch children tested.	w	71	1.3
	c	2	0.04

(Lawson, 1945); 508 c (Gray, 1945); 64 c (Ellis, 1947); 41 c (Feacher, 1947); 27 c (Younge, 1947); 96 c (Lewis, 1947); 182 c (McClain, 1948); 100 c (Petway, 1948); 194 c (Fallin, 1949); 134 c (Hunt, 1950); 55 c (Reese, 1951); 173 c (Brown, 1951); 45 c (Dendy, 1952); 457 c (Allman, 1953); 50 c (Berry, 1954); 20 c (Sutton, 1954); 420 c (Caldwell, 1954); 32 c (Wade, 1954); and 1800 c (Kennedy, Van De Riet, and White, 1963).

[2]The majority of percentages reported in this table were calculated by the reviewer from authors' frequency tables.

[3]About 4/5 of w Ss were of foreign-born parents.

[4]Pintner-Cunningham, Pintner-Durost, and Pintner Intermediate.

TABLE

THE

AUTHOR DATE	LOCATION	TEST	N	SUBJECTS	
				AGE	GRADE
Cliff, E. M. (1949)	Atlanta, Ga.	CTMM[5] Otis Q-S, Beta	c- 116		7
Lawrence, W. C. (1951)	Anderson, Blount, and Knox Counties, Tennessee	Chicago Non-Verbal	c- 923	6-14	
Osborne, R. T. (1960)	County in a Southeastern State	CTMM	w-815 c- 446		6, 8, 10 6, 8, 10
Lindner, R. S. (1962)	Alabama, Florida, Georgia, South Carolina, Tennessee	Draw-a-Man	c- 1800		1-6
Swan, D. A. (1964)	Jackson, Miss.	SRA Primary Mental Abilities	w-5299 c- 3659		2, 5, 7, 10 2, 5, 7, 10
Lacy, L. D. (1926)	Oklahoma City, Okla.	Stanford-Binet, 1916	w-4874 c- 817		Kg-3 Kg-3
Strachan, L. (1926)	Kansas City, Mo.	Stanford-Binet, 1916	w-20,526 c- 984		Kg-3 Kg-3
Proctor, L. S. (1929)	Washington, D. C.	Dearborn, Stanford-Binet, 1916	c- 8178[9]		Elem
Long, H. H. (1933)	Washington, D. C.	Kuhlmann-Anderson	c- 4684		1A, 3A, 5A

[5]*California Test of Mental Maturity.*
[6]This is an IQ of 135.
*No c child earned an IQ of more than 119 on any of the 3 testings; the whites averaged slightly better than one child with an IQ of 140 or more on the testings.
[7]None of the 1800 Ss earned an IQ of over 130 when tested by *Stanford-Binet, 1960 Form* (Kennedy, Van De Riet, and White, 1963).

NINE *(continued)*

GIFTED

METHOD OF SELECTION		IQ's 140 and Over	
		N	PER CENT
Normative survey.	c	0	0.0
	c	1[6]	0.9
All of age range if present on testing days. Included cities except Knoxville.	c	2	0.2
All who were in 6th grade in '54, 8th grade in '56, & 10th in '58 and present on testing days.*	w	1	0.1
	c	0	0.0
Stratified random sampling.	c	19	1.1
Testing program administered to all present.	w	90	1.7
	c	3	0.1
All children tested.	w	38	0.8
	c	1	0.1
All kg tested if present; others tested in first 3 grades.	w	82[8]	0.4
	c	1	0.1
Ss in 26 schs, varied neighborhoods, given *Dearborn;* of these, selected 219 higher scoring Ss for *S-B.* Also tested some recommended by teachers.	c	13[10]	0.2
All children in these grades tested in 1930.	c	10	0.2

[8]Author did not classify the high IQ's further than "above 135".

[9]Elementary sch pop covered in survey. Not all of these children tested.

[10]Used Terman's scale of minimum score for inclusion in main group of gifted (Terman, 1925, Ch. 3), thereby including IQ's a little lower than 140 for those Ss over 11 years of age.

TABLE

THE

AUTHOR DATE	LOCATION	TEST	N	SUBJECTS		
				AGE	GRADE	

AUTHOR DATE	LOCATION	TEST	N	AGE	GRADE
Gound, H. D. (1938)	Bryan County, Okla.	*Otis Group, Form B*	w-190 c- 38		4-12 4-11
Ries, A. J. (1940)	Louisville, Ky.	*Otis S-A, Form B*	w-1871 c- 380		6A 6A
Jones, R. H. (1948)	Baltimore, Md.	*Kuhlmann-Anderson*	c- 2000[11]		7
Lucas, A. H. (1948)	Washington, D. C.	*ACE, CTMM, K-A, Otis, Pintner, S-B*	c- 20,000[12]		12
Clark, W. W. (1923)	Los Angeles, Cal.	*National*	all-4326 c- 510		Elem
Luckey, B. M. (1925)	Cleveland, Ohio	*Stanford-Binet, 1916*	w-10,447[14] c- 1574	5-16 5-16	
Terman, L. M. (1925)	Los Angeles, San Francisco, Oakland, and other California Cities	*Stanford-Binet, 1916*	w-164,640[9] c- 3360		1-8 1-8
Adler, H. M. (1925)	DuPage and Alexander Counties, Ill.	*Otis Primary, Haggerty Delta*	w-11,357 c- 1192		1-8 1-8

[11]Number estimated from reviewer from data supplied by Assistant Director of Dept. of Education in personal communication.

[12]Estimated by reviewer; in 1945-46 there were 49 elem & 12 secondary schs for Negroes in D.C. with 40,747 pupils enrolled. Author must have surveyed at least half of these schs.

[13]These percentages are higher than those obtained by Terman in Cal.; Clark, in personal communication, said that the *National* IQ secured on these children was about 5 points too high.

NINE (continued)
GIFTED

METHOD OF SELECTION		IQ's 140 and Over	
		N	PER CENT
Tested about two thirds w and one third c enrolled in two schs.	w	2	1.1
	c	0	0.0
All children entering 7th grade in Sept '38 who had been tested in 6A in preceding Spring.	w	7	0.4
	c	0	0.0
All lower 7th grades tested by Research Dept. Selected the 23 Ss with IQ's above 119 from 4 of the 5 Negro junior high schs.	c	0	0.0
Files of Research Dept, Div 10-13, searched for records of pupils who had earned IQ's of 120 or higher on initial test. Pupils from 2 nursery schs, 24 elem, 5 junior high sch, 3 senior high schs represented.	c	25	0.1
All c from 5 mixed schs; the 4326 includes total pop of 15 representative elementary schs, Negroes and Mongoloids as well as whites.	w	163	4.3[13]
	c	12	2.4
Board of Educ Clinic cases from preceding 2 years. Ss brought to clinic because of unusual slowness or great ability in sch.	w	43	0.4
	c	0	0.0
1. From each class teacher named most intelligent, next, third; youngest; brightest in bldg during previous semester. 2. Nominees given group test. Retained those scoring in top 5-20% of unselected samples. 3. Gave abbreviated S-B. 4. Complete S-B to all earning IQ of 120 or more on abbrev S-B.[15]	w	641	0.4
	c	2	.06
All public sch children in the two counties tested if present when tests given.	w	198	1.7
	c	0	0.0

[14]Number includes 2964 Ss of Amer-born parents and 7483 of foreign-born parents.

[15]Terman noted that by his technique he probably missed about 20 per cent of qualified cases; inclusion of these would increase the percentage of gifted from 0.4 to 0.5.

IQ of 140 was lower limit for inclusion of Ss under 11 years of age; for those from 11-14, the lower limit was decreased; among his gifted group he included 21 whose IQ's were between 135-139 and one case whose IQ was between 130-134.

TABLE

THE

AUTHOR DATE	LOCATION	TEST	N	SUBJECTS		
				AGE	GRADE	
Wallace, E. B. (1932)	Cincinnati, Ohio	*Detroit Alpha, Otis, Adv.*	c- 465		5-6	
Terwilliger, A. J. (1934)	New York,[16] Yonkers, and Mt. Vernon, N. Y.	*Stanford-Binet, 1916*	c- 7057[9]		Elem	
Canady, H. G. (1936)	Evanston, Ill.	*Stanford-Binet, 1916*	w-25 c- 48		Kg-8 Kg-8	
Jenkins, M. D. (1936)	Chicago, Ill.	*Stanford-Binet, 1916*	c-8145[9]		3-8	
Lichtenstein, M., and Brown, A. W. (1938)	Chicago, Ill.	*Kuhlmann-Anderson*	w-480 c- 178		4-6 4-6	
Tanser, H. A. (1939)	Kent County, Ontario	*National*	w-386 c- 103		1-8 1-8	
		Pintner Non-Lang.	w-387 c- 102		3-8 3-8	
		Pintner-Paterson (short)	w-211 c- 162		1-8 1-8	

[16]Roselle, N. J. was also surveyed, but high IQ's in this city were listed only as "over 125"; consequently they are not included in this table. In the other three cities (N.Y., Mt. Vernon, and Yonkers) no child of 11 or more earned an IQ of 130 or more.

[17]The area in which these 7 schs were located was in general of somewhat higher

NINE *(concluded)*

GIFTED

METHOD OF SELECTION		IQ's 140 and Over[1]	
		N	PER CENT
From 4 publ schs, 2 of them elementary and 2 junior high schs; does not give method of selection.	c	5	1.1
Three schs in Harlem surveyed in addition to those in 3 other cities. Technique like that of Terman (above). In one sch there was a file of IQ's determined by group tests; gave S-B to all having scored above 125 on group.	c	2	0.03
Selected groups tested 2 times, once by c and once by w examiner; method of selection not given. Results in this table of first test only.	w c	3 1	12.0 2.1
Surveyed 7 elementary public schs; method like[17] that of Terman (above).	c	30	0.4
All children in 4 public schs in deteriorating neighborhood.	w c	1[18] 0	0.2 0.0
As far as practicable tested all pupils in the one urban and six rural schs.	w c	7 0	1.8 0.0
	w c	25 0	6.5 0.0
	w c	19 0	9.0 0.0

socioeconomic level than average Negro residential section. Wilkerson (1936) questioned the assumption that the populations of these 7 schools were representative of the total c elementary population in Chicago.

[18]This S's IQ was merely located as being between 130-140.

were canvassed.[9] Of the 187 whose IQ's were 120 or more, there were 25 with IQ's of 140 or above. This estimated 0.1 per cent, while higher than that found for colored children in California, is but half the percentage secured by Proctor. Regarding the latter point, we would remind the reader that the size of Lucas' total group surveyed was merely estimated by the reviewer, and that Lucas included high school pupils whereas Proctor limited her investigation to elementary school children. Relative to the point that larger percentages of gifted Negroes were located in the District schools than in California, we wish to note that: (1) due to the relatively complete group testing program in Washington probably fewer of the gifted colored children were missed than in California;[10] and (2) it is not unlikely that the California teachers (who were white) were less likely to name a colored than a white child as "most intelligent", etc.

New York City Area. Terwilliger (1934) made a study of Negro children with IQ's above 125 in the New York City area. Altogether, there were 5481 Harlem school children canvassed, 500 Negro children in the public schools of Yonkers, 1076 colored pupils in the Mt. Vernon public schools, 465 in the public schools of Roselle, New Jersey, and an unreported number in Tarrytown, New York. The author cited two methods by which he selected the gifted. In one, there was a file of IQ's of children who had been tested either by the *Pintner Rapid Survey* or the *National;* from this Terwilliger selected approximately 45 children whose IQ's were above 125. These children were then tested by the *Stanford-Binet.* The other method, which he used where there were no available data on the children's IQ's, required administering the *Stanford-Binet* to the three youngest children in the high section of each grade and to from one to three additional children from each grade selected by their respective teachers. Among the 7057 New York City, Yonkers, and Mt. Vernon pupils surveyed there were eleven with IQ's of 125 or over.[11] The IQ's of the eleven children ranged from 125 to 157 with two of the number earning 140 or more.[12] The gifted in the New York area comprised .03 per cent of the school populations surveyed.

Chicago. Jenkins (1935, 1936) conducted a systematic search for superior children among 8145 Negroes in Grades 3 to 8 in seven Chicago public schools. Using a method similar to Terman's, he asked classroom teachers to nominate the child thought to be the most intelligent, the child doing the best classroom work, and each child one or more half-years "under age" for his grade. Jenkins administered the *McCall Multi-Mental Scale* to the 539 nominated; and to all

---

[9]Since the 1945-46 enrollment comprised 40,747 pupils attending 49 elementary and 12 secondary schools for Negroes in the District, we have estimated that at least 20,000 pupils of this racial group were contained in Lucas' survey.

[10]Terman estimated that about 20 per cent of the cases who could have qualified were omitted by his technique.

[11]In addition, there was one child in Roselle who had a *Binet* IQ "above 125", but since there was no indication as to how much above 125, the Roselle group had to be excluded.

[12]No child scoring above 129 was as old as 11 years when tested.

earning an IQ of 120 or more on this test, and to several who scored below 120, he gave an abbreviated form of the *Stanford-Binet*. By this technique, Jenkins located 96 colored children with *Stanford-Binet* IQ's of 120 or more; seven additional subjects were found by testing siblings of these children and other children not recommended by their teachers, the entire group of 103 Ss including three who were not in the grades or schools surveyed. Of these superior children, 29 had IQ's of 140 or more, making up approximately 0.3 per cent of the school populations surveyed. Since Terman would have included one of the children who had an IQ of 137 in his gifted group due to the fact that he was over 11 years of age, the total gifted Negro group may be said to have consisted of 30 Ss, or about 0.37 per cent of the school populations.

This percentage is higher than that found for Negroes in California, the District of Columbia, and the New York City area, and compares favorably with the percentage of gifted (0.4) reported for white children in California. However, Jenkins' schools were probably not representative of the Negro child population of Chicago. E. F. Frazier, in an earlier study of the Chicago Negro population, had divided the South Side (where Negroes are largely concentrated) into seven concentric zones varying in socioeconomic level. Jenkins chose for his seven schools only one located in an inferior zone, two located in an average zone, and four located within the two superior zones. "The residential area in which the typical subject of this study lives is of somewhat higher socio-economic level than the area occupied by the average Negro school child of Chicago." (1935, p. 9)

Wilkerson (1936), in a review of the dissertation, observed that the value of the research would have been enhanced had Jenkins so selected his samples as to be in a position to generalize relative to the total elementary school population of Chicago, and that while Jenkins' race should have served as a positive factor in establishing rapport, "It would have been well, however, had he guarded against the influence of possible unconscious bias, together with other factors, by having his IQ ratings checked, at least in part, by another competent person." (p. 129)

Later, in referring to the upper limit of ability of Negroes, Jenkins (1948) wrote: "I am not attempting here to show that approximately as many Negro children as white are to be found at the higher levels of psychometric intelligence. There appears little doubt that the number of very bright Negro children is relatively smaller than the number of bright white children in the total American population. Nevertheless, it is apparent that children of very superior psychometric intelligence may be found in many Negro populations, and that the upper limit of the range attained by the extreme deviates is higher than is generally believed." (p. 400) Garrett (1947) pointed out that in a sample of 8000 white school children at least 800 can be expected to possess IQ's of 120 or higher, as contrasted with the 103 Negro school children having IQ's of 120 or higher found by Jenkins in Chicago. Hollingworth, likewise, observed that the American Negro is one of the groups thus far yielding few superior deviates.

However, ... "superior deviates apparently may arise from any ethnic stock at present existing in the United States—a feature of the situation as important as are the differences in central tendency among stocks." (1940, p. 57)[13]

Baltimore. R. H. Jones (1948), in an effort to find superior children, examined the records of all pupils in the lower seventh grade in four of the five Negro junior high schools in Baltimore. While she discovered 23 pupils whose *Kuhlmann-Anderson* IQ's were 120 or more, she reported none obtaining an IQ of more than 132. Unfortunately, Jones omitted the names of the junior high schools where her subjects were enrolled and did not give the total number in the lower seventh.[14]

SUMMARY

Terman, Proctor, Lucas, Terwilliger, Jenkins, and Jones, in searching for high-scoring children among a combined school population of nearly 49,000 Negroes, found a total of 72 gifted children. This number comprised approximately 0.15 per cent of the colored populations surveyed.

Of the 33,293 colored tested by various investigators who were not primarily interested in finding the gifted but who, nevertheless, reported IQ frequency distributions, 41, or *0.12 per cent,* tested 140 or above. And if one were to include Clark's twelve gifted Negroes, the total number and percentage become respectively, 53 and *0.16.*[15]

These two estimates of the gifted among colored school children, *i.e., 0.15* and *0.12 per cent* (or *0.15* and *0.16*) are very similar in spite of the fact that the methodology by which they were selected differed, in spite of the fact that the former was determined by the *Stanford-Binet* generally and the latter by a variety of tests, and in spite of the fact that the former was based upon city surveys in the Northern and Border areas whereas the latter included smaller cities and towns and Southern as well as Border and Northern sections of the country.

THE RETARDED

Fifty-five of the studies included in Table 10 have been more fully summarized in Tables 2 to 5 where the measures of central tendency were of primary consideration. Wherever the frequency distributions were recorded we have

---

[13]10,447 white (including 7483 of foreign-born parents) and 1574 colored children were brought to the Cleveland Board of Education Clinic during a 2-year period, either because of unusual slowness or marked ability in school; 0.4 per cent of the white and none of the colored earned IQ's above 139. (Luckey, 1925)

[14]Upon inquiry, the Assistant Director, Dept. Education, in personal communication, gave 5253 as the number of c enrolled in the five junior high schools in Oct., 1947. It seems probable that at least 2000 children's records were examined by Jones.

[15]As compared with *1.03* or *1.22 per cent* among white children—depending upon whether or not Clark's gifted were included.

attempted to give the percentages of IQ's below 70. In certain instances the IQ's were reported as "below 65" and in these cases they have been so noted.

In addition, we have included in this section ten special studies relating to mental health surveys, clinical and institutional groups, or to special classes for the retarded. See: St. Louis *Report to the Superintendent . . .* (1925), Luckey (1925), Stowell (1931), Town (1938), Wagner (1938), Engel (1941-42), Lemkau, Tietze, and Cooper (1942), Malzberg (1943), Atchison (1955), and Webb (1963).

Unselected Samples

An examination of Table 10 will show that the percentages of low IQ's earned by both white and colored samples are by no means constant, a fact which may be related to a number of variables, such as geographic location, size of community, number of cases, age and grade, method of selection, and test employed. With very few exceptions, however, the percentages of low IQ's are higher for the Negro than for the white groups examined. In order to make an overall comparison of deficiency rates among the racial groups, we have combined all of the studies in the table, with the exception of institutional, clinical, and other special studies listed above. The numbers exclude duplicates. Wherever the same children have been tested more than once (Thurmond, 1933; Tanser, 1939; Cliff, 1949; Osborne, 1960; Lindner, 1962, and Kennedy, Van De Riet, and White, 1962, 1963) the number of cases has been recorded once and the number of retarded averaged.

Of 33,979 colored children tested, 5469 of them, or *16.10 per cent,* secured IQ's below 70. Similarly, among 64,834 white children examined, 1667, or *2.57 per cent,* earned IQ's at this relatively low level. Therefore, the percentage of low-scoring deviates among Negroes tested was *more than six times* that found among whites. It should be borne in mind, of course, that these percentages are not estimates of the retarded in the general populations but refer to the retarded in grade and high schools. It may be presumed, moreover, that these figures probably underestimate the percentages of retarded among school children because: (1) children absent on testing days would probably have obtained lower IQ's than those present; (2) in certain instances the experimental design limited the Ss to those who had had all of their education within one city school system (thereby eliminating transients) or to those who over a period of time had been neither accelerated nor failed; and (3) in other instances those children who had been identified as retarded had been previously placed in special schools, or else the teachers were asked not to include those considered to be retarded. However, we have found no reason to believe that these factors operated more to the advantage of the white than of the Negro groups tested.[16]

---

[16]Some years ago, Pintner reported that *1.3 per cent* of a random sampling of 4925 American school children (excluding those in special classes) earned *IQ's below 60,* with *6.6 per cent*

Special Studies of the Retarded

One of the early special studies of retarded children was made in St. Louis (1925). One hundred twenty-six colored and 1398 white problem children, including those who were considered (by their teachers) eligible for schools for the mentally deficient and boys who had been suspended and were possible "candidates" for the Boys' Class, were given either the *Pintner-Cunningham* or the *Terman Group* test. Although the number of Negro problem children was proportionally larger than the number of Negroes in the school system, a higher percentage of this group was found to have inferior IQ's than the white problem children; *35.7 per cent* of the Negro cases, as opposed to *7.6 per cent* of the white cases, secured IQ's below 65.

During the same year, Luckey reported on 10,447 white and 1574 colored children who had been brought to the Cleveland Board of Education Clinic during the preceding two years, either because of unusual slowness or exceptional ability in school. The percentage of colored with IQ's below 65 proved to be two or three times that of the whites with IQ's below this point.[17]

Stowell (1931) found the mean IQ of the colored inmates of the District of Columbia Training School for Feebleminded to be 48.1; and that of the whites, 39.4. The higher mean of the colored is probably not significant in view of the fact that the colored in the District contributed about twice as many institutional cases as one would expect from their numbers in Washington. In 1930, Negroes comprised *27.1 per cent* of the population of the District of Columbia, whereas the number of colored feebleminded in the Training School was nearly the equal of the whites.[18]

Wagner (1938) presents diagnoses of the 705 whites and the 240 Negroes who made up the total of the new resident admissions to the Psychiatric Pavilion of the Cincinnati General Hospital for one year, beginning July, 1936. Eleven of the colored and 33 of the white admissions were described as mentally deficient. Since at the time of the study the population of Cincinnati included approximately 418,000 whites and 57,000 Negroes, the patients diagnosed as feebleminded represented an incidence of 7.8 per 100,000 for the whites and 19.2 per 100,000 for the Negro population.

---

achieving *IQ's below 70*. (1931, p. 340) However, he did not give the location of his sample, the age range, nor the proportions of colored and white composing it. Other investigators have more recently estimated the mentally retarded to include about *4.36 per cent* of the Baltimore, Md., school children between Ages 10-14 (doubtless all races—mainly Negro and white—combined). It is interesting that our estimate of *2.57 per cent* retardation (below 70 IQ) among American white school children is the same as that reported among English school children, 10-14 years of age, i.e., *2.56 per cent*. (*The Baltimore and English studies reported in* Tyler, 1965, p. 369)

[17]Depending upon whether or not the comparable white groups included those of foreign-born parents or only those of American-born parents. More than 70 per cent of the white children were of foreign-born parents.

[18]Ths study has not been included in Table 10.

Town (1938) selected all persons belonging to four racial or nationality groups who were examined at the Psychological Clinic of the Children's Aid Society of Buffalo over a five-year period. The 1673 cases included a large number of American-born children who had at least one parent born in the United States, a Polish group, an Italian group, and a colored group. The percentages of retardation for these groups were, respectively, 10.5, 22.5, 24.5, and 23. Because of the largely verbal content of the tests and the fact that the Polish and Italian children were bilingual, the author was of the opinion that the percentages of feeblemindedness among the two foreign groups could not be directly compared with the percentages among the native white and native colored groups. Among the two native groups, however, the white group contributed less than half as many retarded as the Negro group in proportion to their representation in the clinic and in proportion to their numbers in the Buffalo population.

Engel (1941-42) reported that 3169 children of school age were enrolled in the Detroit special public school classes for the retarded during 1938-39. The pupils, all of whom had attended these special classes for one or more years, had been given mental ratings obtained from the *Stanford-Binet* and the *Detroit Learning Aptitude Tests,* supplemented by tests such as *Picture Completion, Pintner-Paterson* or form boards. The percentage of colored children in these classes was *21.4* which was almost twice that found in the general school enrollment. Engel observed that many of the families had come from Southern rural areas where schooling was so limited that their children presented a serious retardation problem when they entered a well-organized city school system.[18]

Lemkau, Tietze, and Cooper (1942) made a survey of mental hygiene problems in the Eastern Health District of Baltimore, an area with a population of 57,000—*77 per cent* of whom were white and *23 per cent* colored. In addition to studying the results of the two special censuses in 1933 and 1936[19] the authors examined the records of various agencies—such as special classes for the retarded, state training schools, various courts, private and public hospitals, and child welfare organizations. Mental deficiency among Negro children was reported to be prevalent; in fact, one out of every 12 colored children as compared with one white child out of every 43 was found to be retarded (Table 10). On the other hand, the adults of the two races showed almost equal mental deficiency rates, *i.e., 0.65* and *0.72 per cents.* The authors were of the opinion that this finding suggested that certain behavior patterns which would be called socially incompe-

---

[19]Conducted by the Department of Biostatistics of the School of Hygiene and Public Health, Johns Hopkins University, 1933; and the National Health Survey, 1936. The Eastern Health District was described as an urban residential district whose economic status was somewhat less favorable than that of the general urban population.

TABLE

THE

AUTHOR DATE	LOCATION	TEST	N	SUBJECTS	
				AGE	GRADE
Arlitt, A. H. (1921)	Not given	*Stanford- Binet, 1916*	w-124[2] c- 71		Primary Primary
Arlitt, A. H. (1922)	New Orleans and near Philadelphia	*Stanford- Binet, 1916*	c- 243	5-15	
Garth, T. R., and Whatley, C. A. (1925)	Dallas and Fort Worth, Tex.	*National*	c- 1272		3-8
Hirsch, N. D. M. (1926)	Massachusetts Mill Towns and Nashville, Tenn.	*Dearborn A, Dearborn C, Pintner- Cunningham*	w-5055 c- 449		1-9 1-9
Goodenough, F. L. (1926)	Chattanooga, Mt. Pleasant, Tenn., Natchitoches, La., and California Cities	*Draw-a-Man*	w-1262 c- 682		1-4 1-4
Patrick, J. R. (1926)	Athens, Ga.	*Otis S-A, Intermediate*	w-47 c- 47		7 7
Hewitt, A. (1930)	South	*Illinois General*	w-85 c- 90		7 7
Farr, T. J. (1931)	Newton County, Tenn.	*Illinois General*	c- 200		All

[1]The majority of the studies included in this table have been more fully summarized in Tables 1-5. The percentages reported were generally calculated by the reviewer from authors' frequency tables.

TEN
RETARDED

METHOD OF SELECTION		IQ's below 70[1]	
		N	PER CENT
	w	18	14.5
	c	8	11.2
From NO publ & private schs & playgrounds; Pa Ss all in publ schs. Method of selection not given.	c	21	8.6
	c	516	40.5
White Ss from the mill towns; c from Nashville. Unselected.	w	310	6.1
	c	77	17.1
Bulk of w in foreign sections of cities. All c tested who were enrolled in the grades; all w tested who were enrolled if facts regarding racial stock available.	w	68	5.4
	c	231	33.9
All c in one sch in Grade 7; 42% w in Grade 7, does not say how selected.	w	1	2.1
	c	21	44.7
Three groups from one w sch, 5 groups from 2 c schs. All from same sch system. All in attendance tested.	w	0	0.0
	c	12	13.3
Selected the 2 largest village schs & tested the 200 in attendance.	c	118	59.0

[2]This number includes 81 of Italian parents (and therefore presumably bilingual) and 43 of native-born parents, all of whom were selected from a larger number on the basis of their inferior or very inferior social status. The 71 include the total group of c, 88% of whom were of inferior or very inferior status. Location not given.

| AUTHOR DATE | LOCATION | TEST | N | SUBJECTS | |
				AGE	GRADE
Thurmond, S. (1933)	Clarke County, Ga.	*Illinois General*	c- 40	12	
		Arthur Point Scale			
		Stanford-Binet, 1916			
Mazique, E. C. (1934)	Atlanta, Ga.	*Otis S-A, Intermediate*	c- 125		Elem and 7
Beavers, L. L. (1935)	Atlanta, Ga.	*Otis S-A, Intermediate*	c- 100		9
Williams, L. B. (1938)	Mexia, Tex.	*Otis S-A, Intermediate*	c- 300		8-11
Bice, H. V. (1938)	A North Carolina County	*Kuhlmann-Anderson*	w-438 c- 457		1-11 1-11
Marks,[3] E. (1941)	Alabama, Georgia, Mississippi, North Car, Tennessee	*Kuhlmann-Anderson*	c- 2250		
Tomlinson, H. (1944)	Austin, Tex.	*Stanford-Binet, 1937*	c- 150	4-9	
Gray, W. H., Jr., (1945)	Louisiana	*Otis S-A, Higher*	c-508		Senior
Jordan, A. M. (1947)	North Carolina County	*Pintner Gen'l Ability: Verbal Series*	w-1980 c- 1214		1-8 1-8

[3]*In* Johnson, C. S. (1941).

TEN *(continued)*

RETARDED

METHOD OF SELECTION		N	IQ's below 70	
				PER CENT
All 12-year-olds tested who were present on testing days.	c	26		65.0
	c	7		17.5
	c	7		17.5
Two private schs; method of selection not given.	c	5		4.0
Ss in 2 publ jr high schs selected at random; whole class in Atlanta University Laboratory High Sch.	c	16		16.0
Method of selection not given.	c	8		2.7
All pupils in attendance in the 2 schs tested.	w	18		4.1
	c	70		15.3
Rural c children in 8 counties: 2 Ala, 1 Ga, 2 Miss, 1 NC, & 2 Tenn.	c	408		18.1
All available pairs of c sibs at the 2 age levels of 4-6 and 7-9.	c	1[4]		0.7
29 high schs representing 22 parishes.	c	14		2.8
Every sch surveyed in a predominantly rural county. All pupils present tested.	w	170		8.6
	c	418		34.4

[4]Number and percentage of cases below IQ of 65.

TABLE

THE

AUTHOR DATE	LOCATION	TEST	N	SUBJECTS	
				AGE	GRADE
McClain, B. M. (1948)	Waugh, Ala.	Otis Q-S, Gamma	c- 182		7-12
Jordan, A. M. (1948)	Winston-Salem, N. C.	P-Cunningham, P-Durost, Pintner Intermediate, Form A	w-5429 c- 4856		1-8 1-8
Fallin, W. (1949)	Bessemer, Ala.	California Capacity Questionnaire	c- 194		10-12
Cliff, E. M. (1949)	Atlanta, Ga.	California Test of Mental Maturity Otis Q-S, Beta	c- 116		7
Hunt, W. B. (1950)	Hardeman County, Tenn.	Otis Q-S, Beta	c- 134		4-5
Reese, H. S. (1951)	Wetumpka, Ala.	California Test of Mental Maturity	c- 55		10-12
Brown, A. S. (1951)	Pike County, Ala.	California Test of Mental Maturity	c- 173		
Lawrence, W. C. (1951)	Anderson, Blount, and Knox Counties, Tenn.	Chicago Non-Verbal	c- 923	6-14	
Dendy, A. P. H. (1952)	Landrum, S. C.	California Test of Mental Maturity	c- 45		7

TEN *(continued)*

RETARDED

METHOD OF SELECTION		N	IQ's below 70
			PER CENT
Jr & senior high sch pupils of Montgomery County Training School.	c	19	10.4
More than 95% of all elementary sch children tested.	w	218	4.0
	c	878	18.1
Test administered to Dunbar High School pupils. Method of selection not given.	c	27	13.9
Normative sampling indicated.	c	8	6.9
	c	34	29.3
Fourth- & 5th-grade pupils in 6 of the 38 county schs.	c	59	44.0
Normative sampling indicated. One senior high sch.	c	3	5.5
Pupils from 8 junior high schs. Method of selection not given.	c	85	49.1
All of age range tested if in attendance; included cities except Knoxville.	c	340	36.8
Tested all present.	c	9	20.0

TABLE

THE

| AUTHOR DATE | LOCATION | TEST | N | SUBJECTS | |
				AGE	GRADE
Sutton, L. J. (1954)	Duplin County, N. C.	*California Test of Mental Maturity*	c- 20		8
Berry, B. Y. (1954)	Brundidge, Ala.	*Otis Q-S, Gamma*	c- 50		10-12
Wade, A. C. (1954)	Candor, N. C.	*Otis Q-S, Alpha*	c- 32		1
Caldwell, M. B. (1954)	Alabama, Florida, Georgia, North Carolina, South Carolina	*WISC*	c- 420		1-7
Osborne, R. T. (1960)	County in a Southeastern State	*California Test of Mental Maturity*	w-815 c- 446		6, 8, 10
Lindner, R. S. (1962)	Alabama, Florida, Georgia, South Carolina, Tennessee	*Draw-a-Man*	c- 1800[7]		1-6
Kennedy, W. A., Van De Riet, V., and White, J. C., Jr. (1962, 1963)	Alabama, Florida, Georgia, South Carolina, Tennessee	*Stanford, Binet, 1960*	c- 1800		1-6
Swan, D. A. (1964)	Jackson, Miss.	*SRA Primary Mental Abilities*	w-5299 c- 3659		2, 5, 7, 10

[5]The experimental designs of Caldwell (1954) and Osborne (1960) served to reduce the number of mentally deficient tested.

TEN *(continued)*

RETARDED

METHOD OF SELECTION		N	IQ's below 70 PER CENT
Tested all 8th-grade pupils in one sch.	c	2	10.0
Random sampling among girls of Pike County Training School.	c	5	10.0
Method of selection not given other than that Ss were from Brutonville Elem Sch where author taught first grade.	c	1	3.1
Random sampling within community; all schs urban. *No S tested who was suspected as being mentally deficient.*[6]	c	26	6.2
All who were in 6th grade in 1954, in the 8th grade in '56, & in 10th grade in '58 (*i.e.* regular promotions, remained in county, & present on 3 testing days).[6]	w c	3 73	0.37 16.4
Stratified random sampling.	c	222	12.3
Stratified random sampling.	c	331	18.4
Testing program administered to all present in the 4 grades in 1960.	w c	36 600	0.68 16.4

[6]The w and c *IQ's below 70* in this study represent the averages of the three tests.
[7]The same subjects were tested by the *Draw-a-Man* and the *Stanford-Binet, 1960 Form.*

| AUTHOR DATE | LOCATION | TEST | N | SUBJECTS | |
				AGE	GRADE
"Report to the Superintendent ......" (1925)	St. Louis, Mo.	*Pintner-Cunningham, Terman Group*	w-1398 c- 126		
Lacy, L. D. (1926)	Oklahoma City, Okla.	*Stanford-Binet, 1916*	w-4874 c- 817		Kg-3 Kg-3
Strachan, L. (1926)	Kansas City, Mo.	*Stanford-Binet, 1916*	w-20,526 c- 984		Kg-3 Kg-3
Long, H. H. (1933)	Washington, D. C.	*Kuhlmann-Anderson*	c- 4684		1A 3A 5A
Charles, C. M. (1936)	St. Louis, Mo.	*Kuhlmann-Anderson*	w-172 c- 172	12-16 12-16	
Vernon, J. O. (1936)	Muskogee County, Okla.	*Otis Primary*	w-123 c- 154		1-4 1-4
		McCall Multi-Mental	w-250 c- 200		3-12 3-10
Gound, H. D. (1938)	Bryan County, Okla.	*Otis Group, Form B*	w-190 c- 38		4-12 4-11
Ries, A. J. (1940)	Louisville, Ky.	*Otis S-A, Form B*	w-1871 c- 380		6A 6A
Lemkau, P., Tietze, C., and Cooper, M. (1942)	Baltimore, Md.	Not given	w-43,890 c- 13,110	3-65 & over 3-65 & over	

[8]Number & percentage of cases below 65 IQ. C comprised 6.7 per cent of all first-grade children in 1924-25 and 8.2 per cent of those considered eligible for special schools.

TEN *(Continued)*

RETARDED

METHOD OF SELECTION		N	IQ's below 70 PER CENT
Children given tests who were thought to be eligible for special schs for mentally deficient; also boys who had been suspended & were possible candidates for the Boys' Class. All were problem cases.	w	106	7.6[8]
	c	45	35.7
Tests given to all Ss.	w	99	2.0
	c	70	8.6
All kg Ss tested if present; those absent or not attending kg, tested in first 3 grades.	w	165[9]	0.80
	c	43	4.4
All children in these grades tested in 1930.	c	338	7.2
Schs in diff parts of city; method of selection within schs not given. W & c boys of about same social status.	w	2	1.2
	c	6	3.5
Tested all w and c present in the 2 schs.	w	1	0.81
	c	11	7.1
	w	2	0.80
	c	8	4.0
Tested about ⅔ w and ⅓ c enrolled in the 2 schs.	w	12	6.3
	c	16	42.1
All children entering 7th grade, Sept '38, who had been tested in the Louisville 6A the preceding spring.	w	75	4.0
	c	53	13.9

Survey of mental hygiene problems found in Eastern Health Dist of Baltimore.		*10-14 Years*	
	w	108	2.6
	c	131	9.8
		7-16 Years	
	w	187	2.3
	c	216	8.2
		20 Years & Over	
	w	178	0.65
	c	59	0.72

[9]IQ's of *65 and below* reported by Strachan. With the inclusion of "foreign" w Ss, the number is 206, the per cent, 1.0.

TABLE

THE

AUTHOR DATE	LOCATION	TEST	N	SUBJECTS	
				AGE	GRADE
Schwegler, R. A., and Winn, E. (1920)	Lawrence, Kan.	*Stanford-Binet, 1916*	w-58 c- 58		7-8 7-8
Barnes, J. R. (1923)	Lawrence, Kan.	*Stanford-Binet, 1916*	c- 210		1-Jr H.S.
Clark, W. W. (1923)	Los Angeles, Cal.	*National*	all-4326 c- 510		Elem
Luckey, B. M. (1925)	Cleveland, Ohio	*Stanford-Binet, 1916*	w-10,447[10] c- 1574	Mainly 5-16	
Adler, H. M. (1925)	DuPage, Alexander Counties, Ill.	*Otis Primary, Haggerty Delta*	w-11,357 c- 1192		1-8 1-8
Wallace, E. B. (1932)	Cincinnati, Ohio	*Detroit Alpha, Otis Advanced*	c- 239 c- 226 •		5 6
Doran, A. T. (1934)	Chicago, Ill.	*Otis S-A, Intermediate*	c- 212		8
Williams, H. J. (1935)	Milwaukee, Wis.	*Otis S-A, Intermediate*	w-133 c- 137		6 6
Canady, H. G. (1936)	Evanston, Ill.	*Stanford-Binet, 1916*	w-25 c- 48		Kg-8 Kg-8

[10]The number of w Ss includes 2964 of American-born parents & 7483 of foreign-born parents.

[11]N and percentages of IQ's below 65; 9% of w of American-born parents had IQ's below 65.

TEN *(Continued)*
RETARDED

METHOD OF SELECTION		N	IQ's below 70 PER CENT
All c in the 2 grades; random sampling of w.	w	4	6.9
	c	6	10.4
	c	29	13.8
All c from 5 mixed schs; the 4326 includes total pop of 15 representative elementary schs.	"w"	45	1.2
	c	14	2.7
Board of Educ Clinic cases from preceding 2 yrs; Ss brought to clinic because of unusual slowness or great ability in sch.	w	1663[11]	15.9
	c	456	28.9
All publ sch children in the 2 counties tested if in attendance.	w	386	3.4
	c	338	28.4
From 4 publ schs, 2 of them elem & 2 junior high schs. Does not give method of selection within schs.	c	41	17.2
	c	57	25.2
From one jr high sch; all Ss had been continuously enrolled in Chicago schs from about age of 6.	c	12	5.7
Intelligence test scores obtained on the 6th-grade pupils in 3 schs.	w	0	0.0
	c	1	0.76
Selected groups tested 2 times, once by c and once by w examiner; method of selection not given. Results in this table of 1st test only.	w	1	4.0
	c	7	14.6

[12] 33 of 705 w admissions were diagnosed as mentally dificient; 11 of the 240 c so diagnosed. The estimated incidence of mental deficiency (with or without psychoses) per 100,000 of the city's population was 7.8 for w and 19.2 for c.

TABLE

THE

AUTHOR DATE	LOCATION	TEST	N	SUBJECTS	
				AGE	GRADE
Wagner, P. S. (1938)	Cincinnati, Ohio	**Not given**	w-705[12] c- 240		
Lichtenstein, M., and Brown, A. W. (1938)	Chicago, Ill.	*Kuhlmann-Anderson*	w-480 c- 178		4-6 4-6
Town, C. H. (1938)	Buffalo, N. Y.	*Stanford-[13] Binet, 1916, Gesell*	w-1146[14] c- 112		
Tanser, H. A. (1939)	Kent County, Ontario	*National*	w-386 c- 103		1-8 1-8
		Pintner Non-Language	w-387 c- 102		3-8 3-8
		P-Paterson (short)	w-211 c- 162		1-8 1-8
Jones, H. L. (1940)	Denver, Colo.	*Terman Group*	c- 100		7-9
Fensch, E. A. (1942)	**Mansfield,** Ohio	**Not given**	c- 31		7-9
Griffith, W. R. (1947)	Portland, Ore.	*Otis S-A, Intermediate*	w-39 c- 76		6-8 6-8
Boylan, F. T., and O'Meara, R. B. (1958)	Chicago, Ill.	*Kuhlmann-Anderson, Thurstone PMA, et al*	c- 1868		

[13]*Binet* in translation to foreign-speaking Ss, *Gesell* to those under 2 years.
[14]*w* in this table includes all American-born w who had at least one parent born in US; 248 Polish & 167 Italian who were either born in Poland or Italy or had both parents born in

TEN *(Concluded)*

RETARDED

METHOD OF SELECTION		N	IQ's below 70[1] PER CENT
Total of new resident admissions to psychiatric pavilion of Cincinnati General Hospital, July '36 to July '37.	w	33	4.7
	c	11	4.6
Tested all pupils in 3 grades in 4 publ schs in poor neighborhood. *Mental defectives had been removed* from schs.	w	27	5.5
	c	16	8.9
Ss included all persons belonging to w & c native-born and to Polish and Italian Ss who were examined at the Psychol Clinic of Children's Aid Soc over 5-year period (1930-34).	w	120	10.5
	c	26	23.2
As far as practicable, tested all pupils in the one urban and 6 rural schs.	w	9	2.3
	c	12	11.7
	w	6	1.6
	c	2	2.0
	w	3	1.4
	c	23	14.2
Random sampling of 100 cases of c and 100 "Spanish-American" boys in a junior high sch.	c	4	4.0
31 of the 74 c in Simpson Jr High Sch; method of selection not given.	c	1	3.2
Eliot Elem Sch; apparently tested all present.	w	0	0.0
	c	5	6.6
Survey of Victor F. Lawson Sch in middle-class Negro neighborhood on South Side; 2300 pupils enrolled. Method of selection not given.	c	0	0.0

these countries are omitted from the table. Their %ages below 70 IQ were 22.5 & 24.5, resp. However, these Ss were bilingual & results not directly comparable acc to Town.

tent in whites are accepted by social workers as within the normal range in colored persons.[20]

Malzberg (1943) was of the opinion that, for legitimate comparisons of mental deficiency rates among races, one must turn to states having large enough populations to provide stable rates and adequate institutional facilities, admissions to which are on a basis free from prejudice. Since he considered these criteria to be met in New York, Malzberg analyzed the rates of first admissions to the New York State schools for mental defectives, 1929 to 1931. He found the average annual rate of Negro first admissions per 100,000 Negroes living in the state to be 12.2 as compared with the average annual rate of 8.9 for the white population. Correcting the figures for age differences, Malzberg reported that the rates become 16.1 and 9.4 for Negroes and whites per 100,000 of their respective populations. If one were to include the private institutions for mental defectives, admissions to which are almost entirely white, the white mental deficiency rate would be increased about ten per cent. On the other hand, Malzberg pointed out that correction should be made to include the first admissions to state schools for defective delinquents, among whom there is a great excess of Negroes.[18]

Malzberg considered it unlikely that factors determining admission to the state schools operate to the statistical disadvantage of the Negroes, for among children less than five years of age there were no Negro first admissions to the state schools. This could not mean that there were no Negro mental defectives in this age group. "Thus, despite a selective factor which operated statistically in favor of Negroes, they showed a significantly higher rate of first admissions to the State schools for mental defectives." (p. 330)

"Neither the results of intelligence testing, nor of institutional statistics, are conclusive by themselves. Taken together, however, they do seem to show some significant differences with respect to the relative distribution of mental deficiency. We may agree with Klineberg that the differences in this respect between whites and Negroes have undoubtedly been exaggerated. There does remain evidence, nevertheless, of a higher rate among Negroes, especially female Negroes . . . . ." (Malzberg, pp. 332-333)[21]

Atchison (1955) reported findings resulting from a three-year period of screening retarded children for special class placement in the Charlotte, North Carolina public schools.[18] From the case record files he selected the *WISC* records of 80 colored children, including 54 males and 26 females, none of whom had secured a *Full Scale* IQ of more than 69. These children had been classified

---

[20]Referring to the lower rates of mental deficiency among adults as reported both in England and in the United States, Tyler (1965, p. 370) observes: "Thus the problem with which we are concerned takes on a new aspect. Specifically and more precisely, the deficiency consists of inability to profit by education, as this is ordinarily provided in schools."

[21]Similarly, in a review of the research on mental deviates, Hollingworth (1940) referred to the American Negro as one of the distinguishable groups yielding disproportionately large numbers of deviates scoring low on intelligence tests.

as familial defectives; there was no evidence among them of organic pathology or sensory incapacity in the evaluations made by the public health authorities, nor was there anyone with a handicap or disability in the upper extremities of the body. Atchison was particularly interested in comparing the *Verbal* and *Performance* scores of the retardates. The mean *Verbal* IQ of the group was 66.3, the mean *Performance* IQ was 56.8, the difference between the means being highly significant ($t = 9.79$). He concluded that equal *Verbal* and *Performance* IQ's on *WISC* may not be characteristic of Negro children classified as familial defective.[22]

The *WAIS* was administered to 20 colored pupils as part of a routine re-examination of children enrolled in special classes for the mentally retarded in Southern California. All subjects had been tested by *WISC* between 13-1 and 15-8 years of age and were examined by *WAIS* approximately two years later when they were between 16-0 and 18-5 years of age.[18] Webb (1963) reported the mean *WAIS* IQ's to be about 9 to 10 points above the *WISC* means; the *WAIS* *Verbal, Performance,* and *Full Scale* IQ's were respectively, 76.93, 83.75, and 78.62, whereas the *WISC* IQ's were correspondingly, 68.37, 73.63, and 67.87. The three *WISC-WAIS* differences were significant at the .02 level or better, and, according to Webb, may reflect differences in the standardization populations for the two tests. Both tests included mental defectives in their sampled populations but only *WAIS* included Negroes in the standardization. While he considered that his findings cast some doubt upon the validity of both tests, Webb was of the opinion that the *WAIS* might give a more representative picture of Negro intelligence.[23]

It will have been observed that the *Performance* means were higher than the *Verbal* in both the *WISC* and *WAIS*. Good correlations were reported between the two scales and between the various subtests of the two scales.[24] On both *WISC* and *WAIS* the *Similarities* and *Vocabulary* subtests proved the most difficult of the *Verbal Scale* and the *Digit Span* and *Comprehension* the least difficult. On the *WISC*, the *Block Design* and *Picture Arrangement* were the most difficult of the *Performance* subtests, on the *WAIS, Block Design* and *Picture Completion* the most difficult. The least difficult test on *WAIS Performance Scale* was *Object Assembly* which was one of the three least difficult of the *WISC* for these subjects.

In our survey we have found that Negroes contribute proportionately more inferior deviates than do whites. An excess of retardation appears in this racial group among relatively unselected samples of school children, among children in special classes for the retarded, among those tested in psychological clinics and

---

[22]See pp. 54-57 for *WISC Performance* and *Verbal* IQ's obtained on several groups of Southern and Southern-born Negro school children.

[23]Because Negroes were included in the normative sample. And, by the same token, it may be that the *WISC* more accurately represents the intelligence of white children (reviewer's comment).

[24].91 between the *Performance Scales* and .80 between the *Verbal Scales.*

mental health surveys, and among children in institutions for the mentally deficient.

SUMMARY

From a combination of relatively unselected samples of white and colored school children, it appears that proportionally the *colored gifted* have been reported about one sixth as often as the *white gifted* and that the *colored retarded* have been reported about six times as often as the *white retarded*. In the special studies of gifted, the colored were found about one third as frequently as were whites in proportion to the numbers surveyed. Among the special studies of the mentally deficient, the rate for the retarded colored was approximately twice that of the rate for the retarded white.

Chapter VIII

DELINQUENTS AND CRIMINALS

Delinquents and criminals are among deviant groups typically excluded in the testing of school children, high school and college students, men enlisted in the Armed Forces, and veterans. While in this review we have used the term *criminal* to apply to *felons* — those individuals convicted of gross violation of human law and serving prison sentences — we have been obliged to employ the term *delinquent* to cover a rather large range of meanings. It includes not only those groups designated by the investigators as delinquent or misdemeanant,[1] those youths examined in reformatories or in industrial schools, those tested by Juvenile Court psychologists, but also those adolescents and adults apprehended or incarcerated for chronic antisocial behavior.

The majority of the studies dealing with the intelligence of Negro delinquents and criminals were conducted in the Northern states; in fact of the forty-four investigations reported in Tables 11 and 12, thirty-two were located in the North.[2] Twenty-two different psychometric tests were employed, the *Stanford-Binet* and *Army Alpha* having been used in thirteen and ten comparisons, respectively.

DELINQUENTS

Southern. Daniel (1932), Lewis (1947), and M. G. Caldwell (1953) secured average IQ's on Virginia and Alabama delinquents. Daniel administered the *Haggerty, Delta 2* to 100 Negro boys committed by the courts to the Virginia Manual Labor School. The mean IQ was reported to be 74.8, the *s*, 10.6.

Lewis limited her study to sixty colored boys of Grades 7 and 8 in the Alabama Reform School at Mount Meigs, all of the subjects being among the 100 who had been tested by the *Revised Army Beta* and the *California Test of Mental Maturity, Intermediate Short-Form.* The delinquents were described as severely handicapped in problem solving due to inadequate language development, lack of experiences, and retarded mental development. The language handicap was evidenced in the low *California* mean of 73.83 as compared with the *Beta* mean of 92.83, and in the low *California Language* IQ of 71.34 in contrast to the *California Non-Language* mean of 81.02. The ability to "sense spatial relations" was greater in the delinquent than in a control group of

---

[1]Fernald *et al.* (1920) entitled their work "A Study of Women Delinquents . . . ." although their cases were drawn from a state reformatory, a state prison for women, a workhouse, and probationers from a night court.

[2]In addition to two investigations which included reformatory and state penitentiary inmates in both Northern and Border states.

nondelinquent colored boys, Lewis suggesting that many authorities accept this ability as indicative of ability to manipulate tools and to succeed in industrial and manual arts.

Caldwell (1953) attempted to analyze the relationships existing between delinquency and type of community, race, intelligence, grade completed in school, and age at "instant conviction". He studied the records of 1183 youthful male offenders, 16-23 years of age, all of whom were incarcerated in four Alabama correctional institutions or in 27 correctional camps during the first six months of 1950. The source materials included case histories, IQ scores on *Army Beta*, and scores on the Minnesota Multiphasic Personality Inventory. The white offenders had completed 7.3 school grades on the average, the colored, 6.6, a *t* of 5.00 indicating a highly significant difference between the mean number of grades completed by the two racial samples. The mean IQ's of the white and colored delinquents were 87.1 and 70.4, respectively, the *t* being 18.15. When the offenders were grouped according to the type of community in which they were living at time of conviction, the white and colored Ss from *urban areas* earned respective mean IQ's of 91 and 73; the white and colored from *villages* (rural-nonfarm areas) achieved mean IQ's of 85.4 and 67.6; and the two groups from *farms* (rural-farm areas) averaged respective IQ's of 81.2 and 63.8. All of these differences between the white and colored groups were significant. Caldwell concluded that his investigation revealed functional relationships existing between intelligence, grade completed in school, type of community, and race.

In a second analysis of his data,[3] Caldwell (1954) presented the mean IQ's of 63 white and 34 colored delinquents from rural-farms, all of them having been included within the above group of 1183 offenders. In the 1953 report the white rural-farm delinquents had completed 6.5 school grades on the average as opposed to a mean of 5.7 grades completed by the Negro rural-farm group. In the second report he probably selected his white and Negro groups so that the Negro Ss would have attained a grade level at least the equal to that of the whites. The mean school grade completed by the 63 rural-farm whites was 7.1, by the 34 rural-farm Negroes, 7.6. The mean IQ of these respective white and colored groups proved to be 87.4 and 72.5.

In a third report (1959), Caldwell indicated that he had selected 231 white and 228 colored offenders from the original 1183, these being subjects of the *MMPI* analysis. The white and colored misdemeanants selected for this analysis were very similar in a number of variables such as their respective mean ages of 19.6 and 19.5 years; their mean number of convictions which were respectively 2.0 and 1.85; their percentages in urban residence at time of first offense, 57 and 70.6 (this difference being advantageous to the colored); and mean school grade completed, 8.3 and 8.6, respectively. These offenders were separated into eight major offense patterns and mean IQ's reported.[4] In every instance the

---

[3]The second and third analyses of Caldwell's data have not been tabulated by reviewer.

[4]Caldwell does not report the number of delinquents committing each offense.

mean IQ of the whites was above that of the colored, the t ratios being significant at the .05 level or better in all patterns except for *forgery*. The respective IQ's of the white and Negro Ss for this crime were 90.2 and 83.0. The listed offenses and critical ratios between the mean IQ's of the two races are as follows: *murder*, 3.22; *assault*, 2.38; *robbery*, 3.64; burglary, 5.0; *grand larceny*, 4.80; *auto theft*, 2.74; *other offenses*, 2.70. The respective mean IQ's of the selected groups of 231 white and 228 colored offenders were 92.8 and 80.2, the difference of 12.6 being highly significant.[5]

Border. Henderson obtained a mean of 86.00 and a standard deviation of 12.80 on the *Stanford-Binet* administered to 100 Negro delinquents at the Blue Plains Industrial School in the District of Columbia. (*in* Beckham, 1933)

Charles (1936) found lower *Kuhlmann-Anderson* IQ's on both white and colored boys than reported by Henderson. Three hundred fifty-two white and 176 colored boys between 12 and 16 years of age, who were confined to the four reform schools located in St. Louis and Boonville, Missouri; Greendale, Kentucky; and St. Charles, Illinois; secured respective mean IQ's of 76.74 and 70.18. The variability of the whites' scores was greater than that of the Negroes, as evidenced by their standard deviations and ranges.

Watts (1941) tested 92 boys committed by a juvenile court to the Industrial Home for colored children in Washington, D. C. The boys were examined on the *Minnesota Paper Form Board*, the *Healy Picture-Completion Test II*, and the *Otis S-A, Form A*. The results on the *Otis* were given in terms of IQ units, the mean being 77.3 and the standard deviation, 14.1. Since the subjects were from 14 to 16 years of age and in the sixth grade, on the average, the author concluded that the delinquents in his study were both intellectually and educationally retarded.

Franklin (1945) analyzed the *Wechsler-Bellevue* test scores made by 276 individuals committed to a Maryland state institution for delinquent Negro boys. The *Full Scale* IQ mean was 76.5, the *Verbal* mean being four points below the *Performance* mean. The boys scored best, on the average, on the subtests of *Object Assembly, Picture Arrangement*, and *Picture Completion;* their performances were worst on the subtests of *Arithmetic, Information*, and *Block Design*.

Weitz and Rachlin (1945) gave the *Otis Quick-Scoring, Beta Test*, Forms A and B, to 340 white and 160 Negro females who were between the ages of 12 and 47. All were venereally infected girls and women who had been apprehended by the health officers and were being treated at a United States Public Health Service Center in St. Louis between February and August, 1944. No voluntary patients were included in the survey. In general, the subjects were products of urban homes in the states of Missouri, Illinois, Arkansas, Mississippi, Kentucky, and Tennessee, with Missouri having contributed 461 of the total number. The schooling of the two racial samples was approximately the same, the whites having

---

[5] $t = 10.6$.

spent, on the average, 9 years and 4 months in school, and the colored, 9 years and 8 months. The median IQ of the whites was 84, that of the colored, 70. About 25 per cent of the whites and slightly more than 50 per cent of the colored were found to be mentally deficient.

Northern. Several California investigations were reported by Mathews (1923) including her own survey of 341 delinquents in the California School for Girls. The *Stanford-Binet* was administered to all girls enrolled in the school in January, 1920, and to all entering from this time to and including January, 1923. The median IQ of the 311 white girls was 81, that of the 19 colored girls, 72[6]; the range of scores secured on the former group was 51 to 118, on the latter, 55 to 97.

Mathews referred to two studies of Williams (see Table 11), both of them from the Whittier School for Boys. In the 1919 research, there were 470 Ss tested, the median IQ of the whites being 82, that of the colored, 77. In the second study of Williams, described by Mathews as "soon to be published," 1250 boys were tested; the median of the whites was 81 (or 83), the median of the colored was 79.[7] Mathews also mentioned an unpublished report by Popenoe in which 467 Preston School of Industry boys were examined. The median of the whites was between 80 and 84; that of the colored, between 70 and 75.

Two early Midwest studies were those of Stone (1921-22) and Hamill (1923). The *Stanford-Binet* test records of 299 white and 100 colored inmates of an Indiana reformatory comprised the data examined by Stone. Except for 16 cases of epileptics and psychotics, all were consecutive entries of boys and young men admitted to the reformatory between September, 1916, and July, 1917.[8] All Ss had been tested within the third or fourth week after their arrival at the institution; since the ages ranged between 16 and 30 years, 16 was used in calculating the IQ. As will be noted in Table 11, the colored were found to have earned lower IQ's on the average and to be less variable. The mean IQ's of the respective white and colored delinquents were 79.05 and 68.85, the respective standard deviations being 13.33 and 10.3.

Securing her data from the Psychopathic Clinic of the Recorder's Court of Detroit, Hamill presents the results obtained from testing 710 native white, 476 foreign-born white, and 154 native colored misdemeanants. A group of misdemeanants, averaging about 11 and "preferably the first arrivals" was examined each day for the early sessions court while awaiting trial by that court; these men were brought in from various precincts on such charges as drunkenness, disturbing the peace, vagrancy, and drunken driving. The main purpose of the

---

[6]The median ages at commitment for the white and colored girls were 16.6 and 16.7, respectively.

[7]In neither of the Williams studies nor in the Popenoe work was the number of colored cases or the name of the mental test given by Mathews. The reviewer infers that the test was the *Stanford-Binet.*

[8]No commitments were for a period of less than one year and none were for as much as *life.* The records indicate that the whites committed relatively fewer crimes against the person but more against property and public order.

testing was to supply the judge with data concerning the accused. The median scores of the native whites and colored tested on the *Pintner Non-Language* during a 7-months period were 259.6 and 146.6, respectively. Among the native whites, 19.5 per cent were described as *inferior,* 72 per cent as *average,* and 8.3 per cent as *superior;* as for the colored, 49.7 per cent were identified as *inferior,* 48.4 per cent as *average,* and 1.8 per cent as *superior.* Hamill attributed the low scores to several factors including: being under the influence of liquor when tested, lack of interest in the test, anxiety, and mental inferiority.

In a survey of women convicted of serious crimes or minor offenses in New York State, Fernald, Hayes, and Dawley (1920) gave various tests to inmates of the New York State Reformatory in Bedford Hills, the State Prison for Women at Auburn, the New York Magdalen Home, the New York County Penitentiary, the New York City Workhouse, and probationers from the New York City Night Courts. Their practice was to take consecutive commitments within each institution with some supplementation as time permitted. Comparisons between from 447 to 478 white and from 107 to 129 colored women were made on the *Yerkes-Bridges-Hardwick Point Scale,* the *Stanford-Binet,* and a *performance test.*[9] On these three tests the respective white means were 71.80, 73.25, and 73.78; the respective colored means were 65.4, 65.4, and 69.26. The groups did not seem to differ consistently in variability.

Slawson (1926) administered two group tests and the *Stanford-Binet* to boys in the New York House of Refuge at Randall's Island, the State Agricultural and Industrial School, the Berkshire Industrial Farm, and the Hawthorne School for Jewish boys. Since there were no Negro boys enrolled in two of these schools and only 15 in a third, Slawson tabulated averages, *etc.,* on the colored for the House of Refuge alone.[10] Slawson's method was to test all boys already in the institution when the program started and to continue with new arrivals during the remainder of the 4-month period. On all three tests employed the means of the whites were significantly above those of the Negroes (.01 level); on the *National,* the respective white and colored means were 203.96 and 171.56; on the *Thorndike Non-Verbal* the white and colored means were 117.65 and 96.33, respectively;[11] and on the *Stanford-Binet,* the mean MA's for the two respective groups were 153.68 and 140.24.

Armstrong (1933) compared the *Stanford-Binet* IQ's of 100 white and 100 colored New York City delinquents of American-born parents; all of these children had been among the 421 Ss on whom clinical examinations had been requested by the Children's Court in 1932. The mean IQ's of the white and colored delinquents were 83.8 and 73.9, respectively. Later, Armstrong and

---

[9]Included in the performance test series were the following: (1) card sorting, (2) memory for digits, (3) Knox cubes, and (4) cancellation of unfamiliar figures.

[10]In this survey the 155-176 whites and the 46-53 colored were all tested in the House of Refuge.

[11]Test scores, not IQ's.

TABLE

THE

AUTHOR DATE	LOCATION	TEST	N	SUBJECTS AGE	GRADE	METHOD OF SELECTION
Daniel,[1] R. P. (1932)	Richmond, Va.	*Haggerty, Delta 2*	c- 100	9-16		Va Manual Labor Sch; all boys committed by court rulings.
Lewis, M. L. (1947)	Mount Meigs, Ala.	*Beta,[2] CTMM*	c- 60	13-20	7-8	Ala Reform Sch; selected only those boys in Grades 7 & 8.
Caldwell, M. G. (1953)	Alabama	*Army Beta*	w-453 c- 730	16-23 16-23	7.3 (M) 6.6 (M)	Male offenders, 16-23, incarcerated in 4 correctional institutions & 27 correct camps during first 6 months of 1950.
Beckham,[4] A. S. (1933)	Washington, D. C.	*Stanford-Binet, 1916*	c- 100	12-16		From Blue Plains Industrial School
Charles,[5] C. M. (1936)	Boonville, St. Louis, Mo., Greendale, Ky., St. Charles, Ill.	*Kuhlmann-Anderson*	w-352 c- 176	12-16 12-16		Four reform schs for boys sentenced by courts; does not give method of selection nor percentage of boys tested.

[1]For results on problem and nonproblem c children in Richmond public schools, see Table 4.
[2]*Revised Beta, California Test of Mental Maturity, Intermed.* See Tables 3 and 4 for results on nondelinquents.
[3]*Village* is identified as 'rural nonfarm'; *farm* as 'rural farm'.

ELEVEN

DELINQUENTS

RESULTS	COMMENTS OF AUTHOR

	IQ	
	c	
M	74.8	
s	10.6	

	IQ		Delinquents showed severe language interference.
	Beta	CTMM	
	c	c	
M	92.83	73.83	
s	14.22	12.55	
Range	59-120	54-109	

		IQ		Race appears to be a dynamic factor in the complex of factors associated with delinquency and crime.
	w		c	
M				
Urban[3]	91.0		73.0	
Village	85.4		67.6	
Farm	81.2		63.8	
Total	87.1		70.4	

	IQ	
	c	
M	86.00	
s	12.80	

		IQ		Diff bet mean IQ's of w and c sch boys of same social status is much less than bet sch boys and delinquent boys of same race.
	w		c	
M	76.74		70.18	
s	13.00		10.45	
Range	45-114		45-99	
$t =$		6.31		

[3]See Table 2 for studies on nondelinquents. Author indicated that for his delinquent group he drew upon the unpubl Master's thesis of T. Henderson, Howard Univ.

[5]See Table 4 for results on St. Louis school boys; t calculated by reviewer.

TABLE

THE

AUTHOR DATE	LOCATION	TEST	N	SUBJECTS AGE	GRADE	METHOD OF SELECTION
Watts, F. P. (1941)	Washington, D. C.	*Otis S-A Form A*	c- 92	14-16		All boys committed by Juvenile Court to Industrial Home. In Home not over one yr. Incompl testing on others due to illness, "absconding from the institution", *etc*. Various test results compared with those of nondelinquent c boys of same IQ, age, & from same publ schs delinquents had attended.
		Healy Picture-Completion Test II				
		Minn Paper Form Board				
Weitz, R. D., and Rachlin, H. L. (1945)	St. Louis Mo.	*Otis Q-S, Beta*	w-340 c- 160	12-47 12-47		All were venereally infected females apprehended by health officers & were being treated at Publ Health Center, 1944. Eliminated 22 cases because of illiteracy.
Franklin, J. C. (1945)	Cheltenham, Md.	*Wechsler-Bellevue*	c- 276	9-20		State institution for delinquent c boys; all routinely tested when admitted during 1943-44. All Ss native-born.
Williams,[7] J. H. (1919)	California		470			From Whittier School for Boys.
Williams,[7] J. H.	California		1250			From Whittier School for Boys.

[9]Difference bet *Verbal* and *Performance* IQ's significant at .01 level; $t=3.00$ (calculated by reviewer).

ELEVEN *(continued)*

DELINQUENTS

	RESULTS		COMMENTS OF AUTHOR
	IQ		Findings indicate that delinquent Negro boys, as a group, are both intellectually and edu-
	c		cationally retarded.
M	77.3		
s	14.1		
Range	50-114		
	Score		
	c		
M	47.65		
s	17.20		
	Score		
	c		
M	22.70		
s	12.05		
	IQ		In general Ss products of urban centers in Mo
	w	c	and surrounding states. Both groups averaged
Mdn	84	70	bet 9-10 yrs formal schooling. Four % c and 16% w reached or exceeded 100 IQ.
	IQ[6]		Performance materials more efficiently handled
	M	*s*	than verbal; best on subtests of *Object As-*
		c	*sembly, Pict Arrangement,* and *Pict Completion;*
Verb	76.2	14.45	worst on *Arith, Inform,* and *Block Design.*
Perf	80.4	18.19	
Full	76.5	15.39	
	IQ		
	w	c	
Mdn	82	77	
	IQ		
Mdn	w	c	
	81-83	79	

[7]Reported by Mathews (1923); Mathews did not give name of test nor method of selection. Number of cases includes all boys.

TABLE

THE

AUTHOR DATE	LOCATION	TEST	N	SUBJECTS		METHOD OF SELECTION
				AGE	GRADE	
Fernald, M. R., Hayes, M. H. S., and Dawley, A. (1920)	NY State Reform, Bedford Hills; Women's State Prison, Auburn; NY Magdalen Home; NY Co Peniten; NYC Workhouse; NYC Night Courts Probationers	*Point Scale* *Stanford-Binet, 1916* *Performance Test*	w-478 c- 129 w-447 c- 118 w-453 c- 107	27[s] 27		Practice to take consecutive commitments within each institution; some additional supplementation of cases.
Stone, C. P. (1921-22)	Indiana	*Stanford-Binet, 1916*	w-299 c-100	16-30 16-29		Data from tests given reformatory inmates, Sept '16-July '17; all consecutive entries except for 16 epileptics, psychotics, *etc.*, who were eliminated.
Hamill, G. (1923)	Detroit, Mich.	*Pintner Non-Language*	w-710 c- 154			At Psychopathic Clinic of Recorder's Court; unselected misdemeanants (generally first arrivals) brought to court from various precincts. Study includes all males tested during 7-month period.
Mathews, J. (1923)	California	*Stanford-Binet, 1916*	w-311 c- 19	12-20 13-19		Includes Ss enrolled in School for Girls, Jan '20 & all succeeding entrants to Jan '23.

[s]Age here indicates mean age when tested; based on 287 native white and 98 native colored cases. English-speaking Ss only included in table.

ELEVEN *(continued)*
DELINQUENTS

	RESULTS			COMMENTS OF AUTHOR
		IQ		All were women convicted of offenses against the law. A decided difference in mental capacity bet these colored and white women as measured by these tests.
	w		c	
M	71.80		65.4	
s	13.29		14.82	
		IQ		
M	73.25		65.4	
s	14.01		11.90	
		IQ		
M	73.78		69.26	
s	8.08		8.04	

		IQ		Large diff bet mean IQ of c and w probably arises in part from a real racial diff in intelligence.
	w		c	
M	79.05		68.85	
s	13.33		10.3	
t =		7.91*		

		Scores		Group as unselected as possible; weighting of scores at lower end of scale may be accounted for by drunkenness, lack of interest, anxiety, "but mostly in terms of the general inferiority of the group."
	w		c	
Mdn	259.6		146.6	

		IQ		W group includes 11% of foreign-born parents.
	w		c	
Mdn	81		72	
Range	51-118		55-97	

TABLE

THE

AUTHOR DATE	LOCATION	TEST	N	SUBJECTS AGE	SUBJECTS GRADE	METHOD OF SELECTION
Slawson, J. (1926)	Randall's Island, N. Y.	*NIT, A or B*	w-160 c- 48	10-20 12-19		Tested all boys in House of Refuge when program started. Continued with new arrivals during the 4-month period.
		Thorndike Non-Verbal	w-155 c- 46	10-20 12-19		
		Stanford-Binet, 1916	w-176 c- 53	10-20 12-19		
Armstrong, C. P. (1933)	New York City	*Stanford-Binet, 1916*	w-100 c- 100	8-15 8-15		From the Children's Court; the 200 Ss were among the 421 delinquents on whom clinical examinations had been requested in 1932.
McClure, W. E. (1933)	Toledo, Ohio	*Stanford-Binet, 1916*	w-530 c- 72	7-17[10]		All who were brought before Judge of Juvenile Court, Lucas Co & given *S-B* during a 2½-year period.
Dombey,[11] E. H. (1933)	Cleveland, Ohio	*Stanford-Binet, 1916*	c- 466	10-17		Selected Juvenile Court records covering a 2-year period.
Lane, H. A., and Witty, P. A. (1935)	St. Charles, Ill.	*Otis Group*	699[12]	15.8 (M)		Analyzed records of mental test that had been given to approx 700 delinquents in the School for Boys.

[9]Ss native-born of native parents; *t*'s calculated by reviewer.
t calculated by reviewer.
[10]Age range for total group; c and w not separated acc to CA's. Mean IQ of w Ss and *t* calculated by reviewer.

ELEVEN *(continued)*

DELINQUENTS

	RESULTS		COMMENTS OF AUTHOR
	Scores[9]		On whole a better performance is manifested when tasks are nonverbal and concrete than when they consist of manipulating abstractions.
	w	c	
M	203.96	171.56	
s	75.24	73.08	
t =		2.68	
M	117.65	96.33	
s	46.67	47.97	
t =		2.71	
	MA		
M	153.68	140.24	
s	33.36	25.92	
t =		3.10	
	IQ[9]		Delinquent c children outnumber their city quota by nearly 3 to 1.
	w	c	
M	83.8	73.9	
s	15.44	13.63	
t =		4.71	
	IQ		About 12% of delinquents were colored. General intelligence of these c slightly lower than that of group as a whole.
	w	c	
M	79.61	77.32	
s	13.0	13.3	
t =		1.38	
	IQ		
	c		
M	75.1		
	IQ		
	w	c	
Fathers			
Native	89	83.16	
Foreign-b	89.68		

[11]A part of study on intelligence of Northern- and Southern-born Negroes living in Cleveland, See Table 14.

[12]Numbers of c and w not given separately; this number includes all delinquents whose test papers were examined.

TABLE

THE

AUTHOR DATE	LOCATION	TEST	N	SUBJECTS		METHOD OF SELECTION
				AGE	GRADE	
Hill, G. E. (1936)	Pontiac, Ill.	*Army Alpha*	1285[12]	16-26		All inmates tested when admitted to state reformatory; analyzed scores of 1285 of last 1500 commitments, some of the last admitted not being available.
Doll, E. A., and Fitch, K. A. (1938)	Jamesburg, N. J.	*Morgan Mental Test, Myers Mental Measure*	w-58 c- 33	10-17 10-17		91 juv delinquent boys selected as representative sample of State Home for Boys (total pop about 600) acc to color, life age, & mental age.
Tulchin, S. H. (1939)	Pontiac, Ill.	*Army Alpha*	w-2143[14] c- No-257 So -509	19.5[15] 19.0 19.6		Survey state reformatory, 1920-27; tests given routinely to every man. All classed as inferior recalled for individual exam. In these cases final classification made on basis of indiv exam.
Springer, N. N. (1941)	Brooklyn, N. Y.	*Stanford-Binet*	w-80 c- 50	16-18 16-18		Random selection of 130 male adolescent delinquents, 16-18 yrs, awaiting sentence in Adolescents' Court.

[13]Calculated by reviewer from author's data.
[14]Native-born of native parents.
[15]Median age.

ELEVEN *(continued)*

DELINQUENTS

RESULTS				COMMENTS OF AUTHOR

		Scores		White offenders are significantly more intelligent than Negro offenders.
	w	c		
Mdn	77.46	51.49		
P	$\langle .001$			
28% c above w *mdn*				

Test	*Mdn*	MA[13]	No significant difference bet social competencies of w and c in spite of a 10% advantage in mental scores on part of whites. Both strikingly low.
	w	c	
Verbal	9.7	8.7	
Nonverb	10.9	9.9	

		Scores			Acc to 1920 Census, c comprised 2.8% state population and 16.1% of reformatory inmates.
	w		c		
		No	So[16]		
Mdn	64	43	30		
Class		*Percentage*			
Sup	15.6	6.6	1.6		
Aver	74.4	68.0	55.8		
Inf	10.0	25.4	42.6		

	Maximum Sch & Score[17]				
Grade	*N*		*Mdn*		
	w	c	w	c	
8	507	44	82	62	
7	344	36	64	62	
6	344	32	58	48	
5	245	38	48	39	
4	175	26	39	38	
3	100	22	32	25	

	IQ		Recidivists about 5 IQ points below first offenders.
	w	c	
M	90.63	88.50	
s	12.88	12.00	
t =	.95*		

[16]Northern-born, Southern-born.
[17]*N* refers to number having completed each grade; *c* here incl only Northern-born.

AUTHOR DATE	LOCATION	TEST	N	SUBJECTS AGE	GRADE	METHOD OF SELECTION
Armstrong, C. P., and Heisler, F. (1945)	New York City	*Stanford-Binet, 1916*	w-200 c- 200	14-15 14-15		Native-born delinquent boys examined in Psychiatric Clinic of Children's Court, 1938-40.
Diggs, M. H. (1946)	Philadelphia, Pa.	*Otis*[18] *S-A*	c- 100	Under 18		Negro boys who had been brought more than once before Juv Div Municipal Court for theft, or were known to have participated in more than one thieving episode.
DeStephens, W. P. (1953)	Ohio	*Wechsler-Bellevue, I* and *II*	w-200 c- 100	22.0 (M) 22.7 (M)		Project involved testing every person entering reformatory from Feb '51-until 300 protocols were secured; 344 admitted but 44 could not be tested during program.
Fisher, G. M. (1961)	Costa Mesa, Cal.	*Wechsler-Bellevue, I*	w-177[19] c- 42	16-19 16-19		From Fairview State Hospital. Adolescent male sociopaths incarcerated because of chronic antisocial & delinquent beh.

[18]*Otis S-A* merely a supplementary test. Author did not name the test by which the most of the IQ's were determined.

ELEVEN *(continued)*

DELINQUENTS

	RESULTS			COMMENTS OF AUTHOR
		IQ		
	w		c	
M	83		79	
		IQ		Most of boys in 14-15 yr age groups. They had committed from 2-11 offenses each, all but 26 having 3 or more offenses to their credit.
		c		
M		76.8		
s		6.1		
		IQ		t	Sig diffs bet w and c samples in: Arith, Picture Completion, Block Design, Object Assembly, and Digit Symbol.
	w		c	
M				
Verbal	90.13		86.70	2.10
Perf	98.30		91.20	3.60
Full Sc	93.55		87.90	3.14
		IQ		Mean *Performance IQ* sig higher than mean *Verbal IQ* in w but not in Negro group.
	w		c	
M				
Verbal		95.58		83.71
Perf		101.70		87.79
Full Sc		98.71		84.45
s				
Verbal		14.65		12.36
Perf		13.52		13.29
Full Sc		13.70		11.59

[19]A group of 55 Mexican-Americans also tested; results omitted by reviewer.

TABLE

THE

AUTHOR DATE	LOCATION	TEST	N	SUBJECTS		METHOD OF SELECTION
				AGE	GRADE	
Rozynko, V. V., and Wenk, E. (1965)	Tracy, Cal.	*California Test of Mental Maturity* *General Aptitude Test Battery*	w- 178 c- 178 MexAm-178	17-25 17-25 17-25	10.2 (M) 10.2 (M) 9.1 (M)	Three independent studies done on new & returned inmates of Cal Youth Authority processed through Reception-Guidance Center at Deuel Vocational Inst. All Ss were randomly selected from inmates tested during a 10 consec- or two 5 consecutive-week-periods. First study contained 78 Ss in each of 3 subgroups; 2nd & 3rd had 50 in each. All subgroups equated for age. Mean age, 19.24 years.[20]

[20]Reviewer has combined the 3 white subgroups and the 3 colored subgroups, omitting the Mexican-American data. The means, s's, and t's were calculated by reviewer from the subgroup means and s's reported by authors.

ELEVEN *(concluded)*

DELINQUENTS

	RESULTS		COMMENTS OF AUTHOR

		IQ		
		CTMM		
	w		c	
Lang				
M	91.99		80.59	
s	16.21		16.71	
t =		6.55		
Non-1				
M	92.75		80.01	
s	15.10		16.01	
t =		7.72		
		GATB		
	w		c	
"G"				
M	95.82		81.39	
s	17.26		14.33	
t =		8.59		
"V"				
M	91.20		80.94	
s	15.33		11.75	
t =		7.08		
"N"				
M	92.86		80.93	
s	19.74		18.63	
t =		5.88		
"S"				
M	108.85		92.20	
s	18.88		18.92	
t =		8.32		
"P"				
M	105.60		93.20	
s	17.15		18.76	
t =		6.49		
"Q"				
M	98.18		91.03	
s	14.54		14.71	
t		4.61		
"K"				
M	97.33		93.32	
s	19.39		16.19	
t =		2.12		
"F"				
M	98.06		89.41	
s	19.18		22.20	
t =		3.93		
"M"				
M	109.36		100.65	
s	20.81		22.17	
t =		3.82		

GATB consists of nine factors:
G—Intelligence
V—Verbal Aptitude
N—Numerical Aptitude
S—Spatial Aptitude
P—Form Perception
Q—Clerical Perception
K—Motor Coordination
F—Finger Dexterity
M—Manual Dexterity

The results support the idea that inadequate motivation is an extremely important factor in Negro inmates' intellectual test performance.

Heisler (1945) found the mean IQ of 200 delinquent white and 200 delinquent colored boys[12] examined in the Psychiatric Clinic of the Children's Court of New York City between 1938 and 1940 to be, respectively, 83 and 79.

Two Ohio studies were reported in 1933; in both, the *Stanford-Binet* was the measuring instrument. From January, 1929, to July, 1931, approximately 1000 children, Age 7 to 17, appeared before the judge of the Juvenile Court of Lucas County at Toledo (McClure). The charges brought against these children were destruction of property, vagrancy, stabbing, holdup, assault, running away, immorality, *etc.*; 602 of these delinquents were tested by court psychologists on the *Stanford-Binet*. The mean IQ of the 72 colored Ss was 77.32, that of the 530 whites was 79.61. Each group showed about the same amount of variability in IQ. Dombey selected test records of 466 colored delinquents who were brought before the Juvenile Court of Cuyahoga County in Cleveland. They comprised the records of all colored tested at the age of 10 and above from June, 1931, to March, 1933.[13] Stealing, burglary, and shop-lifting constituted the largest number of offenses committed by the boys; being away from home and immorality, the principal offenses committed by the girls. The mean IQ of Dombey's Ss was 75.1; when Dombey separated the Northern- and Southern-born, she found the mean IQ of the former to be about six points higher than the mean of the latter.

Lane and Witty (1935) analyzed the *Otis Group* test scores of 699 delinquents in the St. Charles, Illinois, School for Boys.[14] The mean IQ of the Negro boys was 83.16, the mean of the whites was 89.

Hill (1936) and Tulchin (1939) analyzed the test scores of colored and white inmates of the Pontiac, Illinois, State Reformatory. Hill compared the *Army Alpha* records of 1285 young men who were among the latest 1500 commitments, the records of a number of the last admitted not having been made available for examination.[14] The median score of the colored (51.49) was reported to be significantly below that of the whites (77.46); 28 per cent of the colored overlapped the median of the whites.

Tulchin presented the *Alpha* distributions of 257 Northern-born Negroes and 509 Southern-born Negroes who had been tested routinely in the reformatory between 1920 and 1927. The *Alpha* distributions of several groups of white inmates were included with them. The median score of the 2143 native whites of native parents was 64; that of the Northern Negro, 43; that of the Southern Negro, 30. As will be observed from the table, *superior Alpha* ratings were earned by 15.6 per cent of the whites, 6.6 per cent of the Northern-born colored, and 1.6 per cent of the Southern-born colored; on the other hand, the percentages of *inferior* scores secured by the white, the Northern-born colored, and the Southern-born colored were 10.0, 25.4, and 42.6, respectively. When the scores of the whites

---

[12]The 400 were all native-born.

[13]In 1930 the colored population of Cleveland was 8 per cent; in 1932, 21 per cent of the cases heard in the Juvenile Court were Negro.

[14]Number of cases was not given separately for colored and white.

and *Northern-born* Negroes were categorized according to maximum grade completed in school, the several white medians were higher than the corresponding medians of the colored, with the differences ranging from one to 22 points.

Doll and Fitch (1938) were primarily interested in studying the social competence of delinquent boys. They selected a sample of 58 white and 33 colored boys between Ages 10 and 17 with a median age of 14 as representative of the total population of 600 living in the State Home for Boys in Jamesburg, New Jersey. In addition to the Vineland Social Maturity Scale two mental tests had been administered to these boys, the *Morgan Mental Test* (a verbal test) and the *Myers Mental Measure* (a nonverbal scale). The total mental ratio was estimated to be 70 for the 91 juveniles, with retardation present in both racial groups.[15] Doll and Fitch commented that on each test the median MA was one year higher for the white than for the colored boys. It is interesting that the authors found no difference in the social competencies of their groups, in spite of a 10 per cent advantage the white boys had in mental scores.[16]

Springer (1941) attempted to determine the social competence scores of delinquents on the Vineland Social Maturity Scale by means of interviews with their parents.[17] The subjects of his research consisted of a random selection of 130 males between the ages of 16 and 18 who were awaiting sentence in the Adolescents' Court. Eighty of the boys were white and 50 were Negroes, half of each group being first offenders and half recidivists; all lived in the East New York and Brownsville sections of Brooklyn. IQ's were determined by the *Stanford-Binet,* based on a chronological age of 14 years. As will be noted in Table 11, the mean IQ's of the white and colored delinquents were 90.63 and 88.50, respectively, the difference between the means not being significant.

In a comparative study of delinquent behavior manifestations in delinquent and nondelinquent Negro boys, Diggs (1946) selected 100 nondelinquents to *match the delinquents in age, general intelligence, and type of residential area.* The 100 delinquents had either been brought more than one time before the Juvenile Division of the Municipal Court of Philadelphia for theft, or else they were known to have participated in more than one thieving episode. All were drawn from the regular list of complaints made to the Court between September, 1942, and May, 1943; no boy was included in the study if he was as old as 18 years or if he had an IQ under 70; each qualifying Negro boy was included until a total of 100 had been selected. Of those delinquents participating in the study, 84 were born in Philadelphia, 4 elsewhere in the North, 11 in the South, and one in a Border state. The mean IQ was reported to be 76.8, the *s* 6.1, the small size of the standard deviation being due in part to the elimination of cases at the lower end of the scale.

---

[15]The mental ratio as reported by the authors, obtained by dividing median pooled MA by median LA (life age).

[16]The median social quotient (SQ) was 73, there being no racial difference.

[17]Mean social quotients for the white and colored delinquents were 92.38 and 95.60.

DeStephens' report (1953) was based upon a project which involved testing every person entering the Ohio State Reformatory beginning in February, 1951, until 300 protocols were secured. Three hundred forty-four young men were admitted before the data could be completed because, for various reasons listed by the author, 44 entrants could not be tested during the program. During the first half of 1951 all admissions to the reformatory included approximately one third colored and two thirds white offenders; hence it was to be expected that of his 300 cases about 100 would be colored. DeStephens considered his sampling to be representative of Ohio's reformatory population since each county was allowed to send no more than a given number of offenders to it each month.

From Table 11 it will be observed that the *Wechsler-Bellevue, Form I or II* was administered and that the mean IQ's have been tabulated according to *Verbal, Performance,* and *Full Scale.* All three differences favor the whites, the difference between the *Verbal* means being significant at the .05 level of confidence, the differences between the *Performance* means and the *Full Scale* means being significant at the .01 level.[18] The author, in addition, gives the means attained by the colored and white entrants on each of the following subtests: *Information, Comprehension, Digit Span, Arithmetic, Similarities, Picture Arrangement, Picture Completion, Block Design, Object Assembly,* and *Digit Span.* The means of the whites were higher than those of the colored on all subtests, the differences being significant in four *Performance* tests (*Picture Completion* .01, *Block Design* .01, *Object Assembly* .01, and *Digit Symbol* .05) and in one *Verbal* test (*Arithmetic* .05). While both groups did better on the *Performance* than on the *Verbal Scale* the colored offenders benefited less from its inclusion than did the white. The author concluded that the significant differences between the IQ's of the white and colored inmates may be a function of the standardization of the *Wechsler-Bellevue* test itself and not a function of any *true* demonstable difference between the two races.

Fisher (1961) was interested in the reported discrepancies between the *Wechsler-Bellevue Verbal* and *Performance* IQ's obtained on sociopaths. He selected for study 177 white, 55 Mexican-American, and 42 Negro male adolescents, Ages 16 to 19 years, all of whom were incarcerated in the Fairview State Hospital in California because of chronic antisocial and delinquent behavior. The mean *Wechsler Verbal* IQ's obtained on the white and colored sociopaths were 95.58 and 83.71, respectively; the mean *Performance* IQ's obtained on these two groups

---

[18]Dreger and Miller (1960, p. 371), after listing the mean *Verbal, Performance,* and *Full Scale* IQ's separately for the two racial samples as reported by DeStephens, add the following *incorrect* statement: "On the basis of the standard deviations reported none of these differences between groups is significant."

The present writer has checked DeStephens' calculations with the *s*'s provided in his article (but not given by Dreger and Miller) and finds all three *t* ratios to be significant. For the reader who may wish to verify the size of the *t*'s, the reviewer here includes the standard deviations (in order of *Verbal, Performance,* and *Full Scale;* in each pair the *s* of the white group is given first)—14.45, 12.65; 17.55, 15.32; 15.85, 14.05.

of sociopaths were 101.70 and 87.79; while the respective mean *Full Scale* IQ's on the sociopaths were 98.71 and 84.45. These means, as well as the standard deviations, are included in Table 11. From these data the present writer calculated the significance of the three mean differences; in each comparison the *t* ratios proved to be significant at the .01 level. As in the DeStephens study both white and Negro groups earned higher mean IQ's on the *Performance* than on the *Verbal Scale,* with the greater difference between their means occurring among the white deviants.[19]

Rozynko and Wenk (1965) administered the *California Test of Mental Maturity* and the *General Aptitude Test Battery* to saturated and random samples of delinquent white, Negro, and Mexican-American youths processed through the Reception-Guidance Center at Deuel Vocational Institution in California. Altogether there were 178 whites, 178 Negroes, and 178 Mexicans equated as to age, the whites and Negroes having completed the same average number of school grades, *i.e.,* 10.2.

As will be seen in Table 11, the Negroes scored consistently below the whites in both the language and the nonlanguage portions of the *CTMM* and on all nine factors of the *GATB* (Intelligence, Verbal Aptitude, Numerical Aptitude, Spatial Aptitude, Form Perception, Clerical Perception, Motor Coordination, Finger Dexterity, and Manual Dexterity)—a test used by the United States Department of Employment to assess a person's work aptitudes. In all, with the exception of Motor Coordination, the differences between the Negro and white means proved to be highly significant.

The Mexican-American samples scored about equal to the Negroes on the verbal portions of the tests but occupied an intermediate position between the Negro and white groups on the nonverbal portions. In general, as the authors had anticipated, the Mexican-Americans performed *best on nonacademic tasks* and *poorest when the tasks required a knowledge of academic material.* "This group performed best on the Motor Coordination, Finger Dexterity and Manual Dexterity factors and poorest on the General Intelligence, Clerical, Vocabulary and Numerical factors." (p. 5, extended report)

The Negro group, on the other hand, scored lower than the whites on all of the tests and lower than the Mexican-Americans on the nonverbal ones; and the authors, not being able to explain the latter difference on the basis of educational level or socioeconomic status, concluded that inadequate motivation is an extremely important factor in the mental test performance of Negro inmates. In the opinion of the reviewer, it is unnecessary to introduce motivation as an explanation of the position of the Negro delinquent relative to that of the white and Mexican. An examination of the several means included in Table 11 reveals the fact that the whites and Negroes (as well as the Mexican-Americans) achieved

---

[19]The Mexican-Americans (who may have been bilingual, but the author does not mention this point) scored about the same as the Negro sociopaths on the *Verbal Scale* but higher on the *Performance* and *Full Scales.*

higher average IQ's on the three tests of *Motor Coordination, Finger Dexterity,* and *Manual Dexterity* than they did on the academic tests of *General Intelligence, Clerical Perception, Vocabulary,* and *Numerical Aptitude.* The Negro groups earned combined mean IQ's of *94.46* and *83.75,* respectively, on these *non-academic* and *academic factors;* the white groups achieved a *nonacademic* mean of *101.58,* as compared with an *academic* one of *94.51.*

Instead of comparing randomly selected groups of Negro and white delinquents, Clarke (1941) examined the racial samples after they had been matched for IQ.[20] Since his purpose was to analyze Negro and white "response patterns", Clarke analyzed the *Stanford-Binet, Form L* records of 116 white and 116 colored boys, 14 to 16 years of age, who had been admitted to the New York State Training School for Boys between 1937 and 1939. Not only were the white and colored boys of the same chronological and mental ages, but they were all from marginal and submarginal backgrounds of New York City and had been examined by either Negro or white psychologists. The two groups were found not to differ significantly in scatter along the test scale. However, the author reported strong tendencies in the direction of Negro superiority in *verbal* functions and white superiority in *reasoning* and *number* functions.

No implications as to racial differences can be derived from Clarke's study since the author included among his white boys those whose parents were foreign-born and in whose homes a foreign language was spoken. These boys were likely handicapped in verbal facility and, owing to the fact that they were matched in total score with a native American colored group, would be expected to have excelled in numerical or other ability. In addition, about 25 per cent of the 116 colored Ss had earlier migrated from Southern sections of the United States. The author anticipated a greater verbal facility among these Ss — to another group matched for IQ — since he believed proficiency with words to be less dependent upon formal schooling than facility with numbers and abstract reasoning. It is unfortunate, particularly in view of Machover's subsequent analysis of response patterns in criminal groups, that Clarke did not eliminate all subjects of foreign-born parents and all Ss who had received their education outside of New York City.

SUMMARY

In all twenty-eight of the above studies (with the exclusion of Clarke's matched groups) the colored averaged below the white norms or below the white delinquents with whom they were compared. In the twenty-two studies where the results were given in IQ, the average of the approximately 3480 Negroes was 74.44; in the 15 researches where IQ's were reported on comparable groups of white delinquents, the average IQ was 80.64. Therefore, the average IQ of the white misdemeanants examined was about 20 points below

---

[20]Clarke's work has not been included in Table 11.

that of the average white nondelinquent, and about six points above the average obtained on Negro delinquents. From statistics presented by several investigators, it seems that in proportion to their number in the total population of the United States the Negroes have contributed from two to five times their "share" of delinquency.

CRIMINALS

Southern. The *Army Beta Examination,* revised for civilian use by Kellogg and Morton in 1943 and restandardized by Lindner and Gurvitz in 1946 was administered to 991 white and 769 Negro male prisoners admitted to the Reception Center of the North Carolina Prison Department during 1958. The mean ages of the white and colored men were 27.88 and 28.43, their mean school grade completed, 7.37 and 6.82, respectively. The mean *Beta* IQ's earned by the white and colored prisoners were 94.55 and 78.29, respectively, the *t* ratio being 23.91.[21] (Panton, 1960)

Samples of 100 white and 100 colored males were subsequently drawn from the clinical files in accordance with the distribution of the white and colored *Beta* IQ's among the 1958 admissions. As will be observed in Table 12 the *Beta* IQ's of these selected men were within one point of the mean IQ's of the two original unselected samples. The 200 men comprising the selected samples had been administered the *WAIS* as well as the *Beta* and had been diagnosed as *Sociopathic Personality, Anti-Social Reaction* during the initial processing. Panton analyzed the *WAIS* protocols of the white and Negro prisoners in order to determine whether or not there are important characteristics that distinguish personality patterns generally associated with indices of sociopathy.

The mean *WAIS Verbal* IQ's obtained on the white and colored sociopaths were respectively, 90.75 and 77.20; their respective mean *Performance* IQ's were only slightly higher, *i.e.*, 91.60 and 78.55; the *Full Scale* IQ's for the two comparable groups were 90.55 and 76.45. The three differences proved to be highly significant, the *t* ratios being consistently above 7. Likewise, each of the six *Verbal* and the five *Performance* subtest means was significantly higher for the white sociopaths, all 11 differences being significant at the .01 level of confidence.

Panton observed that one of the most interesting aspects of the Negro profiles was the consistently high rank of the *Digit Span* subtest in comparison with its fluctuation of position among the white subjects. He noted that Siegman (1956) had shown that the *Digit Span* scores are affected by anxiety; and that Wechsler had found that low *Digit Span* scores, when not associated with organic defects, might be attributable in part to anxiety and inattention. Since among the Negro sociopaths the *Digit Span* appeared to be the easiest of the *Verbal* subtests, there may be implied a lesser degree of anxiety for the Negroes than

---

[21] All of these specific *t*'s mentioned in reference to Panton's study were calculated by the reviewer.

for the whites. The author remarked that this interpretation supported his previous findings that Negro inmates demonstrated considerably less anxiety than white inmates. (Panton, 1959) The relatively high ranking of the white sociopaths in *Picture Completion* subtest (for all subsamples) appeared to Panton to indicate greater ability to differentiate essential from nonessential details when performing a visual motor task than is demonstrated by the Negroes. Also the fact that both Negro and white samples scored relatively well (within the respective subsamples) on *Comprehension* and relatively poorly on *Vocabulary, Information,* and *Digit Symbol* was interpreted as supporting the clinical impression of the sociopath that he attempts to receive immediate gain by "feeding back" to the examiner socially acceptable answers.

Border. In one of the earlier studies dealing with the relationship between mental defect and delinquency among American Negroes and whites, Groves Smith included a table showing the percentages of lower level *Alpha* grades earned by white and colored individuals admitted to the St. Louis City Jail and to the City Workhouse in 1922.[22] Although he omitted the number of men examined by the "Army Tests" and excluded all percentages scoring at the several levels above *Alpha C—,* Smith nevertheless made it clear (see Table 12) that about 73 per cent of the colored and 32 per cent of the whites in the City Workhouse scored below the level of *C;* and 78 per cent of the colored and about 21 per cent of the white men in the City Jail scored below this level. Smith called attention to other factors besides intelligence test level that should be considered in classifying delinquents and criminals, such as: lack of cooperation due to attitudes of prisoner and examiner; impression that the tests are being used to obtain information about his crime; the idea that the testing is "foolishness"; inability of foreign-born to speak the language and their different racial customs, habits, and attitudes; "nervousness" incident to being apprehended, imprisoned, tried, and sentenced; and the presence of underlying psychopathic, or at least antisocial, personality deviations among those apprehended.

Roebuck (1963) analyzed a sample of 400 arrest histories selected at random from 1155 Negro cases admitted to the District of Columbia Reformatory at Lorton, Virginia, between January, 1954, and November, 1955.[23] The author constructed an arrest-history typology of 13 criminal patterns, such as: robbery, violations of narcotics laws, burglary, sex offenses, auto theft, confidence games, numbers games, check forgery, a triple pattern of drunkenness, assault, and larceny, *etc.* A major part of the study involved various comparisons between the 16 *numbers game operators* and the 384 criminals making up the remainder of the sample. In addition to various social and background characteristics which distinguished the two groups, they differed significantly on *Revised Beta Exami-*

---

[22]The jail population was composed primarily of those awaiting trial; while the workhouse inmates were mainly those who had been sentenced.

[23]Although called a "reformatory" Roebuck reported it to be actually a penitentiary.

nation. The median IQ obtained on the numbers laws violators was 105, that on all other offenders, 86.

Northern. Doll (1920-21) studied the first 152 cases examined individually at the New Jersey State Prison following the initiation of a program of psychiatric and psychological examining in the correctional institutions of this state. About half of the cases were unselected from new admissions, while the other half were unselected cases considered for parole. The median schooling achieved by the 66 native-born whites was between the sixth and seventh grades; the median schooling of the 36 colored Ss was between the second and third grades. The *Army Alpha* scores were tabulated in terms of mental age, the ranges of the respective native white and colored groups being from *under 8 to 18,* and from *8 to 9 to 16 to 18.* The median mental ages of these white and colored prisoners were 14 and 11 years, respectively.[24]

Wickman (1922) described briefly the results of an intelligence survey of men incarcerated in the Warrensville Workhouse in Cleveland, Ohio. About one fifth of the 450 inmates were tested on *Army Alpha* after they had been selected by taking every fifth man in an assembled line; to this number were added all men detained on federal charges and the group of *long termers.* Of the 126 men thus selected, 32 claimed to be unable to read and write and were thereby excused from *Alpha,* another was not tested because of his poor vision and four others were found to have omitted some pertinent fact from their records. The mental test records of the remaining 57 native and foreign-born whites and the 32 colored men are given in Table 12 in terms of percentages achieving the several grade levels between *B* and *E.* It will be noted that one third of the white men and none of the colored earned Alpha grades of C+ or B; and that 26.3 per cent of the white inmates and 71.9 per cent of the colored earned grades of D or E.

Murchison and Burfield (1925) reported the results of *Army Alpha* as given to 1351 Negro prisoners in state penitentiaries and reformatories of Ohio, Illinois, Maryland, and New Jersey. These prisoners were categorized according to birthplace as *South, Border,* and *North,* and the percentage of each group making letter grades from *A* to *E* recorded. Murchison and Burfield concluded that the average intelligence of the Negro criminal was above that of the average of the Negro draft.[25]

In studying the degree of mental deficiency of criminals and delinquents in Illinois prior to 1924, Adler and Worthington (1925) examined the *Army*

---

[24]Doll reported that Negroes comprised 23.6 per cent of the state prison population and 3.7 per cent of the population of the State of New Jersey (1910 census).

[25]See letter-grade distribution of the Negro draft on the *Combined Scale* in Table 7 of this review. (Yerkes, 1921 and Wallis, 1926) In Ohio prison Murchison tested all who could be spared from their duties; in the Illinois prison *Alpha* was given to one half of the men. Many known to be inferior in intelligence may have been kept out by officials who selected the subjects. (L. D. Zeleny, *reported* by Tulchin, 1939)

Alpha records of 4315 men imprisoned in the State Reformatory at Pontiac, the State Penitentiary at Joliet, and the State Penitentiary at Menard. Those Ss who scored below *C—* on *Alpha* had been given individual examinations and the results "were considered in the statistical reports." Besides comparing the intelligence distributions in the several penal and corrective institutions with the Army draft findings, Adler and Worthington, among other things, compared the test records of the Negroes and whites and of the Southern-born and Northern-born Negroes with the several groups of Negro criminals in Murchison's study. As will be noted in the table, the Northern-born Negroes generally scored between the white prisoners and the Southern-born Negroes.[26] At the superior level, the percentages of the whites, Northern-born colored and Southern-born colored were respectively, 24.4, 17.2, and 2.6, with the Northern-born colored having the highest percentage of men at the *A* level; at the *inferior* level (including Grades of C—, D, and E) the percentages of white, Northern-born colored and Southern-born colored men were respectively, 50.5, 61.4, and 86.2. The authors believed the Negro criminal in Illinois to be quite comparable in mental ability to the Negro draft and agreed with Murchison that "the problem of negro intelligence should always be stated as negro intelligence *where.*"

Cox (1930) tabulated the *Stanford-Binet* test results of 742 native white and 258 colored prisoners who were inmates of the Western State Penitentiary at Pittsburgh. The test had been given routinely to the majority of the literate felons of this institution. Cox found the Negroes to be inferior to the white prisoners in 47 of the 50 subtests and significantly inferior to the whites in 31 of them. He divided the subtests at the upper levels in accordance with W. T. Root's analysis of the *Binet*. In all of the Reasoning subtests there were significant differences in the passes by the Negroes and whites; in all of the *Immediate Associative Memory* subtests there were significant differences in the Negro and white passes; in 90 per cent of the subtests placed under the caption of *Educational and Cultural Setting* there were significant differences in the number of Negro and white passes; in 85 per cent of the subtests placed under the heading of *Social and Common Sense Comprehension* there were significant differences in the percentage of passes; and in 70 per cent of the *Language* subtests there were significant differences between the passes of the Negroes and native whites. Cox argued that since many subtests deal with material acquired from the environment and since the environment of the native white convicts was probably superior to that of the Negro convicts, the findings would seem to support the opinion that the superiority of the native whites in the *Stanford-Binet* in an indication of the difference in environmental opportunity. Conversely, he

---

[26]Delinquents at the State Training School for Boys in St. Charles, at the State Training School for Girls in Geneva, at the State Woman's Prison in Joliet, and at the City House of Correction in Chicago were also included in the Adler and Worthington report, but their records were not analyzed according to race.

believed that the superiority of the native whites was not due entirely to innate differences.

Spirer (1940) discusses briefly the unpublished dissertation of G. I. Giardini in which he compared native white and Negro convicts of the Western Penitentiary of Pennsylvania on the *Stanford-Binet*. The median IQ of the whites was reported to be 81, that of the Negroes, 65, the *t* ratio being 11.94. When the Negro prisoners were separated according to school systems under which they received their education, Giardini found the colored who came from states where the school index was 50 or more to have a mean IQ of 71, and those Ss from states where the school index was less than 35 to have a mean IQ of 63.

In a study of New Jersey homicides, Frankel (1939) tabulated various characteristics of 1000 convicted murderers committed to the State Prison at Trenton between 1908 and 1936. Seven hundred twenty-two of these men, including 244 Negroes, 233 native-born whites, and 245 foreign-born whites, had been given mental tests the results of which were recorded in terms of *mental age*. The median MA's of the native-born whites and the colored were 12.7 and 10.6, respectively. The percentages of these two groups ranging from *8 years and below* to *18 years and over* are given in Table 12. It will be noted that up to but not including a mental age of 11 years the colored murderers far exceeded the whites, but the reverse occurred from the mental age of 12 on.[27]

Tulchin (1939) included in his data the *Alpha* medians of 330 Northern-born and 972 Southern-born Negroes in addition to those of 1545 native whites of native parents, all of the men having been tested in the state prison at Joliet, Illinois, between 1920 and 1927. All classified as inferior on *Alpha* had been recalled for individual examinations and for these men the final classification was made on the basis of the individual tests. The median of the whites was at 67; that of the Northern-born Negroes, at 41, that of the Southern-born Negroes, 27. As will be noted in the table, *superior* ratings were earned by 19.8 per cent of the whites, by 6.1 per cent of the Northern-born Negroes, and by 0.9 per cent of the Southern-born Negroes. The percentages of *inferior* ratings secured by the white criminals was 8.5, by the Northern-born Negroes, 24.2, and by the Southern-born Negroes, 47.5.

An attempt was made by Tulchin to rule out the differential of schooling by comparing white and Northern-born colored felons of the same educational attainment. In Table 10 are presented the median scores of the two groups of Ss for each maximum school grade completed from 3 to 10. All eight colored medians were lower than the corresponding white medians, the differences ranging from 5 points at Grade 3 to 27 points at Grade 8.

A total of 96 white and 57 colored women were tested by the *Stanford-Binet* on being admitted to the Women's Prison during the period covered in the survey, 1920-1927. Due to the small number of cases, Tulchin did not attempt to

---

[27]The Negro murder commitment rate was over twelve times that of the native whites from 1915 to 1924 and over thirteen times that of the native whites from 1925 to 1934.

TABLE

THE

AUTHOR DATE	LOCATION	TEST	N	SUBJECTS AGE*	GRADE	METHOD OF SELECTION
Panton, J. H. (1960)	North Carolina	*Revised*[1] *Beta*	w-991 c- 769	27.9 28.4		White and Negro male prisoners admitted to Reception Center, N.C. Prison Dept. in 1958.
		Revised Beta	w-100 c-100	28.1 28.2		Samples of 100 w & 100 c from clinical files in accordance with distribution of *Beta* IQ's on total '58 admissions of each race. All had been administered *Beta* & *WAIS* & had been diagnosed as *Sociopathic Personality, Anti-Social Reaction* in initial processing.
		WAIS				
Smith, G. B. (1924)	St. Louis, Mo.	*Army*[2] *Tests*	Not given			St. Louis Jail and City Workhouse Survey in 1922. Jail pop composed primarily of those awaiting trial; workhouse inmates mainly those who had been sentenced.
Roebuck, J. B. (1936)	Lorton, Va.	*Revised*[4] *Beta*	c- "Numbers"- 16 Others- 384	38 33		Sample of 400 arrest histories selected at random from 1155 Negro cases who entered reformatory bet 1-5-54 and 11-8-55.[5]

*Mean age when tested.
[1]Revised for civilian use by Kellogg and Morton, 1934; restandardized by Lindner & Gurvitz, 1946. Used Wechsler's method for calculating IQ.
All *t*'s in this study calculated by reviewer.

TWELVE

CRIMINALS

	RESULTS		COMMENTS OF AUTHOR

	Beta IQ		Interesting aspect of Negro profiles is consistently
	w	c	high rank of Digit Span subtest in comparison with
M	94.55	78.29	its fluctuation of position among whites. Implies a
s	14.39	13.87	greater freedom from anxiety on part of colored.
t =	23.91		

	Beta IQ	
M	93.50	78.55
s	14.13	14.24
t =	7.44	

	Verbal IQ	
	w	c
M	90.75	77.20
s	14.02	10.63
t =	7.70	

	Perform IQ	
M	91.60	78.55
s	14.14	14.21
t =	6.52	

	Full Scale IQ	
M	90.55	76.45
s	13.61	12.04
t =	7.75	

	Workhouse	
	w	c
Alpha level[3]	%	%
C—	14.3	30.1
D	8.8	20.6
E	8.8	21.9
	Jail	
C—	16.9	26
D	1.3	22
E	2.6	30

	IQ		Reformatory was actually a penitentiary and housed
	Numbers	*Others*	a heterogenous group of felons serving sentences
	c	c	ranging to life imprisonment.
Mdn	105	86	

[2]While author tabulated scores acc to *Alpha*, he indicated that Army Tests were used. Probable that Ss may have been examined by *Beta, Individual Tests,* and/or *Alpha*.

[3]Author omitted classifications above C—.

[4]Lindner and Gurvitz *Revised Beta*.

[5]Although located in Virginia the reformatory housed felons from the District of Columbia.

TABLE

THE

AUTHOR DATE	LOCATION	TEST	N	SUBJECTS		METHOD OF SELECTION
				AGE	GRADE	
Doll, E. A. (1920-21)	New Jersey	*Army Alpha*	w-66[6] c- 36		36[7]	Analysis of first 152 cases examined at N.J. State Prison; half were new admissions & half were un-selected cases considered for parole.
Wickman, E. K. (1922)	Cleveland, Ohio	*Army Alpha*	w- Native 44 Foreign- born 13 c- 32			An intell survey of Warrensville Workhouse in-cluding about 450 men. About 1/5 were tested by assembling men in file & selecting every fifth. To these were added all who were there on federal charges & the group of "long termers."
Murchison, C., and Burfield, H. (1925)	Ohio, Illinois, New Jersey, Maryland	*Army Alpha*	c- 1351			Negro prisoners in state penitentiaries & reformatories. Divided Ss acc to section of country where born: South, Border, North.
Adler, H. M., and Worthington, M. R. (1925)	Joliet, Menard, Pontiac, Ill.	*Army Alpha*	4315[8]			A study of the records of mental testing surveys made prior to 1924. Those who scored below C— on *Alpha* were given individual examinations & these results recorded.[9]

[6]All native-born.
[7]Median of 36 applies to all 152 cases including foreign-born.
[8]Number of c and w not given separately. This number includes all criminals whose test papers were examined.

TWELVE (continued)

CRIMINALS

RESULTS			COMMENTS OF AUTHOR
	MA		Excessive number of Negroes & foreign-born among the prisoners.
	w	c	
Mdn	14	11	

	All w	c	Of the 126 selected, 32 were illiterate and did not take the examination, one was excused because of poor vision, and 4 did not indicate birth or race.
	%	%	
Level			
A	—	—	
B	5.3	—	
C+	28.0	—	
C	24.5	6.2	
C—	15.8	21.9	
D	10.5	28.1	
E	15.8	43.8	

	Birthplace			Average intelligence of Negro criminal above that of the Negro draft.
	c	c	c	
	So	Bor	No	
Level	%	%	%	
A	0.2	0.7	1.2	
B	1.2	1.4	5.0	
C+	2.9	5.3	12.2	
C	15.2	16.8	25	
C—	22.4	25.3	25.1	
D	21.4	17.8	12.1	
E	36.2	33.2	19.1	

		Birthplace		While IQ is relatively stable & the results of mental tests may be accepted as reasonably accurate, nevertheless they cannot be regarded as an absolutely quantitative index of the innate capacity of the individuals.
	w	c	c	
		So	No	
Level	%	%	%	
A	2.4	—	2.9	
B	7.0	0.5	4.3	
C+	15.0	2.1	10.0	
C	25.1	11.1	21.4	
C—	22.7	22.2	24.2	
D	16.7	39.7	22.9	
E	11.1	24.3	14.3	
Sup.[10]	24.4	2.6	17.2	
Inf.	50.5	86.2	61.4	

[9]In addition the author may have included a number of scores from a "cross-section survey made in 1924." This number was not reported and it is possible that none were included in Negro-white comparisons as tabulated.

[10]*Superior* here includes A, B, and C+; *inferior*, C—, D, and E.

TABLE

THE

AUTHOR DATE	LOCATION	TEST	N	SUBJECTS		METHOD OF SELECTION
				AGE	GRADE	
Cox, J. F. (1930)	Pittsburgh, Pa.	*Stanford-Binet, 1916*	w-742 c- 258			Test given routinely to majority of literate inmates of Western Penitentiary. Tabulated test records of 1000 native w & c.
Frankel, E. (1939)	New Jersey	Not given	w-233[6] c- 244			From an analysis of 1000 murderers committed to State Prison at Trenton, 1908-1936.
Tulchin, S. H. (1939)	Joliet, Ill.	*Army Alpha*	w-1545[11] c- No-330 So- 972	28.9[12] 28.6 28.3	7.0[13] 6.3 3.8	Survey state prison, 1920-7; tests given to every man routinely; all classed as inferior on *Alpha* recalled for individual exam. Final classification made on basis of indiv. exam (in case of inferiors).
	Joliet, Ill.	*Stanford-Binet, 1916*	w-96[16] c- 57	28.3[12] 25.8	5-6[13] 5	Intelligence tests to all inmates in Women's Prison in period covered, 1920-7.

[11]Ss native-born of native parents.
[12]Median age at admission to institution.
[13]Median of highest school grade reached.

TWELVE *(continued)*
CRIMINALS

RESULTS	COMMENTS OF AUTHOR
C inferior to w in 47 of the 50 subtests C significantly inferior in 31 of subtests	The superiority of the native whites is so great as to make questionable the explanation that it is due entirely to innate differences in intelligence.

	MA	
	w	c
	%	%
8 & below	2.5	9.1
9	6.0	22.5
10	14.2	32.4
11	15.9	15.6
12	16.3	8.2
13	17.6	4.9
14	7.7	4.1
15	6.4	1.6
16	6.9	0.8
17	4.3	0.4
18 & above	2.2	0.4
	MA	
Mdn	12.7	10.6

Aver annual murder commitment rate during period 1925-1934 was 1.65 per 100,000 male pop 15 years and over for native-born white; the rate was 22.03 per 100,000 male pop 15 yrs and over for colored.

		Scores[14]	
	w	c	
		No	So
Mdn	67	41	27
Sup	19.8%	6.1%	0.9%
Aver	71.7%	69.7%	51.6%
Inf	8.5%	24.2%	47.5%

Maximum Sch & Scores[15]

Grade	N		*Mdn*	
	w	c	w	c
10	92	23	97	73
9	73	20	85	69
8	456	71	73	46
7	168	34	63	55
6	163	30	47	41
5	121	28	53	31
4	108	21	40	33
3	56	26	33	28

Scores

	w	c
Sup	3.1%	1.8%
Aver	68.8%	40.3%
Inf	28.1%	57.9%

Percentages of inferior, average, and superior men in penitentiary and Army very similar.

[14]Northern-born, Southern-born.
[15]*Colored* here includes *Northern-born* only.
[16]Includes all white cases.

TABLE

THE

AUTHOR DATE	LOCATION	TEST	N	SUBJECTS		METHOD OF SELECTION
				AGE	GRADE	
Clemmer, D. (1940)	Midwest[17] State Prison	*Army Alpha*	w-1901 c- 403	17- 17-		Not given; probably whole prison population during testing period.
Machover, S. (1943)	**New York City**	*Wechsler-Bellevue*	cI-50	16-35	0-4	Among criminals who were examined in Psychiatric Clinic of Court of Gen'l Sessions & given psychol tests: *cI*-random selection of criminals provided (1) born in South (2) no sch in North & generally less than 4 grades in South (3) living in NYC fewer than 6 yrs & (4) migrated to NYC at not less than 16 yrs of age.
			cII-50	16-36	3-11	*cII*-selected from large criminal group to match those in cI in CA & in composite of 2 subtests on W-B: Similarities & Comprehension.
			cIII-100	16-26	4-12	*cIII*-random selection of criminals within age range of 16-26.[18]
Corsini, R. (1946)	**New York**	*Alpha,*[19] *Beta*	w-1030 c- 365	40.2* 37.9		All prisoners at Auburn State Prison given mental tests. Author studied records of 1935 inmates in 1943.

[17]The description of the prison identifies it as the Illinois State Prison at Menard.
[18]Reviewer omits from table the summary of scores of w groups matched with c in CA, IQ, and sch grade completed.

TWELVE (continued)

CRIMINALS

	RESULTS			COMMENTS OF AUTHOR
		MA		Those who for any reason failed because of physical
	w		c	defect or illiteracy were individually tested by
Mdn	13-7		11-5	*Stanford-Binet* or a performance test.
Sup	6.7%		0.8%	
Aver	51.8%		19.9%	
Dull	25.2%		35.8%	
Defect	16.3%		43.5%	

	IQ cI	Culturally very restricted Southern Negroes made significantly lower scores on 4 of the 5 performance subtests than matched group (cII). Performance tests such as Digit Symbol, Block Design, & Picture Arrangement are culture-bound and for culturally restricted adults present a less valid index of general intell capacity than the verbal tests of Similarities and Comprehension.
M	66.88	
s	9.51	
Range	48-89	

	IQ cII
M	79.74
s	12.17
Range	58-107

	IQ cIII
M	88.87
s	12.5
Range	64-120

	IQ^{20}			W criminal at Auburn equals intelligence of the
	w		c	w Army draft; the mean Negro IQ is much higher
M	91.4		83.4	than the c Army draft.
s	14.2		13.8	
t =		9		

[19] If scores showed anomalies or if after interviews they appeared to require further testing, the prisoners were retested individually.

[20] In obtaining IQ's, a CA of 15 years was used.

TABLE

THE

AUTHOR DATE	LOCATION	TEST	N	SUBJECTS		METHOD OF SELECTION
				AGE	GRADE	
Malamud, H. R. (1948)	Pennsylvania	*Stanford-Binet 1916*	w Prob-140 Cont-171 c Prob- 74 Cont- 40	23.6 25.4 26.1 25.6		All native w & c inmates of Western State Penitentiary, who, with the exception of about 19 special cases, were admitted to prison during 1930. Cases separated acc to those who were reported as disciplinary (problem) cases in pen & those who were not.
Fry, F. D. (1949)	Pennsylvania	Not given	w-75 c- 22	32.8 29.5		From one penal institution; men secured through supt who asked for volunteers who were willing to participate in research program. Only requirements were that men must be able to read & write with facility & ratio of racial groups in prison pop be maintained.
Stanton, J. M. (1956)	New York	*Army General Classification Test*	w-100 c- 100	31.3 29.0		Ss were the first 100 w & 100 c native-born inmates of Sing Sing received in the prison during a specified period who met certain requirements. They had to be literate, attain a score of 70 or higher on *AGCT*, & men on whom valid Minnesota Multiphasic Inventory profiles had been obtained.

TWELVE *(concluded)*

CRIMINALS

RESULTS				COMMENTS OF AUTHOR
		IQ		Negro inmate is significantly lower in IQ than the w, but the Negro problem case is on average slightly more intelligent than the Negro control case.
	w		c	
M				
Problem	83.79		73.78	
Control	81.49		70.50	
s				
Problem	14.76		15.42	
Control	15.12		13.59	
t				
Problem w-c =		6.80		
Control w-c =		6.79		

		IQ		Negro men made up one third of prison population.
	w		c	
M	100.8		94.6	

Mean *AGCT* score of w group significantly higher at .01 level than that of Negro.

Ss were mainly urbanites from the New York metropolitan area.

separate the foreign-born and native-born whites; neither did he classify the colored according to birthplace. However, the two groups were fairly comparable in chronological age when tested and in the highest school grade completed. All Ss with mental ages below 11 were categorized as *inferior,* and those with mental ages of 16.5 and above were listed as *superior.* As will be observed in the table, 3.1 per cent of the white women and 1.8 per cent of the Negro women were identified by the author as *superior;* while 28.1 per cent of the whites and 57.9 per cent of the colored were found to be *inferior.*

Clemmer (1940) includes in his description of a prison community a comparison between the *Army Alpha* scores of 403 Negro and 1901 white inmates. Although the author did not indicate his method of selection he referred to the fact that 2347 prisoners were in residence on a certain day; it is therefore probable that all prisoners were tested if they were living in the prison during the period surveyed. As will be seen from Table 12, the median mental ages of the racial samples differed by about two years, that of the whites being 13 years, 7 months and that of the colored, 11 years, 5 months. Six and seven tenths per cent of the whites and 0.8 per cent of the colored were placed in the *superior* and *very superior* category; whereas 41.5 per cent of the white and 79.3 per cent of the colored prisoners were classified as *borderline* or *mentally defective.*

In a study of the patterning of abilities measured by the *Wechsler-Bellevue Intelligence Scale,* Machover (1943) selected for his subjects Negro and white criminals who had been examined in the Psychiatric Clinic of the Court of General Sessions. *Group I* consisted of a random sample of 50 Negro criminals, provided: (1) they were Southern-born; (2) they had had no schooling in the North and no more than four grades in the South; (3) they had been living in New York City fewer than six years; and (4) they had migrated to New York City at not less than 16 years of age. Most of the subjects in this group came from rural backgrounds and all had a history of cultural and material impoverishment. *Group II* consisted of 50 Negro criminals selected from a large criminal group to match those of Group I in chronological age and in the composite of raw scores achieved on two of the *Wechsler-Bellevue* subtests: *Similarities* and *Comprehension.* The highest grade completed by members of Group II ranged from 3 to 11, nearly all of the schooling having been received in New York City. Thirty-two of these men had been born and continuously reared in New York City, or had received the major part of their schooling there; only three were born in small Southern towns. *Group III* consisted of 100 Negro felons selected randomly from the files of criminals provided they were within the age range of from 16 to 26 years. The highest school grade reached by this group ranged from 4 to 12. Sixty-eight of these subjects had been born and reared in New York City; 20 had been born in the South but were brought to New York at not more than

7 years of age; the others had come from other large urban areas in the North.[28]

Probably the most important finding of Machover relates to the differential scoring of the Negro *Groups I and II* on the *Wechsler-Bellevue* subtests. Group I—selected because of having been culturally restricted—was matched with a culturally less restricted group on the two verbal subtests. It was to be expected that Group I, because of a severe handicap on verbal material which is presumed to be dependent on schooling, would have been less at a disadvantage on the *nonverbal* subtests (the *Picture Arrangement,* the *Picture Completion,* the *Block Design, the Object Assembly,* and the *Digit Symbol*) and would have earned a total higher IQ than Group II. However, the reverse was true. The culturally restricted Group I (in comparison with the Northern-educated Group II) did best in *Verbal Comprehension* and *Similarities,* and worst in the Performance tests of *Digit Symbol, Block Design,* and *Picture Arrangement.* Machover concluded that the Southern-reared *Negroes* showed marked defects in perceptual organization and perceptuo-motor integration, suggesting that the maturation of these functions is in large measure initially dependent on formal schooling, or in experience at a higher level of cultural complexity than that experienced by the Southern Negro.

This test pattern associated with marked cultural restriction in Group I was observed by Machover to be similar to patterns of individuals showing pathological impairment of mental functioning. Therefore, the author suggested that no clinical designation of a particular pattern of mental pathology is safe without reference to the cultural level of the subject.

Corsini (1946) was interested in comparing the intelligence scores of the New York State Prison inmates at Auburn with the season of birth. Accordingly, he examined the *Army Alpha,* the *Army Beta,* or other mental test records of 1395 felons in 1943. Using a CA of 15 years in each case, the mean IQ of the white prisoners was 91.4, a figure not unlike that of the Army draft. The mean of the Negro prisoners was 83.4, which he estimated as being much higher than the colored Army draft mean, in agreement with the findings of Murchison and Burfield.[29]

In an attempt to find ways of distinguishing probable discipline from probable nondiscipline convicts upon their entry into prison, Malamud (1948) selected the records of all native white and colored inmates of the Western State Penitentiary, who, with a few exceptions, were admitted to prison during

---

[28]The white groups consisted of 100 criminals individually matched with the Negroes of Group III in CA, *Wechsler-Bellevue* IQ, and grade level achieved; 25 criminals selected to match in age, grade, and IQ 25 white noncriminals; and 100 native New York noncriminals, 75 of whom were selected to match in age, grade, and IQ a corresponding group of white criminals (and by inference Negro criminals). The *Arithmetic* subtest was the only one in which there was a significant difference (white criminal group superior to matched colored criminal Group III).

[29]Corsini estimated the mean IQ of the Negro draft to be 69, basing his figure on the mean mental age of 10 years, 5 months.

1930. The cases were then separated according to those who were subsequently reported as *disciplinary* while in the penitentiary and those who were not so reported. The colored criminals, both discipline and nondiscipline cases, earned average IQ's in the low 70's on the *Stanford-Binet, 1916 Form,* being 10 or 11 points below the comparable groups of white criminals; these differences were significant at the .01 level of confidence. As will be seen in Table 12, both Negro and white *discipline* or *problem* groups earned mean IQ's that were slightly above the respective means of the Negro and white *nonproblem* cases.

Fry (1949) compared reactions to the Rosenzweig Picture-Frustration Test of white and colored inmates of two penal institutions in Pennsylvania with those of Pennsylvania State College students. IQ's were not reported on the college students nor were the imprisoned women separated according to race; therefore, Fry's study, as it concerns us, deals only with 22 Negro and 75 white male prisoners in one penitentiary. The mean IQ of the white men was 100.8, that of the colored, 94.6. The white criminals were on the average about three years older and had attained 0.8 higher school grade than the colored. Unfortunately, neither the name of the test or tests nor the size of the standard deviations was reported; this study has the added defect, from the point of view of racial comparisons, of subject selectivity, in that the men were secured through the superintendent of the penitentiary who was instructed to ask for volunteers, the only requirements stipulated by Fry being that every man must be able to read and write with facility and that the ratio of racial groups in the prison population be maintained.

Stanton's research (1956) was directed primarily at obtaining personality profiles of convicted men and comparing them with those obtained on the normative sample. In addition to using the Minnesota Multiphasic Personality Inventory, the *Army General Classification Test (AGCT)* was employed, the chief requirements for the inclusion of the convicts as subjects being that they must be literate, have attained a score of 70 or higher on the *AGCT,* and have valid Minnesota Multiphasic profiles.[30] Stanton obtained as subjects the first 100 white and 100 colored native-born men received in Sing Sing Prison on or after a specified date who met the above requirements and could be reasonably well equated in occupational category and school grade completed. The prisoners were described as mostly urbanites from the New York metropolitan area. The white and colored men selected had completed on the average school grades of 8.32 and 8.42; the occupational categories as recommended by Goodenough were used as guides—all of the Ss being placed in one of the lowest categories. The percentages of whites in categories IV, V, and VI were 22, 44, and 34, respectively; the percentages of colored belonging to these three categories were 20, 49, and 31, respectively. In spite of the occupation and grade matchings and in spite of the

---

[30]Thereby increasing the selectivity of the samples, particularly of the Negro sample. A minimum score of 70 on the *AGCT* is slightly above the mean of 2010 colored enlisted men as reported by Fulk (1949) in World War II. See Table 7.

removal of those men with low *AGCT* scores, the mean *AGCT* score of the white sample of convicts proved to be significantly higher than that of the Negro sample.[81]

Summary

The various studies on Negro and white criminals, like those on delinquents, consistently indicate lower means for the Negroes tested. Where the results were reported in terms of IQ, the mean of 1670 colored criminals was 81.26, that of 2407 white felons, 91.84.

In the instances where colored criminals or delinquents were matched with white convicts or delinquents for occupation, school grade completed, and type of community from which they had come, the differences between the mean scores continued to be significant.

Analysis of the *Wechsler-Bellevue* and *WAIS* tests reveals that for both *Negro* delinquents and criminals the *Arithmetic, Block Design,* and the *Digit Symbol* subtests are consistently among the most difficult; whereas *Digit Span, Comprehension,* and *Similarities* are likely to be among the least dfficult of the subtests.

---

[81]Neither the mean scores nor the standard deviations on *AGCT* were included in Stanton's data.

Chapter IX

RACIAL HYBRIDS

Another approach to the problem of Negro-white differences in intelligence has been through the study of racial hybrids. If Negro-white intermixtures are found to score higher than "unmixed" Negroes it is frequently implied that the higher scoring is due to the effect of the white strain. About 40 years ago, Herskovits said that in order to show that Negroes have lower intelligence than whites in a mixed group such as we have in the United States, those Negroes having the largest amount of white ancestry should on the average stand higher in tests, other things being equal, than persons of total or large amounts of Negro ancestry; and that, unless actual genealogical information is at hand, such types should be in the main distinguishable by some physical traits according to the degree of mixture which they represent.

On the other hand, some writers have observed that Negroes who are *less black* or *less Negroid* in features are more acceptable to whites and are likely to be selected for jobs which place them in close contact with members of the white group; similarly, lighter individuals have frequently been described as having a higher social standing *within* the Negro group.[1] If it is true that mulattoes have social prestige then this group can attract to itself superior men of whatever shade who appear among the Negroes—the superior men infrequently marrying into the "black" group. If a constant and selective social factor operates to bring the best intellectual ability of the race into the light group, then even relatively high correlations between lightness of skin color and intelligence score must be viewed with skepticism.

The majority of investigators who have studied the intelligence of Negro-white hybrids have separated the subjects according to skin color. In some cases the authors merely noted the color of their subjects and later categorized them into *light brown, brown, dark brown,* and *black;* or *dark, medium,* and *light;* or merely *dark* and *light.* In other instances, judgments were made by the Milton-Bradley color top method. A small top, with adjustable amounts of colored papers (red, white, yellow, and black), was spun and an attempt was made to vary the relative amount of the colors until the resulting combination matched the skin of the subject. In some cases, measurements of nose width, lip thickness, ear height, interpupillary span, cephalic index, *etc.,* served as criteria for racial mixture; while in other instances, the experimenters obtained genealogies by

---

[1]For discussions relating to this topic the reader may refer to: Burks and Steggerda (1940), Davis and Dollard (1940), Foreman (1932), Herskovits (1926), Klineberg (1944), La Piere (1946), Reuter (1931), and Simpson and Yinger (1953).

questioning the Ss, their parents, their teachers, or "reliable persons in the community".

An early attempt to classify Negroes into shades of skin color was made by Strong (1913). She divided the 122 children tested by the *Goddard Revision of the Binet-Simon* test in Columbia, South Carolina, into *dark, medium,* and *light* groups, the judgments having been made by the method of simple inspection. From Table 13 it will be observed that the *dark* group included the smallest percentage of children who were over one year retarded while the *light* group had the greatest percentage of pupils who were more than one year advanced. This is probably one of the least important of this group of studies, since the numbers were small, the age and grade ranges relatively large, and the test scores crudely classified.

Ferguson (1919) separated 2395 Camp Lee Negroes, who had been tested by *a, Alpha,* or *Beta,* into *lighter* and *darker* shades of skin color. The darker Negroes were found to average consistently below the lighter members of their group on the several tests employed.

Koch and Simmons (1926), using a color card to aid them in making skin judgments, divided the Austin, El Paso, and San Antonio, Texas, Negro school children into groups identified as *light, intermediate,* and *dark.* As will be noted in the table, there was no uniformity in the rankings of the *intermediate* and *dark* groups on the mental tests; however, in three of four tests the light groups scored higher on the average than the other two groups.

Herskovits (1926) measured nose width and lip thickness of 363 Negro male freshmen attending Howard University; he also determined their skin color by the Milton-Bradley color top method. All of the students had taken the *Thorndike College Entrance Examination* and all reported their genealogies as far as they could give them. Although he did not include average scores made on the *Thorndike,* Herskovits secured correlations between test scores of 115 Ss and measurements of nose width, lip thickness, amount of black element, and amount of white element. Except for the correlation between nose width and intelligence score which was zero (.01) the correlations between test scores and "white characteristics" were very low and positive. The author concluded that the relationship between test scores and physical traits indicating greater- or less-Negro ancestry is so tenuous as to be of no value in making comparisons as to the native abilities of Negroes and whites.

If it is true, as Herskovits and other responsible writers have said, that lighter Negroes are given preferment within the race, then it might follow that darker Negroes, or those more Negroid in other features, attending a first-rate Negro college, might be more highly selected and therefore less representative of the darker skinned Negroes, than is the case with the lighter Negroes. If darker Negro college students make a more highly selected group than the lighter ones, then it would be improper to correlate these outward manifestations of racial heredity with intelligence; and if such correlations are made they are of little value in interpreting race differences. It seems to the reviewer that Herskovits goes beyond his data when he concludes that in the light of his findings the basic hypothesis of white superiority in social efficiency and innate intelligence is to be gravely doubted. We grant that it may be reasonable to question white superiority in innate intelligence, but not because of his findings.

Davenport (1928) separated his 200 Negro adult subjects living in Jamaica, British West Indies, into categories of *Browns* and *Blacks*. He obtained their pedigrees from self reports or from information supplied by "reliable persons" in the community. He determined their physical characteristics, such as nasal breadth, hair form (measured by the diameter of the curl), interpupillary span, cephalic index, skin color (determined by the color top method), breadth of pelvis, length of arm span, *etc.* Comparable measurements were made on adult members of an isolated white community whose German ancestors had come to the island about four or five generations ago and who had carefully preserved their genealogical records. To complete the white group, Davenport went to Grand Cayman Island where he tested some whites of English stock. In so far as possible the three groups selected were from the same social stratum, but the investigator believed that the *Browns* were more highly selected than the other groups. On the three performance tests and on *Alpha* both the mixed and unmixed Negroes were below the white average, the *Browns* being intermediate on the three performance tests and below the *Blacks* on the *Alpha*. Davenport considered the inefficiency of the adult *Browns* as depending upon the presence of an excessively large number of persons in that group who were incapable of making any progress at all with the tasks before them. "One gets the impression that the blacks may have on the average the inferior capacity but are able to use what they have. The browns, as a whole, have a superior capacity to the blacks, but there is a much larger proportion of them who through becoming rattled or through general muddleness are unable to make any score; while, on the other hand, a large number do brilliant work." (p. 236) These statements have a highly subjective tinge and appear to the reviewer not to have been adequately supported by the evidence presented.

Klineberg (1928) found negligible relationships between Negroid traits and intelligence scores. He correlated lip thickness, nose width, and amount of black pigment as measured by the Milton-Bradley color top method with the *Pintner-Paterson* scores of 139 Negro children in villages of West Virginia. With age factors held constant, these coefficients ranged from -.06 to -.12. Using Ferguson's technique, Klineberg divided the 200 Negro boys from Grades 7 and 8 of a New York City public school into two groups, the *More Negroid* and the *Less Negroid*. As will be seen from the table, the former group scored on the average only two points below the latter group on the three form boards used to measure their intelligence. Klineberg concluded from these studies that there was, on the whole, no definite evidence of an inverse relationship between the test score and degree of Negro blood as indicated either by measurements (skin color, hair texture, general facial and cranial conformation) or by general Negroid appearance.

Young (1929) selected for study all Negro 9- and 10-year-olds in the third grade and above in Baton Rouge and Lake Charles, Louisiana. With the aid of the Negro principals and teachers the children were divided into two groups, the one including the darker and the more Negroid and the other the lighter and the less characteristically Negroid. The mean *National* scores of the *light* 9- and 10-year-olds were above those of the *dark* groups; in fact, the mean of the *light* 9-year-olds was one point above that of the *dark* 10-year-olds. At ten years, the median of the *light* group was above that of the *dark,* but at nine years the two medians were identical. In three of the four comparisons, therefore, the *light* Negroes proved to be superior to the *dark.*

Peterson and Lanier (1929) obtained several physical measurements on a group of 75 Negro 12-year-old boys from an elementary and a junior high school in New York City. These measures included nose width, lip thickness, ear height, and interpupillary span. As will be noted in the table, all of the correlations between these several traits and intelligence as measured by the *Yerkes Pre-Adolescent Point Scale* clustered around zero. In Nashville and Chicago they used skin color as the criterion of amount of Negro ancestry, dividing the subjects into *lighter* and *darker* groups after they had rated them on a 7-point scale from *very light* to *very dark*. The medians of the lighter group were superior to those of the darker on the *Stanford-Binet* and the *Myers Mental Measure*.

The correlations between lightness of skin and scores on the tests were positive but low, *i.e.,* .18 and .30. "The facts that all the coefficients were positive and that four out of five of the differences in median scores favored the lighter-skinned group indicate strongly superior ability in the children with the lightest color and therefore probably with the most white blood. This may be interpreted as evidence that the race differences found in this investigation are in part at least due to innate factors; for educational opportunities and other environmental factors might not to a very great extent favor one of these groups of negroes over the other . . . ." (p. 87)[2] Peterson and Lanier recognized a considerable element of truth in Herskovits' theory that greater ability in light colored children is due to a selective process among the male Negroes and not necessarily to the presence of white ancestry in the children. However, they found the theory not to be incompatible with the view that white ancestry in children makes for greater ability, observing that the effect of genes from the white race depends upon whether whites are natively superior and also upon the selection of whites who interbreed with the Negroes.

Jenkins (1936) asked the parents of 63 superior Negro children, who had been located in the Chicago survey, to state the racial composition of their

---

[2]In their comparisons the authors include (in addition to *Stanford-Binet* and *Myers*) a test of *Rational Learning*, a *Five Disc Transfer* test and a *Mental Maze*. The darker was superior to the lighter group on *Mental Maze*.

TABLE

RACIAL

AUTHOR DATE	LOCATION	TEST	N	SUBJECTS AGE	SUBJECTS GRADE	METHOD OF SELECTION
Strong, A. C. (1913)	Columbia, S. C.	*Goddard-Binet*	c- 43 45 34	6-15	1-5	From all grades in one c sch.
Ferguson, G. O., Jr. (1919)	Camp Lee	*Army a*	c- 657	Draft		Literates of 8 companies classed acc to lighter or darker skin.
		Army a	c- 667	Draft		Literates of 8 other co's classed as: yellow, brown, or black.
		Alpha	c- 344	Draft		Literates classed acc to lighter and darker.
		Beta	c- 727	Draft		Illiterates classed acc to lighter and darker.
Koch, H. L., and Simmons, R. (1926)	Austin, El Paso, and San Antonio, Tex.	*MMM*[2] *NIT* *Det* *P-C*	c- 613 246 132 87	6-15 8-14 6-10 7-11	1-4 3-5 1 2	Ss divided into light, intermediate & dark. Judgments made on faces with use of color card.
Herskovits, M. J. (1926)	Washington, D. C.	*Thorndike College Entrance*	c- 115			All c entering *Howard* in '22 & '23 tested; measured nose width, lip thickness; estimated amt bk & w element in skin.

[1]Retarded or advanced more than one year.

THIRTEEN

HYBRIDS

	RESULTS				COMMENTS OF AUTHOR
	Retarded	*Advanced*[1]			
	%	%			
Light	44.2	11.6			
Med	31.1	6.6			
Dark	14.4	8.8			

	Mdn				
Light	51				Urban companies had a greater percentage of lighter men.
Dark	40				

	Mdn	
Yellow	59	
Brown	45	
Black	39	

Dark scored 60% of Light

Dark scored 80% of Light

	M Scores				No consistency in ranking of dark and intermediate.
	MMM	*NIT*	*Det*	*P-C*	
Light	22.7	58.2	39.5	37.2	
Inter	19.9	51.9	35.8	40.7	
Dark	21.2	53.1	35.3	39.3	

Correlation with test score:

Nose width	.01
Lip thickness	—.20
Black element	—.14
White element	.17

Lighter Negroes given preferment within race, making dark show up to ill advantage on tests.

---

[2]*Myers Mental Measure, National Intelligence Test, Detroit First Grade,* and *Pintner-Cunningham.*

TABLE

RACIAL

AUTHOR DATE	LOCATION	TEST	N	SUBJECTS AGE	GRADE	METHOD OF SELECTION
Davenport, C. B. (1928)	Jamaica and Grand Cayman, B. W. I.	*Cube,*[3] *Knox, Manikin, Alpha, Draw-a-Man*	w- 100 br- 100 bk-100	Adults		Attempted to select whites, browns, & blacks from same social stratum. All 3 groups from several towns in Jamaica. Some w in addition from Grand Cayman Isl.
Klineberg, O. (1928)	Northeastern West Virginia	*Pintner-Paterson*	c-139	7-16		House-to-house canvass of villages. Skin color measured by Milton-Bradley color top.
Klineberg, O. (1928)	New York, N. Y.	*Mare-Foal, Casuist, Healy A Form Boards*	c-200	11-16	7-8	Boys from PS 139; c divided into 4 groups using Ferguson's technique.
Young, P. C. (1929)	Baton Rouge and Lake Charles, La.	*NIT*	c-277	9-10	3-	All 9- & 10-yr-olds in 3rd gr & above. With aid of c teachers & principals Ss divided into darker & lighter.
Peterson, J., and Lanier, L. H. (1929)	New York, N. Y.	*Yerkes Pre-Adolescent Point Scale*	c-75	12		Boys from an elementary & a junior high sch.

[3]*Cube Imitation, Knox Moron Test, Manikin, Army Alpha,* and Goodenough *Draw-a-Man* Test.

THIRTEEN *(continued)*
HYBRIDS

RESULTS	COMMENTS OF AUTHOR
Cube-w best, br interm *Knox*-w best, br interm *Mani*-w best, br interm but more failures than bks *Alpha*-w best, bk interm *Man*-w best, others same	*Browns* perhaps were more highly selected than others. *Browns* more variable and generally made somewhat better scores than *Blacks*.

Correlation with test score:[4]
  Nose width   —.06
  Lip thickness —.10
  Black pigment —.12

On whole, no definite evidence for inverse relation bet test score and degree of Negro blood indicated.

	Scores	
	Mdn	*Q*
Less Negroid	99	29
Most Negroid	97	30

No correspondence bet Negro blood, as judged by inspection and general Neg appearance and test results.

	Scores	
9 years	*Mdn*	*M*
Light	35	42
Dark	35	30
10 years		
Light	45	46
Dark	35	41

Correlation with test score:
  Nose width   —.11
  Lip thickness   .07
  Ear height   —.15
  Interpupillary span .01

Only slight evidence that these Negro traits correlate negatively with intell. Possibly skin color may be best criterion of degree of Negro blood.

[4]Holding age constant.

TABLE

RACIAL

| AUTHOR DATE | LOCATION | TEST | N | SUBJECTS | | METHOD OF SELECTION |
				AGE	GRADE	
Peterson, J. and Lanier, L. H. (1929)	Nashville, Tenn., and Chicago, Ill.	*Stanford-Binet, 1916, Myers Mental Measure*	c-83 c-75	12 12		*Na-* all 12 yr olds in 2 c elem schs & 9 from a jr high sch. *Ch-* from parks & playgrounds in summer.
Jenkins, M. D. (1936)	Chicago, Ill.	*McCall, Stanford-Binet, 1916*	c-63		3-8	Gifted had been selected from 7 schs. Parents asked to state racial composition of children.
Bruce, M. (1940)	Rural County in Virginia	*Kuhlmann-Anderson, Stanford-Binet, 1916 Arthur*	c-li- 23 dk-49	6-13		Representative sample from original 432 by taking every 5th in IQ order. E rated each S acc to skin color.
Tanser, H. A. (1939)	Kent County, Ontario	*Pintner-Cunningham*	c-54		1-2	Identification on basis of information given by teachers & local residents, some of them colored.

[5]Lanier rated all Ss according to skin color on a 7-point scale from very light to very dark. Color groups 1, 2, 3 included the lighter Negroes.

[6]A study of racial composition of the c children with IQ's of 125 or above (see Table 9)

THIRTEEN *(continued)*

HYBRIDS

RESULTS				COMMENTS OF AUTHOR
		Mdn^5		Indication of superior ability in children with lightest color and therefore probably with most w blood.
Skin color	S-B		MMM	
1-2-3	17.0		35.8	
5-6-7	14.2		25.8	
Correlation with lightness:				
S-B	.18			
MMM	.30			

	J^6	H		Chicago %ages strikingly similar to those of Herskovits for general population. These superior c children are not atypical in racial composition.
	%	%		
N	22.2	28.3		
NNW	46.1	31.7		
NW	15.9	25.2		
NWW	15.9	14.8		

	IQ			41% of *dark* equals or surpasses median of *light* Negroes.
	Mdn	M	s	
Light	76.0	78.7	9.61	
Dark	73.0	74.35	14.59	
t =	1.32			

Mdn	IQ
Mixed-Bloods	86.4
Full-Bloods	79.1

compared with 1551 cases reported by Herskovits and separated into four groups according to anthropometric and genealogical data. The Herskovits' sample was unselected.

TABLE

RACIAL

AUTHOR DATE	LOCATION	TEST	N	SUBJECTS		METHOD OF SELECTION
				AGE	GRADE	
Tanser, H. A. (1941)	Kent County, Ontario	NIT[7] P Non-L P-P	c-103 102 162		3-8 3-8 1-8	See above.
Codwell, J. E. (1947)	Houston, Tex.	Otis, S-A	c- DN- 176[8] I- 210 SEW- 94		High Sch	480 of 680 boys in P. Wheatley High Sch. Age range of the 480, 11-18.
Grinder, R. E., Spotts, W. S., and Curti, M. W. (1964)	Jamaica, B. W. I.	Draw-a-Man	c- li- 106 mix-197 dk- 638	7.5-10.5		Ss drawn from approx 50 schs throughout island after schs had been rated on basis of social class milieu.In the main, every child "who was in middle child-hood" was used as S, except in large schs where number of children tested was about 35. Color rating assigned to each S based on observation of skin color, hair texture, & nose breadth.

[7]*National Intelligence Test, Pintner Non-Language,* and *Pintner-Paterson* (Short Form) tests.
[8]DN, I, and SEW refer respectively to groups classified as *Dominantly Negroid, Intermediate,* and *Strong Evidence of White.* Primary purpose of study was to compare motor functioning of hybrids.

THIRTEEN (concluded)
HYBRIDS

RESULTS				COMMENTS OF AUTHOR

		IQ		On all 3 tests the mixed surpass the full-
M	*NIT*	*P Non-L*	*P-P*	bloods, and ¼-bloods surpass all c groups.
Mixed	91.7	97.0	96.7	However, ½-bloods below ¾-bloods in two
Full	87.0	94.5	87.8	of the tests.

		IQ		Except for capacity to learn new motor skills
	M		*s*	(where SEW's were superior to DN's) DN's
SEW	91.9		11.6	excelled in most factors of motor function
I	90.9		13.7	and were most inferior in intelligence.
DN	87		13.2	
SEW sig superior to DN				

		Scores[9]		Socioeconomic status was evaluated by writ-
All Ss	*Low*	*High*	*Total*	ten report on number of sibs at home,
Light	29	77	106	presence or absence of electricity or tele-
Mixed	89	108	197	phone, parents' occupation and own voca-
Dark	387	251	638	tional ambitions. Five-point scale was used in
$X^2 = 47.76$	p ⟨ .01			which occup of father was weighted heavily.

Middle Class			
	Low	*High*	*Total*
Light	23	64	87
Mixed	53	76	129
Dark	208	158	366
$X^2 = 29.92$	p ⟨ .01[10]		

[9]*Low* refers to *below Jamaican median* on *Draw-a-Man* and *high* indicates *above Jamaican median* on this test.

[10]This X^2 calculated by reviewer.

children. About 22 per cent of the subjects were said to have all Negro ancestry, 46 per cent to have more Negro than white ancestry, 16 per cent to have about equal Negro and white ancestry, and 16 per cent to have more white than Negro ancestry. These several percentages were observed by Jenkins to be strikingly similar to those reported by Herskovits on an unselected sample of the colored population, indicating that these superior Negro children were not atypical in racial composition.

In her study of the intelligence of children in a rural Virginia county, Bruce (1940) rated a random sample of 72 Negro subjects on a 5-point color scale. Of the four categories represented among her Negro Ss, *i.e., light brown, brown,* and *black,* only two children were *light brown* and two were *black.* Hence, she divided them into only two groups, which she identified as *light* and *dark.* A small and insignificant difference favoring the *light* group was found when a combination of IQ's based upon *Kuhlmann-Anderson, Stanford-Binet,* and *Grace Arthur* were compared, with 41 per cent of the *dark* group equaling or exceeding the median of the *light* group.

In the Kent County, Ontario, research Tanser (1939) classified the Negro school children as *mixed* or *full-bloods* on the basis of information given by teachers and other residents of the community. The small groups of *full-* and *mixed-bloods* secured median IQ's on the *Pintner-Cunningham* of 79 and 86, respectively; while larger groups of *full-* and *mixed-bloods* had respective mean IQ's of 87 and 92 on the *National,* 95 and 97 on the *Pintner Non-Language,* and 88 and 97 on Short Form of the *Pintner-Paterson.* In all of these tests, therefore, the hybrids excelled the unmixed Negro groups. When he separated the cross-breeds into *quarter, half,* and *three-quarters* mixtures, Tanser found the first of these to surpass the other colored groups; however, he reported the *mulattoes* to be below the *three-quarters* group in two of the tests.

In attempting to determine the kind and amount of change in motor function as the amount of Negro element increases or decreases in the Negro-white hybrid, Codwell (1947) tested 505 adolescent boys of the Phillis Wheatley High school in Houston, Texas. The *Otis Self-Administering Test, Form A* was given to a large number of these boys, in addition to a variety of motor tests such as: Sargent Jump, Iowa Revision of the Brace Test, the Burpee Test, Sixty Yard Dash, Running High Jump, *etc.* Codwell employed painstaking techniques in classifying the Negro racial composition of the pupils into three groups; he described these as *Dominantly Negroid, Intermediate,* and *Strong Evidence of White.* These techniques included measures of skin color of hips as determined by the Van Luschan Color Scale, lip thickness, nasal width, stature, sitting height, leg length, and total arm span, as well as careful appraisals of eye color and form of hair. The author, who was Director of the Department of Testing and Measurement at the high school, administered all tests, including the *Otis.* As will be noted in the table, the *Dominantly Negroid* group earned an average IQ of 87, which was about four points below that of the average of the

Intermediate and about five points below that of the *Strong Evidence of White* group. The difference between the means of the *Strong Evidence of White* and the *Dominantly Negroid* was significant at the one per cent level; while the difference between the means of the *Intermediate* and the *Dominantly Negroid* was significant at the .02 level of confidence.

Grinder, Spotts, and Curti (1964) studied the relation between skin color and intelligence as measured by the Goodenough *Draw-a-Man Test*. The subjects consisted of 941 children drawn from approximately 50 Jamaican public and private schools; all island schools had been previously rated on the basis of social standing and these 50 schools representing all of the designated social classes were chosen by random selection. Generally, every child in the selected schools "who was in middle childhood" (age range from $7\frac{1}{2}$ to $10\frac{1}{2}$ years) served as a subject, except in the "large schools" where about 35 children were tested.

One of the authors, with some aid from her Jamaican assistants, assigned a color rating to each S, each rating being based upon observations of his skin color, hair texture, and nose breadth. The rating categories ranged from *very black* at one end of the scale to *very white* at the other, but, as employed in this research, the color scale was reduced from six classes to three: *light, mixed light-dark,* and *dark.*

Each child's socioeconomic status was evaluated (see Table 13) on a five-point scale, with the resulting *lower class,* three *middle classes,* and the *upper class.* The *Draw-a-Man* instructions were carefully followed both as to administration and scoring; the children were tested in groups with one assistant for every ten children and the tests were administered by colored native examiners who spoke the Jamaican dialect.

The scores on *Draw-a-Man* appeared to be extremely skewed toward the lower end of the distribution making a comparison with Goodenough's norms inadvisable; the authors accordingly divided all scores at the Jamaican median, identifying the two groups as *high* and *low.*

As will be seen from the table, when the 106 *light,* the 197 *mixed,* and the 638 *dark* Ss were respectively separated into *low* and *high* on the *Draw-a-Man,* analysis by chi-square indicated a significant relation between skin color and intelligence, with those of light skin obtaining the higher scores.

Noting that very few children rated as *dark* were in the *upper class* and very few *light* pupils were from the *lower* or laboring class, the authors compared skin color within *each of the three middle* socioeconomic groupings. The obtained chi-squares for the *low-middle,* the *middle-middle,* and the *high-middle* classes proved to be 5.54, 5.25, and 3.93, respectively; none of these were significant at the .05 level, since, for two degrees of freedom, X^2 should equal 5.99 to be significant at this level. Following these analyses the authors observed that when social class is controlled "the magnitude of apparently innate differences in intellectual function is decreased to insignificant proportions." And they conclude, after agreeing with Klineberg that it is very difficult to prove the absence of something, with "however, the present study at least lends support to those who contend that the notion of white intellectual superiority is patently erroneous."

The present writer combined the authors' *three middle classes* into one group and separated the children as they had done according to skin color and to *high* and *low* on *Draw-a-Man*, the results of which are included in Table 13. The value of chi-square was 29.92, showing a highly significant relation between skin color and intelligence (according to the authors' criteria) when the *middle-class* group of 582 Ss was singled out for analysis. In fact, if one were to combine any two of the middle-class groups he would find a significant relation between skin color and intelligence.[3] It is evident to this writer that chi-square became insignificant when the authors analyzed *separately* the three middle-class groups because of the reduction in the number of cases (*e.g.,* there were only 3 *low* and 13 *high* Ss of the *light* group included in the *middle-middle* class) and that the data as presented in the article do not warrant their conclusions.

SUMMARY

Among the studies dealing with the intelligence of racial hybrids, we find that in 12 of the 18 comparisons, the *lighter* in color, or those identified as *mixed,* scored higher than the darker, those most Negroid in features, or the unmixed;[4] in four other studies, the *lighter or hybrid* groups scored the higher in the *majority* of the test situations, *i.e.,* three out of four or three out of five;[5] and in two comparisons, there was no evidence of a relationship existing between the amount of white ancestry or absence of Negroid characteristics and test score.[6] Therefore, in the majority of the above studies, it appears that racial hybrids have an advantageous position over the darker and so-called unmixed groups in psychometric tests. The differences are not typically large, however, and in the opinion of this writer these studies make no important contribution to the problem of race differences in intelligence.

---

[3]Combining *low-middle* and *middle-middle*, $X^2 = 11.61$; *low-middle* and *high-middle*, $X^2 = 28.79$; and *middle-middle* and *high-middle*, $X^2 = 12.57$. In each case df $= 2$ and p $<$ .01.

[4]Ferguson (4 separate groups), Klineberg (W. Va.), Klineberg (New York), Peterson and Lanier (Nashville), Peterson and Lanier (Chicago), Bruce, Tanser, Codwell, and Grinder, Spotts and Curti.

[5]Koch and Simmons, Herskovits, Davenport, and Young.

[6]Strong, and Peterson and Lanier (New York).

CHAPTER X

SELECTIVE MIGRATION

For a number of years selective migration has been an area of interest to investigators dealing with the problem of Negro intelligence. Certain authorities hold that the test superiority of the Northern over the Southern Negro is not due to the northward migration of the more able Negroes but rather to the greater equality of education and opportunity offered them in the North; whereas others believe that the more able and energetic Negroes, anticipating greater freedom and the advantages the North presents to them, migrate in that direction.[1] The latter point of view appears to be the more commonly held by early writers, and the former interpretation the one more recently accepted, particularly following Klineberg's publication (1935).

Trabue, for example, wrote in 1919: "It is quite clear that those negroes who live in the North are a selected group. It seems probable, that the negro may not have the ambition to leave his southern environment unless he has somewhat more intelligence and ability than his fellows, and that after arriving in the North, he is not able to compete with the white laborer and to make a living for himself and his family unless he has a degree of intelligence which is fairly comparable with that of the whites among whom he is living." (p. 4)

Wells, likewise, in 1923 expressed this point of view when he said: "The not unimportant part which Oberlin as a community and as a college has historically taken in the emancipation propaganda attracted many colored residents both before and after the war, a species of selection probably operating to choose the more intelligent and energetic members of the race." (p. 52)

Treacy (1926), in referring to the Minneapolis colored pupils of Southern parentage, indicated that the fact that they moved North showed superiority to the typical Southern Negro. Brigham (1923) believed that selective migration accounted for some of the differences found between Northern and Southern Negro troops but included environmental factors and the greater admixture of white blood as other factors responsible for this difference. Popenoe and Johnson (1935), in addition to mentioning the inferior educational opportunities and home backgrounds of rural Southern Negro children in contrast with those of Negroes in a Northern city, said that the fact that some were enterprising, *etc.*, enough to leave the cotton fields and move to a Northern city might also indicate that they were of superior stock.

---

[1] Morris (1947), in questioning 49 Southern administrators, found they believed social and economic opportunities for advancement of Negro youth to be more abundant outside of the South.

I. C. Brown (1942) implied selective migration of Negroes from Texas to California in World War II when she described the majority of this racial group as having left Texas to engage in semiskilled and skilled occupations in California.

On the other hand, such authorities as Sorokin, Zimmerman, and Galpin (1932) were critical of the selective migration argument. These writers cite the work of Carter Woodson who, in 1918, attempted to prove that migrants represent the "talented tenth" rather than a random sampling of the total Negro population. They found that Woodson's theory was contradicted by his own data which seem to indicate that the social rank of Negroes in the North, where more opportunities are open to them than in the South, shows practically the same distribution, ranging from domestics and menials, of whom the proportion is high, to successful persons in the upper classes, of whom the proportion is low. Further, Sorokin *et al.* stated that one must consider the fact that Negro tenancy in the South is decreasing as fast as is Negro farm ownership, or faster, and that the migration seems to be proportionately greater from the tenant class than from the owner class.

Obviously anyone who considers selective migration vital to a discussion and appraisal of race differences in intelligence must assume not only that whites score higher than Negroes but that Northern Negroes are significantly superior to Southern Negroes on the tests. It is true that in both World Wars the Southern Negro was found to score far below the Northern Negro. That this difference was due in considerable part to the inapplicability of the tests used and to the inferior education and limited experience of the Southern Negro soldier is unquestioned. The intelligence scores of Northern and Southern Negro school children, however, appear to differ by smaller amounts than those usually found between Northern and Southern Negro recruits. We have previously estimated the average IQ of Southern Negro children to be 80.6, and that of Northern Negro children to be 87.6. How much of this probable difference of seven IQ points is due to a migration of the more talented Southern Negroes and how much of it to a combination of environmental factors? We will attempt to answer this question after examining the experimental literature pertinent to the problem.

AMOUNT OF SCHOOLING

Gee and Corson (1929) and Raper (1930) have made comparisons between the amount of formal schooling of Negro migrants and sedents. From ten counties in the Tidewater and Piedmont sections of Virginia, Gee and Corson selected for study 143 colored farm families whose schooling had been completed; 675 persons were still living on the farms and 580 had migrated away from the counties. As will be seen from Table 14, the migrants had on the average somewhat more education than the sedents. The authors concluded that in so far as education is a measure of superior ability and ambition their results indicate a cityward selective migration.

In his study of Negro migration from two Georgia counties between 1920 and 1925, Raper compared the maximum schooling attained by 420 adult migrants with that reached by 617 adult sedents. The author found evidence of selective migration, since the education of the migrants from both counties was superior, on the average, to that of the sedents. In Greene County, for example, 12.4 per cent of the migrants as compared with 17.6 per cent of the sedents had not gone beyond the third grade in school, whereas 40.6 per cent of the migrants and 27.3 per cent of the sedents had had at least some high school education. In Macon County, 14.2 per cent of the migrants and 28.8 per cent of the sedents attained less than a fourth-grade education, while 35.8 per cent of the migrants and 18.0 per cent of the sedents had had a minimum of some high school training.

Kiser (1932) commented upon the fact that the Penn Normal, Industrial and Agricultural School had not succeeded in keeping the inhabitants on St. Helena Island (South Carolina). He implied an absence of selective migration when he stated that the school records of 158 living Ss who had been graduated prior to 1929 showed that the proportion of Penn School alumni who had migrated was about the same as that of the island population in general. No analysis of data supported his statement, the fact being reported merely as a comment.

C. S. Johnson (1941) observed that while Negroes in general are leaving the rural South, the migration rate is clearly higher for those of the upper economic and educational levels. He found about one fourth of the Southern-born Negro college graduates living in the North. In addition, Johnson related the desire to migrate from the rural South to the father's education; of the youth whose fathers had completed only the second grade or less, 45.8 per cent wished to live in the North or West, compared with 70.5 per cent of those whose fathers had completed the tenth grade or more.

In a recent survey of Negro migration, Hamilton (1964) includes a table from the *United States Census Population: Life Time and Recent Migration,* 1960. In this table are presented data pertaining to the migration of Negroes from the South Atlantic Division during the period between 1955 and 1960 along with their years of schooling completed. The statistics are tabulated for young Negroes who were between 20 and 24 years of age in 1955. The net migration rate (loss of population) is indicated in terms of the ratio of net migration to the 1955 Negro population in the area. As will be observed in Table 14, the loss in the Negro population of this age group increases consistently from a low of 1.9 per cent for those who had completed fewer than five years of schooling to a high of 9.5 per cent for those who had completed four or more years of college.

School Marks

Klineberg (1935) and Goldstein (1944) have made comparisons between the average school grades of Negro migrants and sedents. The former investigator compared the school marks of 562 Southern Negro children who had left their homes in Nashville, Birmingham, and Charleston (South Carolina) to come North with their parents, with the grades of their sedentary classmates from these three cities. All school grades were expressed on a scale in which 50 was taken as an average performance. The migrating children from Nashville and Charleston achieved somewhat higher averages than the nonmigrating Ss, their respective mean records being 54 and 55.6; whereas the migrants from Birmingham averaged 44.8 and thus were below the sedentary group. For the total group of migrants the mean grade was 49, indicating no evidence of selective migration.

Hollingworth (1940) criticized Klineberg's use of grades as a criterion of intelligence. She pointed out that a difference of 20 to 25 points in IQ is usually necessary before teachers recognize the gap in mental ability between children and record this difference in their school marks. The difference between Northern and Southern average IQ's is considerably less than the 20 to 25 points needed for a valid comparison of grades of migrating and nonmigrating groups. "The school marks of children clustering at 80 IQ, the median for southern Negroes, would not be likely to differ materially from those of children clustering at 87 IQ, the figure representing the extreme of the long-residence groups studied." (p. 47)

Hollingworth's criticism would be similarly applicable to Goldstein's research (1944), since the latter compared grades of migrants and sedents. Using a more highly selected group than Klineberg's, Goldstein secured the school records of every student who had attended the Fred Douglass High School of Columbia, Missouri, between 1920 and 1938 for a year or more. After she had eliminated Ss who had died, were in prison, in sanitariums, and those who had less than five recorded grades, Goldstein was able to secure information about the present location of 501 Negroes, including 224 sedents and 277 migrants, from Negro ministers, teachers, friends, or relatives. The mean scholastic index of the migrants (2.69) was higher than the mean index achieved by the sedents (2.47), the difference being significant at the .01 level of confidence. Goldstein concluded that Columbia was losing the intellectually more alert and enterprising members of her Negro community. It is interesting to observe that the migrations were in the direction of large cities and away from the South; only fifteen per cent of the migrants had moved to cities or towns under 50,000, and only 2.47 per cent of the migrants had moved southward.

In the five reports of Gee and Corson, Raper, Hamilton, Klineberg, and Goldstein, where either the amount of formal schooling or a form of scholastic index was used as the criterion of ability, a total of approximately 20,000 Negro migrants from one Border and various Southern states were compared, directly or by inference, with large numbers of sedents in these areas. Except for the 300 Birmingham subjects the migrants earned higher grades or completed more schooling on the average than the nonmigrants. If these criteria are valid indices of intelligence, it would seem that the studies taken as a whole indicate the *presence* rather than the *absence* of selective migration.

INTELLIGENCE TESTS

District of Columbia

McAlpin (1932) and Long (1934), both comparing *Kuhlmann-Anderson* IQ's earned by Negro children born in the District of Columbia with those of Negro children born outside the District, show considerable agreement in their findings. Without giving the number of subjects, McAlpin reported the mean IQ's of the 3A and 5A children born in the District to be about six points higher than those of children born outside the District. Long, basing his means on a total of 4684 colored Ss in Grades 1A, 3A, and 5A, found those born in Washington to score, respectively, about three, six, and four points higher than those born outside the District. Since measures of variability were not reported it is impossible to determine the significance of the differences obtained; however, it would seem that Long's differences are probably significant, owing to the large number of cases included. Long selected for special study smaller groups of 3A and 5A children who were either in their first year of residence or in their eighth year of residence in Washington. Large differences of 12 and 15 points separated the respective mean IQ's of these groups; however, no measures of variability were reported and the significance of these data was not statistically determined. Both McAlpin and Long correlated test score and length of residence in the city, obtaining low but positive coefficients of .15, .14, .24, and .30. These correlations and the higher mean IQ's of the Ss born in the District were accounted for by the relatively favorable environment of Washington.

Cleveland

Dombey (1933) selected for study the Juvenile Court case records of 466 Negro children who had been given the *Stanford-Binet* test between 1931 and 1933; she found the mean IQ of the Northern-born to be 79.5, which was about six points above the mean of the Southern-born. For several specific age groups she calculated the mean IQ's of Ss born in the North, those who had spent half or more than half of their lives in the North but had not been born there, and those who had spent less than half of their lives in the North. These mean IQ's for subjects of Ages 15, 16, and 17 are presented in the table. Although no measures of reliability were included, it seems evident that there is a trend toward improvement of IQ with increase in time spent in the North.

R. M. Clark (1933) studied the effect of schooling on the intelligence quotients of Negro children in Cleveland and Detroit. As will be noted in Table 14, these children had been given a variety of tests, individual and group, and many of them had been tested twice either by the school psychologists or by Clark. The experimental Ss had moved from the Southern States to the Northern urban centers where the school year was longer, where teachers' salaries and the per capita expenditure were higher, where school attendance was more regular, and where educational opportunities in general were greater than for any of the

Southern States from which the Ss came. Some of these Negro children had attended school in the South before moving North, others had moved before reaching school age, or had reached school age before migrating but had never attended school in the South. All of the controls were born in the North and in most cases had had their entire schooling in either Cleveland or Detroit.

In one of Clark's investigations, 751 Negro children and 130 whites, all living in inferior environments and attending the seven Black Belt schools of Cleveland, had been given a group intelligence test and later the same or a different group test. The first two groups of colored children were Southern-born, one of them having been retested on the average 3.36 years after the first testing, the other after an average interval of 1.55 years. The third group included colored children who were Cleveland-born and who were retested 1.59 years after the first testing; finally there was a group of whites who were retested after an average interval of 1.80 years.[2] As will be observed in the table, the average increase in IQ for the first group was 2.75, whereas there was but negligible improvement from the first to the second testing among all of the other groups. From these results the author concluded that schooling in Cleveland does not materially affect the size of the intelligence quotient changes.

Clark questioned the children in Group I (the Southern-born Negroes who had been retested on the original test 3.36 years, on the average, after the first examination) concerning their age of migration and their route taken from the South. He secured 160 replies which indicated with "reasonable certainty" the age of migration. Almost all of these came directly from the South of Cleveland. Dividing them according to the age at which they had migrated, *i.e.,* up through 2 years, 3 to 5 years, 6 to 8, and 9 years and over, Clark found the mean IQ's to improve by 2.62, 1.93, 1.85, and 3.40 points, respectively. As will be noted in the table, none of the means on the second test were significantly higher than those obtained on the first. He tentatively concluded from these results that the age at the time of migration is not a significant factor in determining constancy of IQ. "So far as the capacity to learn is concerned the age at which Southern Negroes migrate to the North is not a significant factor." (p. 178)

Detroit

In one of his Detroit studies, Clark examined 205 third grade Southern-born colored children who had been previously tested in the first grade. The *Detroit Primary Group Test* was used for both test and retest, the results being given in terms of the percentage of children rating A, B, C+, C, C−, D, and E. As will be noted in Table 14, there was no general improvement from test to retest, in spite of the fact that the two schools from which these children were chosen were

---

[2]Since the seven schools included a high school, two junior high schools, two elementary schools, one school for over-age boys, and one for problem girls, there were several uncontrolled variables in this study. Among these variables were Age and Grade, the character of the Ss, the test and retest used, and the interval of time between the tests.

superior schools and the children themselves were living in the prosperous and "elite" Negro sections of the city. Clark found no point in the scale to have been affected by either increments or decrements, when the second test was given. In the Sampson School, as in the less-favored schools, where both white and Negro pupils were in attendance, the intelligence quotient of the average Negro pupil was found to be lower than that of the average white pupil.

Another of Clark's experiments dealt exclusively with problems cases, 452 of them being Detroit Negroes, 167 of them Cleveland Negroes, and 20 Cleveland whites. All of the children had been tested twice by the *Stanford-Binet*. The Cleveland and Detroit Negro children were divided into Southern-born and Northern-born groups, the former showing a drop in mean IQ of 1.44 points from the first to the second test, the latter showing a corresponding drop of 3.44 points.

From his various analyses Clark concluded that Southern-born Negro boys and girls have intelligence quotients that are somewhat lower than those of Northern-born Negroes and Northern-born whites when they enter the schools of Detroit and Cleveland. Retests failed to show more significant increases or decreases in intelligence quotients for the Southern-born than for the Northern-born. "Any philosophy based on the assumption that the intelligence quotients of Negroes improve directly as their educational opportunities improve is not substantiated by this study." (p. 178)

New Orleans, Atlanta, and Nashville

Instead of studying environmental effects by the testing-retesting program employed by Clark, Klineberg (1935) compared test scores of Negro children who had lived in a city for varying lengths of time. While his main research was conducted in New York City, one study was made in the three Southern cities of New Orleans, Atlanta, and Nashville. Klineberg presented the average score earned on the *National Intelligence Test, Scale A, Form I* by 359 boys who were born in these three cities and compared it with the mean achieved by 165 boys who had lived seven or more years in these cities and with the several means of 252 boys who had lived in the cities from one to six years (Table 14). Although he does not report the number of schools canvassed, the number of Ss in each of the three cities, the method by which his 12-year-old boys were selected, or any measure of variability, the study is interesting in view of the fact that higher average test scores have generally been secured on Southern Negro children from urban areas than from rural districts. As will be seen in the table, the averages, except for the four-year group, show a consistent rise with increase in length of time spent in the city. The author reports the city-born group to be reliably superior to all of the country-born groups; the mean of all Ss who had lived in the cities for four or more years is likewise significantly above the mean of Ss who had lived in the cities for three years or less. He concludes that his results suggest that migrants to a city are not superior at the outset to those remaining

TABLE

SELECTIVE

AUTHOR DATE	LOCATION	TEST	N	SUBJECTS AGE	METHOD OF SELECTION
Gee, W., and Corson, J. J., 3rd. (1929)	Tidewater and Piedmont, Va.		c- sed- 675 migr-580		From 10 counties. Selected members of 143 c farm families who had completed schooling.
Raper, A. F. (1930)	Greene and Macon Counties, Ga.		c-sed Gr- 194 Ma-423 c-migr Gr- 202 Ma-218	18- 18-	Negro migration from 2 counties, 1920-25. All Ss were 18 years & over.
Hamilton, C. H. (1964)	South Atlantic Division		c-'55 pop 37,229 73,109 35,815 96,510 69,379 17,531 16,941	20-24	From 1960 US Census report on Life Time and Recent Migration. The statistics are for Negroes, 20-24 yrs old, whose net migration rate for 1955-60 is compared with pop for '55 of same race, age, & education.
Klineberg, O. (1935)	Nashville, Tenn., Birmingham, Ala., Charleston, S. C.		c-migr 184 303 75		Examined sch records of c who had left for Northern cities with parents; compared them with records of sedents. Aver grade for each class placed at 50.
Goldstein, S. D. (1944)	Columbia, Mo.		c- sed- 244 migr-277		Sch records of all c who had attended high sch for a year or more bet 1920-38; of 580 Ss, 45 eliminated who had fewer than 5 grades, & 34 who were dead, in prison or hosp. Information about location from teachers, ministers, *etc.* Grades given numerical values & averaged.

[1]12.4 per cent of c migrants (over 18 years) from Greene County and 17.6 per cent of c (over 18 years) remaining in Greene Co. in 1920-25 had not gone beyond the third grade; 40.6 per cent of the c migrants and 27.3 per cent of sedents had completed Grade 6, *etc.*

FOURTEEN

MIGRATION

	RESULTS		COMMENTS OF AUTHOR
Maximum	c	c	Migration from farm owners heavier than from
Schooling	*Migrant*	*Sedent*	tenants. In that education is measure of ability,
	%	%	ambition and character, results indicate selective
Grade 4	56.9	65.1	migration in favor of city.
Grades 5-7	31.5	27.0	
High Sch	6.5	4.4	
Above High Sch	5.1	3.5	
Maximum	c	c	In both counties, the illiterate and poorly edu-
Schooling[1]	*Migrant*	Sedent	cated tend to remain in home county more
	%	%	often than those with better education.
Greene			
Grade 3	12.4	17.6	
Grade 6	40.6	27.3	
High Sch	37.1	26.3	
Above HS	3.5	1.0	
Macon			
Grade 3	14.2	28.8	
Grade 6	35.8	18.0	
High Sch	30.3	17.3	
Above HS	5.5	0.7	
Maximum	*Net Migration*		Migration of Negroes from the South has been
Schooling	*Rate*		selective of the best educated.
Below Grade 5	—1.9		
5-7	—3.1		
8	—5.1		
9-11	—5.5		
12	—7.5		
College 1-3	—8.9		
College 4 or more	—9.5		
	Sch Records		May be different factors operative in diff com-
	c Migrants		munities so that from one the superior Ss,
	M	*s*	from another the inferior, will tend to migrate.
Nash	54.0	20.2	Sch records of the group as whole give no
Birm	44.8	19.5	evidence of selective migration.
Charl	55.6	20.2	
	Scholastic Index		Columbia losing the intellectually more alert
	c	c	and enterprising of its Negro community.
	Migr	*Sedent*	
M	2.69	2.47	
s	0.79	0.74	
t =	3.25		

TABLE

SELECTIVE

AUTHOR DATE	LOCATION	TEST	N	SUBJECTS AGE	METHOD OF SELECTION
McAlpin, A. S. (1932)	Washington, D. C.	*Kuhlmann-Anderson*			All c in 3A & 5A had been tested by Research Dept, Div. 10-13; separated Ss into groups born in & outside D.C. Numbers & ages not given.
Long, H. H. (1934)	Washington, D. C.	*Kuhlmann-Anderson*	c- 1A-2103 3A-1323 5A-1258		All c tested by Dept of Research in 1930. Separated into groups born within and outside of D.C.
			c- 3A-283 5A-255		Questionnaires on birth & length of residence in D.C. Used every other test blank. Eliminated pupils who were in D.C. 9 years or more.
Dombey, E. H. (1933)	Cleveland, Ohio	*Stanford-Binet, 1916*	c- 466[2]	10-17	From Juvenile Court records, Cuyahoga County, 1931-33.

[2]Of these, 319 were Southern-born and 147 Northern-born. Missouri was included with Southern states & W.Va. with the Northern. Division made acc to slave populations of states as shown in 1960 census.

FOURTEEN *(continued)*

MIGRATION

	RESULTS	COMMENTS OF AUTHOR
Birthplace *3A* D.C. Outside *5A* D.C. Outside	*M IQ* c 98.1 92.1 95.1 89.7	Capacities need appropriate stimulation in order that consequent abilities may be realized.
Birthplace *1A* D.C. Outside *3A* D.C. Outside *5A* D.C. Outside	*M IQ* c 94.20 91.35 97.59 91.61 94.56 89.19	Decrease in IQ from 3rd to 5th explained by assuming that in early childhood a simple, underprivileged envir may be adequate. With incr in age, the community, home and sch activities become increasingly inadequate.
Residence in D.C. *3A* 1st yr 8th yr *5A* 1st yr 8th yr	 85 97 80 95	Does not believe results indicate poorer calibre of recent migrants.

Birthplace	*M IQ* c			IQ increases steadily in each age group with greater percentage of life spent in North.
South	73.1			
North	79.5			

	M IQ & % Life in North[3]			Assume that intelligence test scores affected by previous environmental conditioning.
Age	c	c	c	
	1-49	50-99	100	
	%	%	%	
15	68.3	73.9	79.3	
16	68.0	76.0	75.2	
17	64.5	73.3	77.8	

[3]We omit mean IQ's for various age groups below 15, since the number of younger children at each age group is small, *i.e.* between 6-13 in the 1-49% groups.

TABLE

SELECTIVE

AUTHOR DATE	LOCATION	TEST	N	SUBJECTS AGE	METHOD OF SELECTION
Clark, R. M. (1933)	Cleveland, Ohio	NIT[4] Haggerty D, Cleveland, Otis S-A, Terman Group	w- 130 c- 1) 381 2) 201 3) 169	1st test 5-15 M-11.39 M-12.96 5-16	7 Black Belt schs of inferior envir. Groups 1) & 2) were Southern-born c; Group 3) Cleveland-born c; w pupils Cleveland-born & attending Black Belt Schools.
		NIT, Haggerty D, Cleveland, Otis S-A, Terman	c- 160		Of 381 (Group 1), E secured 160 replies indicating reasonable certainty of age when migrated. Nearly all came directly from South to Cleveland.
Clark, R. M. (1933)	Detroit, Mich.	Detroit Primary	c- 205[5]		From Sampson & Wengert schs, in "elite" & prosperous Negro sections. Schs good. All c born in South.
	Detroit and Cleveland	Stanford-Binet, 1916	w- 20 c- 1) 382 2) 70 3) 87 4) 80	5-10 5-15 5-15 5-14 5-14	Problem cases.[6] Groups 1) & 2) from records of Det Clinic; random sampling of c who had had at least 2 tests with Binet. Groups 3) & 4) & w from Black Belt schs of Cleveland; all had been tested twice by Binet.

[4]*National Intelligance Test, Haggerty Delta 2, Cleveland Classification, Otis Self-Administering*, or *Terman Group Test*. Group 1) had been tested by sch authorities and retested by Clark on same test on average of 3.36 yrs later. Groups 2) & 3) and w group tested and retested by sch authorities with same or different group test. Average of 1.55 yrs between tests for Group 2), 1.59 yrs bet tests for Group 3), and 1.80 yrs bet tests for w group.

FOURTEEN *(continued)*
MIGRATION

	RESULTS			COMMENTS OF AUTHOR

	First Term			Study shows that schooling in Cleveland or Detroit does not materially affect the size of intelligence quotient changes.
	M IQ	s		
w	95.19	16.60		
c				
1)	90.52	15.88		
2)	93.17	13.90		
3)	93.80	13.61		
	Retest			
w	95.62	15.57		
c				
1)	93.27	14.98		
2)	93.42	13.82		
3)	94.48	14.85		

Age when migrated	M IQ		t	Tentative conclusion that age at time of migration not significant factor in determining constancy of IQ.
	Test I	Retest		
0-2	94.74	97.37	0.87	
3-5	96.31	98.30	0.98	
6-8	93.48	95.33	0.28	
9-	88.21	91.61	1.15	

	% Receiving Ratings		Any philosophy based on assumption that the IQs of Negroes improve directly as their educational opportunities improve is not substantiated by this study.
	Test	Retest	
A	3.90	2.93	
B	7.80	8.29	
C+	14.15	12.68	
C	26.33	27.80	
C—	16.59	18.05	
D	15.61	15.61	
E	15.12	14.64	

	First Test IQ	
	M	s
w-	80.25	10.45
c-		
So-born	67.55	13.63
No-born	76.27	12.11

	Retest IQ	
	M	s
w-	78.25	9.73
c-		
So-born	66.11	11.13
No-born	72.83	10.78

---

[5]In Grade 1 when first tested. Retested in Grade 3.

[6]Colored Group 1) included Southern-born; Group 2) the Northern-born; Group 3) Southern-born and Group 4) the Northern-born.

TABLE

SELECTIVE

AUTHOR DATE	LOCATION	TEST	N	SUBJECTS AGE	METHOD OF SELECTION
Klineberg, O. (1935)	New Orleans, Atlanta, Nashville	*NIT*	c- 39 25 36 47 52 53 165 359	12	Negro boys in publ schs of 3 cities tested in 1930.
Peterson, J., and Lanier, L. H. (1929)	New York, N. Y.	*Yerkes-Bridges-Hardwick Point Scale*	c- 99	12	Boys from 2 publ schs in Harlem; none born in NYC.
Klineberg,[8] O. (1935)	New York, N. Y.	*NIT*	c- 150 125 136 112 157 1017	12	Attempted to secure every 12-yr-c S at certain Harlem elem & jun high schs.
Klineberg,[9] O. (1935)	New York, N. Y.	*Otis S-A, Interm.*	c- 28 37 45 19 23 18 243	12	Girls in Harlem publ schs in 1931.
Klineberg,[10] O. (1935)	New York, N. Y.	*Stanford-Binet, 1916*	c- 62 60 40 65 67 127	10	Both sexes, Harlem publ schs.

[7]Author does not say how many schs were canvassed or how the boys were selected. Statistically significant superiority of city-born group over all country-born; and significant diff bet groups which had been in city four or more years and those in city three years or less.

[8]Includes combined studies of G. Lapidus, C. Yates, and E. Marks supervised by Klineberg.

FOURTEEN *(continued)*

MIGRATION

	RESULTS		COMMENTS OF AUTHOR
Years in City	*Scores[7]* *M*		Results suggest that migrants to city not superior at outset to those remaining in country but later superiority due to influence of better environment.
1	38.3		
2	43.2		
3	44.7		
4	62.5		
5	56.2		
6	62.2		
7 up	68.7		
City-born	74.6		

	Test Score & Yrs in NYC	
r	.20	
PEr	.065	

Years in NYC	*Scores* *M*	Results suggest that IQ remains constant only when there is a relative constancy in the environment.
1-2	72	
3-4	76	
5-6	84	
7-8	90	
9 up	94	
No-born	92	

Years in NYC	*Scores* *M*	*s*	Northern-born reliably superior to 1-2, 3-4, and 5-6 yr groups, also to S-born as a group. In general, results corroborate the NIT findings.
1-2	22.8	12.6	
3-4	22.5	9.6	
5-6	21.5	10.6	
7-8	26.2	13.7	
9-10	33.1	13.7	
11 up	31.4	13.8	
Total	25.1	13.0	
NY-born	30.9	15.1	

Years in NYC	*IQ* *M*	Evidence for an environmental effect is unmistakable.
Under 1	81.5	
1-2	84.7	
2-3	84.5	
3-4	86.9	
4 up	89.4	
Total	85.6	
NY-born	89.8	

[9]This study of I. Traver's, made under Klineberg's direction.

[10]Includes studies of J. Skladman, E. Wallach and H. Rogosin. The reviewer has combined the results of all three studies.

TABLE

SELECTIVE

AUTHOR DATE	LOCATION	TEST	N	SUBJECTS AGE	METHOD OF SELECTION
Klineberg,[11] O. (1935)	New York, N. Y.	*Minnesota Paper Form Board*	c- 27 25 30 23 25 41 265	12	Harlem publ-sch boys.
Klineberg,[12] O. (1935)	New York, N. Y.	*Pintner-Paterson* (short)	c- 20 20 20 50	10	Harlem publ-sch boys.
Lee, E. S. (1951)	Philadelphia, Pa.	*Phila,[13] Chicago, Minn.*	c- sed- 424 migr-930		9 jr or senior high schs in diverse socioeco sections, having 23-92% c. From records selected each c who came to Phila from a Southern state; random sample of Phila-born c from same schs. *Phila tests* given in 1A, 2B, 4B, 6B, 9A; *Chicago & Minn* tests given in 9A. All Ss had reached 9th grade & had never missed any of the tests after entering sch. In this way, excluded ¼ to ⅓ of the high-sch pupils otherwise eligible.
Boylan, F. T., and O'Meara, R. B. (1958)	Chicago, Ill.	*Kuhlmann-Anderson, Thurstone Primary Mental Abilities, and Stanford-Binet, 1937*	c- sed- 1201 migr- 667		V. F. Lawson Sch located in middle-class Negro neighborhood on South Side. Tabulated & compared IQ's of Southern-born & native Chicago pupils, using latest test scores when Ss tested more than once.[14]

[11]Work of E. Horowitz under Klineberg's direction. Tests given acc to directions in Manual but scoring method was altered because Minnesota method too drastic for younger Ss.

[12]Study of B. H. Brown under Klineberg's direction.

[13]*Philadelphia Tests of Mental and Verbal Ability, Chicago Primary Mental Abilities Test,*

FOURTEEN (concluded)

MIGRATION

RESULTS			COMMENTS OF AUTHOR

	Scores		The 2 performance tests fail to demonstrate any
Years in NYC	Mdn	Q	definite environmental effect.
1-2	39.00	30.0	
3-4	26.67	33.34	
5-6	31.88	24.14	
7-8	37.50	17.79	
9-10	37.50	24.25	
11 up	37.50	38.44	
Total	35.22	24.52	
No-born	42.63	26.83	

	Mental Age		No completely reliable diff bet groups, but fairly
Years in NYC	M	s	clear evidences of environmental effect.
Under 2	7.25	3.03	
2-5	7.65	1.85	
5 up	7.50	2.29	
Total	7.47	2.44	
No-born	8.65	2.17	

Phila Test	When Given		Scores on Chicago subtests (totals not given)
	First	Last	indicate that with one exception a diff exists at
	M IQ	M IQ	.05 level bet mean of migrants entering Grade
Sed (no kg)	92.1	93.7	1A & mean of migrants entering at 7A-9A.
Migr. entering			Substantiates work in NYC.
Grade 1A	86.5	92.8	
2B	86.7	90.5	
4B	86.3	89.4	
6B	88.2	90.2	

Minn Test	Score	
	M	
Sed (no kg)	30.3	
Migr entering		
Grade 1A	28.8	
1B-2B	26.6	
3A-4B	23.4	
5A-6B	24.8	
7A-9A	20.6	

	IQ		After considering the distribution of IQ's, have
	c	c	reason to doubt the ready answer that the
	Migrant	Sedent	sch-wide reading problem can be explained by
M	94.29	95.15	the inferior mental ability of the Southern-born
s	11.8	11.9	among the pupils.

Diff bet means not sig

	IQ	
Distrib	Migr	Sed
Above 130	1.5%	1.7%
120-129	6.8	9.3
110-119	25	34
90-109	30	29
80-89	22.8	19.6
70-79	13.3	6.4

and *Minnesota Paper Form Board*. Groups not intended to be representative of c sch population of Philadelphia in that all had reached the ninth grade at least and had never been absent when any of the tests were administered subsequent to their enrollment.

[14]This study has been included in Table 4.

in the country but that their later superiority is due to the gradual influence of the better urban environment.

New York City

Peterson and Lanier (1929), after having tested 99 twelve-year-old Negro boys in New York City by means of the *Yerkes-Bridges-Hardwick Point Scale,* correlated their test scores with the number of years spent in the city. None of these boys were born in New York City. A small and unreliable correlation of .20 was obtained.

Klineberg compared the average *National Intelligence Test, Scale A, Form I* scores of 1017 twelve-year-old Negro children living in New York City and born in the North with the test scores of 680 colored Ss from the same city who were Southern-born. The latter group was subdivided into five categories according to their years of city residence, *i.e.,* 1 to 2 years, 3 to 4 years, 5 to 6 years, 7 to 8 years, and 9 years and over. An attempt was made to secure every twelve-year-old Negro attending certain Harlem elementary and junior high schools. With the exception of the *9 and over group,* which obtained a higher mean than the Northern-born, a consistent improvement in average score characterized a longer city residence. As will be observed in Table 14, the mean of 92 (*score,* not IQ) earned by the Northern-born was 20 points above that obtained by the children who had lived in the city for two years or less.[3]

The *Otis Self-Administering Test, Intermediate Form,* was given under Klineberg's direction to 413 New York City Negro girls, Age 12, all of whom were enrolled in the Harlem public schools in 1931. More than half of the total number were New York-born; 18 to 45 Ss comprised each of the Southern-born groups, the girls having lived in the city from 1 to 2 years, 3 to 4 years, 5 to 6 years, 7 to 8 years, 9 to 10 years, and 11 years and over. When ranked according to average score (from low to high) the groups scored as follows: 5-6, 3-4, 1-2, 7-8, New York-born, 11 and over, and 9-10. Although the increase in average score did not parallel increase in length of city residence, the Northern-born group was found to be reliably superior to those groups who had lived in the city less than seven years and to all Southern-born groups when combined into one.

We have combined the results of the three *Stanford-Binet* investigations made under Klineberg's supervision. Four hundred twenty-one 10-year-old colored children of both sexes were tested; this number includes 127 New York-born Ss and from 40 to 67 in each of the Southern-born groups. When the groups are ranked in average IQ (from low to high) they are as follows: under one year in the city, 2 to 3 years, 1 to 2 years, 3 to 4 years, over 4, and the New York-born. Except for the 2 to 3 year group which averaged slightly below the 1 to 2 year group, an increase in average IQ coincides with increase in length of city residence.

---

[3]In Marks' study (one of the three on which Klineberg's *NIT* discussion is based) the 1-2 year group earned an average score of 88. This average was higher than that earned by the 3-4, 5-6, and 7-8 year groups.

Klineberg observed that the *Stanford-Binet* results were even clearer than the results on the *National* and *Otis* and that the evidence for an environmental effect is unmistakable.[4] These observations, in our opinion, are not warranted in view of the following facts: (1) the author includes no measure of variability in two of the three studies, nor in a combination of these two;[5] (2) although he notes that in the combined Wallach-Rogosin studies there is a significant difference favoring the New York-born group over the less-than-one-year group, and that the mean of the more-than-four-year group is significantly above that of the less-than-one-year group, Klineberg reports that none of the other mean differences were significant and he includes no reliability statistics on the three studies combined; (3) Klineberg obtained only a 5-point difference in mean IQ between the total New York City-born group and the group that had lived in the city from one-to-two years; and (4) the mean IQ of his Southern-born subjects is just four points below that of his New York-born group.

Klineberg likewise discusses the results of the testing of 110 ten-year-old Negro boys attending the Harlem public schools in New York City by means of an abbreviated form of the *Pintner-Paterson Performance Tests.* The subjects included 50 Northern-born children and 20 in each of the three Southern-born groups. The latter consisted of those who had lived in New York less than 2 years, those who had lived in New York from 2 to 5 years, and those who had lived in the city for more than 5 years. The groups ranked as follows in average mental age (from low to high): under 2 years, over 5 years, 2 to 5 years, and Northern-born. The standard deviations which were included in these data may be noted in Table 14. Klineberg observed that for this test there were no significant differences obtained between any of the groups but that, nevertheless, there was evidence of some environmental effect.

The last of the New York series of studies made use of the *Minnesota Paper Form Board Test.* Four hundred sixteen 12-year-old Negro boys, 265 of whom were Northern-born, served as subjects; in addition there were six Southern-born groups with from 23 to 41 Ss in each. The various groups ranked as follows in obtained medians (from low to high): 3 to 4, 5 to 6, 7 to 11 and the over-11 groups, 1 to 2, and the Northern-born. Klineberg included the quartile deviations which will be observed to be generally large, in certain instances larger than the medians (Table 14). None of the differences between the medians were significant.

Klineberg concluded from his researches that there is no evidence to support selective migration, that school records of those who migrated do not demonstrate any superiority over those who remained behind, and that intelligence tests show no superiority of recent arrivals in the North over those of the same age

---

[4]In this connection, he noted that the *Binet,* as opposed to linguistic group tests, is generally considered to be relatively free from the influence of nurture and background.

[5]Wallach's and Rogosin's.

who are still living in Southern cities.[6] He believed that the superiority of the Northern over the Southern Negro could be adequately explained by the more favorable Northern environment rather than by the hypothesis of selective migration.

A number of authors, including Marcuse and Bitterman (1946), Murphy (1951, p. 29), Guilford (1952, p. 515), Morgan (1961, pp. 457-458), and Wickens and Meyer (1961, pp. 451-452), have uncritically accepted Klineberg's findings and conclusions on selective migration and have quoted him as the final authority on the subject. In fact, Klineberg's work and none other was discussed by these writers. Others, such as Thomas (1938), Hollingworth (1940), Florant (1942), Malzberg (1943), Garrett (1947), and Tyler (1965), have either accepted his findings with reservations or have been critical of his technique and interpretation. Thomas, for instance, referred to the general excellence of the study but believed that Klineberg put undue reliance on the small differences in averages; she was critical of the fact that he included no distribution of cases and frequently took no account of variability—which may have been so great as to invalidate some of his observed differences.

Hollingworth found Klineberg's attempt to prove that the superiority of the Northern Negro over the Southern Negro is not a function of selective migration "unconvincing". We have already cited her criticism of his use of grades as a criterion of intelligence. In addition, she was of the opinion that in migratory movements, such as the northward cityward migration of Negroes, very probably the most intelligent come first, i.e., take the initiative; if so, the fact that those of longest residence have more-intelligent children is due to genetics rather than to environment as Klineberg supposed. She argued further that if different environments produce differences found between ethnic groups, why are not the second generation Japanese handicapped in comparison with the generality of Americans? This last point is one that is frequently overlooked by students of race differences and, in the opinion of the reviewer, is worthy of consideration. The few published studies on Japanese-American and Chinese-American children indicate that they tend to score above the American norms on performance tests.

Florant wrote that further research is needed on the topic, that in most of the literature on migration there is the assumption that people migrate in the direction of what they consider to be greater opportunities, and that analysis has often been in terms of the objective conditions rather than from the point of view of the migrant.

Malzberg expressed the belief that Klineberg's conclusion, i.e., the improbability of there being any real quantitative differences in intelligence between Negro and white children, goes beyond the facts of the case. He said it is clearly possible that the trend Klineberg noted will finally level off and approach

---

[6]The reader may check the accuracy of this statement by consulting tables in Chapter III of this review for results on Southern Negroes tested by *Stanford-Binet, National Intelligence Test,* etc.

some asymptote, and it may well be that after a rise due to better adjustment the average intelligence of Negro children will become constant at some value below that of the white children. Malzberg added that the burden of proof would seem to rest on Klineberg, for though he and others have shown that correction must be made for the adverse effect of poor environments they have not shown that such corrections will eliminate all racial differences in intelligence.

Garrett, in much the same vein, wrote that while improvement in environment did raise the scores of the Negro children it did not bring them up to the white standards.

Tyler considered it unfortunate that sampling factors were not better controlled so that a reader would have definite evidence as to whether or not any one or all of the schools in which the investigators worked were representative of the New York Negro population. She indicated that there seemed to be as much fluctuation from school to school as from North to South and questioned the meaning of the large differences between Negro schools in the North.

Philadelphia

Lee (1951), like Clark, compared *test* and *retest scores* obtained on Negro children, some of whom were born in a Northern city, others having migrated to the city from the South. The scores on the *Philadelphia Tests of Mental and Verbal Ability* formed the chief source of material for Lee's analysis. These tests are described as a series of group intelligence tests that have been standardized on Philadelphia school children and are somewhat similar to the *Otis* series of tests. For a number of years they have been given regularly to all pupils in attendance in Grades 1A, 2B, 4B, 6B, and 9A of the Philadelphia public schools and the several group IQ's are inscribed on each pupil's cumulative record card.

Lee selected nine junior and senior high schools in different parts of Philadelphia, a major criterion in the selection of schools being the percentage of Negro students, which varied from 23 to 92 among the high schools chosen.[7] From the nine schools he selected for his experimental group the records of all Negro children: (1) who had come to Philadelphia from a state south of D.C. and east of the Mississippi River, (2) who had reached at least the ninth grade, and (3) who had not missed any of the *Philadelphia* tests in the years subsequent to their arrival in the city. A control group was chosen by taking the record of every fifth Philadelphia-born Negro from alphabetical listings of each class, provided the S had reached at least the 9th grade in school, and provided there were records of his having been tested in Grades 1A, 2B, 4B, 6B, and 9A.[8] The *Chicago Tests of Primary Mental Abilities* and the *Minnesota Paper Form Board*

---

[7]Lee indicated that he made no claim as to the schools being truly representative of the Philadelphia public schools.

[8]About one fourth of the records of the migrants and about one third of the records of the sedents were eliminated because they had missed one or more of the tests.

test were administered in Grade 9, and as with the *Philadelphia* tests Lee separated the nonkindergarten from the kindergarten group and then compared the Philadelphia-born of the former with migrants entering the school system of Philadelphia in Grades 1A, 1B to 2B, 3A to 4B, 5A to 6B, and 7A to 9A.

As will be observed in Table 14, on the *Philadelphia* test the sedents (tested five different times) gained an average of 1.6 points from the first testing in 1A to the last in 9A; those migrants entering Grades 1A to 6B averaged from 86.5 to 88.2 when first tested but when they were examined in 9A they averaged 89.4 to 92.8, gaining on the average from 2 to 6 points, depending on whether they entered the Philadelphia schools in Grade 6B or in Grade 1A. Allowing for about one point in IQ attributable to practice effect, the migrants may be said to have improved from one to five group IQ points, the amount of improvement varying directly with length of time spent in the Philadelphia school system. Lee reported a significant difference (at the .05 level of confidence) for each of the three groups of migrants *entering before Grade 5A* between the first mean IQ obtained and the mean IQ secured in Grade 9A (*i.e.*, the last rating obtained).

In commenting upon this study, Hilgard (1962, p. 440) remarked that the effects (improvement) can hardly be due to *schooling* for the sedents were superior to the migrants even in the first grade; also the sedents improved only slightly in their years in the Philadelphia schools.[9] He concluded, therefore, that the ultimate level was apparently affected by the general increase in environmental stimulation that came with the move to a large city.

On the *Minnesota Paper Form Board* the mean score of the 9A Philadelphia-born pupils was 30.3; for those who had migrated and entered the Philadelphia schools between Grades 9A and 1A the mean scores ranged from about 21 to about 29, indicating a marked relationship between year of entering the school system and the test scored earned when in the ninth grade.

The mean scores on the six subtests of the *Chicago Tests of Primary Abilities,* *i.e.*, number facility, verbal comprehension, spatial orientation, word fluency, inductive reasoning, and rote memory showed a tendency for the earlier the entrance into the Philadelphia school system the higher the subtest score subsequently earned at Grade 9A.[10] Lee found for all the subtests except the last a significant difference between the means of the migrant group entering in Grade 1A and the means of the migrant group entering in Grades 7A to 9A.[11] He concluded that the Philadelphia research had in the main substantiated Klineberg's

---

[9] On the other hand, several authors of textbooks (Geldard, 1962, p. 319; Kimble and Garmezy, 1963, pp. 127-128; and Ruch, 1963, p. 482) have acclaimed this study as being "a crucial test", "an even more impressive demonstration . . ." (than Klineberg's research), and the like.

[10] Except for the rote memory subtest where there was no evidence of this trend. In none of the other five subtests was there complete consistency.

[11] Probably at the .05 level since this was the criterion used in the analysis of *Philadelphia Tests*.

hypothesis that there is an increase in the intelligence scores of Southern Negro migrants to New York with an increase in length of residence in New York.[12]

Chicago

Following a 1957-58 survey of the Victor F. Lawson School which showed retardation in reading in all of its grades, Boylan and O'Meara (1958) questioned 50 Negro and 58 white teachers of the Negro pupils as to possible explanations for it. The teachers, without exception, attributed the low achievement of their pupils chiefly to the presence of a large number of Southern-born children.[13] The school, located in a middle-class Negro neighborhood on the South Side of Chicago, had an enrollment of 2300 pupils including 667 Southern-born and 1201 Chicago-born children who had been given mental tests. Although there were proportionally twice as many Southern-born as Chicago-born Negro children earning IQ's between 70 and 80 (Table 14) yet the mean IQ's of the two groups differed by only one point and the standard deviations were the same. The authors therefore doubted that the inferior mental ability of the Southern-born explained the school-wide reading problem.

CONCLUSION

In the researches reported by Klineberg, McAlpin, Long, Dombey, Clark, Lee, and Boylan and O'Meara in the Northern and Border cities of New York, Washington, D. C., Cleveland, Detroit, Philadelphia, and Chicago, some of the major findings were presented in terms of IQ. This summary will deal only with these results. In the combined *Binet* studies included in Klineberg's data it appears that four points separated the Northern- and Southern-born. This difference may be compared with the six points (McAlpin) and the 3-6 points (Long) which separated the District of Columbia-born from the migrant groups on the *Kuhlmann-Anderson* and with the one point (Boylan and O'Meara) which separated the Chicago-born and the Southern-born on this test. Dombey found the Northern-born and the Southern-born Cleveland delinquents differed on the *Stanford-Binet* by six points. Likewise, in his various studies, Clark found some evidence to indicate that the IQ's of the Southern-born tended to increase a little more, or to decrease a little less, than those of the Northern-born children in Cleveland and Detroit. Finally, from Lee's tables it seems that when tested by the *Philadelphia* examination in the ninth grade, the Southern-born averaged three IQ points below the Philadelphia-born. In general, therefore, it seems that

---

[12]Lee draws no conclusion concerning the presence or absence of selective migration from his results. By inference one might assume the presence of some selective factor since the group IQ's of the Ss migrating from the South averaged between 86 and 88 when they entered the Philadelphia publ schs—regardless of what grade they entered (Table 14).

[13]For more complete description of this study see pp. 128-129 of this book.

Negro children born in the Border and Northern metropolitan centers averaged from three to four IQ points higher than Negro children living in the same cities and attending the same public schools who were born in the South. In the opinion of the reviewer these investigations have not disproved the hypothesis of selective migration, but have shown that selective migration does not account for *all* of the difference between Northern and Southern Negroes. Our single best estimate was that approximately seven points separate the average IQ of Southern colored children from Northern children of their race. If this is correct, then about half or possibly a little more than half of this difference may be accounted for by environmental factors and the remainder by selective migration.

Chapter XI

SUMMARY AND CONCLUSIONS

We have attempted to assemble and evaluate critically the research in the field of Negro intelligence as determined by psychometric tests. The survey covers a span of more than 50 years. Approximately 382 studies have been examined in which 81 tests were administered, and hundreds of thousands of Negro children and adults from various sections of the United States, as well as some 1600 from Ontario, Canada, and the West Indian islands of Jamaica and Grand Cayman, served as subjects.

The research has been summarized in fourteen tables. Three of these include studies of school children, ten of the others deal, respectively, with the testing of young children, high school pupils, college students, members of the Armed Forces, veterans and other civilians, the gifted, the mentally retarded, delinquents, criminals, and racial hybrids; and the last one with the special studies on selective migration. Within each table the researches have usually been grouped according to the test employed, with the Southern studies appearing first in chronological order, followed in turn by those from the Border and Northern states. We have, whenever possible, attempted to include the following items for each work examined: author; date, location of study; number of subjects, age, grade (if in school, or highest grade completed if not in school), and method by which selected; results; and some comment of the investigator. If white subjects were included in the research, comparable data on these were tabulated.

Young Children

Approximately 1700 colored and 13,900 white children between the ages of two and six years served as subjects in 17 studies reported between 1922 and 1965. Ten mental tests were administered, the results of eight of them being recorded in IQ units.[1] The majority of the children were attending kindergartens or nursery schools, or were enrolled in day nurseries; some had been brought regularly to a free clinic for a period of three years; others were examined relative to the appraisal of a preschool special training program; some were tested to determine if they were ready for first grade before the age of six, some participated in a voluntary testing program in a first-grade preregistration period, and a few were already enrolled in the first grade although under six years. Still others were selected from city playgrounds or served as subjects because they were within a

---

[1]The eight tests included: *Stanford-Binet, 1916, 1937, and 1960 Forms, Draw-a-Man, WISC, Lorge-Thorndike, Peabody Picture Vocabulary,* and *Ammons Full-Scale Picture Vocabulary.* These tests were administered in 15 of the studies.

given age range and had siblings within another age range. The children lived in eight Southern, three Border, and four Northern states.

The average IQ's of the various groups of colored children ranged between 83 and 101; the average IQ's of the white groups with whom they were compared ranged between 102 and 113. The combined average IQ of the colored subjects was 94, or approximately 12 points below that of the white Ss.

The combined average IQ's of colored and white children whose test scores were reported prior to 1945 were 96.28 and 105.22, respectively, a difference of nine points; in the 1945 to 1965 period, the respective colored and white IQ's were 90.79 and 107.33, a difference of 16.5 points.

In general, the colored children obtained their highest scores on *Full-Range Picture Vocabulary* (106 IQ) and their lowest on *Lorge-Thorndike* (83 IQ) and *WISC* (83 IQ); the white samples earned their highest scores, on the average, on *Full-Range Picture Vocabulary* (118 IQ) and their lowest on *Lorge-Thorndike* (102 IQ) and *Draw-a-Man* (102 IQ).

It appears evident, therefore, that not only have young white children scored consistently above colored children, on the average, but that young children, both white and colored, have earned higher IQ's than school children of their respective racial groups. The higher IQ's obtained for young children may be attributed in large part to the fact that they do not represent a random sampling of their age group, since the brighter of 2- to 6-year-old children are more likely to be present (and therefore available for testing) in nursery schools, kindergartens, playgrounds, first grades, *etc.*, than are the duller children. It has also been pointed out that preschool tests are not considered to be as reliable nor as valid as tests designed for school children.

School Children   Individual Tests

The review includes 43 investigations in which fourteen individual tests were administered to 9925 colored school children. In 23 of these researches white subjects were also tested; in two of them the colored average equaled that of the compared white groups. However, one of the two studies (Peterson and Lanier, 1929) included white children from non-English-speaking homes. Excluding the records of the whites who spoke a foreign language at home, the median of the remainder is significantly above that of the colored. The other study (Higgins and Sivers, 1958) involved a comparison of test scores of pupils attending schools *serving the lowest socioeconomic* areas of a Northeastern city, and may be presumed to have included children from non-English-speaking homes.[2]

In the 20 investigations which included no white Ss, 17 authors report averages that were below the white norms. Of the three in which the results

---

[2]In the opinion of the reviewer. The authors have made no comment upon this point. Also, their method of selection may have had the effect of excluding some gifted children, particularly among the whites. See pp. 41-42.

compare favorably with the white norms, only Graham's Atlanta group (1926) and one of Long's Washington, D. C., groups (1933) were described as unselected. The other group examined by Long and those included in Beckham's data (1933) were not randomly selected.

In 26 studies the colored subjects were selected at random within the conditions of the experiment and the results presented in terms of IQ. The average IQ of these Negro children tested in the rural South was 77; in the Southern cities and towns, 83; in three Border cities, 90; and in the Northern cities and towns, 86. In the Border cities only children in the lower elementary grades were examined.

The average IQ's of colored and white children who were examined between 1921 and 1944 were 85 and 99, respectively, a *difference of 14 points;* in the period between 1945 and 1964 the respective colored and white averages were 82 and 96, a *difference of 14 points.*

In the ten studies in which whites and Negroes were selected from the same neighborhoods, where mill whites were compared with Negro children of varying status, and where white and colored subjects were matched for occupational status of father or socioeconomic status of the home, with one exception the colored have scored the lower.[3] Where comparisons were made in terms of IQ the colored averaged about nine points below the matched white groups.

School Children   Non-Verbal Group Tests

Forty-one studies which utilized seventeen nonverbal group tests in the examination of about 14,800 colored school children have been reviewed. White children were included in 22 of the investigations. In all of these the white subjects secured higher averages than the colored of the same localities or cities.

In the nineteen experimental studies where the scores of the Negroes were compared with white norms, all except Long (1933) reported inferiority of the colored. In general, the children seem to have been selected by random or stratified sampling or else saturated samples were obtained.

In 28 of the investigations, including 9300 colored children, the results were given in terms of group IQ's. The combined average was approximately 85, ranging from 77 in the rural North, through 80 in the rural South, 83 in the urban North, 86 in the urban South, to 91 in the urban Border states and the District of Columbia. The Negro children tested in the Border cities (St. Louis and Washington) were all in the lower elementary grades.

The combined average IQ's of colored and white children who were examined between 1925 and 1944 were 83 and 99, respectively, a *difference of 16 points;* for the period between 1945 and 1964 the respective colored and white averages proved to be 88 and 101, a *difference of 13 points.*

---

[3]The exception was reported by Higgins and Sivers previously noted.

We have reviewed 103 studies of colored school children in which 18 or more psychometric verbal group tests were administered. Altogether, about 60,850 colored children were examined by these tests, about four fifths of whom were living in urban areas and one fifth in villages or on farms. Approximately 64 per cent of the subjects were tested in the South, the other 36 per cent being about equally divided between the Border and Northern states.

White children were also tested in 58 of the researches, the whites achieving higher scores on the average than the Negroes in every investigation except one.[4]

In 45 studies the colored averages were compared only with established norms. In 44 of these the averages were found to be inferior to the norms, the exception being Long's District of Columbia group of 100 selected subjects (1933).

Group IQ's have been reported by the investigators on approximately 50,000 Negro school children. Separating the studies into South, Border, and North, the respective combined averages were approximately 81, 90, and 90, the overall average being 84.

The average IQ's of colored and white children whose scores were reported between 1923 and 1944 were 85 and 98, respectively, a *difference of 13 points;* in the period between 1945 and 1965 the respective colored and white averages were 83 and 99, a *difference of 16 points.*

HIGH SCHOOL STUDENTS

Twenty intelligence tests administered to approximately 23,600 colored high school students have been reported in the 55 studies included in this review. About 85 per cent of the pupils were tested in the South. In 26 of the investigations white students were also examined, the whites always obtaining higher average scores than the colored Ss with whom they were compared. In 29 studies the colored averages were compared with the test norms rather than with particular white groups; among these studies there were 45 separate means reported, 43 of which were below the norms.[5]

IQ's have been secured on about 13,250 Negro high school pupils whose combined average proved to be 83.5, about the same as the combined mean IQ obtained on Negro school children.[6] The average IQ of the Southern Negro high school pupils was 82, that of the Border and Northern colored students, 91.

---

[4] For review and appraisal of the McCord and Demerath study, see pp. 129-130.

[5] One of Oldham's Chicago groups, identified as of good socioeconomic status, earned a mean IQ of 101 (1935); Anderson's Okmulgee, Oklahoma, Ss achieved a mean of 103 (1947).

[6] *i.e.,* 84.2; this figure is based upon the examination of more than 66,000 colored school children by the various individual and group tests.

The combined average IQ's of colored and white high school subjects whose test scores were reported prior to 1945 were 86 and 97, respectively, *a difference of 11 points;* in the 1945 to 1965 period, the respective colored and white IQ's were 83 and 102, *a difference of 19 points.*

COLLEGE STUDENTS

About 61 per cent of the 24,640 Negro college students included in the survey have been examined on the *American Council Psychological Examination for College Freshmen;* 10 per cent have been tested on the *Higher Form* of the *Otis Self-Administering Test of Mental Ability;* 21 per cent have been examined by the *School and College Ability Tests,* the *College Board Scholastic Aptitude Test,* or the *Medical College Admission Test;* and about nine per cent have been given some other test. Ninety-eight per cent of the subjects were enrolled in colleges for Negroes.

The obtained averages are typically much lower than the norms provided and below the averages of the specific white groups with whom they were compared. On the *Otis S-A* the colored students earned an average score which placed them at about the *13th percentile rank* of the norms distribution; on the *ACE* the colored achieved an average score located at about the *12th percentile rank;* and on the *SCAT,* the *SAT,* and the *MCAT* the Negro students attained average scores placing them at about the *6th percentile rank* according to the norms.

THE ARMED FORCES   WORLD WAR I

A review of the research on the Army data of World War I indicates that white officers scored markedly above colored officers and that white enlisted men were consistently superior to Negro enlisted men. Using the white draft as a frame of reference with a mean of 100 and a standard deviation of 16, the *Combined Scale*[7] scores of about 23,500 colored recruits (selected on prorata bases) were converted into standard-score IQ's. The mean IQ of the colored enlisted men was 83 (Johnson, 1948), slightly more than one point below the combined average IQ's obtained on colored school children and high school pupils.

The Army data also indicate that Northern whites of the draft were unequivocally superior to Northern Negroes of the draft and that Southern white recruits were clearly superior to Southern Negro recruits. The position of the Northern Negro soldier relative to that of the Southern white, however, has been the subject of debate. Instead of comparing relatively limited numbers of *Alpha* or *Alpha only* scores as a number of investigators had done, a more comprehensive and accurate picture of the relative intelligence of the Southern

---

[7]The *Combined Scale* was a device whereby test scores could be converted into a common scale, whether they were scores on *Alpha* only, *Alpha* and *Beta, Beta* only, or *Beta* and some individual test.

white and the Northern Negro recruits was obtained from data on the *Combined Scale*. A comparison of scores on the *Combined Scale* of about 10,000 Negro and 17,000 white enlisted men from the four Northern states where Negroes were reported to have scored their best and the four Southern states[8] where whites were reported to have scored their worst shows the four groups to rank in order of: Northern whites, Southern (and Border) whites, Northern Negroes, and Southern (and Border) Negroes.

THE ARMED FORCES   WORLD WAR II

Four studies have indicated that total rejection rates were higher for Negroes than for whites in World War II and that the rejection rates due to *educational and mental deficiency* were markedly different for the two races. Likewise, six investigations dealing with relatively small samples of enlisted men who were admitted to mental hygiene clinics or hospitalized in psychiatric or neuropsychiatric wards have consistently found the Negro recruit to test below the white.

A number of authors have discussed the Special Training Program designed to qualify intelligent illiterates for induction into the Army. Eighty-four per cent of the whites and 87 per cent of the colored who were admitted to this program completed the course satisfactorily in 8 to 13 weeks time and were assigned to regular Army service, the men having to demonstrate a degree of military proficiency and an achievement of at least a fourth-grade standard in reading and arithmetic. In the opinion of this writer the several studies of enlisted men sent to the Special Training Centers do not contradict, but probably support, the findings of other Army studies. Some of the important points to be considered in the evaluation of the Negro-white comparisons are as follows: the large percentage of Negroes as compared with whites who qualified for the program, the fact that the brighter of the illiterates were directed to the training centers, the fact that about one third of the men sent to the training centers were literate when they arrived (could pass the necessary tests at the fourth-grade level), the point that the ability to adjust was considered as particularly important in the disposition of Negroes of intermediate literacy, the inference that the English-speaking whites needed a higher aptitude score to graduate than did the Negroes, and the fact that about 99 per cent of the men released for assignment to regular training scored in the two lowest classes of the *AGCT,* increasing the Army manpower but not affecting the intermediate or higher levels from which leaders could be drawn.

Several studies, including many thousands of Negroes inducted into the Armed Forces, were based upon data from the Adjutant General's Office.[9] From these it is evident that the colored enlisted man averaged from 25 to 30

[8]The four listed as *Southern* include three Southern and one Border state, Kentucky.
[9]Davenport (1946), Stewart (1947), Star, Williams, and Stouffer (1949), and Fulk (1949).

standard score points below the white recruit on the *Army General Classification Test;* that significant differences occurred when colored and white men of the same Military Occupational Specialty were compared; that the differences were present when men of equivalent education were compared;[10] and that the differences persisted when whites from an all-Southern Command were compared with Negroes from their best Northern Command. Significant differences were also found between Negro and white aviation cadets of World War II and between Negro and white soldiers (post-Korean War) who had been carefully matched on a number of variables.

In making comparisons between the intelligence of enlisted Negroes and whites, one must accept certain pertinent facts that are unfavorable to the Negro: (1) the consistently lower scores earned by the Negroes, (2) the failure of relatively large numbers of Negroes to be inducted, the higher rejection rates not having been due to the presence of more physical defects, (3) the relatively smaller number of occupational deferments given to Negroes because of special abilities or skills, and (4) the smaller percentage of superior colored men drawn into the officer group and thereby eliminated from the comparisons.[11] On the other hand, it seems highly probable that: (1) the lives of relatively more Negroes than whites were culturally impoverished, (2) proportionally more of the Negroes were not as test-sophisticated, were less well oriented to the testing situation, were less aware of the need for speed and attentiveness to the tasks required, were less interested in the tests, had a greater tendency to relax, even to sleep, and (3) relatively more Negroes were uninterested in fighting a war a long way from home, felt themselves completely uprooted from their families, and anticipated little advancement, arduous work, and white antagonism. Before one concludes that these cultural-motivational-personality factors are or are not sufficient to explain away the Armed Forces findings, it is suggested that he consider these studies not in isolation but in conjunction with the research on other Negro and white samples.

SPECIAL GROUPS OF VETERANS AND OTHER CIVILIANS

In all nine of the researches dealing with the testing of special groups of veterans and other civilians, the colored averaged below the whites with whom they were compared. In six of the studies, the results were reported in terms of IQ with the colored averaging from 11 to 17 points below the white subjects and from 16 to 32 points below the white norms.

---

[10]Colored men who had completed as much as 10 grades of schooling earned lower *AGCT* scores than whites with little or no schooling. (Fulk, 1949; Fulk and Harrell, 1952)

[11]Ginzberg observed that at the *end of WW II* there was one Negro officer for approximately every 100 Negro enlisted men while the ratio for the Army as a whole was nearly one officer to 8 men. (1956, p. 85)

The Southern states may have contributed proportionally more white officers than did the Northern states in WWI. See Chap. 5, fn. 30.

DEVIATES

From a combination of relatively unselected samples of white and colored school children, it appears that proportionally the *colored gifted* have been reported about one sixth as often as the white gifted and that the *colored retarded* have been reported about six times as often as the white retarded. In the special studies of gifted, the colored were found about one third as frequently as were whites in proportion to the numbers surveyed. Among the special studies of the mentally deficient, the rate for the retarded colored was approximately twice that of the rate for retarded white.

DELINQUENTS AND CRIMINALS

In all 28 of the studies reviewed, excluding Clarke's groups matched for IQ, the colored delinquents averaged below the white norms or below the white delinquents with whom they were compared. Where the results were given in IQ units the average of the Negro delinquents was 74, the average of the white delinquents, about 81.

The Negro criminals likewise earned lower means than the white criminals in the 16 investigations tabulated. Where the results were given in terms of IQ, the average of the Negro felons was 81, that of the white convicts, 92. When the Negroes were classified according to birthplace, the Northern-born scored higher than the Southern-born but below the native white criminals.

In the instances where colored criminals or delinquents were matched with white convicts or misdemeanants for occupational category, school grade completed, and type of community from which they had come, the differences between the respective means were significant.

RACIAL HYBRIDS

Racial hybrids have a tendency to score higher on psychometric tests, on the whole, than Negro groups described as unmixed.

SELECTIVE MIGRATION

Northern Negroes, both children and adults, have been frequently reported as achieving higher averages on intelligence tests than Southern Negroes of the same grade or age. Some psychologists attribute the Northern-Southern difference to superior education and the more complex, less constrictive environment afforded Negroes in the Northern states; others believe that the more able and energetic Southern Negroes are likely to appreciate the advantages of living in the North and consequently migrate in that direction.

We have separated the research in this field into three categories. In the first two are included five studies where either the amount of formal schooling or a form of scholastic index was used as the criterion of mental ability. Records of approximately 20,000 Negro migrants when compared with those of Negro sedents indicate that migration was generally selective. In the third category, Negro children living in five Northern cities or in the District of Columbia were given intelligence tests and divided into Northern-born and Southern-born (or within the District and outside the District), were separated into various groups according to length of residence in the cities, or were retested after they had lived for a period of time in these cities. The test scores of more than 15,000 Negro children were thus compared. From these researches it appears evident: (1) that the Northern-born secure higher average scores than the Southern-born living in the North, (2) that the District of Columbia-born on the whole earn higher scores than those born outside the District, (3) that there is a tendency for the IQ to improve with increase of time spent in the North, at least up to five or six years, and (4) that when retested the IQ's of the Southern-born seem to increase a little more, or to decrease a little less, than do those of the Northern-born Negroes.

In the studies where IQ's were obtained, Negro children born in the Border and Northern metropolitan centers average from one to six IQ points higher than Negro children living in the same cities and attending the same public schools who were born in the South. In the opinion of the reviewer, these investigations have not disproved the hypothesis of selective migration but have shown that selective migration does not account for *all* of the difference between Northern and Southern Negroes. Our single best estimate is that between seven and ten points separate the average IQ of Southern colored children from Northern and Border children of their race. If this is correct, then about half of this difference may be accounted for by environmental factors and half by selective migration.

Some North-South Urban Comparisons

Recognizing the fact that urban children in general average higher in test performance than rural children and that any comparison between Negroes and whites from the Northern and Southern states is vitiated by the urban-rural variable, we have attempted to control this variable by *comparing only urban children with urban children.* We have, therefore, using Tables 1 to 5, tabulated the means of all preschool children, school children, and high school pupils tested in Northern or Southern towns or cities, provided their selection appeared to have been unbiased and the records were presented in IQ units.[12]

---

[12]Where authors included both rural and urban Ss and treated their scores separately, we included the appropriate statistics; if they specified *county* as source of data, or indicated that rural children attended the consolidated or village schools, the study was excluded. We likewise excluded some Northern urban studies on whites and colored, identified as follows by the investigators: Clark (1923) who later reported that the IQ's obtained were too high; Beckham (1933) whose Ss were not selected at random; W. W. Brown (1955) who reported IQ's only on Ss who had failed one or more grades or one or more high school subjects; and McCord and Demerath (1958) who gave no exact means or medians.

The combined mean IQ of approximately 27,441 Northern white children was 101.7, that of the 25,641 Southern whites, 102.2; while the combined mean of the 15,017 Northern colored subjects was 88.7, and that of the 32,382 Southern Negroes, 82.6.[13] None of the specific Northern white- or Southern white- means were below the combined mean of the Northern colored; and in only one of the 49 studies including Northern Negroes was a mean reported which was above the combined mean of either the Southern or the Northern whites.[14]

In so far as these groups adequately represent their *urban school-age* populations,[15] it is apparent that the whites in the South and North average about the same, that the Northern Negro averages 13 points below the whites, and that the Southern Negro averages between 19 and 20 points below them. It does not lend support to the view (frequently reinforced by test results which have included rural and village Ss) that Northern whites earn higher mental test scores on the average than Southern whites; nor does it support the generalization (based upon tenuous World War I findings) that Negroes from some Northern states are superior on the average to whites from some Southern states.

VARIABILITY

Variability appears to have been the greater among the white than among the Negro subjects examined. Where samples of both racial groups were tested and comparable *s's* or Q's reported, the white subjects proved to have been the more variable in 67 per cent of the 200 comparisons, the colored the more

---

[13]Probably Mermelstein's study of number development in 6- and 9-year-old Negro children living in Flint, Michigan, and Prince Edward County, Virginia, may be of interest to the reader at this point. Investigating developmental changes in children's thinking as a function of school background, Mermelstein (1965) tested their conceptions of *conservation of substance* both by standard Piaget experiments and by a nonverbal technique identified as the *Magic Experiment.* He found no evidence that the Flint children were superior to the Prince Edward children at either age level, despite the fact that one was a Northern group and one a Southern group, and despite the fact that two thirds of the Prince Edward 9-year-olds (on whom there were records) had had but 8 months of formal schooling prior to the testing. Mermelstein concluded that "the results are consistent with the claim that school experiences are not of sufficient moment to alter the natural processes of adaptation which take place in the child's adjustment to his objective world . . ." (p. 60)

[14]A Minneapolis sample of 20 Ss. See Bird, Monachesi, and Burdick (1952). This statement does not mean, of course, that there were no other Northern colored groups above the means of *any* Northern or Southern white groups.

[15]Northern white children tested were likely unrepresentative of the Northern white population, since in more than half of the studies including them the researchers planned to reduce environmental and educational differences between *w* and *c* by selecting children from mixed schools and similar neighborhoods. Further, relatively more *retarded children* in Northern cities have been enrolled in special classes and have seldom been included in testing programs. (See K. B. Clark's reference to the number of classes for retarded children in the Harlem schools alone, 1963.)

variable in 26 per cent of them, and no appreciable difference[16] was found in the remaining seven per cent. The differences in the sizes of the quartile or standard deviations were usually small and the significance of the differences between them rarely determined.

OVERLAPPING

There were 37 studies of school children in which the amount of overlapping was reported by the researchers or could be determinated by the reviewer. The overlapping ranged from 0 to 44 per cent, the average being *approximately 12 per cent.*[17]

At the high school level the average overlap, based on 26 comparisons in 23 studies was *10 per cent,* the range of overlapping being from 0 to 69 per cent. At the college level the average overlap, based on 18 comparisons in eleven studies, was *7 per cent,* the range being from less than one to 55 per cent. Our calculation of the average amount of overlapping, using available data from 34,784 colored school children, high school pupils, and college students examined in 71 studies is *11 per cent.*

The reader may compare the *11 per cent overlap* so determined with the schematic distributions used by Anastasi (1958, p. 549) to illustrate a *30 per cent overlap* which she noted is "close to that usually found between psychological test scores of Negroes and whites in the United States." This authoritative statement made without supporting references is shortly followed with: "If 30 per cent of the Negroes reach or exceed the white median . . . . ." and: "Under these conditions, therefore, the ranges will overlap almost completely." While she does not use the expression *intelligence test scores* but *psychological test scores* it is probable that many persons would infer that her assumption had become a fact and that she was referring to *intelligence testing.* Certainly Klineberg (1963, p. 202) who quotes the passage beginning: "If 30 per cent of the Negroes . . . . . ." and Ingle (1964, p. 378) who does not quote but who writes: "If the 30 per cent overlap usually found between the test scores of whites and Negroes in the United States . . . . ." were inferring that Anastasi implied the presence of a *30 per cent overlap in intelligence test performance.*

Pettigrew (*J. Negro Educ.,* 1964, p. 22) likewise must have been influenced by Anastasi's schematic distributions (fig. 84) cited above and her comments, for he includes a duplicate of the drawing with a few additions to make it easier for the layman to understand and with the substitution of *25 per* cent for the *30 per cent overlap.* Citing no authority for his premise (nor does he in the

---

[16] Assuming ± .20 to be "no appreciable difference", except in a very few instances where the means and standard deviations were very small.

[17] By *overlap* we refer to the percentage of Negroes' scores that equaled or exceeded the median or mean test score of the compared white group. Attention may be called at this point to the fact that in WW I slightly more than *13 per cent* of the 23,596 colored recruits earned scores on the *Combined Scale* equal or superior to the average of the white draft, based on 93,955 cases. (Brigham, 1923)

same discussion accompanying the same figure in his book, *A Profile of the Negro American,* 1964, p. 131) he continues with the statement: "Figure 2 shows two typical intelligence test distributions with an overlap of 25 per cent, that is, 25 per cent of the Negroes tested (shaded area) surpass the performance of half of the whites tested. Notice how the ranges of the two distributions are virtually the same, even though the means are somewhat different."[18]

The reviewer has found the overlap to be *25 per cent or more* in ten of the 71 studies, involving 3039 of the 35,107 Negro Ss,[19] six of the ten researches reported before 1945 and only two of them after 1950. Furthermore, if one looks for the investigations that produced a *30 or more per cent overlap* he would find (according to the information available to the reviewer) five studies, including 872 colored cases. They are as follows: Murdoch (1920) 227; Peterson and Lanier, New York (1929) 187; Graham (1930) 181; Byrns (1936) 124; and Anderson (1947) 153. All but one of them would be called "earlier, less sophisticated investigations" according to Pettigrew, since they were dated prior to World War II. (*J. Negro Educ.,* p. 6; also *A Profile . . .,* p. 102)

On the other hand, there are 35 of the 71 studies in which the overlap was less than 10 per cent; these 35 included 23,222 Ss, nine of the researches dating before the close of World War II and *17 after 1950.*[20]

There seems to be no doubt that writers on the subject have assumed a much greater percentage of overlapping than the research warrants.

STABILITY OF IQ

IQ's of Negroes enrolled in the American public schools have proved to be relatively stable. In the first place, the combined mean IQ's of Negro elementary

---

[18] Pettigrew without doubt impressed the editor of the *J.Negro Educ.* with the truth of a 25 per cent overlap as well as with his scholarship for he commented as follows in an editorial in the same issue: "Fortunately, there are objective investigations available. The research by Thomas Pettigrew of Harvard makes clear the great amount of overlapping in the performance of Negroes and whites on intelligence tests. He shows by facts and figures that 25 per cent of the Negro subjects reach or exceed the median score of the whites, and thereby exceed the performance of 50 per cent of the total white population tested." (Daniel, 1964, p. 97)

Similarly, after having previously (p. 366) called attention to McGurk's statement of a *25 per cent overlap,* Dreger and Miller thought as social scientists they should "set forth the full picture. The wide overlap between white and Negro distributions of scores should be pointed out so that it is evident that within group differences are far greater than between group differences." (1960, p. 374)

It might be noted at this point that Sherwood Washburn, anthropologist, while not committing himself on the *amount* of overlap, thinks of it as *tremendous.* "If one looks at the degree of social discrimination against Negroes and their lack of education, and also takes into account the tremendous amount of overlapping between the observed IQ's of both, one can make an equally good case that given a comparable chance to that of the Whites, their IQ's would test out ahead." (*in* Tumin, 1964, pp. 7-8)

[19]See fn. 95, Chap. 3.

[20]For identification of the 71 investigations, see pp. 205-206, 256, and 305.

school children range between 84 and 85 on Individual tests, on Nonverbal Group, and on Verbal Group tests; (2) the combined mean IQ of Negro high school pupils proved to be 84.1; a large unbiased sample of Negro recruits in World War I earned a combined mean IQ of 83;[21] (4) there seems to be no evidence that in World War II the mean test score of the Negro enlisted man is closer to the white mean than in World War I; (5) colored children at several educational levels have earned average IQ's of comparable size—groups of Northern and Southern children tested in Grades 1 to 3 having earned a combined mean IQ of 83.1, as compared with a mean of 84.5 achieved by other Negro children tested from these regions but in Grades 4 to 7;[22] (6) the Northern Ss in Grades 1 to 3 earned a combined mean of 87.8, those in Grades 4 to 7, a combined mean of 88.2, practically the same as the combined mean IQ of 87.6 secured from the testing of many thousands of Northern Negro school children; (7) elementary school children of Ages 6 to 9 from Northern and Southern states earned a combined mean IQ of 84.0, whereas other Negro children from these areas between the Ages of 10 to 12 attained a combined mean of 83.0; (8) Negro elementary school children tested between 1921-1944 earned a combined mean of 84.8, whereas those tested between 1945-1965 earned a combined mean IQ of 83.6; and (9) high school pupils examined in the earlier period achieved a combined mean IQ of 86.2, while those tested between 1945-1965 proved to have obtained a mean of 83.[23]

ANALYSIS OF TEST ITEMS

In general, Negroes have been reported as earning their best scores in tests identified as purposeful, practical, and concrete, and as achieving their lowest scores in tests that involve logical analysis, abstract reasoning, and certain perceptual-motor functions. Although these findings have been made over a period of many years and have seldom been contradicted, some additional support for them has followed the administration of the *Wechsler* tests to colored subjects of varying ages and circumstances.[24] Among the *Wechsler* subtests,

---

[21]Using the white draft as a frame of reference with a mean of 100 and s of 16, Brigham's Negro scores on the *Combined Scale* were converted into standard-score IQ's. A mean of 83 was secured on the 23,596 colored enlisted men. (D. M. Johnson, 1948)

[22]K. B. Clark (1965) however, reported a drop in median IQ of Central Harlem school children from 90.6 at Grade 3 to 86.3 at Grade 6, followed by a slight rise to 87.7 at Grade 8. These averages are based upon the following tests administered throughout New York City at Grades 3, 6, and 8, respectively: *Otis Q-S Alpha, Otis Q-S Beta,* and *Pintner General Ability and Intermediate Test, Form A.*

[23]Means based upon 4068 and 9156 records of colored Ss, respectively. The 66,000 colored elementary school pupils tested were about equally divided in the two time intervals.

[24]Approximately 21 studies have been reviewed in which Negroes have been tested by the *Wechsler-Bellevue,* the *WISC,* or the *WAIS;* three of these were reported before 1950, the others between 1950 and 1964.

Negroes have appeared to their best advantage on *Comprehension*,[25] and have made their poorest showing on *Block Design, Arithmetical Reasoning,* and *Digit Symbol*. Likewise, Negro college students have shown the least amount of over-lapping in the relatively abstract tests of *SAT, SCAT,* and *MCAT*. Negro pupils have also been described as being more rigid in their responses and less able to organize the elements of the *Rorschach* into a meaningful context than white children. In a recent analysis of the responses of underprivileged Negro and white children to a series of tests, Deutsch (1965) reported the Negro sample as performing poorly in areas including abstraction and verbalization, the language deficiency being evident in the use of abstractions and knowledge of categories rather than in the use of labels and word meanings.

Certain of the early investigators noted that the colored were at their best in the rote or immediate memory type of test, the more recent work of Kennedy, Van De Riet, and White tending to support this view.[26] However, the *Digit Span* subtest of the *Wechsler* has not generally proved to be an easy test for the various groups of Negroes tested on it.

There is a difference of opinion as to the difficulty Negroes have with verbal as compared with nonverbal test material. It has been generally assumed that underprivileged groups such as the Negro are particularly handicapped on verbal tests. A number of investigators, mainly before 1934, have described the language difficulties of their colored subjects. However, Yerkes reported that Negroes at Camp Dix, matched with white recruits for intelligence, did relatively better in situations dealing with *words* as determined by the *Devens Literacy Test*. In more recent years psychologists have compared Verbal (or Language) and Per-formance (or Non-Language) IQ's on the *Wechsler* tests and the *California Test of Mental Maturity*. In fifteen studies in which these tests were employed, the Negro children and adults achieved higher scores or IQ's on the *Verbal* section of the test, in seven studies their Verbal IQ's were the lower, and in four there was practically no difference between the mean Verbal and Performance IQ's.[27]

RACE OF EXPERIMENTER

In searching for an explanation of the inferior performance of colored sub-jects on mental tests, several critics have called attention to the fact that the examiners were usually white and therefore unlikely to motivate the testees as effectively as would a member of their racial group. Canady (1936) attempted to test this hypothesis by having some Negro and white children of Evanston, Illinois,

---

[25]Designed to measure practical judgment and common sense.

[26]Kennedy, Van De Riet, and White (1961) reported that an analysis of item difficulty and biserial item correlation of the data indicated that, in general, the *abstract* verbal items appear at too low a level on the *Stanford-Binet, 1960 Revision* and the *rote memory* items are placed too high on the scale.

[27]Colored school children scored no higher, on the average, on the *Nonverbal* than on the *Verbal Group* tests (Chap. 3).

examined twice on the *Stanford-Binet*, once by one of 20 white students and once by himself (a Negro), all of the twenty-one testers having had a course in the measurement of intelligence and all working in the Northwestern University clinic. About half of the children were tested first by a white and subsequently by the colored student, the other half having the testing procedure reversed. The average IQ of the colored children when examined by Canady was 86.79, their average when tested by a white E was 84.31. Unfortunately, it is not clear whether this difference of 2.48 points was due to rapport established between examiner and colored S, to some unrecognized bias on the part of the examiner, or to some other factor.

Subsequent investigators have related the performance of colored subjects to the *race of the examiner* in conjunction with certain other variables, such as: difficulty of task, belief that the task was (or was not) an intelligence test, and type of incentive employed.

Katz, Roberts, and Robinson (1965), for example, administered digit-symbol substitution tests of three levels of difficulty to six groups of Southern Negro college students, the subjects having been informed that the investigator was studying *eye-hand coordination*. Half of the Ss were tested by a white person and half by a Negro. The students tested by a *white examiner* did better on the average than those tested by a Negro when they were working on *the most difficult* of the three substitution levels. When other groups of Negro students were tested on the *most difficult task* presented as a *test of intelligence* rather than a *study in eye-hand coordination*, there was no longer a significant difference in mean performance of the students, whether the tester was white or colored.[28]

Vega (1964) studied the behavior of Negro pupils in some discrimination situations, relating speed of reaction to the *race of the examiner*, to the type of incentive employed, and to other variables. The tasks were presented as a game

---

[28]Following *eye-hand coordination instructions*, the respective means on the most difficult task under white and Negro examiners were: 28.96 and 21.39; following *intelligence test instructions* the respective means under white and colored testers were: 22.91 and 23.48. The former difference, *but not the latter*, was significant.

In describing this research, Katz (1964, p. 393) indicated that when the task was presented as a *test of intelligence* the Ss did not attain higher scores in the presence of a white E; ". . . . the effect of the IQ instructions was to slightly elevate performance with a Negro tester and to lower scores markedly in the white-tester group, so that the means for both testers were at about the same level."

In another reference to the same study, however, Katz, Robinson, Epps, and Waly (1964, p. 54) say: "But when the same task was described as an intelligence test, there was marked impairment of performance with the white tester, while subjects who were tested by the Negro experimenter showed a slight improvement." Notice that these authors *omitted*: ". . . so that the means for both testers were at about the same level," *probably giving a misleading impression to persons reading this report alone.*

Millman and Glock (1965, p. 19) likewise appear to be misleading in their one-statement review of this same research; "Katz (1964) quoted a study of his which indicated that, especially with difficult intellectually oriented tasks, Negro students perform less well with white than with Negro administrators."

in which the subject was instructed to press one of four keys, depending upon which of four designs simultaneously presented was different from the other three. Twenty-four cards, each containing four designs, were presented successively to each of the 324 Negro pupils selected from Grades 2, 6, and 10 in two schools located in Havana, Florida. Two trials were administered at a given sitting, Trial 2 being a duplicate of Trial 1; between the trials, one third of the children were praised, one third reproved, and one third neither praised nor reproved. Half of the subjects at each of the third grades were examined by one of three Negroes and half by one of three whites, all six E's being male graduate students. Combining Trials 1 and 2, the author found the mean of the pupils tested by a Negro to be 6.00 seconds and the mean of the pupils tested by a white man to be 6.34 seconds. The small difference appears to have been due to the operation of the reproof condition; for the children allocated to the praise- or to the control-condition reacted slightly faster on the average in the presence of a white examiner, the respective mean reaction times being 5.79 and 5.78 seconds (white examiner) *vs.* 5.94 and 6.19 seconds (colored examiner). The children allocated to the reproof condition, however, averaged 7.46 seconds on the combined trials when the examiner was white, in contrast to 5.87 seconds when the examiner was colored.

Katz, Robinson, Epps, and Waly (1964) used an hostility questionnaire which they administered on successive days to male Negro high school students, each of whom was paid one dollar for an hour's participation. On the first day the test was administered under neutral instructions by a Negro. On the second day it was given to the same subjects, half of whom were tested by white and half by a Negro stranger, half of each of these groups being given the hostility questionnaire under *neutral instructions* (task described as a research instrument), and half of them with *intelligence test instructions* ("I am interested in this vocabulary test because it will show me how intelligent you are . . . . I want to see how bright you boys are at .... School . . . . .") The authors report that in the neutral condition the changes in hostility scores (from the previous day) of those who had a white administrator were only slightly different from those who had a Negro administrator. "But when test instructions were used, the White Tester group expressed *less* hostility than previously, while the Negro Tester group showed an *increase* in hostile expression." (p. 57)[29]

The reviewer has selected the nineteen studies made on Negro elementary school children in the South where the results were given in IQ units and where the tester was Negro (either the fact was specifically mentioned or else the research was produced in a Southern Negro college, the author being a candidate for the Master's degree) and compared the combined mean IQ obtained from

---

[29]The authors interpret their findings as follows: both administrators instigated hostility in Ss when they announced that they were testing intelligence on the second day; however, when E was a Negro they revealed their annoyance by forming aggressive concepts, but when he was white the need to control hostile feelings resulted in their avoidance of aggressive words.

the Negro examiners with that secured on all Southern Negro school children. The 2360 elementary school children tested by Negroes earned a mean IQ of 80.9 as compared with a combined mean of 80.6 earned by more than 30,000 Southern Negro school children, an undetermined but probably a large number of whom were tested by white investigators.[30] The present writer also calculated the combined mean IQ achieved by 1796 Southern colored high school pupils who were tested by Negro adults. This was 82.9 as compared with a mean of 82.1 secured by nearly 9000 Southern colored high school students, many of whom were examined by white researchers.

From these comparisons it would seem that the intelligence score of a Negro school child or high school pupil has not been adversely affected by the presence of a white tester.

MOTIVATION

Hurlock (1924), Klugman (1944), and Tiber (1963) have investigated the relative effect of certain incentives upon mental test performance of Negro as compared with white school children. The results of their combined studies suggest that for the average Negro child pennies or candy mints serve as the strongest incentive, followed by praise, followed by reproof. For the white child none of these incentives seems to be favored over another. In the best designed of the three studies, Tiber found none of the differences between the Negro groups to be significant; in fact, the colored group (as was true of the white) *unmotivated by specific incentive*—candy, praise, or reproof—scored as well as any of the *experimentally motivated* groups.

In Vega's study (1964) briefly summarized on the preceding pages, Negro children were reported to have responded, when Trials 1 and 2 were combined and no differentiation was made as to race of examiner, to *praise* (mean of 5.86 seconds), followed closely by *neither praise nor reproof* (mean of 5.98 seconds), followed by *reproof* (mean of 6.66 seconds). As was suggested previously, Negro children allocated to the "cell" combining *reproof and the presence of a white examiner* were slower in reaction time than Negro children allocated to "cells" combining other conditions. Thus, his findings would (1) tend to support those of Tiber who concluded that children unmotivated by specific incentive (candy, praise, or reproof) do about as well in a testing situation as the experimentally motivated; and (2) suggest that at least in the presence of a white examiner the colored child may be better motivated by praise than by reproof.

Katz, Epps, and Axelson (1964) reported that students in a Florida college for Negroes did better on digit-symbol tests when informed that their scores would be compared with *their own college norms* than other students at the college who were told that their scores would be compared with *national norms*.

---

[30]Two of the 19 investigators (Mazique, 1934 and Younge, 1947) included private school children. If one eliminated the private school Ss tested on the basis of their selectivity he would obtain a combined mean IQ of 80.4 on Southern colored children tested by members of their race.

Groups of white students from a Florida university, on the other hand, did equally well under either set of instructions, *i.e.,* comparison with their own college or comparison with national norms. The motivation of these white and Negro students cannot be compared effectively, however, for the testing conditions were different for the two groups. It is interesting that immediately after the testing session the Negro students in the *national-norms condition cared significantly more about doing well* than did those Negro students who received *local-norms instructions.*[31]

It may be appropriate to note here that a number of investigators have found the educational and occupational aspirations of Negro elementary and high school children to be as high as or higher than those of comparable groups of white children. They include: Witty, Garfield, and Brink (1941), Gray (1944), Boyd (1952), Geisel (1962), Smith and Abramson (1962), Gist and Bennett (1963), Gottlieb (1964), and R. G. Brown (1965).[32]

Probably more research is needed before one can be reasonably certain that inferior motivation or depressed educational aspiration has not influenced the mental test performance of Negro subjects.

SELF-ESTEEM

It is not uncommon for students in the area of race or ethnic differences to refer to the *low self-esteem* of Negroes, this characteristic being attributed to their inferior caste status and one of the several nonintellectual factors sometimes held responsible for their lower mental test scores. Various investigators, including K. B. and M. P. Clark (1939, 1940, 1950), Landreth and Johnson (1953), and Morland (1962), have reported racial recognition and preference for white skin, frequently accompanied by some reluctance to acknowledge themselves as Negro, as appearing during the preschool period. Citing the early Clark work and that of Ruth Horowitz (1939), who also reported the presence of correct self-identification of Negro children of nursery school age but did not investigate their preferences, E. L. Horowitz (1944) observed that at the preschool level children learn that they are Negroes and come in contact with the culture pattern which says they are inferior; they may either accept the

---

[31]As indicated on a self-rating scale.

[32]Levin (1964) found the concept *school* to be more favorably evaluated by Negro boys and girls than by white boys and girls attending three integrated New Jersey junior high schools, the Negro boys evaluating the concept significantly more favorably than the white boys.

On the other hand, Mingione (1965) reported that white rural North Carolina elementary and high school pupils were more concerned with achieving high standards of excellence than Negro children in the same grades, living in the same area, and of the same socioeconomic status. And Mussen (1953), using the Thematic Apperception Test cards, reported that lower-class Negro and white New York City boys differed significantly in their *achievement need,* the stories of the Negroes including relatively few responses that indicated striving for accomplishment and success.

cultural evaluation of the Negro and consequently low *self-evaluation* or else there will develop in them an internal conflict between acceptance of the cultural pattern and an attempt at self-evaluation.

From their analysis of 25 New York Negro cases, some of whom were patients in psychotherapy and all of whom were given psychoanalytic interviews supplemented with projective tests, Kardiner and Ovesey (1951) concluded that a direct effect of discrimination on the Negro is frustrated hostility toward whites and *low self-esteem* (or a tendency toward exaggerated self-hatred), these effects being manifested, altered, or concealed in a variety of ways. Dai (1949), from a study of about 80 Negro youths by means of auto-biographies and clinical interviews, attributed a *feeling of unworthiness* to the Negro, due in part to his having absorbed the white person's evaluation of his dark skin and hair form.

Allport *et al.,* referring to the report submitted to the Mid-century White House Conference on Children and Youth, "a fact-finding report on the effects of prejudice, discrimination and segregation on the personality development of children . . . ." said: "The report indicates that as minority group children learn the inferior status to which they are assigned . . . . . they often react with *feelings of inferiority* and *a sense of personal humiliation.* Many of them become confused about their own personal worth."[33] (1953, p. 69) Ausubel (1956) likewise, describing the home and community environment of Harlem children, said that the lower-class Negro child inherits an inferior caste status and almost inevitably acquires *negative self-esteem* that is the realistic ego reflection of such status.

The opinion that Negroes feel inferior has been substantiated by several researches. Anderson (1947) indicated that his Okmulgee, Oklahoma, high school Ss scored at the 35th percentile on the *sense of personal worth* norms when they were tested by the California Test of Personality; Grossack (1957), having administered the Edwards Personal Preference Schedule to Philander Smith College students, reported that both males and females evidenced significantly greater needs for *deference* and *abasement* than the normative groups; Boykin (1959) stated that more than 700 Negro college students[34] who had completed the Bernreuter were *less self-sufficient* and *less self-confident* than the norms group; Katz and Benjamin (1960), selecting 32 Negro and 32 white male students attending New York City colleges or universities and placing them in 16 groups each consisting of two Negro and two white Ss who were matched for intelligence, required them to work for pay under different combinations of group- or individual-reward and high- or neutral- group prestige. Combining the biracial groups, the authors reported that the Negroes spoke significantly less than the whites, that they spoke more to whites than to one another, that they ranked the whites higher than themselves on mental ability, but that they favored one another as future

---

[33]Italics supplied by reviewer.
[34]College or colleges unidentified.

work companions. "These results indicate that even when Negroes are given objective evidence of equal mental ability in a relatively brief interracial contact they tend to feel inadequate and to orient compliantly toward whites." (p. 456)[35]

Roen, having closely matched 50 white and 50 colored soldiers on ten variables, compared their mean scores on the *Army Classification Battery,* the Taylor Manifest Anxiety, the Bernreuter, and the California Test of Personality. The only significant difference between the racial samples, in addition to the difference in mean intelligence, was *lack of self-confidence,* the Negro soldiers obtaining the higher scores. Roen concluded that further research is warranted on the proposition "that Negroes as a group, lacking support from pride in significant historical achievement, and developing in an environment of negative experiences, incorporate intellectually defeating personality traits that play a significant role in their ability to score on measures of intelligence." (1960, p. 150)

Deutsch (1964), comparing 400 Negro and white school children in Grades 4 to 6 in two schools,[36] reported that in all comparisons the Negro children had significantly more *negative self-images* than the white children.

On the other hand, some investigators have found the self-esteem of the Negro subjects to equal, if not exceed, that of the whites. Hurlock (1927) administered the first of the Downey Will-Temperament tests to more than 400 white and colored Ss of the same mean IQ who were in two grades of one New York City public school. This test required the underlining of one word in each of 30 pairs which the pupil thought more nearly described himself. The percentage of *undesirable responses* underlined by the white Ss was 7.3 as compared with 4.6 underlined by the colored, indicating that the colored *overrated themselves on desirable qualities* slightly more often than did the whites.

Patrick and Sims (1934) found samples of Northern and Southern Negro and white college students tested on the Bernreuter to differ in self-sufficiency. The Negroes proved to be the *more self-sufficient,* with the difference between the means of the males being significant. Bayton (1936), testing about 200 Howard University Negro students with this measure, reported that both sexes scored higher in *feeling of superiority* and *self-sufficiency* than the respective standardization groups. Comparing the mean scores on the Bernreuter of 200 Agnes Scott College and Spelman College women, Eagleson (1938) noted that the Negro students were the *more self-sufficient,* the only significant difference obtained.

Administering the *California Test of Personality* to approximately 400

---

[35]The white group was composed of 22 Jewish, 5 Catholic, and 5 Protestant Ss. It would be interesting to replicate this study but using primarily non-Jewish Ss as the white members of the teams. New York City Jewish college students have been reported by several researchers to be somewhat more dominant than NYC non-J students. It is possible that the authors' Jewish subjects may also have been relatively dominant, thus serving to induce or increase a negative self-feeling on the part of their colored team members. (For pertinent studies by Eisenberg, Vetter, Sperling, and Shuey, *see* Shuey, 1944.)

[36]Location of the schools not given.

Negro, Amish, and non-Amish white children in Northern Indiana, Engle (1945) indicated that the colored girls and boys scored higher on the average on *sense of personal worth* than the girls and boys of either of the white groups. Day (1949) reported the mean of 40 fifth-grade colored pupils in Atlanta to be at the 60th percentile of the norms group on *sense of personal worth;* Flemister (1950), testing 100 Negro pupils in a Raeford, North Carolina high school, found that their average score on the *sense of personal worth* was at the 50th percentile of the normative group. Likewise, Outlaw (1950) reported that 100 Negro rural teachers in a Tennessee county in general earned their highest scores on *sense of personal worth,* their median falling at the 75th percentile of the norms group.

Two studies which utilized the California Test of Personality were reported from Hampton Institute. The 300 students entering this college in 1950 received their highest scores, on the average, on *sense of personal worth,* their mean falling at the 76th percentile of the norms distribution. (Walker, 1951) Reporting on the results of the test administered to 330 students entering the college in 1959, Roth (1961) indicated that the colored Ss were more *self-reliant* (mean at the 72nd percentile) and had a greater *sense of personal worth* (mean at the 61st percentile) than the normative samples.

Geisel (1962) compared more than 2000 colored and white junior and senior high school students of a Southern city in reference to a number of variables, one of them being the *concept of self.* Having adopted Osgood's Semantic Differential as his measure of self-concept and using the factor loadings given by Osgood, Geisel selected 18 words having the highest loadings on the three major factors: 10 for the evaluative, 4 for the potency, and 4 for the activity factor. A column of these words was set up on one side of the page and a column of their opposites on the other, the Ss instructed to mark a place on the line connecting each pair of opposites according to the position that very closely described himself. Geisel found that the self-concept scores did not support the hypothesis of a greater proportion of Negroes having low evaluations than whites. In fact, the Negro mean scores were significantly *higher* than those of the whites on the *evaluative factor of self.*

Levin (1964) also employed Osgood's Semantic Differential as a measure of 15 concepts, including that of *self,* selecting 16 words believed to be highly loaded on the evaluative, potency, and activity factors. Following the standard procedure a column of the 16 words was set up on one side of a page and a column of their opposites on the other, the students being instructed to mark a place on the line connecting each pair of opposites according to the position that most closely described how he felt about himself.

Approximately 400 colored and white junior high school students attending two schools in Trenton, New Jersey, and one school in a suburb in this state, were tested under conditions of anonymity. All three schools were integrated; in Trenton, the colored comprised 30 per cent of one school and 70 per cent of the other, both Negro and white children enrolled in these schools coming from the lower socioeconomic classes. Like Geisel, Levin obtained *higher self-evaluations among the Negro than among the white children,* the differences between the Negro-white male suburban children and between the Negro-white female city children being significant.[37]

McDonald and Gynther (1965) attempted to relate race, sex, and social class variables to *self- and ideal-self-concepts* of adolescents. Obtaining *Interpersonal Check List* data from 261 Negro and 211 white high school seniors from segregated schools in a Southern city, these authors reported, together with other findings, the following: (1) as compared with the self-descriptions of the white pupils, the self-descriptions of the Negro subjects yielded significantly higher scores in dominance and love (warmth, friendliness, and cooperation); and (2) as compared with the self-descriptions of the white pupils, those of the colored were *significantly closer to their descriptions* of the *ideal-self.*

Basing our opinion on the results of the various studies noted above, we would conclude that at the preschool level there seems to be some evidence of awareness of color differences and a feeling of inferiority associated with dark skin, but at the grade school level and continuing through high school and college there is no consistent evidence of lower self esteem in Negroes; if there is a difference, it would appear to be more likely that Negroes have a *greater sense of personal worth,* rather than the reverse.

Enriching School Programs

Hoping to aid underprivileged children in a systematic and constructive manner, several professional people—psychologists, teachers, and school superintendents—have initiated school programs aimed primarily at developing *middle-class attitudes toward achievement* (motivation, persistence, ability to delay gratification, and interest in academic studies) and *certain school aptitudes* (perceptual development, concept formation, and language development). Only those projects which have included deprived Negro children examined by mental tests will be reviewed here.

As reported in Wade's thesis (1954), 32 first-grade North Carolina Negro children, mainly from large families of tenant farmers, were given a program of stimulating and varied activities for a period of three months.[38] The author, who was also the first-grade teacher, administered the *Otis Quick-Scoring, Alpha* and other tests before and after the program. She observed that the mean IQ of these children dropped very slightly, from 82.8 to 82.2.

Other attempts at stimulating the intellectual development of the im-

---

[37]The high self-evaluative factor indicating the tendency to score oneself in the direction of *good, kind, clean, successful, wise,* and *healthy,* rather than in the direction of *bad, cruel, dirty, etc.*

[38]Her program of activities was taken from "recognized authorities in child development". For review of this research, see pp. 106-107 and 116.

poverished, however, have produced more favorable results. Gray and Klaus (1963, 1964)[39] found that their 22 subjects composing Group I (those Negro children given intensive training during three successive summers and in addition special work *via* home visitors throughout the intervening school years) advanced in IQ from *85.6* in the early summer of 1962 to *95* in the late summer of 1964. This increase might be attributed to some cumulative practice effect as at the last testing the children had been examined *five times* on the *Stanford-Binet, Form L-M,* except for the fact that the two control groups of colored children dropped about 5 points from the first to fifth testing.

It seems unfortunate that in these excellent studies of Gray and Klaus there could be no control of examiner's bias. Although the psychometrists were apparently not a part of the working project and had not been informed which third of the Murfreesboro children were *control,* it is likely that they knew a good deal about the project, that the enthusiasm of the various college students, teachers, and supervisors working with the experimental group aroused their interest, and that, in any event, it would have been almost impossible for them not to detect from the behavior of the child tested whether or not he was a participant in the training program.

In a very brief and enthusiastic report, Brazziel and Terrell (1962) indicated that they organized a six-weeks enriched program and administered it to one first-grade group of 26 Negro children in Millington, Tennessee.[40] These children were described as being culturally disadvantaged as were the three other groups of Negro first-graders in the same town who made up the control groups. In the spring, at the end of seven months of schooling, the experimental group was given the Detroit Intelligence Test.[41] The authors do not tell us which of the Detroit intelligence tests was employed (presumably the *Detroit First Grade*), who administered and scored the tests, why it was not given *before* the children started on the program, and why it was not also administered to any of the three control groups. They report that the mean IQ was 106.5 and the standard deviation, 13.2, refer to Cronbach's indices for underprivileged children, and cite some miscellaneous IQ means reported on Negro and white groups (not first grade) in the state of Virginia. They conclude with this statement: "An efficacious combination consisting of a direct parent-teacher partnership, per-

---

[39]Experimental Group II (20-22 Ss) improved *5 points* from the first to fifth testing. In between the first and final testings the colored children had experienced two summer sessions of special training and one winter of home contacts.

[40]The authors specifically mention: discussing the program with parents at weekly intervals, use of a 30-minute educational television program which was watched by the children **daily** in their homes, and a six-weeks period of intensified activity to develop perception, vocabulary, word reasoning, ability and will to follow directions.

[41]It is not clear to the reviewer whether or not the enriched program continued beyond the six weeks of "readiness" up to the time the children were tested in the spring; but since the junior author was the classroom teacher (E group) it is probable that she interested them as much as possible in a variety of objects and events throughout the seven months.

missive regimentation, test wisdom development, excellent materials and energetic uninhibited teaching seems to have been the main discovery of this study."
(p. 6)

The last of these programs, generally called the Banneker School Project,
attacked the complacent attitude toward low achievement prevalent among
city slum children and vigorously attempted to develop middle-class attitudes
"through motivation, drives, desires for success". The driving force behind
this achievement project was Samuel Shepard, Jr., an assistant superintendent
of one of St. Louis' five elementary school districts which in 1959 was composed
of 23 schools whose combined enrollment was 95 per cent Negro.[42] Following
the city superintendent's announcement in 1957 that all children *entering the
St. Louis high schools* would have to be certified (by achievement tests) on one
of three tracks: I (high achievers), II (average), III (low achievers), and being
fully aware from previous testings that the Banneker District would contribute
about 47 per cent of its 8th grade graduating class to the third track, Shepard
challenged the Banneker children to come up to the national averages on the
tests. Not only did he meet frequently with groups of children throughout his
district—and with teachers (showing them charts indicating the standing of their
pupils on tests, advising them to help the children by visiting their homes, and the
like), parents, librarians, principals, and business men—but he urged them to
adopt action-arousing mottoes, such as "Success in School is My Most Important
Business!"[43]

In the two years between 1957-58 and 1959-60, the 8th graders from Banneker
District accepted on Track I *increased from 7 to 16 per cent,* and those entering
Track III *dropped from 47 to 24 per cent.*[44] That this improvement was characteristic of the city as a whole (and not solely of Banneker) may be inferred from
a report of W. C. Kottmeyer in 1960, Assistant Superintendent for Elementary
and Special Education at that time. He said that the proportion of children
entering Track I from all St. Louis elementary schools had nearly doubled during
this period (13.5 per cent to 24 per cent) and the proportion entering Track III

---

[42]Shepard's speech before the Division of School Psychologists of the American Psychological
Association (1962) has been multilithed and made available through George Peabody College.
The reader may also refer to various issues between 1959-1964 of the *Southern School News.*
For warm appraisal of the Banneker work, see Pettigrew (1964) and McCullers and Plant (1964).

[43]Implementing his drive to help children "climb out of poverty" Shepard used many
devices, such as: hanging prints of great art works in classrooms, sending children on first
visits to the city art museums, and organizing "operation dineout", the meals being financed
by Banneker businessmen and chaperoned by teachers. (*Southern School News,* 1964, *10,* April,
p. 13)

[44]The median IQ of the Banneker high-8th-graders in 1952-53 was reported to be 84.9,
and in 1958-59 it was 90.5. (*Southern School News,* 1959, *5,* Jan., p. 12) Name of test not indicated, nor standard deviation. Notice that the *terminal program,* which removed those with
IQ's between 48-78 from the regular public schools, began in 1955. The removal of these low-
scoring children, many of whom were in the Banneker District, produces an erroneous impression
of improvement in IQ.

had declined to less than half (33 per cent to 15 per cent). Also, during this same interval, the proportion of pupils from *Long District* (one of the five elementary school districts, and the one nearly all white during these years) entering high school on Track I *advanced from 26 to 39 per cent* and the proportion of its pupils going into Track III *decreased from 12 to 5 per cent.*

Obviously, the Banneker improvement must be considered in its proper perspective, *i.e., the improvement throughout the St. Louis elementary schools.* Proceding under this assumption, the reviewer examined issues of the *Southern School News* between the Summer of 1957 and the Spring of 1965 for articles on this city's public schools, and has noted three items that seem to pertain to the issue in question. (1) The *median IQ of Long District* pupils entering Track I in 1957-58 was 118.3, and in 1959-60 it was 118.7; however, the *median IQ of the Banneker* pupils entering Track I in the earlier period was 109.1, and in the more recent, 105.8.[45] In other words, if these statistics are correct, the median IQ's of children who enter Track I *from the five school districts in different years* are not necessarily the same and may not be directly comparable. (2) The writer does not know the percentage of St. Louis 8th grade children who were retained in 1957-58 for lack of promotion; but Kottmeyer has indicated that 6.6 per cent of the "eight high" pupils in the Banneker District were retained in the elementary school at the end of 1959-60, whereas 0.2 per cent of the Long District pupils were retained at that time. This *relatively large percentage of Banneker children who failed to be promoted* would have served to reduce the percentage of this district entering Track III. (3) There was an increase in the proportion of children not admitted to Track III because of their going into *terminal education.*[46] After the terminal program was initiated in 1955 some children between 48 to 78 IQ continued in the regular classrooms and subsequently went into Track III automatically; these were children who could not be enrolled in special classes for the retarded because of a lack of facilities and therefore did not go as a matter of course into the two-year terminal high school program. By 1959-60 they were being identified by tests and diverted into terminal education. During the period from the beginning of 1957-58 to the end of 1959-60 the proportion of pupils from the city schools entering terminal education in high school and *thereby withdrawn from Track III* increased from 1.2 per cent to 8.2 per cent.[47] As Kottmeyer observed: "This should make teaching of Track III students in the high schools easier than it has been in the past."[43] This withdrawal in increasing numbers of mentally retarded children from the regular classrooms has no doubt given artificial support to the evidence that St. Louis high school children are becoming more intelligent.

---

[45]*Southern School News*, 1960, 6, May, p. 6.

[46]Terminal education for the retarded children. It consists of two years of schooling beyond elementary grades for children who earn *Binet* IQ's of 48-78.

[47]No percentage figures were reported for the Banneker District alone. In the opinion of the reviewer, a conservative estimate of increase in this interval would be from 5 to 20 per cent.

Because of incomplete data the reviewer cannot report with reasonable assurance the effect an intensive educational program has had on the IQ of underprivileged Negro children exposed to it. A fair estimate is that it is far less than that depicted by dedicated and enthusiastic social workers, teachers, psychologists, and news reporters.

Controlling Education and Socioeconomic Environment

May investigators have attempted to control environmental factors by selecting white and colored subjects of the same socioeconomic status, those living in the same neighborhood and attending the same schools, white and colored children whose parents were of the same occupational class, and whites and colored matched for school grade completed and age, as well as father's occupation, residence and other variables. It is obvious that the following researchers have in general compared disadvantaged whites with disadvantaged Negroes and that the former are unrepresentative of their racial group while the latter are probably racially representative.

Strong (1913), for example, compared white cotton mill children with the total group of Negro Ss tested in Columbia, South Carolina; Phillips (1914) equated colored and white Philadelphia pupils according to home rating; Arlitt (1921) compared a group of white children of native-born parents whose fathers were either semiskilled or unskilled laborers with the total Negro group, 88 per cent of whom were of low status; Pintner and Keller (1922) selected for comparative purposes three Youngstown, Ohio, schools from relatively poor neighborhoods in which a large majority were foreign-speaking; Hurlock (1924, 1930) selected two New York City schools, 40 per cent of the enrollments being Negro, and the children in attendance described as of the same social status; Hirsch (1926) compared a "representative sampling" of Nashville Negro children with white Massachusetts mill town Ss of below-average status; Kempf and Collins (1929) compared average IQ's of Southern Illinois white Ss of native-born parents of the unskilled laboring group with the total group of colored from the same urban and rural localities.

R. M. Clark (1933) tested colored and white pupils living in the inferior environment of Cleveland's Black Belt; H. J. Williams (1935) obtained IQ's on pupils attending three Milwaukee schools, a larger percentage of the white than the colored being from families on county relief; Charles (1936) selected St. Louis schools in which the social environment of the two racial samples was reported to be similar; Lichtenstein and A. W. Brown (1938) examined colored and white public school children in a Chicago area characterized by physical deterioration, a decreasing population, and high rates of dependency, crime and delinquency; Tanser (1939) compared rural colored and white school children in a county of Ontario, Canada, both racial samples considered to be of approximately equal socioeconomic status and in a community where racial prejudice was at a minimum; Bruce (1940) matched colored and white pupils in a rural Virginia county according to their Sims socioeconomic scores; Ries (1940) compared white pupils from the poorest junior high school district of Louisville (where living conditions approximated those of the Negro) with the total Negro group (enrolled in the two Louisville junior high schools for Negroes); Shuey (1942) matched New York University white and colored students according to occupation of father, age and amount of previous education of Ss, and other factors; F. Brown (1944) tested white children of Minneapolis living in a Negro neighborhood and attending the same school where most of the Negro Ss were enrolled.

The colored and white subjects studied by Rhoads, Rapoport, Kennedy, and Stokes (1945) were from the three lowest occupational groups in Philadelphia; Garrett (1945) compared Northern colored enlisted men on *Alpha* with whites of considerably less educational attainment; Griffith (1947) examined colored and white children of the same average socioeconomic status who were attending one school in a predominantly Negro district of Portland, Oregon; Jordan (1948) compared Winston-Salem Negro and white school children whose parents were employed in the same occupations; Slivinske (1949) asked Virginia county classroom teachers to rate the homes of their pupils, and he made comparisons between colored and white children from "inferior" and from "superior" homes; Fulk (1949) and Fulk and Harrell (1952) have tabulated the mean *AGCT* scores of Negro and white enlisted men in the Army Air Force Service Command according to school grade completed; Davidson, Gibby, McNeil, Segal, and Silverman (1950) matched groups of white and colored psychoneurotic patients at the Detroit Mental Hygiene Clinic for diagnosis, age, and school grade completed; McPherson (1951) selected two public schools in East Waco, Texas, from the same neighborhood; McGurk (1951) matched colored and white seniors in fourteen high schools of New Jersey and Pennsylvania for school, curriculum, age, and eleven items of the Sims scale; Bird, Monachesi, and Burdick (1952) compared colored and white middle and lower-middle class children from two Minneapolis public schools, the racial samples reported as not differing significantly in social status.

Hess (1955) compared the test scores of groups of low-status white and Negro public school children in Chicago; McCary and Tractir (1957) tested white and colored pupils of middle middle-class families attending the same Pittsburgh high school; G. E. Clark (1957) examined colored and white children of the same socioeconomic class areas in St. Louis but attending separate schools; Sperrazzo and Wilkins (1958, 1959) classified their colored and white subjects who were enrolled in both mixed and separate public schools in St. Louis into three groups according to their fathers' occupational level; McCord and Demerath (1958) compared the test scores of Cambridge and Somerville, Massachusetts, colored and white children from lower and lower-middle socioeconomic levels, half of whom were believed to be predelinquent; Higgins and Sivers (1958) examined colored and white children attending public schools serving the lowest socioeconomic areas of a "northeastern city"; Fowler (1959) compared colored and white Detroit and Hamtramck, Michigan, school children of lower-lower socioeconomic level who had been thus classified on the basis of parental occupation, house type, and neighborhood type; McQueen and Churn (1960) compared colored and white children living in a "Western community" who had been matched for school grade, age, years in the school system, residential area, type of house, and father's occupation; Roen (1960) matched colored and white soldiers stationed in an Army post in the Southwest (after eliminating those of extremely low mental test scores) according to age, education, parental occupation and income, geographic area of childhood, Army rank and number of years in service, urban or rural background, and other variables.

Geisel (1962) separated his colored and white subjects enrolled in junior and senior high schools in a "Southern City" into two sociostatus groups according to the schooling of their parents, the school authorities having previously selected for each racial group one junior high school whose pupils were on the whole from lower socioeconomic backgrounds and one whose pupils were from upper socioeconomic backgrounds; Semler and Iscoe (1963) tested colored and white children from two public schools in Austin, Texas, selected to minimize socioeconomic differences between the racial samples; Tiber (1963), using the McGuire-White Index, identified the social status of his subjects enrolled in a "Southeastern public school system", and tabulated the mean IQ's of middle-class whites, lower-class whites, and lower-class Negroes; Wylie (1963) rated the occupations of the fathers of all children enrolled in the only junior high school in a "small, highly industrialized, Pennsylvania city" according to Hollingshead and Redlich's socioeconomic scale positions, permitting one to compare the IQ's of Negro and white pupils at either the higher or lower occupational level; Hickerson (1963, 1965) compared San Francisco-Bay Area Negro and non-Negro high school students whose fathers were employed in similar occupations, i.e., all were skilled or semiskilled laborers or were first grade noncommissioned officers in the Armed Forces; and Deutsch and B. Brown (1964) compared colored and white children from an unidentified urban school system after selecting a sample stratified by race, grade level, and occupational class, the latter being based upon a scale derived from the education of the main family breadwinner and his occupation.

With two exceptions, the colored averaged below the white groups in mental test performance in all of the 42 investigations.[48] Average IQ's were reported in

---

[48]McCord and Demerath reported no essential difference in mental ability between their groups but so tabulated their results that a reader could not verify their statistics. For detailed comments upon this research, see pp. 129-130.

Higgins and Sivers secured inconclusive results, the colored being the equal of the white Ss on one test but significantly below the whites on the other. The mean difference on the two tests combined was 5.3 IQ points in favor of the white Ss. For other comments on this research, see pp. 40-41 and 117-118.

33 of the studies including a total of about 7900 colored and 9300 white Ss, and from these a mean difference of *11 points* favoring the whites was obtained.[49]

Twenty-five of the 41 studies were located in the North, and in at least fourteen of the researches the colored and white children were not only attending the same schools but were living in the same district or neighborhood.[50] The combined mean difference in IQ between the 2760 colored subjects tested in the North[51] and the whites of comparable socioeconomic status or occupation was 7.6. Nearly all of these Ss in the eighteen studies were of school age, the whites and Negroes attending the same school and living in the same areas, many with large Negro populations.

Where Negro pupils have been compared with whites of the same occupational or socioeconomic class and where children from two or more classes have served as subjects, a greater difference has been found between the racial samples at the upper than at the lower level. McGurk and Sperrazzo and Wilkins, for example, have reported large differences between the means of their Negro and white Ss identified as belonging to the *high* socioeconomic group and smaller differences between the means of their samples belonging to the *low* socioeconomic group. Comparable results have been obtained in the studies where mean IQ differences were reported.[52] The *higher status* white groups averaged the following number of IQ points above Negro groups of comparable status: Jordan (1948) 21.9; Slivinske (1949) 19.8, G. E. Clark (1957) 19.7, Geisel (1962) 21.2, Wylie (1963) 22.6, and Deutsch and Brown (1964) 12.4; whereas the *lowest* (or *lower*) status white groups scored on the average the following number of IQ points above comparable Negro groups of low status: Jordan 12.3, Slivinske 12.6, Clark 8.1, Geisel 11.4, Wylie 8.1, and Deutsch and Brown, 6.0.[53] The combined mean difference in IQ between the 617 colored Ss of higher status and their 1504 white counterparts is 20.3, in contrast with a combined mean difference of 12.2 between the 3374 colored and 2293 white children of low status. The latter difference is very close to that calculated by this writer between the combined groups of colored *v.* white (based upon 32 studies) where the various investigators attempted to control several aspects of the socioeconomic environ-

[49]In contrast with a mean difference of 15-16 IQ points when random or stratified samples have been used.

[50]See: Pintner and Keller; Hurlock; R. M. Clark; Williams; Lichtenstein and A. W. Brown; Tanser; F. Brown; Griffith; Bird, Monachesi, and Burdick; Higgins and Sivers; Fowler; McQueen and Churn; Wylie; and Deutsch and B. Brown (whose research is presumed to have been conducted in a Northern city.)

[51]See: Pintner and Keller; Kempf and Collins; Hurlock; R. M. Clark; Williams; Lichtenstein and Brown; Tanser; F. Brown; Rhoads, Rapoport, Kennedy, and Stokes; Griffith; Bird, Monachesi and Burdick; McCary and Tractir; Higgins and Sivers; Fowler; McQueen and Churn; Wylie; Hickerson; and Deutsch and Brown.

[52]Or IQ's tabulated, from which the present writer calculated mean differences.

[53]Researches of McGurk, Wylie, and Deutsch and Brown (probably) were conducted in the North; those of Clark and Sperrazzo and Wilkins in a Border state; and those of Jordan, Slivinske, and Geisel in the South.

ments of their subjects.[54] This agreement is no doubt due to the fact that in the great majority of the 32 researches the colored and white groups compared were of relatively low socioeconomic status.

The consistent and surprisingly large difference of 20.3 IQ points separating the high-status whites and the high-status colored is accentuated by the finding that the mean of the latter group is *2.6 points below* that of the low-status whites.[55] It is probable that the home, neighborhood, and school environments of the white and colored lower-class children tested are more nearly alike in their stimulating qualities[56] than are the home, neighborhood, and school environments of the white and colored upper and middle-class children; but *it seems improbable that upper and middle-class colored children would have no more cultural opportunities provided them than white children of the lower and lowest class.* The reviewer offers two possible (and to her, reasonable) explanations of the above findings: (1) The likelihood that status-bearing positions open to Negroes in the United States have not required as high a level of intelligence as the much larger number of status-bearing positions open to whites.[57] If this is true, they have not served equally as selective agents in recruiting the most able colored from the laboring class as is true with whites. The continual drawing of the more intelligent from the lower classes would in time produce a difference in the mental test scores of the divergent classes; if this drain is not equally present in the colored and white races one would expect greater differences in the testing of high-status groups and lesser differences when low-status groups are compared. (2) The probability that the disadvantaged living in integrated neighborhoods may not be equally representative of their respective racial groups. Living in these mixed neighborhoods being more prestigious for colored than for whites, a form of selective migration may be presumed to operate, "positively" for the Negroes and "negatively" for the whites. If this hypothesis is correct, it would account for the leveling tendencies observed in the test performances of the two lower-class groups whenever the samples tested are drawn from mixed neighborhoods.

Concluding Statement

The remarkable consistency in test results, whether they pertain to school or preschool children, to children between Ages 6 to 9 or 10 to 12, to children in Grades 1 to 3 or 4 to 7, to high school or college students, to enlisted men or officers in training in the Armed Forces—in World War I, World War II, or the

---

[54] A difference of 12.2 as compared with one of 11.0.

[55] The combined means of the *upper-status white and colored* groups were, respectively, 111.88 and 91.63; the respective mean IQ's of the *lower status white and colored* were 94.22 and 82.04.

[56] *i.e.,* culture-enriching experiences provided.

[57] Dreger and Miller (1960), holding the view that whites and Negroes comprise separate castes, indicate that they do not see how the nature-nurture issue can be resolved by any number of ingenious methods of equating for social and economic variables.

Post-Korean period—to veterans of the Armed Forces, to homeless men or transients, to gifted or mentally deficient, to delinquent or criminal; the fact that differences between colored and white are present not only in the rural and urban South, but in the Border and Northern states; the fact that the colored preschool, school, and high school pupils living in Northern cities tested as far below the Southern urban white children as they did below the whites in the Northern cities; the fact that relatively small average differences were found between the IQ's of Northern-born and Southern-born Negro children in Northern cities; the fact that Negro school children and high school pupils have achieved average IQ's slightly lower in the past twenty years than between 1921 and 1944; the tendency toward greater variability among whites; the tendency for racial hybrids to score higher than those groups described as, or inferred to be, unmixed Negro; the evidence that the mean overlap is between 7 and 13 per cent; the evidence that the tested differences appear to be greater for logical analysis, abstract reasoning, and perceptual-motor tasks than for practical and concrete problems; the evidence that the tested differences may be a little less on verbal than on nonverbal tasks; the indication that the colored elementary or high school pupil has not been adversely affected in his tested performance by the presence of a white examiner; an indication that Negroes may have a greater sense of personal worth than whites, at least at the elementary, high school, and college levels; the unproved and probably erroneous assumption that Negroes have been less well motivated on tests than whites; the fact that differences were reported in practically all of the studies in which the cultural environment of the whites appeared to be similar in richness and complexity to that of the Negroes; the fact that in many comparisons, including those in which the colored have appeared to best advantage, Negro subjects have been either more representative of their racial group or more highly selected than the comparable whites; all taken together, inevitably point to the presence of native differences between Negroes and whites as determined by intelligence tests.

REFERENCES

Adjutant General's Office. Official Army Register. U. S. Govern. Print. Off., Washington, D. C., 1924. Pp. 814.

Adjutant General's Office. Official Army Register. U. S. Govern. Print. Off., Washington, D. C., 1940. Pp. 1252.

Adler, Herman M. Report of the Survey of the Specially Handicapped Children in the State of Illinois. Dept. Publ. Welfare, Springfield, 1925. Pp. 30.

Adler, Herman M., and Worthington, Myrtle R. The scope of the problem of delinquency and crime as related to mental deficiency. *J. Psycho-Asthenics,* 1925, *29,* 47-56.

Allinger, Dorothy A. Comparison of Negro and white pre-school children in performance on specific items of the Revised Stanford-Binet Test. Unpubl. Master's thesis, George Washington Univ., 1954.

Allman, Reva W. A study of selected competencies of prospective teachers in Alabama. *J. Negro Educ.,* 1953, *22,* 136-144.

Allport, Floyd H., *et al.* The effects of segregation and the consequences of desegregation: a social science statement. *J. Negro Educ.,* 1953, *22,* 68-76.

Alper, Thelma G., and Boring, Edwin G. Intelligence-test scores of northern and southern white and Negro recruits in 1918. *J. Abnorm. & Soc. Psychol.,* 1944, *39,* 471-474.

Altus, Grace T. Some correlates of the Davis-Eells tests. *J. Consult. Psychol.,* 1956, *20,* 227-232.

Altus, William D. A note on group differences in intelligence and the type of test employed. *J. Consult. Psychol.,* 1948, *12,* 194-195.

Altus, William D. Racial and bi-lingual group differences in predictability and in mean aptitude test scores in an Army Special Training Center. *Psychol. Bull.,* 1945, *42,* 310-320.

Altus, William D. The validity of the Terman Vocabulary for Army illiterates. *J. Consult. Psychol.,* 1946, *10,* 268-276.

Altus, William D., and Bell, Hugh M. The validity of a general information test for certain groups of Army illiterates. *J. Consult. Psychol.,* 1947, *11,* 120-132.

Altus, William D., and Clark, Jerry H. Some sectional differences among Negro and white illiterate soldiers. *J. Soc. Psychol.,* 1949, *30,* 97-104.

Anastasi, Anne. Differential Psychology. New York: Macmillan, 1958. Pp. 664.

Anastasi, Anne. Psychological Testing. New York: Macmillan, 1961. Pp. 657.

Anastasi, Anne, and D'Angelo, Rita Y. A comparison of Negro and white pre-school children in language development and Goodenough Draw-a-Man IQ. *J. Genet. Psychol.,* 1952, *81,* 147-165.

Anderson, Leroy F. The analysis of differences in performance over a two year period on ACE of Negro college women students, "North" and "South". Unpubl. Master's thesis, Fisk Univ., 1948.

Anderson, Thelma H. Dimensions of the characteristics related to the high- and low-achievement of a selected group of Negro college students. Unpubl. Doctor's dissert., Univ. Oklahoma, 1961.

Anderson, Tommie M. The achievement in mathematics and science of students in the Negro schools and colleges in Mississippi. Unpubl. Doctor's dissert., Indiana Univ., 1958.

Anderson, W. E. The personality characteristics of 153 Negro pupils, Dunbar High School, Okmulgee, Oklahoma. *J. Negro Educ.*, 1947, *16*, 44-48.

Aptheker, Herbert. Literacy, the Negro and World War II. *J. Negro Educ.*, 1946, *15*, 595-602.

Arlitt, Ada H. Further data on the influence of race and social status on the intelligence quotient. *Psychol. Bull.*, 1921, *18*, 95-96.

Arlitt, Ada H. On the need for caution in establishing race norms. *J. Appl. Psychol.*, 1921, *5*, 179-183.

Arlitt, Ada H. The relation of intelligence to age in Negro children. *J. Appl. Psychol.*, 1922, *6*, 378-384.

Armstrong, Clairette P. Juvenile delinquency as related to immigration. *Sch. & Soc.*, 1933, *38*, 61-64.

Armstrong, Clairette P., and Heisler, Florence. A note on the attainments of delinquent boys. *Sch. & Soc.*, 1945, *61*, 29-31.

Atchison, Calvin O. Use of the Wechsler Intelligence Scale for Children with eighty mentally defective Negro children. *Amer. J. Ment. Def.*, 1955, *60*, 378-379.

Ausubel, David P. Ego development among segregated Negro children. *Mental Hygiene*, 1956, *42*, 362-369.

Bagley, William C. The Army tests and the pro-Nordic propaganda. *Educ. Rev.*, 1924, *67*, 179-187.

Ball, John C. Comparison of MMPI profile differences among Negro-white adolescents. *J. Clin. Psychol.*, 1960, *16*, 304-307.

Barnes, John R. The intelligence of Negro children. Unpubl. Master's thesis, Univ. Kansas, 1923.

Bayton, James A. Personality traits of Negro college students. Unpubl. Master's thesis, Howard Univ., 1936.

Bean, Kenneth L. Negro responses to certain intelligence test items. *J. Psychol.*, 1941, *12*, 191-198.

Bean, Kenneth L. Negro responses to verbal and non-verbal test materials. *J. Psychol.*, 1942, *13*, 343-353.

Beavers, Lillian L. A study of the intelligence, vocational interests and vocational possibilities of Negro junior high school girls. Unpubl. Master's thesis, Univ. Cincinnati, 1935.

Beckham, Albert S. A study of the intelligence of colored adolescents of different social-economic status in typical metropolitan areas. *J. Soc. Psychol.*, 1933, *4*, 70-91.

Beckham, Albert S. The intelligence of a Negro high school population in a northern city. *J. Genet. Psychol.*, 1939, *54*, 327-336.

Bender, Lauretta. Behavior problems of Negro children. *Psychiat.*, 1939, *2*, 213-228.

Benedict, Ruth, and Weltfish, Gene. The races of mankind. Publ. Affairs Committee, 1943. Pamph. No. 85. Pp. 31.

Berry, Beatrice Y. A study of the relationship among tested mental ability, tested mechanical aptitude, and tested art ability. Unpubl. Master's thesis, Atlanta Univ., 1954.

Berry, Charles S. The classification by tests of intelligence of ten thousand first-grade pupils. *J. Educ. Res.*, 1922, *6*, 185-203.

Bice, Harry V. A comparison of white and Negro pupils in North Carolina. *Proc. Amer. Assoc. Ment. Def.*, 1938, *43*, No. 2, 72-77.

Bice, Harry V. A study of Negro and white pupils in Piedmont North Carolina. N. C. Board of Charities and Public Welfare, Special Bull., No. 16, 1938. Raleigh, N. C.

Bindman, Aaron M. Participation of Negro students in an integrated university. Unpubl. Doctor's dissert., Univ. Illinois, 1965.

Bingham, Walter V. Personnel classification testing in the Army. *Science*, 1944, *100*, 275-280.

Bird, Charles, Monachesi, Elio D., and Burdick, Harvey. Infiltration and the attitudes of white and Negro parents and children. *J. Abnorm. & Soc. Psychol.*, 1952, *47*, 688-699.

Boger, Jack H. An experimental study of the effects of perceptual training on group I. Q. test scores of elementary pupils in rural ungraded schools. *J. Educ. Res.*, 1952, *46*, 43-52.

Bond, Horace M. An investigation of the nonintellectual traits of a group of Negro adults. *J. Abnorm. & Soc. Psychol.*, 1926, *21*, 267-276.

Bond, Horace M. Cat on a hot tin roof. *J. Negro Educ.*, 1958, *27*, 519-525.

Bonds, Alfred B., Jr. The President's Commission on higher education and Negro higher education. *J. Negro Educ.*, 1948, *17*, 426-436.

Boone, Elwood B. A study of the relationship between recreational interest, intelligence, scholastic achievement, personality and vocational interest. Unpubl. Doctor's dissert., Univ. Michigan, 1945.

Boots, Willis E.   A study in the intelligence of white and of colored grade school children, high school students, and college freshmen. Unpubl. Master's thesis, Univ. Wisconsin, 1926.

Bottosto, Samuel S.   Relationships between county-wide measures of certain socio-economic factors, intelligence, and academic achievement of high school seniors in Florida. Unpubl. Doctor's dissert., Univ. Florida, 1959.

Bousfield, M. B.   The intelligence and school achievement of Negro children. *J. Negro Educ.*, 1932, *1*, 388-395.

Boyd, George F.   The levels of aspiration of white and Negro children in a non-segregated elementary school. *J. Soc. Psychol.*, 1952, *36*, 191-196.

Boykin, Leander L.   Personality aspects of counseling the Negro college student. *Quart. Rev. Higher Educ. Negroes,* 1959, 27, 64-73.

Boylan, Francis T., and O'Meara, Ruth B.   Stereotype and inquiry concerning southern born Negro pupils in Chicago. *J. Educ. Sociol.*, 1958, *32*, 76-82.

Brazziel, William F., and Terrell, Mary.   An experiment in the development of readiness in a culturally disadvantaged group of first grade children. *J. Negro Educ.*, 1962, *31*, 4-7.

Brigham, Carl C.   A Study of American Intelligence. Princeton: Princeton Univ. Press, 1923. Pp. 210.

Brigham, Carl C.   Intelligence tests of immigrant groups. *Psychol. Rev.*, 1930, *37*, 158-165.

Brooks, Lyman B.   A socio-economic and educational study of Negro high-school and junior-college students. Unpubl. Doctor's dissert., Univ. Michigan, 1942.

Brown, Addie S.   An attempt to determine the relationship between mental ability, general silent reading ability, and scholastic achievement in the junior high school of Pike County, Alabama. Unpubl. Master's thesis, Alabama State Coll. for Negroes, 1951.

Brown, Fred.   An experimental and critical study of the intelligence of Negro and white kindergarten children. *J. Genet. Psychol.*, 1944, *65*, 161-175.

Brown, Ina C.   Socio-economic Approach to Educational Problems. Washington, D. C.: U. S. Off. Educ., 1942. Pp. 65-99.

Brown, Ina C.   The Testing of Negro Intelligence. Audrey M. Shuey. *Amer. Anthropologist,* 1960, *62,* 544.

Brown, Robert G.   A comparison of the vocational aspirations of paired sixth-grade white and Negro children who attend segregated schools. *J. Educ. Res.,* 1965, *58*, 402-404.

Brown, Woodrow W.   An application of selected related factors to the incidence and cost of non-promotion in the public schools of York, Pennsylvania. Unpubl. Doctor's dissert., Univ. Pittsburgh, 1955.

Bruce, Myrtle. Factors affecting intelligence test performance of whites and Negroes in the rural South. *Arch. Psychol.*, 1940, No. 252. Pp. 99.

Brunschwig, Lily. Psychological misconceptions of a group of Negro college students and their relationship to some other factors. *J. Soc. Psychol.*, 1943, *18*, 111-126.

Bryan, J. Y. The mental ability of literate transients. *J. Abnorm. & Soc. Psychol.*, 1936, *31*, 276-290.

Buck, James R., Jr. Some identifiable characteristics of students entering Negro senior colleges in Mississippi. Unpubl. Doctor's dissert., George Peabody Coll., 1964.

Burket, George R. Identification, development, and utilization of human talents. Selected pupil and school characteristics in relation to percentage of Negroes in school enrollment. Project Talent Monogr. Ser., U. S. Off. Educ. Project No. 635, Univ. Pittsburgh, 1963.

Burks, Barbara S., and Steggerda, M. Potential marital selection in Negro college students. *Sociol. & Soc. Res.*, 1940, *24*, 433-441.

Buros, Oscar K. (Ed.) The Fifth Mental Measurements Yearbook. Highland Park, N. J.: Gryphon, 1959. Pp. 1292.

Buros, Oscar K. (Ed.) The Fourth Mental Measurements Yearbook. Highland Park, N. J.: Gryphon, 1953. Pp. 1163.

Buros, Oscar K. (Ed.) The Nineteen Forty Mental Measurements Yearbook. Highland Park, N. J.: Gryphon, 1941. Pp. 674.

Buros, Oscar K. (Ed.) The Nineteen Thirty Eight Mental Measurements Yearbook of the School of Education Rutgers University. New Brunswick, N. J.: Rutgers Univ. Press, 1938. Pp. 415.

Buros, Oscar K. (Ed.) The Third Mental Measurements Yearbook. New Brunswick, N. J.: Rutgers Univ. Press, 1949. Pp. 1047.

Byrns, Ruth. Intelligence and nationality of Wisconsin school children. *J. Soc. Psychol.*, 1936, *7*, 455-470.

Caldwell, Marcus B. An analysis of responses of a southern urban Negro population to items on the Wechsler Intelligence Scale for Children. Unpubl. Doctor's dissert., Pennsylvania State Coll., 1954.

Caldwell, Morris G. Case analysis method for the personality study of offenders. *J. Crim. Law, Criminol. & Police Sci.*, 1954, *45*, 291-298.

Caldwell, Morris G. Personality trends in the youthful male offender. *J. Crim. Law, Criminol. & Police Sci.*, 1959, *49*, 405-416.

Caldwell, Morris G. The youthful male offender in Alabama. A study in delinquency causation. *Sociol. & Soc. Res.*, 1953, *37*, 236-243.

Caliver, Ambrose. A Background Study of Negro College Students. *U. S. Off. Educ. Bull.*, 1933, No. 8. Pp. 132.

Caliver, Ambrose. A personnel study of Negro college students. *Teach. Coll. Contrib. Educ.*, 1931, No. 484. Pp. 146.

Calvin, Allen D., Scriven, Michael, Gallagher, James J., Hanley, Charles, McConnell, James V., and McGuigan, F. J. Psychology. Boston: Allyn and Bacon, 1961. Pp. 571.

Canady, Herman G. A study of sex differences in intelligence—test scores among 1306 Negro college freshmen. *J. Negro Educ.*, 1943, *12*, 167-172.

Canady, Herman G. Individual differences among freshmen at West Virginia State College and their educational bearings. *W. Va. State Coll. Bull.*, 1936, Ser. 23, No. 2. Pp. 42.

Canady, Herman G. The American caste system and the question of Negro intelligence. *J. Educ. Psychol.*, 1942, *33*, 161-172.

Canady, Herman G. The effect of "rapport" on the I. Q.: a new approach to the problem of racial psychology. *J. Negro Educ.*, 1936, *5*, 209-219.

Canady, Herman G. The problem of equating the environment of Negro-white groups for intelligence testing in comparative studies. *J. Soc. Psychol.*, 1943, *17*, 3-15.

Cavins, Lorimer V. Survey of Education in West Virginia. Vol. II. State Board Educ., Charleston, W. Va., 1928. Pp. 160.

Chant, S. N. F., and Freedman, S. S. A quantitative comparison of the nationality preferences of two groups. *J. Soc. Psychol.*, 1934, *5*, 116-120.

Chapanis, Alphonse, and Williams, W. C. Results of a mental survey with the Kuhlmann-Anderson intelligence tests in Williamson County, Tennessee. *J. Genet. Psychol.*, 1945, *67*, 27-55.

Charles, C. M. A comparison of the intelligence quotients of incarcerated delinquent white and American Negro boys and of groups of St. Louis public school boys. *J. Appl. Psychol.*, 1936, *20*, 499-510.

Cheers, Arlynne L., and Sherman, Dorothy M. Response pattern differences of selected Negro and white subjects on S. C. A. T. *Personnel & Guid. J.*, 1963, *41*, 582-589.

Clark, Glynn E. A comparison of the performance of selected pupils on the Davis-Eells Test and the Otis Test of Mental Ability. Unpubl. Doctor's dissert., Washington Univ., 1957.

Clark, Kenneth B. Dark Ghetto: Dilemmas of Social Power. New York: Harper & Row, 1965. Pp. 251.

Clark, Kenneth B. Segregated schools in New York City. *J. Educ. Sociol.*, 1963, *36*, 245-250.

Clark, Kenneth B., and Clark, Mamie P. Emotional factors in racial identification and preference in Negro children. *J. Negro Educ.*, 1950, *19*, 341-350.

Clark, Kenneth B., and Clark, Mamie K. Segregation as a factor in the racial identification of Negro pre-school children: a preliminary report. *J. Exper. Educ.*, 1939, *8*, 161-163.

Clark, Kenneth B., and Clark, Mamie P.   Skin color as a factor in racial identification of Negro preschool children. *J. Soc. Psychol.,* 1940, *11,* 159-169.

Clark, Raymond M.   The effect of schooling upon intelligence quotients of Negro children. Unpubl. Doctor's dissert., Western Reserve Univ., 1933.

Clark, Willis W.   Los Angeles Negro children. *Educ. Res. Bull., Los Angeles City Schools,* 1923, *3,* No. 2, 1-2.

Clarke, Daniel P.   Stanford-Binet Scale "L" response patterns in matched racial groups. *J. Negro Educ.,* 1941, *10,* 230-238.

Clemmer, Donald.   The Prison Community. Boston: Christopher, 1940. Pp. 341.

Cliff, Emellen M.   A comparative study of the performance of one hundred sixteen seventh grade students in power and speed situations. Unpubl. Master's thesis, Atlanta Univ., 1949.

Clinton, R. J.   A comparison of white and Negro children: norms on mirror-drawing for Negro children by age and sex. *J. Educ. Psychol.,* 1931, *22,* 186-190.

Codwell, John E.   A study of the kind and amount of change in motor function as the amount of Negro increases or decreases in the Negro-white hybrid. Unpubl. Doctor's dissert., Univ. Michigan, 1947.

Collum, Marion C.   Comparative capacities and achievements of white children in Woodville and Negro children in Ardmore, Oklahoma. Unpubl. Master's thesis, Univ. Oklahoma, 1937.

Congehl, Irene H.   Withdrawal from high school before graduation by Negro girls in St. Louis City. Unpubl. Master's thesis, Washington Univ., 1946.

Cooperative Test Division, Educational Testing Service. American Council on Education Psychological Examination for College Freshmen, 1949 Edition. Norms Bull., Princeton, N. J., 1950. Pp. 25.

Cooperative Test Division, Educational Testing Service. American Council on Education Psychological Examination for College Freshmen, 1952 Edition. Norms Bull., Princeton, N. J., 1953. Pp. 26.

Cooperative Test Division, Educational Testing Service. Cooperative School and College Ability Tests. Manual for Interpreting Scores. Princeton, N. J., 1957. Pp. 49.

Coppinger, Neil W.   The Full-Range Picture Vocabulary Test: a normative study of southern Negro children. Unpubl. Master's thesis, Tulane Univ., 1949.

Coppinger, Neil W., and Ammons, Robert B.   The Full-Range Picture Vocabulary Test: VIII. A normative study of Negro children. *J. Clin. Psychol.,* 1952, *8,* 136-140.

Corsini, Raymond.   Season of birth and mental ability of prison inmates. *J. Soc. Psychol.,* 1946, *23,* 65-72.

Cox, John F. Differences between Negro and native white convicts tested with the Stanford-Binet and retested with a reorganized form of this scale. Unpubl. Master's thesis, Univ. Pittsburgh, 1930.

Craft, Pearlie M. A comparative study of the scores made by two hundred fifty-one Morehouse College students on the Psychological Examination for College Freshmen. Unpubl. Master's thesis, Atlanta Univ., 1943.

Crandall, Virginia C., and Crandall, Vaughn J. A Children's Social Desirability Questionnaire. *J. Consult. Psychol.*, 1965, *29*, 27-36.

Cronbach, Lee J. Essentials of Psychological Testing. New York: Harper, 1949. Pp. 475.

Cronbach, Lee J. Essentials of Psychological Testing. New York: Harper & Row, 1960. Pp. 650.

Cummings, John. Negro Population: 1790-1915. Dept. Commerce, Bureau of the Census, Washington, D. C., 1918. Pp. 844.

Dai, Bingham. Some problems of personality development among Negro children. *In* Kluckhohn, C., and Murray, Henry A. (Eds.) Personality in Nature, Society, and Culture. New York: Knopf, 1949. Pp. 437-458.

D'Angelo, Rita Y. A comparison of white and Negro pre-school children in Goodenough I.Q. and language development. Unpubl. Master's thesis, Fordham Univ., 1950.

Daniel, Robert P. A psychological study of delinquent and non-delinquent Negro boys. *Teach. Coll. Contrib. Educ.*, 1932, No. 546. Pp. 59.

Daniel, Walter G. A memorandum on the education of Negroes. *J. Negro Educ.*, 1964, *33*, 97-102.

Davenport, Charles B. Race crossing in Jamaica. *Scient. Month.*, 1928, *27*, 225-238.

Davenport, Roy K. Implications of military selection and classification in relation to universal military training. *J. Negro Educ.*, 1946, *15*, 585-594.

Davidson, Kenneth S., Gibby, Robert G., McNeil, Elton B., Segal, Stanley J., and Silverman, Herbert. A preliminary study of Negro and white differences in Form I of the Wechsler-Bellevue Scale. *J. Consult. Psychol.*, 1950, *14*, 489-492.

Davis, Allison, and Dollard, John. Children of Bondage. Washington, D. C.: Amer. Counc. Educ., 1940. Pp. 299.

Davis, Allison, and Eells, Kenneth. Davis-Eells Test of General Intelligence or Problem-Solving Ability. Manual. Tarrytown-on-Hudson, N. Y.: World Book, 1953. Pp. 72.

Davis, Julian C. The scatter pattern of a Southern Negro group on the Wechsler-Bellevue Intelligence Scale. *J. Clin. Psychol.*, 1957, *13*, 298-300.

Davis, Robert A., Jr. Some relations between amount of school training and intelligence among Negroes. *J. Educ. Psychol.*, 1928, *19*, 127-130.

Davis, Roland C. Ability in Social and Racial Classes. New York: Century, 1932. Pp. 114.

Davis, Thomas E. A study of Fisk University freshmen from 1928 to 1930. *J. Negro Educ.*, 1933, *2*, 477-483.

Day, Willie V. A study of the relationship between personality and reading comprehension. Unpubl. Master's thesis, Atlanta Univ., 1949.

Dendy, Abbie P. H. A study of the tested differences and relationship in intelligence, personality, and academic achievement of forty-five seventh grade pupils in the Mountain View Elementary School, Landrum, South Carolina, 1951-1952. Unpubl. Master's thesis, Atlanta Univ., 1952.

Derrick, S. M. A comparative study of the intelligence of seventy-five white and fifty-five colored college students by the Stanford Revision of the Binet-Simon Scale. *J. Appl. Psychol.*, 1920, *4*, 316-329.

DeStephens, William P. Are criminals morons? *J. Soc. Psychol.*, 1953, *38*, 187-199.

Deutsch, Martin. Minority group and class status as related to social and personality factors in scholastic achievement. *In* Grossack, Martin M. (Ed.) Mental Health and Segregation. New York: Springer, 1963. Pp. 64-75.

Deutsch, Martin. The role of social class in language development and cognition. *Amer. J. Orthopsychiat.*, 1965, *35*, 78-88.

Deutsch, Martin, and Brown, Bert. Social influences in Negro-white intelligence differences. *J. Soc. Issues*, 1964, *20*, 24-35.

Diggs, Mary H. A comparative study of delinquent behavior manifestations in 100 delinquent and 100 non-delinquent Negro boys. Unpubl. Doctor's dissert., Bryn Mawr Coll., 1946.

Dinitz, Simon, Kay, Barbara A., and Reckless, Walter C. Group gradients in delinquency potential and achievement scores of sixth graders. *Amer. J. Orthopsychiat.*, 1958, *28*, 598-605.

Doll, Edgar A. A study of multiple criminal factors. *J. Crim. Law & Criminol.*, 1920-21, *11*, 33-46.

Doll, Edgar A. The comparative intelligence of prisoners. *J. Crim. Law & Criminol.*, 1920-21, *11*, 191-197.

Doll, Edgar A., and Fitch, Kathryn A. Social competence of delinquent boys. *Amer. Assoc. Ment. Deficiency, Proc. and Addr.*, 1938, *43*, 137-141.

Dombey, Edith H. A comparison of the intelligence test scores of southern and northern born Negroes residing in Cleveland. Unpubl. Master's thesis, Western Reserve Univ., 1933.

Doran, Alicia T. Retardation among Negro pupils in the junior high school. Unpubl. Master's thesis, Univ. Chicago, 1934.

Dozier, Mae C. A study of the relationship between intelligence, reading, and problem solving ability. Unpubl. Master's thesis, Fisk Univ., 1946.

Dreger, Ralph M., and Miller, Kent S. Comparative psychological studies of Negroes and whites in the United States. *Psychol. Bull.*, 1960, *57*, 361-402.

Droughn, Kathleen P. A study of one hundred freshmen students at Virginia State College. Unpubl. Master's thesis. Virginia State Coll., 1946.

Dunn, Faustine H. A study of the group characteristics of the State Teachers College Laboratory High School pupils in regard to intelligence, achievement, and leisure time activities. Unpubl. Master's thesis, State Teachers Coll., Montgomery, Ala., 1946.

Eagleson, Oran W. A racial comparison of personality traits. *J. Appl. Psychol.*, 1938, *22*, 271-274.

Eells, Kenneth, Davis, Allison, Havighurst, Robert J., Herrick, Virgil E., and Tyler, Ralph. Intelligence and Cultural Differences. Chicago: Univ. Chicago Press, 1951. Pp. 388.

Ellis, Pearl D. A comparative study of social development and intelligence of sixty-four first-grade children in Eden Park Elementary School, Baton Rouge, Louisiana. Unpubl. Master's thesis, Atlanta Univ., 1947.

Engel, Anna M. A study of 3,169 retarded pupils in the Detroit public schools. *Amer. J. Mental Def.*, 1941-1942, *46*, 395-401.

Engle, T. L. Personality adjustments of children belonging to two minority groups. *J. Educ. Psychol.*, 1945, *36*, 543-560.

Erickson, Ralph W. On Special-Training-Unit performance as an index of Negro ability. *J. Abnorm. & Soc. Psychol.*, 1946, *41*, 481.

Evans, Caswell A. A study of the effects of environment on intelligence test scores of seventh grade Negro children. Unpubl. Master's thesis, Columbia Univ., 1934.

Fallin, Wilson. Socio-civic and religious attitudes of the Dunbar High School pupils, 1948-1949, Bessemer, Alabama. Unpubl. Master's thesis, Alabama State Coll. for Negroes, 1949.

Farr, T. J. The intelligence and achievement of Negro children. *Educ.*, 1931, *51*, 491-495.

Feacher, Jessie P. A study of behavior traits of 517 Negro pupils in grade one Jacksonville, Florida, and a program of planned activities for improvement of 41 pupils, Lavilla School. Unpubl. Master's thesis, Hampton Institute, 1947.

Feingold, Gustave A. Intelligence of the first generation of immigrant groups. *J. Educ. Psychol.*, 1924, *15*, 65-82.

Fensch, Edwin A. A critical study of Negro students in the John Simpson Junior High School, Mansfield, Ohio. Unpubl. Doctor's dissert., Ohio State Univ., 1942.

Ferguson, George O., Jr. The intelligence of Negroes at Camp Lee, Virginia. *Sch. & Soc.*, 1919, *9*, 721-726.

Fernald, Mabel R., Hayes, M. H. S., and Dawley, A. A Study of Women Delinquents in New York State. New York: Century, 1920. Pp. 542.

Fisher, Gary M. Discrepancy in Verbal and Performance IQ in adolescent sociopaths. *J. Clin. Psychol.,* 1961, *17,* 60.

Flemister, Rachel C. A study of the personality adjustment, the intelligence, and the achievement of one hundred Negro high school pupils. Unpubl. Master's thesis, Atlanta Univ., 1950.

Florant, Lyonel C. Negro internal migration. *Amer. Sociol. Rev.,* 1942, *7,* 782-791.

Foreman, Clark. Environmental Factors in Negro Elementary Education. New York: Norton, 1932. Pp. 96.

Fortson, Charles B. A study of the comparability of Forms I and II of the Wechsler-Bellevue Intelligence Scale when used with clinically normal Negro adults. Unpubl. Master's thesis, Atlanta Univ., 1956.

Fowler, William L. A comparative analysis of pupil performance on conventional and culture-controlled mental tests. Unpubl. Doctor's dissert., Univ. Michigan. Summary in: *4th Yearbk. Nat. Coun. Meas. Educ.,* 1959, 8-19.

Frank, Jerome D. Some psychological determinants of the level of aspiration. *Amer. J. Psychol.,* 1935, *47,* 285-293.

Frankel, Emil. One thousand murderers. *J. Crim. Law & Criminol.,* 1939, *29,* 672-688.

Franklin, Joseph C. Discriminative value and patterns of the Wechsler-Bellevue scales in the examination of delinquent Negro boys. *Educ. & Psychol. Meas.,* 1945, *5,* 71-85.

Freedman, Harry L., and Rockmore, Myron J. Marihuana: a factor in personality evaluation and Army maladjustment. *J. Clin. Psychopath. & Psychother.,* 1946, *7,* 765-782; *8,* 221-236.

Freeman, Frank S. Theory and Practice of Psychological Testing. New York: Holt, 1950. Pp. 518.

Freeman, Frank S. Theory and Practice of Psychological Testing. New York: Holt, Rinehart & Winston, 1963. Pp. 697.

Freeman, Robert L. An analysis of levels of intelligence, achievement and personality of seventh grade pupils of the McCoy Hill Elementary School, Americus, Georgia as a basis for instructional procedure during the school term 1953-1954. Unpubl. Master's thesis, Atlanta Univ., 1954.

Fry, Franklyn D. A study of reactions to frustration in 236 college students and in 207 inmates of state prisons. *J. Psychol.,* 1949, *28,* 427-438.

Fulk, Byron E. A comparison of Negro and white Army General Classification Test scores. Unpubl. Master's thesis, Univ. Illinois, 1949.

Fulk, Byron E., and Harrell, Thomas W. Negro-white test scores and last school grade. *J. Appl. Psychol.,* 1952, *36,* 34-35.

Furlow, Florine D. An analysis of the tested differences and correlations in intelligence as measured by the Detroit Test of Learning, the California Test of Mental Maturity, and the Davis-Eells Intelligence Test manifested by sixth grade pupils of E. R. Carter School, Atlanta, Georgia, 1953-1954. Unpubl. Master's thesis, Atlanta Univ., 1954.

Gardner, George E., and Aaron, Sadie. The childhood and adolescent adjustment of Negro psychiatric casualties. *Amer. J. Orthopsychiat.*, 1946, *16,* 481-495.

Garn, Stanley M. (Ed.) Readings on Race. Springfield, Ill.: Charles C. Thomas, 1960. Pp. 281.

Garrett, Henry E. A note on the intelligence scores of Negroes and whites in 1918. *J. Abnorm. & Soc. Psychol.*, 1945, *40,* 344-346.

Garrett, Henry E. Comparison of Negro and white recruits on the Army tests given in 1917-1918. *Amer. J. Psychol.*, 1945, *58,* 480-495.

Garrett, Henry E. "Facts" and "Interpretations" regarding race differences. *Science,* 1945, *101,* 404-406.

Garrett, Henry E. Negro-white differences in mental ability in the United States. *Scient. Month.*, 1947, *65,* 329-333.

Garrett, Henry E. The SPSSI and racial differences. *Amer. Psychol.*, 1962, *17,* 260-263.

Garrett, Henry E., and Schneck, Matthew R. Psychological Tests, Methods, and Results. New York: Harper, 1933. Pp. 372.

Garth, Thomas R. Race Psychology—A Study of Racial Mental Differences. New York: McGraw-Hill, 1931. Pp. 260.

Garth, Thomas R., Lovelady, Bert E., and Smith, Hale W. The intelligence and achievement of southern Negro children. *Sch. & Soc.*, 1930, *32,* 431-435.

Garth, Thomas R., and Whatley, C. A. The intelligence of southern Negro children. *Sch. & Soc.*, 1925, *22,* 501-504.

Gee, W., and Corson, J.J., III. Rural depopulation in certain Tidewater and Piedmont areas of Virginia. Univ. Virginia: Inst. Res. Soc. Science Monogr. No. 3, 1929. Pp. 104.

Geisel, Paul N. IQ performance, educational and occupational aspirations of youth in a southern city: a racial comparison. Unpubl. Doctor's dissert., Vanderbilt Univ., 1962.

Geldard, Frank A. Fundamentals of Psychology. New York: John Wiley, 1962. Pp. 437.

Gini, Corrado. The Testing of Negro Intelligence. By Audrey M. Shuey. (J. P. Bell Company, pp. 341.) *Amer. J. Psychiat.*, 1961, *118,* 954-956.

Ginzberg, Eli. The Negro Potential. New York: Columbia Univ. Press, 1956. Pp. 144.

Gist, Noel P., and Bennett, William S., Jr. Aspirations of Negro and white students. *Soc. Forces,* 1963, *42,* 40-48.

Goldstein, Sylvia D. Social selection in the migration and occupational choices of Negroes. Unpubl. Master's thesis, Univ. Missouri, 1944.

Goodenough, Florence L. Mental Testing. New York: Rinehart, 1949. Pp. 609.

Goodenough, Florence L. New evidence on environmental influence on intelligence. *39th Yearbk. Nat. Soc. Study Educ.,* 1940, Part I, 325-326.

Goodenough, Florence L. Racial differences in the intelligence of school children. *J. Exper. Psychol.,* 1926, *9,* 388-397.

Goodenough, Florence L., and Harris, Dale B. Studies in the psychology of children's drawings: II 1928-1949. *Psychol. Bull.,* 1950, *47,* 369-433.

Gottlieb, David. Goal aspirations and goal fulfillments: differences between deprived and affluent American adolescents. *Amer. J. Orthopsychiat.,* 1964, *34,* 934-941.

Gound, Hanford D. A comparative study of the mental abilities and achievements of the white children in Achille, Oklahoma and the Negro children in Shoemake School in Colbert, Oklahoma. Unpubl. Master's thesis, Univ. Oklahoma, 1938.

Graham, James L. A quantitative comparison of rational responses of Negro and white college students. *J. Soc. Psychol.,* 1930, *1,* 97-121.

Graham, Virginia T. Health studies of Negro children I. Intelligence studies of Negro children in Atlanta, Ga. *Publ. Health Rep.,* 1926, *41,* 2759-2783.

Grandison, Francis L. The relationship of level of aspiration to Negro and white differences on Form I of the Wechsler-Bellevue Intelligence Scale. Unpubl. Master's thesis, Ohio State Univ., 1951.

Gray, C. T., and Bingham, C. W. A comparison of certain phases of musical ability of colored and white public school pupils. *J. Educ. Psychol.,* 1929, *20,* 501-506.

Gray, Susan. The vocational preferences of Negro school children. *J. Genet, Psychol.,* 1944, *64,* 239-247.

Gray, Susan W., and Klaus, Rupert A. An experimental preschool program for culturally deprived children. Unpubl. paper, 1964.

Gray, Susan W., and Klaus, Rupert A. Early training project: interim report, November, 1963. Unpubl. paper, 1963.

Gray, W. Herbert, Jr. Needs of Negro high school graduates. Unpubl. Doctor's dissert., Univ. Pennsylvania, 1945.

Green, M. W., and Ewert, Josephine C. Normative data on the Progressive Matrices (1947). *J. Consult. Psychol.,* 1955, *19,* 139-142.

Griffith, William R. A study of Negro children in the upper grades of a Portland elementary school. Unpubl. Master's thesis, Washington State Coll., 1947.

Grigsby, J. E.   A comparative study of Negro freshmen with white freshmen of equal intelligence. Unpubl. Master's thesis, Ohio State Univ., 1929.

Grinder, Robert E., Spotts, Wendy S., and Curti, Margaret W.   Relationships between Goodenough Draw-a-Man Test performance and skin color among preadolescent Jamaican children. *J. Soc. Psychol.*, 1964, *62,* 181-188.

Grossack, Martin M.   Some personality characteristics of Southern Negro students. *J. Soc. Psychol.*, 1957, *46,* 125-131.

Guilford, J. P.   General Psychology. New York: Van Nostrand, 1952. Pp. 587.

Haggerty, Melvin E.   Virginia Public Schools Education Commission's Report to the Assembly of Virginia. Part II. Educational Tests. Yonkers, N. Y.: World Book, 1921. Pp. 335.

Hamill, Grace.   The application of the Pintner Group Test to misdemeanants. *J. Delin.*, 1923, *8,* 158-168.

Hamilton, C. Horace.   The Negro leaves the South. *Demography,* 1964, *1,* 273-295.

Hammer, Emanuel F.   Comparison of the performances of Negro children and adolescents on two tests of intelligence, one an Emergency Scale. *J. Genet. Psychol.*, 1954, *84,* 85-93.

Harms, Herbert E., Kobler, Frank J., and Sweeney, Francis J.   Negro Army psychiatric casualties. *War Med.*, 1945, *7,* 309-312.

Harper, Ruth M.   A comparative study of the intelligence and personality traits of pupils who attend school regularly with those who attend irregularly in the Bush Mountain School, Atlanta, Georgia. Unpubl. Master's thesis, Atlanta Univ., 1950.

Harris, Bernett V.   A standardization of Kohs' Design Block Test on a group of Negro children. Unpubl. Master's thesis, Ohio State Univ., 1929.

Hartill, Rufus M., and Loretan, Joseph O.   An experiment in the improvement of retarded and maladjusted children. *Bull. Dept. Elem. Sch. Prin.*, 19th Yearbk, 1940, *19,* 458-465.

Havighurst, Robert J.   Editorial news and editorial comment. *Sch. Rev.*, 1949, *57,* 187-189.

Havighurst, Robert J. (Ed.)   Studying children and training counselors in a community program. *Suppl. Educ. Monogr.*, 1953, No. 78.

Herskovits, Melville J.   On "Racial" differences. *Science,* 1945, *101,* 200.

Herskovits, Melville J.   On the relation between Negro-white mixture and standing in intelligence tests. *Ped. Sem.*, 1926, *33,* 30-42.

Hess, Robert D.   Controlling culture influence in mental testing: an experimental test. *J. Educ. Res.*, 1955, *49,* 53-58.

Hewitt, Alden. A comparative study of white and colored pupils in a southern school system. *Elem. Sch. J.*, 1930, *31,* 111-119.

Hickerson, Nathaniel. Comparisons between Negro and non-Negro students in participation in the formal and informal activities of a California high school. Unpubl. Doctor's dissert., Univ. California, Berkeley, 1963.

Hickerson, Nathaniel. Some aspects of school integration in a California high school. *J. Negro Educ.*, 1965, *34,* 130-137.

Higgins, Conwell, and Sivers, Cathryne H. A comparison of Stanford-Binet and Colored Raven Progressive Matrices IQs for children in low socioeconomic status. *J. Consult. Psychol.*, 1958, *22,* 465-468.

Hilgard, Ernest R. Introduction to Psychology. New York: Harcourt, Brace & World, 1962. Pp. 678.

Hill, G. E. The intelligence of young male offenders. *J. Juv. Research,* 1936, *20,* 20-27.

Hills, John R., Klock, Joseph A., and Bush, Marilyn L. Freshman Norms for the University System of Georgia, 1962-63. Regents of the University System of Georgia, Atlanta, Ga., 1964. Pp. 65.

Hills, John R., Klock, Joseph A., and Bush, Marilyn L. Freshman Norms for the University System of Georgia, 1963-64. Regents of the University System of Georgia, Atlanta, Ga., 1965. Pp. 65.

Hirsch, Nathaniel D. M. A study of natio-racial mental differences. *Genet. Psychol. Monogr.*, 1926, *1,* 231-406.

Hollingworth, Leta S. Children above 180 IQ. Yonkers: World Book, 1942. Pp. 332.

Hollingworth, Leta S. The significance of deviates. I. Review of research. *39th Yearbk Nat. Soc. Study Educ.*, 1940, Part I, 43-66.

Holston, Oliver L. A study of the personality characteristics of a group of eighty-five first summer graduate students of the State Teachers College, Montgomery, Alabama. Unpubl. Master's thesis, State Teachers Coll. at Montgomery, 1946.

Horowitz, Eugene L. Attitudes of Negroes and whites. *In* Klineberg, Otto (Ed.) Characteristics of the American Negro. New York: Harper, 1944. Pp. 215-221.

Horowitz, Ruth E. Racial aspects of self-identification in nursery school children. *J. Psychol.*, 1939, *7,* 91-99.

Horton, Carrell P., and Crump, E. Perry. Growth and development XI. Descriptive analysis of the backgrounds of 76 Negro children whose scores are above or below average on the Merrill-Palmer Scale of Mental Tests at three years of age. *J. Genet. Psychol.*, 1962, *100,* 255-265.

Howard, Mittie E. A comparative study of the extent to which day high school and night high school students in the public schools of Atlanta, Georgia have achieved with relationship to their ability to achieve. Unpubl. Master's thesis, Atlanta Univ., 1947.

Hunt, William A. Negro-white differences in intelligence in World War II—a note of caution. *J. Abnorm. & Soc. Psychol.*, 1947, *42*, 254-255.

Hunt, William B. An investigation of reading achievement, intelligence, personality adjustment, and home background of fourth and fifth grade pupils in Hardeman County Negro schools. Unpubl. Master's thesis, Tennessee Agricul. & Indus. State Coll., 1950.

Hurlock, Elizabeth B. A study of self-ratings by children. *J. Appl. Psychol.*, 1927, *11*, 490-502.

Hurlock, Elizabeth B. The suggestibility of children. *Ped. Sem. & J. Genet. Psychol.*, 1930, *37*, 59-74.

Hurlock, Elizabeth B. The value of praise and reproof as incentives for children. *Arch. Psychol.*, 1924, No. 71. Pp. 78.

Hyde, Robert W., and Chisholm, Roderick M. Studies in medical sociology: III. The relation of mental disorders to race and nationality. *New Engl. J. Med.*, 1944, *231*, 610-618.

Ingle, Dwight J. Racial differences and the future. *Science,* 1964, *146*, 375-379.

Iscoe, Ira, and Pierce-Jones, John. Divergent thinking, age, and intelligence in white and Negro children. *Child Develop.*, 1964, *35*, 785-797.

Jenkins, Martin D. A socio-psychological study of Negro children of superior intelligence. *J. Negro Educ.*, 1936, *5*, 175-190.

Jenkins, Martin D. A socio-psychological study of Negro children of superior intelligence. Unpubl. Doctor's dissert., Northwestern Univ., 1935.

Jenkins, Martin D. The intelligence of Negro children. *Educ. Meth.*, 1939, *19*, 106-112.

Jenkins, Martin D. The upper limit of ability among American Negroes. *Scient. Month.*, 1948, *66*, 399-401.

Jenkins, Martin D., and Randall, Constance M. Differential characteristics of superior and unselected Negro college students. *J. Soc. Psychol.*, 1948, *27*, 187-202.

Jenkins, Trixie A. Intelligence and language ability of white and colored children. Unpubl. Master's thesis, George Peabody Coll. for Teachers, 1932.

Jensen, Arthur R. A statistical note on racial differences in the Progressive Matrices. *J. Consult. Psychol.*, 1959, *23*, 272.

Johnson, Catherine N. The intelligence and achievement of the sixth grade Negro children in the rural schools of Comecuh County, Alabama. Unpubl. Master's thesis, State Teachers Coll., Montgomery, Ala., 1948.

Johnson, Charles S. Growing up in the Black Belt. Washington, D. C.: Amer. Council Educ., 1941. Pp. 360.

Johnson, Charles S. The Negro college graduate: how and where he is employed. *J. Negro Educ.*, 1935, *4*, 5-22.

Johnson, Donald M.   Applications of the standard-score IQ to social statistics. *J. Soc. Psychol.*, 1948, *27*, 217-227.

Johnson, Minerva H.   An evaluation of certain tests as predictive measures of scholastic success at the end of the freshman year. Unpubl. Master's thesis, Fisk Univ., 1940.

Johnson, S. T.   Information, intelligence and their relation for first grade pupils. Unpubl. Master's thesis, Fisk Univ., 1954.

Johnson, Walter L. D., Jr.   An investigation in pupil achievement in relation to intelligence and personality patterns of two hundred twenty-eight pupils of Jack Yates High School, Houston, Texas. Unpubl. Master's thesis, Prairie View Univ., 1946.

Jones, Arlynne L.   An investigation of the response patterns which differentiate the performance of selected Negro and white freshmen on SCAT. Unpubl. Doctor's dissert., Univ. Colorado, 1960.

Jones, Hubert L.   A comparison of physical skill and intelligence of Negro and Spanish American boys of junior high school age. Unpubl. Master's thesis, Univ. Denver, 1940.

Jones, Ruth H.   A study of the socio-economic status and the educational and personality adjustments of superior children of Baltimore. Unpubl. Master's thesis, Howard Univ., 1948.

Jordan, Arthur M.   Efficiency of group tests of intelligence in discovering the mentally deficient. *High School J.*, 1948, *31*, 73-94.

Jordan, Arthur M.   Notes on racial differences. *Sch. & Soc.*, 1922, *16*, 503-504.

Jordan, Arthur M.   Testing the intelligence of the children of a rural county. *High School J.*, 1947, *30*, 35-45.

Kanner, Leo.   Child Psychiatry. Springfield, Ill.: Thomas, 1937. Pp. 527.

Kardiner, Abram, and Ovesey, Lionel.   The Mark of Oppression: a psychosocial study of the American Negro. New York: Norton, 1951. Pp. 396.

Katz, Irwin.   Review of evidence relating to effects of desegregation on the intellectual performance of Negroes. *Amer. Psychol.*, 1964, *19*, 381-399.

Katz, Irwin, and Benjamin, Lawrence.   Effects of white authoritarianism in bi-racial work groups. *J. Abnorm. & Soc. Psychol.*, 1960, *61*, 448-456.

Katz, Irwin, Epps, Edgar G., and Axelson, Leland J.   Effect upon Negro Digit-Symbol performance of anticipated comparison with whites and with other Negroes. *J. Abnorm. & Soc. Psychol.*, 1964, *69*, 77-83.

Katz, Irwin, Roberts, S. Oliver, and Robinson, James M.   Effects of task difficulty, race of administrator, and instructions on Digit-Symbol performance of Negroes. *J. Personal. & Soc. Psychol.*, 1965, *2*, 53-59.

Katz, Irwin, Robinson, James M., Epps, Edgar G., and Waly, Patricia.   The influence of race of the experimenter and instructions upon the expression of hostility by Negro boys. *J. Soc. Issues*, 1964, *20*, 54-59.

Katzenmeyer, William G.   Social interaction and differences in intelligence test performance of Negro and white elementary school pupils. Unpubl. Doctor's dissert., Duke Univ., 1962.

Kempf, Grover A., and Collins, Selwyn D.   A study of the relation between mental and physical status of children in two counties of Illinois. *U. S. Publ. Health Rep.*, 1929, *44*, 1743-1784.

Kendler, Howard H.   Basic Psychology. New York: Appleton-Century-Crofts, 1963. Pp. 750.

Kennedy, Wallace A., and Lindner, Ronald S.   A normative study of the Goodenough Draw-a-Man Test on Southeastern Negro elementary school children. *Child Develop.*, 1964, *35*, 33-62.

Kennedy, Wallace A., Van De Riet, Vernon, and White, James C., Jr.   A normative sample of intelligence and achievement of Negro elementary school children in the Southeastern United States. *Monogr. Soc. Res. Child Develop.*, 1963, *28*, No. 6. Pp. 112.

Kennedy, Wallace A., Van De Riet, Vernon, and White, James C., Jr.   The standardization of the 1960 Revision of the Stanford-Binet Intelligence Scale on Negro elementary-school children in the Southeastern United States. Cooperative Research Program, Off. Educ., U. S. Dept. Health, Educ. & Welfare, 1961. C.R.P. 954. Pp. 176.

Kennedy, Wallace A., Van De Riet, Vernon, and White, James C., Jr.   Use of the Terman-Merrill Abbreviated Scale on the 1960 Stanford-Binet Form L-M on Negro elementary school children of the Southeastern United States. *J. Consult. Psychol.*, 1963, *27*, 456-457.

Kennedy, Wallace A., and Vega, Manuel.   Negro children's performance on a discrimination task as a function of examiner race and verbal incentive. *J. Personal. & Soc. Psychol.*, 1965, *2*, 839-843.

Kenyon, Harry C.   The relation between intelligence quotient and teachers' marks: a study of freshmen at Prairie View University, Prairie View, Texas. Unpubl. Master's thesis, Prairie View Univ., 1946.

Kimble, Gregory A., and Garmezy, Norman.   Principles of General Psychology. New York: Ronald Press, 1963. Pp. 655.

Kiser, Clyde V.   Sea Island to City. New York: Columbia Univ. Press, 1932. Pp. 272.

Klineberg, Otto.   An experimental study of speed and other factors in "racial" differences. *Arch. Psychol.*, 1928, *15*, No. 93. Pp. 111.

Klineberg, Otto.   (Ed.) Characteristics of the American Negro. New York: Harper, 1944. Pp. 409.

Klineberg, Otto.   Negro Intelligence and Selective Migration. New York: Columbia Univ. Press, 1935. Pp. 66.

Klineberg, Otto. Negro-white differences in intelligence test performance: a new look at an old problem. *Amer. Psychol.*, 1963, *18*, 198-203.

Klineberg, Otto. Race Differences. New York: Harper, 1935. Pp. 367.

Klineberg, Otto. The intelligence of migrants. *Amer. Sociol. Rev.*, 1938, *3*, 218-224.

Klugman, Samuel F. The effect of money incentive versus praise upon the reliability and obtained scores of the Revised Stanford-Binet Test. *J. Gen. Psychol.*, 1944, *30*, 255-269.

Koch, Helen L., and Simmons, Rietta. A study of the test-performance of American, Mexican, and Negro children. *Psychol. Monogr.*, 1926, *35*, Pp. 116.

Krech, David, and Crutchfield, Richard S. Elements of Psychology. New York: Alfred A. Knopf, 1958. Pp. 736.

Lacy, L. D. Relative intelligence of white and colored children. *Elem. Sch. J.*, 1926, *26*, 542-546.

Lambeth, Martha, and Lanier, Lyle H. Race differences in speed of reaction. *J. Genet. Psychol.*, 1933, *42*, 255-297.

Landreth, Catherine, and Johnson, Barbara C. Young children's responses to a picture and inset test designed to reveal reactions to persons of different skin color. *Child Develop.*, 1953, *24*, 63-79.

Lane, Howard A., and Witty, Paul A. The mental ability of delinquent boys. *J. Juv. Res.*, 1935, *19*, 1-12.

La Piere, Richard T. Sociology. New York: McGraw-Hill, 1946. Pp. 572.

Lawrence, William C. Chicago Non-Verbal Examination normative data on East Tennessee Negro school children, ages six to fourteen. Unpubl. Master's thesis, Univ. Tennessee, 1951.

Lawson, Robert E. The relationship of intelligence, achievement in general science, and superstitious beliefs in ninth grade pupils of East Highland High School, Sylacauga, Alabama. Unpubl. Master's thesis, Fisk Univ., 1945.

Lee, Everett S. Negro intelligence and selective migration: a Philadelphia test of the Klineberg hypothesis. *Amer. Sociol. Rev.*, 1951, *16*, 227-233.

Leggett, James L. Relative intelligence of white and Negro children. Unpubl. Master's thesis, George Peabody Coll. for Teachers, 1921.

Lemkau, Paul, Tietze, Christopher, and Cooper, Marcia. Mental-hygiene problems in an urban district. *Mental Hygiene*, 1941, *25*, 624-646; 1942, *26*, 100-119, 275-288; 1943, *27*, 279-295.

Levin, Hannah A. A psycholinguistic investigation: Do words carve up the world differently for Negro and white boys and girls from city and suburban jr. high schools? Unpubl. Doctor's dissert., Rutgers—The State Univ., 1964.

Levinson, Boris M. A comparative study of the WAIS performance of native-born Negro and white homeless. *J. Genet. Psychol.*, 1964, *105*, 211-218.

Levinson, Boris M.   The "beat" phenomenon in Wechsler tests. *J. Clin. Psychol.,* 1964, *20,* 118-120.

Lewis, Mary L.   A comparative study of the intelligence of sixty students at the Alabama Reform School, Mount Meigs, Alabama and the intelligence of sixty students at Booker T. Washington High School, Montgomery, Alabama. Unpubl. Master's thesis, Atlanta Univ., 1947.

Lichtenstein, Maurice, and Brown, Andrew W.   Intelligence and achievement of children in a delinquency area. *J. Juv. Res.,* 1938, *22,* 1-24.

Lindner, Ronald S.   The Goodenough Draw-a-Man Test: its relationship to intelligence, achievement, and cultural variables of Negro elementary school children in the Southeast United States. Unpubl. Doctor's dissert., Florida State Univ., 1962.

Littell, William M.   The Wechsler Intelligence Scale for Children: review of a decade of research. *Psychol. Bull.,* 1960, *57,* 132-156.

Long, Howard H.   Analyses of test results from third grade children selected on the basis of socio-economic status. Unpubl. Doctor's dissert., Harvard Univ., 1933.

Long, Howard H.   The intelligence of colored elementary pupils in Washington, D. C. *J. Negro Educ.,* 1934, *3,* 205-222.

Lott, Albert J., and Lott, Bernice E.   Negro and White Youth. A Psychological Study in a Border-State Community. New York: Holt, Rinehart and Winston, 1963. Pp. 236.

Love, Mary I., and Beach, Sylvia.   Performance of children on the Davis-Eells Games and other measures of ability. *J. Consult. Psychol.,* 1957, *21,* 29-32.

Lowry, Carmen E.   The prediction of academic success in a private liberal arts college for Negroes. Unpubl. Doctor's dissert., Univ. Texas, 1957.

Lucas, Archie H.   Trends in the performance of superior Negro children on follow-up tests of mental ability. Unpubl. Master's thesis, Howard Univ., 1948.

Luckey, Bertha M.   Racial differences in mental ability. *Scient. Month.,* 1925, *20,* 245-248.

Machover, Karen.   Human Figure drawings of children. *J. Project. Techniques,* 1953, *17,* 85-91.

Machover, Solomon.   Cultural and racial variations in patterns of intellect. *Teach. Coll. Contrib. Educ.,* 1943, No. 875. Pp. 91.

MacPhee, Halsey M., Wright, Herbert F., and Cummings, Samuel B., Jr.   The performance of mentally subnormal rural southern Negroes on the Verbal Scale of the Bellevue Intelligence Examination. *J. Soc. Psychol.,* 1947, *25,* 217-229.

Malamud, Harold R. A study of Negro and white discipline cases in the Western State Penitentiary of Pennsylvania. Part I. *J. Clin. Psychopath.*, 1948, *9*, 108-127.

Malzberg, Benjamin. The racial distribution of mental defectives in New York State. *Amer. J. Ment. Def.*, 1943, *47*, 326-333.

Marcuse, Frederick L., and Bitterman, Morton E. Notes on the results of Army intelligence testing in World War I. *Science*, 1946, *104*, 231-232.

Mathews, Julia. A survey of 341 delinquent girls in California. *J. Delin.*, 1923, *8*, 196-231.

Mazique, Edward C. A comparative study of the performance of two groups of Negro school children—one hundred and twenty-five in each group—on the New Stanford Achievement Test, the Multi-Mental Scale, and the Otis Self-Administering Tests of Mental Ability. Unpubl. Master's thesis, Atlanta Univ., 1934.

McAlpin, Alice S. Changes in the intelligence quotients of Negro children. *J. Negro Educ.*, 1932, *1*, 44-48.

McCary, J. L., and Tracktir, Jack. Relationship between intelligence and Frustration-Aggression patterns as shown by two racial groups. *J. Clin. Psychol.*, 1957, *13*, 202-204.

McClain, Bertha M. Intelligence and school achievement of pre-adolescent, adolescent, and post-adolescent Negro students in the Montgomery County Training School, Waugh, Alabama, 1947-1948. Unpubl. Master's thesis, State Teachers Coll., Montgomery, 1948.

McClure, W. E. Intelligence of 600 juvenile delinquents. *J. Juv. Res.*, 1933, *17*, 35-43.

McCord, William M., and Demerath, Nicholas J., III. "Negro versus white intelligence: a continuing controversy." *Harvard Educ. Rev.*, 1958, *28*, 120-135.

McCullers, John C., and Plant, Walter T. Personality and social development: cultural influences. *Rev. Educ. Res.*, 1964, *34*, 599-610.

McDonald, Robert L., and Gynther, Malcolm D. Relationship of self and ideal-self descriptions with sex, race, and class in Southern adolescents. *J. Personal. & Soc. Psychol.*, 1965, *1*, 85-88.

McGurk, Frank C. J. Comparative test scores of Negro and white school children in Richmond, Va. *J. Educ. Psychol.*, 1943, *34*, 473-484.

McGurk, Frank C. J. Comparison of the performance of Negro and white high school seniors on cultural and non-cultural psychological test questions. Washington, D. C.: Catholic Univ. Amer. Press, 1951 (microcard).

McGurk, Frank C. J. "Negro vs. white intelligence"—an answer. *Harvard Educ. Rev.*, 1959, *29*, 54-62.

McGurk, Frank C. J. On white and Negro test performance and socio-economic factors. *J. Abnorm. & Soc. Psychol.*, 1953, *48,* 448-450.

McPherson, Lois A. A study of the responses of Negro and white children on the Wechsler Intelligence Scale for Children. Unpubl. Master's thesis, Baylor Univ., 1951.

McQueen, Robert, and Churn, Browning. Intelligence and educational achievement of a matched sample of white and Negro students. *Sch. & Soc.*, 1960, *88,* 327-329.

Mermelstein, Egon. The effect of lack of formal schooling on number development. Unpubl. Doctor's dissert., Michigan State Univ., 1965.

Michael, William B. Factor analyses of tests and criteria: a comparative study of two AAF pilot populations. *Psychol. Monogr.: Gen. & Appl.*, 1949, *63.* Pp. 55.

Millman, Jason, and Glock, Marvin D. Trends in the measurement of general mental ability. *Rev. Educ. Res.*, 1965, *35,* 17-24.

Miner, John B. Intelligence in the United States. New York: Springer, 1957. Pp. 180.

Mingione, Ann D. Need for achievement in Negro and white children. *J. Consult. Psychol.*, 1965, *29,* 108-111.

Montagu, M. F. Ashley. Intelligence of northern Negroes and southern whites in the First World War. *Amer. J. Psychol.*, 1945, *58,* 161-188.

Morland, J. Kenneth. Racial acceptance and preference of nursery school children in a Southern city. *Merrill-Palmer Quart. Beh. & Develop.*, 1962, *8,* 271-280.

Moore, Joseph E. A comparison of Negro and white preschool children on a vocabulary test and an eye-hand coordination test. *Child Develop.*, 1942, *13,* 247-252.

Morgan, Clifford T. Introduction to Psychology. New York: McGraw-Hill, 1961. Pp. 727.

Morris, J. Russell. The social-economic background of Negro youth in California. Unpubl. Doctor's dissert., Stanford Univ., 1947.

Morse, Josiah. A comparison of white and colored children measured by the Binet Scale of Intelligence. *Pop. Sci. Month.*, 1914, *84,* 75-79.

Moynihan, Daniel P. The Negro family: the case for national action. U. S. Dept. Labor, Office of Policy Planning and Research. Washington, D. C., 1965. Pp. 78.

Munn, Norman L. Psychology. Boston: Houghton Mifflin, 1961. Pp. 812.

Murchison, Carl, and Burfield, Helen. Geographical concomitants of Negro criminal intelligence. *Ped. Sem.*, 1925, *32,* 26-44.

Murdoch, Katherine. A study of race differences in New York City. *Sch. & Soc.*, 1920, *11,* 147-150.

Murphy, Gardner. An Introduction to Psychology. New York: Harper, 1951. Pp. 583.

Murray, Walter I. The intelligence-test performance of Negro children of different social classes. Unpubl. Doctor's dissert., Univ. Chicago, 1947.

Mursell, James L. Psychological Testing. New York: Longmans, Green, 1949. Pp. 488.

Mussen, Paul H. Differences between the TAT responses of Negro and white boys. *J. Consult. Psychol.*, 1953, *17*, 373-376.

Myrdal, Gunnar. An American Dilemma. New York: Harper, 1944. Pp. 1483.

National Survey of the Higher Education of Negroes, General Studies of Colleges for Negroes, II. U. S. Off. Educ., Washington, D. C., 1942.

Newland, T. Ernest, and Lawrence, William C. Chicago Non-Verbal Examination results on an East Tennessee Negro population. *J. Clin. Psychol.*, 1953, *9,* 44-47.

Nicholson, Lula W. A study of the performance and sex differences of a group of rural children of homogeneous background on the Pintner-Cunningham Primary Tests. Unpubl. Master's thesis, Fisk Univ., 1949.

Odum, Howard W. Negro children in the public schools of Philadelphia. *Ann. Amer. Acad. Pol. & Soc. Sci.*, 1913, *49,* 186-208.

Oelke, Merritt C. Performance of Negro veterans on nine tests. *Personnel & Guid. J.*, 1959, *38,* 322-325.

Oldham, Ernestine V. The socio-economic status and personality of Negro adolescent girls. *J. Negro Educ.*, 1935, *4,* 514-522.

Osborne, R. Travis. Racial difference in school achievement. *Mankind Monogr.*, 1962, No. 3. Pp. 18.

Osborne, R. Travis. Racial differences in mental growth and school achievement: a longitudinal study. *Psychol. Reports*, 1960, *7*, 233-239.

Osborne, R. Travis. School achievement of white and Negro children of the same mental and chronological ages. *Mankind Quart.*, 1961, *2*, 26-29.

Otis, Arthur S. Otis Self-Administering Tests of Mental Ability. Manual of Directions and Key (rev.). Yonkers-on-Hudson: World Book, 1928.

Outlaw, Algee C. A study of personal and professional characteristics of the Negro rural public school teachers in Haywood County, Tennessee. Unpubl. Master's thesis, Tennessee Agric. & Indus. State Coll., 1950.

Palmer, Robert R., Wiley, Bell I., and Keast, William R. The procurement and training of Ground Combat Forces. Washington, D. C.: Historical Div., Dept. Army, 1948, 53-58.

Panton, James H. Beta-WAIS comparisons and WAIS subtest configurations within a state prison population. *J. Clin. Psychol.*, 1960, *16,* 312-317.

Panton, James H. Inmate personality differences related to recidivism, age and race as measured by the MMPI. *J. Correct. Psychol.*, 1959, *4*, 28-35.

Parker, Lilla M. C. A study of the tested differences in home-status, intelligence, achievement, and personality of the seventh grade graduates from M. M. Burdell, B. S. Ingram, and L. H. Williams schools, Macon, Georgia, 1953-1954. Unpubl. Master's thesis, Atlanta Univ., 1954.

Pastore, Nicholas. A fallacy underlying Garrett's use of the data of the Army Alpha and Beta tests—a comment. *Scient. Month.*, 1949, *69*, 279-280.

Patrick, James R. A study of ideals, intelligence and achievements of Negroes and whites. *Bull. Univ. Ga.*, 1926, *27*, No. 1, Pp. 48.

Patrick, James R., and Sims, Verner M. Personality differences between Negro and white college students, North and South. *J. Abnorm. & Soc. Psychol.*, 1934, *29*, 181-201.

Pennington, Leon A., Hough, Romeyn B., Jr., and Case, Harry W. The Psychology of Military Leadership. New York: Prentice-Hall, 1943. Pp. 288.

Peters, James S., II. A study of the Wechsler-Bellevue Verbal Scores of Negro and white males. *J. Negro Educ.*, 1960, *29*, 7-16.

Peterson, Joseph. The comparative abilities of white and Negro children. *Comp. Psychol. Monogr.*, 1923, *1*, No. 5. Pp. 141.

Peterson, Joseph, and Lanier, Lyle H. Studies in the comparative abilities of whites and Negroes. *Ment. Meas. Monogr.*, 1929, No. 5. Pp. 156.

Peterson, Joseph, and Telford, Charles W. Results of group and of individual tests applied to the practically pure-blood Negro children on St. Helena Island. *J. Comp. Psychol.*, 1930, *11*, 115-144.

Pettigrew, Thomas F. A Profile of the Negro American. New York: Van Nostrand, 1964. Pp. 250.

Pettigrew, Thomas F. Negro American intelligence: a new look at an old controversy. *J. Negro Educ.*, 1964, *33*, 6-25.

Petway, Joseph K. Correlation between the intelligence quotient and the vocational interest of ninth grade pupils. Unpubl. Master's thesis, Fisk Univ., 1948.

Phillips, Byron A. The Binet tests applied to colored children. *Psychol. Clin.*, 1914, *8*, 190-196.

Phillips, Mabel V. The characteristics of superior Negro college students. Unpubl. Master's thesis, Howard Univ., 1946.

Pintner, Rudolf, and Keller, Ruth. Intelligence tests of foreign children. *J. Educ. Psychol.*, 1922, *13*, 214-222.

Pintner, Rudolf, and Maller, Julius B. Month of birth and average intelligence among different ethnic groups. *J. Genet. Psychol.*, 1937, *50*, 91-107.

Popenoe, Paul, and Johnson, Roswell H. Applied Eugenics. New York: Macmillan, 1935. Pp. 429.

Powers, Edwin, and Witmer, Helen. An Experiment in the Prevention of Delinquency. The Cambridge-Somerville Youth Study. New York: Columbia Univ. Press, 1951. Pp. 649.

Pressey, Sidney L., and Teter, G. F. I. A comparison of colored and white children by means of a group scale of intelligence. *J. Appl. Psychol.*, 1919, *3*, 277-282.

Price, A. Cooper. A Rorschach study of the development of personality structure in white and Negro children in a southeastern community. Unpubl. Doctor's dissert., Univ. Florida, 1953.

Price, J. St. Clair. The intelligence of Negro college freshmen. *Sch. & Soc.*, 1929, *30*, 749-754.

Proctor, Lillian S. A case study of thirty superior colored children in Washington, D. C. Unpubl. Master's thesis, Univ. Chicago, 1929.

Queen, Phyllis M. J. A comparison of the verbal intelligence, non-verbal intelligence, and problem-solving abilities of a selected group of sixth graders. Unpubl. Master's thesis, North Carolina College at Durham, 1954.

Raper, Arthur F. Two Black Belt counties. Changes in rural life since the advent of the boll weevil in Greene and Macon counties, Georgia. Unpubl. Doctor's dissert., Univ. North Carolina, 1930.

Reese, Harry S. The relationship between general reading ability, English, general intelligence and achievement in mathematics. Unpubl. Master's thesis, Alabama State Coll. for Negroes, Montgomery, 1951.

Reitzes, Dietrich C. Negroes and Medicine. Cambridge, Mass.: Harvard Univ. Press, 1958. Pp. 400.

Report of the President's Committee. To Secure these Rights. Washington, D. C.: U. S. Gov. Print. Off., 1947. Pp. 178.

Report to the Superintendent of Instruction by the Division of Tests and Measurements. Mental testing in St. Louis. *Publ. Sch. Messinger*, 1925, *23*, 45-57.

Reuter, Edward B. Race Mixture. New York: McGraw-Hill, 1931. Pp. 224.

Rhoads, Teresa F., Rapoport, Milton, Kennedy, Ruth, and Stokes, Joseph, Jr. Studies on the growth and development of male children receiving evaporated milk II. Physical growth, dentition, and intelligence of white and Negro children through the first four years as influenced by vitamin supplements. *J. Pediat.*, 1945, *26*, 415-454.

Richardson, John F., III. A comparison of certain characteristics of a group of Negro Education and non-Education college students: an investigation to determine the nature and significance of the differences in various characteristics between Negro college students who select teaching and those who choose other vocational goals. Unpubl. Doctor's dissert., New York Univ., 1963.

Ries, Arthur J. A survey of the intelligence and achievement scores of white and Negro children entering the junior high schools of Louisville in September, 1938. Unpubl. Master's thesis, Univ. Louisville, 1940.

Roberts, S. Oliver. Socio-economic status and performance of Negro college women, North and South, on the ACE. *Amer. Psychol.*, 1946, *1*, 253.

Roberts, S. Oliver. Socio-economic status and performance on the ACE of Negro freshman college veterans and non-veterans, from the North and South. *Amer. Psychol.;* 1948, *3*, 266.

Roberts, S. Oliver. Socio-economic status and performance over a four-year period on the ACE of Negro college women from the North and South. *Amer. Psychol.*, 1950, *5*, 295.

Roberts, S. Oliver. The measurement of adjustment of Negro college youth: personality scales for whites versus criteria intrinsic to Negro group. Unpubl. Doctor's dissert., Univ. Minnesota, 1944.

Robinson, Mary L., and Meenes, Max. The relationship between test intelligence of third grade Negro children and the occupations of their parents. *J. Negro Educ.*, 1947, *16*, 136-141.

Roebuck, Julian B. The Negro numbers man as a criminal type: the construction and application of a typology. *J. Crim. Law, Criminol. & Police Sci.*, 1963, *54*, 48-60.

Roen, Sheldon R. Personality and Negro-white intelligence. *J. Abnorm & Soc. Psychol.*, 1960, *61*, 148-150.

Roland, H. M., and Swan, Donald A. Race, psychology, and education: Wilmington, North Carolina. *Mankind Quart.*, 1965, *6*, 19-36.

Rooks, Alberta R. Socio-economic status and performance on the A.C.E. of freshman women students, "North" and "South." Unpubl. Master's thesis, Fisk Univ., 1946.

Roth, Robert M. The adjustment of Negro college students at Hampton Institute. *J. Negro Educ.*, 1961, *30*, 72-74.

Rowntree, Leonard G., McGill, Kenneth H., and Edwards, T. I. Causes of rejection and the incidence of defects among 18- and 19-year-old selective service registrants. *J. Amer. Med. Assoc.*, 1943, *123*, 181-185.

Royster, Earl W. The intelligence and mathematical achievement of Negro high school seniors in the rural areas compared with that of the urban areas in four counties in Alabama. Unpubl. Master's thesis, Alabama State Coll., Montgomery, 1954.

Rozynko, Vitali, and Wenk, Ernest. Intellectual performance of three delinquent groups of different ethnic origin. *J. Consult. Psychol.*, 1965, *29*, 282. (Extended report, No. 8386, Amer. Documentation Institute, Library of Congress, Washington, D. C.)

Ruch, Floyd L. Psychology and Life. Chicago: Scott, Foresman, 1963. Pp. 685.

Sanford, Fillmore H. Psychology: A Scientific Study of Man. Belmont, Cal.: Wadsworth, 1965. Pp. 627.

Sartin, James L. A study of Negro responses in items on the Wechsler Intelligence Scale for Children. Unpubl. Master's thesis, Florida State Univ., 1950.

Scarborough, B. Barron. Some mental characteristics of Southern colored and white venereal disease patients as measured by the Wechsler-Bellevue test. *J. Soc. Psychol.*, 1956, *43*, 313-321.

Schwegler, R. A., and Winn, Edith. A comparative study of the intelligence of white and colored children. *J. Educ. Res.*, 1920, *2*, 838-848.

Sears, Pauline S. Levels of aspiration in academically successful and unsuccessful children. *J. Abnorm. & Soc. Psychol.*, 1940, *35*, 498-536.

Semler, Ira J., and Iscoe, Ira. Comparative and developmental study of the learning abilities of Negro and white children under four conditions. *J. Educ. Psychol.*, 1963, *54*, 38-44.

Shepard, Samuel, Jr. The Banneker School Project. Proceedings Section II, Seventh Annual Professional Inst., Div. School Psychologists, Amer. Psychol. Assoc. Nashville, Tenn.: George Peabody College for Teachers, 1962. Pp. 9-16.

Shuey, Audrey M. A comparison of Negro and white college students by means of the American Council Psychological Examination. *J. Psychol.*, 1942, *14*, 35-52.

Shuey, Audrey M. Personality traits of Jewish and non-Jewish students. *Arch. Psychol.*, 1944, No. 290. Pp. 38.

Shuey, Audrey M. The Testing of Negro Intelligence. Lynchburg, Va.: J. P. Bell, 1958. Pp. 351.

Siegman, Aron W. The effect of manifest anxiety on a concept formation task, a nondirected learning task, and on timed and untimed intelligence tests. *J. Consult. Psychol.*, 1956, *20*, 176-178.

Silverglied, Edith. The relation of intelligence to school withdrawal among Negro boys. Unpubl. Master's thesis, Columbia Univ., 1940.

Simpson, George E., and Yinger, J. Milton. Racial and Cultural Minorities: an Analysis of Prejudice and Discrimination. New York: Harper, 1953. Pp. 773.

Slawson, John. The Delinquent Boy. Boston: Gorham Press, 1926. Pp. 477.

Slivinske, Alec J. A comparative study of the effects of certain environmental factors on I. Q. scores. Unpubl. Master's thesis, Univ. Virginia, 1949.

Smart, Mollie S. Confirming Klineberg's suspicion. *Amer. Psychol.*, 1963, *18*, 621.

Smith, Groves B. Comments on the relationship of mental defect to the problems of delinquency and crime. *Proc. & Addr. Amer. Assoc. Study Feeble Minded,* 1924, *29,* 325-343.

Smith, Howard P., and Abramson, Marcia. Racial and family experience correlates of mobility aspiration. *J. Negro Educ.,* 1962, *31,* 117-124.

Smith, Mamie. The intelligence and achievement status in social studies of two hundred fifth and sixth grade pupils in selected elementary schools in Chambers County, Alabama. Unpubl. Master's thesis, Alabama State Coll. at Montgomery, 1953.

Smith, Mapheus. Occupational differentials in physical status. *Amer. Sociol. Rev.,* 1948, *13,* 72-82.

Smith, W. N. A comparative study of the educational achievement and intelligence of the senior high school students of Atlanta University Laboratory High School, May, 1942. Unpubl. Master's thesis, Atlanta Univ., 1942.

Soifer, Meyer W. A comparison of the mental and physical abilities of white and Negro children. Unpubl. Master's thesis, Temple Univ., 1937.

Solomon, Philip. Narcolepsy in Negroes. *Diseases Nerv. System,* 1945, *6,* 179-183.

Solomon, Sylvia J. A study of certain national and racial groups in the University of Toledo. Unpubl. Master's thesis, Univ. Toledo, 1941.

Sorokin, Pitirim A., Zimmerman, Carle C., and Galpin, Charles J. A Systematic Source Book in Rural Sociology. Minneapolis: Univ. Minnesota Press, 1932, Vol. 3. Pp. 752.

Sperrazzo, Gerald, and Wilkins, Walter L. Further normative data on the Progressive Matrices. *J. Consult. Psychol.,* 1958, *22,* 35-37.

Sperrazzo, Gerald, and Wilkins, Walter L. Racial differences on Progressive Matrices. *J. Consult. Psychol.,* 1959, *23,* 273-274.

Spirer, Jess. Negro crime. *Comp. Psychol. Monogr.,* 1940, *16,* No. 2. Pp. 64.

Springer, N. Norton. The social competence of adolescent delinquents: a comparative study of white and Negro first offenders and recidivists. *J. Soc. Psychol.,* 1941, *14,* 337-348.

Stainbrook, Edward, and Siegel, Paul S. A comparative group Rorschach study of southern Negro and white high school and college students. *J. Psychol.,* 1944, *17,* 107-115.

Stalnaker, John M. Identification of the best southern Negro high-school seniors. *Scient. Month.,* 1948, *67,* 237-239.

Stanton, John M. Group personality profile related to aspects of antisocial behavior. *J. Crim. Law, Criminol. & Police Sci.,* 1956, *47,* 340-349.

Stewart, Naomi. Relationship between Military Occupational Specialty and Army General Classification Test Standard Score. *Educ. & Psychol. Meas.,* 1947, *7,* 677-693.

Stone, Calvin P. A comparative study of the intelligence of 399 inmates of the Indiana Reformatory and 653 men of the United States Army. *J. Crim. Law & Criminol.,* 1921-22, *12,* 238-257.

Stouffer, Samuel A., Suchman, Edward A., DeVinney, Leland C., Star, Shirley A., and Williams, Robin M., Jr. The American Soldier: Adjustment during Army Life. Vol. I. Princeton, N. J.: Princeton Univ. Press, 1949. Pp. 600.

Stowell, Geraldine. Comparative study of certain mental defects found in institutionalized whites and Negroes in the District Training School. *Proc. & Addr. Amer. Assoc. Stud. Feeblemind.,* 1931, *36,* 267-281.

Strachan, Lexie. Distribution of intelligence quotients of twenty-two thousand primary-school children. *J. Educ. Res.,* 1926, *14,* 169-177.

Strayer, George D. (Dir.) Report of the Survey of the Public School System of Baltimore, Maryland, 1920-21. Baltimore, 1921, Vol. 2, 239-244.

Strong, Alice C. Three hundred fifty white and colored children measured by Binet-Simon measuring scale of intelligence: a comparative study. *Ped. Sem.,* 1913, *20,* 485-515.

Sumner, Francis C. Mental health statistics of Negro college freshmen. *Sch. & Soc.,* 1931, *33,* 575-576.

Sunne, Dagny. A comparative study of white and Negro children. *J. Appl. Psychol.,* 1917, *1,* 71-83.

Sunne, Dagny. Comparison of white and Negro children in verbal and non-verbal tests. *Sch. & Soc.,* 1924, *19,* 469-472.

Sunne, Dagny. Comparison of white and Negro children by the Terman and Yerkes Bridges revisions of the Binet tests. *J. Comp. Psychol.,* 1925, *5,* 209-219.

Sutton, Luther J. A study of the relationships between the occupational choices, and the interests, achievements, mental maturity, and other factors of the seventh and eighth grade pupils in the Chinquapin Elementary School. Unpubl. Master's thesis, North Carolina Coll. at Durham, 1954.

Swan, Donald A. Comparison of the relation between mental maturity and academic achievement among white and Negro school children in a South Louisiana parish. Unpubl. Monogr., 1965.

Swan, Donald A. Race, psychology, and education: Jackson, Mississippi. Unpubl. Monogr., 1964.

Tanser, Harry A. The Settlement of Negroes in Kent County, Ontario, and a Study of the Mental Capacity of their Descendants. Chatham, Ont.: Shepherd Publ., 1939. Pp. 187.

Tanser, Harry A. Intelligence of Negroes of mixed blood in Canada. *J. Negro Educ.*, 1941, *10*, 650-652.

Tate, Merle W., and Voss, Charlotte E. A study of the Davis-Eells test of intelligence. *Harvard Educ. Rev.*, 1956, *26*, 374-387.

Teahan, John E., and Drews, Elizabeth M. A comparison of northern and southern Negro children on the WISC. *J. Consult. Psychol.*, 1962, *26*, 292. (Extended report, No. 7120, Amer. Documentation Institute, Library of Congress, Washington, D. C.)

Teicher, Morton I., and Singer, E. A report on the use of the Wechsler-Bellevue scales in an overseas general hospital. *Amer. J. Psychiat.*, 1946, *103*, 91-93.

Terman, Lewis M. Genetic Studies of Genius. Vol. I. Mental and Physical Traits of a Thousand Gifted Children. Stanford: Stanford Univ. Press, 1925. Pp. 648.

Terwilliger, A. Janet. A study of Negro children of I. Q. above 125. Unpubl. Master's thesis, Teachers Coll., Columbia Univ., 1934.

Thomas, Dorothy S. Research Memorandum on Migration Differentials. New York: Soc. Sci. Res. Counc., Bull. No. 43, 1938. Pp. 423.

Thomas, Tena E. S. J. A study of the tested differences in intelligence, achievement and personality of two selected groups of ninth grade pupils enrolled in Peabody High School, Alexandria, Louisiana. Unpubl. Master's thesis, Atlanta Univ., 1954.

Thompson, Charles H. The relative enrollment of Negroes in higher educational institutions in the United States. *J. Negro Educ.*, 1953, *22*, 432-441.

Thompson, Charles H. The relative status of the Negro population in the United States. *J. Negro Educ.*, 1953, *22*, 221-231.

Thorndike, Edward L. Intelligence scores of colored pupils in high schools. *Sch. & Soc.*, 1923, *18*, 569-570.

Thorndike, Robert L., and Gallup, George H. Verbal intelligence of the American adult. *J. Gen. Psychol.*, 1944, *30*, 75-85.

Thurmond, Sarah. A comparison of the intelligence and achievement of twelve-year-old Negro children in the rural schools of Clarke County, Georgia. *Bull. Univ. Georgia*, 1933, *33*, No. 11c. Pp. 44.

Thurstone, L. L. Norms for the 1927 Psychological Examination. *Educ. Rec.*, 1928, *9*, 102-107.

Thurstone, L. L., and Thurstone, Thelma G. The American Council on Education Psychological Examinations. *Amer. Council on Educ. Studies*, 1941, *5*, 1-41; 1942, *6*, 1-42; 1946, *10*, 1-34.

Thurstone, L. L., and Thurstone, Thelma G.   The Psychological Examination. *Educ. Rec.,* 1929, *10,* 105-115; 1930, *11,* 101-128; 1931, *12,* 160-178; 1933, *14,* 183-197; 1934, *15,* 161-175; 1935, *16,* 226-240; 1936, *17,* 296-317; 1937, *18,* 252-273; 1938, *19,* 209-234.

Tiber, Norman.   The effects of incentives on intelligence test performance. Unpubl. Doctor's dissert., Florida State Univ., 1963.

Tiber, Norman, and Kennedy, Wallace A.   The effects of incentives on the intelligence test performance of different social groups. *J. Consult. Psychol.,* 1964, *28,* 187.

Tomlinson, Helen.   Differences between pre-school Negro children and their older siblings on the Stanford-Binet scales. *J. Negro Educ.,* 1944, *13,* 474-479.

Town, Clara H.   Research Studies from the Psychological Clinic of the Children's Aid Society of Buffalo and Erie County. II. A comparative Study of United States white, United States Negro, Polish and Italian Groups. Children's Aid Soc., Buffalo, 1938.

Trabue, Marion R.   Intelligence of Negro recruits. *Nat. Hist.,* 1919, *19,* 680-685.

Treacy, John P.   The educational status of colored children in the Minneapolis public schools. Unpubl. Master's thesis, Univ. Minnesota, 1926.

Trudeau, Arthur G.   Army experience and problems of Negro education. *Educ. Victory,* U. S. Off. Educ., Fed. Sec. Agency, 1945, *3,* No. 20, 13-16.

Tulchin, Simon H.   Intelligence and Crime. Chicago: Univ. Chicago Press, 1939. Pp. 166.

Tullis, David S.   A comparative study of Negro, Latin, and Anglo children in a West Texas community. Unpubl. Doctor's dissert., Texas Technological Coll., 1964.

Tumin, Melvin M. (Ed.)   Race and intelligence: an investigation. *University: a Princeton Magazine,* 1964, No. 20, 3-8.

Tuttle, Lester E., Jr.   The comparative effect on intelligence test scores of Negro and white children when certain verbal and time factors are varied. Unpubl. Doctor's dissert., Univ. Florida, 1964.

Tyler, Leona E.   The Psychology of Human Differences. New York: Appleton-Century-Crofts, 1965. Pp. 572.

Vane, Julia R., and Kessler, Rosalyn T.   The Goodenough Draw-a-Man Test: long term reliability and validity. *J. Clin. Psychol.,* 1964, *20,* 487-488.

Vega, Manuel.   The performance of Negro children on an oddity discrimination task as a function of the race of the examiner and the type of verbal incentive used by the examiner. Unpubl. Doctor's dissert., Florida State Univ., 1964.

Vernon, James O.   A comparison of the achievements of Negro and white children in the schools of Boynton, Oklahoma. Unpubl. Master's thesis, Univ. Oklahoma, 1936.

Vernon, Philip E.   Race and intelligence. *Eugen. Rev.,* 1959, *51,* 99-101.

Wade, Alberta C.   A critical study of the social maturity of thirty-two first grade pupils entering Brutonville School, Candor, North Carolina, August 28, 1953. Unpubl. Master's thesis, North Carolina Coll. at Durham, 1954.

Wagner, Philip S.   A comparative study of Negro and white admissions to the psychiatric pavilion of the Cincinnati General Hospital. Unpubl. Master's thesis, Univ. Cincinnati, 1938.

Walker, Audrey J.   A study of the personal and social adjustment of 300 college freshmen. Unpubl. Master's thesis, Hampton Institute, 1951.

Walker, Margaret B.   A comparative study of the achievement, intelligence, and personality traits of thirty problem and thirty nonproblem children of the sixth- and seventh- grades in the Orange Street Elementary School, Fayetteville, North Carolina. Unpubl. Master's thesis, Atlanta Univ., 1946.

Wallace, Elneita B.   A study of the relationship between the socio-economic background, intelligence and educational progress of Negro children. Unpubl. Master's thesis, Univ. Cincinnati, 1932.

Wallis, Wilson D.   Race and culture. *Scient. Month.*, 1926, *23*, 313-321.

Watts, Frederick P.   A comparative clinical study of delinquent and non-delinquent Negro boys. *J. Negro Educ.*, 1941, *10*, 190-207.

Webb, Allen P.   A longitudinal comparison of the WISC and WAIS with educable mentally retarded Negroes. *J. Clin. Psychol.*, 1963, *19*, 101-102.

Weitz, Robert D., and Rachlin, H. L.   The mental ability and educational attainment of five hundred venereally infected females. *J. Soc. Hyg.*, 1945, *31*, 300-302.

Wells, George R.   The application of the Binet-Simon tests to groups of white and colored school children. *Psychol. Monogr.*, 1923, *32*, 52-58.

Wheatley, Luis A., and Sumner, Francis C.   Measurement of neurotic tendency in Negro students of music. *J. Psychol.*, 1946, *22*, 247-252.

Whittaker, James O.   Introduction to Psychology. Philadelphia: W. B. Saunders, 1965. Pp. 631.

Wickens, Delos D., and Meyer, Donald R.   Psychology. New York: Holt, Rinehart & Winston, 1961. Pp. 771.

Wickman, E. K.   Intelligence survey of the Cleveland Workhouse *and* Report of intelligence survey of the Cleveland police department. *In* Pound, Roscoe, and Frankfurter, Felix (Eds.) Criminal Justice in Cleveland. Reports of the Cleveland Foundation Survey of the Administration of Criminal Justice in Cleveland, Ohio. Cleveland, The Cleveland Foundation, 1922, 687-695.

Wilkerson, D. A. Review of M. D. Jenkins: A socio-psychological study of Negro children of superior intelligence. *J. Negro Educ.*, 1936, *5*, 126-131.

Williams, Halcyonnee S. The relationship between intelligence and achievement in English training of a selected group of senior high school pupils of Alabama. Unpubl. Master's thesis, State Teachers Coll., Montgomery, 1946.

Williams, Howard J. The educational status of colored children in the Garfield Avenue, Ninth Street, and Fourth Street public elementary schools of Milwaukee, Wisconsin. Unpubl. Master's thesis, Marquette Univ., 1935.

Williams, Lenora B. Relationship of certain factors to superstitious beliefs of Negro and white high school pupils in Texas. Unpubl. Master's thesis, Univ. Colorado, 1938.

Willis, L. J. A comparative study of the reading achievements of white and Negro children. *Peabody J. Educ.*, 1939, *17*, 166-171.

Witty, Paul. Research upon the American Negro. *39th Yearbk Nat. Soc. Study Educ.*, 1940, Part I, 261-269.

Witty, Paul. New evidence on the learning ability of the Negro. *J. Abnorm. & Soc. Psychol.*, 1945, *40*, 401-404.

Witty, Paul. Reply to Mr. Erickson. *J. Abnorm. & Soc. Psychol.*, 1946, *41*, 482-485.

Witty, Paul, Garfield, Sol, and Brink, William G. A comparison of the vocational interests of Negro and white high-school students. *J. Educ. Psychol.*, 1941, *32*, 124-132.

Witty, Paul A., and Jenkins, Martin D. The case of "B"—a gifted Negro girl. *J. Soc. Psychol.*, 1935, *6*, 117-124.

Woods, Walter A., and Toal, Robert. Subtest disparity of Negro and white groups matched for IQ's on the Revised Beta test. *J. Consult. Psychol.*, 1957, *21*, 136-138.

Woodworth, Robert S., and Marquis, Donald G. Psychology. New York: Holt, 1947. Pp. 677.

World Almanac and Book of Facts for 1926. New York: The World, 1926. Pp. 912.

Wylie, Ruth C. Children's estimates of their schoolwork ability, as a function of sex, race, and socioeconomic level. *J. Personal.*, 1963, *31*, 203-224.

Yerkes, Robert M. (Ed.) Psychological Examining in the U. S. Army. *Mem. Nat. Acad. Sci.*, 1921, *15*, Pp. 890.

Yerkes, Robert M., and Foster, Josephine C. A Point Scale for Measuring Mental Ability, 1923 Revision. Baltimore: Warwick & York, 1923. Pp. 219.

Young, Florene M., and Bright, Howard A. Results of testing 81 Negro rural juveniles with the Wechsler Intelligence Scale for Children. *J. Soc. Psychol.*, 1954, *39*, 219-226.

Young, Florene M., and Collins, John J. Results of testing Negro contact-syphilitics with the Wechsler-Bellevue Intelligence Scale. *J. Soc. Psychol.*, 1954, *39*, 93-98.

Young, Florene M., and Pitts, Virginia A. The performance of congenital syphilitics on the Wechsler Intelligence Scale for Children. *J. Consult. Psychol.*, 1951, *15*, 239-242.

Young, Paul C. Intelligence and suggestibility in whites and Negroes. *J. Comp. Psychol.*, 1929, *9*, 339-359.

Younge, Samuel L. The interrelationship of socio-economic status, intelligence and achievement of sixth grade Negro pupils. Unpubl. Master's thesis. Tuskegee Institute, 1947.

AUTHOR INDEX

SUBJECT INDEX

Composed, printed, and bound by
J. P. Bell Company, Inc.,
Lynchburg, Virginia